Principles of Naval Weapons Systems

Principles of Naval Weapons Systems

Edited by David R. Frieden
Lieutenant Commander
U. S. Navy

Revision and new material by
Gene P. Bender, Commander, USN
Leslie R. Carter, Lieutenant Commander, USN
Rodger B. Carter, Lieutenant Commander, USN
Michael B. Candalor, Lieutenant Commander, USN
Hugh C. Dawson, Lieutenant Commander, USN
David R. Frieden, Lieutenant Commander, USN
Maurice A. Gauthier, Commander, USN
Gary J. Magnuson, Captain, USMC
John H. McKim, Lieutenant Commander, USN

Naval Institute Press
Annapolis, Maryland

Fundamentals of Naval Science Series

Library of Congress Cataloging in Publication Data
Main entry under title:

Principles of naval weapons systems.

    Includes bibliographies and index.
    1. Weapons systems.   I. Frieden, David R.,
1948 –   II. Bender, Gene P.
VF346.P75 1985   623.4   85-4777
ISBN 0-87021-537-X

Printed in the United States of America

Contents

Preface

This text and its associated workbook were written in support of the education of NROTC and U.S. Naval Academy midshipmen by providing entry-level knowledge of the theory and principles of weapons systems encountered in Navy and Marine Corps operations. The original *Principles of Naval Weapons Systems* was published by the United States Naval Academy in 1976 in response to a major change in educational philosophy that occurred when Rear Admiral Kinnard R. McKee, USN, was superintendent. Previously, education in weapons was accomplished by describing and explaining specific existing hardware, which obviously could not apply to every midshipman's ultimate duty assignment. Rear Admiral McKee directed that weapons be presented from a systems viewpoint, de-emphasizing specific platforms and hardware and emphasizing theory and principles of operation. Hardware was used to explain theory rather than the reverse. The purpose of the text then and now is to provide sufficient background in theory and principles to enable the reader to readily understand a weapon system or sensor once its operational parameters are determined from technical manuals, warfare publications, or other sources. This should include an understanding of a potential adversary's capabilities as well.

This text is the result of a zero-based, two-year effort to revise and update undergraduate weapons systems education. Each chapter of the earlier book was examined for applicability, accuracy, and clarity. Extensive changes were made in several chapters, and many were totally rewritten. The book includes numerous photos and diagrams not previously presented as well as older material that has been updated.

It is hoped that the text will exceed its stated purpose by supporting an individual through commissioning and his or her active-duty career, because little change is expected in theory and principles except in the total amount of knowledge required and areas of emphasis. No matter what degree of detailed knowledge is required in an officer's future assignments, these basic principles will still apply. Since all the information contained herein could not be covered in a one-semester or two-quarter college-level course, instructors and curriculum managers should establish the level of knowledge required for their students and select the material for study accordingly. The mathematical derivations included exceed requirements in some areas in order to provide a means with which those with more advanced engineering or scientific backgrounds can relate the material presented to their own areas of expertise. Most goals of this text can be accomplished completely by a reader with a background in algebra and trigonometry. In most cases, the explanations are too simplistic from an engineering point of view; however, it should be pointed out that the book was intended to provide undergraduates in any major with a survey of the subject in one semester or less and to provide a basis for follow-on training after commissioning.

This text should be used with the loose-leaf workbook, which contains sample problems, learning objectives, and programmed instructions. It is hoped that those with some knowledge of physics, chemistry, and engineering can use the text and workbook without access to an instructor.

Those involved in the production of this publication are indebted to the following members of the Task Force 3000 team that produced the first edition of *Principles of Naval Weapons Systems* during 1975–1976: Lieutenant Commander P. M. Quast, Lieutenant Commander R. Twaddle, Lieutenant Commander R. T. Sollenberger, Lieutenant W. T. Ober, Lieutenant D. P. Gunn, Lieutenant P. H. Scherf, Lieutenant N. P. Walsh, Captain M. F. Shields, USMC, and Associate Professor K. A. Knowles. Over the years revisions of the text were conducted by U.S. Naval Academy ES-300 course coordinators: Commander J. A. Roux, Captain C. N. Blair, USMC, and Lieutenant Colonel A. Ranizewski, USMC. This steadily improved the basic text until the present effort began in June 1983.

We are grateful for the assistance provided by other military and civilian faculty of the Department of Weapons and Systems Engineering, especially its chairman, Professor Charles F. Olsen, without whose support and encouragement production of this book would have been impossible. Special thanks are extended to Lieutenant Commander Gary Harrel of the NROTC unit at the University of Washington for his efforts to ensure that the special requirements of officer candidates outside the Naval Academy were met by the basic text and workbook; further, Lieutenant Commander Harrell deserves thanks for his major contribution to the standardization of education throughout naval officer procurement programs.

The patience and perseverance of Ms. Donna Scarborough and Ms. Virginia Christiansen in typing hundreds of pages of new material and changes to the manuscript despite the marginal legibility of submitted material was the major reason that any production deadlines were met. Whatever resemblance exists between the text and correct, readable English prose was due to Naval Institute editor Carol Swartz, who managed to bring order to the jungle of equations and disjointed paragraphs provided her. The artistic efforts of Mr. Bill Clipson of the USNA Educational Resources Center in preparing many of the diagrams presented have certainly decreased the length of written explanations by many "thousands of words."

The list of individuals at various commands and agencies who provided information, critical review, diagrams, and photos is so long that mentioning all who are due thanks would be impossible. However, specific mention of the following organizations is in order: Naval Sea Systems Command, Naval Weapons Systems Engineering Station, Naval Air Systems Command, Naval Surface Weapons Center, White Oak, Maryland, and Dahlgren, Virginia, Johns Hopkins University Applied Physics Laboratory, the Naval Weapons Center, China Lake, California, and the Chief of Naval Education and Training.

David R. Frieden
Lieutenant Commander, USN

Principles of Naval Weapons Systems

Introduction

The term *weapons systems* is a generalization encompassing a broad spectrum of often dissimilar components and subsystems. These components range from simple offensive or defensive devices, through delivery platforms, to the strategic integration and direction of complex weapons systems or more intangible technologies designed to defeat an adversary or deny enemy objectives. The principles addressed in this text are drawn from diverse practical experience and a wide range of academic disciplines to provide present and future officers with a basic foundation in weapons systems. By no means should it be considered all-encompassing or the definitive word concerning the principles addressed. Rather, the reader should view it as a basis for subsequent functional training and continuing education in the art and science of naval weapons systems and their applications.

A target can be either stationary or mobile; it may travel in the atmosphere, in space, on the surface, or below the sea. It may be guided or unguided, maneuverable or fixed in a predetermined flight path. It may vary in configuration and may travel at speeds that range from a few knots to several times the speed of sound. In order to achieve neutralization or destruction of the target, the weapons system must accomplish many separate but interrelated functions. These functions involve target detection, resolution, classification, localization, tracking, and ultimately neutralization. As can be deduced, an accurate solution to a fire control problem requires the careful interaction and integration of many subsystems.

Detecting subsystems must be designed to cope with countless target and environmental characteristics. These include target location, speed, direction, size, and aspect. There are three phases involved in the sensing of a target by a weapons system. The first phase is surveillance and detection, the purpose of which is to search a predetermined area for a target and to detect its presence. The second phase is target location, during which the target position is accurately fixed as to its bearing, range, depth, or elevation. Finally, the target must be classified as to its category, number, size, and identity. Special consideration must be applied to multiple targets. A measure of the quality of a detecting device is its ability to distinguish among, or resolve, individual targets in a multi-target group. Once individual targets are resolved, appropriate action can be taken. The detection of single or multiple targets by any system is complicated by noise, which is any energy sensed other than that attributed to the target. Noise is generated within the circuitry of the detecting system, as well as being a constituent of the environment surrounding the target. Detection systems must, therefore, be designed to minimize noise and to distinguish target signals from noise.

Sensing the presence of a target is obviously essential to subsequent neutralization; however, the sensor provides only a periodic update of target information. To solve the fire-control problem successfully, continuous or periodic updates of the target's position and its velocity relative to the weapon platform must be provided for computational purposes. To achieve this, methods must be devised to enable the sensor to follow the target. The generation of continuous target data by a weapons system is called *tracking*. In the generic sense, any system that follows an input is said to *track* that input. For example, the output of a home thermostat temperature-control system can be said to track the input temperature setting. Inherent in this process of control is the concept of feedback. In control systems (or in this context, tracking systems), feedback provides information to the system itself on how well the output is being controlled. Weapons systems employ feedback that shows how well the sensor system is following (tracking) a target. In general, feedback provides the tracking system with the difference between where the sensor is actually pointing and where the target is actually located. This difference is designated as *system error*. It is the goal of any tracking system to reduce this error to zero, at which time the sensor is said to be on target. This text will discuss the various methods of target tracking employed in modern weapons systems. Regardless of the method used, the purpose of target tracking is to provide a more or less continuous input of target parameters to a computational system.

Although it has been implied thus far that a weapons system responds only to a single target, in reality information regarding numerous targets, friendly and hostile, is being continually gathered. In order to direct the weapons system in a logical and timely response to the voluminous data acquired by electronic sensors, there must be the capability to compile, coordinate, and evaluate the data, and then initiate the appropriate response. To process all the data manually would be difficult and reaction times greatly lengthened. A computer can relieve the operator of this burdensome and time-consuming task.

The extremely high speed, precision, reliability, and flexibility of the computer has allowed us to remain abreast of current developments. Three basic types of computers—analog, digital, and hybrid (a combination of analog and digital)—will be discussed, along with their inherent advantages and applications. Special-purpose and general-purpose computers enable a weapons systems to detect, track, and predict target motion automatically. These factors establish the target's presence and define the circumstances of engagement; however, neutralization of the target requires that a destructive mechanism (i.e., the warhead) be delivered to the vicinity of the target by a weapon. Weapon effectiveness is a combination of the explosive used, the fuzing mechanism, and the warhead design. Delivery is a broad category, encompassing launching systems and the propulsion, guidance, and control of the weapon.

The fire-control problem from target detection to neutralization is, therefore, a complex integration of numerous subsystems operating in concert to achieve a common goal. This text will provide the reader with the basic principles and facts with which to analyze a weapons system's performance. Although the mathematical analyses appearing throughout this text are not comprehensive or precise to engineering accuracy, they do furnish the reader with basic thumbrules for evaluating or predicting weapon and sensor performance as an aid to imaginative use of tactics. Without a thorough understanding of the physical processes that alter the performance of equipment, the tactician is unable to make full use of his assets or exploit the limitations of his adversary.

1

Energy Fundamentals

Introduction

A paramount requisite of a complete weapons system is that it have some means of detecting a target. In order to accomplish this, the weapons system must be capable of sensing some unique characteristic that differentiates or identifies it as a target. One such characteristic is the energy that is either emitted or reflected by the target. This energy may be in several forms, including electrical, audio, heat, or visible light. A characteristic common to all the energy forms listed above is their manner of propagation. That is, they all propagate in the form of traveling waves and as such can be defined and categorized by their frequency and wavelength. It is the function of the sensor system to detect the appropriate energy form and to furnish the information thus obtained to the other components of the weapons system.

This chapter is heavily directed toward the properties of radar energy, but the principles presented here are the same for all other types of electromagnetic energy—such as radio, infrared, visible light, and X rays. Sound energy, though not electromagnetic, also exhibits many of these same properties, as will be described later in this text. It is imperative that a solid foundation in the principles of energy transmission and propagation be acquired in order to fully understand the design and use of various types of modern weapons-system sensors.

Characteristics of Traveling Waves

Energy moves from a source in waves, in much the same way as waves spread out concentrically from the point of impact of a pebble dropped in water. While the waves created by this familiar example are two-dimensional, electromagnetic energy radiated from a point in a vacuum travels in three-dimensional waves—i.e., concentric spheres. In the study of radiated energy, it is often difficult to describe expanding spheres of concentric wave fronts as they propagate through space. It is convenient, therefore, to trace the path of rays rather than waves. A ray is formed by tracing the path of a hypothetical point on the surface of a wave front as it moves through a medium.

Frequency

The principle distinguishing characteristic of any form of radiated energy is its frequency, which is normally measured in cycles per second or hertz (Hz). In the case of sound, it is the rate at which an object vibrates. For electromagnetic energy such as radio, radar, and light, it is the rate at which the electric and magnetic fields of a propagating wave expand and collapse. Since radiated energy is composed of periodic waves, it can be represented by a sinusoid or sine wave. The significance of frequency is clearly evidenced by the fact that the nature of the energy form (i.e., heat, light, electromagnetic, etc.) and its frequency are directly interrelated.

Figure 1–1 shows the electromagnetic spectrum from audio frequencies to gamma rays. Notice that radar energy is normally between 1 GHz and 10 GHz, but there are some exceptions. For example, some long-range air-search radars transmit between 200 MHz and 980 MHz, and over-the-horizon radars at an even lower frequency.

$$\lambda = \frac{c}{f} \qquad (1-1)$$

Wavelength

Wave motion is further described by wavelength (λ). Wavelength is most simply defined as the distance between two identical points on adjacent waves (normally crests). For a traveling wave, it is also a measure of the distance covered by the wave during one complete cycle. From the latter definition, a relationship between frequency and wavelength can be derived.

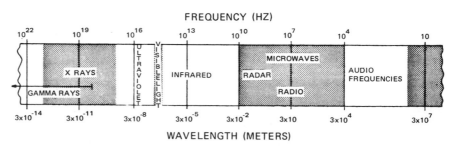

Figure 1–1. The electromagnetic frequency spectrum.

where

λ = wavelength (meters)

c = Wave propagation velocity in a particular medium (meters/sec)

f = frequency (Hz)

Wavelength is important in the design of radio and radar antennas, since *for any given amount of signal directivity, the size of the antenna is directly proportional to the wavelength of the energy being directed.*

Coherency

Any pure energy of singular frequency will have the waveform of a sinusoid and is termed *coherent* energy. Energy that is composed of more than one frequency will have some waveform other than a sinusoid and is considered *noncoherent* energy.

Coherent energy has two major advantages over noncoherent energy when employed in radar systems. First, doppler shift due to moving targets can be measured. Second, radar receivers with superior signal-to-noise ratios can be used. Radars of older design use noncoherent signals, since at the time of their development, the technology was not available to produce a high-powered coherent signal. Most radars produced today are of the more advantageous coherent type.

Velocity

Electromagnetic energy propagates through a vacuum at the speed of light, approximately 3×10^8 m/s. This equates to approximately one nautical mile every 6.81μs. The velocity in other media is less than in a vacuum.

The ratio of the velocity of electromagnetic energy in a vacuum to the velocity in a different medium is called the index of refraction of that medium. At radar frequencies and above, the index of refraction of air is very close to 1.0 and therefore is usually ignored.

Amplitude

A final characteristic of wave propagation is the amplitude. This may be graphically defined as the maximum displacement of any point on the wave from a constant reference value. Displacement is also a direct indication of the level of energy at any point on a propagating wave. In order to derive an equation that completely defines displacement in terms of time and distance, it is helpful to begin by investigating the simplified example of a standing sine wave at a single instant in time (see figure 1–2).

The y displacement of this waveform at any given point along the r axis is:

$$y = a \sin \frac{2\pi r}{\lambda}$$

The y displacement is solely a function of the lateral (r) displacement from the origin since the above waveform is fixed with respect to time.

Now consider a wave that is propagating to the right. To envision this effect, first imagine that the waveform of figure 1–2 is moving to the right at a constant velocity and then focus on the resulting variation in displacement at some fixed distance along the r axis. Figure 1–3 illustrates this variation. In it, the displacement of a point (P) at a fixed lateral position is observed at three successive time intervals.

At time t_1 the displacement of the wave at point P is shown in figure 1–3a. This displacement will vary as the wave propagates in direct proportion to the frequency of oscillation. Figure 1–3b represents some later time, t_2. Finally, time t_3 is chosen such that during the interval $t_3 - t_1$ the distance (Δr) traveled by the wave is equal to one wavelength ($\Delta r = \lambda$). This is illustrated in figure 1–3c. Note that point P has returned to its original position and has thus undergone a complete cycle. The time required for a full cycle is termed

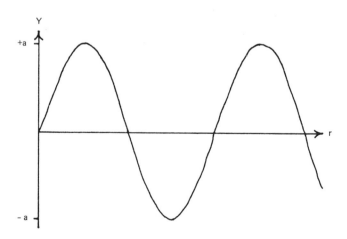

Figure 1–2. Standing sine wave.

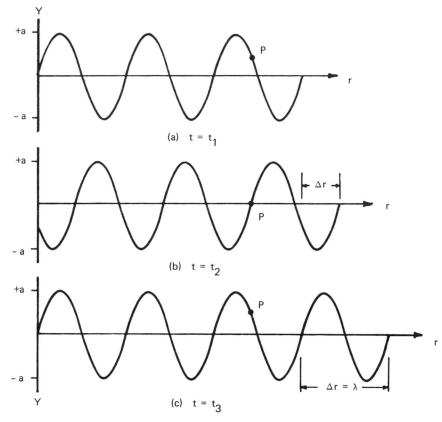

Figure 1–3. Propagating wave.

the period, T, and is mathematically determined as the inverse of the frequency.

$$T = 1/f$$

The number of cycles through which any point will have passed during an elapsed time (t) is equal to the frequency multiplied by elapsed time $(f \cdot t)$. Since a full cycle is equivalent to 360° or 2π radians, the phase angle of any point after an elapsed time (t) is $2\pi ft$.

It is now possible to express the displacement at any point on a propagating wave as a function of distance from the source, elapsed time, and amplitude:

$$y = a \sin \left(\frac{2\pi r}{\lambda} - 2\pi ft \right)$$

and since

$$\lambda = \frac{c}{f} \operatorname{or} f = \frac{c}{\lambda}$$

the equation becomes:

$$y = a \sin \left[\frac{2\pi r}{\lambda} - 2\pi \frac{c}{\lambda} t \right]$$

or   (1–2)

$$y = a \sin \left[\frac{2\pi}{\lambda} (r - ct) \right]$$

where

y = displacement in the y direction
a = amplitude
λ = wavelength (meters)
r = distance from wave origin (meters)
c = velocity of propagation (meters/sec)
t = elapsed time (sec)

Electromagnetic Waves

Maxwell's Theory

An accelerating electric field will generate a time-varying magnetic field. Conversely, a time-varying magnetic field will generate a time-varying electric field. Thus, a changing electric field produces a changing magnetic field that produces a changing electric field and so on. This means that some kind of energy transfer is taking place in which energy is transferred from an electric field to a magnetic field to an electric field and so on indefinitely. This energy transfer process also propagates through space as it occurs. Propagation occurs because the changing electric field creates a magnetic field that is not confined to precisely the same location in space, but extends beyond the limit of the electric field. Then the electric energy created by this magnetic field extends somewhat farther into space than the magnetic field. The result is a traveling wave of electromagnetic energy.

The Generation of Electromagnetic Waves

An elementary dipole antenna is formed by a linear arrangement of suitable conducting material. When the dipole is subjected to an alternating electric force, several phenomena occur that result in electromagnetic radiation.

An electric field is generated in the plane of the conductor that has a maximum intensity at the instant of maximum voltage. The

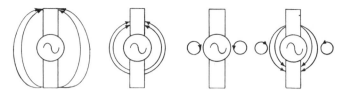

Figure 1–4. Generation of electro-magnetic radiation.

associated lines of electric force are illustrated in the dipole schematic of figure 1–4a. Note that the outer lines are bowed away from the inner ones. This is due to a natural repulsion between lines of force in the same direction. In figure 1–4b the voltage has dropped somewhat, and the separated charges, together with their associated lines of force, have moved closer to the center of the dipole. As the voltage continues to drop, the lines begin to collapse back into the antenna. The outermost lines do not collapse, however, and instead double upon themselves to form a closed loop. At this instant the voltage is zero as shown in figure 1–4c. As the voltage begins to build in the opposite direction, the lines of force reform as shown in figure 1–4d. The interaction between these new lines and the closed loops results in the repulsion of the loops away from the antenna at the speed of light.

It was stated at the beginning of this section that an alternating electric field will produce a magnetic field. The antenna in the preceding example must therefore be surrounded by a magnetic field as well as an electric one. A graphical illustration of this field is shown in figure 1–5. Since the current is maximum at the center of the dipole, the magnetic field is strongest at this point. The field is oriented in a plane at right angles to the plane of the electric field, as may be seen by comparing figures 1–4 and 1–5. Using the "right-hand rule" the magnetic field is as shown in figure 1–5.

The elementary dipole antenna of the foregoing discussion is the

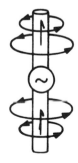

Figure 1–5. Magnetic field about a dipole antenna.

Energy Fundamentals   **11**

basic radiating element of electromagnetic energy. The constantly changing electric field about the dipole generates a changing magnetic field, which in turn generates an electric field, and so on. Because of the repulsion between lines of force in the same direction, the alternating fields thus produced are propagated out into space as electromagnetic waves.

The Electromagnetic Wave

In order to provide further insight into the nature of electromagnetic radiation, two approaches to the graphical representation of electromagnetic fields will be undertaken.

Figure 1–6 illustrates the waveform of both the electric (E) and magnetic (H) fields as they are mutually oriented in space. The frequency of these waves will be identical to the frequency of the voltage applied to the dipole. From previously developed relationships, their field strength at any distance and time may be defined as

$$E = E_0 \sin \left[\frac{2\pi}{\lambda} (r - ct) \right] \tag{1–3}$$

and

$$H = H_0 \sin \left[\frac{2\pi}{\lambda} (r - ct) \right] \tag{1–4}$$

where

E_0, H_0 = maximum field strength
c = speed of light = 3×10^8 meters/sec

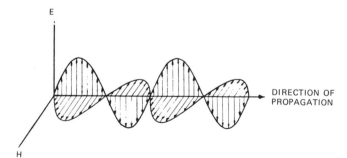

DIRECTION OF
PROPAGATION

Figure 1–6. Electromagnetic wave field orientation.

Frequency and wavelength for various types of energy throughout the electromagnetic spectrum are shown in figure 1–1. Past and present designations for various radar frequency bands are shown in figure 1–7.

12   Principles of Naval Weapons Systems

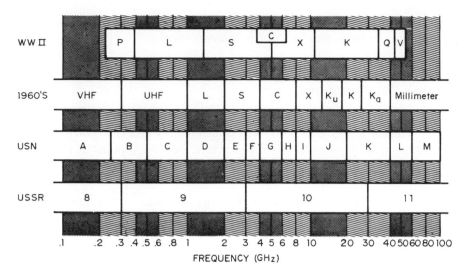

Figure 1–7. Radar frequency band designations.

Figure 1–8 illustrates the orientation of electromagnetic field components about a dipole antenna. The electric field (or flux) lines are represented by closed, vertical loops on either side of the antenna. Lines of magnetic flux are shown as dots and crosses to indicate flux out of and into the plane of the diagram. The darker waves labeled "curves of radial variation of flux density" indicate relative electric field strength at various radial directions from the antenna and would correspond to the E field curve of figure 1–6.

Note that both the E and H fields are strongest in the direction perpendicular to the antenna axis, as the amplitude of the "curves" shows. Conversely, there are only weak E and H fields propagated

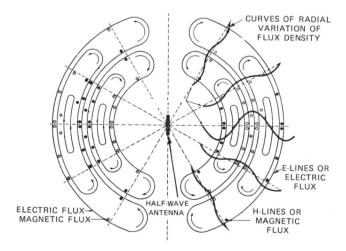

Figure 1–8. Fields in space around a dipole antenna.

from either end of the antenna. Thus, antenna orientation is a major factor in electromagnetic energy transmission.

Phase Relationships

Consider two dipole antennas, each of which is operating at the same frequency, but located such that one antenna is a quarter of the wavelength farther away from a common reference point as shown in figure 1–9a. For simplicity, only the E field from each antenna is shown.

The field strength at point A from antenna 1 is equivalent to $E_0 \sin\left[\dfrac{2\pi}{\lambda}(r - ct)\right]$. For antenna number two, however, the equation becomes

$$E_0 \sin\left[\frac{2\pi}{\lambda}\left(\left(r + \frac{\lambda}{4}\right) - ct\right)\right] \text{ or } E_0 \sin\left[\frac{2\pi}{\lambda}(r - ct) + \frac{2\pi}{\lambda}\left(\frac{\lambda}{4}\right)\right]$$

which can be reduced to

$$E = E_0 \sin\left[\frac{2\pi}{\lambda}(r - ct) + \frac{\pi}{2}\right]$$

where $\pi/2$ is the phase angle shift that would result from a distance increase of 1/4 wavelength. Therefore, rather than displace the antennas, the same effect can be achieved by shifting the initial phase angle of the energy supplied to one antenna by $\pi/2$ radians (figure 1–9b). This might be accomplished by advancing the initial excitation of antenna 2 by 1/4 period.

In general, the form of equation (1–3) that accounts for some initial phase angle, ϕ, other than zero is

$$E = E_0\sin\left[\frac{2\pi}{\lambda}(r - ct) + \phi\right] \qquad (1\text{–}5)$$

or

$$H = H_0\sin\left[\frac{2\pi}{\lambda}(r - ct) + \phi\right] \qquad (1\text{–}6)$$

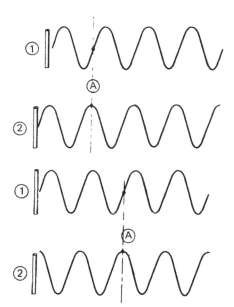

Figure 1–9a. Phase difference due to distance from source.

Figure 1–9b. Phase difference due to time difference.

Interference

Referring again to figure 1–9, it is now appropriate to discuss the total field strength at point A from the two sources. This total field strength is simply the mathematical summation of the instantaneous values of each individual field. This summation can be expanded to any number of sources and is termed interference. If the net field strength is greater than that of the individual fields, the interference is constructive. Conversely, if the net field strength is less than the individual fields, the interference is destructive.

For example, if the antennas of figure 1–9 were exactly in phase, the net field strength would be twice the value as from a single antenna (constructive interference). If the antennas had a phase difference of π radians (180°), the net field strength would be zero (destructive interference). Any other phase relationships will result in some intermediate net field strength.

Example. Consider a system in which two antennas are driven by a common source, except that the voltage reaching antenna number 2 is advanced with respect to that reaching antenna number 1, such that the radiation from antenna 2 is 90° out of phase with that from antenna 1. Determine the field strength of the electric field at a point P, equidistant from both antennas.

Since the antennas are both driven by the same source, the radiation from each antenna will have the same wavelength and amplitude. If point P is located a distance r from both antennas, the electric field at point P due to the radiation from antenna 1 can be represented as

$$E_1 = E_0 \sin \left[\frac{2\pi}{\lambda} (r - ct) \right]$$

Now, the radiation reaching point P from antenna 2 is *90° out of phase* with that from antenna 1, thus the electric field due to antenna 2 at point P is

$$E_2 = E_0 \sin \left[\frac{2\pi}{\lambda} (r - ct) + 90° \right]$$

The total field strength at point P, E_p, due to the interference of these two waves is the algebraic sum of two individual field strengths or

$$E_p = E_1 + E_2$$
$$= E_0 \sin \left[\frac{2\pi}{\lambda} (r - ct) \right] + E_0 \sin \left[\frac{2\pi}{\lambda} (r - ct) + 90° \right]$$

Now, apply the trigonometric identity

$$\sin A + \sin B = 2 \sin \frac{1}{2}(A + B) \cos \frac{1}{2}(A - B)$$

thus

$$E_p = 2E_0 \sin \frac{1}{2} \left[\frac{2\pi}{\lambda} (r - ct) + \frac{2\pi}{\lambda} (r - ct) + 90° \right]$$
$$\cos \frac{1}{2} \left[\frac{2\pi}{\lambda} (r - ct) - \frac{2\pi}{\lambda} (r - ct) - 90° \right]$$

or

$$E_p = 2E_0 \cos (-45°) \sin \left[\frac{2\pi}{\lambda} (r - ct) + 45° \right]$$
$$E_p = 1.414 E_0 \sin \left[\frac{2\pi}{\lambda} (r - ct) + 45° \right]$$

Thus, in order to determine constructive or destructive interference, it is necessary to look at the absolute value of the amplitude of this resultant wave, E_p. In general terms this amplitude can be written

$$2E_0 \cos -\frac{\phi}{2}$$

where ϕ is the phase difference between the radiating elements.

By comparing this amplitude to what would have been received by a single source, we determine the type of interference by:

$$\left|2E_0\cos - \frac{\phi}{2}\right| > E_0 \text{ (constructive)} \qquad (1-7)$$

$$\left|2E^0\cos - \frac{\phi}{2}\right| < E^0 \text{ (destructive)} \qquad (1-8)$$

Electromagnetic Energy Transmission

Wave Polarization

The electromagnetic energy field from a single dipole antenna resembles a huge doughnut with the antenna at the center of the "hole" (figure 1–10). A cross section of the surface of this field, taken perpendicular to the direction of propagation, is termed a wave front. All energy on a wave front is in phase by definition. Since E and H fields are mutually perpendicular, this type of electromagnetic field is described as linearly polarized, with the direction of polarization defined by the orientation of the E field. That is, if the electric field is horizontal (figure 1–11a), then the wave is horizontally polarized.

Wave polarization is particularly important in the consideration of electromagnetic signal reception. For example, a vertically polarized antenna would be largely inefficient in the reception of a horizontally polarized signal.

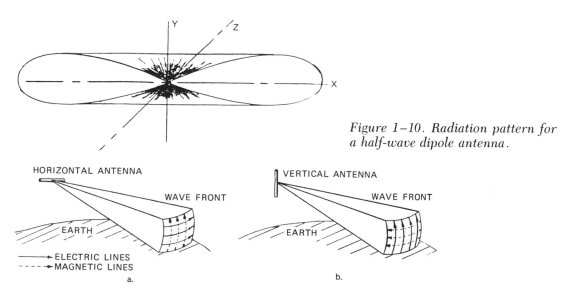

Figure 1–10. *Radiation pattern for a half-wave dipole antenna.*

HORIZONTAL ANTENNA

WAVE FRONT

EARTH

VERTICAL ANTENNA

WAVE FRONT

EARTH

——→ ELECTRIC LINES
– – – –→ MAGNETIC LINES

a.

b.

Figure 1–11. Horizontal and vertical polarization.

Electromagnetic Wave Propagation

Reflection

When a radiated electromagnetic wave encounters a conducting surface, reflection of energy from that surface occurs. This reflection is in accordance with the law that states that the reflected and incident waves travel in directions that make equal angles with the normal to the reflecting surface and are in the same plane. The angles are called the angle of reflection and the angle of incidence, respectively, and are measured from the normal to the reflecting surface. Uneven surfaces reflect a multitude of directions, and such reflection is called diffuse.

Reflection can be expressed in terms of the reflection coefficient of a surface, that is, the ratio of the intensities of the reflected field to the incident field. The most common measure of intensity is defined by the electric field strength. Often energy is lost from the incident wave because of the presence of natural obstacles such as dust, snow, or water vapor. These will cause some degree of diffuse reflection resulting in a loss in beam power. The greatest loss in field strength during reflection, however, occurs from the diffusion caused by the roughness and irregularities in the conducting surfaces themselves (figure 1-12).

Refraction

As an electromagnetic wave travels through the atmosphere, it is also subject to the phenomenon of refraction. When a wave strikes a boundary between two transparent media in which the velocity of light differs, the incident ray will generally divide into a reflected ray and a refracted ray.

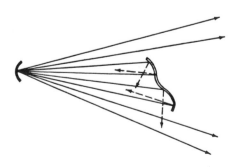

Figure 1-12. Diffusion from an irregular surface.

Figure 1–13 graphically depicts both reflection and refraction.

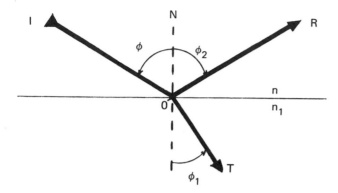

Figure 1–13. Reflection and refraction of an incident ray.

where

IO = Incident ray
OR = Reflected ray
OT = Refracted ray
NO = Normal
 ϕ = Angle of incidence
 ϕ_1 = Angle of refraction
 ϕ_2 = Angle of reflection
n, n_1 = Indices of refraction

The plane of incidence is the plane defined by IO and NO in the above diagram. The law of reflection or Fresnel's Law can be stated as follows:

The angle of reflection equals the angle of incidence, and the reflected ray lies in the plane of incidence.

Thus, the law states the IO, NO, and OR are all in the same plane and that $\phi_2 = \phi$.

The law of refraction, commonly called Snell's Law, states that:

The ratio of the sine of the angle of refraction to the sine of the angle of incidence is constant, and the refracted ray lies in the plane of incidence.

or

$$\frac{\sin \phi_1}{\sin \phi} = \text{constant}$$

If the indices of refraction are known, Snell's Law may be rewritten in the form

$$n \sin \phi = n_1 \sin \phi_1 \qquad (1-9)$$

While there are no clearly defined media "boundaries" in the earth's atmosphere, an electromagnetic wave will encounter several variations in air density. The index of refraction of air increases with density, and thus there is a downward bending of the rays of propagation as shown in figure 1–14. One advantage of such bending of the radar waves is the extension of the radar horizon slightly beyond the absolute line-of-sight.

Diffraction

Diffraction causes plane waves traveling in a straight path to bend around a boundary or obstruction. This may be observed at the end of a breakwater or a solid pier when ocean waves approach from an acute angle to the structure. The waves may be observed to bend around the end of the breakwater resulting in a reduction of the protected area shoreward from it (figure 1–14).

Similar effects can be observed in electromagnetic waves when an obstacle is encountered, such as the edge of an antenna or even large objects such as a mountain or island depending on the wavelength. This phenomenon accounts for some losses in antennas and the fact that radar contact or radio communication can sometimes be achieved behind an object depending on the geometry (figure 1–15).

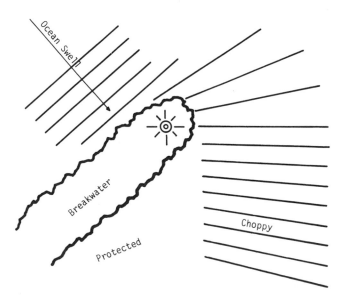

Figure 1–14. Diffraction of ocean swell around a breakwater.

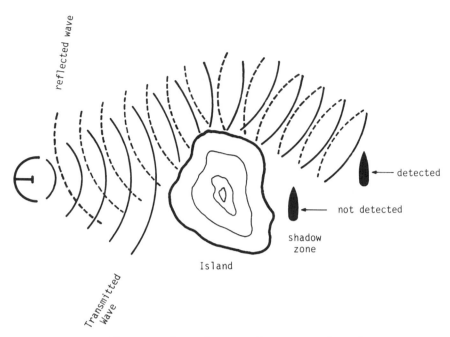

Figure 1–15. Diffraction of a radar wavefront around an obstruction.

Wave Propagation

Ground wave. At lower frequencies (table 1–1) and with vertical polarization, an electromagnetic wave will travel along the earth's surface (figure 1–16). With a highly conductive surface such as that provided by salt water, attenuation will be minimized and ranges will be extended over that experienced over dry ground. Over the horizon, ranges can be achieved due to the tendency of waves at lower frequencies to bend toward the earth's surface enough to follow its curvature. At frequencies above 5 to 10 MHz, excessive bending due to diffraction results in the collapse of the electrical field and complete attenuation. Ground-wave propagation requires wavelengths that are too long for anything but communications in ships and aircraft, but can be used by fixed, ground-based radar.

Sky waves. Layers in the ionosphere of altitudes from 50 to 500 km can be used to refract electromagnetic energy back toward the surface of the earth where it can be reflected to the layer again (figure 1–17). Using a series of these wave reflections and refraction, communications can be established at long ranges, but not with complete reliability. Care must be exercised in selecting the layer to be used and the frequency and the elevation angle of transmission, to ensure

Table 1–1.   Electromagnetic Propagation Characteristics by Frequency (From Leydorf et al.)

Frequency	Wave Type	Comments
20 kHz– 550 kHz	(1) Ground (2) Sky	(1) Effective to ranges of 500 nm (2) Very long range communications
100 kHz– 550 kHz	Sky	Increased ionospheric losses with increase in frequency
550 kHz–1650 kHz	Ground	Range restricted to primary service area
1650 kHz– 30 MHz	Sky	Skip distance, fading, daily and seasonal variations very important, reliability function of direction of transmission. Echoes possible in very long range transmissions.
30 MHz– 30 GHz	Space	LOS restrictions, multi-path, losses due to absorption by water vapor and other atmospheric gases.

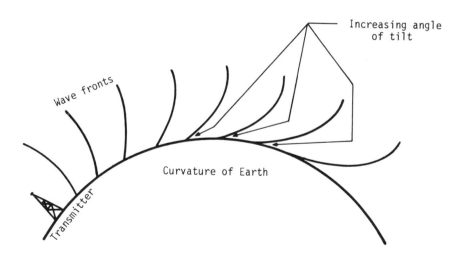

Figure 1–16. Ground wave.

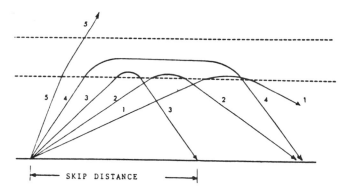

Figure 1–17. Signal paths for different angles of incidence at the ionosphere. (From Leydorf et al.)

SKIP DISTANCE

that refraction occurs in the layer selected and the waveform returns to earth at the desired point. Again, the frequencies involved are too low to be used for anything but communication by ships or aircraft, but may be used by ground stations for over-the-horizon target detection.

Space waves. Above 30 MHz the ionosphere will not refract electromagnetic waves back toward earth, and there is essentially no ground-wave propagation. In a vacuum, energy at these frequencies would travel in a straight line or direct path; however, due to changes in atmospheric density, it is refracted toward the earth, but not sufficiently to follow the earth's curvature. The effect of this is to extend the line-of-sight of the electromagnetic wave over the geometric and visual horizons to some extent.

Radar Line of Sight

At the high-frequency ranges normally used for radar transmission, the propagated energy follows an essentially direct path. Transmission and reception are therefore limited to "line-of-sight." At the earth's surface the "line-of-sight horizon" is the maximum allowable sepa-

RADAR LINE OF SIGHT

Figure 1–18. Extension of radar horizon as the result of atmospheric refraction of space waves.

Energy Fundamentals   **23**

ration between transmitter and receiver and can be readily calculated by the following empirical relationship:

$$d_{max} = \sqrt{17h_t} + \sqrt{17h_r} \qquad (1-10)$$

where d_{max} is the maximum separation in kilometers and h_t and h_r are antenna and receiver heights in meters, respectively. In the case of radar, h_r would represent the height of the target in meters. The above equation takes into account the bending of the ray due to refraction. Analysis of the equation shows an approximate distance increase of 16% over the direct or geometric line of sight that is given by the following relationship:

$$\text{GEOMETRIC } d_{max} = \sqrt{13h_t} + \sqrt{13h_r} \qquad (1-11)$$

Example. Calculate the line-of-sight horizon for a radar with an antenna height of 30 meters against a target at an altitude of 1,500 meters.

Solution: In equation $(1-10)$, the radar antenna can be considered the "transmitter," and the target can be considered the "receiver." Thus, $h_t = 30$ meters, $h_r = 1,500$ meters. Using equation $(1-10)$,

$$d_m = \sqrt{17(30\text{m})} + \sqrt{17(1500\text{m})} = 182.3 \text{ km}$$

Ducting

Unusual ranges for electromagnetic energy transmission at sea may be caused by abnormal atmospheric conditions a few miles above the earth. Normally, the warmest air is found near the surface of the water. The air gradually becomes cooler as the altitude increases. Sometimes, unusual situations develop where warm layers of air are found above cooler layers. This condition is known as temperature inversion. When a temperature inversion exists, channels or ducts are formed that will conduct the electromagnetic waves many miles beyond the assumed normal range.

With certain exceptions, ducts are formed over water where the following conditions are observed aboard ship:

1. A wind is blowing from the land.
2. There is a stratum of quiet air.
3. High pressure, clear skies, little wind.
4. Cool breeze over warm open ocean.
5. Smoke, haze, or dust fails to rise.
6. Received signal is fading rapidly.

Losses

Losses in electromagnetic energy transmission are primarily due to spreading and absorption. As the wave travels outward from its source, its energy is spread over an increasingly larger area, as an expanding circular wave in a pool of water. The energy per unit area of the wave front is proportional to $1/R^2$, where R is the distance from the transmitter. If the transmission is through some medium other than free space, *the molecules of the medium will absorb some of the energy as the wave passes.* The severity of this attenuation due to absorption is dependent on the medium as well as the frequency of the radiation. Atmospheric attenuation is essentially negligible at the lower end of the radar frequency band, but at the high radar frequencies it may become quite significant. This subject will be further discussed in chapter 10.

Summary

The nature of an energy form and its frequency (and therefore wavelength) are directly interrelated. The electromagnetic frequency spectrum covers a range of from less than 100 Hz to over a trillion GHz. The energy forms included in this range begin with audio and end with gamma radiation.

Electromagnetic radiation consists of both an oscillating electric field and an oscillating magnetic field, which, in accordance with Maxwell's theory, are mutually regenerating. The frequency of oscillation of these fields is identical to the frequency of the electromotive force that generates them. The fields are oriented at right angles to one another in a plane perpendicular to the direction of propagation. The orientation of the E field is used to define the polarization of the wave.

References

Bureau of Naval Personnel. *Basic Electronics.* Vol. 1, NAVPERS 1087-C, Washington, D.C.: GPO.

Commander, Naval Ordnance Systems Command. *Weapons Systems Fundamentals.* NAVORD OP 3000, vol. 1, 1st Rev. Washington, D.C.: GPO, 1971.

Fitts, Richard E., ed. *Fundamentals of Electronic Warfare.* Colorado Springs, Col.: U.S. Air Force Academy, 1972.

Ghatak, Ajoy K. *An Introduction to Modern Optics.* New York: McGraw-Hill, 1971.

Leydorf, Glenn E., ed. *Naval Electronic Systems*. Vol. 2, Annapolis, Md.: U.S. Naval Academy, 1971.

Miller, Gary M. *Modern Electronic Communication*. Englewood Cliffs, N.J.: Prentice-Hall, Inc., 1983.

Skilling, Hugh H. *Fundamentals of Electric Waves*. New York: Krieger, 1974.

2

Radar Principles and Systems

Introduction—Radar Principles

Radar is an acronym for Radio Detection and Ranging. Hertz demonstrated in 1886 that radio waves could be reflected by metallic bodies. In 1904 a German engineer by the name of Hulsmeyer patented an obstacle detector and ship navigation device. In 1922 Naval Research Laboratory (NRL) engineers A.H. Taylor and L.C. Young detected a wooden ship using a continuous-wave radar. The first detection of aircraft came in June 1930 by L.A. Hyland of NRL. In England, Sir Robert Watson-Watt was asked by the Royal Academy of Britain in 1932 if a radio ray could be directed as a weapon against enemy aircraft. He answered the question by saying, in effect, "No, but we certainly can locate the aircraft." His answer is the now famous "Death Ray Memo" in which he proposed an air defense system before anyone had built the first radar set.

Through the application of electromagnetic waves, a certain class of objects can be detected and located at far greater distances than that possible for the unaided eye. This seeing is unimpaired by night, fog, cloud, smoke, or most other obstacles to ordinary vision. Moreover, radar permits the rapid, convenient, and accurate measurement of the range to objects that it "sees" in a way unequaled by optical devices and methods. It can also measure the relative velocity of objects in a simple and natural way. Range and range rate information can be fed directly into fire-control systems with a precision unobtainable by a human operator.

Other aspects of radar performance are definitely inferior to that of the eye. The detailed definition of the scene radar offers is very much poorer than that afforded by the human eye. Even the most advanced radar equipment can only show the gross outlines of a large object, such as a ship or a coastline. Two closely spaced small objects, such as aircraft, may appear as one object to the radar. It is therefore best suited to dealing with isolated targets that are against a relatively featureless background, such as ships at sea, airplanes, islands, or any other large terrain features.

Radar systems employ two basic types of energy transmission: pulse and continuous wave (CW). The pulsed radar transmits radio frequency energy in a series of short pulses separated by non-transmission intervals or rest time. Target echoes are processed during these non-transmission intervals, and range is determined based on the total travel time for the pulse/echo. In CW radar, on the other hand, the transmitter sends out a continuous signal. If a non-moving object is in the path of the transmitted wave train, the frequency of the reflected signal will be the same as the transmitted signal. If the object is moving, the frequency of the reflected signal will differ from that of the transmitted signal, and that difference can be used as an indicator of target motion. In CW transmission, either a movement of the radar or the target is necessary to produce an indication of target presence.

Pulse Transmission

The pulse-echo system of detection is used in almost all radar sets. In this system, the transmitter is turned on for short periods and off for long periods. During the period when the transmitter is turned on, it transmits a short burst (pulse) of energy. When a pulse strikes any object, part of the reflected energy returns to the receiver, where it is processed and displayed on the screen of a cathode ray tube. Since the transmitter is turned off after each pulse, it does not interfere with the receiver (as it might if a continuous signal were used).

The elapsed time between the beginning of one pulse transmission and the beginning of the next is called the pulse repetition time (*PRT*) as shown below in figure 2–1.

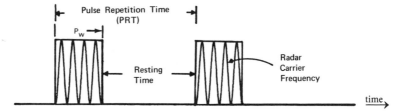

Figure 2–1. Pulse transmission.

This time must be of sufficient duration to allow the echo pulse to return from the maximum range of the system, otherwise the reception of an echo will be obscured by the succeeding pulse. An expression commonly used instead of *PRT* is the pulse repetition frequency (*PRF*), expressed in hertz, where *PRF* = 1/*PRT*.

The minimum range at which a target can be detected is determined by the pulse width, P_w. If a target is so close to the transmitter that an echo is received before the transmitter is cut off (and the receiver turned on), the echo will not be displayed. Because the pulse duration time must be short to increase reception of nearby targets and yet contain sufficient power to ensure a return echo of sufficient magnitude from the maximum range of the set, extremely large transmitted power outputs are required to produce a pulse of sufficient energy. The useful power of the transmitter is contained in the radiated pulses and is termed the peak power of the system.

Since the radar system is not transmitting for a long period of its total cycle, the average power is quite low when compared with the peak power during the pulse time. The relationship between average power dissipated over the entire cycle and peak power developed during the pulse time can be expressed by the following equation:

$$\frac{Average\ Power}{Peak\ Power} = \frac{Pulse\ Width}{Pulse\ Repetition\ Time} = \frac{P_w}{PRT} \qquad (2-1)$$

and, since $PRF = \dfrac{1}{PRT}$, the equation can be alternately expressed as

$$\frac{Average\ Power}{Peak\ Power} = (P_w)\ (PRF)$$

The greater the pulse width, the higher the average power; the longer the pulse repetition time, the lower the average power. The relationship between pulse width and pulse repetition time and between average power and peak power is termed the duty cycle. It represents the ratio of the time that the transmitter is on to one cycle of operation of the transmitter.

$$\frac{P_w}{PRT} = \frac{Average\ Power}{Peak\ Power} = \text{Duty Cycle (or Duty Ratio)} \qquad (2-2)$$

for example; a 2 microsecond (2 μsec) pulse repeated at a PRF of 5,000 Hz represents a duty cycle of .01, since the pulse repetition time is $1/PRF = \dfrac{1}{5000}$ sec or 200 μsec.

$$\frac{P_w}{PRT} = \frac{2}{200} = .01 = \text{duty cycle}$$

assuming an average power of 20 kilowatts, then for 2 microseconds 2,000 kilowatts are available. Peak power $= \dfrac{\text{average power}}{\text{duty cycle}} = \dfrac{20\ \text{kilowatts}}{.01} = 2,000$ kilowatts. The relationship is graphically presented in figure 2–2.

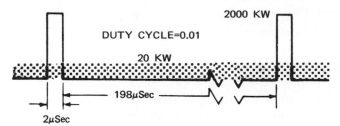

DUTY CYCLE=0.01

2000 KW

20 KW

198μSec

2μSec

Figure 2–2. Transmitted power distribution.

Range Determination

The effectiveness of range determination depends primarily on the ability of the system to measure distance in terms of time. Electromagnetic radiation travels in space at a constant velocity of 3×10^8 m/sec. When it is reflected, there is no loss in velocity, but merely a redirecting of the energy path. Range is then determined by the time required for a two-way energy transmission. The determination of range can be made by using the equation

$$R = \frac{ct}{2} \tag{2–3}$$

where

R = The distance or range from radar set to target
c = The speed of propagation of electromagnetic waves
t = The time required for the two-way trip

The propagation speed of electromagnetic radiation in various other units is approximately

1. 186,000 miles/sec
2. 328 yds/μsec
3. 3×10^8 meters/sec (use for problems)
4. 300 meters/μsec

Since range determinations are based on the measurement of time required for a pulse to travel to a target and return, radio waves traveling 186,000 miles in a second, for example, will travel 0.186 miles in a microsecond. This corresponds to a time of 5.376 microseconds to travel one mile. If the aircraft shown in figure 2–3 exists at a distance of one mile from the radar set, the reflected echo will reach the receiver 10.75 microseconds after transmission. This interval is the round-trip time and can be converted to linear range measurements.

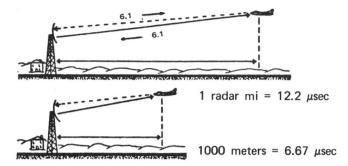

1 radar mi = 12.2 μsec

1000 meters = 6.67 μsec

Figure 2–3. Radar range-time relationship.

In order to use this time-range relationship, a time-measuring device is needed. The cathode ray tube is useful for this purpose. A time base is provided by using a linear sweep to produce a known rate of motion of an electron beam across the screen of the cathode ray tube.

The formation of the time base is shown in figure 2–4a. In (1) a radar pulse is leaving the airplane. At the time the pulse is radiated, the spot on the screen of the cathode ray tube is deflected vertically for a brief instant, then it continues across the screen to the right. In (2) and (3) the pulse is traveling toward the target, and the spot is moving across the screen. When the pulse strikes the target, there is no deflection, since energy is at the target itself. In (4) the reflected

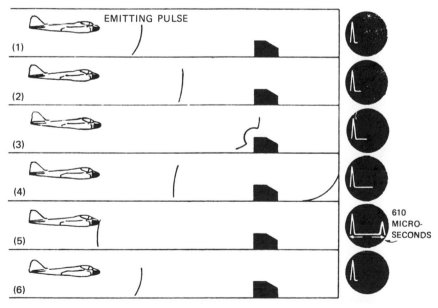

Figure 2–4. Formation of a time base.

pulse is returning. In (5) the reflected energy has returned to the receiver, and there is a second vertical deflection of the spot on the right side of the cathode ray screen. The distance between the two upward deflections serves as the basis for determining the range of the target from the radar antenna. Assume, for example, that the set is designed so that the spot moves across the cathode ray tube in 700 microseconds. The spot was almost to the end before the echo arrived, its position indicating that it took 610 microseconds to reach that point. Since radar waves travel at 3×10^8 m/s, the range of the target in the illustration is $1/2(3 \times 10^8) (610 \times 10^{-6})$ or 91.5 km ($\approx$ 50 miles). The last picture shows another pulse being emitted and the start of the formation of a new time base.

Figure 2–5a. Radar power amplifier klystron tubes. (Left) 1-Mw peak power pulse amplifier at 5400 MHz. (Right) 5-kw CW power amplifier at 10,200 MHz.

Pulse Radar Components

Radar sets vary considerably in detail as well as in the function they are designed to accomplish. The basic principles of operation are essentially the same for all sets, however, and a single radar set can be visualized in which the functional requirements hold equally well for all specific sets.

A typical pulse-echo type radar is composed of seven basic components—synchronizer, transmitter, antenna system, duplexer receiver, indicator, and power supply. The relationship among these components is illustrated in figure 2–5.

The *synchronizer* (also known as the timer, keyer, modulator, or control central) supplies the synchronizing signals that determine the timing of the transmitted pulses and coordinates the action among all circuits in the system.

The *transmitter* is a radio frequency (*RF*) oscillator that makes use of various circuit devices to generate energy having the appropriate frequency.

The *antenna system* receives the radio frequency energy from the transmitter and radiates it in the form of a highly directional beam. Any returning echos are received by the antenna and passed on to the receiver.

The *duplexer*, which consists of a TR (Transmit-Receive) and an ATR (Anti-Transmit-Receive) device, is employed to enable the use of a single antenna for both the transmit and receive cycles of the

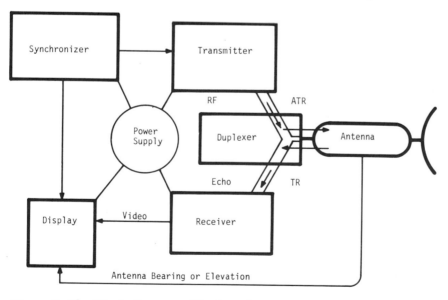

Figure 2–5b. Block diagram of basic radar set.

system. The TR device effectively blocks the transmitter output energy from entering the receiver during the transmit time. The ATR device ensures that all reflected energy is directed to the receiver during receive time.

The *receiver* amplifies the weak, returned *RF* pulses from the target and processes them into video pulses to be supplied to the indicator.

The *display* produces a visual indication of the existence of echo pulses in a manner that furnishes the requisite output information.

The *power supply* furnishes all a-c and d-c voltages necessary for the operation and interaction of the system components.

Continuous-wave Transmission

Rather than transmitting carefully timed pulses of radio frequency energy, a radar transmitter may be turned on and left on to transmit a continuous wave of *RF* energy. A continuous-wave radar cannot use the interval between the time energy is transmitted and the time it is received to measure range; however, it can distinguish moving from stationary targets through the principle of the doppler frequency shift.

Doppler Frequency Shift

When a radar transmitter and target are stationary with respect to one another, the wavelength, frequency, and speed of the transmitted and reflected energy are related by the previously developed equation, $\lambda = c/f$. If, however, there is any relative motion between the source and the target, there will be a shift between the frequencies of the transmitted and received energy. This shift is a function of relative speed and may be determined as follows:

Case I: Source closing on a stationary target.

If the transmitter is moving with speed *s* toward a stationary target, the wavelength of the transmitted energy will be compressed to λ' as shown in figure 2–6a.

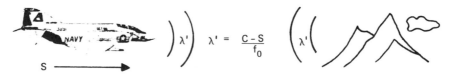

$$\lambda' = \frac{c - s}{f_0}$$

Figure 2–6a. Source moving toward a stationary target.

The target receives and reflects the energy at the new frequency, $f' = c/\lambda'$, due to the compressed wavelength, λ'.

$$f' = \frac{c}{\lambda'} = \frac{c}{\left[\dfrac{c-s}{f_0}\right]} = \frac{c}{c-s}f_0$$

This frequency is returned to the source that is moving with speed s, resulting in still another frequency shift in the energy actually received.

$$f'' = \frac{c+s}{\lambda'} = \frac{c+s}{\left[\dfrac{c-s}{f_0}\right]} = \frac{c+s}{c-s}f_0$$

which reduces to

$$f'' = \left[1 + \frac{2s}{c-s}\right]f_0$$

Since the speed of the fastest aircraft or missile is negligible compared to the speed of light, very little error is introduced by assuming that $\dfrac{2s}{c-s} = \dfrac{2s}{c}$.

Therefore,

$$f'' = \left[1 + \frac{2s}{c}\right]f_0$$

which results in a net difference, or shift, in frequency between f_0 and f'' of

$$\Delta f = \frac{2s}{c}f_0$$

and, since $f_0 = c/\lambda$, then

$$\Delta f = \frac{2s}{\lambda} \qquad\qquad (2\text{--}4)$$

Case II: Source and target moving.

As with the previous example, the transmitted wavelength is equal to λ' due to source speed, s_1

$$\lambda' = \frac{c - s_1}{f_0}$$

This wavelength impinges upon the target, which is moving at speed

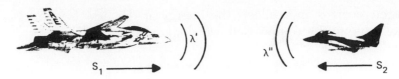

Figure 2–6b. Source and target closing.

s_2 as shown in figure 2–6b. The speed of the target results in a shift in the frequency of the energy received at the target, f'.

$$f' = \frac{c + s_2}{\lambda'} = \frac{c + s_2}{\left[\dfrac{c - s_1}{f_0}\right]} = \frac{(c + s_2)}{(c - s_1)}f_0$$

The target reflects energy at frequency f', but due to speed s_2 the wavelength is again compressed to λ''.

$$\lambda'' = \frac{c - s_2}{f'} = \frac{c - s_2}{\left[\dfrac{c + s_2}{c - s_1}\right]f_0} = \frac{(c - s_1)(c - s_2)}{(c + s_2)f_0}$$

Energy of wavelength λ'' is returned to the source, but the source's speed s_1 results in an increase in the received frequency, f''

$$f'' = \frac{c + s_1}{\lambda''} = \frac{(c + s_1)(c + s_2)}{(c - s_1)(c - s_2)}f_0$$

This equation may be reduced if it is assumed that $s_1 s_2$ is small compared to c.

$$f'' = \frac{c + s_1 + s_2}{c - s_1 - s_2}f_0$$

Letting $s_1 + s_2 = s$, the relative speed of closure is

$$f'' = \frac{c + s}{c - s}f_0$$

which, as shown in case I, reduces to a frequency shift of

$$\Delta f = \frac{2s}{\lambda} \tag{2–4}$$

where

Δf = doppler shift (Hz)
$\quad s$ = relative speed of closure (meters/sec)
$\quad \lambda$ = wavelength of transmitted energy (meters)

Equation (2–4) has been developed by considering the relative speed of closure between target and source. If the distance between target and source is increasing, equation (2–4) may also be used if it is realized that a relative speed of opening is simply a negative relative speed of closure. This means that an opening target will result in a negative frequency shift.

When calculating the doppler frequency shift due to a moving target, s is the relative radial velocity of the target. That is, only relative motion along the line of sight between the source and the target will result in a doppler frequency shift. Relative motion along the line of sight is the algebraic sum of the source velocity component and the target velocity component along the line of sight.

Example. An aircraft flying on a heading of 040°T at 450 knots detects an air contact on a bearing of 080°T closing rapidly. The contact's target angle is 000°. What will the doppler shift be for the onboard CW radar if its carrier frequency is 9.35 GHz and the contact is doing 550 knots?

Solution. It is always easier to draw a diagram first. Using the information available to you (course and speed of your aircraft, relative or true bearing to the target, and his course and speed) construct the following picture.

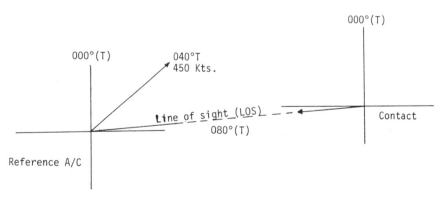

Figure 2–7a. Detector and target relationship.

Note: Target angle of 000° implies the reference aircraft is dead ahead of the contact.

Next, draw in the relative speed vector for both the reference A/C and the target. In this case, all of the target's speed is along the line of sight.

Find the angle between the reference aircraft's true speed vector

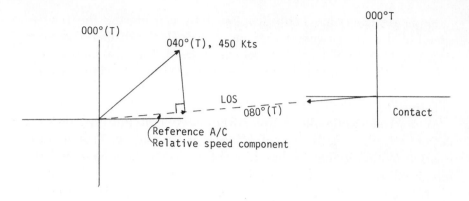

Figure 2–7b. Resolving line-of-sight relative velocity.

and the line of sight. In this case it is 080°T − 040°T, or 40°. The relative speed along the line of sight for the reference aircraft can be calculated by:

$$S_{ref} = V_{ref} \cdot \text{Cos } \theta = 450 \text{ kts} \cdot \text{Cos } 40° = 344.72 \text{ kts}$$

Note that S in the doppler formula must have units of meters/second.

$$\text{Convert: } 344.12 \text{ kts} \times \frac{.508 \text{m/sec}}{\text{kts}} = 175.12 \text{m/s}.$$

$$\text{For the target, } S_{TLT} = 550 \text{ kts} \times \frac{.508 \text{m/s}}{\text{kt}} = 279.40 \text{m/s}.$$

Now the algebraic sum of the relative speed components along the line of sight can be found:

$$S_r = S_{ref} + S_{TGT} = 175.12 \text{m/s} + 279.40 \text{m/s} = 454.52 \text{m/s}$$

Before the doppler formula $\Delta F = \dfrac{2s_r}{\lambda}$ can be used, λ must be calculated

$$\lambda = \frac{c}{f} = \frac{3 \times 10^8 \text{ m/s}}{9.35 \times 10^9 \text{ Hz}} = .0321 \text{ meters}$$

Now the doppler shift, Δf can be calculated

$$\Delta f = \frac{2S_r}{\lambda} = \frac{2(454.52 \text{ m/s})}{.0321 \text{m}} = 28331.7 \text{ Hz} = 28.33 \text{ kHz}$$

Radar systems that use this shift in frequency to detect moving targets are discussed in greater detail in the section on radar systems later in this chapter.

Continuous-Wave Radar Components

An elementary continuous-wave (CW) radar with a minimum of essential components is illustrated in figure 2–8a. The radar continuously radiates energy at a fixed frequency. There is no timing circuit of the sort encountered in pulse-echo radar because there is no pulsing of the signal. Because of the continuous operation, the peak power of the radar is equal to its average power; its duty cycle is unity. Energy is reflected back to the receiving antenna by objects within the beam.

A separate antenna is used for receiving since the receiver and transmitter must operate simultaneously. There is some danger that the transmitted energy will directly enter the receiving antenna. This can be reduced by locating the antennas some distance apart. If displacement is not possible, energy isolation can be provided by making the antennas highly directional or by using metallic baffles with absorbant material.

A weak sample of the transmitted *RF* energy is sent to the mixer where it is combined with the echo signal. The echo signal for a moving target will differ from the sample signal because of the doppler shift. The output of the mixer is a function of the difference, which is then amplified and sent to the indicator. Since there is no blanking of the receiver while the transmitter is on, there is no minimum detection range. However, the radar has no time reference and cannot measure range in a conventional manner. The change in received frequency due to the doppler shift is proportional to the target's

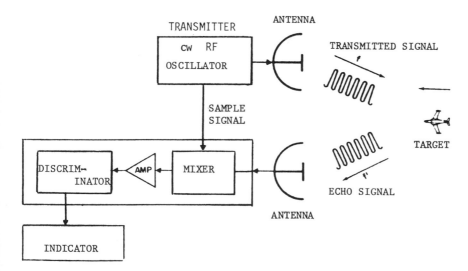

Figure 2–8a. Elementary CW radar.

velocity in the line of sight to the target. The doppler radar only measures radial velocity or that component directly inbound or directly outbound.

The doppler shift frequency band is measured in kilohertz while a typical pulse radar will have a bandwidth measured in megahertz. The comparatively narrow bandwidth of CW radar means a high signal-to-noise ratio. Most of the noise resulting from sea return, land masses, and other such undesirable targets will be rejected by the amplifier. Moreover, the amplifier can be tuned in such a way as to select desired frequency bands in the doppler shift bandwidth so that only the signals from targets of a certain range rate will be amplified. For example, the amplifier could be tuned to accept only frequencies that could be expected from the doppler shift of attacking aircraft. The radar would then single out only targets with those characteristics. This gives the radar a target selection and identification capability that is a distinct advantage in some circumstances.

The elementary CW radar that has been discussed has several inherent disadvantages. It cannot measure range. It is "blind" to targets with no radial relative motion and therefore no doppler shift. A situation where this blindness would be a definite drawback would be in a non-closing "tail chase" between two aircraft. Additionally, the CW radar in this example would require two antennas. The ability to separate moving targets from stationary targets is considered so desirable, however, that ways have been found to modify the more useful form of the pulse radar so that the doppler effect could be used. This merging of continuous-wave and pulse radars is discussed in the next part of the chapter.

Modulation

Radar and communications transmissions are modulated so as to convey information, to enhance signal processing in the receiver, or to deal with countermeasures of various types. Variation of the amplitude of the carrier wave form (Amplitude Modulation, AM), the frequency (Frequency Modulation, FM), or the phase (Phase Modulation, PM) may be employed in CW systems or be superimposed on the output of a pulsed system individually or in combination. Pulsing the output of a transmitter is in itself a means of modulation that can be varied in several ways to provide coding for information security or countermeasures resistance. The duration of a pulse can be varied as well as its position in a pulse train, carrier frequency, or amplitude. Many radars combine several of the above methods as a means of analog or digital communication with a weapon to direct its flight path, to assist its guidance system in target acquisition, or to activate fuzing systems.

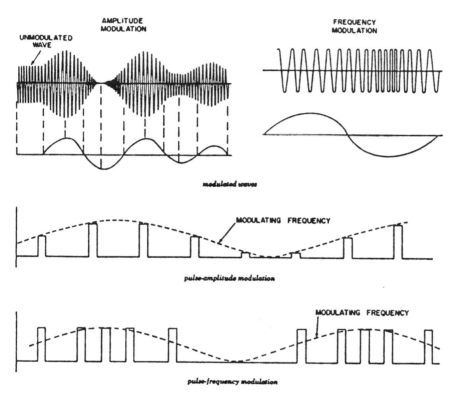

Figure 2–8b. Electromagnetic energy modulation techniques.

Radar Beam Formation and Antennas

In almost all radar systems, it is desirable to concentrate the radiated electromagnetic energy into a directional beam. This makes possible the illumination of a specific area in space and subsequently allows for accurate determination of the location from which the reflected energy is returned. An additional advantage is the obvious power increase in the desired location.

A radar antenna system has two general purposes. It radiates radio frequency energy developed by the transmitter and confines this energy to a narrow beam. Subsequently, the antenna receives the echo signals from targets and supplies them to the receiver. The antenna system must therefore employ some type of a reflector or refractor for beaming radiated energy and for concentrating the received energy.

Radar Principles and Systems   **41**

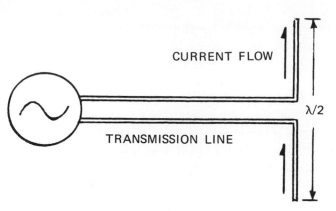

CURRENT FLOW

TRANSMISSION LINE

λ/2

Figure 2–9. Half-wave dipole antenna.

Half-Wave Dipole Antenna

The simplest form of electromagnetic antenna is the half-wave dipole and is illustrated in figure 2–9.

This antenna is created by bending the open ends of the transmission lines 90 degrees. Recall from the discussion of electromagnetic radiation in chapter 1 that this configuration will cause electromagnetic waves to be propagated outward into space. The physical length of this dipole antenna must be equal to one-half the wavelength (or a multiple thereof) of the transmission frequency in order to achieve optimum radiation. Under these conditions the radiation emitted from the antenna is in resonance with the exciting voltage.

A plot of the electric field intensity of a half-wave dipole antenna will produce the radiation pattern graphically illustrated in figure 2–10.

Beam Power Distribution

The radiation pattern for a point source antenna is a sphere surrounding the antenna, with power distribution (in watts/meter^2) that

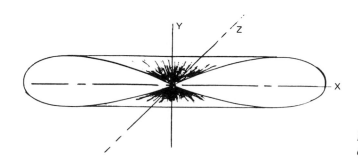

Figure 2–10. Radiation pattern for a half-wave dipole antenna.

is uniform, i.e., the same everywhere. As seen from the radiation pattern of the dipole antenna in figure 2–10, the power is not equally distributed. It is maximum along the X axis and nulls out, or goes to minimum, along the Y axis. If an observer were to walk around the Y axis of a fixed distance on the X-Z plane with a power meter, he would measure one constant value. If he stopped at any point and climbed a "ladder," that is, moved up parallel to the Y axis, he would see the power initially slowly decrease. The higher he went, the more rapidly the power would decrease until it reached almost zero somewhere near the 30–40 degree angle off the horizontal. Thus, for any given distance away from the dipole, the power distribution in height (and depth) is not uniform.

What is needed is a way to concentrate the energy along the X axis and limit it to a small angle away from the axis. Thus, a beam is formed. The power density of the beam would not be uniform, but would change not only in height, as a dipole does, but in width. (See figure 2–11.)

Thus, as the observer walks around the Y axis, at a fixed distance from the axis, and measures the power received, he finds a maximum power point along the X axis. Moving right or left shows the power level dropping off until it goes almost to zero. The width of the beam is measured as the angle between the points where the power has dropped to one-half the maximum (points A and B). The beam width serves as a measure of the angular resolution of the radar.

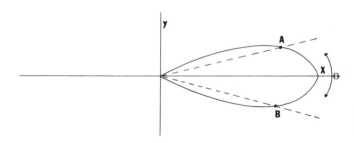

Figure 2–11. Top view of the radiation pattern of a beam, looking at X-Y plane.

Beam Requirements

The tactical application of the radar determines the requirements of the beam. The type of beam required for target search is different from that required for tracking or for in-close intercept applications. Because the purpose of an early-warning radar is to search for and detect a target at maximum ranges, high transmitter power, wide beam patterns, and scan rates that are consistent with the area to be

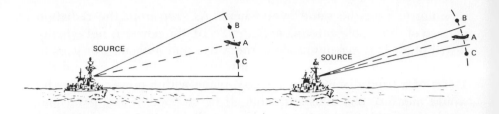

Figure 2–12. Beamwidth and target position accuracy. (Left). Wide beamwidth. The airplane at A can move to B or C without producing a noticeable change on the radar viewing screen. (Right). Narrow beamwidth. If the airplane at A moves to B or C, it can no longer be detected unless the beam is moved.

put under surveillance are the primary requisites. Accuracy of information output is sacrificed for maximum detection probability. When used for tracking or guidance—operations that require extreme accuracy—the radar beam must be a narrow width propagated at higher frequencies and rotated in a chosen segment of the entire search area. The narrowness of the antenna beam determines the accuracy with which the radar can measure azimuth and elevation. It also determines the angular resolution of the radar.

In order to obtain the greatest accuracy in determining azimuth angles, the beam must be as narrow as possible. As shown in figure 2–13, the relative signal strength is a function of angular position of the target from the lobe axis. The maximum signal is received when the axis of the lobe passes through the target.

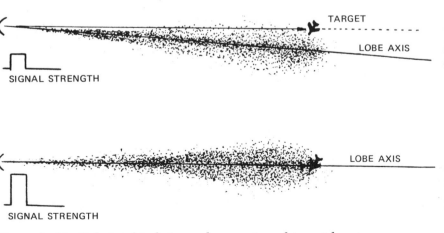

Figure 2–13. Relationship between beam axis and target bearing.

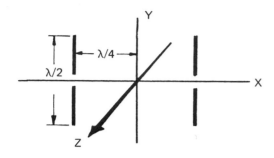

Figure 2–14. Two-element linear array.

Linear Antenna Arrays

There are two basic methods of concentrating radar energy in order to obtain directivity—linear arrays and quasi-optical. The first method is to arrange two or more simple half-wave antennas in such a way that their fields are additive in a specific direction and cancel in others. The principle of field summation and cancellation is the same as discussed in chapter 1 of this text. Such a set of elements constitutes what is referred to as a linear array, of which the two most common types are the broadside and endfire arrays. The second method is to use an antenna type referred to as quasi-optical.

Consider the case of two half-wave dipole antennas spaced one-half wavelength apart and positioned as shown in figure 2–14. An investigation will be made of the radiation patterns from these antennas in the X, Y, and Z directions. The investigation is based upon excitation of both antennas by equal, in-phase voltages.

For clarity of presentation, the Z direction will be investigated first. The diagram of figure 2–15 has been rotated 90° about the X axis in order to present an end-on view of the two dipoles.

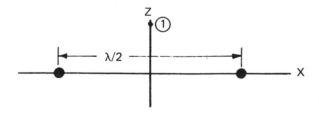

Figure 2–15. End view of two-element array.

Since the dipoles are equidistant from the Z axis, the radiation from antennas A and B arriving at point 1 (or any other point on the Z axis) will be in phase. Each wave will have traveled an identical distance. The field amplitude at point 1 will therefore be a constructive combination of the fields of antennas A and B and will in fact be equal to twice the value resulting from either element alone. A similar analysis holds true for the Y direction. Recall from chapter 1, however, that dipole antennas do not radiate significant amounts of energy along their linear axis and that the field strength will decrease correspondingly in the Y direction as the distance from the Y axis gets smaller.

A significant feature of this antenna becomes more obvious upon investigation of the X direction. Because the antennas are one-half wavelength apart, the waves from antenna A will arrive at a specific point on the X axis exactly 180° out of phase with the waves from antenna B. The resultant combination of the fields will produce a net field strength of zero.

It should now become evident that the proper spacing of multiple dipole antennas accomplishes two distinct means of directing electromagnetic energy in a desired pattern. The first of these is reinforcement of field strength in the desired direction and the second is the cancellation or reduction of field strength in directions where no field is desired. The resulting pattern of electromagnetic radiation from the two-antenna system that has just been described is shown in figure 2–16.

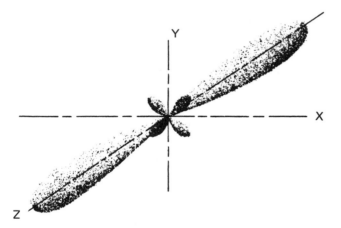

Figure 2–16. Radiation pattern for two-element linear array.

Note that there are main lobes in both directions along the Z axis and several side lobes.

The main lobe is the carrier through which the radar unit sends and receives information. It is therefore desirable to have most of the energy available concentrated into this lobe. Furthermore, since the bearing information provided by the radar is determined by the direction in which the main lobe is pointing, a radar return from a side lobe would be undesirable because erroneous bearing information would be obtained. In order to reduce the possibility that this situation will occur, the side lobes must be reduced in strength as much as possible.

Broadside array. The design of a broadside antenna array is based upon the principles discussed in the preceding section of this text. The directivity pattern of this unit is along the $+Z$ and $-Z$ direction (perpendicular to the page). Since the antennas are excited in phase, the constructive interference occurs in the direction of $\pm Z$, while destructive interference is established along $\pm Y$ and $\pm X$. A schematic of a 16-element (dipole) array is shown in figure 2–17.

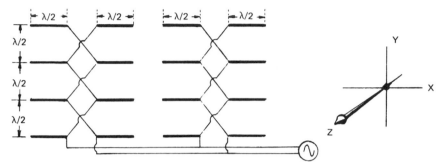

Figure 2–17. Broadside array.

The radiation pattern of this antenna is similar to that of the double half-wave dipole example discussed earlier. Field strength of this pattern along the $\pm Z$ direction will, of course, be greater due to the increased number of radiating elements.

Endfire Array. To this point the discussion of multi-element arrays has dealt only with antenna elements that are stimulated with the same input at the same time—that is, in phase stimulation. Consider what would happen to the broadside array of figure 2–17 if adjacent elements were stimulated 180° out of phase. The constructive interference would now occur along the $\pm Y$ axis instead of the $\pm Z$ axis. The directivity of this antenna will be in the plane of this text and toward the top and the bottom of the page. This discussion of phase shift in antenna excitation leads to a consideration of electronic beam positioning. By shifting the excitation of adjacent elements 180°, the main beam was rotated 90° from the $\pm Z$ direction to the $\pm Y$ direction. It is logical to assume that some intermediate beam directivity can be readily achieved through a suitable phase shift in element excitation. This principle is, in fact, used and will be discussed in greater detail in later chapters.

Parasitic elements. The directivity patterns of both broadside and endfire type arrays are still not optimum, since the main beams go

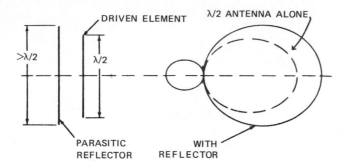

Figure 2–18. Radiation patterns with and without parasitic reflector.

in two directions. It is obviously desirable that the main radar beam be concentrated in one direction only. One method of accomplishing this is through the use of parasitic elements. A parasitic element is simply a conductor of suitable length that is placed in the field near the radiating antenna (driven element) and aligned in the same direction. The field of the radiating (or driven) antenna causes a voltage to be induced in the parasitic element. This voltage will produce a current flow and, if the length of the parasitic element is close to one-half wavelength, the element will generate some electromagnetic radiation of its own. The phase of the voltage induced in the parasitic element is such that there will be some degree of cancellation on the side of the radiating antenna and reinforcement on the opposite side. Figure 2–18 illustrates the radiation patterns from a half-wave antenna alone and from an antenna and parasitic reflector combination. Essentially, the parasitic element serves as a reflector and will modify the radiation pattern accordingly in a specific direction.

Quasi-Optical Systems

Reflectors. Earlier in chapter 1 the reflectivity of electromagnetic waves was discussed. This characteristic is put to use as a method for increasing directivity. Various types and shapes of reflectors can be used with driven elements and feeders to obtain increased directivity and a unidirectional radiation pattern. At radar microwave frequencies, reflectors with parabolic cross sections are used primarily. These include the full paraboloid, the parabolic cylinder, the truncated paraboloid, and the orange-peel paraboloid, in that order of usage. These shapes are illustrated in figure 2–19. The geometry of a parabolic antenna and its associated feed system is illustrated in figure 2–20.

The paraboloid employs a point source of radiation, such as a feeder horn or a dipole antenna with a small auxiliary backup reflector as a feeder, and produces a sharp parallel (pencil) beam. The parabolic

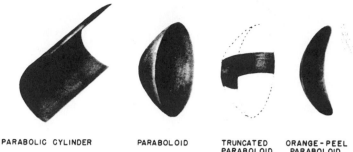

PARABOLIC CYLINDER   PARABOLOID   TRUNCATED PARABOLOID   ORANGE-PEEL PARABOLOID

Figure 2–19. Reflector shapes.

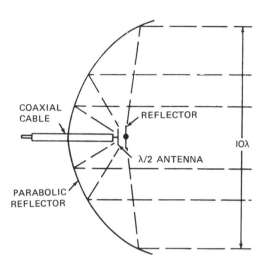

COAXIAL CABLE

REFLECTOR

$\lambda/2$ ANTENNA

PARABOLIC REFLECTOR

10λ

Figure 2–20. Parabolic reflector.

cylinder uses a line source, such as a dipole array, and produces a flat fan-shaped beam to cover greater volume of space for search purposes. The larger the reflector, the sharper the beam. Reflectors are made of sheet metal or wire mesh. Figure 2–21 shows a radiation pattern for a parabolic cylinder. Comparative lengths of the side lobes and major lobes are shown based on a maximum length of one. Angles shown are measured from the centerline of the main beam.

Lenses

In optics, lenses can be functionally interchanged with reflectors. Again, because electromagnetic waves behave similarly to light waves, lenses of various sorts can be used for microwave radar instead of reflectors or in conjunction with them. Some advantages of using lenses are: The feed horn or dipole can transmit directly through the lens towards the target instead of being in the path of a reflected beam, beam aberrations can be reduced, phase relationships can be better controlled, and side lobes can be reduced.

Radar Principles and Systems   **49**

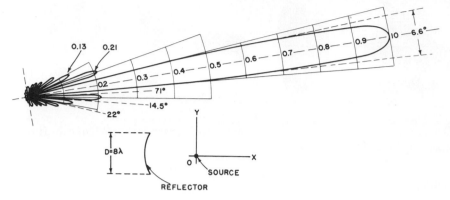

Figure 2–21. Radiation pattern of a parabolic cylinder.

The purpose of any such lens is to refract the diverging beam from a feeder into a parallel beam and vice versa for incoming radiation. Theoretically this can be accomplished by using as a lens material any medium in which the velocity of propagation differs from that in free space. A wave guide, for example, has a velocity of propagation greater than that of free space, while materials such as plastic, with a dielectric constant greater than one, have a lesser velocity.

A wave-guide lens is shown in figure 2–22. It consists of a bundle of wave guides that make it look like a concave egg crate. The reason for this shape becomes more evident when it is realized that the outermost electromagnetic rays must travel a longer distance to pass through the lens than the center waves. They would thus differ in phase if left unaltered. The longer outer wave guides provide a longer high-velocity path for the phase of these outer rays to "catch up" with that of the inner ones. The whole intent of this design is to achieve rays that are all in phase in a plane that contains the line AB in figure 2–22 and is perpendicular to the beam axis.

In the dielectric lens of figure 2–23, the short center waves are slowed down more in relation to the long outer rays to accomplish

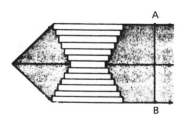

Figure 2–22. Waveform lens.

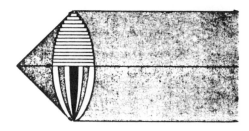

Figure 2–23. Dielectric lens.

the same effect. Such lenses are fabricated from layers of material of varying dielectric constants.

Wave Guide

At extremely high frequencies such as those employed in all but the lowest frequency radars, wire conductors, even coaxial lines, can act like a short circuit across the output of the transmitter. Under these conditions a simple hollow metal tube or *wave guide* containing some type of dielectric gas, such as nitrogen or dry air, provides the most efficient means of connecting the radar transmitter to the antenna. The wave guide can be of rectangular, round, or oval cross section, with the major dimension approximately equal to half the wavelength at the transmitted frequency. In the event that a frequency much lower than designed is employed, cut-off will occur, and transmission will cease. At high power levels, loss of dielectric constant or insulating ability of the gas in the wave guide could result in arcing between regions of opposing charge, ultimately causing catastrophic destruction of the system. Use of a wave guide requires a different concept of transmission of current and voltage because there is no second conductor to complete the electrical circuit. Instead, electromagnetic lines of force circulate across the major dimension of the wave guide with electric lines of force oriented across the minor dimension, inducing propagation the length of the line as depicted in figure 2–24a. When the open end of a wave guide is properly flared, an electromagnetic horn is created. These *feed horns* can be employed to release electromagnetic radiation directly into space. An RF transparent cover is placed over the open end to maintain gas pressure.

Angular Measurements

Determination of Azimuth or Bearing

The measurement of the direction of a target from the radar system is usually given as an angular position. The angle may be measured

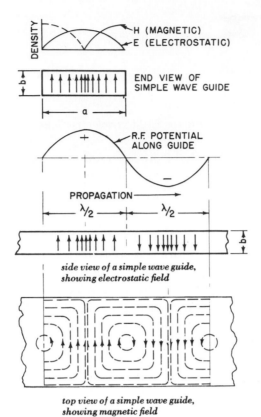

DENSITY

H (MAGNETIC)
E (ELECTROSTATIC)

END VIEW OF
SIMPLE WAVE GUIDE

b

a

R.F. POTENTIAL
ALONG GUIDE

+

−

PROPAGATION

λ/2 — λ/2

b

*side view of a simple wave guide,
showing electrostatic field*

*top view of a simple wave guide,
showing magnetic field*

Figure 2–24a. Wave guide.

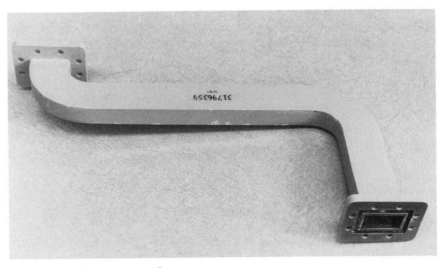

Figure 2–24b. Wave guide.

52   Principles of Naval Weapons Systems

from true north or with respect to the heading of a vessel or aircraft containing the radar set. The angle at which the echo signal returns is measured by using the directional characteristics of the radar antenna system.

Remember that radar antenna systems are constructed of radiating elements, reflectors, and directors to produce a single narrow beam of energy in one direction.

Single-Lobe System

The simplest form of antenna for measuring azimuth or bearing is one that produces a single-lobe pattern. The system is mounted so that it can be rotated. Energy is directed across the region to be searched, and the beam is scanned in azimuth until a return signal is picked up. The position of the antenna is then adjusted to give maximum return signal.

Figure 2–25 shows the receiving pattern for a typical radar antenna. Signal strength is plotted against angular position of the antenna with respect to the target. A maximum signal is received only when the axis of the lobe passes through the target.

The sensitivity of the single lobe depends on the angular width of the lobe pattern. The operator adjusts the position of the antenna system for maximum received signal. If the signal strength changes rapidly with angular rotation, the accuracy with which the on-target

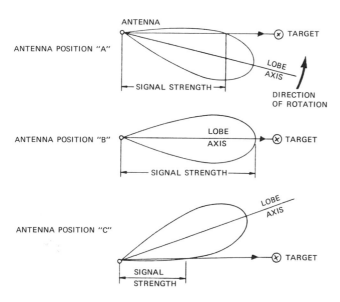

Figure 2–25. Relationship between beam axis and target bearing.

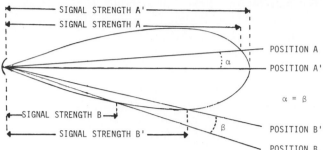

Figure 2–26. Accuracy of single lobe.

rapidly with angular rotation, the accuracy with which the on-target position can be selected is great. Thus, in figure 2–26 signal strengths A and A' have very little difference. If the energy is concentrated into a narrower beam, the difference is greater and the accuracy better.

Beamwidth

As stated above, the angular resolution characteristics of single-lobe radar are determined by the antenna beamwidth. Classical electromagnetic diffraction theory is used to establish the relationship between the physical size of the antenna aperture and its half-power points radiation pattern. Therefore, for a diffraction-limited antenna the beamwidth (radians) would be $\phi = k\lambda/l$, where l is the antenna dimension in the plane of the measured beamwidth, λ is the wavelength, and k is a constant of proportionality depending on the distribution of the electromagnetic energy across the aperture. A k value of $4/\pi$ is sometimes used for an intermediate or typical pattern. A conflicting characteristic arises with narrow beamwidths for good angle resolution. That is, as the beamwidth becomes narrower, by decreasing k, the side lobes generally become more pronounced. This can be a serious problem that will not be discussed, but it indicates that there are limits on beamwidths for a particular antenna.

Double-Lobe Systems

Figure 2–26 shows that the signal strength varies more rapidly on the side of the lobe than near the axis for the same change in angle. The greatest rate of change of signal strength per degree of change in azimuth occurs between the angles that give 50 to 85 percent of maximum. Radar systems designed for such applications as gun laying or fire control require the highest possible accuracy in measuring

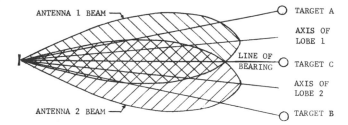

Figure 2–27. Double-lobe pattern.

azimuth. The double-lobe system achieves this accuracy by combining two lobes to form the antenna-system pattern.

The principle of the double-lobe system is illustrated in figure 2–27. Two separate antennas are combined so that their directivity characteristics overlap, but with lobe axes that are displaced by some small angle. In practical operation the antennas would be alternated in their use so that returned signals could be readily compared. Such alternate use of antennas is termed lobe switching and would be resorted to after a target had been located and accurate bearing information was necessary.

In figure 2–27, consider three targets in positions *A, B,* and *C* with respect to the two-lobe pattern. A target in position *A* would produce a much larger output when the antenna with lobe 1 is operated than with that for lobe 2. Thus the echoes, as received by the two antenna patterns, would differ significantly in amplitude. This disparity in outputs would give a clear indication as to the steering operation necessary to bring the echo amplitudes into comparison. When the pattern orientation is such as to place the target in position *C,* the echoes would be comparable. Further, they would change rapidly, and in opposite ways, with change in target bearing. This change would be easily recognizable.

The use of two lobes in this way would therefore serve a dual purpose. Once a target has been detected, lobe switching would greatly increase the accuracy of azimuth information. Secondly, a means to keep the radar "on target" is made available, since any difference in return strength between lobes could be inserted as a steering command to an antenna repositioning device. Although the double-lobe system can detect immediately the direction in which the target is off axis and although it is more accurate due to tracking on the edge of the lobe, the inherent disadvantage of a double-lobe system is that the signal strength is reduced due to the tracking off the beam axis.

It must be pointed out that the preceding discussion of double-lobe systems is primarily theoretical in nature and that such systems are not currently employed. The principles that were introduced, however, have a very definite application to automatic tracking systems, as will be shown by the investigation of conical scan techniques in chapter 5.

Determination of Elevation

The remaining dimension necessary to define completely the location of an object in space can be expressed either as an angle of elevation or as an altitude. If one is known, the other can be calculated from the right-triangle relationship and the slant range (figure 2–28).

The free-space pattern of an antenna array is based on the arrangement of the individual elements within the system. If the same array is placed close to a large conductive surface such as the earth, however, the vertical free-space pattern may be changed by the effect of ground reflection. Figure 2–29 represents an antenna above the earth that has been elevated sufficiently so that significant radiated energy will not be reflected from the earth's surface. Therefore, the only energy that reaches the target is that which comes directly from the antenna system. If the antenna beam is lowered to the position shown in figure 2–30, some of the transmitted energy hits the earth and is reflected back into space. Essentially, the target now receives energy from two separate sources, and the effective field is the resultant of the two fields so produced. The reflected wave travels farther than

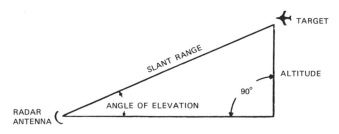

Figure 2–28. Determination of altitude.

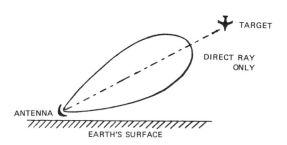

Figure 2–29. Antenna elevated to avoid ground reflections.

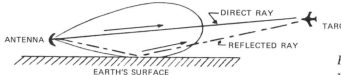

Figure 2–30. *Reflection of transmitted energy by surface of earth.*

Figure 2–31. *Typical vertical-coverage pattern.*

the direct ray in reaching the target. The addition of the fields at the target depends on the difference in the distance traveled. For example, if the path difference for a given target position is a half wavelength, the fields cancel each other—providing, of course, that the antenna and its image are of the same phase. If the position of the target is changed so that the path difference is a full wavelength, the opposite effect is produced. The result of ground reflection is to break the single free-space lobe into a number of smaller lobes, with gaps between them. This effect is illustrated in figure 2–31. The angle (in radians) of the first (lowest) lobe is approximately equal to $\lambda/4h$, where h is the height of the radar.

Height or Elevation Finding Methods

Any method used for determining the angle of elevation or the altitude must either make use of ground reflections or completely avoid them. The threshold-pickup method and the signal-comparison method use the effect of ground reflections to find altitude. The tilted-antenna method avoids ground reflections and depends upon the measurement of the angle of elevation.

Threshold pickup. This method uses an antenna system whose lobe axis is parallel to the earth. The positions of the lobes and gaps of the antenna pattern are determined by flying an aircraft toward the radar installation at known altitudes and recording the ranges at which a minimum usable signal is returned. A typical plot of this data (fade

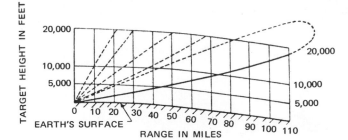

Figure 2–32. Typical fade chart for estimating aircraft altitude.

chart) is shown in figure 2–32. The chart obtained in this way is used by observing the range at which the unknown target first appears and then reading its altitude from the chart. This method is very inaccurate, primarily because the graph of the antenna pattern is determined by the use of a single aircraft, while the target may be any number of planes. In general, the greater the number of planes, the greater is the strength of the returned signal. Therefore, a large flight of planes at a given altitude will be detected at a greater range than a single plane.

Signal comparison. This method is simply an extension of the threshold-pickup method. Two antennas are placed one above the other to give slightly different vertical-coverage patterns. Although the lobes overlap, they do not coincide. The signals received on the two antennas are compared in magnitude, and their ratio, together with the range of the target, is applied to a height-range chart from which altitude is read. Under favorable conditions, the altitude can be determined within 500 feet. Inaccuracies due to the number of planes in a given target are largely eliminated because a ratio is used.

Tilted antenna. This method measures the angle of elevation directly, in the same way that azimuth is measured. Ground reflections are avoided by using the system on targets that are high enough so that transmitted energy does not strike the ground (figure 2–29). The accuracy of this method depends on the free-space pattern and the ability of the operator to locate the on-target position of the antenna array.

Stacked Beam. Some three-dimensional air-search radars find the altitude or height of the target by signal comparison. The beams of these radars are swept from the horizon to near vertical by use of frequency-scanning techniques. This creates in effect a *stacked* layer of beams at different frequencies. (See figure 2–33.) Each frequency produces a beam that is a known angle off the horizon. The target return will normally be in one or more beams. By comparing the return to the known position of the beams, the angle the target makes

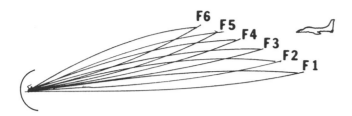

Figure 2–33. Frequency-scanning techniques.

with the horizon can be found. This allows a standard height calculation using slant range.

Radar Performance Factors

A detailed investigation will now be conducted of certain factors that affect radar performance. Such factors are carrier frequency, pulse shape, pulse width and pulse repetition frequency, the power relation (relation between peak and average power), beamwidth, and scan rate. The choices of these constants for any particular system will depend upon the tactical use, required accuracy and range to be covered, practical physical size limit, and the problem of generating and receiving the signal.

Signal Reception

Although the radar antenna transmits powerful pulses of directional electromagnetic energy, only a small part of this energy actually strikes a distant target. Furthermore, since the return energy from the target is reflected over a wide angle, only a minuscule fraction of the transmitted energy returns to the radar antenna. Thus, the function of the radar receiver is to receive the weak target echoes from the antenna and amplify them sufficiently to provide an indication of desired target information. The weaker the signal that the receiver is capable of using, the greater the effective range of the radar set. It is the steady improvement in receiver design that has made a greater contribution to the usefulness of radar than any other single development. Present day receivers are extremely sensitive, having been perfected to the point where they will discriminate signals on the order of a PICOwatt (10^{-12}) and will amplify and display them in many useful ways.

Signal-To-Noise Ratio

The absolute lower limit to the sensitivity of a radar receiver is set by a phenomenon called noise. Noise consists of any of several unwanted voltage inputs to the receiver that may ultimately obscure a weak target return signal. Noise may be attributed to many external sources, ranging from atmospheric disturbances to deliberate attempts made by opposing forces to saturate or jam the return radar echo. These are transitory in nature, however, and are less critical to the determination of system performance than the noise generated by the circuitry of the system itself.

A radar receiver has a means of setting the "threshold level," a level a signal must exceed to be seen on an indicator or be used in some other manner. Unfortunately, noise signals are not at one constant level and can vary as illustrated in figure 2–34. If a threshold level is set high enough to prevent any noise signals from appearing, the radar's sensitivity is reduced considerably. If the threshold is set too low, then too many false indications are seen, and the noise signals tend to complicate detection of the desired information. Therefore, a compromise level is selected by adjusting manually or automatically for specific operating conditions. The threshold level can then set the "false-alarm rate" of the radar, which is simply the number of false-alarm signals that appear in a given time period, such as one minute. The probability of a false-alarm signal occurring depends upon the threshold setting. The ratio of the return radar signal input to the noise voltage is called the signal-to-noise ratio.

It is a fundamental fact of electronic systems that there will always be some noise present. If nothing else, the fact that systems are not operated at absolute zero ($-273°C$) guarantees that there will be random electron motion in all electronic components. Electron movement constitutes a current, and this random current through any resistance produces a "noise" voltage in the system.

Receiver Bandwidth

The pulse-modulated carrier wave form consists of a series of sine waves having odd harmonic relationships that combine to form the nearly square pulse amplified by the transmitter. Thus, though the preponderance of energy transmitted by the radar is at the intended

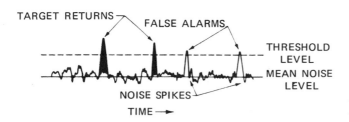

Figure 2–34. Comparative signal amplitudes and threshold levels.

frequency, the process of achieving nearly vertical leading and trailing edges results in inclusion in the pulse of additional wave forms other than the carrier frequency. The receiver must therefore be designed to detect and amplify a band or range of frequencies above and below the transmitted frequency. This bandwidth must be sufficiently large to accommodate all frequencies included in the transmitted pulse, or the pulse shape will be distorted by the receiver and degradation of performance will result. The presence of doppler shift in returning echos further increases the bandwidth requirements whether or not the radar includes doppler processing capability.

Typical bandwidths for radar receivers range from one to five megahertz. The gain of the receiver should be as uniform as possible over the entire bandwidth. If the receiver bandwidth is too wide, too much noise will be amplified. The result of this is that the minimum detectable signal (MDS) is increased. A high signal-to-noise ratio is required so that the receiver can detect a weak signal from a distant target and override the noise generated in the receiver. The amount of noise that will pass through the receiver is a function of the band-width of the receiver. In general, a reduction of the bandwidth of the receiver reduces the noise in the output, but does so at the expense of distortion of the pulse shape. The amount of distortion that can be tolerated is the limiting factor in increasing the signal-to-noise ratio by reducing the bandwidth.

Receiver Sensitivity

The need for the radar receiver to be sensitive enough to detect weak echoes from distant targets has been discussed earlier in this chapter. The sensitivity of a radar is measured by the smallest input signal (reflected energy from target) that can produce an internal electrical signal to the indicator (scope) that is discernible against the noise background.

Receiver sensitivity figures prominently in the radar range equation. The smallest discernible signal is denoted as S_{min} and is usually measured in milliwatts. S_{min} is sometimes referred to as Minimum Detectable Signal (MDS). The relationship between receiver sensitivity and S_{min} (MDS) is given by:

$$\text{receiver sensitivity (dbm)} = 10 \log_{10} \left[\frac{S_{min}}{1 \text{ milliwatt}} \right]. \quad (2\text{--}5)$$

For example, a receiver sensitivity of -87 dbm corresponds to a minimum discernible signal of 2×10^{-9} milliwatts.

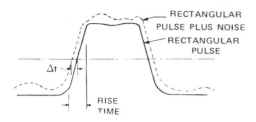

RECTANGULAR
PULSE PLUS NOISE
RECTANGULAR
PULSE

Δt

RISE
TIME

Figure 2–35. Noise-distorted radar pulse. (From Leydorf et al.)

Pulse Shape

The shape of the pulse determines range accuracy, minimum and maximum range, and resolution or definition of the target. The pulse shape is of little importance in the detection of a target as long as there is sufficient energy in the return pulse to cause a detectable echo at the receiver. However, the shape of the pulse is very important with regard to range and doppler velocity measurements.

The ideal pulse would have perfectly vertical leading and trailing edges. To do so in practice, however, would require an infinite bandwidth. This is because a square pulse would contain the carrier frequency plus all odd harmonics of that frequency. In actual practice, rise times (the time for the pulse to reach maximum amplitude) of 0.05 microseconds are commonplace. The steepness of the leading edge is a predominant factor in the accuracy of range determination. Slope of the trailing edge causes the receiver to remain blanked longer than necessary, reducing minimum range performance and target resolution.

Noise may also affect the shape of the pulse, thereby affecting the accuracy of range measurements. Figure 2–35 illustrates a typical pulse shape, with a pulse corrupted by noise superimposed (shown by dotted line). The time delay from transmitted pulse to receiver will, in effect, be shortened by Δt.

Pulse Width

The width of the pulse determines the radar's range resolution, maximum detection range, and minimum range. For good range resolution—that is, the ability to separate two targets at nearly the same range—a narrow pulse width is required. To calculate radar range resolution, use the radar range formula:

$$\text{RANGE RESOLUTION} = \frac{ct}{2}, \text{ where } t \text{ is the pulse width}$$

(*Note*: This is the same formula used to calculate minimum range.)

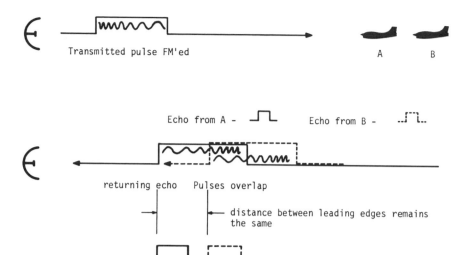

Figure 2–36. Pulse compression.

This determines the actual length of the pulse as it propagates through the air, from leading edge to trailing edge. Figure 2–36 illustrates that when two targets are separated by a distance less than the range resolution, the leading edge of the pulse will be striking the farthest target, while the trailing edge of the pulse is approaching the closest target. As the two pulses return to the radar, the leading edge of pulse B is hidden in pulse A.

Since the radar timer stops when the leading edge of the returning echo is detected and both pulses overlap, only one target would be displayed on the radar scope. A pulse width of 5 microseconds means a range resolution of 750 meters. Narrowing the pulse width to 0.1 microseconds gives a range resolution of 15 meters. Thus, the narrower the pulse, the better the range resolution.

From the foregoing it would seem that an extremely narrow pulse would be desirable. This is not always the case. In order to be detected, a target must return an echo that is strong enough to be indicated on the scope. The energy in the returned echo may be increased by increasing the peak transmitted power or by increasing the pulse width. The peak power that a radar transmitter may produce is limited by the size and quality of its power supply, power amplifier, and other components. Therefore, it is usually more practical to design a radar with a lower peak power, increasing the pulse width to

Radar Principles and Systems   **63**

maintain a sufficient total energy level. The important criterion in the detection of echoes is the amount of energy in the radiated pulse.

Another factor affected by pulse width is the minimum range. As previously stated, if a target is so close to the transmitter that its echo is received before the transmitter is completely off, the echo reception will not be processed. For good detection of close targets, small pulse widths are necessary, but again the limitations mentioned above come into play.

Pulse Compression

The amount of energy in a rectangular pulse is given by the product of peak power and pulse width. Thus, for a radar system that is peak-power limited, an increase in pulse width would lead to increased detection capability. It is also known from the previous discussion that increased pulse width reduces range resolution. Pulse compression is a signal-processing technique that allows the use of wide pulses to enhance detection capability while maintaining the range solution of short pulsed transmissions.

One method of pulse compression uses a transmitted pulse that is increased in frequency over the duration of the pulse width. When the reflected pulse is received, it is passed through a pulse compression filter through which lower frequencies pass more slowly than higher frequencies. Thus the frequency variation of the returning pulse results in the trailing edge of the pulse moving through the filter faster than the leading edge. This results in the pulse "piling-up" on itself. The output of this filter is a pulse of greater power amplitude and narrower pulse width. This modified pulse is then processed in the normal manner.

Figure 2–36 shows the effect of using pulse compression in signal processing. Notice that the energy or area contained by the pulses is the same in both cases. In the receiver, pulse compression circuits cause the leading edges of both echos to be delayed at the same time, with decreasing delay toward the trailing edge of the pulse, resulting in each echo becoming shorter and effectively increasing the amplitude.

Power Relation

Remember that in equation (2–2) the relationship between average power and peak power is expressed as

$$\frac{average\ power}{peak\ power} \qquad \frac{pulse\ width}{PRT}$$

High peak power is desirable to produce a strong echo over the maximum range of the equipment. Low average power enables the transmitter tubes and circuit components to be smaller and more compact. Thus, it is advantageous to have a low duty cycle. The peak power that can be developed is dependent upon the interrelation between peak and average power, pulse width and PRT, or the duty cycle.

Scan Rate and Beam Width

Another factor that enters into the PRF is the rate of angular motion of the antenna in searching extensive regions. If the antenna is moved through too large an angle between pulses, not only will the number of pulses per target be too low, but there may even be areas in which targets may exist without their being detected. In this connection, still another factor to consider is the sharpness of the antenna beam. A sharp beam must be pulsed more often than a wide beam to avoid skipping over targets.

The following equation shows the relationship of the antenna beam-width, PRF, and antenna scan rate:

$$N_B = \frac{\Theta_B PRF}{\dot{\Theta}_s} \qquad (2-6)$$

where

Θ_B = antenna beamwidth in degrees
$\dot{\Theta}$ = antenna scanning rate in degrees per second
N_B = the number of pulses returned from a point target as the antenna scans through its beamwidth. (Generally, at least 10 pulses must be returned from a point target for reliable detection probability.)

Pulse Repetition Frequency

As stated earlier in this chapter, the pulse repetition time (PRT) largely determines the maximum range of the radar set. If the period between successive pulses is too short, an echo from a distant target may return after the transmitter has emitted another pulse. This would make it impossible to tell whether the observed pulse is the echo of the pulse just transmitted or the echo of the preceding pulse. Such a condition is referred to as range ambiguity.

Although the pulse repetition frequency must be kept low enough to attain the required maximum range, it must also be kept high enough to avoid some of the pitfalls a single pulse might encounter. If a single pulse were sent out by a transmitter, atmospheric conditions might attenuate it; the target might not reflect it properly, or moving parts—such as a propeller—might throw it out of phase or change its shape. Thus, information derived from a single pulse is highly unreliable. By sending many pulses, one after another, the probability of detection is increased. Radar equipment is therefore designed in such a way that many pulses (10 or more) are received from a single object. In this way, the effects of transmission anomalies and pulse-to-pulse variations are averaged out.

Tactical employment of a radar set determines, to a large degree, the *PRF* to be used. Long-range search sets require a pulse rate slow enough to allow echoes from targets at the maximum range to return to the receiver before the transmitter is again pulsed. Higher pulse rates are used in aircraft interception sets where the maximum range is less.

The following equation will readily determine either the *PRF* or the maximum unambiguous range if one of them is known:

$$PRF = \frac{\text{Speed of Light}}{2 \times R_{unamb}} \qquad (2-7)$$

Thus, a radar with a *PRF* of 800 hertz could operate to a maximum range of about 187.5 kilometers without range ambiguity.

In theory, it is desirable to strike a target with as many pulses of energy as possible during a given scan. Thus, the higher the *PRF* the better. A high *PRF* combined with a narrow pulse improves angular resolution and range rate accuracy by sampling the position of the target more often. It was shown, however, that maximum range limits the *PRF*. A compromise is reached by selectively increasing the *PRF* at shorter ranges in order to obtain the desired accuracy of measurements.

Carrier Frequency

The selection of an appropriate carrier frequency is contingent upon several factors, including the directivity and resolution desired and the existing design limitations on electronic equipment.

For quasi-optical antenna systems, the higher the frequency, the shorter the wavelength and therefore the smaller the antenna required. Conversely, for an antenna of fixed dimensions, the directivity can be increased by using higher frequencies. Higher frequencies also provide for increased target resolution and enable the detection of much smaller sized targets because of the shorter wavelength.

The disadvantages of high frequencies include greater propagation loss (energy dissipation) and the inherent difficulties of generating and amplifying this *RF* energy. Frequencies from 100 to 20,000 megahertz are in general use, with the majority of the higher ranges being used in aircraft and missile fire-control radars.

Antenna Gain

A most important characteristic of any radar set is its antenna gain. It is a measure of the ability of an antenna to concentrate energy in a particular direction. Two different but related definitions of antenna gain are the *directive gain* and the *power gain*. The former is sometimes called the *directivity*, while the latter is often simply called the *gain*. The directive gain is descriptive of the antenna radiation pattern, whereas the power gain is an indication of antenna efficiency.

Directive gain. The directive gain of a transmitting antenna may be defined as

$$G_D = \frac{Maximum\ Radiation\ Intensity}{Average\ Radiation\ Intensity}$$

where the radiation intensity is the power per unit solid angle radiated in the direction (Θ, ϕ) and is denoted $P(\Theta, \phi)$.

As one might expect, the directive gain and the beamwidth bear an intimate relationship to each other. If Θ_B and ϕ_B are the azimuth and elevation half-power beamwidths, then the relationship is

$$G_D = \frac{4\pi}{\Theta_B \times \phi_B} \tag{2-8}$$

As an example; for a 3° beamwidth

$$G_D = \frac{4\pi}{(3/57.3)^2} \approx 4600$$

where Θ_B and ϕ_B are measured in radians.

Power gain. The definition of directive gain is based primarily on the shape of the radiation pattern. The power gain, which will be denoted by G, includes the effects of antenna losses and any other loss that lowers the antenna efficiency. The power gain is defined as

$$G = \frac{\substack{Maximum\ Radiation\ Intensity \\ from\ the\ Antenna\ of\ Interest}}{\substack{Radiation\ Intensity\ from\ Omnidirectional \\ Source\ with\ same\ Power\ Input}} \tag{2-9}$$

Because of the losses, this gain is always smaller than the directive gain. If there were no losses, the two gains would be identical.

It should be noted that although the power gain of an antenna may exceed unity by a considerable amount (because of the way it is defined), the efficiency of the antenna is always less than 100%.

Antenna Aperture

A secondary effect of antenna design is that which determines its effectiveness as a collector of energy. The amount of power available to the receiver is a function of the energy density of the returning echo (watts per m^2) and the effective area of the antenna in m^2. The antenna effective area or aperture (A_e) is related to the carrier frequency of the radar, the construction of the antenna, and the antenna physical size. The difference between the physical area of the antenna and A_e is a measure of its efficiency (typically 65 to 85%), thus:

$$A_e = \rho_a A$$

where:

ρ_a = antenna efficiency
A = physical area of the antenna (m^2)
A_e = antenna aperture in m^2

Antenna aperture and power gain (G) are related by the following:

$$G = \frac{4\pi A_e}{\lambda^2} \tag{2-10}$$

or

$$G = \frac{4\pi \rho_a A}{\lambda^2}$$

Notice that antenna gain, and thus directivity, increases as wavelength decreases for a fixed antenna size. Stated another way: *for a specific frequency, increased directivity (narrower beamwidth) requires a larger antenna.*

Radar Cross Section of Targets

The radar cross section of a target is defined as the area intercepting that amount of power which, when scattered equally in all directions, produces an echo at the radar.

The radar cross section is, of course, a characteristic of the target and as such is not actually one of the radar performance factors. However, it is one of the major factors affecting the strength of a radar echo. For most common types of radar targets such as aircraft, ships, and terrain, the radar cross section does not bear a simple relationship to the physical area, except that the larger the target size, the larger the cross section is likely to be.

When an object is illuminated by an electromagnetic wave, a portion of the incident energy is absorbed as heat, and the remainder is reradiated (scattered) in many different directions. The percentage of incident energy directed back toward the radar site varies greatly as the target aspect varies (often by a factor of 1,000 or more). Major factors determining the radar cross section are target size, shape, skin material, aspect angle, and radar carrier frequency. There is no simple formula that will give the cross section of an actual target such as a ship or aircraft. Thus, cross-sectional data is experimentally obtained, and the results are valid only for a specified frequency.

Figure 2–37 is a polar representation of the radar cross section of a typical aircraft. Notice the very large changes in cross section that occur as the view angle changes. Nulls and maxima are closely spaced. The variations shown are of greater magnitude than one may realize at first. Inspection of the scale in figure 2–37 reveals an overall change of approximately 33db. Recall, from equation (2–5), that a 33db change is the equivalent of a power ratio of 2,000!

Observe, also, that the relative size of the radar cross section ob-

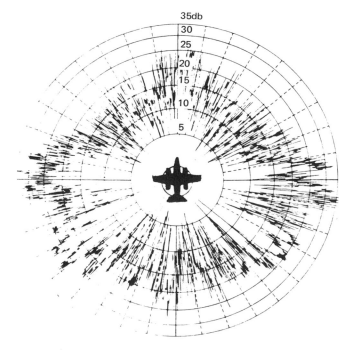

Figure 2–37. Experimental cross section of a tactical bomber-sized aircraft as a function of azimuth angle. (From Merrill I. Skolnick, courtesy Ridenour)

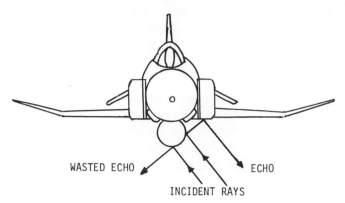

WASTED ECHO

ECHO

INCIDENT RAYS

Figure 2–38. Illustration of the manner in which the junction of wings and fuselage, and curved surface of aircraft, modify radar cross section.

tained from a broadside view of the aircraft is much larger than that corresponding to other views. Two factors are responsible for this. When viewed at 90 degrees:

1. the aircraft appears physically larger
2. the junction of wings and fuselage functions as a multiplicity of corner reflectors.

These effects combine to greatly enhance the radar echo. Figure 2–38 illustrates this effect. Many other portions of the aircraft serve as large convex mirrors that simply deflect the incident energy off into undesirable directions. This energy is wasted. There are important correlations between these conditions and a similar situation that will be encountered in sonar work shown in a subsequent section of the text.

Table 2–1. Summary of Radar Performance Factors

Factor	*Radar Characteristics Affected*
Pulse shape	Range accuracy; range resolution; minimum range
Pulse width	Range resolution; minimum range; maximum detection range
Pulse repetition frequency	Maximum unambiguous range; range rate accuracy; angular resolution; detection probability
Carrier frequency	Directivity; target resolution; propagation loss; size of equipment
Scan rate and beamwidth	Probability of detection; angular resolution
Receiver sensitivity	Maximum range
Transmitter power	Maximum range; physical size
Antenna gain	Maximum range

Indicators

The purpose of the indicator and its associated components is to display target information supplied to the receiver from the antenna system.

In most cases the indicator is a cathode ray tube (CRT) type. These may vary considerably in complexity and may display numerous data simultaneously to the operator. Some data that might be presented include:

1. Target range
2. Target bearing
3. Target range rate (velocity)
4. Target elevation
5. Useful symbology such as:
   a) artificial horizon
   b) steering references
   c) target designation symbols, etc.

The indicators commonly used along with displayed parameters are shown in figure 2–39.

The Simplified Radar Range Equation

Several of the aforementioned factors affecting radar performance can now be combined to develop the basic radar range equation.

If the peak power output of a radar transmitter is denoted by P_t and is radiated uniformly in all directions, the power density (power per unit area) at any distance R from the radar can be determined by dividing the transmitted power by the surface area of an imaginary sphere of radius R.

$$\text{POWER DENSITY FOR AN OMNIDIRECTIONAL ANTENNA} = \frac{P_t}{4\pi R^2} \qquad (2\text{--}11)$$

It has been shown, however, that radars employ directional antennas rather than omnidirectional ones. The power output of a directional antenna is related to P_t by the power gain.

$$\text{POWER DENSITY FOR A DIRECTIVE ANTENNA} = \frac{P_t G}{4\pi R^2} \qquad (2\text{--}12)$$

The above relationship defines the power that will reach a target at a distance R from the radar. The power that is reradiated by the

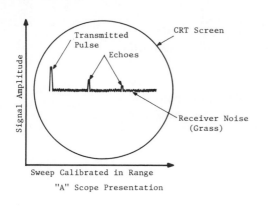

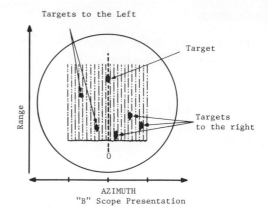

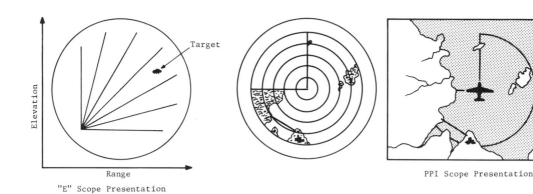

Figure 2–39. Radar indicator displays.

target is a function of the radar cross section of the target, σ,

$$\text{POWER RERADIATED BY TARGET} = \frac{P_t G \sigma}{4\pi R^2} \qquad (2\text{--}13)$$

The power that returns to the radar is again a function of the surface area of a sphere of radius R.

$$\text{POWER DENSITY OF ECHO AT RADAR} = \frac{P_t G \sigma}{(4\pi R^2)^2} \qquad (2\text{--}14)$$

Finally, only a portion of this echo power is captured by the antenna. If the effective area of the antenna is A_e, then the echo power, P_r, received at the radar is

$$P_r = \frac{P_t G A_e \sigma}{(4\pi R^2)^2} \qquad (2\text{--}15)$$

where

P_t = power transmitted by radar
G = antenna power gain
A_e = antenna effective area
σ = radar cross section of target
R = distance from radar site to target

If the smallest magnitude of echo power that the receiver is capable of resolving from input noise (S_{min}) is equated to P_t, then it becomes a simple matter to solve for maximum range of the radar. Since

$$S_{min} = \frac{P_t G A_e \sigma}{(4\pi R^2_{max})^2} \tag{2-16}$$

then

$$R_{max} = \left[\frac{G\sigma A_e P_t}{(4\pi)^2 S_{min}} \right]^{1/4} \tag{2-17}$$

This is the simplified radar equation. This equation was derived by considering only peak transmitter power. A more detailed analysis of the factors determining radar range would have shown that the maximum range of a pulse radar is dependent on the amount of energy contained in a pulse. Intuitively, it makes sense to say that if a radar transmits a greater amount of energy, the maximum range at which a target may be detected will be greater. The one-fourth power relationship occurs because the signal is twice subjected to the inverse-square law relationship that governs free-space transmission of electromagnetic waves having spherical waveform: the relationship applies first to power transmitted in the forward path and again in the return path. This fourth-root relationship between power and maximum range is the explanation of why long-range radars require such powerful transmitters. The following numerical example will illustrate this.

Example: A 100-kw radar can detect a specified target at a maximum range of 100 km. How much transmitter power would be required to detect the same target at 500 km (neglecting the effect of earth curvature)?

Solution:

$$\frac{R_2}{R_1} = \sqrt[4]{\frac{P_2}{P_1}}$$

$$P_1 = \left(\frac{R_2}{R_1} \right)^4 P_1 = \left(\frac{500}{100} \right)^4 \times 100\,\text{kw} = 62{,}500\,\text{kw} = 62.5\,\text{Mw}$$

The 62.5-megawatt transmitter does not exist. To make this possible would necessitate significant improvements in the efficiencies of transmitter and waveguide components to avoid serious losses in this part of the system. Evidently, to extend the range of this radar to 500 km, even with the aid of a more practical ½- to 2-megawatt transmitter, would require vast improvements in receiver gain, or large increases in antenna gain and/or effective area. Improved receiver gain implies maximum effort in noise reduction. It should now be clear why it is so important to reduce the noise to as low a level as technologically possible. It should also be evident that the cost of a radar is exponentially proportional to the range required.

Use of The Simplified Radar-Range Equation

This expression of the radar-range equation does not include terms for the values of the various losses associated with specific equipment, nor does it completely account for applicable statistical theory associated with detection. The term S_{min} assigns a detection probability of .5 to a situation where the returning echo power at the receiver (first preamplifier) just equals the noise level. While this chapter was not intended to provide sufficient range prediction accuracy for engineering purposes, it can provide to the tactician significant data concerning sensor performance where the actual detection range has been experimentally established for a target of known radar cross section (σ). Under conditions where the actual detection range has been established and a new range is to be determined for a given change in target size, gain, antenna size, power, or S_{min}, the terms for the non-included variables can be assumed to drop out when using ratio and proportion methods of problem solving. The assumed accuracy of the range determined in this way is sufficient for rough tactical decision making when used for that radar in the context of the equipment manufacturer's instructions and directives from higher authority.

Example: Recent fleet exercises have shown that your AEW aircraft radar can detect a target drone ($\sigma = 1$ m^2) at a range of 75 km. What range could a cruise missile be detected by the same radar if its radar cross section is .5 m^2?

Solution:

$$\frac{R_2}{R_1} = \sqrt[4]{\frac{\sigma_2}{\sigma_1}}$$

$$R_2 = \sqrt[4]{\frac{\sigma_2}{\sigma_1}} \times R_1 \qquad R_2 = \sqrt[4]{\frac{.5}{1}} \times 75$$

$$R_2 = 63 \text{ km}$$

Example: During operations in the Mediterranean Sea, the on-station E-2C detects a large contact to the north at 400 km with the AN/APS 125 radar (peak power 1 Mw). A power fluctuation causes the low-voltage protection circuits to shut down the radar. When operation is restored, it is discovered that MDS is degraded by 3dBm, and peak power is reduced to 750 kw. At what range will the target be detected?

Solution:

$$R_2 = \sqrt[4]{\frac{\dfrac{P_{T2}}{S_{min2}}}{\dfrac{P_{T1}}{S_{min1}}}} \times (R_1)$$

MDS degraded by 3dBm
means $S_{min2} = 2 \times S_{min1}$
$P_{T1} = .75\, P_{T1}$

$$R_2 = \sqrt[4]{\frac{\dfrac{.75}{2}}{\dfrac{1}{1}}} \times (400)$$

$$R_2 = 313.02 \text{ km}$$

Millimeter Wave Radar

This topic is presented because of the increased interest in these systems in recent years and also to demonstrate how one parameter (frequency) can affect the capability of a radar system. Somewhat arbitrarily defined, millimeter waves range from 1 mm to 10 mm wavelengths, or from 300 GHz to 30 GHz, respectively.

Extremely short wavelengths of millimeter radar cause certain fundamental, operational characteristics to be more extreme. For example, practical millimeter radars have narrower antenna beamwidths than do microwave radars. This should allow better angle resolution with relatively small equipment. Small beamwidths not only imply high accuracy, but also reduced vulnerability to jamming (enemy must detect beam) and the ability to track at low altitudes without multipath interference from earth reflections.

Another way that radar performance is affected is in doppler shift from moving targets. From equation (2–4) it should be obvious that as the wavelength decreases, the doppler frequency shift will increase. This makes it easier to detect targets with small relative speeds.

One major limitation of millimeter wave radar is that high frequencies are much more susceptible to atmospheric absorption and propagate only a fraction of the distance of lower frequencies. In fact, the absorption is so severe that to obtain reasonable propagation ranges (20 km) the operating frequency must be selected from bands centered at approximately 35, 95, 140, or 220 GHz. These regions are called propagation "windows" (windows will be discussed further in chapter 10). Within these windows, propagation through dry contaminants such as dust and smoke is good as compared to infrared systems. However, this "limitation" may also be used to an advantage. For example, if short-range operation is required to avoid detection, then a frequency outside a window may be suitable.

This discussion of millimeter radar is not complete, but hopefully has provided the student with some appreciation of how a single parameter can change the operational capability of the radar.

Environmental Considerations

When operating high-energy *RF* sources, care must be exercised because of the possibility that mutual influence among various transmitters and receivers exists. In many cases signals from other similar systems can constitute a serious interference threat. This interference can be divided into two broad categories: antenna-to-antenna coupling and non-antenna coupling.

Antenna-to-Antenna Coupling

High levels of energy coupled into a receiving antenna pose a severe interference threat. In addition, reception of these high-energy signals can cause degradation or burnout of crystal detectors.

Non-antenna Coupling

Anomalous detection. Anomalous detection of *RF* signals can occur in a variety of equipment: public address systems, motion picture sound systems, hi-fi systems, etc. In addition, lifelines and other metallic standing rigging aboard ships can act as receiving antennas for this energy. If not properly grounded, or if corrosion results in poor metal-to-metal contact, arcing can occur, which would degrade radio communications and could result in an electrical shock hazard.

Hazards to ordnance (HERO). RF energy coupled into the circuit wiring of electrically fired ordnance can create fields high enough to cause premature ignition of rocket motors or dud the weapon. In most cases specific distance requirements between the transmitter and the ordnance are specified.

Hazards to personnel (RADHAZ). Human tissue absorbs the energy present in these *RF* waves with a resultant temperature rise. Frequency ranges beween 1–3 GHz can result in as high as almost 100% absorption. Below 1 GHz, absorption is less than 40%; however, a new danger exists. Because of the longer wavelength, penetration into the body is deeper. As a result, heating of internal organs occurs, which is not as apparent as the rise in skin temperature. When operating high-energy devices, care must be taken to prevent accidental irradiation of personnel close to the transmitter. Above 3 GHz, much of the energy is reflected, but absorption still accounts for about 40% of this energy.

Introduction—Radar Systems

In the first part of this chapter, the basic principles of radar operation were discussed. Two basic types of radar were introduced, pulse-echo and continuous wave. Historically, the first radars used CW transmission, but the inability to measure target range served as an impetus for the development of pulse-echo radar sets. More advanced radar technology led to the development of radars that combine the advantages of range determination with those of velocity discrimination.

In this part of the chapter, some more advanced radar technology will be discussed. It will be shown how a CW radar can be made to measure range through the use of frequency modulation. Then a common signal processing scheme known as pulse compression will be discussed. Finally, this part will conclude with a discussion of pulse doppler and MTI radar systems.

Frequency Modulated CW Radars

In addition to the classic pulse-echo techniques, radar systems may employ an alternate means to detect target range. A method in common use is the frequency modulation technique. An example of a frequency-modulated output signal is plotted against time in the frequency modulation chart of figure 2–40. As shown, the frequency of the output signal is caused to increase linearly from 420 MHz to 460

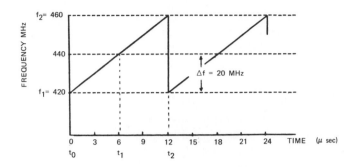

Figure 2–40. Frequency modulation chart. (From Leydorf et al.)

MHz and then quickly return to 420 MHz. The sequence begins again at 420 MHz and repeats continuously.

Since the frequency changes regularly through a range of 40 MHz as a programmed function of time, its value at any instant in the cycle can be used as the basis for computing the time elapsed after the start of that sequence. For example, at time t_0, the transmitter sends out a 420 MHz signal that travels toward an object. It strikes the object and returns to the receiver at time t_1. At this time, the transmitter is sending out a new frequency of 440 MHz. Thus, since f changes from 420 to 460 MHz in an interval of 12.0 microseconds, the time required for the 420 MHz signal to change from 420 to 440 MHz is 20/40 of 12.0 or 6.0 microseconds. (Recall that this round-trip time is equivalent to a radar range of one-half mile.)

In the frequency modulation system, when an echo is received, two separate signals are supplied to the receiver simultaneously. For example, at t_1, both the 440 MHz transmitted signal and the 420 MHz reflected signal are fed to the receiver. When these two signals are

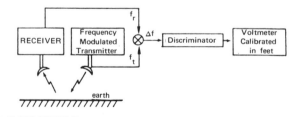

A. BLOCK DIAGRAM

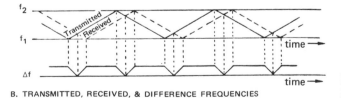

B. TRANSMITTED, RECEIVED, & DIFFERENCE FREQUENCIES

Figure 2–41. Radar altimeter. (From Leydorf et al.)

mixed in the receiver, a beat note results. The frequency of the beat note varies directly with the distance to the object, increasing as the distance increases. A device that measures frequency can be calibrated to indicate range (distance to object).

The best example of a frequency modulated (FM) radar is the common radar altimeter found on board some aircraft and cruise missiles. Its function is to measure the absolute altitude of the aircraft, i.e., to measure the range of the earth from the aircraft. A simple block diagram of a typical radar altimeter is shown in figure 2–41.

In this example the frequency of the transmitted output is swept from f_1 to f_2 and back again, both excursions being executed at a linear rate. The reflected wave from a point on the earth's surface is identical to the transmitted wave except for a time delay, and hence frequency difference, which depends on altitude. Inside the radar, the transmitted and received frequencies beat together to produce a difference frequency Δf. Several possibilities exist for displaying the output data. One such system produces a direct output voltage proportional to frequency difference.

Combination Systems

A nuisance factor that sometimes seriously degrades the performance of search radar (and pulse radar in general) is clutter. Clutter is produced by echoes from stationary or low-velocity targets such as trees, waves, buildings, terrain features, etc. The effect of stationary targets is to clutter up the scope and make the detection of ships and aircraft more difficult. A system that will reject clutter but accept moving targets is often highly desirable.

As an example, consider a target aircraft flying close to the ground in order to avoid detection. Echoes from the target and any nearby terrain features would arrive simultaneously. If a conventional radar were in use, the target return would be masked by the return from the larger terrain features. A radar system sensitive to moving targets, however, would reject the ground return and thereby highlight the target.

The purpose of this section is to examine the methods that allow the rejection of stationary targets by a pulse radar. The fundamental principle of operation depends upon the fact that echoes from a nonmoving target will return to the radar site after a fixed delay. On the other hand, the delay associated with a moving target will vary from pulse to pulse. It will increase or decrease depending upon whether target range is increasing or decreasing.

Velocity-discriminating radar sets may be designed either as a pulse-modulated doppler radar or as a moving target indicator (MTI) radar. Both types of radar operate under the same physical principles, and the distinction is generally based upon the fact that pulse doppler radars provide better velocity discrimination and clutter rejection, whereas MTI radars provide more accurate range resolution.

Velocity Discrimination

If a basic CW radar system were modified to pulse the transmitted energy instead of transmitting continuously, a simple system for detecting moving targets would be the result. A diagram of such a system is shown in figure 2–42. Essentially, the system is a pulse-echo system, with one important difference; the receiver is sensitive to frequency shifts within the echo pulse.

For a non-moving target, the phase *difference* between pulses transmitted from this system and echo pulses would be constant. If the target has a relative velocity, however, the phase difference between successive pulses will vary. This variation is due to the changing distance that must be traveled by each pulse. Since the target moves a distance equal to $V_t T$ between pulses (where V_t = target velocity and T = pulse repetition time), the round-trip distance will change by $2V_t T$. This distance change is alternately expressed as $2V_t T/\lambda$ wavelengths, which equates to a phase angle difference of $2\pi \dfrac{2V_t}{\lambda} T$. Note that $\dfrac{2V_t}{\lambda}$ is the frequency shift due to the doppler effect.

Successive return pulses are sent from a receiver to a phase detector where they are compared to a sample of the transmitted signal. The output of the phase detector for both fixed and moving targets is shown in figure 2–43. Since there is a constant phase difference for fixed targets, the output is a constant amplitude. The output for a moving target fluctuates in amplitude because of the change in phase difference. However, this fluctuation in voltage amplitude is not easily

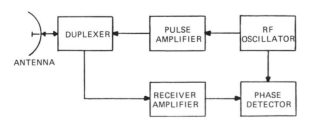

Figure 2–42. Elementary pulse-modulated doppler system.

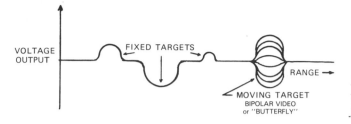

Figure 2–43. An "A" scope presentation of phase detector output for fixed and moving targets.

implemented into a meaningful indicator display. Therefore, further processing is normally performed on this doppler information.

Pulse-Doppler Radar

The phase-detector output may be processed in at least two distinctively different ways in order to eliminate the stationary targets. The first technique stems from the fact that the rate of change in phase between the transmitted signal and the echo is simply the doppler frequency, as previously shown. Thus, by routing the return signal through a frequency-filtering device, any unwanted echoes can be selectively eliminated. Such a device is called a *bandpass filter*. It will allow passage of only those signals that possess frequency characteristics within the narrow band for which it was designed. The filters in current use are sensitive to velocity changes on the order of 3 meters/sec. Signals from stationary targets can therefore be blocked from reaching the indicator. A series of bandpass filters can be used to provide a means of distinguishing between targets of different velocity characteristics as shown in figure 2–44. For airborne applications, stationary targets would appear to close with a relative velocity equal to the velocity of the target aircraft. It is a fairly simple matter to selectively "turn off" the appropriate bandpass filter that corresponds to this velocity.

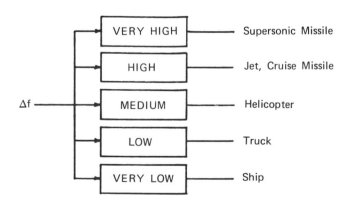

Figure 2–44. Doppler frequency gates for separation of targets.

Radar systems that derive target velocity information in this manner are designated as pulse-doppler radars. These radars possess two advantages over CW systems. Since they are pulse-modulated, they can measure range as well as velocity. Secondly, the pulse-doppler system requires only one antenna instead of two.

In actual practice, pulse-doppler radars use several banks of band-pass filters whose outputs are linked to the indicator. Target relative velocity and azimuth are thereby displayed in the same manner that range and azimuth are displayed for pulse-echo type radar sets.

MTI System

Another way to eliminate stationary targets is by using a delay line and canceler. Figure 2–45 illustrates this technique.

With this system, the output of the phase detector is delayed one pulse repetition time and then subtracted from the next pulse. The signals that appear the same for all pulses are those from stationary targets and are therefore canceled. Signals from moving targets are not canceled and may, in fact, be enhanced. The outputs of the phase detector and the delay-line canceler are compared in figure 2–46.

If the signals of sweep 1 are delayed for an interval equal to the *PRT* and then subtracted from the signals of sweep 2, all signals of constant amplitude are canceled, and only variations between successive pulses remain. The last three traces show the canceled signals.

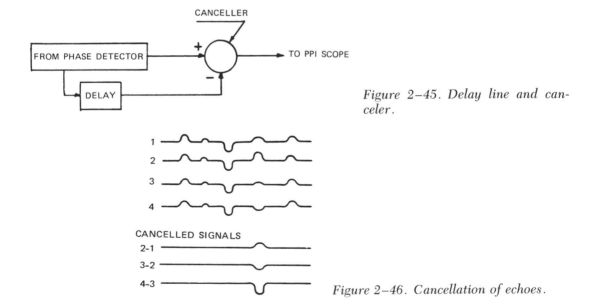

Figure 2–45. *Delay line and canceler.*

Figure 2–46. *Cancellation of echoes.*

Radars that employ this type of signal processor are called MTI radars to differentiate them from the pulse-doppler systems.

Blind Speeds

If a target is moving at such a speed that the phase change from consecutive pulses is 360°, or an exact multiple of 360°, then the target echo will not fluctuate. This occurs when the doppler frequency, f_D, is exactly equal to the *PRF* or a multiple thereof. This can be shown by looking at the distance a target travels, ΔR, for a given velocity, V_t, for two consecutive radar pulses. This distance traveled can be found from

$$\Delta R = 2V_t PRT$$

If this distance is exactly equal to a wavelength or multiple thereof, then there will be no phase change observed at the radar. Mathematically this statement is written

$$2V_t PTR = n\lambda \qquad \text{or} \qquad (2\text{–}18)$$

$$V_t = \frac{N\lambda}{2PRT} = \frac{n\,PRF\,\lambda}{2}$$

These target speeds are called blind speeds, since a delay-line canceler would detect no pulse-to-pulse changes in phase. Further, using equation (2–4) and assuming a stationary source ($V_t = s$) then

$$f_D = n\,PRF$$

Example: Calculate the blind speeds for a 10-cm radar that has a *PRF* of 200 Hz.
Solution:

$$V_t = \frac{n}{2} \times \frac{200}{\text{sec}} \times 10^{-1}\,\text{meters} = 10n\,\frac{\text{meters}}{\text{sec}}$$

Therefore, the radar (in the MTI mode) would be blind to all targets having relative radial velocities of $n = 10, 20, 30 \ldots$ meters/sec. Converting to knots, the values of target speeds extending from 0 to 600 knots would contain 31 blind speeds each occurring at integer multiples of 19.3 knots.

For a search radar, this multiplicity of blind speeds is of little consequence since they fall within a narrow range and are sharply defined. It is unlikely that a target on any normal trajectory would approach the site for more than a few seconds at one of the blind speeds. In fact, this represents such a highly unlikely possibility that

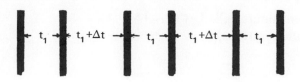

Figure 2–47. Staggered pulse repetition frequency.

the probability of detection of such targets would remain quite high. If, however, it is deemed necessary to minimize the blind speeds within a specified range of possible values, it is possible to do this by varying the pulse repetition rate of the radar. One method of accomplishing this, in practice, is to have every second pulse delayed by a small time interval. The result is a staggered *PRF* as shown in figure 2–47.

The shorter interval, t_1, produces a blind speed that is higher than that associated with the longer interval $t_1 + \Delta t$. It is possible to choose t_1 and Δt such that a blind speed due to one of these intervals will usually not be blind for the other.

One might think that these blind speeds could be avoided with pulse-doppler techniques. Not so! The Fourier series for a pulsed radar wave reveals that the spectral lines in the sidebands that are responsible for the amplitude variations are spaced at integer multiples of the pulse repetition frequency on either side of the carrier frequency. This whole set of *PRF*-related doppler frequencies is always present in the signal returns for stationary targets. Thus the pulse-doppler system must reject all doppler frequencies that are integer multiples of the *PRF*. The pulse-doppler system is therefore blind to the same target speeds as the MTI radars that use delay lines and cancelers.

Most pulse-doppler systems avoid the problem of blind speeds by making the *PRF* high enough so that the first blind speed is higher than the highest target velocity likely to be encountered in practice.

Example: What *PRF* is needed if a 10-cm radar is to have no blind speeds under 600 knots (relative radial speed)?

Solution: Convert 600 knots to 304.8 meters/sec.

$$PRF = \frac{2V_t}{\lambda} = \frac{609.6}{10^{-1}} = 6{,}069 \text{ Hz}$$

Such high pulse repetition rates introduce yet another problem— that of ambiguous range. For example, a pulse-doppler radar with a *PRF* of 4,000 Hz ($T = 250$ μsec) would have a maximum unambiguous range of only about 37.5 kilometers. Range ambiguities can be resolved through the use of a staggered *PRF*. For this reason some long-range missile fire-control radars may operate with many different pulse repetition rates. Another method involves the use of frequency agility. In this method the frequency of the set is changed from pulse to pulse so that each echo can be identified with a particular outgoing transmitted pulse.

Both types of radar described in this section are, of course, pulse-doppler radars in that they are pulsed and use the doppler shift. The terms pulse-doppler and MTI are sometimes used interchangeably. In general, pulse-doppler radars have a series of frequency gates to process the phase detector output, while MTI radars use a delay line and canceler. MTI radars are normally search radars with a low *PRF*, whereas the high-*PRF* pulse-doppler radars are more suited for fire-control. Usually pulse-doppler radars have duty cycles above 10%, while MTI radars have duty cycles considerably less than 10%.

Over The Horizon (OTH) Radar

As discussed in the previous chapter, lower frequencies in the HF region can be used for target detection with some limitations. Though the band between 1.8 and 40 MHz is subject to high noise levels and interference from long-range communications, it can provide detection ranges up to several thousand km with the sky-wave propagation path or several hundred km when the ground-wave path is used.

Sky-wave radar. Use of refraction layers in the ionosphere can extend radar range to 4,000 km on a single hop; however, the long wavelengths required dictate the use of antennas 300 m or more in length. Obviously this limits OTH radar to fixed land-based sites if the entire HF portion of the spectrum is to be employed. The actual range is determined by the frequency and elevation angle of the transmitted beam. The ionizing layers in the atmosphere change with time of day, season, and solar activity, which can result in multiple propagation paths or no refraction at all, degrading or eliminating employment of the radar in this mode. Elevation beamwidths must be very narrow in order to avoid multiple path propagation; however, this requirement tends to increase the already large vertical dimension of the antenna. Precise selection of frequency can allow the operator to select the specific refracting layer desired. Because of the large angle of incidence, considerable backscatter results when the beam returns to earth. This clutter is stronger than the returns from all aircraft and most ship targets. For this reason the OTH radar must employ MTI, pulse-doppler, CW, or FM-CW methods to allow the target to be resolved in velocity and to reject non-moving land or sea clutter. Detection of ships requires more sophisticated processing techniques and longer observation times because their velocities closely approximate that of sea return or weather. Multiple hop propagation will result in increased clutter and degraded operation, but the range is increased by 100% with each hop. Use of a single frequency under optimum conditions could illuminate a range interval 1,000 km deep starting at 1,000 to 4,000 km. Using multiple frequency transmissions can increase the depth of this range interval, or if conditions are poor, it may require as many as six frequencies in one transmission just to cover the 1,000 km interval.

Ground-wave radar. With slight modification the radar just described can be employed at frequencies that propagate as ground waves. The beam is transmitted at zero elevation and has a detection range against low-flying aircraft of 200 to 400 km. Again, the long wavelength employed restricts its use to shore sights, but it is able to maintain surveillance down to the surface of the earth, assuming land and sea clutter rejection features similar to those employed in sky-wave radars are used. In actuality detection is easier than with sky-wave radars, because the angle of impingement with the earth's surface is smaller and backscatter is less.

Summary

Although radar is by no means the ultimate solution to the target sensing and detection problem, it has become an integral factor in the development of advanced weapons systems. Radar is extensively used not only for target detection, but for target tracking and weapon guidance to intercept as well. It is not limited in suitability to any single environment and is equally effective on land, sea, and airborne weapons systems.

A typical radar is made up of six basic components. These are the synchronizer, transmitter, antenna system, receiver, indicator, and power supply. Although all components share an equal importance to overall radar effectiveness, the antenna system is unique in that it serves in a multiple capacity. First of all, it serves as both the transmitter and receiver of broadcast energy. In a pulsed system this dual role is accomplished by the same antenna through the employment of a duplexer to isolate the receiver during the transmit cycle. Secondly, the antenna design directly determines the shape of the radar beam and thus the accuracy of target positioning. This shaping is accomplished through design applications that incorporate the subjectivity of electromagnetic waves to reflection, refraction, and interference.

Practical limitations on minimum radar return signal detection are set by noise. Noise may be environmental radiation, system noise, or the result of thermally induced electronic fluctuation within the input circuitry of the receiver.

Radar performance is determined by many factors, several of which are closely interrelated. Among these are pulse shape, width and repetition frequency, antenna gain, and target reflectivity. The absolute maximum range of a radar is determined by transmitter power, antenna gain and reception area, target radar cross section, and receiver sensitivity. A change in any of these factors will alter maximum range in accordance with a one-fourth power relationship.

There are three basic types of radar systems in current use: pulse-echo, continuous wave, and pulse-doppler/MTI. Pulse systems are of value because of an ability to measure target range, whereas the value of continuous-wave systems lies in velocity discrimination. Pulse-doppler systems are essentially pulse systems that are modified to be sensitive to the doppler shift of the echo pulse. A fourth type of system that uses a frequency modulation technique to measure range is widely employed as a radar altimeter in modern aircraft.

Pulse range determination is based simply on the fact that a transmitted radar pulse travels at the speed of light, and therefore range is a function of pulse round-trip time. The accuracy of target bearing information is based on sensitivity to changes in return signal strength. The more accurately these changes can be calibrated, the more accurate the bearing information. Target elevation is determined by three basic methods. The threshold-pickup method and the signal-comparison method use the interference that results when the radar beam contacts the earth's surface. The tilted-antenna method determines elevation in a manner similar to azimuth determination.

Continuous-wave radar systems have the principal advantage of being able to output selectively for display targets that meet certain velocity characteristics. This selection is possible because the CW radar components allow for the comparison of transmitted and echo signals and because an amplifier can be tuned to accept only the doppler frequencies of particular interest.

Pulse-doppler and MTI radars offer the features of range determination and velocity discrimination. Both are sensitive to the doppler shift within returned pulses, and both make use of the fact that the amplitude of returned pulses from targets with no relative velocity will not vary with time. Thus, a fluctuating output from a pulse phase detector would indicate a moving target. Pulse-doppler radars use a series of frequency gates to process the phase detector output, while

MTI radars use a delay line canceler. Two problems inherent to these systems are blind speeds and range ambiguity. Blind speeds can be eliminated by making the *PRF* high enough so that the slowest blind speed is higher than a target could exhibit. Higher *PRFs* mean lower unambiguous ranges. This problem can be counteracted by frequency agility in transmitted pulses, enabling the "tagging" of a particular pulse to be used for range measurement. Finally, a staggered *PRF* can be used as a solution to both the blind speed and ambiguous range problems.

References

Bureau of Naval Personnel. *Aviation Fire Control Technician 3 & 2*. NAVPERS 10387-A. Washington, D.C.: GPO, 1971.

Bureau of Naval Personnel. *Aviation Fire Control Technician 1 & C*. NAVPERS 10390-B, Washington, D.C.: GPO, 1969.

Bureau of Naval Personnel. *Basic Electronics*. Vol. 1., NAVPERS 10087-C, Washington, D.C.: GPO.

Commander Naval Ordnance Systems Command. *Weapons Systems Fundamentals*. NAVORD OP 3000, vol. 1, 1st Rev. Washington, D.C.: GPO, 1971.

Corse, Carl D., and William R. Barnett. *Introduction to Shipboard Engineering and Naval Weapons*. Vol. 2. Annapolis, Md.: U. S. Naval Academy, 1971.

Leydorf, Glenn E., ed. *Naval Electronic Systems*. Vol. 4. Annapolis, Md.: U.S. Naval Academy, 1971.

Operations Committee, Naval Science Department, U.S. Naval Academy. *Naval Operations Analysis*. Annapolis, Md.: Naval Institute Press, 1972.

Ridenour, L. N. *Radar System Engineering*. MIT Radiation Lab Series. Vol. 1. New York: McGraw-Hill, 1949.

Skolnik, Merrill I. *Introduction to Radar Systems*. New York: McGraw-Hill, 1980.

———. *Radar Handbook*. New York: McGraw-Hill, 1970.

Terman, Frederick E. *Electronic and Radio Engineering*. New York: McGraw-Hill, 1955.

3

Elements of Feedback Control

Introduction

The elements of feedback control theory may be applied to a wide range of physical systems. However, in engineering this definition is usually applied only to those systems whose major function is to dynamically or actively command, direct, or regulate themselves or other systems. We will further restrict our discussion to weapons control systems that encompass the entire series of measurements and computations, beginning with target detection and ending with target interception. But before discussing control systems, we must first define several key terms.

Control System Terminology

Input. Stimulus or excitation applied to a control system from an external source, usually in order to produce a specified response from the system.

Output. The actual response obtained from the system.

Feedback. That portion of the output of a system that is returned to modify the input and thus serve as a performance monitor for the system.

Error. The difference between the input stimulus and the output response. Specifically, it is the difference between the input and the feedback.

A very simple example of a feedback control system is the thermostat. The *input* is the temperature that is initially set into the device. Comparison is then made between the input and the temperature of the outside world. If the two are different, an *error* results and an *output* is produced that activates a heating or cooling device. The comparator within the thermostat continually samples the ambient temperature, i.e., the *feedback*, until the *error* is zero; the *output* then turns off the heating or cooling device. Figure 3–1 is a block diagram of a simple feedback control system.

Other examples are:

(1) Aircraft rudder control system

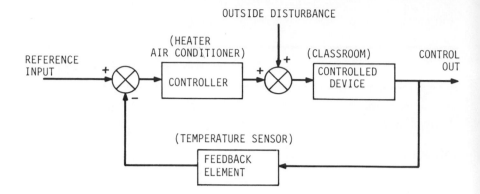

Figure 3–1. Negative feedback control system.

(2) Gun or missile director
(3) Missile guidance system
(4) Laser-guided projectiles
(5) Automatic pilot

Discussion

Feedback control systems employed in weapons systems are classified as *closed-loop* control systems. A closed-loop system is one in which the control action is dependent on the output of the system. It can be seen from figure 3–1 and the previous description of the thermostat that these represent examples of closed-loop control systems.

The result of this closing of the control loop by the feedback is that the system is able to determine by itself the accuracy of the output as governed by the input.

Characteristics of Feedback

The basic elements of a feedback control system are shown in figure 3–1. The system measures the output and compares the measurement with the desired value of the output as prescribed by the input. It uses the error (i.e., the difference between the actual output and desired output) to change the actual output and to bring it into closer correspondence with the desired value.

Since arbitrary disturbances and unwanted fluctuations can occur at various points in the system, a feedback control system must be able to reject or filter out these fluctuations and perform its task with the prescribed accuracies, while producing as faithful a representation of the desired output as feasible. This function of filtering and smoothing is achieved by various electrical and mechanical components, R-C networks, gyroscopic devices, accelerometers, etc., and by using different types of *feedback*. *Position feedback* is that type of feedback employed in a system in which the output is either a linear distance or an angular displacement, and a portion of the output is returned or fed back to the input. Position feedback is essential in weapons control systems and is used to make the output exactly follow the input. For example: if, in a missile-launcher control system, the position feedback were lost, the system response to an input signal to turn clockwise 10° would be a continuous turning in the clockwise direction, rather than a matchup of the launcher position with the input order.

Motion smoothing by means of feedback is accomplished by the use of *rate* and *acceleration feedback*. In the case of rate (velocity) feedback, a portion of the output displacement is differentiated and returned so as to restrict the velocity of the output. Acceleration feedback is accomplished by differentiating a portion of the output velocity, which when fed back serves as an additional restriction on the system output. The result of both rate and acceleration feedback is to aid the system in achieving changes in position without overshoot and oscillation.

The most important features that negative feedback imparts to a control system are:

(1) *Increased accuracy*—An increase in the system's ability to reproduce faithfully in the output that which is dictated by an input.

(2) *Reduced sensitivity to disturbance*—When fluctuations is the relationship of system output to input caused by changes within the system are reduced. The values of system components change constantly throughout their lifetime, but by using the self-correcting aspect of feedback, the effects of these changes can be minimized.

(3) *Smoothing and filtering*—When the undesired effects of noise and distortion within the system are reduced.

(4) *Increased bandwidth*—When the bandwidth of any system is defined as that range of frequencies or changes to the input to which the system will respond satisfactorily.

Block Diagrams

Because of the complexity of most control systems, a shorthand pictorial representation of the relationship between input and output was developed. This representation is commonly called the block diagram. Control systems are made up of various combinations of the following basic blocks.

Element. The simplest representation of system components. It is a labeled block whose *transfer function (G)* is the output divided by the input.

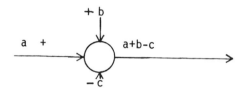

$$c = Gr$$

Figure 3–2a. Element.

Summing Point. A device to add or subtract the value of two or more signals.

Figure 3–2b. Summing point.

Splitting Point. A point where the entering variable is to be transmitted identically to two points in the diagram. It is sometimes referred to as a "take off point."

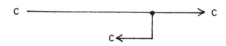

Figure 3–2c. Splitting point.

Control or Feed Forward Elements (G). Those components directly between the controlled output and the referenced input.

Reference Variable or Input (r). An external signal applied to a control system to produce the desired output.

Feedback (b). A signal determined by the output, as modified by the feedback elements, used in comparison with the input signal.

Controlled Output (c). The variable (temp., position, velocity, shaft angle, etc.) that the system seeks to guide or regulate.

Error Signal (e). The algebraic sum of the reference input and the feedback.

Feedback Elements (H). Those components required to establish the desired feedback signal by sensing the controlled output.

Figure 3–3 is a block diagram of a simple feedback control system using the components described above.

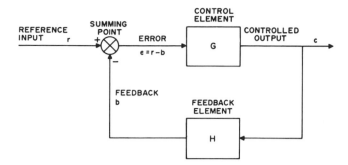

Figure 3–3. Block diagram representation of a control system.

In the simplified approach taken, the blocks are filled with values representative of component values. The output (c) can be expressed as the product of the error (e) and the control element (G).

$$c = eG \qquad (3-1)$$

Error is also the combination of the input (r) and the feedback (b).

$$e = r - b \qquad (3-2)$$

But feedback is the product of the output and of the feedback element (H).

$$b = cH \qquad (3-3)$$

Hence, by substituting equation $(3-3)$ into equation $(3-2)$

$$e = r - cH$$

and from equation $(3-1)$

$$e = c/G$$
$$\therefore c/G = r - cH \qquad (3-4)$$
$$c = Gr - cGH$$
$$c + cGH = Gr$$

$$c = \left(\frac{G}{1 + GH}\right)r \qquad (3-5)$$

It has then been shown that figure 3–3 can be reduced to an equivalent simplified block diagram, $\dfrac{G}{1 + GH}$, shown below.

$$c = \frac{rG}{1 + GH} \qquad (3-6)$$

In contrast to the closed-loop system, an open-loop system does

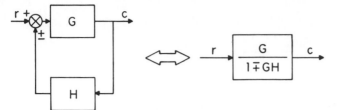

Figure 3–4. Equivalent block diagrams.

not monitor its own output, i.e., it contains no feedback loop. A simple open-loop system is strictly an input through a control element. In this case:

$$c = rG$$

The open-loop system does not have the ability to compensate for input fluctuations or control element degradation.

Motor Speed Control System

If the speed of a motor is to be controlled, one method is to use a tachometer that senses the speed of the motor, produces an output voltage proportional to motor speed, and then subtracts that output voltage from the input voltage. This system can be drawn in block diagram form as shown in figure 3–5. In this example

r = input voltage to the speed control system
G = motor characteristic of 1,000 rpm per volt of input
c = steady state motor speed in rpm
H = the tachometer characteristic of 1 volt per 250 rpm motor speed

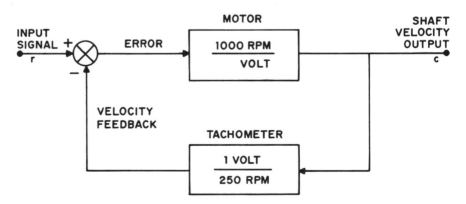

Figure 3–5. Velocity feedback employing a tachometer.

Example.

This example assumes that the input signal does not change over the response time of the system.

Neglecting transient responses, the steady state motor speed can be determined as follows:

$$r = 10 \text{ volts}$$

$$c = (e)(1000) \text{ rpm}$$

$$e = \frac{c}{1000} \text{ volts}$$

$$b = \frac{c}{250} \text{ volts}$$

$$e = r - b$$

$$= 10 - \frac{c}{250} \text{ volts}$$

Equating the two expressions for *e* and solving for *c* as in equation (3–4)

$$\frac{c}{1000} = 10 - \frac{c}{250} \text{ volts}$$

$$c + 4c = 10,000 \text{ rpm}$$

$$c = 2,000 \text{ rpm}$$

Finally the error voltage may be found

$$e = \frac{c}{1,000} = 2 \text{ volts}$$

or by using the simplified equivalent form developed earlier as equation (3–6):

$$c = r\left(\frac{G}{1 + GH}\right) = 10V\left(\frac{1000 \text{ rpm/V}}{1 + 1000\frac{\text{rpm}}{V}\frac{1V}{250 \text{ rpm}}}\right) = 2000 \text{ rpm}$$

$$e = \frac{c}{G} = \frac{2000 \text{ rpm}}{1000\frac{\text{rpm}}{V}} = 2 \text{ volts}$$

Response in Feedback Control Systems

In weaponry, feedback control systems are used for various purposes and must meet certain performance requirements. These requirements not only affect such things as speed of response and accuracy, but also the manner in which the system responds in carrying out its control function. All systems contain certain errors. The problem is to keep them within allowable limits.

Weapons system driving devices must be capable of developing sufficient torque and power to position a load in a minimum time. In a system, a motor and its connected load have sufficient inertia to drive the load past the point of the desired position as governed by the input signal. This *overshooting* results in an opposite error signal reversing the direction of rotation of the motor and the load. The motor again attempts to correct the error and again overshoots the desired point, with each reversal requiring less correction until the system is in equilibrium with the input stimulus. The time required for the oscillations to die down to the desired level is often referred to as *settling time*. The magnitude of settling time is greatly affected by the degrees of viscous friction in the system (commonly referred to as *damping*). As the degree of viscous friction or damping increases, the tendency to overshoot is diminished, until finally no overshoot occurs. As damping is further increased, the settling time of the system continues to increase.

Consider the system depicted in figure 3–6.

A mass is attached to a rigid surface by means of a spring and a dashpot and is free to move left and right on a frictionless slide. A free body diagram of the forces is drawn in figure 3–7.

Newton's laws of motion state that any finite resultant of external forces applied to a body must result in the acceleration of that body, i.e.:

$$F = Ma$$

Therefore, the forces are added, with the frame of reference carefully

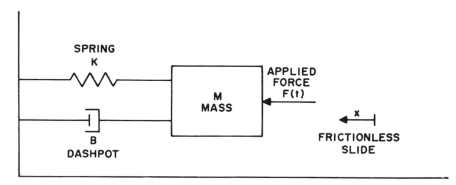

Figure 3–6. Simple transverse mechanical system (accelerometer).

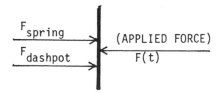

F_spring

F_dashpot

(APPLIED FORCE)
F(t)

Figure 3–7. Free body diagram.

noted to determine the proper signs, and are set equal to the product of mass and acceleration.

$$F(t) - F_{spring} - F_{dashpot} = Ma \qquad (3-7)$$

The force exerted by a spring is proportional to the difference between its rest length and its instantaneous length. The proportionality constant is called the spring constant and is usually designated by the letter K, with the units of Newtons per meter (N/m).

$$\therefore F_{spring} = Kx$$

The force exerted by the dashpot is referred to as damping and is proportional to the relative velocity of the two mechanical parts. The proportionality constant is referred to as the damping constant and is usually designated by the letter B, with the units of Newtons per meter per second $\left(\dfrac{\text{N-sec}}{\text{m}}\right)$.

$$\therefore F_{dashpot} = Bv$$

Noting that velocity is the first derivative of displacement with respect to time and that acceleration is the second derivative of displacement with respect to time, equation (3–7) becomes

$$F(t) - Kx - B\frac{dx}{dt} = M\frac{d^2x}{dt^2} \qquad (3-8)$$

rearranging

$$M\frac{d^2x}{dt^2} + B\frac{dx}{dt} + Kx = F(t)$$

or

$$\frac{d^2x}{dt^2} + \frac{B}{M}\frac{dx}{dt} + \frac{K}{M}x = \frac{F(t)}{M} \qquad (3-9)$$

This equation is called a second-order linear differential equation with constant coefficients.

Using the auxiliary equation method of solving a linear differential equation, the auxiliary equation of (3–9) is:

$$s^2 + \frac{B}{M}s + \frac{K}{M} = 0 \tag{3–10}$$

and has two roots

$$s = \frac{-\dfrac{B}{M} \pm \sqrt{\left(\dfrac{B}{M}\right)^2 - \dfrac{4K}{M}}}{2} \tag{3–11}$$

and the general solution of equations (3–9) is of the form

$$x(t) = C_1 e^{s_1 t} + C_2 e^{s_2 t} \tag{3–12}$$

where s_1 and s_2 are the roots determined in equation (3–10) and C_1 and C_2 are coefficients that can be determined by evaluating the initial conditions.

It is convenient to express B in terms of a damping coefficient ζ as follows:

$$B = 2\zeta \sqrt{MK}$$

or

$$\zeta = \frac{B}{2\sqrt{MK}}$$

Then equation (3–10) can be written in the form:

$$s^2 + 2\zeta\omega_n s + \omega_n^2 = 0 \tag{3–13}$$

where

$$\omega_n = \sqrt{\frac{K}{M}} \text{ and is the natural frequency of the system.}$$

and

$$\zeta = \frac{B}{M(2\omega_n)}$$

$$= \frac{B}{2\sqrt{MK}}$$

For the particular value of B such that $\zeta = 1$ the system is critically damped. The roots of equation (3–10) are real and equal ($s_1 = s_2$),

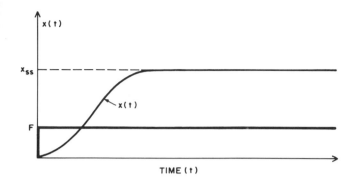

Figure 3–8a. Critically damped motion.

and the response of the system to a step input is of the form

$$x(t) = A(1 - C_1te^{-st} - C_2e^{-st}) \qquad (3\text{–}14)$$

The specific response is shown in figure 3–8a.

For large values of B ($\zeta > 1$), the system is overdamped. The roots of equation (3–10) are real and unequal, and the response of the system to a step input is of the form

$$x(t) = A(1 - C_1e^{-s_1t} - C_2e^{-s_2t})$$

Since one of the roots is larger than in the case of critical damping, the response will take more time to reach its final value. An example of an overdamped system response is shown in figure 3–8b.

For small values of B such that $\zeta < 1$ the system is underdamped. The roots of equation (3–10) are complex conjugates, and the general solution is of the form

$$x(t) = A[1 - e^{-\sigma t}\sin(\omega t + \phi)]$$

where σ is $\dfrac{B}{2M}$, the real portion of s, and ω is the imaginary part of the complex roots.

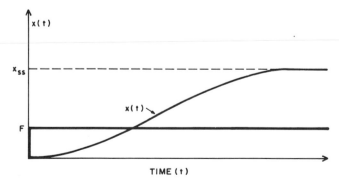

Figure 3–8b. Overdamped motion.

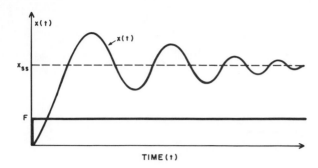

Figure 3–8c. Underdamped motion.

The system oscillates at the frequency ω. For small values of ζ, ω is very nearly the same as ω_n in equation (3–13).

Examples of critically damped, overdamped, and underdamped system response are depicted in figures 3–8a–c respectively.

The previous illustrations are characteristic of the types of motion found in most weapons tracking systems. In the case where the system is *underdamped*, in that the oscillations of overshoot are allowed to continue for a relatively long period of time, the system responds rapidly to an input order, but has relative difficulty in settling down to the desired position dictated by that input. Rapid initial response is a desirable characteristic in weapon control tracking systems if the system is to keep up with high-speed targets. However, the long settling time is an undesirable trait in a dynamic tracking system because during the settling time, the target will have moved, thus initiating a change in the system input prior to the system's responding adequately to the previous stimulus. It should be easy to extrapolate this condition over time to the point where the system can no longer follow the target and the track is lost.

Some of the more common methods of achieving damping are the employment of friction (viscous damping), feeding back electrical signals that are 180° out of phase with the input, or returning a DC voltage that is of opposite polarity to that of a driving voltage.

When the damping in a system becomes too great, the system will not overshoot, but its initial response time will become excessive. This condition is known as *overdamped*. It is generally an undesirable condition in weapons systems because of the relatively slow initial response time associated with it.

When a system responds relatively quickly with no overshoot, the system is *critically damped*. In actual practice, systems are designed to be slightly underdamped, but approaching the critically damped condition. This accomplishes the functions of minimizing the system response time while at the same time minimizing overshoot. Figure

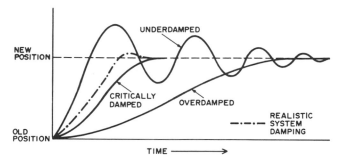

Figure 3–9. Comparison of system response with varying degrees of damping.

3–9 is a graphical representation of the relationships among the different conditions of damping.

Example. To illustrate the basic concepts of feedback control, consider the simple mechanical accelerometer that is employed in various configurations in missile guidance systems and inertial navigation systems. In this example, the accelerometer is employed in a guided-missile direction-control system. It is desired to hold the missile on a straight-line course. To accomplish this, lateral accelerations must be measured and compensation made by causing the steering-control surfaces to be actuated to produce a counter acceleration, thus assisting the overall guidance system in maintaining a steady course. This example depicts the system for left and right steering only; however, the up/down steering control is identical.

The accelerometer consists of a spring, a mass, and a damping fluid all contained within a sealed case, with the entire assembly mounted in the missile.

The position, x, of the mass with respect to the case, and thus with respect to the potentiometer, is a function of the acceleration of the case. As the mass is moved by the results of lateral acceleration, motor drive voltage is picked off by the wiper arm of the potentiometer. The system is calibrated so that when no acceleration exists, the wiper arm is positioned in the center of the potentiometer and no drive voltage is fed to the motor.

As lateral accelerations of the missile occur, the mass is moved by the resulting force in a manner so as to pick off a voltage to steer the missile in a direction opposite to that of the input acceleration. As the missile is steered, an acceleration opposite to that initially encountered tends to move the mass in the opposite direction. The motion of the mass is opposed by the damping action of the fluid and the spring. To achieve a relatively rapid response and a minimum of overshoot, the choice of the viscosity of the fluid and the strength of the spring is critical.

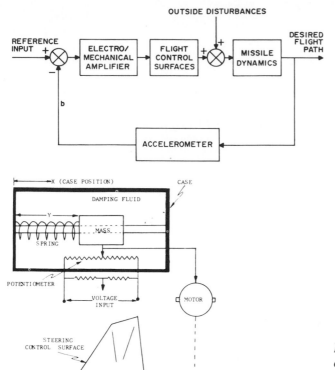

OUTSIDE DISTURBANCES

REFERENCE INPUT

ELECTRO/ MECHANICAL AMPLIFIER

FLIGHT CONTROL SURFACES

MISSILE DYNAMICS

DESIRED FLIGHT PATH

b

ACCELEROMETER

X (CASE POSITION)

CASE

DAMPING FLUID

Y

MASS

SPRING

POTENTIOMETER

VOLTAGE INPUT

MOTOR

STEERING CONTROL SURFACE

Figure 3–10. Accelerometer steering control.

Summary

This chapter has presented a broad overview of the basic concepts of feedback control systems. These concepts are employed over a wide range of applications, including automatic target tracking systems, missile and torpedo homing systems, and gun and missile-launcher positioning systems.

A feedback control system consists of an input, an output, a controlled element, and feedback. System response should be as rapid as possible with minimum overshoot. To accomplish this, some means of damping is employed. If damping is weak, then the system is underdamped. This condition is characterized by rapid initial response with a long settling time. If damping is too strong or the system is overdamped, then the system response time is excessively long with no overshoot. The critically damped condition occurs when damping is weak enough to permit a relatively rapid initial response and yet strong enough to prevent overshoot. Control systems employed in modern weaponry are designed to be slightly underdamped but approaching the critically damped case. The result of this compromise in design is the achievement of rapid initial response with a minimum of overshoot and oscillation.

References

Bureau of Naval Personnel. *Aviation Fire Control Technician 3 & 2*. NAVPERS 10387-A. Washington, D.C.: GPO, 1971.

Commander, Naval Ordnance Systems Command. *Weapons Systems Fundamentals*. NAVORD OP 3000, vols. 2 & 3, 1st Rev. Washington, D.C.: GPO, 1971.

H.Q., U.S. Army Material Command. *Servomechanisms*. Pamphlet 706-136, Sec. I. Washington, D.C.: GPO, 1965.

Spiegel, Murry R. *Applied Differential Equations*. Englewood Cliffs, N.J.: Prentice-Hall Inc., 1967.

Weapons and Systems Engineering Dept. *Weapons Systems Engineering*. Vol. 2, Annapolis, Md.: USNA, 1983.

4

Computational Systems

Introduction

As discussed in this text, computers will be categorized as digital, analog, or hybrid. The digital computer performs arithmetic and logic operations with discrete values. The analog computer represents mathematical or physical relationship with electronic analogies. The hybrid computer is actually a combination of analog and digital design that is connected by converters to permit communication between them.

Digital Computers

Between 1937 and 1944, Aiken built the first general-purpose automatic digital computer, called the "Mark I." It was electromechanical, using relays as one of the major calculating devices. Between 1939 and 1945, Eckert and Mauchly built the "ENIAC," also a digital computer. It consisted of 18,000 electron tubes, weighed 30 tons, and dissipated 150 kilowatts. The time required for an adding operation was only 0.21 msec compared to 300 msec for the Mark I. These early computers are presently displayed at the Smithsonian Institution in Washington, D.C. In 1951 Eckert and Mauchly built the first "UNIVAC" for the United States Census Bureau. The "EDVAC," completed in 1952, was the first computer to use internally stored instruction (program).

Electronic digital computers became more common during the early 1950s, and military and industrial applications grew as their capabilities expanded. The AN/FSQ-7 computer was developed in 1954 for the USAF SAGE (Semi-Automatic Ground Environment) air defense system. A typical installation weighed nearly 300,000 pounds and occupied 40,000 square feet of floor space.

During the 1970s computer development and miniaturization have accelerated at an unbelievable rate. Integrated circuits using semiconductor technology have led to smaller and smaller "chips," such that the wire size to use with them has become a major problem.

Figure 4–1 shows one entire 32-bit central processing unit of a

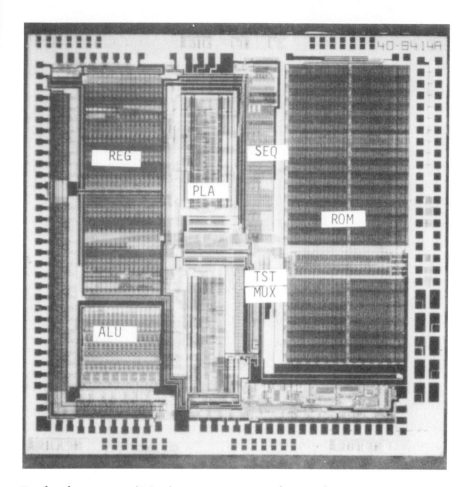

Read-only memory (ROM) - Stores 9,216 38-bit words
Test multiplexer (TST MUX)
Sequencing stack (SEQ) - Used to address the ROM
Programmable logic array (PLA) - Decodes micro instructions
Arithmetic and logic unit (ALU)
28 32-bit registers (REG) - For temporary storage

Figure 4–1. 32-bit central processing unit on 0.25 × 0.25-inch die.

computer containing 450,000 transistors on a 0.25×0.25-inch silicon die. Devices as small as 1.5 micrometers (micron) and line separations as small as 1.0 micron are employed. This computer operates at an 18-MHz clock frequency and makes use of pipelining or gang execution of instructions, arithmetic and logic operations, and memory operations.

Digital computer systems consist of hardware and software components. The physical components are the hardware. The programs and files that govern the hardware are the software.

Hardware

The basic sections of a digital computer are shown in figure 4–2. The digital computer hardware has three major groups of devices: input/output devices, storage devices (memory), and the central processing unit. Another grouping is to refer to all input/output and auxiliary memory devices that can be connected to a basic computer (CPU and its original memory) as peripherals.

(1) Central Processing Unit (CPU)

This portion of the computer hardware is the heart or central brain of a computer. It is often referred to simply as the processor, and it contains the arithmetic and logic unit and the control unit as well as a permanent memory (called ROM) containing its operating instructions, software interpretation instructions, and additional temporary storage registers.

(a) Arithmetic and logic unit (ALU). This portion of the computer hardware is where arithmetic and logical operations are performed. The ALU generally consists of an accumulator and registers for storage of operands and results. Also there is shifting and sequencing circuitry for implementing multiplication, division, and other desired operations. In computers, multiplication usually is done by a series of additions, and division by a series of subtractions.

(b) Control unit. This is the part of the digital computer or central processing unit that determines the execution and interpretation of instructions in proper sequence, including the decoding of each in-

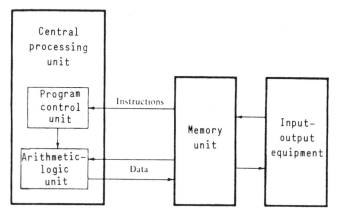

Figure 4–2. Digital computer organization.

struction and the application of the proper signals to the arithmetic unit and other registers in accordance with the decoded information.

The information read into the control unit from memory is in the form of voltage levels that make up a "binary word," and represents a specific operation that is to be performed. The location of the data to be processed is generally a part of the instruction. The control unit then energizes circuitry that causes the specified operation (add, subtract, compare, etc.) to be executed. Subsequently, the control unit reads the next instruction or jumps as directed to find the next instruction to execute.

The four major types of instructions are:

(1) Data transfer
(2) Arithmetic
(3) Logic
(4) Control

Data transfer commands are those whose basic function is to transfer data from one location to another.

Arithmetic instructions are those that combine two pieces of data to form a single piece of data by using one of the arithmetic operations.

Logic instructions make the digital computer into a system that is more than a high-speed adding machine. By using logic instructions, the programmer may instruct the system on various alternate sequences through the program. The choice of which sequence to use will be made by the control unit under the influence of the logic instruction. Logic instructions provide the computer with the ability to make decisions based on the result of previously generated data.

Control instructions are those that are used to send commands to devices not under the direct command of the control unit, such as input/ouput units and auxiliary memory devices.

(c) Read only memory (ROM). This memory is used to store information on a permanent basis. Typically, when power is first supplied to a computer, the computer reads its ROM and sets itself up as a computer ready to operate. The ROM will also contain standard interpretation instructions to convert from higher to lower software languages. For computers with a specific application or for computer training, a PROM (Programmable ROM) might be employed to retain the program with power off. There are also EPROMs (Erasable PROM), which can be erased with ultraviolet light and re-programmed.

(2) Storage (Memory)

(a) Primary storage (main memory). Primary storage is immediate

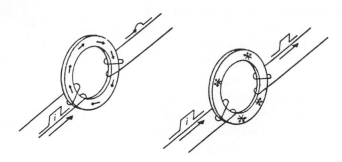

Figure 4–3. Ferrite core memory.

access memory and is used to store data, instructions, and intermediate results in a manner that permits them to be made available for quick access and processing. It is random access memory (RAM).

One type of primary storage is the ferrite or magnetic core memory. The core consists of a ferrite toroid with at least two windings. A positive pulse through the input winding will create a magnetic field in the core, in a clockwise direction (figure 4–3).

When the pulse is removed, the magnetic field will remain. The core "remembers" that is has been set. If a negative pulse is sent through the input winding, the magnetic field will be reversed. The rapid reversal of the magnetic field will induce a current in the output winding. The pulse that sets the core is called the write pulse. A pulse in one direction will write 1; a pulse in the other direction (or a pulse through a separate winding wound in the opposite direction) will write 0. Once the core is set, it can be "interrogated" by sending a pulse in the same direction as is used to write 0, called a "read" pulse. If the core is set to 1, there will be a pulse induced in the output line. If it is set to 0, there will be no output pulse. Note that readout is destructive. The process of interrogating the core resets it to 0, regardless of the information content.

Another type of main memory is semiconductor memory. This technique basically relies on a switchable on-off circuit to store and maintain either of two bit states. After the circuit is set to one state it can then be read by testing its ability to carry a current; if it can carry one, it is "on," if not, it is "off." This read process does not require a restore cycle as core does; however, most types of semiconductor (often called silicon) memory are "volatile." If the system suffers a power failure, the bit values will not be maintained in a volatile memory. Therefore, a back-up system is usually provided for power or a hasty copy in such an event. Semiconductor memory costs less than ferrite core memory. Table 4–1 shows a comparison of various memory types.

Table 4-1. A Comparison of Various Memory Characteristics

(1977 Data) Memory Technology	Average Capacity -Unformatted- (Kilobits)	Data Rate (Bits per Second)	Average Access Time (milliseconds)	Price Per Bit (Cents)	Random Access	Non-volatile
Drums (Fixed head, first drive)	1.0×10^5	6.0×10^6	8.5	2.0×10^{-5}	Block Access	Yes
Tapes (Mass storage system)	1.1×10^9	1.2×10^6 (Bytes per second)	1.4×10^4	2.5×10^{-5}	No	Yes
Cores (Single module)	6.4×10^2	2.0×10^4	2.5×10^{-4}	1.9×10^{-1}	Yes	Yes
Disks (Moving head, first drive)	6.0×10^1	1.2×10^4 (Bytes per second)	3.7×10^1	7.7×10^{-4}	Block Access	Yes
Cartridge (Single drive with electronics)	2.4×10^4	4.8×10^4	2.0×10^4	1.0×10^{-1}	No	Yes
Cassette (Single drive with electronics)	5.8×10^3	2.4×10^4	2.0×10^4	1.3×10^{-2}	No	Yes
Bipolar Random Access Memory (per chip)	4.0	1.3×10^7	6.0×10^{-5}	5.0×10^{-1}	Yes	No
Metal-Oxide-Semiconductor (MOS) (per chip)	1.6×10^1	2.0×10^6	2.7×10^{-4}	3.0×10^{-1}	Yes	Few
Floppy Disk (one) (Single drive with electronics, double density)	6.4×10^3	5.0×10^5	2.6×10^2	1.0×10^{-2}	Block Access	Yes
Magnetic Bubbles (per chip)	1.0×10^2	5.0×10^4	4.0	1.1×10^{-1}	Block Access	Yes
Charge-coupled Devices (per chip)	1.6×10^1	2.0×10^6	6.5×10^{-2}	1.3×10^{-1}	Block Access	Few
Video Disks (Ready-only-memory, single disk medium)	1.0×10^7	7.2×10^6	5.0×10^3	1.0×10^{-5}	Block Access	Yes

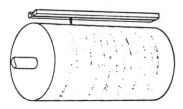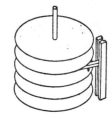

Figure 4–4. Magnetic drum and disk.

(b) Secondary storage (auxiliary memory). The function of secondary storage (auxiliary memory) is to store data that is not presently being used by the computer. The access time of this secondary storage may vary from several seconds to several minutes depending on the storage device used. Many secondary storage devices are based on the familiar magnetic tape recording principle. When a strip of plastic, coated with iron oxide or some similar magnetic material, is passed close to the field of an electromagnet, the particles are oriented or polarized. The orientation is retained after the field that created it is removed, and the particles themselves form a miniature magnet. When this magnetized section of tape passes a gap similar to the one that generated it, it will create a magnetic flux, whereby it can be read. In practice, several channels are recorded across the width of the tape. The form of the memory is sometimes a tape recorder, but it is often in the form of a drum or a series of disks. There is no basic difference in principle between these forms; the drum can be thought of as a series of tape bands, and the disks as a series of tape rings. (See figure 4–4.)

Drum memories and disk memories may read and write one bit at a time, or have several heads in parallel, as is the practice with tape. Some drum memories and disk memories have two or three sets of read/write heads. While one word is being read, another head moves to address the next word.

The tape memory has an infinite capacity if allowance is made for changing tapes, and has the largest capacity of all memory devices, even if only the tape actually on the machine is counted. Unfortunately, the access time (i.e., the time it takes to move the tape until the word addressed is under the read head) may be very long, since the entire length of the tape may have to be traversed. For this reason, tape is not used for storing intermediate data, although it is often used for storing program or operating instructions and files since the machine usually runs through them one at a time, in the order in which they occur. The drum type improves the access time at the expense of capacity. The disc type also sacrifices capacity for improved access time. The capacity of the disc type is greater than that of the drum type, and its access time is about the same if several read/write heads are used, but its cost is greater. The access time for drum-type and disk-type memories can be reduced by optimum coding. This is the practice of storing the instructions in such a way that the material addressed will come under the read head just at the time it is required. This is not practical for general-purpose computers. Since the time required for each computer operation must be calculated to determine what position the read head will be in, the process is costly and usually requires several trial runs on the computer. For a special-purpose computer, however, optimum coding can often permit the use of a much less expensive memory than would otherwise be required.

(3) Input/Output

The category of input/output (I/O) equipment includes all devices necessary to communicate with the computer. The function of this equipment is to convert instructions and data into whatever form is required by the computer, and to convert the results into a usable form.

Some of the more common input/output devices are: keyboard, teletypes, paper tape readers, paper tape punches, high-speed line printers, magnetic tape units, cathode ray tubes, card readers, magnetic discs, and optical mark readers. (See figure 4–5b.)

Often the largest part of a computer (such as your hand-held calculator) consists of input/output equipment. In a military computer, where data is not available in advance and is obtained from a variety of sources, the speed and accuracy requirements of this equipment are often more demanding than those of the computer itself. Generally speaking, the I/O devices are much slower than the speed of the central processor.

Computer Software

Once the "hardware" or circuit wiring of a digital computer is completed and the desired external equipment or peripherals is attached, it must be given a detailed, complete, and unambiguous set of instructions to carry out after it is set into operation. These instructions are called the "program" or "software" and are as important to the functioning of a digital computer as the electronic expertise that went into its internal design.

Because a digital computer performs its computations on numbers, some method of electronically representing numbers must be used to enter data into the computer and to manipulate the data internally. Most data representation systems that are used with digital computers require only the gross recognition of the presence or absence of data. This is sometimes known as yes/no, on/off, true/false, or 1/0 data representation. The binary number system, which only uses the digits 1 and 0, is a natural method to use to represent numbers within the computer, since any number may be represented by the correct sequence of 1s and 0s.

Within the computer, each digit of a binary number is known as a "bit" (binary digit). Most computers use a fixed number of bits to represent numbers. These groupings of bits are called computer "words" and are the basic units of manipulation within the computer. Typical word lengths are from 8 to 32 bits, although longer word lengths are possible and some computers are able to address every bit. Computer memories, in turn, are capable of storing or filing a fixed number of words at any one time, which is frequently used to denote the computer size. That is, a 48K computer would have immediate access memory (RAM) to store 48K words of whatever length that computer uses. It should be noted that $1K = 1024 = 2^{10}$. The arithmetic accuracy of a computer using longer words is greater.

Programming is done on three broad levels: (1) Machine language, (2) Assembly (or symbolic) language, and (3) High-level (or compiler) language. The term "language" arose because of the similarity between communicating with a computer and communicating with someone who only understands a different language. In either case, it is necessary to translate your ideas or instructions into a form understandable by the other. Machine language is the most rudimentary form of programming. Since digital computers are binary machines, data and instructions are represented internally by binary numbers—either in memory or in the various registers. Machine language programming requires that the binary numbers representing the desired sequence of events to be performed by the computer be entered into the appropriate memory locations within the computer. This is usually done by manually setting an input register to the binary number desired, specifying the memory location for that number and entering the number into memory at that location. This is time consuming for a person to do and is subject to error because humans do not think in binary. In addition it requires the programmer to be present at the computer in order to enter the data.

For example, to program a typical general-purpose digital computer in machine language, all programs consist solely of binary numbers as shown below:

$$1\ 0\ 0\ 1\ 1\ 1\ 0\ 0\ 1\ 1\ 0\ 1$$
$$0\ 1\ 1\ 0\ 1\ 1\ 1\ 0\ 0\ 0\ 0\ 1$$

The entire program would be extremely difficult to write since all operations would require the programmer to think in binary. In order to eliminate this problem, translators are used that convert higher level languages or mnemonics into the machine language that the computer "understands."

The next higher language—assembly language—allows a programmer to use a specified alphanumeric code for his program. This code uses alphabetic and hexidecimal mnemonics instead of binary numbers. For example, ADD would mean add, and could represent the binary number 00110110—obviously more easily understood. Also, memory locations could be assigned a name instead of a binary number—for instance, ADD X instead of 00110110 and 1101110011111—and any further references to X would specify that same location. When symbolic language is used, the computer must already have had a translator program put in it—usually written in machine language and stored in its ROM—that will interpret each symbolic code and translate it to the corresponding machine language code that eventually gets stored in its memory. Usually, symbolic language programs are translated on a one-for-one basis, i.e., each mnemonic instruction generates only one machine language instruction. Sometimes, however, there are certain symbolic instructions that generate a long sequence of machine language instructions.

Machine languages and symbolic languages are applicable only to a specific model of a computer. They will differ from computer to computer because of internal design differences, i.e., the same binary code may mean different things to two different computers. When writing software to control the operation of the computer, assembly language offers the programmer complete control of the machine. Usually, only professional programmers use machine or symbolic language for programming because it is so machine oriented and can be extremely tedious and detailed.

In an attempt to alleviate this difficulty, many high-level languages have been developed. All of them attempt to aid the programmer by allowing him to state his problem in simple English language phrases or mathematical notation. Like any language, each has its own peculiar grammar and format that must be followed for it to be successfully understood by the computer. An important feature of high-level languages is that a program written in a high-level language is not machine dependent. However, the translator/compiler for a given language is machine dependent, and the high-level language program must be converted by the translator/compiler into the machine language for that specific computer. The most common compiler languages today in the U.S. are: BASIC—used primarily with time-shared systems, FORTRAN—oriented toward scientific problem solving, COBOL—aimed at business applications, and PL/I (Programming Language I)—an effort to combine scientific problem solving and business applications. There are many other languages in existence, but not as widespread or in common usage. The language used for the Navy and Marine Tactical Data systems is a compiler language called CMS-2.

Since no one language could meet all DOD programming requirements, there are many languages in use in DOD. Supporting so many languages is a severe software maintenance problem. In addition, system integration becomes a critical issue when computers can't communicate via the same language. To alleviate these problems, DOD commissioned the creation of a high-level language called ADA. ADA's "mission" is to be a standard language, capable of fulfilling all of DOD's programming needs. As a result, it is a huge and complicated language, but should simplify programming, software support, and systems integration over the long term.

Classes of Digital Computers

Purpose. Digital computers may be divided into two broad classes—special purpose and general purpose. As the name implies, *special-purpose computers* are designed for individual, specific applications where no flexibility is required. Only that amount of hardware or circuitry necessary to accomplish its purpose is used, and the design is optimized in terms of size, power, cost, or any other relevant criteria. Since the application and design of each special-purpose computer is unique, no attempt will be made to discuss all the possible techniques used in their construction.

The solution of the fire control problem must be accomplished in a "real time" environment; that is, it must proceed fast enough so as to permit the results to influence the related process that is underway. The same is true for command and control systems. Herein lies the main difference between special-purpose and general-purpose computers. The military special-purpose computer must function in the "real time" environment with sufficient speed to accomplish this mission.

Some applications of special-purpose computers are: Poseidon guidance, cryptographic decoding, AN/TPQ-27 radar-directed bombing systems, and radar tracking systems. Applications of the computers to command and control systems will be discussed later. In almost any of the above applications, the computer is a part of some larger overall system, and its design is conditioned by the need to be integrated with the rest of the hardware.

On the other hand, the *general-purpose computer* is produced for a large range of potential applications and is designed to be as flexible as possible in order to accommodate a maximum number of uses. Because of this, for any single use, a general-purpose computer will normally not be required to use all of its potential capability. Very few programs require the full use of all the instructions, the memory storage space, the input/output capability, or the high processing speed of the modern computer. Because of the rapid advances in today's weapons systems, the general-purpose computer offers the advantage of being able to be reprogrammed to accommodate changes in both our systems and those of our adversaries.

The current general-purpose computer of the Navy and Marine Corps tactical data systems and fire control systems is the UNIVAC AN/UYK-7 computer.

Architecture. One way to solve a bigger problem is to build a bigger, faster computer. Another way is to use more than one computer. How the computers in a multi-computer system are organized is called the system architecture. Two terms often used in describing such architectures are *distributed processing* and *parallel processing*. Not all references agree on the definitions, and computer systems are built to purpose, not to definition. In general terms, a computer system is *distributed* if it is more than one computer working on parts of the same problem in coordination with each other (whether located remotely from each other or not). This type of computer system is *loosely coupled*. A *parallel-processing* computer system is one in which more than one computer is working on parts of the same problem (whether located remotely from each other or not) under a hierarchical structure where some computers are subordinate to others. This is a *closely coupled* system.

Still another way to look at computing is whether the computer is a separate entity from the system it serves, or is an integral part of that system. When the computer is an integral part of a system, it is considered *embedded*, as are computers in many weapons systems. Embedded computers may be either general or special purpose and could have any appropriate architecture.

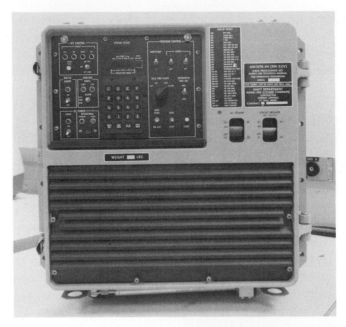

Figure 4–5a. The AN/UYK-44 digital computer configured for use as a stand-alone computer (top) or as separate circuit cards for use as an embedded installation (bottom). (Courtesy Sperry Corporation)

Figure 4–5b. Magnetic tape drive for P-3C Orion.

Analog Computers

Perhaps the first analog computation was the graphic solution of surveying problems. The first actual analog computer was probably the slide rule, which was developed about 1600.

The next analog computational device of importance was the nomogram. A nomogram is a chart on which some functional relationship of three or more variables is represented in such a way that it is possible to determine the values of one variable corresponding to given values of the other variables. Descartes was apparently the first to use graphs to represent functional relations between two variables.

Another analog-computing aid is the plainimeter, which was developed about 1814 by J. H. Herman. The plainimeter is an integrating device used to measure the area bounded by a closed curve on a two-dimensional plot such as a map.

In 1876 Lord Kelvin applied the ball-and-disk integrator to the construction of a harmonic analyzer. This machine was used to analyze and predict the height of tides in various ports.

Invented independently by Abdank Abakanoviez in 1878 and C. V. Boys in 1882 is the integraph, another integrating device of the same family, which can be used to obtain the integral of an arbitrary function from a two-dimensional plot. By proper manipulation of the integral curve and by successive approximations, it is possible to solve certain classes of differential equations with the integraph.

No really major breakthroughs were made in the area of analog devices until the early 1940s. During the Second World War many special-purpose electronic analog computers were built, and components were developed that made possible the construction of general-purpose analog computers. The most significant development, perhaps, was that of the voltage operational amplifier. Designs came out of the war that made possible the construction of an amplifier with extremely high gain and input impedance and near-zero output impedance. This brought about the construction of a quite accurate analog computer in 1947. Since that time many developments have taken place. The general-purpose computer has been improved with respect to accuracy, preciseness, and ease of problem setup. Machines have grown from 20 amplifiers to 500 and 1,000 amplifiers. Many problems are solved every day on analog computers involving 100 to 500 amplifiers.

Basic Features of an Analog Computer

The analog computer provides the following five essential functions required for the solution of differential equations:

(1) Addition (subtraction is merely inverse addition).
(2) Multiplication (division is merely inverse multiplication).
(3) Integration (solution of differential equation is essentially an integration process).
(4) Function generation: i.e., the ability to produce inputs such as step functions, ramps, sinusoidal functions, impulse functions.
(5) Display: i.e., the values of variables can be taped and measured on voltage-sensitive meters, chart recorders, or $X-Y$ plotters.

Removable patch boards are used to wire up connections between components so as to represent the equation being solved. When satisfied with the circuitry, the patch board is then plugged into the computer and activated to solve the equation.

Hardware Components

The basic computing element of the electronic analog computer is the high-gain directly coupled amplifier. For purposes of analysis the high-gain amplifier is assumed to have an infinite input impedance and a zero output impedance. The symbol for the high-gain amplifier is shown below in figure 4–6. The output for most laboratory analog computers is limited by amplifier design to the range ±13 volts. Since the gain (K) is of the order 10^8, this requires that the input voltage (E_{input}) must remain less than 10^7 volts. This results in the point being a virtual ground since, for proper amplifier operation, this point must remain near zero, or ground. This fact is used in the analysis of the operational amplifier.

The high-gain amplifier can be used for addition, subtraction, inversion of sign (inverter), and for integration. In order to accomplish any of these functions, a feedback loop must be connected as shown in figure 4–7. When the amplifier is so connected, it is normally referred to as an operational amplifier. Simply by changing the feedback element, the amplifier can be changed to build a summing amplifier or integrating amplifier, etc.

Summing amplifier. For the case where the feedback element is purely resistive, the circuit can be analyzed using Kirchoff's current law at the point in figure 4–8 marked *SJ* (summing junction). Since the gain across the amplifier is 10^8, the current, i_b, must approach zero, which will be assumed, and E_B must be at virtual ground or zero.

Therefore

$$i_{input} + i \nearrow_B^0 + i_f = 0$$

and

$$\frac{(E_{IN} - E_B)}{R_{IN}} + \frac{(E_O - E_B)}{R_f} = 0$$

$$\frac{E_{IN}}{R_{IN}} + \frac{E_O}{R_f} = 0$$

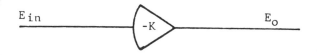

E in   -K   E$_O$

Figure 4–6. High-gain DC amplifier.

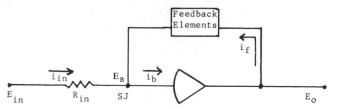

Figure 4–7. Operational amplifier.

solving for E_O

$$E_O = -\left(\frac{R_f}{R_{IN}}\right) E_{IN} \qquad (4-1)$$

Note that the output of an operational amplifier always experiences a sign reversal and is dependent upon the ratio of the feedback resistor to the input resistor.

Using equation (4–2)

$$\frac{R_f}{R_{IN}} = \frac{100K\Omega}{100K\Omega} = 1 \qquad \begin{array}{l} E_O = -E_{IN} \\ \text{a gain of 1} \end{array}$$

$$\frac{R_f}{R_{IN}} = \frac{100K\Omega}{10K\Omega} = 10 \qquad \begin{array}{l} E_O = -10\,E_{IN} \\ \text{a gain of 10} \end{array} \qquad (4-2)$$

Whenever the input and feedback resistors are of the same value, the coefficient by which the output is related to the input is unity, and the device is a simple inverting amplifier or inverter. It should be remembered that all amplifiers invert the signal, but an amplifier that only changes the sign of the input is given the special name of inverter. If this analysis is extended to the case where there is more than one input (hence more than one R_{IN}), then the device is called a summing amplifier or *summer*. By modifying the feedback elements, one can cause an operational amplifier to act as an integrating amplifier, a differentiating amplifier, or an inverter. From this analysis it is obvious that one use of the analog computer is to solve differential equations. Figure 4–9 summarizes the symbols used in analog com-

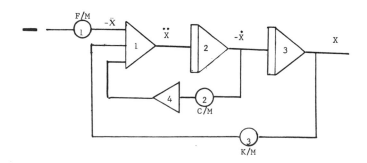

Figure 4–8. Analog flow diagram for accelerometer.

Linear Computing Element	Symbol		Mathematical Operation Performed
	Input	*Output*	
Potentiometer (pot)	x_i ──◯── K	$x_o = Kx_i$	Multiplication by a constant
Inverter	x_i ──▷──	$x_o = -x_i$	Sign reversal
Summer	x_1 ──▷── x_2	$x_o = -(x_1 + x_2)$	Addition
Summer	x_1 ──▷── $-x_2$	$x_o = -(x_1 - x_2)$	Subtraction
Integrator	$\pm$ as per $\mp$ IC ◯ $\lvert x_o(0)\rvert$ x_i ──▷──	$-\left(\int_0^t x_i\,dt - x_o(0)\right)$	Integration

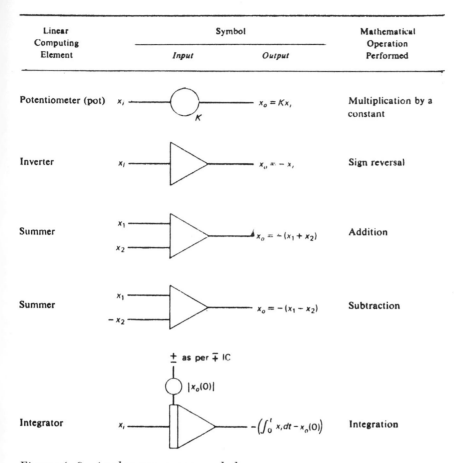

Figure 4–9. Analog computer symbology.

puter flow diagrams for the linear computing elements described in this chapter. Amplifier gains are unity in all examples depicted.

Applications of Analog Computers

The uses of analog computers fall into three general categories: solution of equations, simulation, and control. The difference is more in the method by which the analog is arrived at than in the actual nature of the analog. For example, if analog devices were used to simulate a mechanical system piece by piece, it would be called simulation. If the differential equations for the system were obtained and analog devices used to solve the equations, it would be called solution of equations, yet the analogs resulting from both processes might be identical.

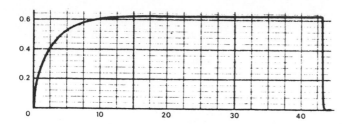

Figure 4–10. Graph of distance vs time for an accelerometer S&A device.

Solution of equations. Most projectiles and missiles use some type of accelerometer safety and arming (S&A) devices. The equation of motion of the mass or *g*-weight in an accelerometer is given as

$$M\ddot{X} + C\dot{X} + KX = F(t) \qquad (4\text{–}3)$$

This equation can be solved quite easily using the analog computer. The analog flow diagram is shown in figure 4–8. Normally the coefficient of the acceleration term is made equal to 1, so the equivalent equation is

$$\ddot{X} + \frac{C}{M}\dot{X} + \frac{K}{M}X = \frac{F}{M}(t) \quad \text{Solve for} -\ddot{X} \qquad (4\text{–}4)$$

$$-\ddot{X} = \frac{C}{M}\dot{X} + \frac{K}{M}X - \frac{F(t)}{M} \qquad (4\text{–}5)$$

If the output of amplifier 3 is placed on an *X–Y* recorder, a graph of the displacement of the *g* weight as a function of time is produced. For appropriate values for *F*, *K*, *C*, and *M*, the solution for *X* can be either critically damped, overdamped, or underdamped. If the system is to be critically damped, the graph would be as shown in figure 4–10.

Simulation. Consider the accelerometer S&A devices previously discussed. If the accelerometer is to be modeled and the analog computer is to be the vehicle on which the system is represented, the modeling is called a simulation. By simply varying either pots 1, 2, or 3, it is possible to vary the force, degree of viscous damping, or spring constant and thereby vary the performance of the system without having to build several different accelerometers. In this manner, many simulations can be performed in a minimal amount of time.

Although this is a simplistic treatment of a very rudimentary system, the student can easily realize the tremendous cost savings using the analog to model more complex systems.

Control. In addition to performing calculations, analog devices are frequently used to translate the results into action. The most common application of this type is the area of weapons control and system control.

In most weapons control systems, the object is to cause the input to exactly match the output and respond at a predetermined rate. The analog can be efficiently used first to simulate the physical system and then to determine the type and magnitude of feedback necessary to have the system respond as desired.

In most cases, the data from analog computers used in weapons systems will be data that must be translated into action. In this case, the output is usually connected to some form of control system. For example, if the output were a gun elevation, the signal would be used as the order to a servomechanism that would elevate the gun.

Hybrid Computers

In the 1940s, computer engineers tended to specialize in either analog or digital computers, rather than in both. But by the late 1950s the trend towards specialization ended as engineers began to realize the advantages/disadvantages of both types of computers, depending on the specific problem the computer was used to solve. The hybrid computer is a combination of both digital and analog design.

Since the hybrid computer can handle any problem or physical process described by a set of simultaneous ordinary or partial differential equations, it makes possible an accurate, truly representative simulation. Dynamic problems that once took too long or were too difficult to handle became solvable in a reasonable length of time. Figure 4–11 shows the flow of information in a hybrid computer composed of a general-purpose digital computer and a general-purpose analog computer.

The analog computer excels in solving dynamic problems and simulating complex physical systems. It has no equal for man-machine interaction, recording and graphic display, and repetitive or iterative multivariable problem solution at real-time and faster than real-time speeds. High-speed computing elements, used to simulate mathematical functions, physical systems, and dynamic processes, are arranged in much the same pattern as the physical system they represent. In contrast to a sequential digital computer, the analog machine is a parallel system, performing all computations simultaneously, and is therefore capable of producing continuous solutions to dynamic problems. It has no need for numerical approximations, since its mathematical functions are carried out directly. Precision is limited to 1 part in 10,000, which is sufficient for accurate simulation of scientific and engineering problems.

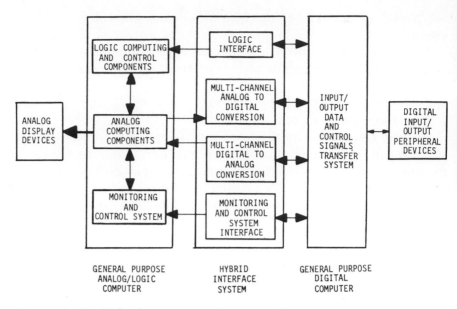

Figure 4-11. Hybrid computer information flow.

The digital computer is good at solving algebraic equations and even better at manipulating numbers. It is unbeatable for high-speed precision in arithmetical operations, data storage, and documentation. Because it is a sequential machine, however, it can perform only one calculation at a time and thus cannot solve even simple multivariable problems all at once. It must break them up into segments, store the results, and recall them as needed. The basic sequential nature of the digital computer is retained even in the multiprocessor environment. The documentation capability of the digital computer is unmatched by any other system. Results are available in a variety of forms, such as printed tables, magnetic or punched tape, and the familiar punched cards. Properly used in high-accuracy, high-volume numerical calculations, the digital computer is extremely economical, and its assets are desirable for much engineering and scientific work, such as stress analysis of static structures.

Hardware

Analog to digital (A/D) converters. An "analog to digital" converter (ADC) is an electronic device that accepts an analog or continuous input voltage from some source and determines the value of that voltage for eventual input to a computer. The analog input in figure 4-12 is converted within the ADC to a coded digital output, where

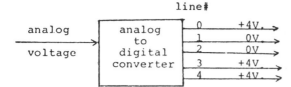

line#

Figure 4–12. Analog to digital converter.

the presence or absence of a voltage on any of the lines 0 through 4 signifies a binary 1 or 0.

The process of analog-to-digital conversions is not uncommon. Our minds make hundreds of analog-digital conversions each day. For example, if you ask a young child what time it is, he will probably look at a clock and tell you that the long hand is near the six and the short hand is between the four and the five. The child is performing the function of data transmission, not data conversion. He is accepting the instantaneous value of the constantly moving hands of the clock, but he is transmitting the information in analog, not digital, form. The data that the child transmitted is converted into numerical values, in this case, four thirty. You, the inquirer, are therefore performing the analog-to-digital conversion; the child is not.

Care must be taken to avoid confusing truly digital readouts with others that merely appear to be digital. The needle of a voltmeter or the pointer on an automobile speedometer provides analog data by indicating the instantaneous value of volts or miles per hour in a constantly changing manner. It is only by reading these meters and assigning numerical values that a truly digital readout is obtained. Just as in the example of the clock, the human observer is serving as the analog-to-digital converter. Similarly, the type of data that is obtained from a micrometer scale or from the mercury column of a thermometer is analog in nature, until converted by the reader. The accuracy of each of these devices is in large measure a function of the ability of the reader to convert the information accurately from analog to digital form.

On the other hand, mechanical counters such as those commonly used to count the number of people entering a building provide a true digital readout. No great amount of skill is required for reading such a device because its accuracy does not depend on the reader, but upon its design. If each click of the counter corresponds to a count of one, no amount of skill on the part of the reader will increase its inherent precision.

Digital to analog (D/A) converters. A digital-to-analog converter performs the reverse operation, accepting a digital input on a parallel group of input lines and transforming that into an output voltage proportional to the digital input. This output voltage may then be used for any desired purpose.

Digital-to-analog conversion, like analog-to-digital conversion, can be accomplished by both mechanical and electrical methods. The purpose of mechanical digital-to-analog conversions is to convert digital information into a mechanical movement or shaft position as is common in weapons systems.

Scope of Hybrid Computation

Hybrid computation offers the most economical and efficient means of solving a broad spectrum of problems that arise in many fields of science and engineering. Some classes of applications related to specific fields are shown in table 4–1. The major applications in aerospace have been for vehicle simulations. The objectives of these simulations have been to train pilots, design and evaluate automatic control systems, determine fuel requirements for optimal space missions, etc. In addition, special studies such as nose-cone ablation of a re-entry vehicle have arisen that require the solution of partial differential equations.

In the chemical field, the major applications involve the solution of partial differential equations for chemical reactors, heat exchangers, etc. Also, various types of optimization problems have been solved using hybrid techniques. In all of these problems, the analog computer accuracy is adequate, and the high speed is employed very effectively.

In the biomedical field, the most significant applications have been for analysis and identification of signals derived from sensors attached to humans and animals. In most cases, this has been done to determine abnormalities due to disease or the introduction of drugs into the subject. Considerable experimental work has been done in the simulation of physiological function on the analog computer. The hybrid computer offers a convenient means of automatically relating the results of these simulations to actual data.

The applications for hybrid computation in the communications field have been rather specialized, as can be seen in the list in table 4–1. Some of these have been research studies, such as the Ionospheric Ray Tracing that involved the solution of the equations of the path of a radio wave under the influence of a changing refractive index. In this problem, the analog computer solved all of the equations defining the ray path, and the digital computer provided the complex function generation to represent the ionosphere. The overall economic savings in solving this problem on the hybrid computer was

Table 4–1.   Classes of Hybrid Computer Applications

Field of Application	Type of Problem	
Aerospace	1.	Aerospace vehicle mission simulations
	2.	V/STOL vehicle simulations
	3.	Aircraft adaptive control
	4.	Control system studies
	5.	Boundary value problems
	6.	Nose-cone ablation
	7.	Launch window studies
	8.	Terrain avoidance simulation
Chemical	1.	Chemical reactor simulations
	2.	Heat-exchanger simulations
	3.	Distillation columns
	4.	Kinetics curve fitting
	5.	Process optimizations
	6.	Plant optimization
	7.	Process control simulation
Bio-Medical	1.	EKG and EEG data analysis
	2.	Physiological simulation
Communication	1.	Wave propagation
	2.	Ionospheric ray tracing
	3.	Antenna pattern calculations
	4.	Radio signal data processing
	5.	Learning and recognition studies
Others	1.	Submarine simulations
	2.	Nuclear reactor simulations
	3.	Gas pipeline analysis

approximately 600/1 over an all-digital solution. The learning and recognition studies used the hybrid computer to analyze the spectrum of a voice signal and to develop functions that would permit recognition of arbitrary words within a given vocabulary.

The other applications listed in table 4–1 represent specific studies that have been performed in various fields.

Typical Hybrid Computer Application

As mentioned earlier, one of the major uses of hybrid computation has been in the combined simulation of an aerospace vehicle. One example of this type of problem is the simulation of a space vehicle re-entering the atmosphere under control of a temperature rate sensing system. In this type of control system, temperature sensors are placed on the wing-tips and nose of the vehicle to sense those points that are subject to the greatest aerodynamic heating during re-entry. The control system operates on the rate of change in the temperature of these points to control the attitude of the vehicle to ensure safe limits in the skin temperature peaks. This control will override the guidance system commands if the integrity of the vehicle is in danger.

An overall block diagram of this simulation is shown in figure 4–13. As in all simulations of this type, the translational equations of motion are solved on the digital computer for precision, and the attitude equations are handled on the analog computer due to the lower precision requirements and higher frequencies.

The digital computer is also used to simulate the guidance system and the temperature sensors, since these are related only to the lower frequency variables generated from the translational equations. In addition, the digital computer is used to compute the aerodynamic force and moment coefficients that include four functions of one variable and four functions of two variables using stored tables in the digital memory. The patchable logic is used to simulate the reaction jet control system used to maintain vehicle attitude based on commands from the temperature rate flight control program.

It should be noted that a complete system simulation such as this encompasses a number of the standard operations listed in the basic

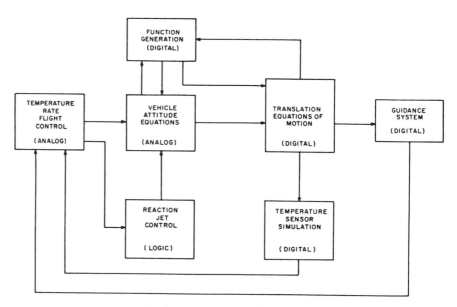

Figure 4–13. Space vehicle re-entry simulation.

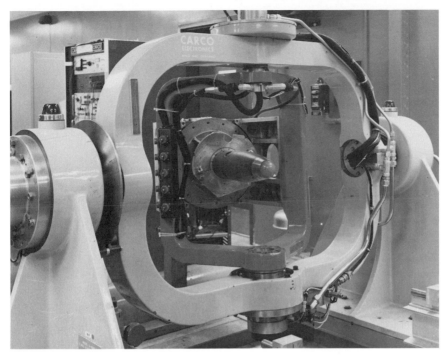

Figure 4–14. Hybrid computer flight simulation system for a Sidewinder missile.

functions. This simulation was very successful, and an efficiency of at least 20 to 1 over all-digital computation was realized.

Summary

The most significant feature that distinguishes analog computation from digital computation is continuity; analog computations imply continuous computation—that is, the variables involved in a calculation appear as continuous or smooth functions, whereas digital computations are separate, discrete manipulations of numbers producing numerical results similar to a cash register receipt.

Digital computers are electronic devices that manipulate individual numbers in much the same fashion as you would if you were solving a problem step by step with a pencil and paper. However, each step is performed in an extremely short time—typically 1 or 2 microseconds to add two numbers. In addition, digital computers are more flexible than analog computers, in that any numerical manipulation desired may be performed. Also, the precision of digital calculations may be to any desired number of significant digits. The most powerful capability of the digital computer, the step that separates it from an adding machine or desk calculator, is its ability to make decisions and decide between alternatives, adjusting to situations as they occur. For instance, when you perform a calculation of the price of a new car, you then compare that price to your budget and make the decision to buy or not to buy the car. Your subsequent actions and decisions will then be based on that decision, perhaps examining finance charges in one case and considering a different car in the other. A digital computer is capable of performing the same type of decisions, and because of this simulation of human thinking processes, there is a feeling that the digital computer is capable of thinking or acting as an "electronic brain." In fact, in order for a digital computer to do anything, it must be given a set of operating instructions that describe in minute detail what operations, decisions, etc., it is supposed to perform. Perhaps the greatest advantage is that of the stored memory. This, coupled with the logic capability, has enabled the digital computer gradually to replace the analog in weapons systems.

Analog computers employ electronic circuits or mechanical systems to create an electrical or mechanical analogy (analog) of a mathematical problem or physical process. As an example, the relationship $V = L\ di/dt$ indicates that voltage across an inductor (coil) is proportional to the derivative of the current through the inductor. Therefore, a circuit that measures the voltage across an inductor that results from a known applied current would provide an electrical analogy of the mathematical process used to solve differential equations. Common mechanical analogs include that provided by combining moving and stationary logarithmic scales, as on a slide rule, to perform multiplication, division, etc. A large number of mathematical operations may similarly be performed by appropriate electrical circuits or mechanical devices that are interconnected to represent a complex mathematical formula. The primary limitation of analog computers is loss of accuracy due to difficulty in manufacturing circuit elements or mechanical devices to the extremely close tolerances required and in maintaining those tolerances while in use. Another problem is that not all problems have electrical or mechanical analogies such as sorting a list of numbers into ascending order. Analog computers can typically provide answers to three significant figures.

This precision is sufficient for most computations, where the precision of the input data is of the same order of magnitude. Because both the input and output of the analog computer are usually electrical quantities (either voltage or current), the analog computer has great application in systems requiring continuous electrical control for operation. The use of an analog computer to compute the lead angle required for an antiaircraft gun system is a typical example.

The fundamental characteristic of the analog is simulation, i.e., it duplicates the geometry, dynamic behavior, or some other aspect of the problem. The basic operating principle of analog devices is continuous measurement of quantities. Analog computers can be employed in weapons systems wherever problems of calculations from continuous data, simulation, or control are encountered.

Hybrid computers have a parallel analog processor, a serial digital processor, and a hybrid interface that allows these dissimilar systems to interact and communicate with each other. Such a combination of analog and digital equipment allows the capabilities of one system to compensate for the limitations of the other, thus yielding the best of both worlds.

Comparison

1. Digital Computers
   a. Advantages:
      Precision limited only by size of computer word
      Ability to store large amounts of information
      Ability to perform logic functions
      Ability to handle non-numerical data
   b. Disadvantages:
      Cannot perform "real-time" calculations
      Limited to discrete input/output
2. Analog Computers
   a. Advantages:
      Dependent variables within computer treated in continuous form
      Parallel operation, with all computational elements operating simultaneously
      Ability to perform efficiently such operations as multiplication, addition, integration, and non-linear function generation
      High-speed or "real-time" operation, with computing speeds limited primarily by the characteristics of the computing elements and not by the problem
   b. Disadvantages:
      Accuracy limited by the quality of computer components
      Limited ability to make logic decisions, store numerical data, provide extended time delays, and handle non-numerical information

Differentiation is difficult to realize in practice

The summing amplifiers and integrators almost always introduce a change in algebraic sign

The useful frequency range of the computer is limited at low frequencies by drift and at high frequencies by phase shift and attenuation

The amplitude scale of the computer is limited by amplifier saturation

3. Hybrid Computers

Some of the reasons for combining digital and analog computers are listed below.

To obtain the accuracy of the digital and the speed of the analog

By employing digital memory, to increase the flexibility of an analog simulation

To permit the processing of both discrete and continuous data simultaneously

To increase digital speed by using analog subroutines

The results of this combination are:

Accurate simulation

High-speed man-to-machine interactions

Precise numerical and algebraic calculations

Mass memory

Graphic display

Automatic documentation

References

Bekey, G. A., and W. J. Karplus. *Hybrid Computation*. New York: Wiley and Sons, 1968.

Blum, Joseph L. *Introduction to Analog Computation*. New York: Harcourt, Brace, & World, Inc., 1969.

Commander, Naval Ordnance Systems Command. *Weapons Systems Fundamentals*. NAVORD OP 3000, vol. 1, 1st Rev. Washington, D.C.: GPO, 1971.

Commander, Naval Ordnance Systems Command. *Weapons Systems Fundamentals*. NAVORD OP 3000, vol. 2, 1st Rev. Washington, D.C.: GPO, 1971.

Durling, Allen. *Computational Techniques*. New York: Educational Publishers, 1974.

Harrison, H. L., and J. G. Bollinger. *Introduction to Automatic Control*. Scranton, Pa.: International Text Book Co., 1963.

Headquarters, U.S. Army Material Command. *Servomechanisms*. AMC pamphlet 706-136, April, 1965.

Landauer, J. Paul. *Spectrum of Applications for the Modern Hybrid Com-*

puter. Electronic Associates, Inc. Bulletin No. 66460, Applications Reference Library, 1970.

Mader, Chris. *Information Systems: Technology, Economics Applications*. Science Research Associates, Inc., Chicago: 1975.

Naval Education and Training Command. *Digital Computer Basics*. NAV-TRA 10088-A, Washington, D.C.: GPO, 1973.

Stone, Harold S. *Introduction to Computer Architecture*. Science Research Associates, Inc. Chicago: 1975.

5

Automatic Tracking Systems

Introduction

In any fire control system, *target tracking* is the means by which target parameters are measured with respect to the tracking station. These parameters, *azimuth, elevation, range,* and relative target *velocity* are ultimately employed to predict the collision point between the target and whatever weapon is launched against it. Before any computation or launching can be accomplished, however, the critical target parameters must be continuously and accurately measured. This process of continuous measurement is not exact and some *error* is always present.

The line-of-sight (LOS) between the sensor and target, along which radiant energy from the target is received by the sensor, is used to track the target. If the tracking element were at all times pointed directly along this line-of-sight, tracking would be perfect and no error would exist. In reality, however, error is always present, and therefore a second line, the *tracking line*, is defined as the line that forms the axis of symmetry of the radiated energy, commonly called the antenna boresight axis. When error exists, the line-of-sight and the tracking line are not coincident; usually the tracking line lags the line-of-sight by some small amount, due to the general inability of mechanical tracking systems to anticipate target movements. This error defines the central problem of any tracking system: How can

Figure 5–1. Relationship between the line-of-sight and the tracking line.

the error between the line-of-sight and the tracking line be reduced to an acceptable minimum average value?

This problem of minimizing the error between the LOS and the tracking line is further complicated by the fact that weapon platforms are not generally stable. The combined effects of weapon platform roll, pitch, and yaw produce a disturbance in the tracking system that is not related to target motion. These rotational motions not only affect the tracking element's ability to hold the target, but also generate erroneous output data. Since the basis of relative target velocity computation is an accurate measurement of target position over time, the uncompensated rotational motions of the weapon platform would result in erroneous target velocities being generated. As will be seen in a later chapter of this text, target velocity data is a major input for the computation of the weapon launch lead angle.

Tracking radars require separate components for range and angle tracking of a specific target. These functions were performed manually in early radars by operators watching target video, then positioning handwheels to maintain markers over the desired target blip on each scope. The handwheels positioned potentiometers, which adjusted voltages analogous to target azimuth, elevation, or range that were supplied to fire control computers and lead-computing gun sights. As target speeds and operator workloads increased, automatic tracking circuitry was developed that maintained tracking efficiency over sustained periods and made possible the later development of unmanned homing weapons.

Angle-tracking Servo System

Once a target position error signal has been extracted from the returning energy, it forces input to the azimuth and elevation-drive servo systems. These systems keep the antenna pointing at the target; i.e., they serve to minimize the error between the LOS and the tracking line.

In general, all angle-tracking servo systems function conceptually in the same manner. In this regard, practical tracking servo systems accomplish the following functions:

(1) They sense position error magnitude and direction.
(2) They provide for position feedback.
(3) They provide for data smoothing/stabilization.
(4) They provide for velocity feedback to aid in achieving a smooth track.

(5) They provide a power driving device.

It must be emphasized that the concepts discussed here are applicable to the following diverse systems:

- Shipboard fire control mono-track systems (single target capability)
- Homing missiles
- Acoustic homing torpedoes
- Aviation fire control tracking systems (single target capability)

This discussion will be developed from a viewpoint of how the servo system illustrated in figure 5–2 satisfies each of the functions (1) through (5) above.

Position error magnitude and direction. This function is performed by the radar itself in conjunction with circuitry that has been designed specially for the type of radar employed. From the study of sensor subsystems, recall that generally the output of a sensor is target position data, and that this data is available only when the sensor is pointing at the target. Since target position data should be available to the weapon control system at all times, some means of detecting target motion is required if the sensor is to follow the target. Recall also that target information enters the sensor from a beam of energy,

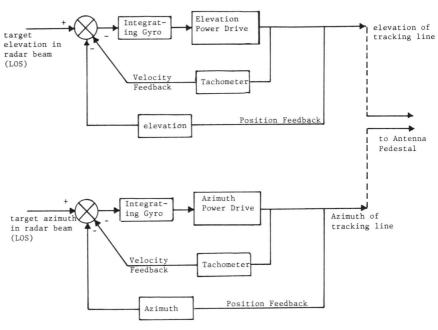

Figure 5–2. Block diagram of a typical automatic tracking system employing a radar sensor system.

with the energy concentrated along the axis of the beam. For example, using a radar sensor, target information is available when the target is within the radar's beam of energy and is strongest when the target is on the beam axis. As the target moves to the periphery of the beam, the return signal level begins to diminish. The amount of signal reduction can therefore be used as a measure of how far the target is away from the beam axis and ultimately can be employed to position the radar antenna back on the target automatically. However, the return signal level will diminish by the same amount regardless of which direction the target takes with respect to the beam axis. For this reason a means of sensing direction is required in addition to that of sensing magnitude. If the target is not exactly in the center of the radar beam, then an error exists between the direction that the radar antenna is pointing and the true line-of-sight to the target. Several methods of determining position error are presented below.

(1) *Sequential lobing*—One of the first tracking methods developed was lobe switching or sequential lobing, which is still in use today in some countries. Recall from chapter 2 that direction (in one axis) can be determined by a double lobe system very rapidly. If the angular error in the orthogonal coordinate is desired simultaneously, the beam could be stepped in a minimum of three (usually four) positions for signal comparisons in a process called sequential lobing. The stepping process is limited by the *PRF* of the system in that beam position must be stopped long enough for at least one transmission and received echo, and probably more prior to switching to the next position. Four separate antennas or four separate feed horns are required in addition to very complex waveguide plumbing and switching techniques. Because three horns or antennas are shorted at any one time, considerable scanning losses occur, and the data rate is extremely low unless sophisticated electronic lobing systems are used.

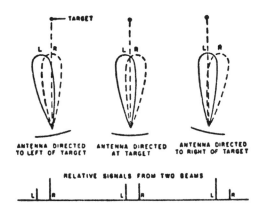

Figure 5–3. Lobe switching. (From Fox et al.)

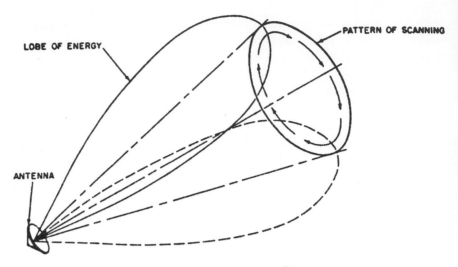

LOBE OF ENERGY

PATTERN OF SCANNING

ANTENNA

Figure 5–4. Conical scanning. (From Fox et al.)

(2) *Conical Scan*—The natural extension of this beam-stepping process in four positions is to rotate the beam continuously in a circular fashion. The error between the tracking axis and the line-of-sight can then be sensed in magnitude and direction by causing the radar beam to be rotated rapidly about the axis of the antenna, thus producing a narrow cone of energy in space. This is generally accomplished mechanically by nutating the feed point (rotating the feed horn) in a small circle around the focal point of a fixed paraboloid; thus, the antenna beam will lie along the axis of the reflector. If the feed point is moved transversely slightly away from the focus, the beam will be at an angle with the axis. If the feed point is oscillated back and forth, the beam will swing from side to side. If the feed point is moved (nutated) in a circle about the axis, a conical scan will result.

Now examine figure 5–6. In this case the antenna axis is pointed directly at the target, so no matter where the transmitted lobe is in the nutation cycle, the echo received by the radar is always of the same amplitude. Although maximum possible energy return is never received, the resulting echoes are all equally strong, and target tracking is very accurate. In actuality, a pulsed radar is employed with a *PRT* less than the nutation period.

The rate of beam rotation must be such that several pulses of radiated energy are exchanged with the target during each period of beam rotation. In actual practice, the ratio PRF/f_s is approximately 40 to 1, where f_s is the scan frequency and *PRF* is the pulse repetition frequency of the radar.

When the LOS and the tracking line are coincident—i.e., the

Figure 5–5. Mk 68 gun director with AN/SPG-53A conical-scan fire control radar. Note the nutating feed horn in the center of the parabolic antenna.

target is exactly on the tracking line—successive target echoes received by the system will be of equal amplitude since the beam center is at all times equidistant from the target during each scan period. However, if the target is not exactly on the antenna axis, an error exists between the line-of-sight and the tracking line. This error is immediately detectable because as the beam rotates, the return pulses are amplitude modulated due to the varying proximity of the target and the beam center. The frequency of modulation is the scan frequency of the system f_s.

This concept of amplitude modulating the sensor input signal is not limited in application to active radar systems. Any system whose function it is to track an energy source can be made to do so by employing the conical scan concept, i.e., laser, infrared, and sonic sensors.

Using the error signal generated from the amplitude modulated input signal in figure 5–7, the radar will be repositioned to cause the returning input signal to again equalize as in figure 5–6.

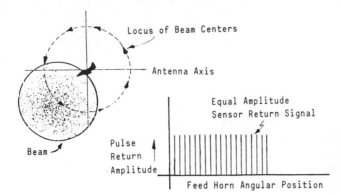

Equal Amplitude
Sensor Return Signal

Pulse
Return
Amplitude

Feed Horn Angular Position

Figure 5–6. Relationship of target position and return pulse amplitude when the target is on the tracking line.

For a system using conical scan techniques, the actual movement of the beam through space is easily detected by the target. Since the error signal is computed directly from the varying amplitude of the return energy, it is possible for the target to use a transponder, which samples the incoming energy and then rebroadcasts it. When the target senses maximum incoming energy, the transponder rebroadcasts an amount equal to or slightly greater than it sensed. As the energy falls off in amplitude due to the major axis of the beam moving

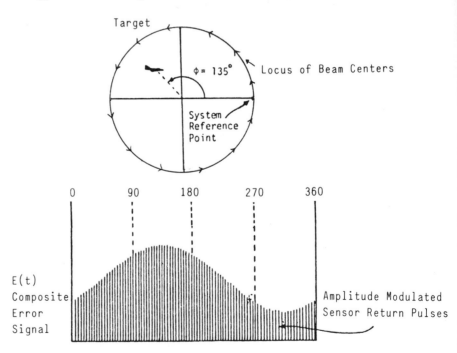

Figure 5–7. Relationship of target position and return pulse amplitude when the target is displaced from the tracking line.

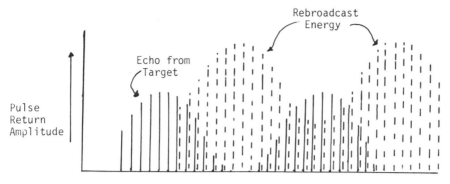

Figure 5–8. Returning "skin" echo with jammer signal superimposed.

away, the transponder will broadcast a signal with proportionally greater amplitude (dotted line in figure 5–8).

When the incoming energy increases with the approach of the main beam axis, the transponder will broadcast a signal with less and less enhancement, until at maximum it is again equal to or slightly greater than the radar echoes. As a result, the radar's tracking system drives the radar away from the target. This technique is referred to as inverse conical scan and is a common means of deceiving conical scan tracking systems.

(3) *COSRO*—As a means of achieving a degree of immunity to deception from inverse conical scan ECM, a system known as COSRO was developed. COSRO, meaning Conical Scan on Receive Only, employs a non-scanning transmit beam and a rotary (nutating) scanner in the waveguide between the duplexer and the receiver to extract elevation and azimuth angle error. A receiver in a target being tracked by the COSRO radar would detect a steady, non-scanning, pulse radar beam that would provide no information that would assist in determining deception techniques beyond the radar performance parameters listed in chapter 2.

During the rest time between pulses, the duplexer switches the antenna to the COSRO scanner (figures 5–9 and 5–10) and receiver. The COSRO scanner has the effect of shifting the axis of greatest sensitivity to echo reception similar to the slight change in the direction of the transmitted beam of a conical scan radar caused by nutation of the feed horn. One could imagine a receive "beam," similar in shape to a transmitted beam, being nutated about the radar boresight axis. The COSRO scanner determines the distribution of signal strength in the received energy by use of an *RF* signal detector rotated by a motor tachometer. The location of the greatest amount of returned energy is determined, and signals are sent to the elevation

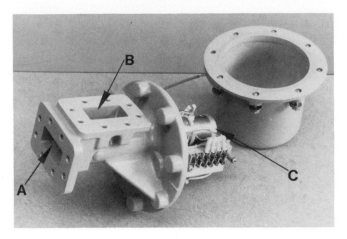

Figure 5–9. COSRO scanner. A— input from duplexer; B—output to receiver; C—scanner motor.

and azimuth power drives to reposition the antenna on the center of the target. When the target is centered, the COSRO scanner will sense equal signal strength throughout the rotation of the *RF* signal detector. This concept can be employed with sequential lobing radars to produce a Lobe on Receiver Only or LORO radar. While there are techniques to deceive these types of radars, as presented in chapter 11, much more sophistication, complexity, and expense are involved.

(4) *Monopulse*—Conical scanning and sequential lobing techniques determine the target's position relative to the radar's main beam axis. If the target is on axis, its amplitude for the return pulse is maximized. If the target is off axis, the return pulse's amplitude is

Figure 5–10. COSRO scanner with motor removed showing RF detector.

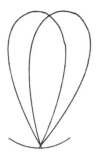

REFLECTOR

Figure 5–11. Simultaneous beam formation.

less. The amount of decrease is dependent on how far off axis the target is. Using this idea and moving the beam through space, the radar amplitude modulated a train of pulses coming back to the receiver. An error signal is extracted from the train of pulses and is used to position the radar. Serious tracking errors can be generated in such a system if the return of any one pulse is markedly increased or decreased in amplitude as compared to the next pulse in the train. Such a fluctuation could easily occur if there were a sudden change in the target's radar cross section (or any number of other reasons). To avoid these errors, a tracking system determines the amplitude modulation using only one pulse instead of a train of pulses. To accomplish this, the target must be located in two or more beams simultaneously—and a comparison made between the return pulse in each beam. This technique is known as simultaneous lobing, or since the tracking error signal is derived from a single pulse, it is also called monopulse. The comparison of the return echo in each beam can be done either in amplitude or phase. We will concentrate on amplitude comparison.

Let's look at two beam systems. These beams can be generated simultaneously in space by a single reflector, and two adjacent feed horns fed by one transmitter. Figure 5–11 shows these beams slightly overlapped.

If an observer were to actually move across the beam paths in figure 5–11 with a power meter, the meter would sense the algebraic sum of the electromagnetic energy produced by the two beams. If the power meter is moved about to various positions in front of the reflector and the measured power levels graphed, a plot as depicted in figure 5–12 would be produced. Notice that the radiation pattern appears as one lobe, though it is really the sum of two separate lobes.

The monopulse radar is designed so that each beam can be identified separately by employing different polarization or some other tagging process. For this reason the beams can be examined together

Automatic Tracking Systems   **143**

REFLECTOR

Figure 5–12. Sum pattern of two beams.

(sum) as depicted in figure 5–12 or separately. By summing the beams, the monopulse radar will receive a large return from a target centered between the two beams just as if it were tracking with the center of a strong single beam. This aspect is employed by the monopulse radar for target detection and range determination. For angle tracking, the radar receiver will invert the value of the energy from one beam, thus changing the sign (figure 5–13), and sum that negative value with the positive value from the other beam. It can be shown that if the target is on the boresight axis of the reflector, there will be equal reflected energy in the two beams. Thus, their algebraic sum would be zero. If the target were to the right of the boresight axis, the sum would be positive, and if it were to the left, the sum would be negative. A graph of the algebraic sum or difference of energy from the two beams is depicted in figure 5–14.

This is how the monopulse radar determines the amount and di-

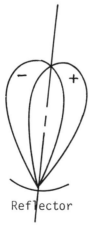

Reflector

Figure 5–13. Difference pattern for two beams.

144 Principles of Naval Weapons Systems

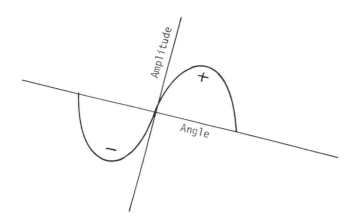

Figure 5–14. Output versus angular displacement for the two beams in figure 5–13.

rection of angular error in one axis. For example, any target to the left of center would have a negative amplitude, and any target to the right of centerline a positive amplitude. The farther from centerline, the greater the magnitude of the signal. This can easily be used as an error signal to drive a servomotor to keep the antenna pointed at the target, thereby reducing the error to a very small value. Figure 5–15 depicts a simplified block diagram of a monopulse system.

This diagram depicts the microwave comparator circuit shown in figure 5–16. The microwave comparator circuit is composed of waveguide and hybrid junctions called "magic tees." The hybrid junctions have two inputs and two outputs. One output is the sum of the inputs, and one is the difference of the inputs. Four hybrids can be connected as shown in figure 5–15 to provide azimuth and elevation error. In this case a cluster of four feed horns producing four beams, indicated by the letters *A*, *B*, *C*, and *D*, are used. To determine azimuth, the sum of the *C* and *D* horn outputs are subtracted from that of the *A* and *B* horns. If the result is positive, then the target is to the right of the boresight axis, assuming the horns at the top of the diagram are facing the reader. If the result is negative, then the target is to the left of the boresight. Elevation error is determined by subtracting the sum of the outputs of the *B* and *D* horns from the sum of the outputs of the *A* and *C* horns, a positive value indicating that the target is above the boresight and a negative value indicating that the target is below the boresight. The tracking circuit and power drives will attempt to equalize the amplitude of the target echo in all four horns, which would result when the target was on the boresight axis.

The signal-to-noise ratio for a monopulse tracker would generally be higher than that of a conical scan system, since the target is tracked

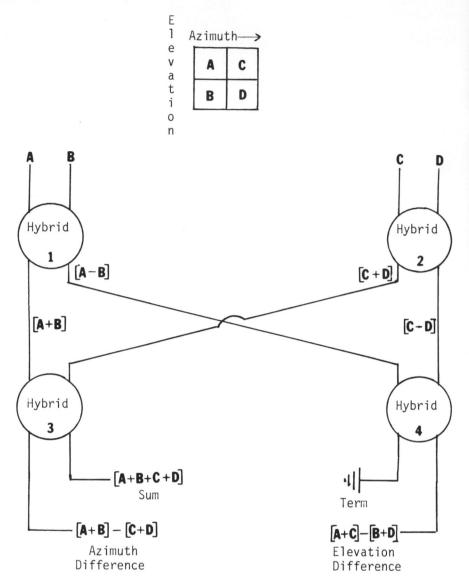

Figure 5–15. Monopulse radar signal comparator circuit. (From Skolnick et al.)

on the axis of summation of the beams rather than on the edge. The target would not be able to sense whether it was being tracked by a monopulse or a COSRO radar, thus making ECM techniques complicated. It is very difficult to deceive a monopulse radar in angle, but it is as easy (or hard) to deceive it in range as with any other radar. The disadvantages of increased complexity and cost of monopulse over that of other techniques are being reduced by advances

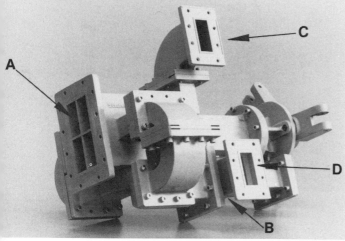

Figure 5–16. Monopulse microwave comparator. A—Antenna feed; B— Hybrid junction; C—Azimuth output; D—Elevation output.

in technology, so that most of today's tracking and homing systems incorporate some variation of this system.

Position feedback. When an error signal is developed and the system is caused to drive in response to it, the system must know when it has reduced the error toward zero. The position feedback is accomplished as an intrinsic part of the error signal generation from the radar. As the system moves in response to the original error, the result is to position the tracking line in coincidence with the LOS. This action by the system reduces the position error signal toward zero, thus providing an indication that the system has responded

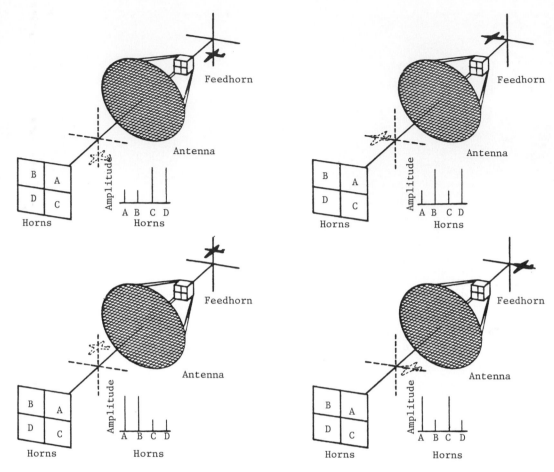

Figure 5–17. Amplitude changes of received energy with target position.

correctly to the error initially measured by the radar. This process is essentially instantaneous and continuous throughout the entire time that the sensor is providing target information to the system. The equilibrium state of the tracking system then is a null composite error signal input to the phase sensitive demodulator ($E(t) = 0$)), resulting in zero DC output to the drive system. It must be understood that the true equilibrium state is *never* achieved while the system is actually tracking, but that if operating properly, the system will always tend toward this state.

Data Smoothing and Stabilization

Stabilization. It should be understood that no single method of compensation for rotational movement exists. Nevertheless, all systems incorporate gyroscopic devices in one way or another. With reference to stabilization, tracking systems can be grouped into three major classes:

(1) *Unstabilized*—The tracking subsystem operates in a totally unstable environment, and therefore its output contains rotational motion components. Gyroscopic compensation is external to the tracking subsystem.

(2) *Partially stabilized*—The tracking member is stabilized along one axis (cross level), and the output contains rotational disturbances associated only with the uncompensated axis. The remainder of compensation is external to the tracking subsystem.

(3) *Fully stabilized*—The tracking member is gimbal-mounted and remains totally unaffected by rotational movement. Its output is completely free of rotational disturbances, and therefore no further compensation need be done prior to computation.

The reference gyro can be dedicated to a specific weapons system, or all weapons and sensors could be served by a single gyro reference. The usefulness of a gyro as a stable reference is due to its tendency to remain in a fixed plane in space if no force is applied to it, and its tendency to turn at right angles to the direction of an outside force applied to it.

Inertia. Gyroscopic inertia enables a gyro to remain at an apparently fixed orientation in space. This property allows it to be used as a directional reference or a vertical reference because it generally remains in the same plane while the vehicle or platform carrying it undergoes roll, pitch, and yaw. This apparent rigidity in space has been used to resist roll in ships; however, this means of direct stabilization required from one to three rotors weighing up to 120 tons each. Modern methods of stabilizing ships, aircraft, and weapons employ very small gyros as vertical and directional references for some type of autopilot. The autopilot senses movement of the gyro, then calculates error and generates a control signal that causes a hydraulic or electrical device to rotate a *Control Surface* that supplies the force to correct the orientation of the ship or aircraft in space or to alter its direction of motion. In each case the gyro (called a free gyro) is permitted to remain fixed in space, thereby moving an attached variable resistor or similar device as the platform rotates under it. In some ships and aircraft, an electrical signal is produced and distributed where needed from a single master gyro for use in navigation, weapons, and sensors, or command and control systems.

Precession. A gyro's spin axis has a tendency to turn at right angles

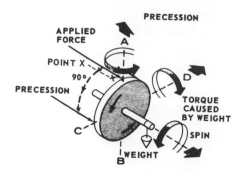

Figure 5–18. The gyroscope.

to the direction of a force applied to it (figure 5–18). This precession causes the flight path of spin-stabilized gun projectiles to curve in the horizontal plane (chapter 19). As depicted in figure 5–19, when a downward force is applied by the weight on the end of the gyro spindle, a torque (*D*) results in precession in a counterclockwise direction. Thus, with a force applied in the vertical plane, the gyro precesses in the horizontal plane. A rate gyro or integrating gyro is fixed in one axis, and the torque of precession is converted to an electrical signal that is used to compute displacement or as a means of controlling gain in an antenna or launcher positioning system.

The integrating gyro. Stabilization and data smoothing can be accomplished with the same equipment. Inputs include roll or pitch angle and target position angle error, which are converted to a single output. The major input is the angle error signal that the gyro smooths to prevent the system from attempting to follow the instantaneous changes in the error signal. The position-error voltage derived from the radar is generally not a smoothly changing signal. If the drive

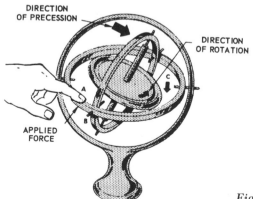

Figure 5–19. Gyro precession.

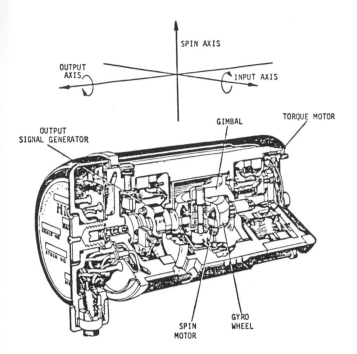

SPIN AXIS

OUTPUT AXIS

INPUT AXIS

OUTPUT SIGNAL GENERATOR

GIMBAL

TORQUE MOTOR

SPIN MOTOR

GYRO WHEEL

Figure 5–20. Integrating gyro, cut-away view.

system were to attempt to follow this signal, the result would be a series of jumps and a relatively rough positioning of the tracking element. The key to this smoothing process is the fact that the gyro cannot respond instantaneously to the changing input signal. This results in an averaging of the small incremental input changes. Figure 5–20 illustrates this electrical input/output relationship.

The governing equation for a gyro device is:

$$T - I\omega dA/dt$$

where

T is torque
ω is the angular velocity of spin
I is the movement of inertia about the spin axis
dA/dt is the angular velocity of precession

The input to the gyro itself is torque caused by the error signal being fed to small coils about the torque axis shaft. When a torque is applied, the response of the gyro is precession, and a signal proportional to the amount of precession is produced by a signal generator mounted on the precession axis shaft. The ability to follow an input signal accurately is governed by the rate of precession.

$$dA/dt = T/I\omega \qquad (5\text{–}1)$$

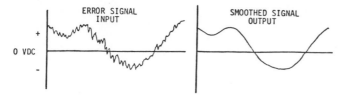

Figure 5–21. Input/output relationship for error signal input to an integrating gyro torque motor and output for signal generator.

Equation (5–1) illustrates that the rate of precession, and ultimately the response of the gyro, are essentially governed by the spin velocity. The slower the spin, the greater will be the response to a given input torque. To achieve a smoothing function, the rate of spin, ω, should be relatively high to prevent the gyro from reacting to all the small changes in the input error signal.

The stabilization process results from the fact that the gyro is mounted in the housing of the tracking element. When the weapon platform pitches and rolls, the gyro reacts to this movement and generates a signal that results in positioning the tracking element in the opposite direction to the rotational motion of the weapon platform.

Limitations. A gyro spinning on earth will appear to tilt with the passage of time without any force applied. In reality the gyro is remaining in its original orientation, and the tilt is due to the rotation of the earth on its axis. Because the gyro does not rotate on frictionless bearings, there is some reaction force that causes the gyro to drift. Both of these phenomena must be taken into account when the gyros are employed.

Velocity feedback. The primary purpose of velocity feedback is to aid in the prevention of a dynamic overshoot. The velocity feedback signal is employed in a degenerative manner; i.e., the feedback voltage is subtracted from the output drive signal of the gyro. This subtraction serves to limit the speed of the output motors at an equilibrium level. This equilibrium level is governed by the ratio of the feedback voltage to the input drive voltage.

Power driving devices. Naval weapons systems generally employ two broad categories of motive devices: electric motors and electrically controlled hydraulic motors. These devices are used to actually move the driven element of the system. The use of two types of motors usually depends upon the physical size of the load to be driven. Smaller loads, such as missile-steering control surfaces and small fire control directors, are driven by electric motors. Electrohydraulic motors are used to position heavy loads such as missile launchers and gun mounts.

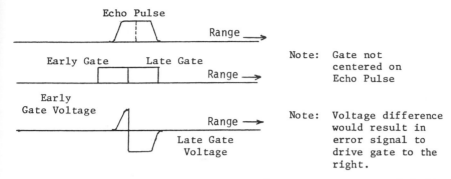

Figure 5–22. Early-late gate range error detector. (From M. I. Skolnik)

Range Tracking

Automatic range tracking has been an objective since the early days of radar. The first range-tracking units, developed during World War II, were electromechanical devices such as the Mechan Range Unit. As target closing speeds increased, electronic analog, digital, and hybrid rangers replaced mechanical units to respond to the threat.

The purpose of the range unit is to follow the target in range and provide continuous distance information or slant range to the target. Timing pulses are sent to the receiver and display unit to provide range gating and allow the angle tracking system to look at only one specific range interval (really a time interval) where the desired target echo pulse will be received. The location of the range gate and that of the target are examined, the amount and direction of error between the center of the gate and the target is determined, error voltages are generated, and circuitry responds by moving the gate to center it on the target. This operation is carried out by a closed-loop feedback system similar to the angle tracking servo system discussed previously.

There are several methods of sensing range-tracking error; however, all implementations involve some method of incrementing the distance to maximum range of the radar such that specific portions of range interval can be examined. One type of range gating system is described below.

(1) Early and late gate—The main range gate is split into early and late gates, each charging a separate capacitor. When target video enters that portion of the gate, each capacitor charges to a voltage proportional to the amount of target video in that half of the gate, such that if the video is centered, each capacitor will have an equal, though opposite, charge. Summing the charges on the two capacitors

will result in a positive or negative error voltage, or in a zero error voltage if the target is centered.

Summary

This chapter has presented an analysis of automatic tracking systems. The tracking function was traced from the generation of position error magnitude and direction to the load-driving device. Two methods of generating position error were investigated in detail, *conical scan* and *monopulse*. Conical scan produces an error signal by causing the beam of sensor energy to be rotated rapidly about the sensor (antenna) axis. Monopulse systems achieve the same result by electronically dividing the radiated energy into four separate parts, which form the beam. The relative amplitudes of the returning energy in the four parts are compared, and an error results when there is an imbalance in signal strength.

A typical tracking servo system was discussed, with emphasis placed on the following characteristics:

(1) Position error magnitude and direction
(2) Position feedpack
(3) Data smoothing and stabilization
(4) Velocity feedback
(5) Power driving device

References

Bureau of Naval Personnel. *Fire Control Technician I & C*. NAVPERS 10175. Washington, D.C.: GPO.

Bureau of Naval Personnel. *Fire Control Technician G 3 & 2*. NAVPERS 10207. Washington, D.C.: GPO, 1969.

Commander, Naval Ordinance Systems Command. *Weapons Systems Fundamentals*. NAVORD OP 3000, vol. 2, 1st Rev. Washington, D.C.: GPO, 1971.

Commander, Naval Sea Systems Command. *Close-In Weapon System MK15 Mds 1-6 (PHALANX)*. NAVSEA OP 4154, vol. I. Washington, D.C.: GPO, 1983.

Dunn, J.H., D.D. Howard, and K.B. Pendleton. "Tracking Radar," Chapter 21 of the *Radar Handbook*, M.I. Skolnik, ed. New York: McGraw-Hill, 1970.

Fox, J. Richard, Lt., USN. *Shipboard Weapons Systems*. Annapolis, Md.: U.S. Naval Academy, 1975.

Skolnik, M.I. *Introduction to Radar Systems*. New York: McGraw-Hill, 1980.

Skolnik, M.I., ed. *Radar Handbook*. New York: McGraw-Hill, 1970.

6

Track-While-Scan Concepts

Introduction

Various surface and airborne radars constitute a major sensor input to computerized command and control systems such as the Marine MACCS and Navy NTDS. These facilities perform multiple functions, including surface, subsurface, and airspace surveillance; identification; threat evaluation; and weapons control. To operate in today's environment, command and control systems require near real-time (as it occurs) target position and velocity data in order to produce fire control quality data for a weapon system. Until recent times, the interface between the raw data supplied by the sensor and the command and control system was the human operator; however, this limited the data rate and target handling capacity. Additional personnel were added as a partial solution to these problems, but even under ideal conditions of training, motivation, and rest, the human operator can only update a maximum of six tracks about once per two seconds and that only for a short time.

To supply fire control quality data, the classical solution has been to provide separate precision tracking sensors, such as those systems discussed in the previous chapter. Although the systems have widespread use, they are limited to tracking at a single elevation and azimuth. Data from these systems were provided to an analog computer to solve the fire control problem and compute launcher and weapon orders. With the advent of the high-speed electronic digital computer, computational capacity exceeded the data-gathering capacity of the fire control sensors; however, target handling continued to be limited by the non-scanning tracking methods employed.

The solution to both problems was to interface a high-scan-rate (15–120 rpm) search radar with the electronic digital computer through a device capable of converting the pattern of echo returns detected by the receiver into usable binary information. In addition, using the digital computer to direct and compose radar beam patterns, as described in the next chapter, created a flexible system capable of multimode simultaneous operation in search, designation, track, and weapon

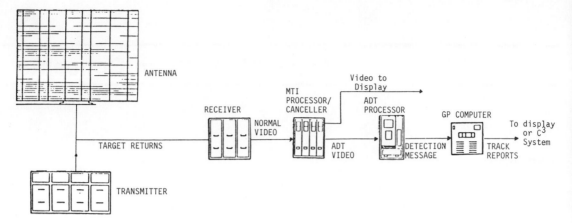

Figure 6–1. Track-while-scan radar block diagram.

control. This ability to perform such functions as multi-target tracking, prediction of future target positions, and terrain avoidance for aircraft navigation is transforming previously fragmented sensor and control capability into a dynamic and powerful sensing, command and control, and weapon employment system. The combination of automatic detection and tracking (ADT) functions within a search radar is sometimes referred to as Track-While-Scan (TWS) (figure 6–1). ADT is being retrofitted into older equipment and is included in most new equipment. *The central concept of TWS is to maintain target tracks in a computer with periodic information updates from a scanning radar.*

Fundamentals of Automatic Detection and Tracking (ADT)

A functional tracking system must provide the basic target parameters of position and rates of motion. In the systems presented earlier in this text, both position data and velocity data were used to maintain the tracking antenna on the target at all times, thus limiting the system to the traditional single-target tracking situation. In a track-while-scan system, target position must be extracted and velocities calculated for many targets while the radar continues to scan. Obviously, in a system of this type, target data is not continuously available for each target. Since the antenna is continuing to scan, some means of storing and analyzing target data from one update to the next and beyond is necessary. The digital computer is employed to perform this function and thus replaces the tracking servo systems previously discussed.

A Tracking Algorithm

The following algorithm for solving the track-while-scan problem is based upon the assumption that the radar furnishes target position information once each scan. The scheme can be implemented with software (computer programs) only, or with a combination of special radar circuits (hardware) and software. Existing systems also allow the operator to modify the system tracking parameters.

Any track-while-scan system must provide for each of the following functions:

(1) Target detection
(2) Target track correlation and association
(3) Target track initiation and track file generation (if no correlation)
(4) Generation of tracking "gates"
(5) Track gate prediction, smoothing (filtering), and positioning
(6) Display and future target position calculation

Target detection. Target detection is accomplished by special circuitry in the receiver of radars designed as TWS systems or by signal-processing equipment in a separate cabinet in retrofit installations. The function of this ADT processing equipment is similar and will be addressed here in general terms. It should be remembered that the ADT processor is not a computer, although it does have some memory capacity. *Its primary function is that of converting data to a form usable by the separate digital computer that actually performs the smooth tracking, velocity, acceleration rate generation, and prediction functions of the TWS system.*

The ADT processor's memory allocates space addressed to each spatial cell that makes up the search volume of the radar. The dimensions of these cells are often defined by the horizontal and vertical angular resolution capability of the radar as well as by a distance in range equal to the pulse compression range resolution. After several scans, the ADT processor contains what amounts to a three-dimensional binary matrix representing the entire search volume of the radar. This matrix or array represents cells with echo returns with a "1" and those without returns with a "0" (figure 6–2).

In some systems, individual beams in the radar are overlapped such that most targets will occupy more than one beam position at any radar range. When employed, this procedure (called *beam splitting*) allows angular resolution less than the beamwidth of the radar. In addition, this avoids gaps in coverage and allows examination of hit patterns among several beams as a means of rejecting clutter or

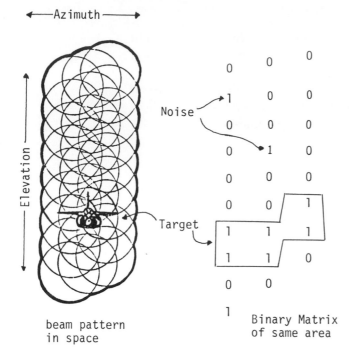

← —Azimuth— →

Elevation

Noise

Target

beam pattern
in space

Binary Matrix
of same area

```
        0      0
   0              0
      1      0    0
   0      0      0
      0      1    0
   0      0      0
   0      0      1
      1   1      1
   1      1      0
      0   0
      1
```

*Figure 6–2. The ADT processor
converts echo-return patterns from
successive positions of the radar beam
into a three-dimensional binary matrix as shown.* (Note: *Only azimuth
and elevation are depicted.) (Courtesy ITT Gilfillan Corp.)*

false targets. A radar may require N hits out of M beams at the same
range interval, with all hits overlapping in elevation and azimuth
before any further consideration is given to initiating a track. N and
M may be operator selectable or preset during the design process.

Most systems employ further means to avoid generation of tracks
on clutter or false returns. These can be grouped into those associated
with conventional radar receiver anti-jamming circuitry and those
exclusive to ADT. It should be obvious that an effective TWS radar
must retain conventional features such as Constant False-Alarm Rate
(CFAR), MTI, and automatic gain-control circuitry. These will help
prevent the processing of obviously false returns, allowing the ADT
system to make more sophisticated decisions between valid and in-
valid targets. The ADT processor will generate a time history of all
echo returns over several radar scans. Stationary targets remaining
within a given resolution cell over a number of scans result in its
identification as a clutter cell. The collected information on all clutter
cells within the radar search volume is referred to as a *clutter map.*
Returns remaining in clutter cells will be rejected as false targets.
Moving targets will not remain in a given cell long enough to be
eliminated. Returns that vary rapidly in strength and centroid location, such as clouds and chaff in high winds, could appear non-sta-
tionary and would cause a track to be established. These returns are

then tested for the known velocity characteristics of valid targets by velocity filters, thus reducing the number of false tracks that would otherwise be generated in this manner.

Target Acquisition, Tracking, and Turn Detection Gates

A "gate" can be defined as a small volume of space composed of many of the cells described previously, initially centered on the target, which will be monitored on each scan for the presence of target information. Gate dimension and position information is generated by the general-purpose digital computer and sent to the ADT processor for application. Action by the clutter map is inhibited inside these gates to avoid generation of clutter cells by valid tracks.

When a target is initially detected, the algorithm receives only the position data for that initial, instantaneous target position. The *acquisition gate* is then generated in the following manner:

	Acquisition Gate	Tracking Gate
Range Gate	$= R$ 2000 yds. (1828.15 meters)	R 120 yds. (109.69 meters)
Bearing Gate	$= B$ 10° (.1745 radians)	B 1.5° (.0262 radians)
Elevation Gate	$= E$ 10° (.1745 radians)	E 1.5° (.0262 radians)

(This is an example only, numbers will vary depending on the actual system.)

The acquisition gate is large in order to allow for target motion during one scan period of the radar. If the target is within the acquisition gate on the next scan, a smaller *tracking gate* is generated that is moved to the new expected target position on subsequent scans. Although figure 6–3 shows only a very small (120 yards by 1.5° by 1.5°) tracking gate, in actual practice intermediate gate size may be generated until a smooth track is achieved. Note that the track and acquisition gate dimensions given in figure 6–3 are representative, but are only an example and may vary for different systems. In the event that a video observation does not appear within the tracking gate on a subsequent scan, ADT will enter some type of turn-detection routine. A common means of dealing with a turn or linear acceleration of the target is the *turn-detection gate*. The turn-detection gate is larger than the tracking gate and is co-located with it initially, employing separate logic and algorithms different from the tracking routine. The turn-detection gate size is determined by the maximum acceleration and turn characteristics of valid tracks. Some systems

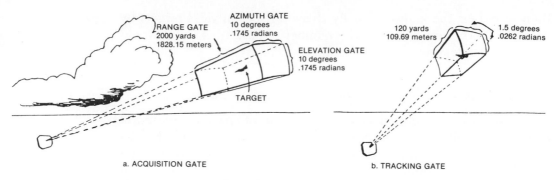

RANGE GATE
2000 yards
1828.15 meters

AZIMUTH GATE
10 degrees
.1745 radians

ELEVATION GATE
10 degrees
.1745 radians

TARGET

120 yards
109.69 meters

1.5 degrees
.0262 radians

a. ACQUISITION GATE

b. TRACKING GATE

Figure 6–3. Track-while-scan acquisition and tracking gates.

will maintain one track with the original tracking gate and one with the turn-detection gate for one or more scans after initial turn detection, allowing for the possibility of inaccurate observation, clutter, or possible decoys prior to the determination of which is the valid track position. Only one of these tracks would be displayed to the operator, that one being determined by a programmed validity routine.

Track Correlation and Association

Target observation on each radar scan that survives hit pattern recognition and clutter rejection functions is initially treated as new information prior to comparison with previously held data. Logic rules established in the digital computer program, which perform correlation and association of video observations with currently held tracks, are the key to preventing system saturation in high-density environments. Generally speaking, target observations that fall within the boundary of the tracking gate are said to correlate with that track. Each observation is compared with all tracks in the computer's memory and may correlate with one track, several tracks, or no tracks. Conversely, a track gate may correlate with one observation, several observations, or no observations. Whenever there is other than a one-to-one correlation of observations with tracking gates, *tracking ambiguity* results.

Resolution of track ambiguity. Track ambiguity arises when either multiple targets appear within a single track window or two or more gates overlap on a single target. This occurrence can cause the system to generate erroneous tracking data and ultimately lose the ability to maintain a meaningful track. If the system is designed so that an operator initiates the track and monitors its progress, the solution is simply for the operator to cancel the erroneous track and initiate a

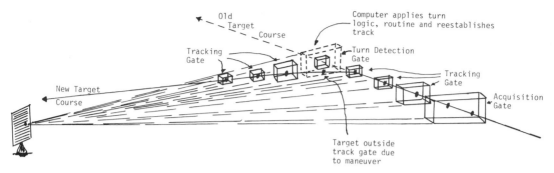

Figure 6–1. TWS processing.

new one. For automatic systems, software decision rules are established that will enable the program to maintain accurate track files, resolve ambiguity, and prevent saturation by false targets.

Depending upon the specific use, many different sets of rules are employed to resolve this ambiguity, an example of which is outlined below:

1. If several video observations exist within one tracking gate, then the video closest to the center of the gate is accepted as valid.
2. If several tracking gates overlap one video observation, the video will be associated with the gate with the closest center.
3. If two contacts cross paths, then the tracking gates will coast through one another, and re-correlation will occur when the gates no longer overlap.
4. If one video observation separates into two or more, rule 1 above is applied until there is clear separation in velocity and position and a new tracking gate is generated for the uncorrelated video. Rule number 2 is then applied until the gates no longer overlap.

Track initiation and track file generation. Concurrent with the generation of the acquisition window, a track file is generated in order to store the position and gate data for each track. In addition to the basic position and window data, calculated target velocities and accelerations are also stored in each track file. For ease of calculation and interchange of information with other systems, all data is converted from polar to rectangular coordinates by the computer, as described in succeeding chapters. Track files are stored within the digital-computer subsystems' memory in rectangular coordinates, and the data are used to perform the various calculations necessary to maintain the track. Figure 6–5 illustrates the data structure of a hypothetical target track file. *Note that within the computer, position*

TRACK NUMBER
(Identifier)

POSITION HISTORY

X_n	Y_n	Z_n
X_{n-1}	Y_{n-1}	Z_{n-1}
X_{n-2}	Y_{n-2}	Z_{n-2}

VELOCITY HISTORY

$\dot{X}_n$	$\dot{Y}_n$	$\dot{Z}_n$
$\dot{X}_{n-1}$	$\dot{Y}_{n-1}$	$\dot{Z}_{n-1}$

ACCELERATION

$\ddot{X}_n$	$\ddot{Y}_n$	$\ddot{Z}_n$
$\ddot{X}_{n-1}$	$\ddot{Y}_{n-1}$	$\ddot{Z}_{n-1}$

WINDOW

Acquisition code Position of gate center	Track code Position of gate center

Figure 6–5. Simplified computer target track file (the subscript n *denotes the most recent radar scan).*

data has been converted from polar coordinates to rectangular coordinates. Each track file occupies a discrete position in the digital computer's high-speed memory. As data are needed for computation or new data are to be stored, the portion of memory that is allocated for the required data will be accessed by the system software (programs). In this manner, tactical data, in addition to the tracking data, may be stored in the "track" file—for example, ESM data, engagement status, and IFF information. (It is equally important to track friendly forces as well as hostile forces.) The generation of the track file begins with the initial storage of position data along with a code to indicate that an acquisition window has been established.

If target position data is obtained on subsequent scans of the radar, the file is updated with the coordinates, the velocities and accelerations are computed and stored, and the acquisition window code is canceled. The acquisition window is then decreased in size relative to that of the tracking window, and the track code is stored, which indicates an active track file. As the radar continues to scan, each input of data is compared with the gate positions of active track files until the proper file is found and updated. The techniques of computer data file sorting and searching are beyond the scope of this text; however, it should be noted that the search for the proper track file is generally not a sequential one-to-one comparison. This method is much too slow to be used in a system where speed of operation is one of the primary goals.

Track gate prediction, smoothing, and positioning. As was discussed in the earlier sections on servo-controlled tracking systems, (*conical scan and monopulse*), tracking errors were generated as a result of the target moving off the antenna axis. It was the task then of the error detectors and servo systems to reposition the antenna axis onto the target. During the process of repositioning the antenna, the system response motion was smoothed by employing rate (velocity) and position feedback. Recall that this feedback was accomplished by electrical and mechanical means within the servo system. Recall also that in general the *system lagged the target*, i.e., the target would move and the system would respond.

In a *track-while-scan system*, tracking errors also exist due to target motion. The tracking gate now has replaced the "tracking antenna," and this gate must be positioned dynamically on the target in a manner similar to that of the "tracking antenna." However, there is no "servo" system to reposition and smooth the tracking gate's motion. This repositioning and smoothing must be done mathematically within the TWS algorithm. To this end, smoothing and prediction equations are employed to calculate the changing position of the tracking window. Instead of the system "lagging" the target *the tracking gate is made to "lead" the target*, and smoothing is accomplished by comparing predicted parameters with observed parameters and making adjustments based upon the errors derived from this comparison.

The classic method of smoothing track data is by the α-β tracker or α-β filter described below. This simple filter is ill-suited to extreme target maneuvers and in most current systems is increased in complexity to what is called the Kalman filter. Among other things, the Kalman filter is capable of dealing with higher order derivatives of target motion (i.e., beyond acceleration).

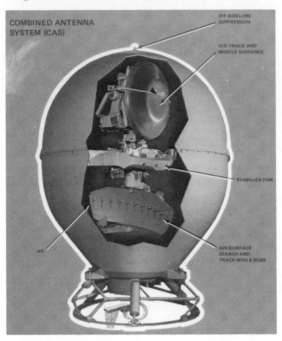

Figure 6–6. Mk 92 fire-control system. (Courtesy Sperry Gyroscope)

In some systems, complete track file information is retained in the separate command and control system computer, with the TWS computer retaining only position data, velocity, and acceleration.

The α–β Tracking Algorithm
SYSTEMS EQUATIONS

Smooth position $P_{sn} = P_{pn} + \alpha (P_n - P_{pn})$ $\hspace{2cm}$ (6–1)

Smooth velocity $V_n = V_{n-1} + A_{n-1}T + \dfrac{\beta}{T}(P_n - P_{pn})$ $\hspace{1cm}$ (6–2)

Smooth acceleration $A_n = A_{n-1} + \dfrac{\gamma}{T^2}(P_n - P_{pn})$ $\hspace{1cm}$ (6–3)

Predicted Position $P_{pn+1} = P_{sn} + V_nT + \dfrac{1}{2}A_nT^2$ $\hspace{1cm}$ (6–4)

(future position)

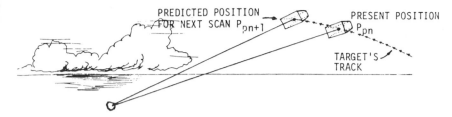

Figure 6–7. Dynamic volumetric gate positioning.

where

P_n is the target's position measured by the radar during scan n.
P_{sn} is the smoothed position after scan n.
V_n is the smoothed velocity after scan n.
A_n is the smoothed acceleration after scan n.
P_{pn} is the predicted target position for scan n.
T is the scan time (1 sec. in this case).
α, β, γ are system constants which determine the system response, damping and gain, etc.

Note: P_n represents the three cartesian coordinates.

Let us now examine equations 6–1 through 6–4 in greater detail and in the process correlate the track-while-scan functions to those of the servo tracking systems discussed earlier.

Equation (6–1)

$$P_{sn} = P_{pn} + \alpha\,(P_n - P_{pn})$$

Equation (6–1) is analogous to the position feedback realized in the servo tracking system by the radar error signal output. The subscript n refers to the current scan of the radar. The predicted position for the current scan P_{pn} is modified by the error between the observed position and the predicted position $(P_p - P_{pn})$; this yields a new updated position P_{sn} for the scan. This updated position is then employed in equation (6–4) to calculate a future target position for the next scan $(n + 1)$.

Equation (6–2)

$$V_n = V_{n-1} + A_{n-1}\,T + \frac{\beta}{T}\,(P_n - P_{pn})$$

Equation (6–2) is analogous to the rate (velocity) feedback achieved by the tachometer loop in the servo tracking sysem. In equation (6–2) the target velocity is updated and modified by comparing the observed position with the predicted position and then dividing the position error by the time of the scan to obtain velocity $(P_n - P_{pn})/T$.

The velocity is further refined by modifying it by the acceleration $A_{n-1}T$.

Equation (6–3)

$$A_n = A_{n-1} + \frac{\gamma}{T^2}(P_n - P_{pn})$$

Equation (6–3) develops the updated target acceleration to be employed in smoothing velocity on the next scan and in predicting the target position for the next scan. The old acceleration value is modified by the tracking error derived from the term $(P_n - P_{pn})/T$.

Equation (6–4)

$$P_{pn+1} = P_{sn} + V_n T + \frac{1}{2}A_n T^2$$

Equation (6–4) is simply the classic displacement equation derived in physics. It is used to predict the future target position for the next scan. The predicted position for the next scan P_{pn+1} is obtained by modifying the smoothed present position P_{sn} by velocity and acceleration obtained from equations (6–2) and (6–3).

Successive applications of this system of equations serves to minimize the tracking error in a manner similar to the repositioning of the "tracking antenna" in the servo tracking system. It should be noted at this point that although the techniques of tracking differ between the two, i.e., servo and TWS, the function and the concepts exhibit a direct correlation.

TWS System Operation

Let us now take the logical components of the TWS algorithm and put together the entire tracking algorithm. The algorithm is described by means of an annotated flow diagram, figure 6–8. The reader should follow the flow through at least three radar scans in order to properly understand the system dynamics. For the purpose of this illustration, assume that the system begins with a new detection and that tracking

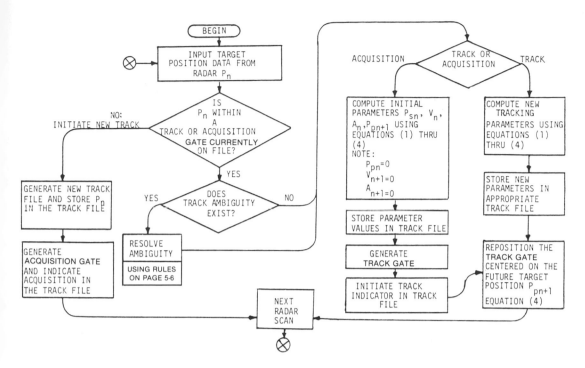

Figure 6–8. Simplified TWS algorithm flow diagram.

can be initiated on the second scan. (In actual practice, three or more scans are usually necessary to establish a valid track.)

The necessity for digital computer control should now be very evident. It should be observed that the entire algorithm is repeated for every target on every radar scan.

Active Tracking Radar

Conventional TWS procedures applicable to mechanically scanned radar systems do not fully exploit the potential of radars employing phased array beam steering in all axes. The ability of these systems to position beams virtually instantly and to conduct many types of scans simultaneously provides great flexibility in planning tracking strategies. These radars conduct what amounts to a random search, employing different pulse widths and PRTs applicable to the situation. When an echo that meets required parameters is observed, the radar immediately transmits several beams in the vicinity of the target while continuing search in the remainder of the surveillance area. This results in the immediate establishment of a track without the relatively long (.5 to 4 seconds) time period waiting for the antenna to return on the next scan, which is experienced in mechanically scanning radars. This technique, called *active tracking*, results in greatly decreased reaction time and more efficient use of the system.

Integrated Automatic Detection and Tracking (IADT)

By extending the concepts described in this chapter and adding additional computer capability, it is possible to combine the outputs of several radars that are co-located, as on ships or at shore-based command and control systems such as MACCS. Systems such as the AN/SYS-2 IADT, now entering limited use aboard missile ships, develop a single track file based on the outputs of several radars. When radars are employed with different scan rates, a separate external timing reference must be employed, which becomes the scan rate for the IADT and the synthetic video display. Track updating and smoothing occur as previously described, except updates are considered relative to narrow sectors of the search volume—typically a few degrees in width. System software updates tracks a few sectors behind the azimuth position of the synthetic scan. Observations are accepted from the radar having the oldest unprocessed position data sector by sector as the synthetic scan passes. This provides the first available position report, no matter which radar produced it. Thus, position reports are used as they occurred in real time, and no position report is accepted out of order. IADT reduces loss of data due to individual radar propagation and lobing characteristics while allowing quality weighting of data relative to its source. IADT systems can accept the output of TWS or non-TWS radars as well as that derived from IFF transponders.

Summary

The central concept underlying any track-while-scan system is that the sensor itself continues to perform its primary function of search (scanning) and data input, while the remainder of the system performs the target tracking function. The sensor simply provides target position data to the computer subsystem where target velocities and position prediction are calculated. In a military application, the major advantage of a TWS system is the elimination of the process of target designation from a search radar to a fire control radar. The tracking information, developed in the TWS system, is used as a direct data input to the computation of a fire control solution. Therefore, as soon as a target is detected, a fire control solution is available without the inherent delay caused by the designation process. The time required from first detection to fire control solution is on the order of seconds for a TWS system, as opposed to tens of seconds or even minutes for a manually designated system employing separate search and fire control sensors.

The focus of this chapter has been to answer the question, "What functions should a TWS system perform in order to combine the search and tracking tasks into one integrated unit?" The functions of (1) target detection, (2) target track correlation and association, (3) track initiation and track file generation, (4) generation of tracking "gates," (5) track gate prediction, smoothing (filtering), and positioning, (6) display and future target position calculations were explained as well as was an explanation of the α-β filter.

An introduction to employment of Integrated Automatic Detection and Tracking was presented demonstrating the performance of a single data processor with many sensor inputs. The single track output combined the best capabilities of all the sensors employed.

References

Benedict, T. R. "Synthesis of an Optimal Set of Radar Track-While-Scan Smoothing Equations." *IRE Transactions on Automatic Control*. July 1962, p. 27.

Binias, Guenter. "Automatic Track Initiation with Phased Array Radar." *The Record of the IEEE International Radar Conference*. New York: April 1975, pp. 423–34.

Cantrell, B. H., G. V. Trunk, F. D. Queen, J. D. Willson, J. J. Alter. "Automatic Detection and Integrated Tracking System." *The Record of the IEEE International Radar Conference*. New York: April 1975, pp. 391–95.

Commander, Naval Ordnance Systems Command. *Gun Fire Control System MK 86 Mod 4*. NAVORD OP 3758. Washington, D.C.: GPO.

Hovanessian, S. A. *Radar Detection and Tracking Systems*. Dedham, Mass.: Artech House, 1978.

Simpson, H. R. "Performance Measures and Optimization Condition for a Third-Order Sample Data System." *IRE Transactions on Automatic Control*, April 1963, p. 182.

Skolnik, M. I. *Introduction to Radar Systems*. 2nd ed. New York: McGraw-Hill, 1980, pp. 183–86.

7

Electronic Scanning and the Phased Array

Introduction

The potential for increased target handling capacity available in Track While Scan radars is limited by the requirement to position the radar antenna mechanically. Existing mechanical scanning methods are inherently slow and require large amounts of power in order to respond rapidly enough to deal with large numbers of high speed maneuvering targets. With mechanically scanned systems, antenna inertia and inflexibility prevent employment of optimum radar beam positioning patterns that can reduce reaction times and increase target capacity. With electronic scanning, the radar beams are positioned almost instantaneously and completely without the inertia, time lags, and vibration of mechanical systems. In an era in which the numerical superiority of adversaries is expected to remain large, electronic scanning can offset that advantage. The specific benefits of electronic scanning include:

(1) increased data rates (reduction of system reaction time),
(2) virtually instantaneous positioning of the radar beam anywhere within a set sector (beam position can be changed in a matter of micro-seconds),
(3) elimination of mechanical errors and failures associated with mechanically scanned antennas,
(4) vastly increased flexibility of the radar facilitating multi-mode operation, automatic multi-target tracking, highly directional transmission of missile guidance and control orders, interceptor and general air traffic control from one radar at virtually the same time.

Principles of Operation

The fundamental principles underlying the concept of electronic beam steering are derived from electromagnetic radiation theory employing constructive and destructive interference.

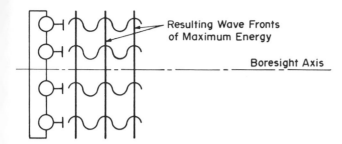

Resulting Wave Fronts
of Maximum Energy

Boresight Axis

Figure 7–1. Wave front resulting from elements radiating in phase. Maximum energy is concentrated along the array boresight axis.

These principles can be stated as follows:

The electromagnetic energy received at a point in space from two or more closely spaced radiating elements is a maximum when the energy from each radiating element arrives at the point in phase.

To illustrate this principle consider figure 7–1. All elements are radiating in phase, and the resultant wave front is perpendicular to the axis of the element array. Figure 7–1 and subsequent diagrams show only a limited number of radiating elements. In actual radar antenna design several thousand elements could be used to obtain a high-gain antenna with a beam width of less than two degrees.

The wave fronts remain perpendicular to the boresight axis and are considered to arrive at a point target in space at the same time. As illustrated in figure 7–2, the path lengths from the elements to point *P* equalize as *P* approaches infinity. Thus, in situations where the target range is very large compared to the distance between elements, the paths from the elements to point *P* are almost parallel. Under these conditions, energy will arrive at point *P* with the same phase relationship that existed at the array.

To achieve beam positioning off the boresight axis, it is necessary to radiate the antenna elements out of phase with one another. Figure 7–3a depicts the phase shift necessary to create constructive inter-

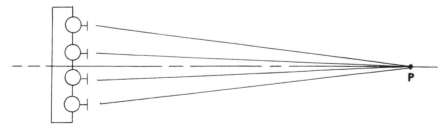

Figure 7–2. Array with elements radiating in phase.

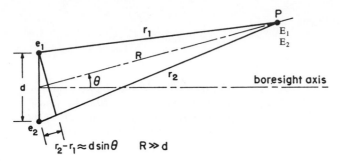

Figure 7-3a. Radiation path length difference for energy arriving at point P from two sources.

ference along a line joining an arbitrary point P with the center of the array. In order to achieve this constructive interference at Point P, the energy arriving from all radiating sources must be in phase and arrive at the same time. The energy from element e_1 must travel a path length r_1, while the energy from element e_2 must travel the longer path length r_2.

The electric field magnitudes from the two elements at point P are given by equation (1–5) as follows:

$$E_1 = E_0 \sin \frac{2\pi}{\lambda} (r_1 - ct) + \phi_1$$

$$E_2 = E_0 \sin \frac{2\pi}{\lambda} (r_2 - ct) + \phi_2$$

Since these two electric fields must be in phase at point P for constructive interference to occur, the arguments of the sine functions must be equal.

$$\frac{2\pi}{\lambda} (r_1 - ct) + \phi_1 = \frac{2\pi}{\lambda} (r_2 - ct) + \phi_2$$

$$\phi_1 - \phi_2 = \frac{2\pi}{\lambda} (r_2 - ct) - \frac{2\pi}{\lambda} (r_1 - ct)$$

thus

$$\phi_1 - \phi_2 = \Delta\phi = \frac{2\pi}{\lambda} (r_2 - r_1)$$

The path length difference, $r_2 - r_1$, approaches the value $d \sin \theta$ as the distance R in figure 7–3a increases. In figure 7–3b, where point P has been moved an infinite distance from the source, the paths from the two sources have become parallel and the path length difference is exactly $d \sin \theta$. For points at a distance R less than infinity, $d \sin \theta$ is still a good approximation for the path length

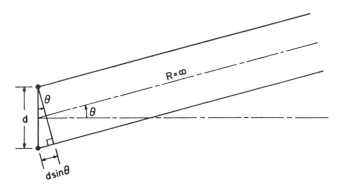

Figure 7–3b. Radiation path length difference for energy arriving at a point an infinite distance from two sources.

difference, $r_2 - r_1$, as long as R is large compared to the element spacing, d. Thus, applying this distance approximation yields

$$r_2 - r_1 \cong d \sin \theta (R > d)$$

For practical radar applications, d (the distance between elements) is on the order of a few centimeters while R is on the order of kilometers, a difference of several orders of magnitude; therefore, the distance approximation is valid for all radar applications in the far radar field (ranges greater than 1 km).

Applying the distance approximation to the expression already obtained for the required phase difference between two radiating elements yields equation (7–1).

$$\Delta\phi = \frac{2\pi d}{\lambda} \sin \theta \qquad (7–1)$$

where:

$\Delta\phi$ = the phase shift between adjacent elements expressed in radians.
λ = the free space wavelength in meters.
d = the linear distance between radiating elements in meters.
θ = the desired angular offset in degrees.

Methods of Beam Steering

The previous discussion addressed the theory required to compute the relative phase shift between adjacent radiating elements in order to position the beam of an array-type antenna to a specific angle off of the antenna boresight axis. In practice there are three methods of accomplishing this phase difference.

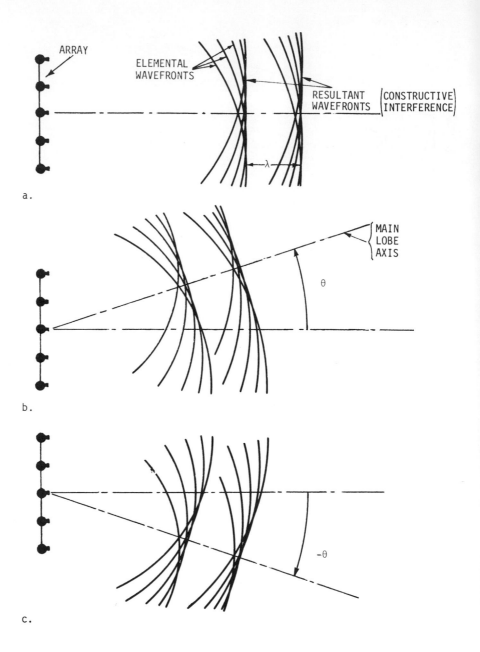

Figure 7–4. a. Beam positioning along the boresight axis; all elements are radiated in phase.
b. Beam positioning above the boresight axis; elements lag in phase by $\Delta\phi$, *with the uppermost element receiving the greatest phase shift.*
c. Beam positioning below the boresight axis; elements lag in phase by $\Delta\phi$, *with the lowermost element receiving the greatest phase shift.*

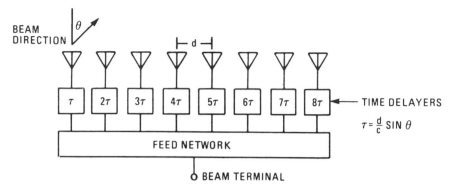

Figure 7–5. Time-delay scanning. (From RCA Review)

Time Delay Scanning

The employment of time delay as a means of achieving the desired phase relationships between elements allows greater flexibility in frequency utilization than other methods. However, in practice the use of coaxial delay lines or other means of timing at high power levels is impractical due to increased cost, complexity, and weight.

To accomplish time delay scanning, variable time delay networks are inserted in front of each radiating element. By proper choice of these time delays, the required effective phase shift can be applied to each element. The time delay between adjacent elements required to scan the beam to an angle, θ, is given by:

$$t = \frac{d}{c} \sin \theta \qquad (7{-}2)$$

Frequency Scanning

One of the simpler methods of phased-array radar implementation is frequency scanning. This method is also relatively inexpensive. Figure 7–6 shows the schematic arrangement of elements when frequency scanning is used to position a beam in either azimuth or elevation. The length of the serpentine waveguide line (ℓ) is chosen such that for some center frequency, f_0, the length of signal travel between elements is an integral number of wavelengths, or

$$\ell = n\lambda \ (n = \text{any integer greater than zero})$$

where

λ_0 = wavelength in the serpentine line at frequency f_0.

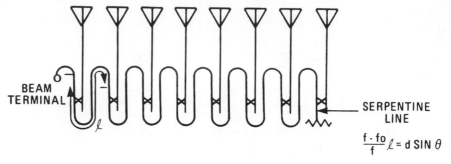

$$\frac{f \cdot f_0}{f} \ell = d \, SIN \, \theta$$

Figure 7–6. Frequency scanning. (From RCA Review)

Thus, when the excitation frequency is f_0, the serpentine line will cause all elements to radiate in phase, and the beam will be formed along the boresight axis. If the excitation frequency is increased or decreased from the center frequency, f_0, the line length, ℓ, will no longer represent an integer number of wavelengths. As the excitation energy travels along the serpentine line, it will reach each successive radiating element with a uniformly increasing positive or negative phase shift. This results in the beam being deflected by an angle θ from the boresight axis. Thus, by varying the radar transmitter frequency about some base frequency, the beam can be positioned in one axis. In figure 7–7 the frequency scanned array has been simplified to a two-element system with the boresight axis normal to the plane of the elements. The feed is folded into a serpentine form to allow close element spacing while maintaining the required line length (ℓ) between elements.

Figure 7–7. Two-element frequency-scanned array.

RF energy at 5,000 MHz is fed at the top of the array, and the elements are separated by distance d equal to (.03 meters). At time $t = 0$, the energy enters the serpentine feed line, and antenna A_1 radiates immediately starting at zero phase. Since the period of the wave form is $T = 1/f$, then $T = 1/5,000$ MHz or 200ρ sec. Therefore, it takes 200ρ sec for one wavelength to propagate from A_1. If the distance ℓ

traveled in the serpentine feed between A_1 and A_2 equals one wave-length or any integer number of wavelength ($L = n\lambda$ where $n = 1$, 2, 3, . . .), then

$$t = \frac{L}{c} = \frac{n\lambda}{c} = \frac{n\left(\dfrac{c}{f}\right)}{c} = \frac{n}{f} = nT$$

where

t = elapsed time, and
T = the period of the wave form

Therefore, the energy from A_2 will always be in phase with A_1. The beam formed by the array will be on the boresight axis. Note that this represents a broadside array (the elements transmit in phase). If the frequency is changed to 5,500 MHz, the period T becomes 181.81p sec; however, the wave form still takes $t = L/c$ or 200p sec longer to reach A_2 than to reach A_1 when fed into the serpentine line as depicted in figure 7–8. Note that the wave form from A_2 is no longer in phase with A_1. Energy from A_2 lags A_1 in phase by 200p sec $-$ 181.81p sec or 18.19p sec. The amount of phase shift can be determined by:

$$\frac{t}{T} = \frac{\Delta\phi}{2\pi(\text{radians})}$$

$$\frac{18.19\text{psec}}{181.81\text{psec}} = \frac{\Delta\phi}{2\pi \text{ radians}}$$

$$\Delta\phi = (.1)(2\pi)$$

$$\Delta\phi = 0.6286 \text{ radians or } 36°$$

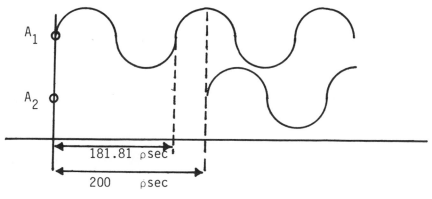

Figure 7–8. *Wave forms with delay in phase.*

Figure 7–9. Beam depression due to phase lag.

Since there is a phase difference, $\Delta\phi$, then the beam axis can be located as follows:

$$\Delta\phi = \frac{2\pi d}{\lambda}\sin\theta$$

$$0.6286 = \frac{2\pi\,(.03\text{m})\sin\theta}{(0.545\text{m})}$$

$$\sin\theta = 0.1817$$

$$\theta = 10.47°$$

Since energy from A_2 lags 36° in phase, the beam will be 10.47° *below* the boresight (figure 7–9).

In this illustration the distance from A_1 to a point in space (R_1) is greater than from A_2 to that point (R_1). The wave forms will arrive in phase at the point because A_2 lags A_1 when the energy is transmitted.

Thus, as frequency is varied, the beam axis will change, and scanning can be accomplished in one axis (either elevation or azimuth). The principles are employed in the AN/SPS-48 and AN/SPS-52 series

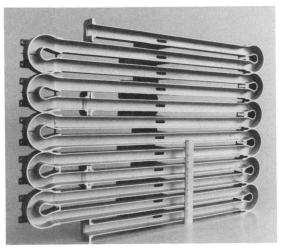
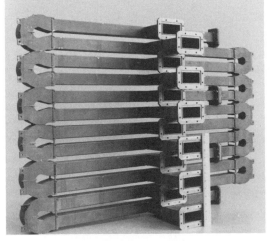

Figure 7–10. Serpentine feed assembly for a frequency-scanning radar, cut away to show internal detail.

radars as well as in the older AN/SPS-39. Variation in frequency tends to make these radars more resistant to jamming than they would be if operated at a fixed frequency, and it also provides a solution to the blind speed problem in MTI systems. Frequency scanning does impose some limitations in that a large portion of the available frequency band is used for scanning rather than to optimize resolution of targets. Additionally, this imposes the requirement that the receiver bandwidth be extremely wide or that the receiver be capable of shifting the center of a narrower bandwidth with the transmitted frequency. Equation (7–3) gives the relationship between the percentage variation in frequency (bandwidth) and the scan angle, which is referred to as the Wrap-up Ratio.

$$\text{Wrap-up Ratio} \left(\frac{f - f_0}{f}\right) \ell = d \sin \theta \qquad (7\text{–}3)$$

or

$$\frac{\ell}{d} = \frac{f \sin \theta}{f - f_0}$$

The wrap-up ratio is the ratio of the sine of the maximum scan angle to the percentage change in frequency required to scan.

Phase Scanning

In a phase-scanned radar system, the radiating elements are fed from a radar transmitter through phase-shifting networks or "phasers." This system is shown in figures 7–11, 7–12, and 7–13. The aim of the system is again to position the beam at any arbitrary angle, θ, at any time. In this case the means of accomplishing the phase shift

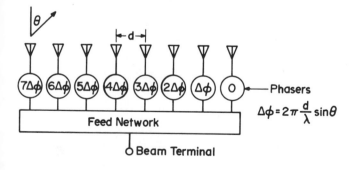

Figure 7–11. Phase scanning. (From RCA Review)

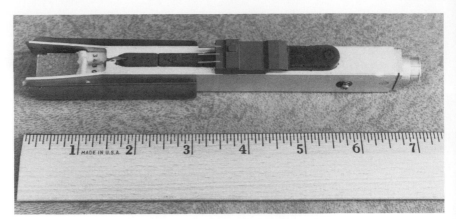

Figure 7–12. A ferrite phase shifter or "phaser."

at each element is simply to shift the phase of the incoming energy to each element. These phasers are adjustable over the range 0 to $\pm 2\pi$ radians. The task of the system is to compute the phase shift required for each element, and set each phaser to the proper value to accomplish the desired beam offset. While phase scanning is more expensive than frequency scanning, it is much less expensive (in dollars, weight, and power losses) than time delay steering. To a first approximation, the bandwidth of a phase-scanning antenna in % is equal to the normal beamwidth in degrees. Thus a 1° beamwidth antenna working at 10 GHz can radiate over a 100 MHz bandwidth (i.e., ± 50 MHz) without distortion.

Energy reception. To receive energy transmitted in a steered beam by any of the three scanning methods, the applied frequency, time,

 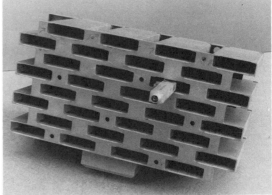

Figure 7–13. A section of a phased-array radar antenna. Note location of phase shifter in the back of the assembly.

or phase relationships are maintained at each element, which has the effect of making the radar sensitive to energy returning from the direction of transmission. *Thus, each of the scanning methods is completely reversible and works equally well in reception of energy as in transmission.* Unfortunately, some beam positions do not have the same phase shift in the reverse direction. When non-reciprocal phase shifters are used, it is necessary to change the phase-shifter setting between transmit and receive to maintain the same phase shift on receive as was used on transmission.

Computation of Required Phase Relationships

No matter which of the three possible methods of phase scanning is used in a phased array system, the objective is a relative phase shift of the energy being radiated by each element in the array. The incremental phase shift required between two adjacent elements is given by equation (7–1). When using this equation it will be assumed for consistency that $\Delta\phi$ represents the phase lead given to each element with respect to its adjacent element in the direction of the chosen reference element. Thus, when positioning the beam to the same side of the boresight axis as the reference element, each array element must lead the next element closer to the reference by the same amount, $\Delta\phi > 0$. When positioning the beam on the opposite side of the boresight axis from the reference, each element must lag the element next closer to the reference by the same amount, $\Delta\phi < 0$ (negative $\Delta\phi$ or effective phase lag). This convention can be extended to include a sign convention for the angle θ. Choose the reference element as the top most element and the farthest right element when looking from the antenna along the boresight axis. Also choose elevation angles as positive above the boresight axis and negative below, and choose azimuth angles as positive in a clockwise direction (scanning to the right) and negative in a counterclockwise direction. (Do not confuse the above definitions of lead/lag in the spatial domain with the electrical definitions of lead/lag in the radian domain.)

Figure 7–14 illustrates this convention. In order to position the beam above the boresight axis, the angle θ will be positive and thus $\sin\theta$ will be positive also. This yields a positive $\Delta\phi$ between elements. To determine the phase applied to each element ϕ_e, simply use the relationship

$$\phi_e = e\,\Delta\phi \quad e = 0,1,2,\ldots \tag{7–4}$$

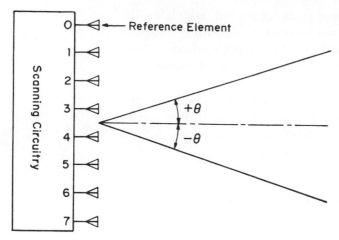

Figure 7-14. *Reference element and sign convention for scanning in elevation.*

or

$$\phi_e = e \frac{2\pi d}{\lambda} \sin \theta$$

Similarly, to position the beam below the boresight axis requires the use of a negative angle θ. This yields a negative Δφ and equation (7-4) again yields the applied phase of each element.

Example 1. Phase Scanning in Elevation

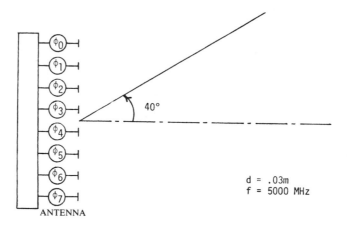

d = .03m
f = 5000 MHz

If the reference element has a phase of zero, compute the phase applied to element five when the beam is scanned 40° above the boresight axis.

$$\text{Find } \lambda: \quad \lambda = \frac{c}{f} = .06 \text{ m}$$

$$\text{Find } \Delta\phi: \quad \Delta\phi = \frac{2\pi d}{\lambda} \sin \theta \qquad\qquad (7\text{--}1)$$

$$\Delta\phi = \frac{2\pi \,(.03)}{.06} \sin 40°$$

$$\Delta\phi = 2.02 \text{ radians}$$

$$\text{Find } \phi_5: \quad \phi_e = e\Delta\phi \qquad\qquad (7\text{--}4)$$

$$\phi_5 = 5(2.02 \text{ radians})$$

$$\phi = 10.10 \text{ radians}$$

Note that this result is greater than 2π radians. In practice, the phasers can only shift the phase of the energy going to an element by an amount between -2π and 2π radians. Expressed mathematically

$$-2\pi \leqslant \phi_i \leqslant 2\pi$$

Thus, the phase shift applied to element five must be

$$\phi_5 = 10.10 \text{ radians} - 2\pi \text{ radians}$$

$$\phi_5 = 3.82 \text{ radians}$$

In other words, element five must lead the reference element (element zero) by an amount of 3.82 radians.

Example 2. A Hypothetical Three-Dimensional Search Radar

In this example, azimuth information is obtained by rotating the antenna mechanically in a continuous full-circle search pattern. Range

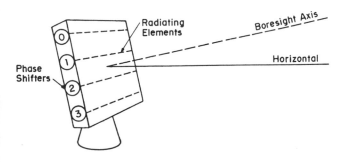

Figure 7–15. Three-dimensional search radar employing phased-array techniques in elevation.

Figure 7–16. The Marine Corps AN/ TPS-59 3-D radar. This radar is mechanically scanned in azimuth and uses phase shifters to scan in elevation.

information is obtained in the standard way by timing the pulse travel to and from the target. The phase shifters (0), (1), (2), (3) control the elevation position of the beam. It is desired to control the elevation of the beam in 0.0872 rad (5°) steps from + 1.047 rad (60°) to − 0.2617 rad (15°) with respect to the antenna boresight axis, which is + 0.2617 rad (15°) displaced from the horizontal. The system operational parameters are as follows:

Antenna rotational speed—10 rpm
Pulse repetition rate (PRR)—400 pps
No. of elevation beam positions—16
No. of pulse per beam position—2

For each beam position the amount of phase shift is calculated for each radiating element. The resultant phase shifts are applied, and then two pulses are transmitted and received. The elevation scan logic is illustrated by the flow diagram, figure 7–17. The resultant scan pattern is illustrated in figure 7–18.

This example is, of course, hypothetical. Some operational 3-D radars, such as the Marine AN/TPS-59 function similarly. It is important to note that the concept of controlling beam position by varying the relative phase of radiating elements is common to frequency-

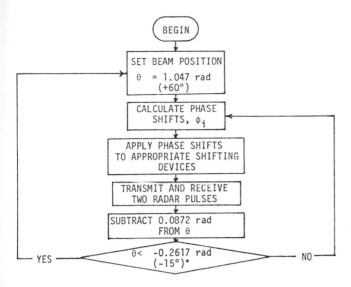

Figure 7–17. Elevation beam positioning logic. (*For antenna whose unshifted beam center is 15° above the horizon.)

scanned, phase-scanned, and time-delay scanned arrays. The difference is in the methods employed to achieve the proper phase relationships between the radiating elements.

Example 3. Full Three-Dimensional Phased-Array Radar

The logical extension of the simple system of example 2 is the realization of a fully operational three-dimensional phased-array radar system to compute direct radar beams in elevation and bearing. Such a system is used in the Ticonderoga-class Aegis cruisers, in the AN/AWG-9 radar for the F-14 aircraft, in the Air Force COBRA DANE

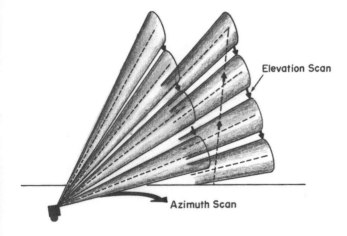

Figure 7–18. Scan pattern for 3-D radar. For simplicity, all beam positions are not shown, and scanning angles have been exaggerated.

Electronic Scanning and the Phased Array   **185**

surveillance system, and in the Army Patriot missile acquisition and guidance radar.

The task now is to position the beam in both elevation and azimuth by electronic means. As in the two-dimensional case, the phase shift for each element in the array must be computed and applied prior to transmitting a pulse of radar energy.

The array is made up of many independent elements. A unique element can be designated by the subscripts (e,a) for the eth row and a^{th} column. The equations governing the positioning of the beam are presented below.

Elevation Above or Below the Boresight Axis (Elevation scan)

$$\phi_e = e\pi 2d \, (\sin \theta_{EL})/\lambda \qquad (7-5)$$

Azimuth to the Right or Left of the Boresight Axis (Azimuth scan)

$$\phi_a = a\pi \, 2d \, (\sin \theta_{AZ})/\lambda \qquad (7-6)$$

The phase shift for each unique element is simply an additive combination of the above equations. Figure 7–19 illustrates the positioning of the beam in the quadrant $(+AZ, +EL)$. The combination of equations is therefore:

$$\phi_{e,a} = \phi_e + \phi_a \qquad (7-7)$$

$$\phi_{e,a} = e\frac{2\pi d}{\lambda}(\sin \theta_{EL}) + a\frac{2\pi d}{\lambda}(\sin \theta_{AZ})$$

$$\phi_{e,a} = \frac{2\pi d}{\lambda}[e(\sin \theta_{EL}) + a(\sin \theta_{AZ})]$$

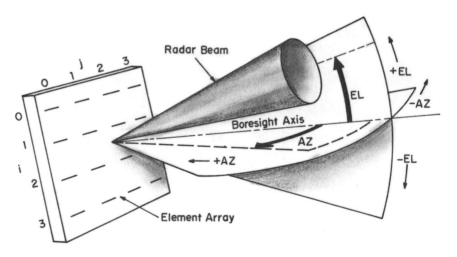

Figure 7–19. Three-dimensional phased-array radar.

The example has been patterned after radars that use phase scanning in both directions (elevation and azimuth). Other systems have been designed using a combination of array scanning systems. The AN/SPS-33 radar, which is no longer in use, was frequency scanned in elevation and phase scanned in azimuth.

Synthetic Aperture Radar

The synthetic aperture radar (SAR) is discussed here because of its similarities with conventional linear array antennas. SAR permits the attainment of the high resolution associated with arrays by using the motion of the vehicle to generate the antenna aperture *sequentially* rather than *simultaneously* as with conventional arrays. As an example of SAR, look back at figure 7–14. The eight elements in the figure will now represent points in space where the platform is located when the radar radiates energy as it travels from point seven to point zero. At each point along the path, data is gathered from the echos received, and this information is stored. Upon collecting the data at position zero, all the stored data from positions one through seven are combined with the data from position zero and processed as the data would be from an eight-element linear array with simultaneous inputs from all elements. The effect will be similar to a linear-array antenna whose length is the distance traveled during the transmission of the eight pulses. The "element" spacing of the synthesized antenna is equal to the distance traveled by the vehicle between pulse transmissions. A common use of SAR is in aircraft, which is known as side-looking radar, or SLR. In SLR, the aircraft travels in a straight path with a constant velocity. Its radar antenna is mounted so as to radiate in the direction perpendicular to the direction of motion. SARs in this configuration can be used to gain imaging data of the earth's surface in order to provide a maplike display for military reconnaissance, measurement of sea-state conditions, and other high cross-range resolution sensing applications.

Other Considerations

This has been a highly simplified treatment of electronic scanning and the phased-array radar. In addition to positioning the main lobe of energy, other considerations are:

(1) The suppression of side lobe interference.
(2) Array element excitation amplitudes and geometry to achieve various beam radiation patterns.
(3) Combining the phased array with a track-while-scan function.

(4) Modulating the radiated energy to transmit information (for missile guidance commands, etc.)

In practice there are limits to the useful angular displacement of an electronically scanned radar beam. One limit is caused by the element pattern. The antenna pattern of an array is the product of the array pattern and the element pattern. In the simple examples given in this section we have assumed that the element pattern was omnidirectional. A practical array element pattern is not omnidirectional, so the elements limit the scan angle. Another limit is caused by the element spacing. A large scan angle requires a close element spacing. If the scan angle exceeds that which can be accommodated by the element spacing, grating lobes will be formed in the other direction.

Summary

In this chapter, electronic scanning and its application to a phased-array system have been presented, focusing upon the concept of beam positioning. The basic concepts of radar beam steering as a result of phase differences among multiple radiating elements were addressed along with equations that determine the direction of a resultant beam. It should be noted that even with the increased complexity of the system, the output of the phased-array radar remains the same as any other basic sensor, i.e., target position. The great advantage of an electronically scanned system is that a single radar can perform multiple functions previously relegated to several separate radar systems.

Phased-array technology is also being applied to non-radar systems such as IFF, communications, EW, and sonar. By changing the phase relationships of the elements of a sonar transducer, the resultant beam of acoustic energy can be positioned downward to take advantage of CZ or bottom bounce conditions.

References

Cheston, T. C. "Phased Arrays for Radars." IEEE SPECTRUM, Nov. 1968, p. 102.

Kahribas, P. J. "Design of Electronic Scanning Radar Systems (ESRS)," Proceedings of the IEEE. Vol. 56, No. 11, Nov. 1968, p. 1763.

Patton, W. T. "Determinants of Electronically Steerable Antenna Arrays." RCA Review, vol. 28, No. 1, March 1967, pp. 3–37.

Sears, F. W., and M. W. Zemansky. University Physics. 4th ed. Reading, Mass: Addison-Wesley, 1970, p. 611.

Skolnik, Merrill I. Introduction to Radar Systems. 2nd ed. New York: McGraw-Hill, 1980.

8

Principles of Underwater Sound

Introduction

The effectiveness of the present-day submarine depends upon its ability to remain undetected for long periods of time while it searches, tracks, or attacks from beneath the sea surface. This medium of concealment, however, is advantageous to the submarine only so long as it is not detected or deprived of its ability to detect. Before a submarine can be attacked, it must be detected and its subsequent positions determined within the requirements of the available weapons system. Detection and position fixing can take place in two ways. There may either be some radiation or reflection of energy from the submarine to the searcher, or else the submarine may disturb one of the natural, static, spatial fields, such as the earth's magnetic field, thereby betraying its presence.

The choice of energy to be used for underwater detection is determined by three factors:

1. Range of penetration in the medium
2. Ability to differentiate between various objects in the medium
3. Speed of propagation

Of all the known physical phenomena, light has excellent differentiation ability and high speed of transmission, but its range in water is very limited, on the order of tens of meters, thereby restricting its operational usefulness. This is not to say that light will never be used in ASW, for continuing experimentation and perfection of laser light detectors might yet add this method to the arsenal. Radio frequency waves also are propagated with extreme rapidity and to great distances through certain mediums, but sea water is essentially impervious to them for most frequencies. VLF signals will penetrate only about 10 meters, whereas higher frequency penetration depths can be measured in millimeters. Magnetic and gravitational field distortions are detectable only at very short ranges because the anomaly diminishes proportionally with the inverse of the range cubed. While their detection range is greater than either light or radio frequency, it is only of the magnitude of several hundred meters and therefore is insufficient for normal surveillance.

Acoustic energy, while lacking the propagation speed of electromagnetic waves, is capable of being transmitted through the sea to distances that are operationally significant. Because of this, sound is the physical phenomenon used for antisubmarine warfare, underwater communications, and underwater navigation. It must not be inferred, however, that sound is a panacea. It too has significant limitations to its effective employment, all of which must be thoroughly understood by the operators of underwater sound equipment. The optimum use of sound requires a thorough understanding of its limitations so that these effects can be minimized. For example, sea water is not uniform in pressure, temperature, or salinity, and all these characteristics have important effects on sound propagation through the sea. The requirement for predicting these effects on sonar performance has become a necessity, and a difficult one at that.

Fundamental Concepts

All sound, whether produced by a cowbell or a complicated electronic device, behaves in much the same manner. Sound originates as a wave motion by a vibrating source and requires for its transmission an elastic medium such as air or water. For example, consider a piston suspended in one of these mediums. As the piston is forced to move forward and backward, the medium is compressed on the forward stroke and decompressed or rarefied on the return stroke. Thus, a wave motion or series of compressions and rarefactions is caused to move from the source out through the medium. In the fluid medium the molecular motion is back and forth, parallel to the direction of the piston's movement. Because the fluid is compressible, this motion results in a series of detectable pressure changes. This series of compressions and rarefactions, such as is produced by the piston, constitutes a compressional wave train. Another way of explaining the phenomenon of acoustic wave propagation is to consider the medium of transmission as a loosely packed collection of mass elements connected by springy bumpers. A disturbance of the elements at some point (e.g., piston motion) moves along in the fluid by the successive extension and compression of the springs as the elements swing back and forth, each communicating its motion to its neighbor through the connecting bumpers. In this way, the agitation of a cluster of elements is propagated through the medium even though the individual ele-

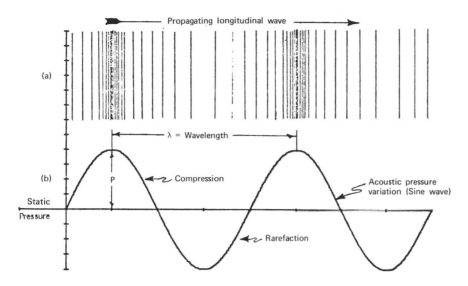

Figure 8–1. Pictorial representation of simple longitudinal wave.

ments do no more than move about their equilibrium positions without actually migrating.

The sine wave of figure 8–1 is a graphical representation of the compressional wave train. As the wave passes a given point, the fluid elements are compressed and extended in the manner depicted by the sine wave's oscillations above and below the static pressure. The compressions and rarefactions are so labeled on the curve. There are two important things to note on this curve. The first is the maximum amplitude of the sine wave, labeled P, which represents the maximum pressure excursion above and below the static or hydrostatic pressure that exists in the fluid at the location of the wave train. The second thing to note is that the wave train would be passing, or propagating, at the speed of sound c in the medium. The units for speed of sound are meters per second. The relationship between the three acoustic quantities that can be derived from figure 8–1 is:

$$\text{Frequency } (f) = \frac{\text{Speed of sound } (c)}{\text{Wavelength } (\lambda).} \qquad (8–1)$$

This is exactly the same as described for electromagnetic energy in chapter 1 and thus will not be elaborated upon.

One final point should be made about the sine wave representation of figure 8–1. Though somewhat difficult to imagine and more difficult to describe pictorially, the displaced parallel lines in figure 8–1a represent the motion of the elements within the field as the wave train passes. As the elements are compressed and extended, their motion can also be mathematically described by a sine wave; however, the elements would be oscillating to and fro about their static position. The maximum amplitude would be the maximum displacement from the static position. To provide an example of the order of magnitude of these displacements, consider that the faintest 1,000 Hz tone that can just be heard in air has pressure variations of only 2/10,000,000,000 of one atmosphere of pressure. The corresponding particle displacement is about 10^{-9} cm. By way of comparison, the diameter of an atom is about 10^{-8} cm.

As this pressure disturbance propagates through the medium, the pressure at any point in the medium can be expressed as a function of the distance, r, from the source and time, t, since a particular wave departed the source,

$$P(r,t) = P(r)\sin\left[\frac{2\pi}{\lambda}(R - ct)\right] \qquad (8\text{--}2)$$

Note how the maximum amplitude, $P(r)$, is dependent on the distance from the source. Neglecting wave interference effects, the amplitude of a pressure disturbance will always diminish, and equation 8–2 therefore represents a decreasing amplitude sinusoid wave. If, however, the distance is fixed, then pressure is solely a function of time, and equation 8–2 simplifies to

$$P(t) = P_A \sin\left[2\pi(ft)\right] \qquad (8\text{--}3)$$

where P_A is now the maximum amplitude at the range r.

A propagating sound wave carries mechanical energy with it in the form of kinetic energy of the particles in motion plus the potential energy of the stresses set up in the elastic medium. Because the wave is propagating, a certain amount of energy per second, or power, is *crossing a unit area* and this *power per unit area*, or *power density* is called the *intensity*, I, of the wave. The intensity is proportional to the square of the acoustic pressure. Before giving the defining relationship for intensity, however, two variables must be explained. The value of peak pressure, P, as shown in figure 8–1 is not the "effective" or *root-mean-square* pressure. An analogy exists between acoustic pressure and the voltages measured in AC circuits. Most voltmeters read the rms voltage. The rms value of a sinusoidal voltage is simply the peak voltage divided by the square root of two. For example, the common 115-volt line voltage has a peak value of about

162 volts. In order to obtain the rms pressure, P must likewise be divided by the square root of two.

$$P_e = P_{rms} = \frac{P}{\sqrt{2}} \qquad (8-4)$$

In this text, the effective or rms pressure as measured by a pressure-sensitive hydrophone will be labeled P_e. The explanation of units for pressure will be fully discussed at a later time.

The second variable that must be explained is the proportionality factor that equates intensity to effective pressure squared. It consists of two terms multiplied together — fluid density, ρ and the propagation speed of the wave, c. The quantity, ρc, is called the *characteristic impedance*; it is that property of a sound medium that is analogous to resistance or impedance in electrical circuit theory, where power equals voltage squared divided by resistance. Additionally, it can be illustrated by a simple example: When two dissimilar mediums, such as air and water, are adjacent to each other, the boundary between the two is called a discontinuity. When sound energy is traveling through one medium and encounters a discontinuity, part of the energy will be transferred across the boundary and part will be reflected back into the original medium. The greater the difference between the characteristic impedances, the greater will be the percentage of energy reflected. (The difference between the ρc values for air and water in SI units is approximately 1.5×10^6.) Thus, when sound is traveling through water and it reaches the surface, only a small amount is transmitted into the air. Most of the energy is reflected by the air/ocean boundary back into the water. Obviously, it is important to maintain a consistent set of units when comparing characteristic impedances, and care must be exercised when dealing with different sources of acoustic information.

With the concepts of rms pressure and characteristic impedance understood, it is now possible to formulate an expression for acoustic intensity, the average power per unit area normal to the direction of wave propagation.

$$I = \frac{P_e^{\,2}}{\rho c} \quad (\rho c_{\text{sea water}} \simeq 1.5 \times 10^5 \text{ dyne-sec/cm}^3) \qquad (8-5)$$

The units of acoustic intensity are normally watts/m². The importance of equation 8–5 is that it clearly shows the dependence of the power transmitting capacity of a train of acoustic waves on the pressure. If the rms pressure in the water can be measured, then the sound intensity can be determined. One way to do this is by means of a hydrophone, an electrical-acoustic device, much like a microphone, that transforms variations in water pressure into a variable electric voltage. Thus, after appropriate calibration, P_e can be read directly from a voltmeter attached to the input of a hydrophone.

Measurement of Acoustic Parameters

A convenient system is needed in order to measure and discuss acoustic parameters. Pressure is defined as a force per unit area. Although many people are familiar with the British units of pounds per square inch (psi), it has long been the convention in acoustics to use metric units, namely newtons per square meter (N/m^2), or dynes per square centimeter ($dynes/cm^2$). Of the two metric units, the dynes/cm^2 has been the most commonly used. It has an alternate name, *microbar* (μbar), and is equivalent to approximately 1/1,000,000 of a standard atmosphere. For underwater sounds, a reference pressure of 1 μbar was established from which all others were measured. The corresponding reference pressure for airborne sounds was 0.0002 μbar, because this was the approximate intensity of a 1,000-Hz tone that was barely audible to human ears. The previously less commonly used N/m^2 also has an alternate name, a *Pascal* (Pa), and the reference standard derived from this was the micropascal (μPa), which is equivalent to 10^6 N/m^2.

With such a profusion of reference standards and measurement systems, there were ample opportunities for misunderstandings as an operator or planner consulted different sources of acoustic information. In 1971 the Naval Sea Systems Command directed that thereafter all sound pressure levels should be expressed in the Systeme Internationale (SI) units of micropascals. Although all new publications contain the updated standards, older references will not until they are revised. To assist in making conversions until all publications are revised, table (8–1) summarizes some conversion values.

Table 8–1.   Acoustic Reference Conversion Factors

1 μbar	$= 1$ dyne/cm^2 $= 0.1$ N/m^2
	$= 10^5$ μPa $\simeq 10^{-6}$ atmospheres
1 μPa	$= 10^{-6}$ N/m^2 $= 10^{-5}$ μbar
	$= 10^{-5}$ dyne/cm^2 $\simeq 10^{-11}$ atmospheres

Throughout this text, the acoustic pressure reference standard, P_0, is 1 μPa unless otherwise noted.

In theoretical investigations of acoustic phenomena, it is often convenient to express sound pressures in newtons/m² and sound intensities in watts/m². However, in practical engineering work it is customary to describe these same quantities through the use of logarithmic scales known as *sound pressure levels*. The reason is related, in part, to the subjective response of the ear. The human ear can hear sounds having pressure disturbances as great as 100,000,000 micropascals and as small as 10 micropascals. A problem is encountered when discussing pressures that vary over so great a range, in that the minimum audible disturbance is one ten-millionth that of the maximum. In underwater acoustics, useful pressures having even greater variations in magnitude are commonly encountered. In order to make the numbers more manageable, both in magnitude and for actual manipulation, logarithms are used rather than the numbers themselves. Suppose two acoustic signals are to be compared, one having a P_e of 100,000,000 μPa and the other a P_e of 10 μPa. Their ratio would be

$$\frac{P_1}{P_2} = \frac{100,000,000\ \mu\text{Pa}}{10\ \mu\text{Pa}} = 10,000,000 = 10^7$$

In underwater acoustics, however, the attribute of primary interest is sound intensity, or power, rather than pressure. As with pressure, acoustic intensities are referenced to some standard intensity, designated I_0, and the logarithm of the ratio taken. Intensity level is therefore defined as

$$IL = 10 \log (I/I_0) \tag{8-6}$$

where IL is measured in dB. However, as there is only one intensity reference (10^{-12} watt/m² in air) and many pressure references, IL must be able to be expressed in terms of pressure. By inserting equation (8–5) into equation (8–6), a new expression of IL can be obtained, which is based on pressure rather than intensity per se.

$$IL = 10 \log \frac{\dfrac{P_e^2}{\rho c}}{\dfrac{P_0^2}{\rho c}} \tag{8-7}$$

or

$$IL = 10 \log \frac{P_e^2}{P_0^2} = 20 \log \frac{P_e}{P_0}$$

Under the assumption that the reference intensity and the reference pressure are measured in the same acoustic wave, then a new sound level can be defined called *sound pressure level*.

$$SPL = 20 \log \left(\frac{P_e}{P_0} \right) \qquad (8-8)$$

As before, *SPL* has the dimensionless units of decibels. Since the voltage outputs of the microphones and hydrophones commonly used in acoustic measurements are proportional to pressure, acoustic pressure is the most readily measured variable in a sound field. For this reason, sound pressure level is more widely used in specifying sound levels, and this is also why only pressure references are used in underwater acoustics. Note that *IL* and *SPL* are numerically equivalent.

$$IL = 10 \log \frac{I}{I_0} = 20 \log \frac{P_e}{P_0} = SPL \qquad (8-9)$$

where

$$I_0 = \frac{P_0^2}{\rho c}$$

In addition to the advantages mentioned above in dealing with logarithms, the use of decibels makes conversions between pressure reference standards very simple. The conversion factors in table 8–1 can in themselves be cumbersome to use, but when expressed in dB, only addition or subtraction is required. When converting from a pressure referenced to 1 μbar to one referenced to 1 μPa, simply add 100dB. When converting from 0.0002 μbar to 1 μPa, simply add 26dB. If converting from 1 μPa to the others, merely subtract the appropriate values. Table 8–2 shows some representative values of conversions between different reference levels.
Note that the new micropascal reference standard is small enough that negative values of decibels are rarely encountered.

As an aid in interpreting and understanding the decibel scale and its relation to intensity and pressure, it is useful to remember that

a factor of 2 in intensity is $+3$ dB
a factor of 0.5 in intensity is -3 dB
a factor of 10 in intensity is $+10$dB
a factor of 0.1 in intensity is -10 dB
a factor of 2 in pressure is $+6$dB
a factor of 0.5 in pressure is -6 dB
a factor of 10 in pressure is $+20$ dB
a factor of 0.1 in pressure is -20 dB

Table 8–2.   Atmospheric Pressure BAR $\simeq$ 14.7 PSI

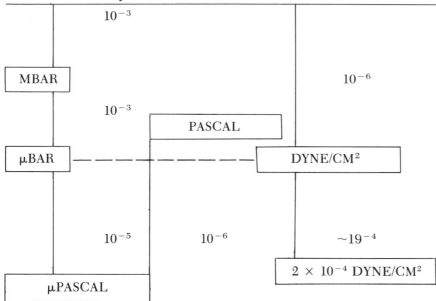

In understanding intensity levels and sound pressure levels, it is important to note that the decibel scale is a *ratio* of power or energy, no matter what quantities are being ratioed. A problem commonly arising in acoustic calculations is that of obtaining the overall intensity level after the individual intensities within the applicable bandwidths have been calculated. Such a situation is encountered in calculating a term in the sonar equations (to be discussed later) called *noise level,* which is actually a combination of ambient noise and self-noise. Because we are dealing with decibels, it is not possible to merely add similar intensity levels together and work with their sum. For example, two 30 dB signals combine to give a total intensity level of 33 dB, not 60 dB as might be expected. The reason for this is that, as shown above, doubling the intensity is represented in decibels by a +3 dB change. The process is more complicated when dealing with levels of unequal value. Although it would be possible, through antilogs, to convert each IL back to its intensity units, add all the intensities together, then reconvert to dB levels, this is a cumbersome process. Figure 8–2 can be used to determine the dB increase above a level of IL_1, in terms of the difference $IL_1 - IL_2$, to be expected when IL_1 and IL_2 are combined. This process can be expanded to include any number of intensity levels.

Although standardization has been reached for measuring intensities, such is not the case for other quantities. Ranges are expressed

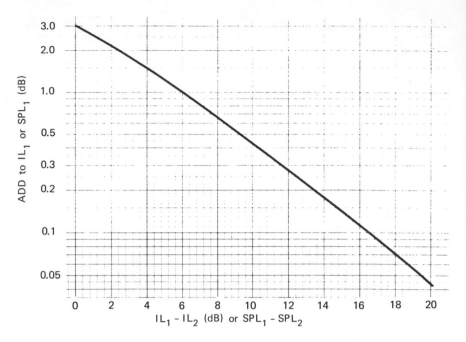

Figure 8–2. Nomogram for combining dB levels.

in yards, kilometers, and nautical miles. Depths are given in feet, meters, or fathoms. Sound speed is stated in feet per second or meters per second and ship speed in knots. Temperatures are commonly specified in degrees Fahrenheit or degrees Celsius. These diverse units should warn the user to exercise due caution when discussing the various facets of underwater sound to ensure that misunderstandings do not occur. In this text, the SI units of measure will be used wherever possible.

Sound Propagation Through the Sea

The sea, together with its boundaries, forms a remarkably complex medium for the propagation of sound. It possesses an internal structure and a peculiar upper and lower surface that create many diverse effects upon the sound emitted from an underwater source. In traveling through the sea, an underwater sound signal becomes delayed, distorted, and weakened. The transmission loss term in the sonar equations expresses the magnitude of these effects.

Consider a source of sound located in the sea. The intensity of the sound can be measured at any point in the sea, near to or far from the source. For purposes of measuring intensity at the source, the intensity measurement is generally taken at one unit distance from the source and labeled I_0. The intensity can then be measured at any distant point where a hydrophone is located and denoted I. It is operationally significant to compare the two values. One way to do this is to form the ratio I_0/I. Note that if the ratio, denoted n, is greater than unity, the intensity at the source is greater than at the receiver, as would be expected. If $n = i_0/I$, then

$$10 \log n = 10 \log I_0 - 10 \log I$$
$$= \text{sound intensity level at the source minus sound intensity level at the receiver.}$$

The value $10 \log n$ is called the transmission loss and, of course, is measured in decibels. Most of the factors than influence transmission loss have been accounted for by scientific research, and can be grouped into two major categories: spreading and attenuation.

Spreading Loss

To understand spreading loss, it is convenient to imagine a theoretical ocean that has no boundaries and in which every point has the same physical properties as any other point—i.e., an infinite, homogeneous medium. In such a medium, sound energy would propagate from a point source in all directions along straight paths and would have a spherical wave front.

Under these conditions the change in power density *with* distance from the point source would be due only to the spherical divergence of energy. Note that there is no true *loss* of energy as might be implied, but rather the energy is simply *spread* over a progressively larger surface area, thus reducing its density. For this model, the amount of power spread over the surface of a sphere of radius r, centered at a point source, is expressed by

$$\text{Power density (watts/m}^2\text{) at } r = \frac{P_t \text{ (watts)}}{4\pi r^2} \qquad (8-10)$$

where P_t is the acoustic power level immediately adjacent to the source.

This concept of power density (watts/m²) was used to develop the radar equation in chapter 2. As stated on page 8–5, the units of acoustic energy are watts/m². Therefore, equation 8–10 can be written

$$I_r = \frac{P_t}{4\pi r^2} \text{ (watts/m}^2\text{)} = \frac{P_e^2}{\rho c} \text{ where } P_e \text{ is}$$

measured at range r, and P_t is the acoustic power level immediately adjacent to the source.

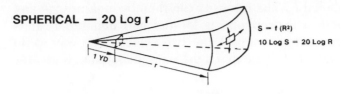

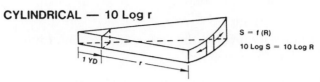

Figure 8–3. Spreading loss. (Courtesy Raytheon Corp.)

The intensity of the sound immediately adjacent to the source is measured, by convention, at a unit distance (1 meter) from the source. It will be labeled I_1 and is given by

$$I_1 = \frac{P_t}{4\pi(1)^2}$$

The acoustic intensity (I_r) at some distance, r, from the source will be less than the acoustic intensity (I_1) at 1 meter from the source. This is the result of spreading a fixed amount of power over a geometrically increasing surface area (a sphere, figure 8–3). The reduction of the acoustic intensity as a function of distance, r, is shown in the ratio

$$\frac{I_r}{I_1} = \frac{\dfrac{P_t}{4\pi(r)^2}}{\dfrac{P_t}{4\pi(1)^2}} = \frac{1}{r^2}$$

However, the ratio I_r to I_1 at any significant range is typically so small that these values are best examined on a logarithmic scale using the decibel.

$$10 \log \frac{I_r}{I_1} = 10 \log \frac{1}{r^2} = 10 \log (1) - 10 \log r^2 = -20 \log r$$

or

$$10 \log I_2 = 10 \log I_1 - 20 \log r$$

The reduction in acoustic intensity (I_1) due to range (spreading) is called the transmission loss (TL), and for spherical spreading

$$TL = 20 \log r \ (r \text{ in meters}) \tag{8–11}$$

and

$$10 \log I_r = 10 \log I_1 - TL$$

The ocean is not an unbounded medium, however, and all sources are not omnidirectional point sources. For sources that radiate energy only in a horizontal direction, sound energy diverges more like the surface of an expanding cylinder. Also, since the ocean is bounded at the surface and bottom, cylindrical divergence is usually assumed for ranges that are large compared to the depth of the water or for when sound energy is trapped within a thermal layer or sound channel. For this model, the acoustic intensity of energy at the surface of a cylinder of radius r is expressed by

$$I_r = \frac{P_t}{2\pi rh} \text{ watts/m}^2 \qquad (8-12)$$

where h is the vertical distance between upper and lower boundaries (see figure 8–3).

The transmission loss is therefore

$$10 \log \frac{I_r}{I_1} = 10 \log \frac{1}{r} = 10 \log (1) - 10 \log r = -10 \log r$$

or

$$10 \log I_r = 10 \log I_1 - 10 \log r$$

or

$$TL = 10 \log r \qquad (8-13)$$

and

$$10 \log I_r = 10 \log I_1 - TL$$

Equation (8–13) represents cylindrical divergence of sound energy, sometimes referred to as inverse first power spreading. Except at short ranges, it is the most commonly encountered type of spreading loss. It should be noted that the loss of intensity of a sound wave due to spreading is a geometrical phenomenon and is independent of frequency. As range increases, the percentage of intensity lost for a given distance traveled becomes increasingly less.

Attenuation Loss

Attenuation of sound energy in seawater arises principally through the action of two independent factors, *absorption* and *scattering*, with an additional contribution from bottom loss.

The primary causes of *absorption* have been attributed to several processes, including viscosity, thermal conductivity, and chemical reactions involving ions in the seawater. While each of these factors offers its own unique contribution to the total absorption loss, all of them are caused by the repeated pressure fluctuations in the medium as the sound waves are propagated. They involve a process of conversion of acoustic energy into heat and thereby represent a true loss of acoustic energy to the environment.

Experimentation has produced a factor α, called the *absorption coefficient*, which when multiplied by the range gives the total loss in dB due to absorption. Water temperature and the amount of magnesium sulphate ($MgSO_4$) are important factors influencing the magnitude of α, because the colder the average water temperature and the greater the amount of $MgSO_4$ present, the greater will be the losses due to absorption. However, it is the frequency of the sound wave that causes the most significant variation in the absorption coefficient. While the formula will change slightly with temperature and geographical location, an equation for the value of α in decibels per meter for seawater at 5°C is

$$\alpha = \frac{0.036 f^2}{f^2 + 3600} + 3.2 \times 10^{-7} f^2 \qquad (8-14)$$

where:

f = frequency in kHz

While this formula is rather cumbersome, the important thing to observe is that α increases roughly as the square of the frequency. This relationship is of major importance to the naval tactician. It tells him that if higher frequencies are chosen for sonar operation in order to achieve greater target definition, the price he must pay is greater attenuation. The higher the frequency, the greater the attenuation and the less the range of detection. For this reason, where long-range operation of sonar equipment is desired, the lower the frequency used the better. Figure 8–4 depicts typical values of the absorption coefficient of seawater at 5°C for varying frequencies.

To obtain the transmission loss due to absorption, α is merely multiplied by the range in meters. Thus,

$$TL = \alpha r \qquad (8-15)$$

Another form of attenuation is *scattering*, which results when sound strikes foreign bodies in the water, and the sound energy is reflected. Some reflectors are boundaries (surface, bottom, and shores), bub-

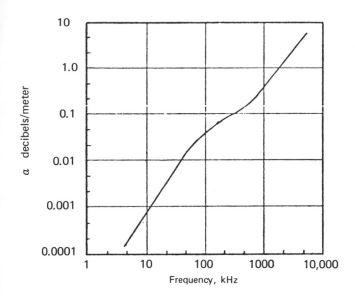

Figure 8-4. Absorption coeffi- cients.

bles, suspended solid and organic particles, marine life, and minor inhomogeneities in the thermal structure of the ocean. The amount of energy scattered is a function of the size, density, and concentration of foreign bodies present in the sound path, as well as the frequency of the sound wave. The larger the area of the reflector compared to the sound wavelength, the more effective it is as a scatterer. Part of the reflected sound is returned to the source as an echo, i.e., is backscattered, and the remainder is reflected off in another direction and is lost energy. Back-scattered energy is known as reverberation and is divided into three types: volume, surface, and bottom.

Volume reverberation is caused by various reflectors, but fish and other marine organisms are the major contributors. Additional causes are suspended solids, bubbles, and water masses of markedly different temperatures. Volume reverberation is always present during active sonar operations, but is not normally a serious factor in masking target echoes. The one exception involves the deep scattering layer (DSL), which is a relatively dense layer of marine life present in most areas of the ocean. During daylight hours, the layer is generally located at depths of about 600 meters and does not pose a serious problem. At night, however, the layer migrates toward the surface and becomes a major source of reverberation. It is rarely opaque to sound when detected with a sonar looking down on it from directly above, as with a fathometer, but this is not the case with a search sonar transmitting in a more or less horizontal direction. By pinging horizontally, the sound waves encounter many more organisms, and the effect can vary from partial transmission of sound to total reflection and scattering, thereby hiding a submarine.

Surface reverberation is generated when transmitted sound rays strike the surface of the ocean, i.e., the underside of the waves. It is always a factor in active sonar operations, and is directly related to wind speed because it controls wave size and the angle of incidence.

Bottom reverberation occurs whenever a sound pulse strikes the ocean bottom. In deep water this condition normally does not cause serious problems, but in shallow water, bottom reverberation can dominate the background and completely mask a close target. The amount of energy lost through scattering will vary with the roughness of the bottom and the frequency of the incident sound.

Sound reflected from the ocean floor usually suffers a significant loss in intensity. Part of this loss is caused by the scattering effects just described, but most of it results from the fact that a portion of sound energy will enter the bottom and travel within it as a new wave, as illustrated in figure 8–5. The net result is that the strength of the reflected wave is greatly reduced. The amount of energy lost into the bottom varies with the bottom composition, sound frequency, and the striking angle of the sound wave. The total of these losses can vary from as low as 2 dB/bounce to greater than 30 dB/bounce. In general, bottom loss will tend to increase with frequency and with the angle of incidence. Soft bottoms such as mud are usually associated with high bottom losses (10 to 30 dB/bounce); hard bottoms such as smooth rock or sand produce lower losses.

While it is possible to derive equations that will compute precise values of *TL* associated with each of these additional scattering and bottom loss factors, the ocean characteristics are so variable that there is little utility in doing so. It is customary, therefore, in operational situations, to make an educated guess as to their values and lump them together into one term "A," known as the *transmission loss anomaly*, which is included in the transmission loss equation.

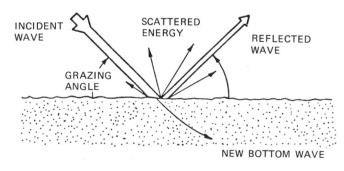

Figure 8–5. Bottom loss.

Total Propagation Loss

It would be useful to have a simple mathematical relationship that would describe all the effects of the various factors influencing transmission loss as they occur in the ocean. But the state of the physical conditions encountered in the ocean are very complex and not at all easy to represent. A few mathematical models do exist that provide close approximations for some sets of conditions, but at present, no single model accounts for all the conditions encountered.

A simplified model used to obtain approximate values of transmission loss for the *spherical spreading case* is

$$TL = 20 \log r + \alpha r + A \qquad (8–16)$$

and for the *cylindrical spreading case*

$$TL = 10 \log r + \alpha r + A \qquad (8–17)$$

It is important to realize that sound transmission in the ocean is three-dimensional and that transmission loss versus horizontal range alone is not sufficient information for most operational situations. Areas of no sonar coverage occur at various intervals of range because of refraction, reflection, and interference between waves traveling via different paths. Therefore, while the *TL* equations are interesting and somewhat useful, they are not always totally accurate.

Sound Sources and Noise

Background noise, like reverberation, interferes with the reception of desired echoes. Unlike reverberation, however, it does not result from unwanted echoes of the transmitted pulse but from active noise-makers located in the ship or in the water.

Noise produced by these sources is classified as self-noise and ambient noise. Self-noise is associated with the electronic and mechanical operation of the sonar and the ship. Ambient noise encompasses all of the noises in the sea.

Self-Noise

Self-noise is produced by noisy tubes and components in the sonar circuitry, water turbulence around the housing of the transducer, loose structural parts of the hull, machinery, cavitation, and hydrodynamic noises caused by the motion of the ship through the water.

The dominant source of *machinery noise* in a ship is its power plant and the power distribution system that supplies power to the other machinery on the vehicle, such as compressors, generators, propellers, etc. Machinery noise is normally always present and is kept to a minimum by acoustically isolating the various moving mechanical components.

The gearing connecting the propellers is an important source of machinery noise. If the engine runs at a relatively low speed, as is the case with a reciprocating heat engine, gears may not be required between the engine and the propeller. High-speed power sources, however, such as steam or gas turbines, usually require reduction gears to the propeller. The frequency of the explosions in the cylinders of a reciprocating engine is not likely to be a source of ultrasonic (above 15 kHz) noise but might be an important source of low-frequency sonic noise. A more crucial source of noise in the reciprocating engine is the clatter of the valves opening and closing. In gas turbines, the noise generated is in the ultrasonic region at a radian frequency equal to the angular velocity of the turbine buckets.

Noise in the ultrasonic region is extremely important in sonar and acoustic torpedo performance. The noise produced by auxiliary units, such as pumps, generators, servos, and even relays, is often more significant than the power-plant noise. The large masses involved in the power plant usually keep noise frequencies relatively low. For this reason, a small relay may interfere more with the operation of a torpedo than an electric motor that generates several horsepower. Small, high-speed servomotors, however, may be serious sources of ultrasonic noise.

Flow noise results when there is relative motion between an object and the water around it. This flow is easiest to understand by assuming that the object is stationary and that the water is moving past it. Under ideal conditions such that the object is perfectly streamlined and smooth, water movement will be even and regular from the surface outward as shown by the flow lines in figure 8–6. This idealized condition is called laminar flow and produces no self-noise. Irregular objects can achieve nearly laminar flow conditions only at very low speeds (i.e., 1 or 2 knots or below).

As flow speed increases, friction between the object and the water increases, resulting in turbulence (figure 8–6) and progressively increasing noise due to fluctuating static pressure in the water. Thus we have, in effect, a noise field. If a hydrophone is placed in such a region, fluctuations of pressure will occur on its face, and result in flow noise in the system.

As pressures fluctuate violently at any one point within the eddy, they also fluctuate violently from point to point inside the eddy.

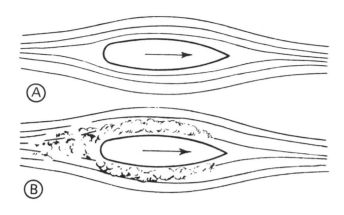

Figure 8–6. Patterns of flow noise.
A: laminar flow; B: turbulent flow.

Moreover, at any given instant the average pressure of the eddy as a whole differs but slightly from the static pressure. Thus, very little noise is radiated outside the area of turbulence, and although a ship-mounted hydrophone may be in an intense flow-noise field, another hydrophone at some distance from the ship may be unable to detect the noise at all. Flow noise, then, is almost exclusively a self-noise problem.

Actually, not much information is known about flow noise, but these general statements may be made about its effect on a shipborne sonar:

1. It is a function of speed with a sharp threshold. At very low speeds there is no observable flow noise. A slight increase in speed changes the flow pattern from laminar to turbulent, and strong flow noise is observed immediately. Further increases in speed step up the intensity of the noise.
2. It is essentially a low-frequency noise.
3. It has very high levels within the area of turbulence, but low levels in the radiated field. In general, the noise field is strongest at the surface of the moving body, decreasing rapidly with distance from the surface.
4. The amount of flow noise can be related to the degree of marine fouling on the ship's bottom and sonar dome.

Fouling is the attachment and growth of marine animals and plants upon submerged objects. More than 2,000 species have been recorded, but only about 50 to 100 species are the major troublemakers. These nuisances can be divided into two groups—those with shells and those without. Particularly important of the shell forms are tube-worms, barnacles, and mollusks because they attach firmly and resist being torn loose by water action. Nonshelled forms such as algae, hydroids, and tunicates commonly attach to relatively stationary objects and therefore do not cause much trouble on ships that frequently get underway.

Most fouling organisms reproduce by means of the fertilization of eggs by sperm, and the resulting larvae drift with the currents. Depending on the species, the larval stage may vary from a few hours to several weeks. Unless the larvae attach themselves to a suitable surface during this period, they will not grow into adulthood.

Geography governs fouling by isolating species with natural barriers. Temperature is the most important factor governing distribution of individual species, limiting reproduction or killing adults.

On a local scale, salinity, pollution, light, and water movement affect the composition and development of fouling communities. Most fouling organisms are sensitive to variations in salinity, developing best at normal seawater concentrations of 30 to 35 parts per thousand. Pollution, depending on type, may promote or inhibit fouling. Fouling algae and microscopic plants, the food supply of many fouling animals, are dependent upon sufficient light for proper growth.

To forestall fouling on ship bottoms and sonar domes, the Navy uses special paints with antifouling ingredients. The most common active ingredient of antifouling paint is cuprous oxide, and the effective life of the paint is from 2 to 2 1/2 years.

Cavitation

As the speed of the ship or object is increased, the local pressure drops low enough at some points behind the object to allow the formation of steam. This decrease in pressure and the resulting bubbles of vapor represent the onset of cavitation. As the ship moves away from the bubbles, however, the pressure increases, causing the bubbles to collapse and produce a continuous, sharp, hissing noise signal that is very audible.

Because the onset of cavitation is related to the speed of the object, it is logical that cavitation first appears at the tips of the propeller blades, inasmuch as the speed of the blade tips is considerably greater than the propeller hub. This phenomenon, known as blade-tip cavitation, is illustrated in figure 8–7.

As the propeller speed increases, a greater portion of the propeller's surface is moving fast enough to cause cavitation, and the cavitating area begins to move down the trailing edge of the blade. As the speed increases further, the entire back face of the blade commences cav-

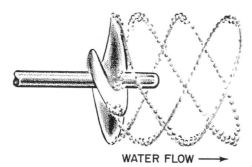

WATER FLOW ⟶   *Figure 8–7. Blade-tip cavitation.*

itating, producing what is known as sheet cavitation, as shown in figure 8–8.

The amplitude and frequency of cavitation noise are affected considerably by changing speeds, and changing depth in the case of a submarine. As speed increases, so does cavitation noise. As depth increases, the cavitation noise decreases and moves to the higher frequency end of the spectrum in much the same manner as though speed had been decreased. This decrease in noise is caused by the increased pressure with depth, which inhibits the formation of cavitation bubbles.

Since all torpedo homing systems and many sonar systems operate in the ultrasonic region, cavitation noise is a serious problem. Torpedoes generally home on the cavitation noise produced by ships, and any cavitation noise produced by the torpedo interferes with the target noise it receives. Because the speed at which a vehicle can operate without cavitating increases as the ambient pressure is increased, some acoustic torpedoes are designed to search and attack from depths known to be below the cavitating depth. In the same way, a submarine commander, when under attack, will attempt to

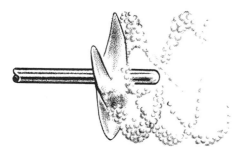

WATER FLOW ⟶   *Figure 8–8. Sheet cavitation.*

Principles of Underwater Sound   209

dive to depths at which he can attain a relatively high speed without producing cavitation.

Ambient Noise

Ambient noise is background noise in the sea due to either natural or manmade causes, and may be divided into four general categories: hydrodynamic, seismic, ocean traffic, and biological.

Hydrodynamic noise is caused by the movement of the water itself as a result of tides, winds, currents, and storms. The level of hydrodynamic noise present in the sea is directly related to the condition of the sea surface. As the surface becomes agitated by wind or storm, the noise level rises, reducing detection capability. Very high hydrodynamic noise levels caused by severe storms in the general area of the ship can result in the complete loss of all signal reception.

Seismic noises are caused by land movements under or near the sea—as, for example, during an earthquake. They are rare and of short duration, and hence will not be elaborated upon.

Ocean traffic's effect on ambient noise level is determined by the area's sound propagation characteristics, the number of ships, and the distance of the shipping from the area. Noises caused by shipping are similar to those discussed under the heading of self-noise, with the frequencies depending on the ranges to the ships causing the noise. Noises from nearby shipping can be heard over a wide spectrum of frequencies, but as the distance becomes greater, the range of frequencies becomes smaller, with only the lower frequencies reaching the ship because the high frequencies are attenuated. In deep water, the low frequencies may be heard for thousands of kilometers.

Biological noises produced by marine life are part of ambient background noise and at times are an important factor in ASW. Plants and animals that foul the ships are passive and contribute to self-noise by increasing water turbulence. Crustaceans, fish, and marine mammals are active producers of sounds, which are picked up readily by sonar equipment.

During and since World War II, a great deal of research on sound-producing marine animals has been carried out. The object was to learn all the species of animals that produce sound, their methods of production, and the physical characteristics of the sounds (frequencies, intensities, etc.). Sounds produced by many species have been analyzed electronically, and considerable physical data have been obtained.

All important sonic marine animals are members of one of three groups: crustaceans, fish, and mammals.

Crustaceans, particularly snapping shrimp, are one of the most important groups of sonic marine animals. Snapping shrimp, about 2 centimeters long, bear a general resemblance to the commercial species, but are distinguishable from them by one long, large claw with a hard movable finger at the end. They produce sound by snapping the finger against the end of the claw. Distribution of snapping shrimp appears to be governed by temperature, and they are found near land in a worldwide belt lying between latitudes 35°N. and 40°S. In some places, such as along the coast of Europe, they range as far north and south as 52°. The largest colonies or beds of snapping shrimp occur at depths of less than 30 fathoms on bottoms of coral, rock, and shell. There are exceptions, however; they may, for example, occur as deep as 250 fathoms, and have been found on mud and sand bottoms covered with vegetation.

A shrimp bed is capable of producing an uninterrupted crackle resembling the sound of frying fat or burning underbrush. Frequencies range from less than 1 to 50 kHz. Noise is constant, but there is a diurnal cycle, with the maximum level at sunset. Over beds, a pressure level of 86 db re 1μ Pa frequently is recorded, and one as high as 146 db re 1μ Pa has been noted. Intensity drops off rapidly as the range from the bed increases. Lobsters, crabs, and other crustaceans may make minor contributions to background noise.

Fish produce a variety of sounds that may be placed in three categories, depending upon how the sounds are caused. The first category includes sound produced by the air bladder, a membranous sac of atmospheric gases lying in the abdomen. The sound is caused by the movement of muscles inside or outside the bladder or by the general movement of the body. The second division includes sounds produced by various parts of the body such as fins, teeth, and the like rubbing together. This noise is called stridulatory sound. The third class includes sounds that are incidental to normal activities, such as colliding with other fish or the bottom while swimming, biting and chewing while feeding, and so on.

The majority of the sonic fish inhabit coastal waters, mostly in temperate and tropical climates. Although fish are the most prevalent, and therefore the most important, sound producers, their activity is not as continuous in intensity as that of snapping shrimp. The level of sound produced by them increases daily when they feed (usually at dawn and dusk), and annually when they breed. Fish sounds range in frequency from about 50 to 8000 Hz. Sounds of air bladder origin have most of their energy concentrated at the lower end of this spectrum, 75 to 150 Hz, whereas stridulatory sounds characteristically are concentrated at the higher end of the spectrum.

Marine mammals, in addition to returning echoes from sonar equipment, produce sound vocally and stridulously. Seals, sea lions, and similar animals possess vocal cords, and bark or whistle or expel air through their mouths and nostrils to produce hisses and snorts. Whales, porpoises, and dolphins force air through soft-walled nasal sacs, and the sounds produced in this way have been described as echo-ranging pings, squeals, and long, drawn-out moans similar to a foghorn blast. Other sounds probably produced by stridulation and attributed principally to whales, porpoises, and dolphins are described as clicking and snapping.

While difficult to determine accurately on an operational basis, ambient noise levels are nonetheless important factors to be considered in determining sonar performance. Figure 8–9 is an example of a set of Wenz curves that can be used to estimate noise levels from a variety of sources within the frequency range of interest. Figure 8–10 is an expansion of the shipping noise/wind noise portion of the Wenz curves.

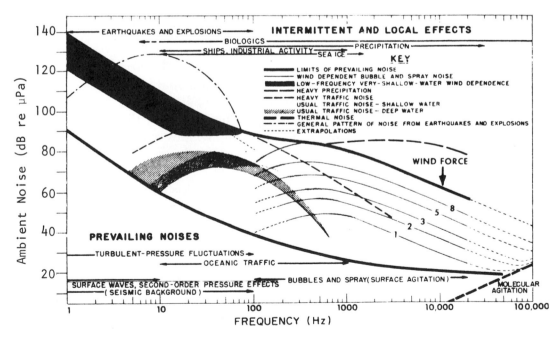

Figure 8–9. Acoustic ambient noise in the ocean.

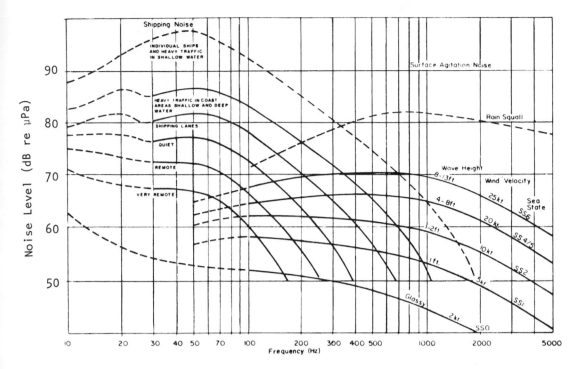

Figure 8–10. Ambient noise levels (simplified Wenz curves).

Sample Problem Using Wenz Curves

A SOSUS station is searching for an enemy submarine known to be producing sound at a frequency of 300 IIz. It is suspected that the sub is patrolling in shipping lanes that currently have 6-ft. seas. Use Wenz curves to determine an approximate value of ambient noise.

From figure 8–9 the ambient noise level due to shipping at 300 Hz is 65 dB and that due to 6-ft. seas is 66 dB.

Using the nomogram, figure 8–2, combine the signals of 65 dB and 66 dB.

$$I_{L1} - I_{L2} = 66-65 = 1$$

From the nomogram add 2.4 dB to 66 dB ∴ 68.4 dB.

The Sonar Equations

The key to success in antisubmarine warfare is initial detection. For this work the major sensor in use today is sonar, both active and passive, and the present state of knowledge of the physical world suggests no change in this situation for many years. An understanding of sonar can only be achieved through a comprehension of the sonar equations and the concept called figure of merit. Many of the phenomena and effects associated with underwater sound may conveniently and logically be related in a quantitative manner by the sonar equations. For many problems in ASW, the sonar equations are the working relationships that tie together the effects of the medium, the target, and the equipment, so that the operator can effectively use and understand the information received and provide prediction tools for additional information. Therefore, the purpose of this section is to spell out the sonar equations and figure of merit, to state the specifics of their usefulness, and to indicate how the various parameters in the sonar equations, including the figure of merit, can be measured.

The sonar equations are based on a relationship or ratio that must exist between the desired and undesired portion of the received energy when some function of the sonar set, such as detection or classification, is performed. These functions all involve the reception of acoustic energy occurring in a natural acoustic background. Of the total acoustic energy at the receiver, a portion is from the target and is called *signal*. The remainder is from the environment and is called *noise*. The oceans are filled with noise sources, such as breaking waves, marine organisms, surf, and distant shipping, which combine to produce what is known as ambient noise. Self-noise, in contrast, is produced by machinery within the receiving platform and by motion of the receiving platform through the water. Further, in active systems, scatterers such as fish, bubbles, and the sea surface and bottom produce an unwanted return called reverberation, which contributes to the masking of the desired signal.

The function of the design engineer is to optimize the signal-to-noise (S/N) ratio for all conditions as detailed in the original design specifications of the sonar set. The operator, using his knowledge of the design specifications, his known ability in certain circumstances, the predicted conditions extrapolated from previously determined measurements, and actual on-board measurements, can then predict the detection probability.

In order to predict performance, the operator's interaction with the sonar set must be defined or quantified in a manner that provides a measure of predictability for varying signal and noise levels. This quantity, known as Detection Threshold (DT), attempts to describe in a single number everything that happens once the signal and its accompanying noise are received at the sonar. Detection threshold is defined as the single minus noise level required inboard of the hydrophone array in order than an operator can detect a target. Actually, the business of detecting a sonar signal is a chance process for several reasons, one of which is that a human being is involved. The decision to call a target may be either right or wrong: if a target is really present, then there is a detection; if a target is not present, then there is a false alarm. Hence, the definition of *DT* is normally qualified by adding the requirement that an operator "can detect a target on 50 percent of those occasions for which a target presents itself." Thus, if the average value of provided signal-to-noise equals the average of required signal-to-noise, a detection occurs in 50 percent of the times that a detection could occur. To summarize:

If average provided = average required, then detection probability is 50%

If average provided > average required, then detection probability is 50% to 100%

If average provided < average required, then detection probability is 50% to 0%

Note that the *instantaneous* value of the provided or required signal-to-noise can vary over a wide range due to the variability of operators, and an individual operator's moods, as well as time fluctuations in propagation loss, target radiated signal, and own ship noise. Hence, while the average value of provided signal-to-noise may be less than the average value of required signal-to-noise, at times the instantaneous value may be greater than the required value, and a detection may occur. Thus, a probability of detection greater than zero exists.

Putting this all together, it can be seen that if detection is to occur with a specified degree of probability, then the signal, expressed in decibels, minus the noise, expressed in decibels, must be equal to or greater than a number, the Detection Threshold, which also is expressed in decibels.

$$S - N \geqslant DT \qquad (8-18)$$

This equation is the foundation upon which all the versions of the sonar equations are based, and is simply a specialized statement of the law of conservation of energy.

The next step is to expand the basic sonar equation in terms of the sonar parameters determined by the *equipment*, the *environment*, and the *target*.

Parameters determined by the equipment:

Own sonar source level: *SL*
Self-noise level: *NL*

Receiving directivity index: *DI*
Detection threshold: *DT*

Parameters determined by the environment:

Transmission loss: *TL*
Reverberation level: *RL*
Ambient-noise level: *NL*

Parameters determined by the target (*for active sonar)

*Target strength: *TS*
Target source level: *SL*

Two pairs of the parameters are given the same symbol (Own Sonar Source Level/Target Source Level, and Self-noise Level/Ambient-noise Level) because they are essentially identical. This set of parameters is not unique, nor is the symbolism the same in all publications, but they are the ones conventionally used in technical literature. It should be noted as the discussion progresses how each of these parameters will fit into the mold of the basic sonar equation.

Passive Sonar Equation

A passive sonar depends on receiving a signal that is radiated by a target. The target signal can be caused by operating machinery, propeller noise, hull flow noise, etc., but the same fundamental signal-to-noise ratio requirement must be satisfied. At the receiver, the passive equation begins as $S - N \geq DT$. If the target radiates an acoustic signal of *SL* (Target Source Level), the sound intensity is diminished while en route to the receiver because of any one or more of the following: spreading, ray path bending, absorption, reflection, and scattering. The decrease in intensity level due to this is called Transmission Loss (*TL*) and is also measured in decibels. Hence the intensity level of the signal arriving at the ship is

$$S = SL - TL \qquad (8-19)$$

Noise, *N*, acts to mask the signal and is not wanted. Therefore, the receiver is composed of many elements, sensitive primarily in the direction of the target so that it can discriminate against noise coming from other directions. This discrimination against noise can be referred to as a spatial processing gain and is called the Receiving Directivity Index, *DI*. *DI* gives the reduction in noise level obtained by the directional properties of the transducer array. Therefore, in

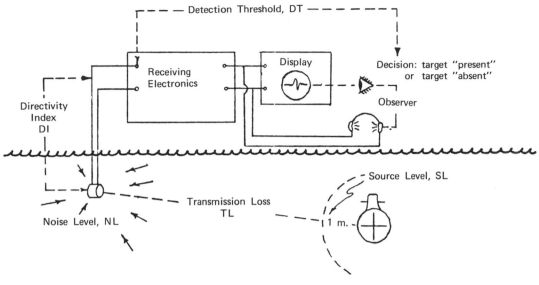

$$SL \ - \ TL \ - \ NL \ + \ DI = DT$$

Figure 8–11. *Diagrammatic view of passive sonar equation.*

the basic equation, noise is now reduced and becomes

$$N = NL - DI \qquad (8\text{–}20)$$

There are two things to note in this simple equation: the first is that *DI* is always a positive quantity, so that $NL - DI$ is always less than or equal to *NL*; the second is that the parameter *NL* represents both Self-noise Level and Ambient-noise Level, for by its definition it is the noise at the hydrophone location and can come from any, or all, sources.

The passive sonar equation can now be constructed in terms of signal and noise. When *S* and *N* are substituted from equations (8–19) and (8–20) into (8–18) the result is

$$SL - TL - NL + DI \geqslant DT \qquad (8\text{–}21)$$

which is the simplest form of the passive sonar equation. In words, equation 8–21 says that the source level of the target minus the loss due to propagation through the medium, minus the sum of all interfering noises plus improvement by the spatial processing gain of the receiver, must be equal to or greater than the detection threshold for a target to be detected with the specified probability of detection. However, the greater-than or equal-to condition is normally written as an equality. It is then understood to mean that if the left-hand side's algebraic sum is greater than DT, detection is possible with a greater probability than that specified by DT. If the sum is less than DT, detection probability decreases. Generally speaking, these two conditions imply that either detection is highly probable or seldom occurs. As a further aid to understanding the passive sonar equation, figure 8–11 illustrates the sonar parameters and indicates where each term involved interacts to produce the desired results.

Active Sonar Equation

In an active sonar, acoustic energy is transmitted, and the received signal is the echo from the target. Two different, but related, equations are needed to describe the active sonar—one for an ambient-noise-limited situation and the other for the reverberation-limited situation. As developed previously, sonar performance is governed by the requirement that signal minus noise must be equal to or greater than detection threshold. The difference in the two active sonar equations that satisfy this requirement depends upon the characteristics of the noise that is actually present at the receiver when the signal is detected. The ambient noise may be described as either *isotropic*—i.e., as much noise power arrives from one direction as from any other—or as *reverberation*, in which noise returns primarily from the direction in which the sonar has transmitted.

Before developing the active sonar equations, the two types of noise should be briefly explained. More detail will follow later in the chapter. Ambient noise consists of those noises present even when no sound is being radiated by a sonar. These include such noises as sea animals, machinery, propulsion noises generated by the echo-ranging platform, and the turbulence generated in the vicinity of the sonar. This type is the same as the noise level term discussed in the passive sonar equation. The second type, reverberation, consists of a multiplicity of echoes returned from small scatterers located in the sound beam and near the target when they reflect the transmitted energy. The combined effect of echoes from all of these scatterers produces a level of noise at the receiver that will tend to mask the returning echo from any wanted target.

The development of the active sonar equation is similar to that for the passive equation. In other words, the formal sonar parameters will be fitted to the signal and noise terms of equation (8–18). If a sonar transmits an acoustic pulse with an initial source level of SL dB, the transmitted pulse will suffer a transmission loss in traveling to the target. The target will scatter acoustic energy, some of which will return to the sonar. The back-scattered intensity is called target strength and is related to the scattering cross section of the target. The returning echo will again undergo a propagation loss, and thus the signal at the sonar will be

$$S = SL - 2TL + TS \qquad (8-22)$$

As long as the source of the radiated energy and the receiver for the echo are located together, the transmission loss experienced is equal to twice the one-way transmission loss.

When the echo returns, under some conditions the reverberation background due to the initial transmission will have disappeared, and only ambient noise will be present. This noise will be identical to that described in the passive sonar equation, modified by the receiving directivity index. The fundamental relationship can then be expressed as

$$SL - 2TL + TS - NL + DI \geqslant DT \qquad (8-23)$$

which is the basic active sonar equation used when the sonar is operating in a *noise-limited* situation.

If, on the other hand, the echo returns when the reverberation background has not decayed to a level below the ambient noise level, the background noise is given by RL. In this case, the parameter DI, defined in terms of an isotropic background, is inappropriate, inasmuch as reverberation is by no means isotropic. For a reverberation background the terms $NL - DI$ are replaced by an equivalent reverberation level observed at the hydrophone terminals, and the sonar equation takes the form.

$$SL - 2TL + TS - RL \geqslant DT \qquad (8-24)$$

which is known as the *reverberation-limited* active sonar equation. Detailed quantification for the new term, RL, is difficult at best, for it is a time-varying function resulting from the inhomogeneities in the medium. One thing to note is that in the normal conversion from the basic equation to the active equations, the inequality again becomes an equality. As discussed under the passive sonar equation, it is understood that when the terms on the left-hand side exceed the detection threshold by a significant amount, detection is highly probable, and when it is significantly less than the detection threshold, detection seldom occurs. Figure 8–12 pictorially depicts the active sonar equations.

Of special interest in the active sonar equations is the term TS,

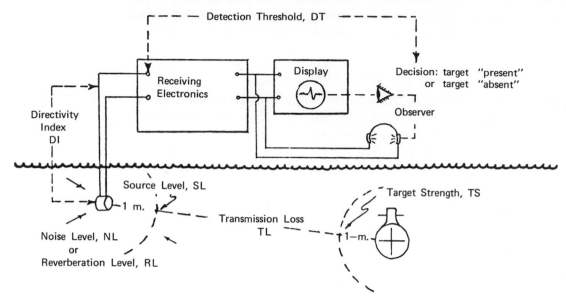

$$SL - 2TL + TS - NL + DI = \underline{DT} \quad \text{or} \quad SL - 2TL + TS - RL = \underline{DT}$$

Figure 8–12. Diagrammatic view of active sonar equation.

and the fact that it usually is on the order of 15 to 25 dB. Because *TS* is 10 times the logarithm of the reflected intensity divided by the inbound intensity, this statement apparently says that more energy is reflected than is incident, a condition clearly not possible. The key lies in the definition of terms:

I reflected is the intensity, *I*, of the reflected signal measured one meter from the target, assuming the target is a point source.

I inbound is the intensity, *I*, of the signal inbound from transmitting ship to the target measured at a point on the target.

Intensity is actually power per unit area striking the target at some point, and thus the total sound power striking the target is *I* inbound times an effective area. It one assumes that the major portion of this power is reflected *not* from the original effective area (which is almost the same as the profile area of the target), but instead from a *point* source, it necessarily follows that the reflected energy computed in this way must be greater because of the reduced area from which the energy emanates. Thus *I* reflected is greater than *I* inbound if both are defined as indicated above.

In this case, there is no such wave as the one that is defined as originating from the point source. This construct is merely a convenient way of duplicating the actual measured value of *I* reflected when the wave is 1,000 meters or more away from the point source en route back to the transmitting ship. Thus, if one were to measure I reflected and I *inbound* both at 1,000 meters from the target, then I inbound would definitely be greater than I reflected. Therefore, I reflected would have been computed to suffer a greater attenuation in traveling 1,000 meters from the constructed point source than I inbound will suffer in going 1,000 meters to the target. The explanation for this is the rapid attenuation due to spreading from the point source as compared to that undergone by the inbound wave, which is very near a plane wave when it is within 1,000 meters of the target.

Figure of Merit

The possible detection range of particular equipment should be known so that a tactician will then have a measure of the sonar's capability and a feel for what the sonar can do in a given tactical situation. Unfortunately, with no change in basic sonar configuration its detection capability measured in terms of range can increase or decrease severalfold simply because the ocean itself has changed. To state this another way, sonar equipment can only be designed to detect the arrival of a certain sound energy intensity. The range from which that sound intensity arrives is highly dependent on how much energy was lost en route, and therefore detection range alone is a poor measure of sonar capability. A better measure is the ability of the sonar to detect a certain level of sound energy intensity just outboard of its receiver. The key to this better measure of performance is to separate the sonar from the ocean in which it must operate. Only then can sonar capability be discussed in terms of the unchanging sonar hardware as distinguished from the ever-changing ocean.

The better measure for sonar capability is called figure of merit (FOM), and it equals the maximum allowable one-way transmission loss in passive sonars, or the maximum allowable two-way transmission loss in active sonars for a detection probability of 50 percent. Therefore, solving equations (8–22) and (8–23) for transmission loss, we get

$$\text{Passive FOM} = SL - NL + DI - DT \qquad (8\text{--}25)$$
$$\text{Active FOM} = SL + TS - NL + DI - DT \qquad (8\text{--}26)$$

This combination of terms is probably the most used performance parameter for sonars, and it is important to understand just what it means. The FOM of a sonar system is the maximum transmission loss that it can tolerate and still provide the necessary detection probability as specified by *DT*. FOM is improved by raising the source level (this can be accomplished by increasing the transmitted power in the active case or finding a noisier target in the passive case), decreasing the ambient noise level, increasing the absolute value of the receiving directivity index, and decreasing the detection threshold. The value of figure of merit is that, with no knowledge of the intervening propagation path between a ship and a target, a quantitative comparison of two different sonars can be made. Naturally, to the tactician, detection ranges are of prime importance, and although FOM can be interpreted in terms of range, it can be done only if the propagation losses involved are known. As will be discussed, this is extremely difficult to determine.

In summary, sonar performance is the key to ASW success, and figure of merit is the key to sonar performance. With knowledge of his sonar's FOM, a commanding officer can ensure that his equipment is peaked, and also predict detection ranges against possible enemy targets. The war planner can do likewise for either a real or hypothetical enemy. Because the changing ocean results in dramatic changes in propagation loss versus range, to state a sonar's capability in terms of range is only half the story, and may even be misleading. Using figure of merit, however, the sonar with the higher FOM will always be the better sonar when comparing sonars in the same mode.

Speed of Sound in the Sea

From physics it will be remembered that when gas is the transmitting medium, the denser the gas, the slower the speed of sound, and yet the speed of sound in water is about four times greater than that in air. Although this seems contradictory, it is not, because there is another more important factor that influences the speed of sound. In truth, the speed of sound is determined primarily by the elasticity of the medium and only secondarily by the density.

Elasticity is defined as that property of a body that causes it to resist deformation and to recover its original shape and size when the deforming forces are removed. Of specific concern is volume elasticity or bulk modulus—that is, the ratio of force per unit area (stress) to the change in volume per unit volume (strain). Thus,

$$\text{Bulk Modulus} = \frac{\text{Stress}}{\text{Strain}}$$

In order to bring about a change in the volume of a liquid, it is necessary to exert a force of much greater magnitude than is required to bring about an equivalent change in the same volume of air. Therefore, the value of bulk modulus is much greater for a liquid than for a gas. This bit of information, however, is meaningless until it is applied in the formula for the speed of sound.

The speed of sound, c, in a fluid is equal to the square root of the ratio of bulk modulus to density. Thus,

$$c = \sqrt{\frac{\text{Bulk Modulus}}{\text{Density}}} \qquad (8\text{--}27)$$

Although seawater is almost a thousand times denser than air, the enormous bulk modulus of water is the more important factor determining sound speed. Of concern, however, are not the differences of the two mediums but the conditions in water that cause changes in sound speed. Contrary to the assumptions made up to this point, the ocean is not a homogeneous medium, and the speed of sound varies from point to point in the ocean. This variation in sound speed is one of the most important characteristics affecting the transmission of sound. The three main environmental factors affecting the speed of sound in the ocean are salinity, pressure, and temperature.

Salinity, which on the average ranges from 32 to 38 parts per thousand (ppt), is fairly constant in the open ocean. A change of salinity will cause a small corresponding change in density with a resulting change in bulk modulus, causing variation of sound speed. The greatest variation in salinity in the open ocean exists in the vicinity of "oceanic fronts," which are narrow zones separating water masses of different physical characteristics, usually exhibiting very large horizontal gradients of temperature and salinity (figure 8–13). Even greater variation in salinity can be expected around the mouths of rivers, heavy ice, and in areas of extraordinary rainfall (e.g., the monsoon) where a layer of fresh water overrides a layer of salt water. A change in salinity of one part per thousand will result in a change in sound speed of approximately 1.3 meters per second.

Pressure in most circumstances is more important than salinity, but in the sea its change is constant and thus predictable. It also causes a change in bulk modulus and density, and the result is an increase in sound speed of 0.017 m/sec for every meter of depth increase. This slight change, which is important when temperature remains constant, causes a sound beam to bend upward at great depths as will be discussed later.

Temperature, the foremost factor affecting sound speed, usually

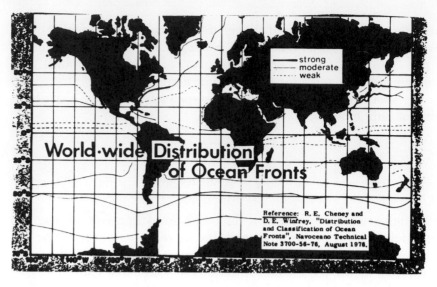

Figure 8–13.

decreases with depth, and this leads to an accompanying decrease in sound speed at the rate of approximately 3 m/sec per degree Celsius. Below a depth of about 1,000 m, however, temperature is fairly constant, and the predominant factor affecting sound speed becomes pressure. At first glance it would seem that a temperature decrease would increase sound speed due to the increased water density, but not so. As the temperature of a medium decreases, bulk modulus decreases while density increases. Considering these effects in terms of the sound speed formula in equation (8–27), it is clear that a decrease in temperature brings an attendant decrease in sound speed. It also should be noted that temperature differs bulk modulus and density at a variable rate. A change in temperature at one point on the scale, therefore, affects sound speed differently than an equal change at another point on the scale. It should be noted that the effect of temperature is relatively large compared to the other factors. It takes a depth change of about 165 meters to cause the same change in sound speed as a one-degree temperature change. As will be discussed, temperature is therefore the only factor normally measured and evaluated under operational conditions.

Dealing with these three factors to arrive at values for bulk modulus and density, and thence sound speed, is very cumbersome. To overcome this, numerous empirical relationships have been developed for converting the three factors directly to sound speed. A simplified version of such sound speed equations developed by Wilson in 1960 is present below.

$$c = 1449 + 4.6T + 0.055T^2 + 0.003T^3$$
$$+ (1.39 - 0.012T)(S - 35) + 0.017d \quad (8\text{--}28)$$

where

T = temperature in degrees Celsius
S = salinity in parts per thousand
d = depth in meters

Given accurate temperature, salinity, and depth data, this equation is accurate within 0.6 meters/sec. 96 percent of the time. By way of contrast, the equation for the speed of sound in air is approximately

$$c = 331.6 + 0.6T$$

In making calculations involving the transmission of sound through the sea, it frequently is adequate to use a standard speed rather than the more accurate value given by equation 8–28. Although in seawater c can vary from a low of about 1,420 m/s to over 1,560 m/s depending on environmental conditions, a standard speed of 1,500 m/s may be assumed for computation purposes unless otherwise noted.

Field Observations of Sound Speed

Knowledge of sound velocity is important to the ASW tactician and physical oceanographer because of the effect that variations in sound velocity have upon acoustic absorption and refraction. Two different devices are in use today for finding the speed of sound in the sea.

The first device is called a *bathythermograph*. As previously stated, temperature is the predominant ocean variable affecting sound speed. Not only is it relatively easy to measure, but when applied to empirical relationships such as equation (8–28), sound speed can be computed. Older BT systems employed a mechanical device that was lowered on a cable and the temperature was scribed on a smoked piece of glass. This had a number of inherent disadvantages that have been overcome through the development of the expendable bathythermograph (XBT), which does not require retrieval of the sensing unit. A cutaway view of an XBT is shown in figure 8–14a. It consists of a thermistor probe that is ejected from the launching platform and sinks at a known non-linear rate. The XBT is connected to a special recorder on board the launching platform by a fine wire. As it sinks, the

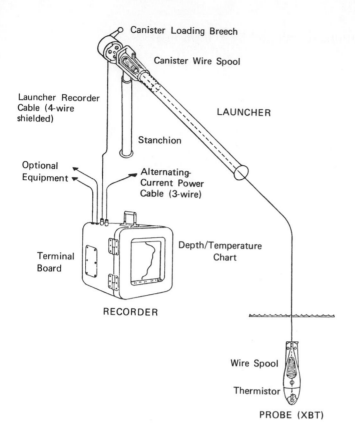

Figure 8–14a. Expendable bathy-thermograph.

thermistor changes its electrical resistance with changing temperature, and as a result a temperature vs. depth trace is obtained. Because
the wire uncoils from both the probe and its launcher, there is no
tension on the wire until the probe has sunk to its full depth. At this
point, the wire snaps and the recording stops. Variants of the basic
XBT have been developed for use aboard submarines and from aircraft
through incorporation into sonobuoys.

When the XBT temperature vs. depth trace is converted to sound
speed vs. depth, it produces a sound speed profile very similar to
that obtainable from a sound velocimeter, and is of sufficient accuracy
for operational requirements.

It is important to remember that while temperature is the dominant
factor, the sound-speed profile is really a composite of the pressure,
salinity, and temperature profiles as shown in figure 8–15. In the
area of ocean fronts, where salinity may vary up to 3 ppt. from assumed
values, the use of temperature data alone may result in an error of
up to 4.2 meters per second in the calculation of sound speed.

A typical composite deep-sea sound-speed profile is shown in greater

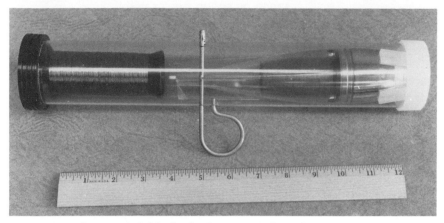

Figure 8–14b. Expendable bathythermograph probe.

detail in figure 8–16. The profile may be divided into four major layers each having different thermal characteristics. Just below the sea surface is the *surface layer*, in which the speed of sound is susceptible to daily and local changes of heating, cooling, and wind action. The surface layer may contain isothermal water that is formed due to mixing by the action of wind as it blows across the water. Below the surface layer lies the *seasonal thermocline*—the word "thermocline" denoting a layer in which the temperature changes rapidly with depth. The seasonal thermocline is characterized by a negative sound-speed gradient that varies with the seasons. During the summer and fall, when the near-surface waters of the sea are warm, the seasonal thermocline is strong and well defined; during the winter and spring, and in the Arctic, it tends to merge with, and be indistinguishable from, the surface layer. Underlying the seasonal thermocline is the *permanent thermocline*, which is affected only slightly by seasonal changes. Below the permanent thermocline and extending to the sea bottom is the *deep isothermal layer*, having a nearly constant temperature of about 4°C, in which the speed of sound

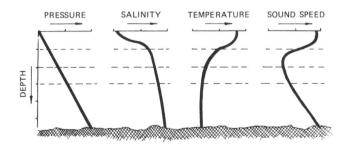

Figure 8–15. Graphical relationship of sound speed to pressure, salinity, and temperature.

Principles of Underwater Sound   **227**

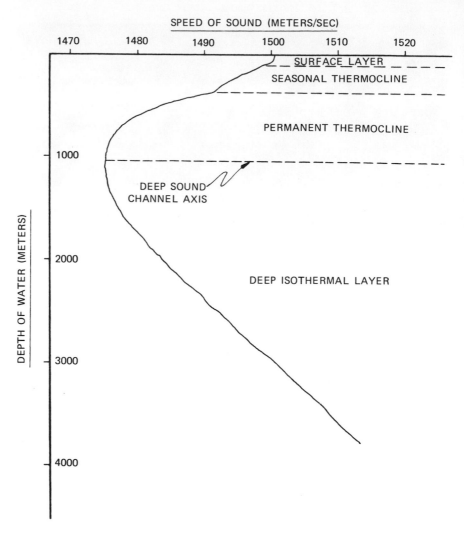

Figure 8–16. *Typical deep-sea speed profile divided into layers.*

has a positive gradient because of the effect of pressure on sound speed. Between the negative speed gradient of the permanent thermocline and the positive gradient of the deep isothermal layer, there is a speed minimum toward which sound traveling at great depths tends to be bent or focused by refraction. This is the deep sound channel and will be discussed later.

The second and most accurate method is the *sound velocimeter.* Its principle advantage is that it can measure sound speed directly, without need for conversions, by transmitting a pulse of sound over a very short path on the order of ½ meter or less. When the pulse arrives at the receiver, another pulse is then triggered from the transmitter; this is known as the "sing-around" or "howler" principle. The faster the speed of sound in the water in which the velocimeter is submerged, the faster the pulse will travel and the sooner it will arrive at the receiver to trigger the succeeding pulse. Since nearly all the time delay between pulses occurs as acoustic delay in the water, the PRF of the pulses is determined by the local sound speed and is directly proportional to it. Thus, knowing the path length and observing the PRF can lead directly to computation of sound speed. Until recently sound velocimeters were expensive and awkward to use, thus eliminating their use tactically. The recent development of the expendable sound velocimeter (XSV) has made it possible to reduce sound velocity measurement errors to less than .25 meters per second at reasonable expense without reduction of the mobility of combatant units. Today's sophisticated sonars and acoustic navigation systems can provide improved information in many oceanic regions when actual sound-velocity profiles are used rather then extrapolated sound velocity values based on temperature profiles and assumed salinity data.

Ray Theory

The propagation of sound in an elastic medium can be described mathematically by solutions of the wave equation using the appropriate boundary and medium conditions for a particular problem. The wave equation is a partial differential equation relating the acoustic pressure P to the coordinates x, y, z, and the time t, and may be written as

$$\frac{\delta^2 P}{\delta t^2} = c^2 \left(\frac{\delta^2 P}{\delta x^2} + \frac{\delta^2 P}{\delta y^2} + \frac{\delta^2 P}{\delta z^2} \right) \qquad (8\text{--}29)$$

There are two theoretical approaches to a solution of the wave equation. One is called normal-mode theory, in which the propagation is described in terms of characteristic functions called normal modes, each of which is a solution of the equation. The normal modes are combined additively to satisfy the boundary and source conditions of interest. The result is a complicated mathematical function which, though adequate for computations on a digital computer, gives little insight, compared to ray theory, on the distribution of the energy of the source in space and time. Normal-mode theory is well suited for a description of sound propagation in shallow water, but will not be discussed in this text.

The other form of solution of the wave equation is ray theory, and the body of results and conclusions therefrom is called ray acoustics. The essence of ray theory is (1) the postulate of wave fronts, along which the phase or time function of the solution is constant, and (2) the existence of rays that describe where in space the sound emanating from the source is being sent. Like its analog in optics, ray acoustics has considerable intuitive appeal and presents a picture of the propagation in the form of the ray diagram.

For almost all operational problems, the sound-speed gradient, with respect to horizontal changes of location, can be assumed to be zero. The major gradient of interest is the vertical gradient, dc/dz, where z is the amount of depth change. If a source of sound at the surface of the sea radiates omnidirectionally, a wave front expanding from this source in all directions transfers energy from one particle in the water to another, and by this means the wave is propagated. If some point on this wave front is selected, and from it a line is drawn in the direction of energy propagation, then connecting these points as the wave expands in space will result in a line called a ray, as illustrated in figure 8–17.

A sound wave, or ray, which enters another medium or layer of the same medium having a different characteristic impedance, will undergo an abrupt change in direction and speed. Depending upon the angle of incidence and the abruptness of change in ρc, a portion of the impinging acoustic energy will be reflected off the medium boundary, and a portion will be refracted or bent passing through the boundary. *A sound ray will always bend toward the region of slower sound speed.*

One of the most important practical results of ray theory is Snell's Law, which describes the refraction of waves in mediums of variable speeds. Snell's Law states that the angle of incidence, ϕ_1, at a boundary is related to the angle of refraction, ϕ_2, by the following expression:

$$\frac{\sin \phi_1}{\sin \phi_2} = \frac{c_1}{c_2} \tag{8–30}$$

where

c_1 = sound speed in medium 1
c_2 = sound speed in medium 2

If the wave is considered to be passing through three horizontal layers or strata, in each of which the sound speed is considered to

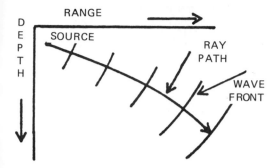

Figure 8–17. Ray theory.

be constant, then Snell's Law can be rewritten as

$$\frac{c_1}{\cos \Theta_1} = \frac{c_2}{\cos \Theta_2} = \frac{c_3}{\cos \Theta_3} = \frac{c_n}{\cos \Theta_n} \qquad (8\text{--}31)$$

where

c_n = speed of sound at any point in the medium
Θ_n = angle made with horizontal at that point

Note that the angle Θ in equation 8–32 is the complement of the angle usually expressed in Snell's basic law. It is commonly referred to as the grazing angle or angle of inclination. This expression is the basis of ray computation used by most computers, since it enables a particular ray to be "traced out" by following it through the successive layers into which the speed profile may have been divided. In a

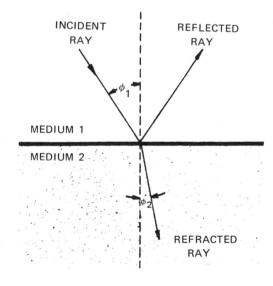

Figure 8–18. Snell's Law.

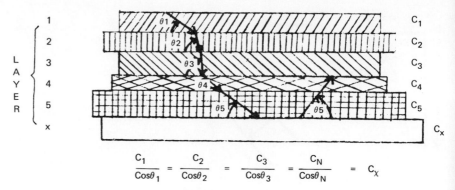

$$\frac{C_1}{\cos\theta_1} = \frac{C_2}{\cos\theta_2} = \frac{C_3}{\cos\theta_3} = \frac{C_N}{\cos\theta_N} = C_\chi$$

Figure 8–19. Snell's Law applied to multiple layers.

layered medium having layers of constant speed, the rays consist of a series of straight-line segments joined together, in effect, by Snell's Law.

In practice, however, temperature does not change abruptly, but rather the gradient will normally decrease or increase at a measurable rate. For such a situation, the sound speed at any depth z would be given by

$$c(z) = c_0 + gz \qquad (8\text{–}32)$$

where

c_0 = speed at the surface or transducer depth
g = speed gradient dc/dz between the surface and depth z

The net result is that, in reality, ray traces appear as curves rather than straight lines. By combining equations (8–31) and (8–32), an expression can be developed for the radius of curvature R of any ray at any point along the ray path, as shown by equation (8–33) and figure 8–20.

$$R = \frac{c_0}{g} = -\frac{c}{g \cos\Theta} \qquad (8\text{–}33)$$

Under operational conditions, values of R are very large, approaching several tens of kilometers.

Propagation Paths

The thermal structure of the ocean governs the refractive conditions for a given water mass. Despite infinite vertical temperature variations in the ocean, the temperature structure normally can be related to

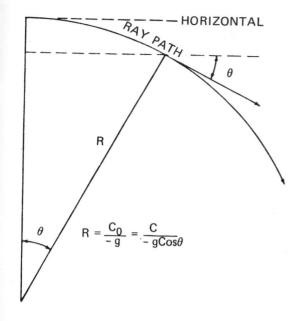

$$R = \frac{C_0}{-g} = \frac{C}{-g\cos\theta}$$

Figure 8–20. Radius of curvature.

three basic types: (1) isothermal, (2) negative temperature gradient, and (3) positive temperature gradient. In discussing sound propagation, it is customary to use the temperature profile as an indicator of sound speed conditions at various depths, because it has the greatest effect. It must be remembered, however, that changes in sound-beam direction result from changes in the sound-speed profile, which is influenced not only by temperature but pressure and salinity as well.

In an isothermal condition, the water's temperature is almost constant. If there is a slight decrease in temperature, and it is just balanced out by the pressure increase, the result is an iso-sound-speed condition. This causes a straight-line ray, leaving the source in lines

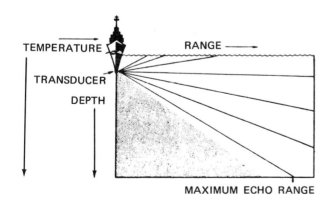

Figure 8–21. Sound travel in isovelocity water.

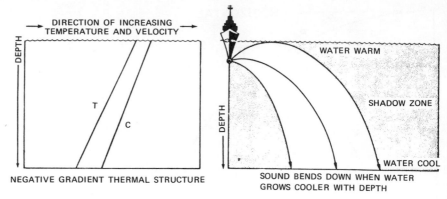

Figure 8–22. Sound travel in water of decreasing temperature.

that continue with little or no change in angle. Long ranges are possible when this type of structure is present.

When there is a negative temperature gradient, sound speed decreases with depth, and sound rays bend sharply downward. This condition is common near the surface of the sea. At some horizontal distance from the sound source, beyond where the rays bend downward, is a region in which sound intensity is negligible (figure 8–22); it is called a *shadow zone*. The magnitude of the temperature gradient determines the amount of bending of the sound beam and thus the range of the shadow zone. For example, if the decrease in temperature to a depth of 10 meters totals 2°C or more, the shadow zone would begin beyond a horizontal range of 1,000 meters due to the sharp curvature of the sound beam.

When the temperature of the water has a positive gradient, sound speed increases with depth, and sound rays are refracted upward.

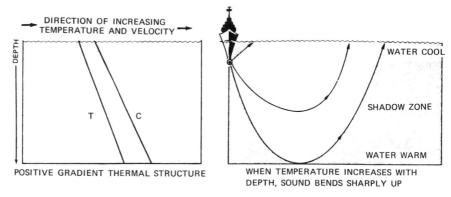

Figure 8–23. Sound travel in water of increasing temperature.

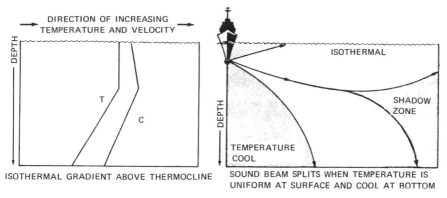

DIRECTION OF INCREASING
TEMPERATURE AND VELOCITY

DEPTH

T

C

ISOTHERMAL GRADIENT ABOVE THERMOCLINE

ISOTHERMAL

SHADOW
ZONE

DEPTH

TEMPERATURE
COOL

SOUND BEAM SPLITS WHEN TEMPERATURE IS
UNIFORM AT SURFACE AND COOL AT BOTTOM

Figure 8–24. Layer depth phenomenon.

Longer ranges are attained with this temperature structure than with a negative gradient because the rays are refracted upward and then reflect off the surface. Unles the surface of the sea is very rough, most of the rays are repeatedly reflected at the surface to longer ranges.

Circumstances usually produce conditions where combinations of temperatures occur. One of these combinations includes a layer of isothermal water over water with a negative gradient. One ray, labeled "the critical ray," becomes horizontal at the boundary or division between the isothermal layer and the negative gradient. The speed of sound is a maximum at this boundary point. Consequently, we define the layer depth (z) as that depth of greatest sound speed (c) above the seasonal thermocline (see figure 8–16). One-half of the critical beam bends toward the upper region at a reduced speed, and the other half bends toward the lower region at a reduced speed. The angle that the critical ray makes with the horizontal at the point of projection is called the critical angle.

All rays in the sound beam directed at an angle less than the critical angle will follow paths entirely within the isothermal layer and will be bent upward to the surface. All rays directed at an angle greater than the critical angle follow paths that penetrate the boundary and are subsequently refracted downward. No rays enter the region bounded by the two branches of the split critical ray, and for this reason it is also called a shadow zone. Sharp shadow zones are not fully developed because of diffraction and other effects, though the sound intensity in this area is quite low. Submarine commanders deliberately use this phenomenon, when it exists, to attempt to escape detection when approaching a target. The optimum depth for close approach to a target with minimum probability of counter-detection is approximately

$$\text{Best depth} = 17\sqrt{Z} \qquad (8-33)$$

where z is the layer depth in meters.

This is accurate down to a layer depth of 60 meters. Below that, the best depth for approach is a constant 60 meters below layer depth.

In the deep ocean, temperature usually decreases with depth to approximately 1,000 meters. Deeper than this, temperature is a constant 4°C and sound speed increases as a result of pressure. Thus it is possible to have equal speeds at two different depths with slower speed conditions in between. When water with a negative speed gradient overlays a positive speed gradient, a *sound channel* is produced. Under these circumstances, any sound signal traveling in this area is refracted back and forth so that it becomes horizontally channeled. Sound rays originating with an initial upward inclination are refracted downward, while those originating with an initial downward inclination are refracted upward. Rays from a sound source in this layer that make a small angle with the horizontal are roughly sinusoidal, crossing and recrossing the layer of minimum speed. This reinforcement of rays within the sound channel can continue until the sound is absorbed, scattered, or intercepted by some obstacle. Sounds traveling in this manner sometimes are received at extremely great distances from the source. These long ranges occur primarily as a result of two factors: absorption is small for low-frequency sound, and most of the sound energy from a sound source at the axis is confined to the channel.

Under certain circumstances, a sound channel can exist near the

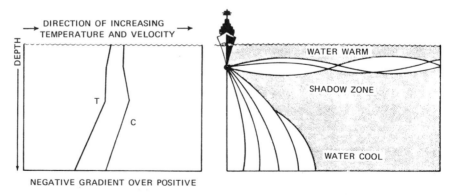

Figure 8–25. Sound channel.

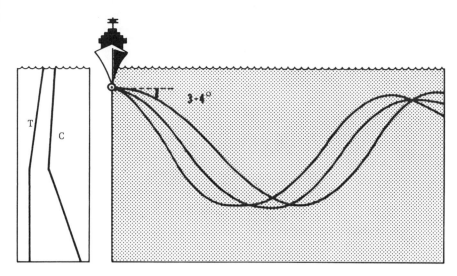

Figure 8–26. Convergence zone.

surface of the sea. In a surface layer with a strong positive temperature gradient the upward bending of sound rays combined with reflections from the surface will form such a channel. Sonar ranges many times greater than normal have been observed where sound channels exist. However, the conditions that produce such sound channels near the surface of the ocean are rare and not very stable.

When a negative gradient exists over a positive gradient in extremely deep water, a situation known as *convergence zone* may occur. Because of the decreasing temperature, the sound beam is initially refracted downward. When the beam goes so deep that pressure becomes the predominant factor, the beam bends upward again toward the surface. About 50 kilometers from the source the beam strikes the surface and is refracted toward the bottom again. Under

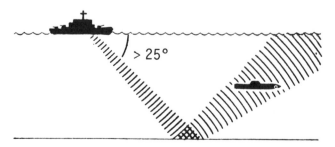

Figure 8–27. Bottom bounce.

Principles of Underwater Sound   **237**

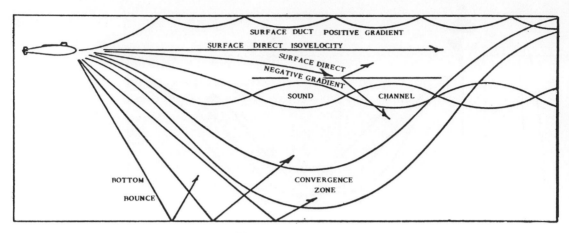

Figure 8–28. Possible propagation paths.

proper conditions it is possible to have multiple convergence zones at approximately 50 kilometer intervals.

In addition to being refracted by varying conditions in the medium, sound can be reflected in the manner of a light beam striking a mirrorlike surface and lose little of its intensity. The two surfaces that can produce this type of reflection are the surface of the water and the bottom of the ocean. Rarely if ever are these surfaces smooth enough to give a mirror reflection, but in many instances the majority of the sound is reflected as a beam. Some sonars make use of this phenomenon which is called *bottom bounce*. A beam is directed against the bottom from which it is reflected to the surface of the water. From the surface it is reflected back to the bottom again. Thus, the ray bounces from one to the other until its energy is dissipated or until it strikes a target and returns to the sonar. As with reflected light, the angle of reflection is equal to the angle of incidence. Obviously, ranging over a fairly flat bottom is more effective than ranging over a rough or sloping bottom.

It is obvious, then, that many sound paths are available, as indicated in the composite drawing in figure 8–28. Only by observing the environment carefully and paying close attention to his equipment will the operator be able to use them to best advantage and not find them a liability.

Summary

Of all the energy forms available, sound, even with its inherent disadvantages, is the most useful for underwater detection of submarines. It travels as a series of compressions and rarefactions at a speed equal to the product of its frequency and wave-length. The pressure of the wave can be expressed as a function of both time and its distance from the source. Acoustic power, called its intensity, is a measure of the amount of energy per unit area and has the units watts/m². Acoustic pressure is expressed in micro-pascals. To make comparisons easier, both are normally converted to the logarithmic decibel system. The active and passive sonar equations are an expression of various factors determined by the equipment, the medium, and the target, which lead to an overall measure of sonar performance called figure of merit. Actual sound propagation through the sea is subject to geometric spreading and attentuation, both of which decrease the acoustic intensity at the receiver. The speed of sound in the sea is related to the bulk modulus and density of the water, which are affected by the temperature, pressure, and salinity. Temperature is the most important of these environmental factors, and therefore the thermal structure of the ocean is of significant tactical importance. The tracing out of sound paths in water is known as ray theory and is governed by Snell's Law. Various unique propagation paths can be identified according to the thermal structure of the water, but in practice such paths are a complex combination of simpler structures.

Sample Figure of Merit Problem

Your sonar is capable of either passive or active operation. You are operating in the shipping lanes with a sea state of 2. Water depth is 200 fathoms. Using the following information, you must decide which mode to use. Intelligence information indicates that the threat will be a Zebra-class submarine (all dB are reference 1μPa).

Target parameters:

radiated noise source level	100 dB
radiated noise frequency	500 Hz
target strength	15 dB
target detection range	10,000 m

Sonar parameters:	Active	Passive
Source level	110 dB	—
Frequency	1.5 kHz	—
Self-noise at 15 kts	50 dB	50 dB
Directivity index	10 dB	8 dB
Detection threshold	−2 dB	3 dB

In order to determine which sonar to use, it is necessary to calculate the FOM and *total* transmission loss for each mode.

First, calculate the total transmission loss for each mode. Since the desired target detection range of 10 km is much greater than the water depth of 200 fathoms, we will use equation (8–17) for cylindrical spreading:

$$TL = 10 \log r + \alpha r + A$$

The quantity A is assumed to be zero since no information is available. The absorption coefficient (α) is calculated by substituting signal frequencies for each mode into equation (8–14):

$$\alpha = \frac{.036 f^2}{f^2 + 3600} + 3.2 \times 10^{-7} f^2 \text{ (where } f \text{ is in kilohertz)}$$

<table>
<tr><td align="center">Active mode</td><td align="center">Passive mode</td></tr>
</table>

$$\alpha = \frac{.036(1.5)^2}{(1.5)^2 + 3600} + (3.2 \qquad \alpha = \frac{.036(.5)^2}{(.5)^2 + 3600} + (3.2$$
$$\times 10^{-7})(1.5)^2 \qquad\qquad\qquad \times 10^{-7})(.5)^2$$

$$\alpha = 2.32 \times 10^{-5} \qquad\qquad \alpha = 2.6 \times 10^{-6}$$
$$TL = 10 \log(10,000) + 2.32 \qquad TL = 10 \log(10,000) + 2.6 \times$$
$$\times 10^{-5}(10,000) \qquad\qquad\quad 10^{-6}(10,000)$$
$$TL = 40 + .232 \qquad\qquad\qquad TL = 40 + .026$$
$$TL = 40.232 \text{ (one way)} \qquad TL = 40.026 \text{dB (Total } TL)$$
$$2 \times TL = 80.464 \text{dB (Total } TL)$$

Note that TL depends only upon the detection range and the frequency of the signal.

Next calculate the FOM using equation (8–26) for the active mode and equation (8–25) for the passive case. Note that the only values that must be determined are the noise levels using the Wenz curves and nomograms for the different frequencies:

<table>
<tr><td align="center">Active Mode</td><td align="center">Passive Mode</td></tr>
<tr><td align="center">$f = 1500$ Hz</td><td align="center">$f = 500$ Hz</td></tr>
</table>

AN(shipping) = negligible   AN(shipping) = 57dB
AN(sea state) = 58dB   AN(sea state) = 61dB
Self-Noise = 50dB   Self-Noise = 50dB

Using the nomogram, combine the signals for each mode:

58–50 = 8dB   61 ≡ 57 = 4
$NL = 58 + .65$ (from nomogram) $AN = 61 + 1.5$ (from nomogram)
$NL = 58.65$ dB $AN = 62.5$ dB
     $62.5 ≡ 50 = 12.5$
     $NL = 62.5 + .25 = 62.75$ dB

Note that when three noise signals are involved, a two-step signal-combining process is required. The resultant is always added to the higher signal level. Determining the FOM is now a simple matter of substituting the calculated and given values into the appropriate equations:

Active Mode

$$FOM = SL + TS - NL + DI - DT$$
$$FOM = 110 + 15 - 58.65 + 10 - (-2)$$
$$FOM = 78.35 \text{ dB}$$

Passive Mode

$$FOM = SL - NL + DI - DT$$
$$FOM = 100 - 62.75 + 8 - 3$$
$$FOM = 42.25 \text{ dB}$$

Compare the FOM of each mode with the total TL for each mode to determine which mode is optimum for this target. The FOM for the active case is less than the total TL. Therefore, the active mode will give your ship less than 50% probability of detection. The FOM for the passive case is greater than the total TL. Therefore, the passive mode will give a greater than 50% probability of detection, which means that the passive mode should be used.

References

Cheney, R. E., and D. E. Winfrey. "Distribution and Classification of Ocean Fronts," NAVOCEANO Technical Note 3700–56–76. Washington, D.C.: GPO, 1976.

Chramiec, Mark A. Unpublished lecture notes on Figure of Merit and Transmission Loss, Raytheon Company, 1983.

Commander, Naval Ordnance Systems Command. *Elements of Weapons Systems.* NAVORD OP 3000, vol. 1, 1st Rev. Washington, D.C.: GPO, 1971.

Corse, Carl D. *Introduction to Shipboard Weapons.* Annapolis, MD: Naval Institute Press, 1975.

Duxbury, Alyn C. *The Earth and its Oceans.* Reading, Massachusetts: Addison-Wesley Publishing Company, Inc., 1971.

Honhart, D. C. Unpublished class notes on *Acoustic Forecasting*, Naval Postgraduate School, 1974.

King, L. F., and D. A. Swift. *Development of a Primer on Underwater Sound for ASW.* Master's thesis, Naval Postgraduate School, 1975.

Kinsler, L. E., and A. R. Frey. *Fundamentals of Acoustics.* 2nd ed. New York: John Wiley and Sons, 1962.

Myers, J. J., C. H. Holm, and R. F. McAllister, eds. *Handbook of Ocean and Underwater Engineering.* New York: McGraw-Hill Book Company, 1969.

Naval Education and Training Command. *Sonar Technical G3 & 2(u)*, NAV-EDTRA 10131-D. Washington, D.C.: GPO, 1976.

Naval Operations Department, U.S. Naval War College. *Technological Factors and Constraints in System Performance Study-Sonar Fundamentals*. Vol I-1, 1975.

Naval Training Command. *The Antisubmarine Warfare Officer (U)*. NAV-TRA 10778-C. Washington, D.C.: GPO, 1973.

Operations Committee, Naval Science Department, U.S. Naval Academy. *Naval Operations Analysis*. Annapolis, MD: U.S. Naval Institute, 1968.

Sollenberger, R. T., and T. R. Decker. *Environmental Factors Affecting Antisubmarine Warfare Operations*. Master's thesis, Naval Postgraduate School, 1975.

Sverdrup, H. U., M. W. Johnson, and R. H. Fleming. *The Oceans*. Englewood Cliffs, N.J.: Prentice-Hall, Inc., 1942.

U.S. Naval Oceanographic Office. *Ocean Thermal Structure Forecasting*. SP 105 ASWEPS Manual Series, vol. 5, 1st ed., by R.W. James. Washington, D.C.: GPO, 1966.

Urick, R. J. *Principles of Underwater Sound*. 2nd ed. New York: McGraw-Hill Book Company, 1975.

9

Underwater Detection and Tracking Systems

Introduction

Antisubmarine warfare, with the exception of fixed systems such as arrays of underwater hydrophones, is waged by various mobile antisubmarine craft: surface, airborne, and undersea. It is imperative that the officers and men of each type of antisubmarine force understand the characteristics, capabilities, and limitations of the other types. Only by such knowledge can they fully understand the basic concept of modern antisubmarine warfare—the integration and coordination of all forces available. Each type has certain advantages and disadvantages, and maximum effectiveness can be achieved only by coordinating all types. The basic characteristics of each force that should be evaluated are its inherent capabilities and limitations, detection methods, fire control systems, and weaponry.

Surface Ship

A principal advantage of the surface ship is its available manpower. It has more men on board than any other type of ASW craft. Greater numbers of personnel not only allow more efficient operation, but also enable the ship to perform other tasks and functions at the same time as it is engaged in ASW operations. The stamina of the surface ship also gives it a marked advantage over aircraft and conventional submarines, making it the most effective craft to implement today's peacetime hold-down tactics. In addition, the surface ship has a great variety of detection equipment, including active and passive hull-mounted sonars, towed arrays, VDS, radar, ESM, and if LAMPS equipped, the sonobuoys, MAD electro-optics, and extended ESM capability that come with the LAMPS helo.

The surface ship has several weapons, such as active and passive homing torpedoes and ASROC, along with its conventional and nuclear payloads. Although not many different weapon types are carried, the surface ship has the advantage of a larger reload capacity. All other ASW craft are somewhat limited in the amount of ordnance they can carry. A further capability of most surface ships is a highly accurate and stabilized fire control system that is equal to or better than that of other ASW craft. Another benefit of the surface ship is its ability to conduct all-weather operations. Except when conditions are extreme, impaired visibility, darkness, storms, or rough seas do not prevent the surface ship from performing its ASW mission.

The final advantage of the surface ship is its prolonged time on station. In this respect, though, and in others such as all-weather operations and accurate fire control systems, the nuclear-powered submarine is challenging the surface ship for the role of the most effective ASW platform.

These characteristics best adapt surface-type vessels to the following ASW functions:

1. Searching for submarines, establishing their location, and engaging in direct attack upon them.
2. Coordinating ASW operations with other ships and aircraft.

The three broad types of ASW operations in which the surface-type vessel may engage are:

1. ASW strike operations.
2. Patrol of assigned areas while continuously searching for submarines.
3. Escort of merchant vessels or other naval vessels not adapted to ASW search and direct attack.

The Aircraft Carrier

The mobile airpower of carriers is used for employment against submarines and their bases, surface ships and their yards, aircraft and their airfields, and for support of amphibious, land, and air operations as well. Its importance in carrying out the mission of the Navy paradoxically makes the carrier an ASW liability because, basically, the carrier has no direct defense against submarine attack. Only one attack carrier was lost to submarines in all of World War II. If the advances made in submarine capabilities since then are considered, however, their menace increases dramatically. The modern carrier must now be protected against a devastating combination of weapons: the fast, quiet submarine armed with antiship cruise missiles (ASCM). To fully protect the fast carrier task force against this threat demands carriers with aircraft designed for ASW operations, a screen of destroyers, supporting friendly submarines, long-range patrol aircraft, and even sophisticated satellite sensor data. While not totally at the mercy of the submarine, the carrier nonetheless is in a very uncomfortable position.

Aircraft

The primary advantage of any aircraft is speed and the ability to deploy sensors over large areas. The most troublesome problem in operations against a known submarine is *time late*, the difference in time between the last contact with a submarine and the arrival of the ASW forces in the contact area. Aircraft speed, therefore, provides the ability to search large areas in a short period of time, helping to reduce the effect of time late and increasing the chance of regaining contact in a long time-late situation.

Another aircraft advantage that can give the ASW forces the element of surprise is that some detection and localization devices, such as magnetic anomaly detectors and some sonobuoys, are passive. Thus, the submarine cannot determine that it is being searched for or that it has been detected. This is not true, however, when active sonar and active sonobuoys are employed by helicopters.

Two basic types of ASW aircraft are available: fixed-wing—typified by the S-3A and P-3C (figure 9–1), and helicopters—typified by the SH-2, SH-60, and SH-3. Of the two types, the fixed wing is faster, and it can make good use of its speed to close the last-known position of a contact or search large areas quickly. Its elevation gives it much longer radar horizons than surface ships. In contrast, the helicopter, although slower than fixed-wing aircraft, has special characteristics that peculiarly adapt it to ASW uses. Its ability to hover and its

Figure 9–1. P-3C ASW aircraft.

maneuverability enable it to maintain continued contact with a submarine. Furthermore, its speed flexibility and its sensor capability allow it to be integrated into a surface-ship screen. Additionally, the helicopter can be sent to investigate a distant contact much more rapidly than a surface ship.

Submarines

The submarine itself is one of the most effective ASW vehicles. It operates in the same medium and shares the target's advantages of concealment and passive detection. It can, like the target, take advantage of the sound-refracting properties of seawater, and it can track the target with less distraction caused by this phenomenon. Like the target submarine, it can go deep enough to escape the effects of surface waves and winds.

The submarine can be employed in protecting the capital ships of a carrier task force and in supplementing and protecting radar picket destroyers. Submarines can precede a carrier strike force into enemy waters to function as ASW screens and as minelayers.

Like any other vehicle, the ASW submarine has limitations. To find the enemy submarine, the ASW submarine must be deep, but to communicate this information to the surface forces it must be shallow. To maintain the silence essential for most effective listening, it must not move, but to get information to someone who can do something about it, the ASW sub must break off the contact or expose its location by coming to periscope depth to communicate. ASW submarines are also faced with the possibility of being mistaken for the enemy. Successful multi-ship coordinated operations depend on reliable communications, and the submarine cannot participate until adequate communications have been developed and made available to the forces afloat.

Nuclear submarines have many advantages. The strong points of these ships are the two major weaknesses of conventional submarines: nuclear ships are fast, whereas conventional submarines must operate at slow speeds unless they will be able to snorkel in a short time; furthermore, nuclear submarines can go out and remain submerged on station for extended periods, whereas diesel-electric submarines must have recourse to the surface to recharge batteries. It should be noted, however, that of the two, *the diesel-electric submarine can operate much more quietly when submerged than the nuclear type, due to the nature of its propulsion plant*.

Shore Installations

The underwater *SO*und *SU*rveillance System (SOSUS) consists of groups of acoustic listening stations strategically located and connected to arrays of hydrophones placed on the ocean floor in a manner best suited to survey the area. They operate in a manner similar to radio direction finding (RDF) stations in that cross bearings, this time acoustic, can be used to determine target location. Such information can then be relayed to ASW forces in the vicinity for further investigation.

Detection Equipment

A submerged submarine can be detected in a number of ways by taking advantage of the fact that the submarine alters the normal properties of its environment. The submarine presents a reflecting surface to an acoustic beam; it distorts a flow of electric current; and it acts as a source of acoustic, electric, and magnetic fields, and of temperature and pressure gradients. Many of these effects have been used in the development of shipborne detectors or droppable detectors for use with aircraft. The first and most important are sonars in their various forms. Others are radar, electronic support measures, magnetic anomaly detectors, and electro-optics.

Sonar uses sound as a means of detecting a submarine. Passive sonars merely listen for externally created sounds, such as those produced by a snorkeling submarine, which can be heard from 100 to 200 kilometers. Active sonars, also called echo-ranging sonars, produce and send out a burst of sound or a ping. The object is to bounce the sound off the submarine, measure the time elapsed between transmission and reception, as well as the angles involved, in order to determine the range and bearing. Both of these basic types are illustrated in figure 9–2. Sonar will be discussed in fuller detail later in this chapter.

Radar, of course, is effective only against surfaced submarines or submarines showing a periscope or snorkel mast. Detection ranges also are limited. For example, typical surface ship detection ranges are 20 to 25 kilometers for a surfaced submarine, about 8 kilometers for a 1 meter snorkel, and about 6 kilometers for a periscope. Further, a sea state of 4 or above reduces radar effectiveness against submarines. Aircraft radar detection ranges are considerably greater than radar detection from a surface ship, but the effect of sea state is similar.

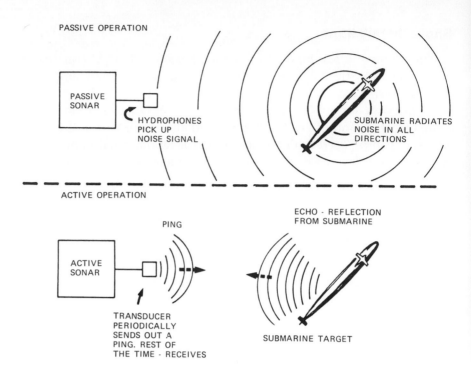

Figure 9–2. Simplified passive and active sonar operation.

Electronic support measure equipment allows the determination of target bearing and provides signal information reliable enough to identify the nationality of the transmitter. RDF stations perform similar functions, except that they operate mainly in the radio frequency bands. The use of cross bearings, as determined by ESM installations and/or RDF stations, provides an accurate location of the transmitter.

Magnetic Anomaly Detection (MAD)

Another method of detecting a submerged submarine is through the use of MAD equipment, which uses the principle that a metallic submarine disturbs the magnetic lines of force of the earth.

Light, radar, or sound energy cannot pass from air into water and return to the air in any degree that is usable for airborne detection. The lines of force in a magnetic field are able to make this transition almost undisturbed, however, because magnetic lines of force pass through water and air in a similar manner. Consequently, a submarine lying beneath the ocean's surface, which causes a distortion or anomaly in the earth's magnetic field, can be detected from a position in

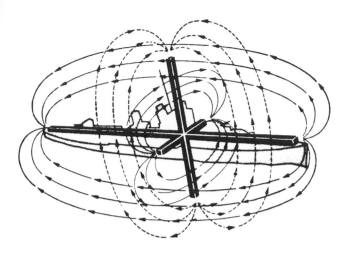

Figure 9–3. Permanent magnetic flux lines about a ship. (From Weapons Systems Fundamentals)

the air above the submarine. The detection of this anomaly is the essential function of MAD equipment.

When a ship or submarine hull is being fabricated, it is subjected to heat (welding) and to impact (riveting). Ferrous metal contains groups of iron molecules called "domains." Each domain is a tiny magnet, and has its own magnetic field with a north and south pole. When the domains are not aligned along any axis, but point in different directions at random, there is a negligible magnetic pattern. However, if the metal is put into a constant magnetic field and its particles are agitated, as they would be by hammering or by heating, the domains tend to orient themselves so that their north poles point toward the south pole of the field, and their south poles point toward the north pole of the field. All the fields of the domains then have an additive effect, and a piece of ferrous metal so treated has a magnetic field of its own. Although the earth's magnetic field is not strong, a ship's hull contains so much steel that it acquires a significant and permanent magnetic field during construction. A ship's magnetic field has three main components: vertical, longitudinal, and athwartship, the sum total of which comprises the complete magnetic field, as shown in figure 9–3.

The steel in a ship also has the effect of causing earth's lines of force (flux) to move out of their normal positions and be concentrated at the ship. This is called the "induced field," and varies with the heading of the ship.

A ship's total magnetic field or "magnetic signature" at any point on the earth's surface is a combination of its permanent and induced magnetic fields. A ship's magnetic field may be reduced substantially by using degaussing coils, often in conjunction with the process of

LINES OF FORCE ENTERING EARTHS SURFACE

ship has greater permeability, therefore
lines of force tend to concentrate in her
causing distortion of Earth's field in that area

Figure 9–4. Effect of ship's hull on earth's magnetic field. (From Weapons Systems Fundamentals*)*

"deperming" (neutralizing the permanent magnetism of a ship); but for practical purposes it is not possible to eliminate such fields entirely.

The lines comprising the earth's natural magnetic field do not always run straight north and south. If traced along a typical 200-kilometer path, the field twists at places to east or west and assumes different angles with the horizontal. Changes in the east-west direction are known as angles of variation, while the angle between the lines of force and the horizontal is known as the angle of dip. Short-trace variation and dip in the area of a large mass of ferrous material, although extremely minute, are measurable with a sensitive magnetometer.

The function, then, of airborne MAD equipment is to detect the submarine-caused anomaly in the earth's magnetic field. Detection ranges are on the order of 500 meters from the sensor. This means that the depth at which a submarine can be detected will be a function both of the size of the submarine and how close the sensor is flown to the surface of the water.

Visual sighting is the oldest, yet the most positive, method of submarine detection. Even in this age of modern submarines, which have little recourse to the surface, the OOD and lookouts of an antisubmarine ship should always be alert for possible visual detection of a submarine. Aircraft, even those not normally assigned an antisubmarine mission, can use visual detection methods to particular advantage as a result of their height above the surface.

Although each of these means of detection are important, this text will discuss in detail only sonar in its several forms.

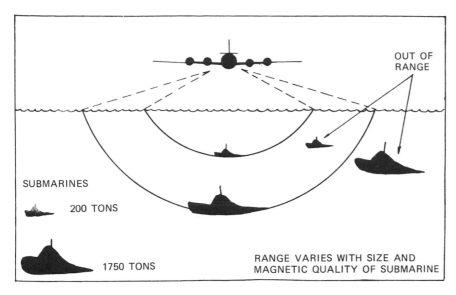

Figure 9–5. Magnetic anomaly detection (MAD) sweep. (From Introduction to Shipboard Engineering and Weapons Systems*)*

Basic Sonar Systems

The various types of sonar used in weapons systems are divided into three basic categories: echo-ranging, listening, and communications systems.

Echo-ranging, or *active*, *systems* are used to detect the presence of submarines, to analyze shoreline and bottom characteristics, and to determine bottom depths. The basic echo-ranging system consists of a transmitter, one or more transducers, a receiver, and displays and controls of various sorts. The transmitter has a source of power and a means for modulating the basic power in a manner suitable for the particular application. The transmitter power is converted from electrical to acoustic energy by means of the transducer for transmission of the sonar signal into the water. Received signals or echoes are converted by the same transducer (or by a different transducer in some sonar systems) from acoustic back to electrical energy. The received signal from the transducer is processed in a receiver, where various amplification, demodulation, and comparison operations are performed. The output of the receiver, in the form for proper presentation of target data, is fed to display and control units. The displays include aural types, such as loudspeakers and earphones, and visual types, including cathode ray tubes, paper recorders, and indicator lamps.

Listening, or *passive*, *systems* use only the receiving elements of the echo-ranging system. These are the transducer, receiver, displays, and controls. The transducer in a listening-only system is generally called a hydrophone. An echo-ranging system would be used on a vessel for passive listening under circumstances in which it was not tactically desirable to make the presence of the vessel known by transmitting; in this case, the transmitter would simply be turned off.

Communications systems are basically similar to the echo-ranging systems, although generally simpler in design. Transmission consists of pulsed-code or voice-modulated ultrasonic power. The reception consists of demodulation and amplification stages. The display portion consists of aural and visual types.

Within each category are many varieties. The several types of echo-ranging systems are divided basically into searchlight and scanning sonar systems, which will be explained later. Many echo-ranging systems also are capable of both direct listening and communications.

Transducers

A device for converting one form of energy to another is a transducer. In sonar, electrical energy is converted to acoustic energy in the form of oscillation of the molecules of the water through which the sound travels. These oscillations cause a synchronous variation of pressure in the water. The signals generated or received by the electronic circuits in sonar equipment are in the form of electrical energy. The sonar transducer acts as the link between the water and the electronic circuits of the sonar equipment.

There are three physical phenomena that exhibit the ability to change electrical to mechanical energy and mechanical to electrical energy, and are employed in sonar transducers. These are the electrostrictive, piezoelectric, and the magnetostrictive effects. Materials exhibiting electrostrictive and piezoelectric properties are generally of crystalline or ceramic nature. They change dimensions when subjected to an electric field and develop a voltage potential between two opposite faces when mechanically stressed. Materials exhibiting the magnetostrictive effect change dimensions when subjected to a magnetic field and change magnetic permeability when subjected to mechanical forces. This change in permeability changes the intensity of any magnetic field in the presence of the material.

Variation in the strength of the electric or magnetic field around such materials will cause them to change dimensions at a frequency identical to that of the field change. When the transducers are placed in water, acoustic waves can then be propagated from the material to the water. When sound waves impinge upon such material after propagation, the pressure variations will cause variations in its dimensions, which in turn cause magnetic or electric field changes that can be detected and displayed.

Crystal Transducers

The piezoelectric effect is the electric polarization produced by mechanical strain in certain classes of crystals. The polarization, and the electric potential induced by it, is proportional to the strain and changes sign with it. In the converse piezoelectric effect, an electric potential across the crystal face produces a mechanical deformation, proportional to the induced electric polarization and of the same sign. The magnitude of this effect varies for crystals of different materials, and for the different axes of the crystal. A crystal transducer is constructed by cementing or mounting a stack of quarter-wavelength crystals to a heavy steel backing resonator plate also one-quarter wavelength thick. The assembly is mechanically resonant at the operating frequency. When used for listening, the maximum electric signal is produced by the crystals if the frequency of the received sound is the same as the resonant frequency of the transducer.

Ceramic Transducers

When an electric field is applied across a dielectric, the dielectric is deformed. This phenomenon of change in dimensions is called electrostriction and is independent of the direction of the electric field and proportional to the square of the field intensity. Ceramic for transducers has an advantage over crystals in that the ceramic can be molded to any desired shape. This property is particularly desirable for making cylindrical scanning or omnidirectional transducers. These types are used in active sonar systems.

Magnetostrictive Transducers

A magnetic field will cause a number of materials to change dimensions in the direction of the applied field. Depending on the material and the strength of the magnetic field, some materials will expand and some will contract, but independently of the direction of the applied field. In one type of transducer, the elements are nickel tubes. To increase the area of the active face in contact with the water in this design, a series of tubes or rods are attached to a diaphragm, and the diaphragm becomes the active face of the transducer. The dimensions of the tubes and the diaphragm plate are designed to make the transducer mechanically resonant at the operating frequency for maximum efficiency. In such a transducer, the sinusoidal magnetic field is obtained by winding coils around the nickel rods and impressing a current at the desired sonar signal frequency through the coils.

Hydrophones

Hydrophones are transducers designed only for reception. They may be either magnetostrictive or electrostrictive and use the same principles as for two-way transducers. However, since they do not handle high transmission power, with its resulting increase in temperature, their construction can be much lighter.

Transducer Directivity

The directivity or beam pattern of a transducer is a function of the mechanical arrangement of the transducer elements and the associated electrical and electronic circuitry. As with radio and radar antennas, where the directivity pattern is caused by interference between electromagnetic radiation from various parts of the antenna, so in transducers the patterns are caused by interference between sound radiated from various points on the transducer surface. Control of transducer beam patterns is needed so that the directivity can be matched to operational needs. They can be designed to exclude noises from directions other than along the transducer beam by suppressing back and side lobes, thus reducing background noises and permitting detection of weaker targets. They also can concentrate transmitted power on the target for stronger echoes and longer ranges.

Directivity patterns can be modified, such as for the reduction of side lobes, by shading a transducer. A transducer is shaded in design if the power projected per unit area is varied over the surface. Shading can be accomplished (1) physically by arranging the spacing, size, or number of elements; (2) electrically by the number of turns on magnetostrictive elements, or by phasing and delay networks; or (3) mechanically by the physical shape of the active surface of the transducer. For circular face, flat transducers, the beam width, Θ, is given by the equation

$$\sin \Theta/2 = 0.61 \, \lambda/D \qquad (9-1)$$

where

    Θ is the angle between half-power points
    λ is sonic wavelength
    D is transducer diameter

For satisfactory operational resolution, the beam width must not be greater than 10 degrees. Therefore, for this width the ratio D/λ must be at least 6, and from this it can be seen that low-frequency operation requires large-size transducers.

Transducer Power

A transducer transforms electrical into mechanical and acoustic energy by generating an alternating sound pressure that is superimposed on the static ambient pressure of the water through which the sound is propagating. The relationship between acoustic power output P of the transducer and the sound pressure is

$$P = P_e^2(A/\rho c) \qquad (9-2)$$

where

    A = area of transducer through which the acoustic energy flows.

The pressure of the sound wave generated at the surface of the transducer is limited by the hydrostatic pressure at the transducer, which in turn is limited by the cavitation pressure, the pressure below which water vaporizes. If the pressure in the rarefaction portion of the sound wave falls below the cavitation pressure, the water vaporizes and small bubbles form that greatly reduce the transducer efficiency. This factor limits maximum transmitted power to about 0.3 watts per square centimeter of the transducer area in the region near the surface of the sea. Maximum transmitted power increases with depth, however, as the square of the ambient pressure. Thus, at a depth where the ambient pressure is doubled, the maximum transmitted power becomes about 1.2 watts per square centimeter of transducer area.

Increasing transmitted power for a given transducer configuration thus normally means increasing transducer array size. Transducer array size is also directly related to signal frequency, and for a reasonable beam width the transducer array face must be 6 to 8 wavelengths wide. Since maximum range is obtained with lower frequencies, long-range sonar requires very large transducer arrays.

This size vs. power and frequency situation presents severe physical and tactical limitations. Large transducer arrays add considerably to drag effects even with streamlined domes. They present problems on how and where to mount them, and require very large power sources as well. They require large ships to accommodate them and their associated electrical and electronic equipment. The total amount of power transmitted by a transducer array of fixed size and frequency is limited, and, therefore, concentrating the power in a beam by control of directivity patterns becomes the more practical method of increasing power to a target.

Active Sonar

In the *early searchlight echo-ranging systems*, a short burst or pulse of sound energy called a ping is transmitted from a highly directional transducer through the water. Range is measured by accurately determining the time interval between the transmitted burst and the instant its reflection returns from a target or discontinuity in the water. Bearing is determined by noting the direction in which the transducer is trained when the intensity of the reflected signal is greatest. The term *searchlight* applied to this type of equipment comes from a comparison of the 5°–10° narrow beam projected by the transducer with the light beam of a searchlight.

The searchlight transducer is generally a flat-faced transducer designed and shaded to produce a very sharp forward directivity pattern. The transducer must thus be physically rotated or trained in order to scan an area or to determine the bearing of a target for which the

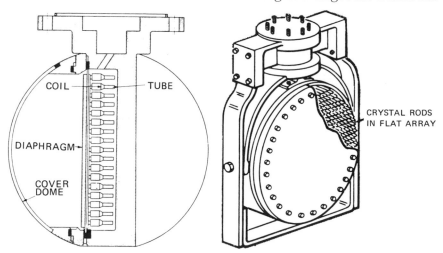

Figure 9–6. Searchlight sonar transducer. (From Weapons Systems Fundamentals)

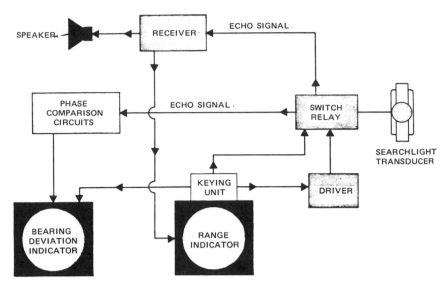

Figure 9–7. Searchlight sonar functional diagram. (From Weapons Systems Fundamentals)

intensity of a reflected signal is greatest. A cycle of operation is initiated with a signal from the keying unit. This unit is usually associated with the range indicator and produces its signals when the range indicator is in the zero range position. Signals are sent to three units to perform the functions indicated in figure 9–7. They are sent to the switching relay, to cause this relay to disconnect the transducer from the receiving circuits and connect it to the driver. At the end of a predetermined length of time, a little longer than the transmitted pulse, this relay reconnects the transducer to the receiving circuits. Signals are sent also to the driver, to trigger it, and to the bearing deviation indicator (BDI). When triggered by a signal from the keying unit, the driver transmits an electrical pulse of the proper amplitude and frequency through the switching relay to the transducer. The transducer converts this pulse of electrical energy to sound and radiates it in a beam.

Any objects in the sound beam will reflect back to the transducer a part of the sound energy falling on them. The transducer transforms this reflected sound energy into electrical energy. This electrical signal goes from the transducer through the switching relay, to the receiver, and then to the phase-comparison circuits of the BDI channel. In the receiver, the received signals are amplified and combined with the output of a local oscillator to give a beat frequency in the audible range of frequencies. The audible output is fed into a loudspeaker or earphones. A part of the received signal, after amplification, is rectified to give a D.C. signal proportional in amplitude to the received signal. This output from the receiver goes to the range indicator.

At the end of a period of time dependent on the distance to which search or ranging is being conducted, the keyer produces another signal, and the cycle is repeated. If search is being conducted to 5,000 meters, then the pulse repetition frequency must allow an interval long enough for sound to travel to a target 5,000 meters away and back to the transducer at an average speed of 1,500 meters per second. For shorter search ranges or when ranging on a target closer than 5,000 meters, the interval may be shortened by increasing the PRF in the keying unit.

Certain limitations of the searchlight sonar severely restrict its operational usefulness. Chief among these are

1. *Slow search.* After transmitting a ping, it is necessary to remain trained on the same or nearby bearing for a length of time equal to that required for sound to travel to a target at the greatest range to which search is being conducted and to return. For a search range of 5,000 meters, this interval is nearly 7 seconds. If search is conducted at 5-degree bearing intervals (advisable for good coverage), 4 minutes will be required to search through a 180-degree sector centered on the bow of the ship. In this time a ship or a submarine traveling at 20 knots will travel over 1 nm. If search range is increased, the time to search a given sector increases proportionately.

2. *Easily saturated.* When the equipment is being used to determine range and bearings on one target, it cannot be used to range on another target on a different bearing, nor can it be used for search.

3. *Necessary to train the transducer.* This requirement is important partly because of the generally heavy and cumbersome training equipment. Of equal or greater importance is the fact that this requirement limits transducers to comparatively small sizes. This limitation on the size of the transducer has two important effects. One, it limits power output due to cavitation. Two, it makes necessary the use of comparatively high frequencies because the diameter of the transducer face must be 6 to 8 wavelengths to achieve the necessary beamwidth. It follows that if the physical size of the transducer is limited, there is a lower limit on the frequencies that can be used. Because of this limitation, searchlight sonar frequencies fall in the range

from 20 kHz to 30 kHz. The absorption coefficient for these frequencies is high, and therefore the effective range of these sonars is limited under most conditions to 1,500 to 2,000 meters.

To overcome some of the limitations of searchlight sonar, the *scaning echo-ranging* sonar was developed. The scanning principle permits 360-degree search on every transmission. Each transmission permits range and bearing information to be obtained on a number of targets. In scanning sonar systems, the transducer is fixed, so this simplifies the mechanical problems encountered in the sonar set and permits the use of larger transducers. The use of greater power is thus possible because of the greater area of the transducer. The scanning transducer is especially useful at lower frequencies because the much lower attenuation of sound at these frequencies makes search possible at much longer ranges.

Although the principles used in the scanning echo-ranging system for the determination of range and bearing are the same as those used in searchlight equipments, the two types differ greatly in the method of presenting range and bearing information, the type transducer used, the method used to sweep the transducer beam, and the rate at which the transducer beam is swept.

In sonar scanning equipments, a nonrotating cylindrical transducer is used. When transmitting, sound energy radiates from the transducer with equal intensity in all directions. When receiving, scanning circuitry causes the transducer to be sensitive only to signals returning from a narrow sector. This sector is electronically sampled at high data rates, and the range and bearing information is presented on a cathode-ray tube as a PPI or B-scan plot. The use of this method makes it possible to obtain range and bearing on every target for every transmission.

One of the principal advantages of a scanning search transducer over a searchlight transducer is that it can scan electronically by means of electronic scanning circuitry, while a searchlight transducer must scan mechanically. To scan the entire area around the ship, the circuits that compensate for the time delays on the individual staves of the transducer due to its cylindrical shape are connected to complex electronic switching networks instead of directly to the transducer stave. This scanning circuitry is designed to sample the acoustic energy impinging upon the transducer as a function of azimuth. This information can be displayed on a CRT that has a light trace rotating at the same frequency and in phase with the electronic scanning rate. The point at which the rotating light trace exhibits maximum intensity is the bearing of the target, as shown in figure 9–8.

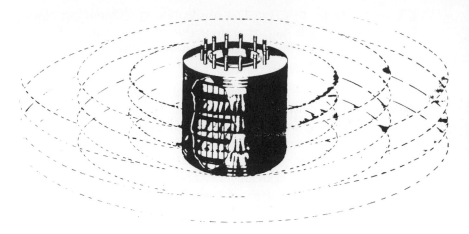

Figure 9–8. Scanning sonar transducer. (From Weapons Systems Fundamentals)

Figure 9–10 shows the main features of a typical sonar CRT display. This is a highly idealized diagram and is not intended to show features realistically.

A line, or cursor, originating at the center of the CRT and parallel to the bearing of the audio scanner, is the first presentation. With this the operator can read on a dial around the CRT face the bearing of echoes he hears.

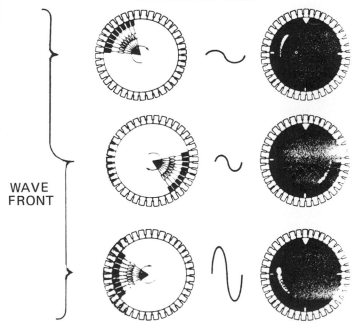

WAVE
FRONT

Figure 9–9. Scanning switch operation. (From Weapons Systems Fundamentals)

Immediately following the printing of the cursor on the CRT, the pulse is transmitted. The electron beam appears and begins the expanding sweep at a rate proportional to the time it takes the transmitted pulse to travel. This expanding sweep is spiral. The electron beam prints as it revolves in synchronization with the electronic scanning circuitry. The angular position of the beam corresponds with the segment of the transducer being electronically scanned. Presence of an echo produces a bright spot on the face of the CRT, at a point corresponding to the range and bearing of the object reflecting the pulse.

As the pulse is transmitted, a broken line is displayed originating at the CRT center and bearing 180° from own ship's heading. This is known as the stern line, and it assists the operator in determining areas for searching.

Since the equipment is alert in all directions because of the rapid scanning feature, a true geographic plot is produced of the area surrounding the ship. The operator can determine range and bearing to a contact by training the cursor to the center of the spot and adjusting its length. Noise sources other than echoes from the transmitted pulse can also be received and are presented as bright spokes or wedges on the CRT aligned on the bearing of the source. Torpedoes thus are easily identifiable.

When searching for a target, the sonar system is set so that the

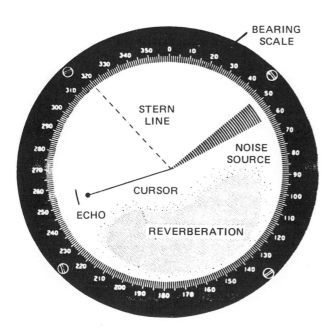

Figure 9–10. Sonar CRT display. (From Weapons Systems Fundamentals)

Underwater Detection and Tracking Systems   **261**

left, center, and right video signals from the scanning circuitry are added or summed. This provides a broad, easily seen pip for an echo. When the target pip has been identified and the sonar system is set to track it, the system is switched for difference operation, in which only the center video signal is displayed, and the target pip becomes small and sharp so that it can be tracked most effectively.

The video presentation is normally oriented to true north, with the CRT display electrically rotated to maintain 000°T at the top of the display. Without gyro input, the presentation is in relative bearing, with ship's head at the top of the CRT. Changes in own ship course will, when the presentation is in relative bearing, cause the entire CRT picture to rotate. The video presentation is also compensated to eliminate the effect of own ship roll and pitch, and to keep the CRT picture stabilized. Reverberation or minor sound reflections from such sources as surface waves, small fish and other sea life, etc., show up as small spots or light patterns. Sonars are responsive to a wide range of frequencies and therefore pick up all kinds of noise sources. This is called hydrophone effect, and it occurs during active mode operation as well as in passive or listening mode. Since the CRT indications of noise sources do not arise from timed echoes of the transmitted pulse, there is no blip that shows range to the noise source. The spoke shows only bearing. The spoke can be made broad or sharp by sum or difference reception.

A functional block diagram of typical scanning sonar equipment is shown in figure 9–11. A cycle is initiated by signal pulses from the keying circuits. These signal pulses go to the following four units, where they perform the functions indicated.

1. *Transmit-receive switch*. Switch the transducer from the receiver circuits to the transmitter circuits.
2. *Transmitter*. Trigger the transmitter and cause the formation of a pulse of the proper length, frequency, and amplitude.
3. *Sweep generator*. Return the sweep generator to zero range conditions and start a new cycle.
4. *Control circuits*. Cause control circuits to disconnect the cathode-ray tube deflection coils from the synchro-generator on the video scanning switch and connect it to the one on the audio scanning switch.

The pulse formed by the transmitter goes through the transmit-receive switching section and is applied to all staves of the transducer with the same phasing. Therefore, the transducer transmits a burst

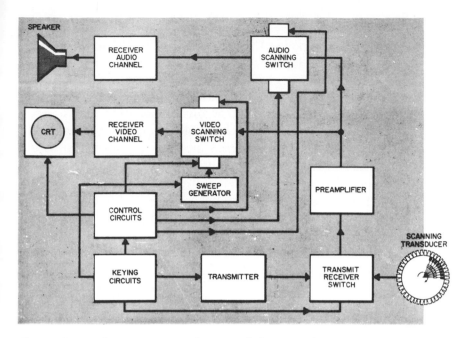

Figure 9–11. Scanning sonar functional diagram. (From Weapons Systems Fundamentals)

of sound of the same duration and frequency as the exciting pulse, disbursed equally in all directions. Target echoes or independently generated sounds of the proper frequency reaching the transducer cause electrical signals to be generated in the staves of the transducer. These signals go through the transmit-receive switching section, now in the listening condition, to the preamplifiers. In the preamplifiers, one for each stave, the signals are amplified and fed to the scanning switches. The video scanning switch, rotating at about 1,800 rpm, takes these inputs and combines them to give a video output equivalent to that of a highly directional, rapidly rotating, flat transducer. The output of the video scanning circuitry is further amplified and is coupled to the grid of the cathode-ray tube in the indicator to produce a brightening of the trace when sound signals are being received.

Signals from the preamplifiers also enter the audio scanning circuitry, where they are combined to give an audio signal. The audio scanning circuitry is adjusted in azimuth manually by the operator. The output of the audio scanning circuitry is amplified and converted to the desired audible frequency range in the receiver audio channel. The output of the receiver audio channel goes to a loudspeaker to permit aural interpretation of received signals.

Modern sonar systems have several operating features that provide for greater transmitted power than the conventional omnidirectional transmission. By using beam-forming techniques, the sonar sound beam can be formed into sectors of less than 40°. At any instant, the signal is the resultant of phased excitation of several adjacent transducer staves and rows (for depression angle), resulting in a source-level improvement that is characteristic of directional transmission. These different types of directional transmissions are called Processed Directional Transmission (PDT), Rotating Directional Transmission (RDT), Convergence Zone (CZ), and Bottom Bounce (BB). CZ and BB are just PDT operations with the beam depressed to some angle.

Sonar equipment mounted to the hulls of ships presents various problems. Self-generated noises due to water action around the sonar dome require that extreme care be exercised in the design of the dome to provide adequate streamlining. Streamlining is also required to minimize drag. The drag of the sonar dome, particularly for large, long-range sonar, can be considerable, so that in some applications retractable domes are used. Shielding is required to block off own ship's propeller noise, and vibration mounts may be needed to isolate the transducer from shipboard vibration. In one application, the problem of the interference of own ship's hull noise with sonar operation has led to placing the transducer in a streamlined dome in the bow of the ship. This application has the disadvantage that the bow dome is easily damaged and requires careful maneuvering of the ship during docking, but its advantages have resulted in this design being the most common in submarines and other naval warships.

Passive Sonar

The propellers, machinery, and varied activities aboard ships and submarines produce sounds that are transmitted to the water, either directly from turbulence or through the ship's hull in contact with the water. These sounds can be detected and identified at considerable distances with suitable equipment. The search for, detection, and identification of noises produced by ships and submarines is termed passive listening.

The receiving channels of echo-ranging equipment can be used for listening. Target bearings are determined in the same manner as for targets detected by echo ranging. However, echo-ranging equipment is needlessly complex for installation where it is to be used solely for listening. Moreover, the frequency range over which echo-ranging

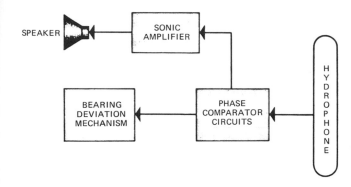

Figure 9–12. Passive sonar functional diagram. (From Weapons Systems Fundamentals*)*

equipment has a good response is not the optimum for general listening, because it is designed to listen primarily at the transmitter frequency.

Equipment intended to be used for listening is in principle the same as the receiving channel of echo-ranging equipment, as may be seen by comparing the functional block diagram of listening equipment shown in figure 9–12 with the functional block diagram of the searchlight echo-ranging system that was shown previously. However, no range indicator is provided, as range cannot be conveniently determined from sounds originating from a target.

Another major difference is in the transducer, called a hydrophone when used for listening exclusively. The construction of hydrophones can be much lighter than that of transducers because they do not have to handle high power. They are generally designed with a flat response over a much wider frequency range than transducers. This frequency range is generally below that of transducers, partly because sound is attenuated less at lower frequencies and partly because the high-intensity sounds produced by machinery and propellers are in the lower frequency ranges. Ships are often detected at long ranges using these equipments. For maximum range sensitivity and bearing resolution, some listening installations use large arrays of hydrophones. For instance, hydrophone arrays are installed in submarines in one of three configurations.

1. The *circular* array is typically enclosed in the bow, and consists of a series of hydrophones arranged vertically in a cylinder much like a surface ship sonar.
2. The *conformal* array consists of groups of hydrophones mounted in a horseshoe-shaped pattern around the bow.

3. The *spherical* array is ball shaped, and actually forms the forward part of the submarine hull, giving the bow its familiar shape.

Other Types of Sonar

Variable Depth Sonar (VDS)

To overcome the difficulty of hunting or watching for submarines that take advantage of shadow zones for hiding, variable depth sonar is used. In this application, a streamlined body containing sonar equipment is towed behind a ship, connected electrically to display and control equipment on the ship. Controllable vanes and depth sensors permit the body to be towed at any desired depth up to a maximum of about 200 meters. Advantages of VDS are:

1. It can operate independently of, or in conjunction with, a hull-mounted sonar.
2. Hull-mounted sonar shadow zones can be ensonified.
3. The transducer can be positioned at selected ocean depths.
4. A deep transducer is not affected by the environmental conditions that limit hull-mounted sonar, e.g., quenching.
5. 360° coverage is provided by placing the transducer below hull baffles, thereby providing detection capability aft of the ship.

Figure 9–13. VDS towed vehicle ready for lowering.

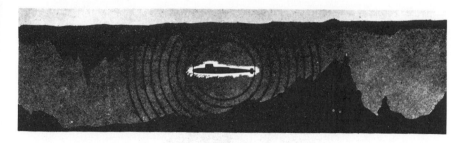

Figure 9–14. High-resolution sonar navigation (From Weapons Systems Fundamentals*)*

High-Resolution Sonar

These sonars are characterized by the use of high frequencies (10 kHz and up), short range, and good resolving capability. Sonars in this grouping are useful in searching for small underwater objects such as mines, or in bottom mapping. The feasibility of making bathymetric maps of the ocean bottom similar to topographical maps of land has been demonstrated and is becoming a useful form of submarine navigation. Observations of bottom contours taken with echosounders are compared with a computer memory, and when a match is obtained, the position is determined. Accuracies on the order of ±1,000 meters are currently possible. High-resolution sonar is also used in polar under-ice operations, in which the transducer is pointed upward to "map" the underside of the ice, thereby avoiding collisions with ridges.

Towed Array Sonar System (TASS)

Exclusive reliance on active sonar has ceased to be the only available or acceptable way for surface combatants to operate. A new family of passive sonars has been developed called towed arrays, in which a line of hydrophones is simply towed astern of the ASW platform. The hydrophones of the array are grouped according to the beam patterns desired and the frequency band to be covered. The principal advantage of the towed linear array from a performance point of view is that the sensing array can be towed more than 1,000 meters astern, far from the machinery noise of the towing vessel.

In addition to the hydrophones themselves, the array consists of heading, water temperature, and depth sensors to enable the towing platform to determine the attitude of the array. This is especially important when determining the bearing from which a sound is originating. This ability is directly related to the *DI* term in the sonar equation and is developed for a line array of sensors as follows.

Consider first that the ambient noise background of the sea arises principally from wave motion, marine creatures, and from the radiated noise of ocean shipping. This component of background noise is isotropic, and thus a single omni-directional hydrophone seeking a directional signal from a target in an isotropic noise field sees noise over an arc of 360°, while the signal sought is available on only a single direction or line of bearing. It is apparent that if one could arrange a number of hydrophones and "steer" them to look in a single direction, noise in all other directions would be rejected and the signal-to-noise ratio in any selected direction would be enhanced.

In figure 9–15 let line E_0-E_5 represent a line of array elements spaced distance d apart. Let lines a-a through f-f represent the successive positions of a plane wave of sound energy as it strikes the hydrophone elements of the array from an angle Θ with respect to the array axis. Let x be the distance the sound wave travels from the time it strikes one array element until the next. Consider that as the sound wave strikes each element, it generates a voltage proportional to the intensity of the incoming signal. It can be seen that the output voltage of element E_1 will be delayed at the processor relative to E_0 by the length of time required for the sound to travel the distance x, which will be equal to $(d \cos\Theta)/c$. For successive elements, the total delay for the nth element with respect to element E_0 will be

$$\text{Delay} = \frac{nd \cos \Theta}{c} \tag{9–3}$$

where c is the sound velocity and n is the number of the element. By electrically delaying the arrival of the signal from each element to the processor according to its position in the array, and then adding these electrical signals, it can be seen that the signal-to-noise ratio for the array input to the processor will be greater than that input by a single hydrophone. This is true because the sinusoidal sound signals added or summed will always be in phase at all the array elements, while the background noise is out of phase. At the same time, the directionality of the array reduces noise arriving from other directions relative to the signal. Note that cosine is used here because the angle Θ is measured from the array axis, not from a line normal to that axis as in electronically scanned radars (Chapter 7).

This process is used to "steer" electronically the receiving beam of the array. Upon reception of a signal from an unknown direction,

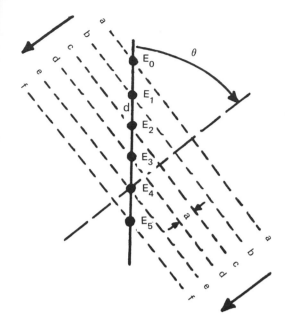

Figure 9–15. Linear array directionality.

the amount of delay amongst equally spaced elements can be varied until a maximum in-phase signal is detected. This delay can then be used to determine the angle of the target off the array axis. It should be obvious that sound from any target off the "beam" of the array will arrive at all the elements simultaneously with no time delay, and any sound from targets off the "bow" or "stern" of the array will arrive at successive elements with a maximum time delay. Target positions intermediate to these two will produce delays between zero and the maximum. A problem of bearing ambiguity arises in that it is not possible to determine from which side of the array the sound is arriving. This can be resolved through cross bearings from an array towed by another platform, or by changing course with the one array to obtain a second set of bearings.

These considerations are the basis for computation of directivity index in the sonar equation. For the simple line array illustrated,

$$DI = 10 \log \left(\frac{2L}{\lambda} \right) \tag{9–4}$$

where

L is the array length (from first to last hydrophone).
λ is the wavelength for the frequency concerned.

Example—Towed Array Sonar System

A passive sonar array consisting of 30 hydrophones is being towed on a course of 090°T. The spacing between the hydrophones coupled with the lowest anticipated frequency of 50 Hz produces a directivity index of 15.87 dB. The speed of sound is 1,500 m/sec at the tow depth. Calculate the delay experienced between successive elements of the array for a signal arriving from 120°T.

Solution—An array of 30 hydrophones has 29 spaces because of a hydrophone at the beginning and one at the end. The total length is therefore 29 d. From equation (9–4)

$$DI = 10 \log \left(\frac{2L}{\lambda}\right) \qquad \lambda = c/f$$

$$15.87 \text{ dB} = 10 \log \frac{2(29\,df)}{c}$$

$$15.87 = 10 \log \frac{2(29)d(50)}{1500}$$

$$d = 20 \text{ m}$$

A signal arriving from 120°T is also 030°R to the array heading, therefore $\Theta = 030°$

Now $n = 1$ for succesive elements

$$\text{delay} = \frac{nd \cos\Theta}{c} = \frac{1(20)}{1500} \cos 30°$$

$$\text{delay} = 11.55 \text{ msec}$$

For most hull-mounted sonars, the active receiving hydrophone arrays are arranged on the surface of a cylinder, although some submarine sonar arrays are installed on the surface of a sphere. Directionality, in these cases, is established by converting the arc of the cylinder or sphere to an equivalent line array electronically by a simple phase delay between the hydrophones followed by summing the hydrophone outputs.

Other systems within the family of the towed array sonars are:

1. Submarine Towed Array Sonar System (STASS)
2. Airborne Towed Array Sonar System (AIRTASS)
3. Tactical Towed Array Sonar System (TACTAS)

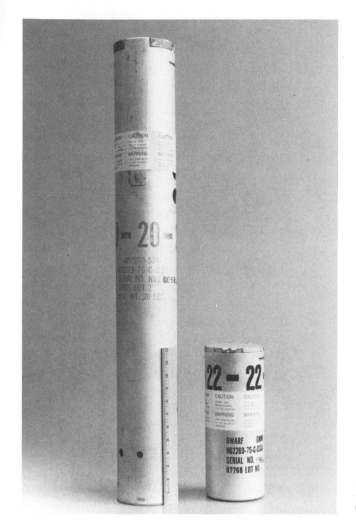

Figure 9–16. Sonobuoys: "A" size (left), "B" size (right).

Sonobuoy

The sonobuoy is an expendable piece of detection equipment, designed to be dropped from helicopters, carrier and patrol-type aircraft, and in some instances from ships. The purpose of the sonobuoy is to detect underwater sounds and to transmit these sounds to nearby aircraft via a low-powered VHF radio transmission.

A surfaced submarine can readily be detected by airborne radar at great distances. However, it is difficult for the aircraft to get within striking range of the submarine without being detected because the submarine is also equipped with search radar and ESM equipment.

The submarine immediately dives when an enemy aircraft is detected. The aircraft arrives in the general vicinity of the submerged submarine a few minutes later and drops sonobuoys in an effort to relocate the submarine.

The sonobuoy is a receiver-transmitter combination designed to float in an upright position in the water. Upon being dropped from an aircraft, the sonobuoy falls through the air in a vertical position, stabilized by a parachute or four small fins, and enters the water in an upright position. Upon striking the water, the stabilizing device is ejected, and a small transmitting antenna erects itself. The impact breaks open a dyemarker container located in the bottom of the sonobuoy, and also releases a hydrophone or transducer that sinks to a predetermined depth. In addition, battery power is activated, and the buoy usually becomes operational within 30 to 90 seconds after impact.

On some sonobuoys, the depth of the hydrophone (or length of hydrophone cable) may be selected before launch, thus allowing the best use of available BT information. In addition to the depth setting, sonobuoys are also available with various operating lives; they are made to sink (scuttle) at the end of their useful life. (This will be short for buoys intended for localization and long in the case of buoys used in large area searches.) Buoys are designed to have a life ranging from several minutes to several days, depending on their intended use. The scuttling of the sonobuoy is accomplished by use of water-soluble plugs. In some buoys, scuttling time can be varied.

Underwater sounds picked up by the hydrophone and the receiver transmitter in the sonobuoy are transmitted to the monitoring receiver in the aircraft. By dropping sonobuoys in a pattern encompassing a large ocean area, the sonobuoy receiver operator can determine the location of the submarine and its course and speed.

A significant difference between most sonobuoys and other types of sonar systems is that because the sonobuoy uses only a single hydrophone as its acoustic array, the directivity index or array gain approaches zero. This means that all other factors being equal, a sonobuoy will be expected to have a smaller figure of merit than sonars having multiple hydrophones in the acoustic array.

Sonobuoys may be grouped into three major categories: passive, active, and special purpose; and two subcategories: omnidirectional or directional.

The omnidirectional passive sonobuoy uses an omnidirectional hydrophone to detect the sounds of a target submarine. A single omnidirectional sonobuoy cannot determine the position of the target;

however, range estimates can be made if the acoustic conditions are known. The directional passive sonobuoy employs both directional and omnidirectional hydrophones, whose output indicates the bearing of the target relative to the sonobuoy position. This is accomplished by a magnetic compass, which, combined with the hydrophones, determines azimuth angle of the target with respect to magnetic north. These inputs are multiplexed and transmitted to the receiving aircraft.

Active sonobuoy pulse initiation and pulse duration are either self-timed or commandable. The sonar transmitter in the self-timed active sonobuoy pulses the transducer at a fixed pulse length and at a fixed pulse interval. The sonobuoy electronics contain a keying circuit that determines the fixed pulse characteristics. In the commandable active sonobuoy, the sonar transmitter pulses the transducers at a specific frequency for a length of time determined by UHF command from the controlling aircraft. Commandable active sonobuoys may be omnidirectional, giving target range only, or directional, producing both range and bearing information. In both the commandable and self-timed sonobuoys, the sonar signal that pulses the transducers is used to establish a time base for target range measurement. The sonar receiver is activated during the interval between sonar pulses in order to receive echoes from the target.

In addition to the active and passive sonobuoys, there are two special-purpose types. The first is used to obtain a temperature vs. depth profile so that sound propagation conditions can be predicted. The depth is determined by timing the descent of the temperature probe, which descends at a constant rate of 1.5 meters per second. The probe uses a thermistor bead to measure temperature. Conceptually, this sonobuoy type is nothing more than an XBT with a radio link to the aircraft.

The second special-purpose type is designed to be a communications link between the aircraft and friendly submarines.

All of the sonobuoy types are generally carried aboard ASW aircraft, with their actual numbers and use being dictated by the tactical situation.

Acoustic Navigation Systems

Echo Sounder

Water depths can be measured in several ways. One method is to drop a weighted, distance-marked line to the bottom and observe the depth directly from the line. The chief disadvantages of this method

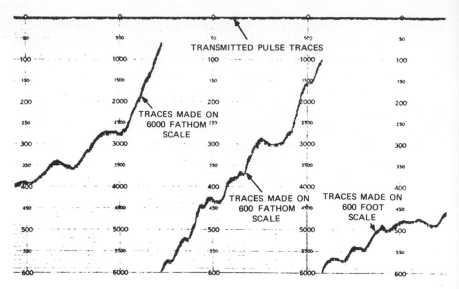

Figure 9–17. Echo sounder recording showing a steady decrease in depth.

are that its use is limited to very shallow water, and operation is slow. The use of sound is the more common method of measuring water depth. A sound pulse, directed toward the bottom, is transmitted, and its echo is received. The time between pulse transmission and echo reception is measured and, based on the speed of sound in water, the depth is thereby determined. Such a device is known as a sonar sounding set, called an echo sounder. Basically it is a navigational instrument, one that operates on acoustic principles rather than by radar or visual means. Its use is especially critical when using bathymetric navigation methods.

Acoustic Log

Conventional methods of determining submarine or ship speed have typically employed a tube or ram pressure orifice that sampled the increased water pressure caused by movement through the water. More recently, equipment measured the current induced by an electrolite (a solution of positive and negative ions, e.g., salt water) flowing past a point. Increased electrolite flow would result in increased current proportional to speed through the water. Each of these methods is dependent on undisturbed water flow at the measurement point. Errors could be caused by hull obstructions, the proximity of the ocean bottom, or wave action, and could result in significant inaccuracy in own ship speed provided for ship and submarine navigation and weapons systems. In recent years, acoustic devices have been employed to measure speed more reliably. These employ a transmitter operating around 100 kHz and a receiver capable of converting doppler shift due to passage of water or the ocean bottom directly to speed accurate within .1 kt. Low power levels and the high frequency employed virtually eliminate detection by hostile forces while measuring speed over the ground in water depths of 200 meters or employing volume back scatter from the water to measure velocity in deeper areas of the ocean.

Underwater Communications

For many reasons it may be necessary for a ship and submerged submarine to communicate with each other. Of paramount importance is the safety of the submarine and its crew. During exercises the ship can advise the submarine when it is safe to surface. Should an emergency arise aboard the submarine, the ship can be so informed. Exercises can be started and stopped, or one in progress can be modified, by using the underwater telephone. Attack accuracy can be signaled by the submarine to the attacking ship. The most widely used underwater telephone installation is the AN/WQC-2 sonar set. Although intended for use by sonar control personnel, most installations provide remote voice operation from the bridge and from CIC.

The range of transmission varies with water conditions, local noise level, and reverberation effects. Under normal sonar conditions, however, communication between ships should be possible at ranges out to 12,000 meters. Under the same conditions, submarines achieve a greater range. If the submarines are operating in a sound channel, the communication range may be many kilometers greater than that achieved by ships. Local noise, caused by ship's movement through the water, machinery, screws, etc., can reduce the range to less than half the normal range. Severe reverberation effects may also cause a reduction in range.

Doppler

In the process of submarine detection, it is desirable to obtain as much information about the target as possible. Such information includes target motion and it is here that sonar operators use the principles of doppler. Because doppler effect varies inversely with the speed of sound, the effect is much less marked in the sea than it is in the air. Doppler can, however, be noted by the operator if he listens carefully.

Operators of newer sonars find it almost impossible to distinguish by ear the effects of doppler because the sonars operate at very low frequencies. Some new sonars, however, incorporate doppler discriminators that determine whether the target is moving slowly or rapidly. Operators on old equipment usually can detect doppler effect by aurally comparing the pitch of the reflection of echo with the pitch of reverberations.

The initial transmission is increased or decreased in pitch by the effect of relative motion. It strikes a target at this changed frequency, and echoes at an altered frequency. As the sound returns, it is again affected by the same factors that acted upon the original sound, and consequently is changed in pitch again. Thus, it is received at the source with a frequency change double what normally would result from the given rate of relative motion.

In echo ranging the operator does not hear the outgoing sound transmission because the receiver is blocked during ping time. For this reason, he cannot compare the frequency of the outgoing ping with that of the returning echo. He can, however, compare the frequency of the echo from the target with that of the reverberations heard immediately before the echo is heard. This comparision is extremely valuable because the difference between the pitch of the reverberations and the pitch of the target echo depends solely on the target's absolute motion in the path of the sound beam. Any change in transmission frequency that may result from source movement has its effect upon reverberation as well as on target echo and, therefore, is undetectable by the sonar operator.

An increased pitch, then, indicates that the target is heading toward the echo-ranging ship; a decreased pitch indicates that the target is heading away from the echo-ranging ship. Both of these indications are independent of source motion and also of the direction of range change. For example, a submarine may be closing in range due to the superior speed of the searching ship, but if the submarine is heading away from the ship, its echo will yield a decreased pitch because the target echo is being compared with the reverberations. Actually, the pitch of both echoes and reverberations will be higher than the frequency of the equipment because of the closing range. But the increase in reverberation frequency will be greater than that in target echo frequency because the range rate between the source and the water particles causing reverberation is greater than that between the source and the target. The net audible effect, therefore, is a decrease in pitch.

Doppler is valuable for more than the assumptions it enables antisubmarine personnel to make about target course and speed. A difference in pitch between two tones aids in hearing them separately. Even a very weak echo can be distinguished if its pitch differs markedly from the pitches of surrounding echoes. Thus, target doppler is a great aid to the operator in detecting echoes against a background of reverberation.

Figure 9–18 shows doppler effect for several different situations. The curved lines indicate reverberations and echoes returned to the ship (source). The encircled dots represent particles in the water that cause reverberations. In all views of the illustration, the transmitted pulse was 14.0 kHz.

In view A, reverberation alone is illustrated. Note the change in frequencies caused by the motion of the ship.

The submarines in view B are moving at right angles to the transmitted pulses, hence they cause no doppler. Notice that the frequencies of the echoes from the submarines are the same as those of the reverberations.

View C illustrates two circumstances that produce *up* doppler. *Up* doppler is a sonar expression indicating that the target echo pitch is

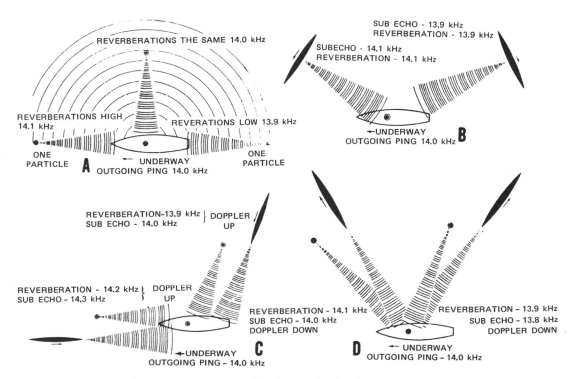

Figure 9–18. Reverberation, transmitted pulse, and echo frequencies.

higher than that of reverberation and that the target is in motion and heading toward the source.

View D is an example of *down* doppler situations, with the target in motion and heading away from the source.

Doppler Degree

Doppler varies in its degree of frequency difference from the surrounding reverberation echoes in a manner dependent on the component of target speed in the line of sound. As figure 9–19 shows, targets coming directly toward the echo-ranging ship yield echoes of increasing pitch as their speeds increase. The doppler of a constant speed target varies with the target's heading relative to the echo-ranging ship's position. Also, a target approaching at a constant speed either increases or decreases its degree of up doppler as it heads toward the ship in a more or less direct manner.

The degree of doppler thus depends on the speed of the submarine and on its target angle or aspect. The resulting component of these forces in the line of sound can be classified in one of three categories, according to the rate of range change.

1. Relative speeds greater than 6 knots toward or away (doppler marked up or down)
2. Speeds between 3 and 6 knots toward or away (doppler moderate up or down)
3. Speeds less than 3 knot (doppler slight up or down).

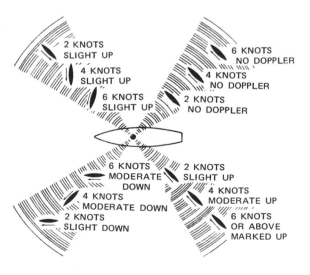

Figure 9–19. Doppler degree.

With the new low-frequency sonars, designed to decrease absorption loss, doppler determination is very difficult, and for most operators, a submarine speed of over 3.6 knots is required for good doppler discrimination. A change of at least 10 Hz is required for the ear to discern a change in frequency. In newer sonars, each knot of target motion results in a doppler shift on the order of 3 Hz, whereas in older, higher frequency sonars, each knot of target motion leads to a 10 Hz shift.

Doppler has another important application in the use of sonar, in addition to the estimation of the factors needed for an accurate solution of the fire control problem. Many echoes are returned from floating debris, kelp, and other inhomogeneous particles suspended in the medium or at rest on the bottom. These echoes show no doppler effect; they are motionless relative to the medium. Therefore, doppler is significant aid in the classification of an underwater contact as being, or not being, a submarine. In this usage, however, a handicap arises. Stationary objects located in a current yield doppler indications. A reef or pinnacle located in a current moving at 3 knots in a westerly direction, for example, appears to be underway at 3 knots in an easterly direction. This effect occurs because the target is not motionless in respect to the medium in this example. Because the sound wave cannot differentiate between relative motion resulting from a stationary target in a moving medium and that resulting from a moving target in a stationary medium, an erroneous indication of target motion is yielded. Conversely, a submarine drifting along with a current may yield no doppler even though it is moving.

Tactical Considerations of Sonar Employment

Table 9–1 is a summary of factors affecting sonar performance and an indication of who or what controls each factor. If the controlling items from the right side are grouped, tactical sonar performance might be considered to be represented by

Tactical Sonar Performance = Sonar design + ship design + ship operation + sonar operation + target design + target operation + sonar condition + sonar operator training + tactical geometry + environment

These controlling items may be further grouped as follows:

1. Items not under the control of the ASW commander:
   own sonar design

own-ship design
target design
target operations
tactical geometry
environment
2. Items under the control of the ASW commander (ship and force respectively):
own sonar conditions
own sonar operator training
own-ship operation
own sonar operation
3. Items the ASW commander can measure:
environment
sonar figure of merit

Several of these factors have been discussed earlier, and some additional ones will now be covered.

Table 9–1.　Factors Affecting Passive Sonar Tactical Performance

Factor	Controlled by
Target Signature	Target Design Characteristics
	Target Speed
	Target Machinery Quieting
Background Noise	
Self-Noise	Own-Ship Speed (Flow Noise)
	Own-Ship Machinery Noise Field
Ambient Noise	Environment (Sea State, Wind, Shipping Noise, Sea Life)
Directivity	Own Sonar Array Design
	Own Sonar Operating Condition
Detection Threshold	Own Sonar Design
	Own Sonar Operating Condition
	Own Operator Training & Condition
Propagation Loss	Environment (Sound Paths Available, Bottom Loss, Layer Depth, Ocean Area)
Attenuation	Own Sonar Design (Frequency)
Additional Factors Affecting Active Sonar Tactical Performance	
Source Level	Own Sonar Design (Power Available)
Target Strength	Target Aspect
	Target Reflectivity
Reverberation	Environment (Sea Structure)
	Own Sonar (Source Level)

Environmental Problems

As has been previously stated, the environment is variable, which contributes to the degree of difficulty of the ASW detection problem. As counter to its variability, the speed profile of the environment is measurable, but it is measurable to both the hunter and the hunted. The understanding and exploitation of that which is measured will probably determine the victor, or at the minimum, determine who holds the edge in detectability vs. counterdetectability in the encounter. It is generally accepted that the advantage belongs to the one who gains the initial detection in the ASW encounter.

Some of the measurable environmental factors that will affect own-ship detectability by the enemy and own-ship capability to detect him are listed below:

sound paths available
shallow water vs. deep water
layer depth
seasonal variation in area (wind, temperature, etc.)
local transient phenomena (rain, afternoon effect, etc.)
currents in area of operations

Understanding of the *sound paths* available is paramount in assessing the counterdetectability situation. This is based on past marine geophysical survey data, correlated with current bathymetry (BT) or sound velocity profile (SVP) measurements. The direct sound path is readily determined from current BT or SVP measurements. The viability of the bottom-bounce sound path is determinable by survey data on bottom reflectivity and bottom absorption loss. The existence of convergence zones is normally based on ocean depth and knowledge of prior surveys. In the absence of prior surveys, ocean depth is an acceptable basis for predicting the absence or presence of a convergence zone. However, even if sound paths prediction is in error, assuming the enemy has the capability to use the sound paths most advantageous to him is a sound tactical decision.

With respect to *detection in shallow water*, it has already been indicated that sonar performance may be enhanced because the ocean bottom and surface boundaries act as a duct for the channeling of sound. Since no precise quantitative measure of the expected improvement is available, the ASW tactical commander could view the shallow water problem as one in which ambiguities may be created by him to mask the real composition and precise presence of his forces. One can even conceive of his active sonars being used in a bistatic mode, i.e., using one ship's sonar as an ensonifying source, and any other ship's sonar or sonobuoys being used as receiving or detecting sensors. Bistatic geometry creates problems in establishing precise target location. On the other hand, an indication of target presence may tip the tactical balance, or at least provide the tactical commander with alternative courses of action, no matter how the target presence was established.

The depth of the bottom of the *surface layer* of water is a great determinant of sonar performance from a hull-mounted surface-ship sonar because the target submarine may choose to proceed below the layer. As was discussed earlier, cross-layer detection is usually limited in range because of the refraction or bending of the sound rays. Shallow layers favor the submarine because by going deep below the layer, he is frequently able to detect the surface ship's radiated noise when its active sonar transmission is trapped in the surface layer and/or refracted sharply downward. The tactical answer to this situation from the escort point of view is to vary the vertical angle of transmission of his sonar projector so as to penetrate the layer, or to deploy a variable-depth sensor below the layer.

Predictions of seasonal *variation* in the area of operations, based on previous surveys and observations of wind action and temperature profile, are basic data for the operational planner. When the ASW force is *in situ*, the tactical commander should validate or verify the predictions by regular periodic measurements of the ocean temperature or sound-speed structure. The length of the period between measurements should be based on observations of current weather phenomena affecting sound propagation conditions, i.e., wind, time of day, etc. It is particularly important to be aware of the surface-heating effect of the sun and of the fact that in areas of little mixing of the sea by wind-driven waves, a positive temperature gradient may be developed between mid-morning and mid-afternoon that could seriously degrade surface-ship sonar performance. Under these conditions, hourly measurements of the environment are in order. Similarly, when conducting operations in the vicinity of currents like the Gulf Stream or the Labrador Current, where "fingers" of water with marked differences in temperature to that of adjacent waters is common, the tactical commander should consider hourly measurements.

Acoustic Emission Control Policy (EMCON)

Acoustic counter detection of active sonars can be accomplished at ranges much greater than that of the active sonar. Therefore, it is safe to assume that an adversary cannot be surprised when active systems are used unless transmission, for purposes of final precision target location, occurs immediately prior to weapon firing. At the same time, it is very important to limit other acoustic emissions to limit an adversary's ability to detect, identify, and target friendly units by sophisticated passive methods. Acoustic emission control (acoustic EMCON) is a method of limiting emitted noises and of using them to create an ambiguous acoustic environment, thus forcing an adversary to come to very close range to resolve his fire control and identification problems prior to firing a weapon. Ships and submarines are designed with noise reduction as a primary consideration. Operating procedures can be modified to control acoustic emissions, including practices such as turn count masking (where a multi-engine ship would operate her main engines at different RPM to confuse an adversary as to its actual speed). Other methods might include the use of sprint and drift tactics to vary the composite radiated noise signal level generated within a group of ships. Acoustic Countermeasures are covered in more detail in chapter 11.

Submarines and Antisubmarine Warfare in the Future

No one can say just what warfare will be like in the future, but it can be conjectured clearly enough to show that submarines will have much to do with determining who has command of the sea. According to past experience and new developments, submarines will likely be used in any or all of the following ways by both sides.

1. To destroy the enemy's navy and merchant marine.
2. To impede or cut off the flow of supplies and troops by threat of attack on merchant shipping.
3. To deny the use of shipping lanes and harbor areas to the enemy's merchant shipping and naval units by submarine-planted mines.
4. To divert the enemy in greater or lesser degree from his primary mission of winning the conflict by causing him to concentrate on antisubmarine warfare.
5. To mount direct attacks by submarine-launched guided missiles and rockets.
6. To function as pickets.
7. To function as transports in situations where the submarine's special characteristics are important.
8. To function as antisubmarine units.

Though in many respects antisubmarine warfare of the future will resemble that of World War II, there will be great differences. The advent of nuclear-powered ships and submarines and nuclear weapons creates a growing challenge in the antisubmarine warfare problem of the modern navy. Detection equipment and tactics are constantly undergoing revision and improvement to keep abreast of this changing technology. The ASW forces of the future will include many ships and weapons now unfamiliar. But the most advanced hardware, alone, will never ensure victory. At the base of the tactical problem are the officers and men who will put this hardware to use.

Summary

Antisubmarine warfare is waged by surface, airborne, undersea, and shore-based forces, each with its own unique capabilities. Methods of detecting submarines include sonar, radar, electronic support measures, and magnetic anomaly detection. Of these, sonar is the most widely used and is capable of the three basic functions of echo-ranging (active), listening (passive), and communications. The device in a sonar for acoustic to electrical (and vice versa) energy conversion is the transducer. Simple versions of transducers, designed for listening only, are called hydrophones. Active sonar transducers fall into two basic types, searchlight and scanning, with the latter being the most useful for tactical detection. Other types of sonars include variable-depth sonar, high-resolution sonar, towed array sonar systems, sonobuoys, echo sounders, and communications systems. The phenomenon of doppler shift due to a moving target is useful for target classification. Tactical considerations in the employment of sonar are grouped into those that the ASW commander can control, those that he cannot, and those that he can measure. The concept of EMCON is as applicable to acoustic emissions as it is to radio and radar. The submarine is a formidable adversary, and sonar remains the best method of detecting it.

References

Bureau of Naval Personnel. *Introduction to Sonar*. NAVPERS 10130-B, 2nd ed. Washington, D.C.: GPO, 1968.

Bureau of Naval Personnel. *Sonar Technician G3&2 (U)*. NAVEDTRA 10131-D. Washington, D.C.: GPO, 1976.

Bureau of Naval Personnel, *Sonar Technician S 3&2 (U)*. NAVPERS 10132-B. Washington, D.C.: GPO, 1971.

Commander, Naval Ordnance Systems Command. *Weapons Systems Fundamentals*. NAVORD OP 3000, vol. 1, 1st rev. Washington, D.C.: GPO, 1971.

Corse, Carl D., and William R. Barnett. *Introduction to Shipboard Engineering and Naval Weapons Systems*, Vol. II. Annapolis, Md.: U.S. Naval Academy, 1971.

Koch, Winston E. *Radar, Sonar, and Holography—An Introduction*. New York: Academic Press, 1973.

Naval Education and Training Support Command. *Principles of Naval Ordnance and Gunnery*. NAVEDTRA 10783-C. Washington, D.C.: GPO, 1974.

Naval Operations Department, U.S. Naval War College. *Technological Factors and Constraints in Systems Performance Study-Sonar Fundamentals*. Vol. I-1, 1975.

Naval Training Command. *The Antisubmarine Warfare Officer (U)*. NAVTRA 10778-C, Washington, D.C.: GPO, 1973.

10

Electro-optics

Introduction

The first optical sensor of importance to the Navy was the human eye. To a large degree the eye still remains the ultimate optical sensor, and most other optical and electro-optical systems can be considered as devices to augment the eye. Generally, it should be understood that we shall be dealing with frequencies within a factor of ten of the visible optical frequencies, which for the eye can be considered as centered in the "green-yellow" range of about 5.4×10^{14}Hz. Frequencies ten times lower than this are in the invisible "infrared," usually thought of as heat radiation, and frequencies ten times higher than this are in the invisible "ultraviolet."

Optics have played a major role in naval problems in the past, and it may be expected that when combined with electronics, as electro-optics, they will play an important role in the future. Prior to World War II, optical systems were important in fire control, weapon delivery, surveillance, reconnaissance, etc. Many of these functions were then taken over by radio frequencies, particularly radar, and optics were eclipsed. Newly developing technology not only includes devices and techniques for passive sensing of light and IR from targets, but also, with the invention and development of the laser—an active device—the techniques of radar can be extended to optical and IR frequencies. Communication devices with very high data rates become feasible at these high frequencies, and radiation weapons that can deliver high quantities of energy to a target for the purpose of damaging it become possible.

It is clear that the use of optics cuts across a wide variety of functions, platforms, and missions. It will be seen that the advantages derived from the use of optical frequencies, which include precision imaging, tracking, location, and ranging, often offset the disadvantages related to limited ranges and weather limitations. Although electro-optical (E-O) systems are not all-weather for us, neither are they all-weather for our adversary. In essence, if we can't see them neither can they see us.

The Electro-optic Spectrum

The expanded scale of figure 10–1 shows a portion of the electromagnetic frequency spectrum significant for this discussion. Because the frequencies in this portion of the spectrum are in the millions of megahertz, it is customary to refer to wavelength rather than frequency when describing the specification of these waves. The unit most commonly used to describe wavelengths of visible and infrared light is the micron (μm or μ) which is 10^{-6} meters long. Visible light extends from 0.4μ to 0.76μ, whereas IR extends from 0.76μ to $1,000\mu$. Visible light can be further broken down into bands according to its color, and IR into bands called near (NIR), middle (MIR), far (FIR), and extreme (XIR). There are, in fact, no clear-cut boundaries to the various portions of the electromagnetic spectrum. Thus, the limits used are somewhat arbitrary, and may vary from publication to publication.

Note that

$$1\text{Å} = 10^{-10} \text{ meter or one angstrom}$$
$$1\ \mu\text{m} = 10^{-6} \text{ meter or one micrometer or micron}$$
$$\text{"Red" Light} = 7,000\ \text{Å} = .7\mu\text{m}$$

Fundamental Concepts of Optical Radiation

Optical radiation will, for the purpose of this discussion, be defined as that between the wavelength limits of 0.3μ and 15μ. The reason for the limitation is that the atmosphere severely attenuates longer

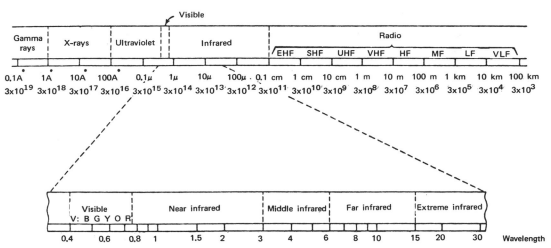

Figure 10–1. The electro-optic spectrum. (From Infrared System Engineering)

and shorter wavelengths, thus wavelengths outside of that band will not generally be tactically useful.

As part of the electromagnetic spectrum, light is a transverse wave and consists of fluctuations in the electric and magnetic fields of the propagating wave. It is interesting to note that the key optical quantity is the electric vector or field. This field defines the direction of polarization and activates optical sensors including photographic film and the human eye. Both fields are quantized, that is, the energy is considered to be carried by particle-like entities called photons, each having allowable energies of hv. The same statement is true for the microwave region, but here the photons are of low relative energy and frequency, thus the particle nature of the field is of less importance. For the RF region the wave characteristic predominates, and quanta or photons need not be considered.

Optical frequencies are generated by two general types of sources, thermal radiators and selective radiators. Figure 10–2a shows the spectral characteristics of each. A thermal source radiates a continuous spectrum of frequencies, with maximum radiated energy occurring at some particular frequency as indicated. Selective sources have an output concentrated in narrow frequency intervals, called line spec-

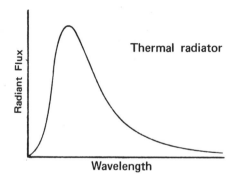

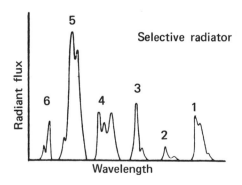

Figure 10–2a. Output of thermal and selective radiators. (From Infrared Systems Engineering)

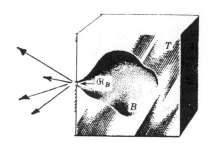

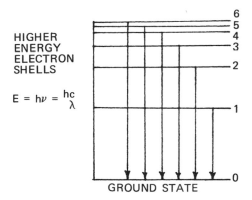

HIGHER
ENERGY
ELECTRON
SHELLS

$E = h\nu = \dfrac{hc}{\lambda}$

GROUND STATE

Figure 10–2b. Thermal and selective sources. (From Infrared Systems Engineering)

tra, caused by the excitation of individual atoms or molecules by various means. Some of the selective radiators that are tactically significant include the stream of hot gases from the exhaust of a jet engine or rocket, the shock-excited layer surrounding a reentry body, and the gas-discharge sources used in flashing light communication systems. Typical thermal radiators include the hot metal of a jet engine or rocket tail pipe, aerodynamically heated surfaces, motor vehicles, personnel, terrain, ships, and space vehicles. A particularly unique selective radiator is a laser that radiates at nearly a single frequency. Its radiation spectrum can be constrained to a single narrow line. In this regard a laser source is very similar to a radar energy source, except that the frequencies are much different. Of course, in the optical wavelengths the most significant source is the sun. The sun's radiation reflected from objects forms the basis for most passive optical sensors. The sun is essentially a thermal source of radiation, not selective as one might expect.

Thermal Radiators

In 1860 Kirchhoff stated that good absorbers are also good radiators at any given wavelength. In addition, he coined the term "blackbody" to describe an object that absorbs all incident radiation, and as a result must also reradiate that energy with complete efficiency. The black-body is the standard with which any other source is compared.

The closest approximation to an ideal blackbody is the entrance to a completely enclosed cavity in an opaque body, as depicted in figure 10–2b. The simplest type is usually an elongated, hollow metal cyl-inder, blackened inside, and completely closed except for a narrow aperture at one end. Light or other radiation entering the opening is almost completely trapped by multiple reflections from the walls, so that the opening usually appears completely black. Experimental study of the spectral distribution of the intensity of blackbody radia-tion yields two important facts: one is that the total intensity, inte-grated over all wavelengths, is proportional to the fourth power of the absolute temperature; the other is that the wavelength at which the maximum value of intensity occurs varies inversely with the ab-solute temperature. These two important findings have been for-mulated as the Stefan-Boltzmann Law and Wien's Displacement Law, respectively.

Total Emissive Power

The Stefan-Boltzmann Law expresses the total emissive power of an ideal blackbody, integrated over all wavelengths, and is stated by the formula

$$E = \sigma T^4 \qquad (10–1)$$

where

E is the power radiated per unit area of the body (watts/cm^2)
σ is a constant of proportionality (5.67×10^{-12} watts/cm^2 °K^4)
T is the absolute temperature of the blackbody (°K = 273 + °C)

From this it can be easily determined that if the temperature of the body is doubled, the radiation emitted will increase by a factor of 16. When the blackbody is radiating in an environment that is at a tem-perature other than absolute zero, the law is written as

$$E = \sigma (T^4 - T_e^4) \qquad (10–2)$$

where

T_e is the temperature of the surrounding environment (°K)

Thus, an object in thermal equilibrium with its surroundings has a net thermal radiative flux of zero. The ideal blackbody is, however, only a theoretical concept, and the Stefan-Boltzmann Law must be further refined to

$$E = \varepsilon \, \sigma \, (T^4 - T_e^4) \qquad (10\text{--}3)$$

where

ε is the emissivity of the grey body, for which $0 < \varepsilon < 1$

Emissivity is the ratio of the total radiant energy emitted by an object at temperature T, to the total energy emitted by an ideal blackbody at the same temperature, and under the same conditions. Its numeric value lies between the limits of zero for a nonradiating source and unity for an ideal blackbody. All bodies emit radiation as a result of the thermal agitation of their molecules or atoms, whether there are other causes of excitation or not.

The value of emissivity for a given object is a function of the type of material and its surface finish. We will neglect variations with wavelength (selective radiation) and the temperature of the material. For metals, emissivity is low, whereas for non-metals it is high. Representative values of emissivity, ε, and reflectivity, ρ, are shown in table 10–1. Defining α = absorbtivity; ε = emissivity; ρ = reflectivity, $\alpha + \rho = 1$ for opaque surfaces that have zero transmission. From Kirchhoff $\alpha = \varepsilon$ for a given wavelength so $\rho = 1 - \varepsilon$.

The radiation from a metal or other opaque material originates within a few microns of the surface; therefore, emissivity of a coated or painted surface is characteristic of the coating rather than the underlying material. However, the visual appearance of a material is

Table 10–1.   Optical Properties of Various Opaque Surfaces

Surface	Absorbtivity, α or Emissivity, ε	Reflectivity, ρ
Blackbody Cavity	1.00	0.00
Lamp Black	.95	.05
Dry Soil	.92	.08
Ocean at Sea State 4	$\simeq.80$	$\simeq.20$
Steel	.60	.40
Aluminum Paint	.25	.75
Stainless Steel	.09	.91
Aircraft Aluminum	.08	.92
Aluminum Foil	.04	.96
Silvered Mirror	.02	.98

not always a reliable guide to its emissivity at infrared wavelengths. For example, snow appears to be an excellent diffuse reflector to the eye, and we might conclude that it has low emissivity. However, since the great bulk of the thermal radiation from a body at the temperature of snow occurs above 3μ, our visual estimate of its appearance based on sensing radiation centered at 0.5μ is meaningless. Snow, it turns out, has a high emissivity of about 0.85. Another example is the emissivity of human skin at 32°C, which is close to unity and is independent of its color.

Emissivity is also used as a basis for defining types of thermal radiation, and distinguishing between thermal and selective radiation. In summary,

1. A blackbody source is a source for which $\varepsilon = 1$.
2. A greybody source (also a thermal source) is a source for which ε is a constant greater than 0 but less than 1.
3. A selective source is a source for which ε is a function of the wavelength.

Spectral Distribution of Power

As stated earlier, thermal radiators emit energy over a broad range of wavelengths, but peak at one particular wavelength. The wavelength at which maximum radiation occurs is a function of temperature and is expressed by the Wien Displacement Law.

$$\lambda_m = \frac{a}{T} \tag{10-4}$$

where

λ_m is the wavelength of maximum radiation (μ)
a is an empirical constant, 2898 (μ°K)
T is the temperature of the body (°K = 273 + °C)

Note that this law locates only the point of maximum radiation and not the radiated energy in other parts of the spectrum.

When the Stefan-Boltzmann Law and Wien Displacement Law are applied to blackbody ($\varepsilon = 1$), radiation at a low temperature range of 500°K to 900°K, figure 10–3 is the result. Greybody ($\varepsilon = .66$) emission from an object at 900°K is depicted by the broken line.

This is an interesting temperature range because it includes the temperature of the hot metal tail pipes of turbojet aircraft. Several characteristics of thermal radiation are evident from these curves. The total output power, which is proportional to the area under the

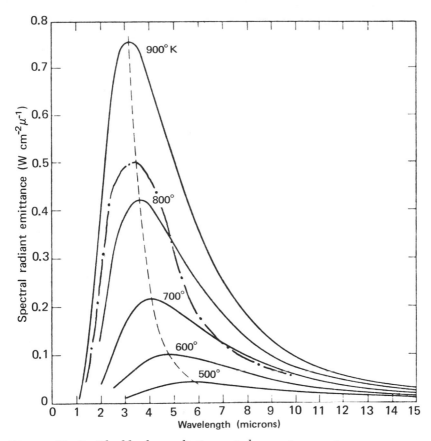

Figure 10–3. Blackbody radiation at lower temperatures. . ———— .
———— . Greybody @ 900°K with ε = .575 + .66. (From Infrared System
Engineering)

curves, increases rapidly with temperature. The wavelength of maximum radiation shifts towards shorter wavelengths as the temperature
increases. The individual curves never cross one another; hence the
higher the temperature, the higher the output power density at all
wavelengths.

If the same spectral distribution of power is plotted against the
product of wave length λ and Kelvin temperature T, the result is
figure 10–4, a universal curve (A) that will suffice at any temperature.
In addition, the integral of curve (A) is plotted as curve (B), which
provides the fraction of energy radiated below a given value of λT.
For example, at a value of $\lambda T = 4000$, 48 percent of the power
radiated occurs below this point. This would be true for $\lambda = 8\mu$ and
$T = 500°K$ ($\lambda t = 4000$), $\lambda = 4\mu$ and $T = 1000°K$, and so on. Note
that the peak of the (A) curve occurs where $\lambda T = 2898$ which is the
constant a in equation (10–4), the Wien Displacement Law.

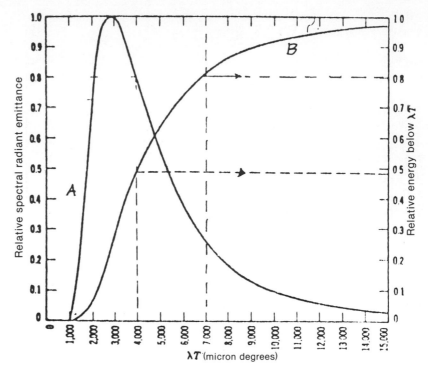

Figure 10–4. Universal blackbody curve. (From Infrared System Engineering)

Curve (B) in figure 10–4 is useful in that it graphically determines the fraction of total power radiated by an object that can be used by a detector of a given band width. From the previous discussion of thermal radiators it should be apparent that the radiated power per unit area E of equation (10–3) is that radiated over all wavelengths, and that a real detector will only respond to a relatively narrow band of wavelengths. For this reason, we must determine the fraction of the radiated power E that is within the band width of a given receiver.

Example: For a detector band width from 8 μ to 14 μ what fraction of the energy radiated from an object at 500°K can be processed by the receiver due to band width limitations?

First obtain λT for the upper and lower limits of the band width:

$$14\mu \times 500°K = 7000\mu°K \qquad 8\mu \times 500°K = 4000\mu°K$$

Entering figure 10–4 we find that .48E is radiated below a λT of 4,000μ°K and .8E is radiated below a λT of 7,000μ°K; therefore, subtracting .48 from .8 we find that .32E is radiated in the band width of this particular receiver.

Selective Radiators

Continuous emission spectra are produced by hot solid objects where the oscillations of each atom or molecule are strongly influenced by its adjacent neighbors, due to the high density of the substance. Line emission spectra are produced from gases at high temperature and low pressure where each element emits its own characteristic pattern of lines, uninfluenced by adjacent atoms or molecules.

Figure 10–5 shows a schematic representation of a hydrogen atom with the nucleus and its associated electron shells or orbits. If a hydrogen electron is excited from its normal energy level (called a ground state) to a higher level, say, for example, the E_0–E_1 transition, then energy must be provided to the atom. The electron returns to its normal level in a very short time (about 10^{-8} sec for most atoms), which is known as the lifetime of the higher energy state. In the transition to the lower energy state, the atom sheds its excess energy in the form of light or other electromagnetic energy.

Quantitatively, the amount of energy absorbed or emitted is given by Planck's Law,

$$h\upsilon = E_1 - E_0 \qquad\qquad (10\text{–}5)$$

where

E is the amount of energy per photon (Wsec)
h is the Planck's constant 6.63×10^{-34}Wsec^2
υ is the frequency of the emitted radiation in Hz.

Example: If a hydrogen atom returns to the ground state from its

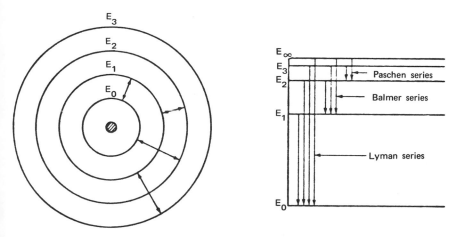

Figure 10–5. Energy-level diagram of a hydrogen atom.

highest state of excitation, it loses 13.6 ev. The wavelength of light emitted is then

$$\lambda = \frac{c}{v} = \frac{hc}{hv} = \frac{hc}{E_{photon}}$$

substituting

$$\lambda = \frac{6.63 \times 10^{-34} \text{Wsec}^2 \times 3 \times 10^8 \text{m/sec}}{13.6 \text{ ev}}$$

and

$$1 \text{ ev} = 1.6 \times 10^{-19} \text{ Joule} = 1.6 \times 10^{-19} \text{Wsec}$$

$$\lambda = \frac{1.99 \times 10^{-25} \frac{\text{Wmsec}}{\text{Wsec}}}{21.8 \times 10^{-19}} = 912\text{Å} = .0912\mu\text{m}$$

This ultraviolet wavelength is the limit of the Lyman series and corresponds to the highest energy photon emitted by a hydrogen atom. The remaining series of figure 10–5 are transitions to other than the ground state.

The spectra of heavier atoms get increasingly complicated with atomic weight. Some elements, such as hydrogen and neon, have relatively few widely spaced lines; iron (gaseous, not solid) has many thousand spectrum lines. Band-emission spectra are molecular spectra seen in fluorescence and phosphorescence. Each band consists of many closely spaced lines that are irregularly distributed with respect to wavelength and intensity. This characteristic is caused by transitions to lower energy states, which take much longer, on the average, than the normal 10^{-8} seconds. In some cases, long-lived states may exist for hours or days following exposure to intense light, giving rise to materials that fluoresce or "glow in the dark" while still at low temperatures. CRT screens, aircraft instrument lighting, and the visual detection of submarines by biological luminescence are three applications of fluorescence in naval weaponry.

Optical Transmission Characteristics

Radiation Spreading or Divergence

The general concept of spherical spreading, waves moving outward in spherical shells, holds true for optics as well as for sound and radar. For a truly spherical wave, it will be remembered that the inverse square law applies—that is, the power density (power per unit area) decreases as the square of the inverse of the range. Mirrors and lenses used as projectors can form plane waves only over short ranges; after those ranges, spherical spreading applies. Laser sources, as described previously, may be constructed to have very small divergence. Narrowing the divergence of a beam further is still, of course, very useful for concentrating power and is equivalent to increasing the antenna gain of a radar system. Just as in the case of radar antenna theory, a narrower divergent beam can only be obtained by increasing the size of the optical lenses or reflectors employed. Thus, lenses or reflectors are the antennas for optical systems.

Atmospheric Propagation

The atmosphere is a significant limiting factor to the tactical employment of optical frequencies. Propagation losses are caused by two mechanisms: absorption and scattering. Absorption lines (or bands in the case of molecular cases) are a direct loss process, mostly attributable to the constituents of air, water vapor, carbon dioxide, oxygen, etc., being cooler than the source of light being absorbed. These constituents have areas of selective absorption, and radiation at these frequencies is absorbed by the molecules and converted into thermal motion, giving rise to an increase in temperature. Figure 10–6 shows the transmission structure of the lower atmosphere. One is thus constrained to work within the available "windows" of relatively high transmission. The windows are generally known well enough to permit system designers to choose optimal frequency bands for the task at hand.

An examination of figure 10–6, together with the target-emission characteristics shows several good transmission windows in the target-emission bands of interest. In particular, a good transmission window exists from about 2.9μ to slightly above the 4.4μ region of HF chemical laser devices. Another good window is located between about 4.4μ and 5.2μ. Finally, from slightly below 8μ to about 14μ is a wide window. [The fact that these windows are in the infrared portion of the spectrum explains why IR is so useful for target detection and tracking.]

Another propagation factor arises from the particulate matter in the air—salt particles, very small water droplets, dust, etc. The phenomenon is called *scattering* and mainly causes a redistribution of light rather than a true loss. It is certainly a loss for light traveling in a particular direction, e.g., from source to detector, and is thus significant as a direct attenuation factor. But the energy lost from the line of sight is sent off in other directions rather than lost as heat. As

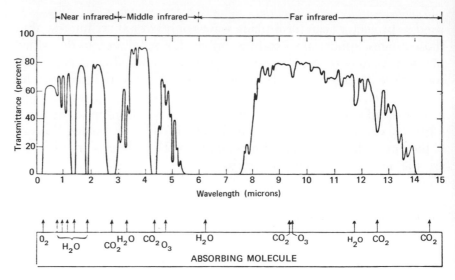

Figure 10–6. Atmospheric transmission windows. Transmittance of the atmosphere for 1,850-meter horizontal path at sea level. (Adopted from Gebbie et al. from Infrared Systems Engineering)

far as attenuation goes, scattering loss is in principle indistinguishable from absorption. One reason for considering it as a separate mechanism is that it is not as selective as absorption, and it is the phenomenon that makes possible the detection of a signal outside the main beam. Since significant side lobes, in the RF sense, do not show up in the optical regime, the major potential for "seeing" a signal outside the main lobe is aerosol scattering.

The scattering phenomenon also leads to a loss of contrast between target and background. Thus, in the visible spectrum, a dark target becomes progressively less black in appearance as it moves away from the observer, until finally it will vanish against the horizon—regardless of its size. This has led to the concept of "visibility," which unfortunately is not as well defined as one might like. Roughly speaking, the visible range for a large dark object against the horizon is the distance at which the brightness difference between the object and sky is 2%. This diminution of contrast is due to scattering and is the limiting factor in visible observation. The use of sensors other than the eye will not change this range by a significant amount.

Ocean Propagation

The ocean is the other major medium in which the Navy operates. It is a very highly attenuating medium as shown in figure 10–7. The only significant "window" is in the visible spectrum and is frequently called the "blue-green" window. It is a relatively "dirty" window, however. The attenuation is so great that underwater ranges are severely limited and may be expected to be measured in tens of meters, with a maximum of perhaps 1,000 meters under highly optimum conditions. Therefore, optics have only very limited potential applications underwater except in air-to-subsurface and subsurface-to-air optical communication links and ASW detection. Morse code light signals have been transmitted about 100 meters underwater to a submerged detector from an aircraft and vice versa. When operationally feasible, optical communication links may change some tactical submarine capabilities.

A second possible use of electro-optics across the air-ocean boundary is the employment of a blue-green laser for active submarine detection. Carried aboard an aircraft, the laser would be pointed downward to sweep back and forth as the aircraft flew a search pattern. Under certain conditions, the laser beam could reflect off the hull of a shallow submarine, thereby revealing its position. Ranges are small when compared with acoustic methods, and therefore tactical applications are limited. It is envisioned that this method could be used

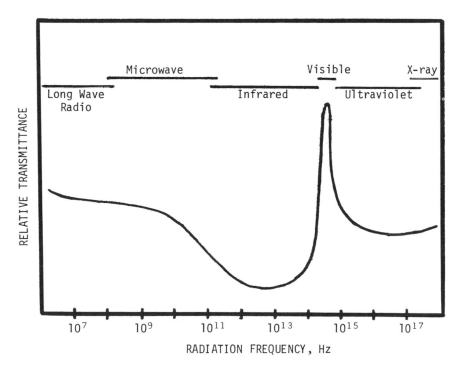

Figure 10-7. Ocean transmission windows.

in the same manner as Magnetic Anomaly Detection (MAD) equipment is presently employed.

Transmission Through Liquids and Solids

Many liquids and solids are employed in optical systems, both as filters and as lenses. Each nongaseous material has its own unique band absorption spectrum, similar in concept to that depicted above for the ocean. To act as a filter of unwanted noise, a material is selected that exhibits a strong transmission window at the desired wavelengths and a minimal transmission elsewhere. Thus, only the desired wavelengths pass through into the detector, blocking out all other unwanted wavelengths. When used as lenses, certain crystalline solids, such as sapphire, lithium fluoride, and quartz, function in the usual optical manner to collect and focus the energy on a detector as well to select a band width of interest.

Although the path lengths that the incoming energy must transit when passing through these various liquids and solids are insignificant when compared to the ranges between the target and detector, the absorption effects are not. This is due to the greater densities of the lens and filter materials compared to the transmitting environment. The intensity of the incoming energy will decrease roughly as an exponential function of the depth of penetration and is highly dependent upon the type of material employed. Because absorption effects are generally the limiting factor in electro-optic transmission, losses through filters and lenses cannot be ignored.

Optical Sources, Targets, and Backgrounds

Any solid object at a temperature above absolute zero is a source of thermal radiation. Other objects or devices that radiate as a result of excitation of their atoms or molecules are sources of selective radiation. Visible and IR sources of radiation are tactically significant in three different senses:

1. A source such as a turbojet exhaust may be a target.
2. A source such as the sun or a laser may serve as an illuminator against tactically significant targets. In the case of the laser, it may serve as a carrier of information in a communication or ranging system or as a carrier of energy for destructive purposes.
3. Sources such as the sun or other celestial bodies may serve as background noise against which a target must compete.

The intent of this section is to review some of these sources and note some of the significant characteristics of their radiation.

The *sun*, of course, is the most significant source of illumination energy. Indeed, for most of man's history the sun has served as an illuminator for man's natural sensor system, his eyes. The primary limitation of the sun as an illuminator is that it is not available (at least directly) at night, and weather can drastically attenuate its radiation. The sun can be approximated as a blackbody at 5,900°K; however, the radiation received on the surface of the earth looks more like selective radiation rather than thermal radiation. This is due to the fact that the radiation must transit the atmosphere, which is a selective transmission medium due to the numerous absorption bands in which various wavelengths are attenuated.

The sun's spectrum has a maximum radiated energy at .5μ, which, unsurprisingly is yellow. This wavelength corresponds to the peak of the response of the human eye to light. Another significant fact is that the atmosphere is an excellent transmission medium at these wavelengths. The sun is also a strong source of IR radiation in the near-infrared region (.7μ to 3μ), and in most of this region the atmosphere is a good transmission medium.

The next most significant illuminator is the *laser*, which is an ac-

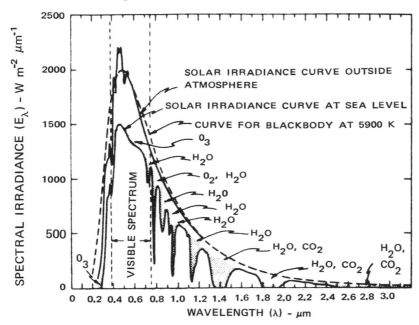

Figure 10–8. Spectral radiance E λ of the sun at mean earth-sun separation, indicating absorption at sea level due to atmospheric constituents shown. (From The Infrared Handbook)

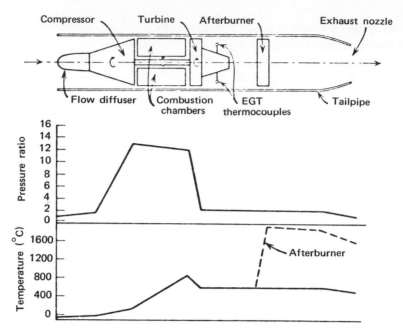

Figure 10–9. The turbojet engine. (From The Infrared Handbook)

ronym for "Light Amplification by Stimulated Emission of Radiation." Laser radiation is, for all practical purposes, concentrated at a single frequency. Lasers have been fabricated to operate at many different frequencies covering the optical and IR region.

The significant feature of lasers is that they provide coherent sources of extremely high radiance in the portion of the spectrum extending from the ultraviolet to microwaves. Research is currently underway to extend their capabilities to gamma and X rays. There are two major tactical implications of these characteristics of lasers. First, due to their coherence (which implies a nearly single frequency source), all the techniques and applications that have been developed in the radio and radar frequency range can be extended to the remainder of the electromagnetic spectrum. Second, because of the extremely high radiance and the extremely short wavelengths available, the laser has the potential of developing into a radiation weapon that can destroy or damage tactical targets. The significance of the short wavelength coupled with the coherence of the beam is that the beam can be focused to small areas on a target at long ranges.

Gas turbine engines such as the turbojet and turbo fan are tactically significant targets that radiate considerable energy due to the combustion process. There are two main sources of radiation from these engines: the hot metal tail pipe is a thermal radiator, and the stream of high-temperature exhaust gases is a spectral radiator. For a non-afterburning engine viewed from the rear, the radiation from the tail pipe is far greater than that from the plane. The tail pipe is effectively a cylindrical cavity that is heated by the exhaust gasses.

For engineering calculations, the non-afterburning turbojet engine can be considered to be a greybody, with an emissivity of 0.9, a temperature equal to the exhaust gas temperature, and an area equal to that of the nozzle. If, however, the afterburner is used, the plume becomes the dominant source. The plume radiance in any given circumstance depends on the number and temperature of the gas molecules in the exhaust stream. These values, in turn, depend on fuel consumption, which is a function of aircraft flight altitude and throttle setting.

Aerodynamic heating is another source of IR radiation. As an object moves at high speed through the atmosphere, it becomes heated, and at speeds above Mach 2, the resulting high temperatures produce sufficient radiation to be of interest. Space vehicles reentering the earth's atmosphere convert an enormous amount of kinetic energy into heat. Surface temperatures of 2,000°C and more can be expected.

Source Geometry

Infrared sources can be classed as either extended sources or point sources, depending on the relationship between their size, distance, and the dimensions of the detector aperture. An extended source is one that produces an image at the detector optics that is larger than the detector itself. A true point source, though imaginary, can be assumed when the range to the source is greater than ten times the largest dimension of the source. It should be clear that a source such as a ship's stack could be considered an extended source while measuring exhaust temperature with a radiometer at a distance of less than one meter, and be considered a point source when employing a tactical infrared device such as FLIR at a range of several kilometers.

Background

All detections of targets that depend on self-emission of the target (i.e., passive detection systems) are accomplished against some background that has a two-dimensional distribution of intensity and frequency. The background sources can be considered as noise that competes with the target source and can cause false alarms. Significant background sources include the earth, the sky, outer space, stars, and planets. During the daytime, the radiation from the surface of the earth is a combination of reflected and scattered sunlight and thermal emission from the earth itself. (When considered as backgrounds, stars and planets are of interest because they may be mistaken for targets.)

Optical Sensors

Visible Region Detectors

As noted earlier, the human eye is a key optical detector in the .4μ to .76μ region. In detecting small target patches against a background, an important factor is the target contrast against the background. Although not uniformly agreed upon, one concept most frequently used is the ratio $\Delta L/L$, where ΔL is the difference in luminance or brightness between target and background, and L is the brightness of the background. Low-light-level TV and starlight scopes are employed to improve the detection capability of the eye (i.e., they reduce the value of $\Delta L/L$ required for detection) in the visible region.

At low light levels, the fovea, or center of vision, is relatively blind, and a faint source can only be seen by looking slightly away from it— a fact well known to experienced night time lookouts. Dark adaptation is said to require up to 30 minutes, is not affected by deep red lights, and is rapidly destroyed by white and blue lights. Observers can see points separated by 1 to 3 minutes of arc, which is frequently cited as the resolution capability or acuity of the human eye. Due to diffraction limiting remarkably, one can see a telephone wire that subtends a size far below the "resolution" for two points. In fact, a line that subtends 0.5 sec of arc can be readily seen. The eye is very good at seeing straight lines, and this fact is frequently used to integrate patterns out of displays. The use of binoculars and telescopes to aid vision is a standard technique, yet for an extended object, such as the moon, the use of a telescope will, in fact, not increase the brightness over that as seen by the naked eye; it may even decrease the brightness. It will, of course, give magnification and permit smaller detail to be seen than with the unaided eye. If the target is a point light source such as a star, then use of a telescope will markedly increase the detectability of the point source over that of the unaided eye. The Navy 7 × 50 "night binoculars" are a familiar example of a device for seeing objects in very low light levels.

In addition to the human eye, another category of devices that are sensitive to visible light are photodetectors. These use the photon energy of the incident light to vary an electrical property of the sensor material. They may be divided into three major types—photoconductive, photovoltaic, and photoemissive. The photoconductive cell makes use of an element whose resistance varies when exposed to radiant energy. The elements usually employed are semiconductors such as lead sulfide and germanium, which may also be used as IR radiation detectors. The photovoltaic cell is used chiefly in photographic light meters. It produces small voltages in low resistance devices when exposed to light. Photoemissive cells produce an electrical charge when exposed to light waves. The photon energy produces a voltage potential that causes an emission of electrons, allowing the intensity to be determined. They are relatively insensitive, but provide high fidelity and low signal-to-noise levels. The exposed surface of the cathode element of a photoemissive cell is coated with cesium oxide or another light-sensitive electron-emitting material. The electrons emitted are collected by a positive anode and the output signal multiplied to a suitable level by subsequent amplifier stages.

Infrared Detectors

There are, in general, two classes of IR detectors—those depending on the heating effect of IR radiation, and those depending on the quantum nature of photons. The first group of sensors are called thermal detectors and are normally categorized as either radiometers, thermocouples, thermometers, or heat cells.

The second group of sensors are called semiconductor detectors, and they are by far the most important type of photon detector in use today. There are basically two types of semiconductor detectors, intrinsic and extrinsic. Intrinsic photodetectors involve "pure" semiconductor materials, while extrinsic photodetectors involve a given semiconductor material doped with specific "impurity" materials. Ex-

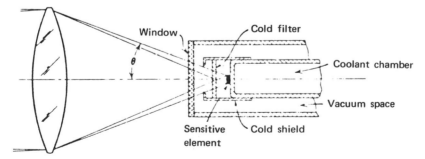

Figure 10–10. A semiconductor radiation-shielded IR detector package. (From Infrared Systems Engineering)

trinsic photodetectors have been made that are sensitive to wavelengths longer than 200μ, while intrinsic semiconductor photodetectors are limited to wavelengths below about 30μ.

Target Detection

The question "What targets can I see with IR viewers or Low-Light-Level (LLL) systems?" is like the question "How far can I see?"; the answer to each is "It all depends . . ." Still, it is possible to indicate a few general order-of-magnitude statements. Various levels of discrimination of targets have been defined by J. Johnson of the Army Warfare Division, Night Vision Laboratory, to be

1. Detection (an object is present)
2. Orientation (longitudinal axis can be sensed)
3. Recognition (class discerned)
4. Identification (types in class can be determined)

In all systems involving transmission or reception of electromagnetic radiation, the undesired factor of noise must be considered. For example, noise sources generated in IR systems are thermal fluctuations in the molecular structure of the detecting surface, or in the electronic circuitry associated with the system. The noise equivalent power (NEP) of a detector is the input radiant flux in watts necessary to give an output signal equal to the detector noise. The detector with the lower NEP has the higher useful sensitivity.

Although the amount of thermal power radiated by a source is important, the really significant quantity for detection is related to the *difference* in temperatures of the source and the thermal detector. The source will contribute power to the detector as a function of the source temperature; the detector will radiate away power in accordance with its temperature.

The difference between source and detector is as important as the difference between source and background. In other words, thermal detection, like all other detection schemes, is a differential process. The general detection problem is somewhat more complicated than suggested here. Not only must the source temperature and its emissivity be considered, but also its reflectivity and the thermal level and gradients in the surrounding environment.

As the wavelength of maximum radiation of the source and the wavelength that characterizes the temperature of the detector approach equality, the sensitivity of the detector is degraded by self-noise. According to Hudson, wavelengths greater than 8μ require progressively lower detector temperatures that approach absolute zero (0°K). Between 3μ and 8μ some cooling is required (to 77°K), and below 3μ (i.e., at very high source temperatures above 700°C) no cooling is required.

Optical and IR Imaging Systems

Image and camera tubes, or video cameras, are relatively important devices. The workhorse of video systems is the vidicon. A particular type of vidicon uses a thin-layer, high-resistivity photoconductive material as its photosensitive element. This layer is deposited on a transparent conducting backplate that in turn is supported by the glass faceplate of the tube. The backplate is maintained at a potential of about 30V more positive than the thermionic cathode, from which the beam electrons used to scan the exposed surface of the photo-conductive layer are emitted. The scanning beam drives the exposed surface to cathode potential at each scan; hence, an electric field is established through the layer. The scene is focused on the layer, and wherever the layer is illuminated, current passes through the layer; its exposed surface potential rises between scans to be driven back to cathode potential by deposition of beam electrons. This electric current that passes in the backplate circuit when electrons are so deposited is used as the output signal.

All other camera tubes operate in the photoemissive mode. The emitted electrons are accelerated by an electric field and impinge on a target that provides a current gain. These tubes lead into the area of Low Light Level Television. They include the Image Orthicon, the Image Isocon, the Silicon Intensifier Target (SIT), the Secondary Electron Conduction (SEC) tube, and the Image Intensifier. The standard vidicon may also be used as the sensor after several stages of intensification. The intensification is usually accomplished by using a photocathode on which the scene is focused, and then by focusing

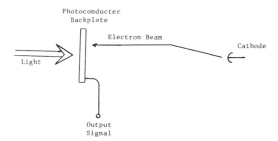

Figure 10–11. Schematic representation of vid-icon camera tube.

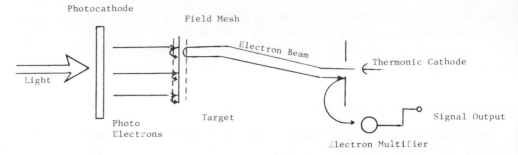

Figure 10–12. Schematic representation of image orthicon camera tube.

the emitted electrons on a phosphor that emits light in the pattern of the scene which is in turn focused on another photocathode, etc. It should be noted that image intensification need not be applied to TV-type systems and that many LLL direct-view systems are in use by the military. In these systems the eye views a phosphor, which is excited by electrons from several stages of intensification. Light gains of 1,000 to 10,000 are readily available. The systems provide the capability of viewing, with the light-adapted eye, a faintly illuminated scene that ordinarily would require the eye to be dark-adapted. Usually, a considerable degree of detail degradation is experienced in these systems.

It might be noted that none of these systems can "see" in complete darkness—some illumination is required from stars, moon, sky, etc. The only systems that can "see" in total darkness are the infrared systems that operate on self-emission and a contrast between targets and their surroundings. There is a continual argument about which is "better"—low-light-level systems or Forward-Looking-Infrared (FLIR) systems. The answer is neither. Under varying conditions, one or the other appears "better."

FLIR imaging sensors use an array of IR photosensitive detectors that are scanned across a scene to provide a TV-type thermal image of the scene. They operate in the $8\mu-14\mu$ spectral region, since as noted earlier, there is a very good atmospheric transmission window in this band. The primary tactical significance of IR imaging systems is that no illumination of the scene is required. Unfortunately, FLIRs are not "all weather." Clouds, rain, humidity, or other moisture absorbs and scatters infrared energy, thus reducing FLIR range compared to that of a microwave sensor, like radar. But in contrast to the human eye or other visual sensors, FLIR can more readily penetrate light fog and especially haze. Under such conditions, infrared range can be three to six times that of visual range.

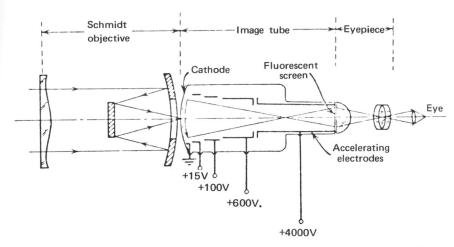

Figure 10–13a. Infrared telescope using an electrostatic image tube. (From Infrared System Engineering)

Figure 10–13b. Infrared seeker head for a Sidewinder missile.

Performance factors of most interest for a FLIR sensor are its thermal resolution and its angular resolution. The thermal resolution is the temperature difference between two adjacent parts of a scene that can just be distinguished on the output image. The angular resolution is the angular separation between two points in the scene (which are temperature resolvable) at which the two points can just be distinguished. The relationship between thermal resolution and angular resolution is an inverse relationship, so that the smaller or better the angular resolution, the larger or poorer the thermal resolution. The angular resolution is simply the field of view of an individual detector, and the smaller the detector, the better the angular resolution. Thus, there is a trade-off between thermal and angular resolutions that is influenced by detector size. With the FLIR systems, angular resolutions of less than a milliradian are readily achievable, while thermal resolutions of hundredths of a degree centigrade can be achieved. Unfortunately, these high-angular and thermal resolutions cannot be achieved with one system.

Since FLIR systems respond to thermal contrasts, they work better at night when warm bodies stand out more clearly against the cooler ambient temperature background. It is also interesting to note that they can detect a submarine periscope in total darkness from the temperature gradient in the periscope's wake.

Example Detection Problem

A NASA substation has been directed to track a space vehicle during reentry. Given the following data, at what range will the target be detected?

Surface area of vehicle: $125m^2$
Detector Bandwidth: 3μ to 5μ
Heat-shield emissivity: .7
Vehicle skin temperature: $575°C$
Environment temperature at re-entry altitude: $-180°C$
IR detector aperture: $1.5m^2$
IR detector MDS: $61.1 \times 10^{-7}w$
$\sigma = 5.67 \times 10^{-12}w/cm^2°K^4$
$A = 2898\mu°K$

Target detection is reasonable (i.e., 50%) when the signal reaching the receiver equals the minimum discernable signal (MDS). The first step is to determine the energy leaving the spacecraft utilizing equation (10–3).

First convert to absolute temperature:
skin temperature: $575°C + 273° = 848°K$
environment temperature: $-180°C + 273° = 93°K$

Equation 10–3 $E = \varepsilon \sigma (T^4 - T_e^4)$

Substituting: $E = (.7)(5.67 \times 10^{-12})(848^4 - 93^4)$
$E = 2.05$ watts/cm^2

Note: This is energy density or energy per unit area. We must convert to total energy by multiplying by the total surface area of the spacecraft. Remember, the surface area of the spacecraft is in m², not cm².

$$E_{TOT} = E \times \text{surface area}$$

$$= 2.05 \text{ w/cm}^2 \times 125\text{m}^2 \times \frac{10^4 \text{ cm}^2}{1\text{m}^2}$$

$$= 2.56 \times 10^6 \text{ watts}$$

This value of E_{TOT} is the total energy radiated by the spacecraft at all wavelengths. The detector in this case will use only that energy within its bandwidth of 3μ to 5μ; therefore, we must employ figure 10–4 to calculate the radiated energy within this band.

For this band $\lambda T = 2,544$ to $4,240$ for the spacecraft at 848°K.

Entering figure 10–4 with 2,544 we find that
.1 of the total energy is below this value and
.5 of the total energy is below the upper value for λT of 4,240.

Subtracting .1 from .5 we have .4, therefore, the total energy within the bandwidth of the detector is:

$$.4 \times (2.56 \times 10^6) \text{ or } 1.024 \times 10^6 \text{ watts}$$

The total energy output of the spacecraft (E_{TOT}) is radiated uniformly in all directions. Therefore, to express the energy density at some range R, we must divide by the surface area of the imaginary sphere of radius R.

$$\text{Energy density at range } R = \frac{E_{TOT}}{4\pi R^2}$$

Total energy available to the IR detector at range R is equal to the energy density at range R times the detector aperture.
Thus:

$$E_{TOT} \text{ at range } R = \frac{1.024 \times 10^6 \text{ watts}}{4\pi R^2} \times 1.5\text{m}^2$$

We can make the assumption that distance in this case is greater than ten times the largest dimension of the spacecraft; therefore, we will assume it to be a point source.

Detection probability is 50% if $E_{TOT} = MDS$, which will occur at some range, thus:

$$61.1 \times 10^{-7} = \frac{1.024 \times 10^6 \text{ watts}}{4\pi R^2} \times 1.5\text{m}^2$$

Solving for R we have:

$$R = \sqrt{\frac{1.024 \times 10^6 \text{w} \times 1.5\text{m}^2}{4\pi \times 61.1 \times 10^{-7}\text{w}}}$$

therefore:

$$R = 141.44 \text{ km.}$$

Laser Fundamentals

There are two basic approaches that can be taken to develop light sources with the power-per-unit frequency of radio frequency devices; either extend electronic oscillator principles to the shorter optical wavelengths, or find some way to get atomic or molecular oscillators to work together.

The first approach requires building resonant structures with dimensions on the order of the wavelength being generated. Electronic resonators have been built to generate wavelengths down to one millimeter, while optical wavelengths are about 1,000 times shorter. It has not been found *feasible* to build resonators down to this size. The second approach is the principle on which first the Maser (for Microwave Amplification by Stimulated Emission of Radiation, by C. H. Townes in 1951) and then the Laser (for Light . . ., etc., by T. H. Maiman in 1960) were conceived and built.

The key to synchronizing the large number of atomic and molecular oscillators available in any given mass of material is the phenomenon, first described by Einstein in 1917, of stimulated emission. Normally when a photon is absorbed by an atom, the energy of the photon is converted to internal energy of the atom, and it is said that the atom is in an "excited" state. Generally, this is not a stable state, having a short lifetime, and the atom will eventually radiate this excess energy spontaneously and revert to the "ground" state (i.e., the stable state). Some atoms, however, retain these electrons in this "excited" state for a much longer period of time.

If the atom can be struck by a photon of energy $h\upsilon$ while in the excited stage, the atom is stimulated to make an immediate transition to the ground state and give off a photon in a process called stimulated emission. This process is shown in figure 10–14.

Note that in our simplified two-level laser, the incident photon must have an energy of exactly $h\upsilon = E_2 - E_1$. Also, in order to have a surplus of atoms in the higher state E_2, a population inversion must

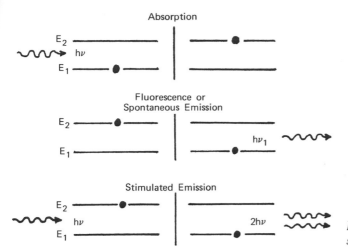

Figure 10–14. Stimulated emission schematic.

take place to cause a majority of atoms to be in the higher state. This "population inversion" normally cannot be achieved in a simple two-level laser system as depicted above. Instead, a three-level system, one ground level and two excited levels, can easily achieve a population inversion if one of the excited states has a lifetime much longer ($\sim$ 1 msec) than the other excited state.

The engineering problem in designing a laser is preparing an "active medium," in which most of the atoms can be placed in an excited state, so that a wave of photons of the right frequency passing through them will stimulate a cascade of photons. There must be an excess of excited atoms to enable stimulated emission to predominate over absorption. In a multistate laser, atoms can be raised to an excited state by injecting into the system electromagnetic energy at a wavelength different from the stimulating wavelength; this activating process is called "pumping."

As an example, the first laser to be constructed by Maiman consisted of a single crystal of synthetic pink ruby, Al_2O_3, doped with the addition of an impurity, Cr_2O_3. The inert aluminum and oxygen atoms suspend the chromium atoms that actually form the active medium. Figure 10–15 shows a ruby laser pumped with a helical flash lamp.

With low levels of pumping energy, coherent fluorescence in the red at $.694\mu$ occurs; however, the line width is rather large, as with most spontaneous secondary emission. Nevertheless, if the pumping energy exceeds a certain threshold, see figure 10–16, the characteristic narrow line of the laser results. This effect is due to the active medium and the fact that the ruby is in an optically resonant cavity.

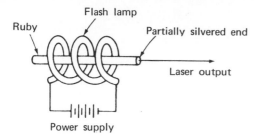

Flash lamp

Ruby

Partially silvered end

Laser output

Power supply

Figure 10–15. Ruby laser with helical flash tube.

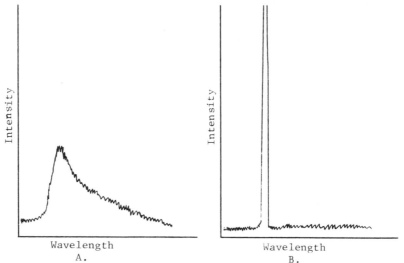

Figure 10–16. Energy emitted from ruby becomes more monochromatic as the pumping energy is increased. A: spectral output below; B: above lasing threshold.

The mirrored end faces are polished flat and parallel to each other while separated by an integral number of half wavelengths. Typically, one end is coated to about 100% and the other to about 50%. A process of multiple reflection called avalanche action, analogous to a ping pong ball and two paddles, one missing 50% of the shots, causes a photon cascade resulting in a pulse of light that is monochromatic, coherent, and has very little divergence.

Optically resonant cavities may use combinations of plane and spherical mirrors or diffraction gratings. The plane parallel cavity in figure 10–17 is found in almost all pulsed solid-state lasers. The field between the mirrors may be regarded as the superposition of plane waves traveling back and forth longitudinally. A standing wave pattern leads to reinforcement when the distance of the mirrors is an integral number of the half-wavelength. Reinforcement takes place when

$$n\lambda = 2L \qquad (10-6)$$

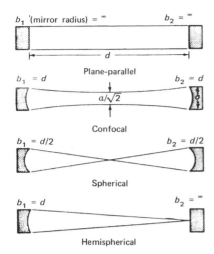

Figure 10–17. Laser cavity configurations.

where

n is an integer, in the order of 100,000 for a ruby laser a few cm long.

λ is the wavelength in the laser material.

L is the distance between mirrors.

The confocal cavity has two identical spherical mirrors separated by a distance equal to their radius of curvature. Confocal configurations are normally used because of their ease of adjustment and high power output (several orders of magnitude over the parallel plane due to diminished off-axis losses). Most continuous wave gas lasers use the confocal configuration, the hemispherical being about one-half as efficient, and the spherical being hard to align.

To operate a laser in a continuous mode, continuous excitation must be provided to maintain the population inversion necessary to replenish those atoms de-excited by stimulated emission. Light that comes from a laser is characterized by the following properties:

(1) Monochromaticity—Laser light comes predominantly from a particular energy level associated with a particular wavelength selected by the optical length of the cavity. Normally it is desirable to have only one line present, thus the light is almost always monochromatic. Thermal vibration of the active medium's atoms will cause doppler broadening of the line width, and the presence of impurities may cause other wavelengths to be present. Temporal (or time) coherence is sometimes used to describe the single frequency characteristic of lasers.

(2) Coherence—Coherence is that property whereby all waves

have fixed phases relative to each other. Laser light is coherent as it emerges from the laser output mirror and remains so for a certain "coherence length." Slight variations in the mechanical, acoustical, and thermal stability of the laser will adversely affect the frequency stability of the laser. The spatial coherence length of a He-Ne gas CW laser, known for its stability, is typically about 30 km for a shift in frequency of 1/2 the line width. The ruby laser is fairly unstable, having a coherence length of about one meter.

(3) Divergence—Because the laser light emerges perpendicular to the output mirror, the beam has very little divergence, typically in the order of one milliradian. These beamwidths are considerably larger than predicted by diffraction theory due to the output mirror's non-uniform illumination. With careful design a laser beam can be made to have a divergence nearly equal to the diffraction limit or

$$\Theta_0 = \frac{1.22\lambda}{d} \qquad (10\text{--}7)$$

where

Θ_0 is the angular distance from the first null to the center of the diffraction pattern.

d is the diameter of the beam emerging from the laser or any subsequent lenses.

Unlike incoherent sources, which cannot be focused to achieve images with higher intensity than originally emitted, the laser can be concentrated into a spot as small as one wavelength in diameter. The nearly parallel beam from a 50-kw infrared neodymium laser can be focused down to a radiant power density of 10^{12} watts/cm², about 100 million times the power density at the surface of the sun.

(4) Power—Most lasers operate at rather low efficiencies, usually

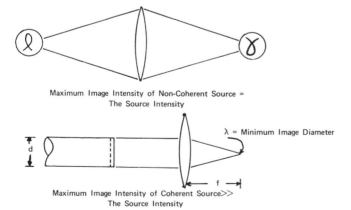

Maximum Image Intensity of Non-Coherent Source =
The Source Intensity

λ = Minimum Image Diameter

Maximum Image Intensity of Coherent Source>>
The Source Intensity

Figure 10–18. Coherent vs non-coherent imaging.

at best only a few percent. Pulsed lasers are no exception. They are able to deliver relatively low energy outputs; however, the very short duration pulses result in very high power outputs. A typical 1-cm-diameter, 4-cm-long ruby laser might be pumped by a xenon flash lamp discharging 1,000 Joules from a capacitor bank. An overall efficiency of $n = .1\%$, which is reasonable, yields an output energy of only 1.0 Joule, although the power output is 2 kw due to the pulse width of .5 milliseconds. A pulsed solid-state ruby laser requires PRTs of the order of ten seconds to allow for heat dissipation. Although pulsed lasers have been built that deliver 250 Joules in 5 nanoseconds for a power output of 50 gigawatts, repeated pulses must be delayed to allow sufficient cooling.

Elemental and molecular gases, liquid chemicals, and fluorescent dyes have been used, both in pulse and continuous wave with flowing active media in liquid states to aid in heat transfer. Typical CW lasers deliver energies comparable to pulsed lasers; however, their power outputs are far lower, normally one watt or less. Very large CO_2 lasers greatly in excess of 1 kw continuous power have been operated for limited durations. Chemical lasers have been operated at power levels over 400 kw.

Example: A satellite-borne IR carbon dioxide laser with an exit diameter of 2 cm, continuous power of 1,000 watts, and a divergence of .1 milliradian is to be targeted against a ballistic warhead 1 km away. Calculate the IR intensity on the target.
The sun delivers about 1,400 W/m² just outside the atmosphere.

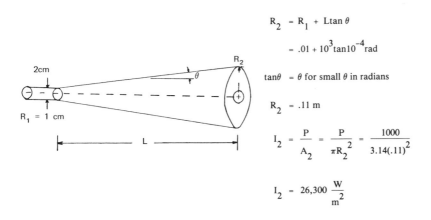

$$R_2 = R_1 + L\tan\theta$$

$$= .01 + 10^3 \tan 10^{-4} \, \text{rad}$$

$$\tan\theta = \theta \text{ for small } \theta \text{ in radians}$$

$$R_2 = .11 \, \text{m}$$

$$I_2 = \frac{P}{A_2} = \frac{P}{\pi R_2^2} = \frac{1000}{3.14(.11)^2}$$

$$I_2 = 26,300 \, \frac{W}{m^2}$$

Table 10–2. Typical Laser Characteristics

Active Ion Host Material	Wavelength (μm)	Power	Applications
Neon/Helium (gas)	0.6328 (red)	0.5 to 100 mW (cw)	General purpose, ranging, alignment, communication
AR/Argon (gas)	0.4880 (green)	0.1 to 5W (cw) 10–100W (pulsed)	Heating, welding, communication
CO_2/Carbon Dioxide (gas)	10.6 (IR)	0 to 1 kW (cw) 0 to 100 kW	Cutting, welding, communication, vaporization, drilling
Chromium/Ruby (solid)	0.6943 (red)	0 to 1 GW (pulse)	Cutting, welding, vaporization, drilling, ranging
Neodymium/ Glass (solid)	1.06 (IR)	0 to 1 GW (pulse)	Cutting, welding, vaporization, drilling, communication, tactical military uses

Laser Applications

Laser Weapons

It was originally thought that the most powerful lasers to be built would be of the solid-state variety; for the simple reason that in a solid the active "lasing" particles are more highly concentrated than in a rarified gas. Instead, the problem limiting the power levels of early lasers was that the process that excited the population inversion within the laser device simultaneously generated considerable waste heat that was difficult to dissipate. This wasted heat adversely affects the performance of the optical medium and poses a fundamental limitation on the attainment of high average power output of any laser device.

Because heat transfer by diffusion and conduction to the cavity walls limited static lasers to a maximum output of about 1 kw/meter in length (independent of CW/pulse mode or diameter), dynamic lasers with flowing active media were developed.

Solid-state and static liquid- and gaseous-state lasers commonly use light, high-voltage electric discharge, or RF energy to pump their nonflowing active media: the ruby laser, helium-neon laser, and the ammonium laser.

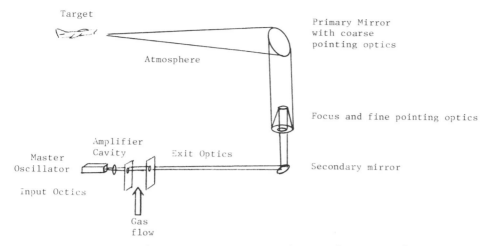

Figure 10–19. Representative high-energy gas dynamic laser optical train.

Three different types of high-energy laser devices are considered potential candidates for continuous wave (CW) and pulsed high-power applications suitable for weapons applications. These devices, which include the Gas Dynamic Laser (GDL), the Electro-Discharge Laser (EL) and the Chemical Laser (CL) use inter-molecular collision, electrical discharge, and the heat of formation of a chemical reaction (hydrogen fluoride) as respective methods of exciting their active media. The gas dynamic laser may operate as either a closed-cycle or an open-cycle device, achieving supersonic flow velocities to aid in both pumping the active medium to an excited state and to rid the device of wasted heat. Figure 10–19 depicts a typical GDL optical train. Note transverse flow, perpendicular to the optical axis, and the fact that all the optical elements are front surface mirrors, necessary to avoid absorption and subsequent heat damage if refractive lenses were used.

A decade ago, it was thought that the only significant obstacle to radiation weapons was achieving sufficiently high energy levels. Today it is recognized that the concept faces a very broad spectrum of technical challenges, possibly more difficult than those that faced the nation's intercontinental ballistic missile and nuclear weapon programs in earlier decades. Foremost of these is that high-energy laser technology is not easily translated from the relatively benign environment of the laboratory to the rigors of military vehicles. Other problems include the extremely precise beam-aiming/tracking system and optical elements that can reflect/pass high-energy laser radiation without damage to themselves, and the development of lightweight power supplies, suitable for military use.

Additionally, there are obstacles to high-energy laser propagation through the atmosphere, imposed by nature, and the complex effects of pulsed radiation on target materials, some of which function to screen the target from the laser. While there is cautious optimism that these problems ultimately can be solved, it is not yet clear whether radiation weapons will be cost-effective in the most promising near-term applications, such as close-in air defense, in competition with more conventional missiles and guns.

High Energy Propagation Effects

When high energy electromagnetic waves are propagated through the atmosphere, there are a number of propagation effects that can present problems. These propagation effects include the following and are discussed from the standpoint of the laser weapon application.

Absorption of beam energy, principally due to water vapor and carbon dioxide for the 10.6μ wavelength, can be a problem. Water vapor absorption is of greater consequence at the surface and at low altitude than at high altitude, where radiation weapons might be used for bomber defense. Also significant, especially at the shorter wavelengths, is scattering due to water vapor and airborne particulate matter.

Turbulence-induced beam spreading, which results from refractive index variations along the laser beam path due to density variations, is also more severe for lasers that operate at shorter wavelengths. The problem is more severe at sea level than at higher altitude.

Thermal blooming is a beam-defocusing effect that occurs because the air in the beam path is heated by radiation energy, changing its index of refraction. Under certain conditions this can waste 90% of the beam energy unless corrective steps are taken. The thermal blooming problem can be eased by using a pulsed-laser whose pulses are sufficiently brief that the air does not have time to heat up sufficiently to cause serious defocusing. If the time interval between successive pulses is sufficiently long, motion of the laser beam as it tracks a moving target in combination with natural air-mass movement will cause the next pulse to transit through a new shaft of cooler air. Apparent motion may also be provided by the movement of the aircraft equipped with the laser.

Rangefinders and Laser "Radars"

Laser radars are, in a systems analysis sense, identical to microwave radars; i.e., the same equations apply in regard to operating range, jamming vulnerability, scanning, etc. The major difference in shorter wavelength has provided better range and angular resolution, due to interferometry techniques and narrow beam divergence. Because of the limited field of view the laser radar can handle, it cannot be considered for the search function, but is better suited to operate as a tracker. The potential exists for laser radars to be used for imaging, although this future application has yet to be realized.

The combination of high peak powers and monochromaticity made the laser rangefinder an instant success in high-resolution distance measurement. The narrowness of the frequency line radiated by the laser greatly enhances the capability of the laser as an optical or IR sensor, since the receiver bandwidth can be correspondingly narrowed to eliminate the wider bandwidth noise. The net effect is an increase in signal-to-noise ratio.

The basic techniques for laser rangefinding include pulse and continuous waveforms as with radio frequency and acoustic ranging devices. The pulse techniques simply involve measuring the time interval between the pulse leaving the laser and a reflected return from some target. Field ranging units have been built that are small, easily portable, and are capable of ranging targets 10 kilometers away with an accuracy of 10 meters. Additional rangefinder functions may include range gating and multiple target recognition. Continuous wave (CW) laser rangefinders use the delay between transmission and reception of a modulated signal to determine the range. The maximum range capability of CW systems is less than the pulsed systems because of their lower peak powers. However, ranges may be improved significantly by using corner reflectors on the target. CW rangefinders may be calibrated to accuracies of about 1 part per million.

Optical heterodyne systems, employed to obtain range rate information, carry the information by slight variations in the frequency of the radiation. The reflected radiation is made to interfere with the transmitted radiation or with some reference radiation on a photodetector. The resulting fringe pattern movement on the detector generates a beat frequency equal to the frequency difference, and can be related to the range rate of the target with respect to the detector.

Laser Target Designators

During the past few years, increasing attention by the military has been given to developing electro-optical techniques to improve weapons guidance and delivery. Use of laser-guided weapons has resulted in an order of magnitude increase in accuracy of weapon delivery, so that direct hits are almost guaranteed.

Target designators are semiactive illuminators used to "tag" a target. Typical designators, like rangefinders, possess high peak power, short pulsewidth, and narrow beam characteristics for precise target designations. Lasers with a train of narrow pulses are generally used. Designators are generally employed by artillery spotters or in conjunction with laser search/track receivers in aircraft or aboard ship.

Laser search/track receivers detect and locate the laser energy being reflected off an illuminated target. Deployed in aircraft, helicopters, and laser-guided weapons, a laser tracker can be expected to have an angle tracking precision of about 20 microradians. Since the target location is unknown, a wide field of view, typically 10 to 20 degrees, must be provided by a large-area detector. In many cases the large-area detector is divided into a quad-cell array to provide angular information for laser tracking.

Typical laser-guided bomb receivers use an array of photodiodes to derive target angular position signals. These signals produce control surface movements to direct the weapon to the target. An airborne detector can provide steering information to the pilot, via his gunsight, for example, and lead him on a direct heading to the target, finally giving him an aim point for a conventional weapon. Alternatively, a laser-guided "smart" bomb or missile may be launched when a pilot is satisfied that the detector head has achieved lock-on and the launch envelope requirements are satisfied. In either of these cases, the pilot may never see the actual target, only the aim point as indicated by the laser. A laser seeker located in the nose of the weapon is used to home in on a target illuminated by a laser designator.

Laser Communication Devices

In the field of communications, the laser offers two unusual advantages. The first of these pertains to the bandwidth. It is known that the rate at which information can be transmitted, or the number of channels that can be multiplexed on an information carrier, is proportional to the bandwidth, which is, in turn, proportional to the carrier frequency. Thus, the step from microwaves to the optical region expands the available bandwidth by a factor of 10,000 or more. By developing and employing the proper methods of modulation and demodulation, a single laser could replace all the present information-carrying systems between the east and west coasts of the United

States. Some laser communications systems are beginning to be employed; however, the full potential for these applications are still in need of further development.

The second immediate advantage of lasers in connection with long-range information transmission is the ability of aiming and concentrating the carrier energy in the proper direction. A point-to-point communication link requires a narrow beam, and the narrowness of a microwave beam is limited by the size of the antennas employed. Antennas of considerable size are required to produce a beam only a few degrees wide in the centimeter wavelength region. For laser light, the dimensions of the radiator required for the same gain are decreased by a factor of 10,000. In fact, at a wavelength of 1 micron or less the practical beamwidth is limited by secondary considerations, not by the size of the radiator. It is not at all difficult to obtain beamwidth of a few milliradians.

One of the important advantages of laser line-of-sight communications is that the laser beam has effectively no sidelobes. This factor, coupled with its narrow beamwidth, should provide covert communications capabilities in tactical situations.

Tactical Considerations

As has already been indicated, the functional use of E-O equipments will frequently parallel and augment the capabilities of other non-E-O equipments, such as RF radar or communication systems. E-O systems will be used, for example, for target detection, tracking and identification, fire control, surveillance, threat warning, damage assessment, communications, etc. It is likely that some new E-O systems will not have only a single function, but will have multifunctional capabilities. For example, a high-energy laser at long ranges could be used as a target designator for E-O homing missiles or projectiles; at intermediate ranges, the same device could serve as an antisensor weapon, whereas at short ranges the equipment could be employed as an antistructure optical radiation weapon. It is probable, however, that most operational functions will be carried out by optimized individual E-O systems, rather than by non-optimal centralized E-O systems.

Also it should be noted that even though E-O systems are designed to perform the same functions as RF and microwave systems, their characteristics will, in many cases, be different because of the much higher frequency of E-O radiation and because of environmental influences. By way of illustration, many military applications require the use of minimally divergent beams; the beam divergence of E-O beams can be one hundred to one thousand times less than that of a high-quality microwave beam. However, the small probability of intercepting the E-O system would be increased if there were present a high aerosol content in the line-of-sight path, which would side-scatter a portion of the optical signals. The range at which this scattered radiation could be detected could depend on environmental conditions.

Passive detection systems for detecting targets in a search mode continue to be of great interest and potential importance to the military planner. The infrared search set is considered a highly desirable device, particularly for use in EMCON conditions and against incoming aircraft. It would make a useful adjunct to radar. Consider that it has the potential for better detection than radar against incoming low-level attacks and that the high resolution may offer an evaluation of the number of incoming targets. The system would not be affected by enemy electronic countermeasures—although IR countermeasures are conceivable. The systems will work at short (25 km) range against low targets; and could work independently of the search radar and during an RF EMCON condition. They are not all-weather and will not detect targets through clouds or fog. The technology for 360° search is under investigation.

The concept of using an active optical illuminator for large-volume search is simply not feasible. The average power required becomes far too large. Accordingly, optical radar should not be expected to play any role in large-volume search. Once the volume has been reduced, optical radar can provide precision bearing, range, and doppler within the smaller volume.

Passive tracking is possible and has been carried out. Daytime tracking in the visible spectrum is possible with TV-type contrast trackers with very high precision. Because the precision is usually obtained with magnification, the target is readily identified. Identification should be readily achievable at 20 kilometers, and tracking to 20 microradians seems quite feasible.

The infrared guided missile is probably the best-known military application of infrared. Laser designation and TV guidance came out of the SEA theater and have slipped over into the Middle East. A review of weapons employing E-O guidance shows that the U.S.S.R. has deployed a sizable array of such weapons. This trend indicates that optical countermeasures are increasingly important.

As discussed previously, the possible application of the laser as a radiation weapon is currently under intensive investigation. There are many technological questions that must be answered before the potential of laser weapons can be properly assessed. The development of such a weapon will undoubtedly revolutionize the tactics in many areas of warfare. Perhaps the primary arena for the laser weapon is in space. In space there is no attenuating atmosphere, and line-of-sight distances are vast.

The requirements for E-O countermeasures are dictated by the severity of the E-O threat. As the tactical deployment of E-O missile seekers, fire control sensors, reconnaissance, surveillance, and other E-O seekers proliferates, the need for an effective means of countering them will become more urgent. These countermeasures can take the form of active or passive devices, techniques, or procedures. Active devices include such items as flare, modulated radiation, and laser jammers. Passive approaches include such items as camouflage, engine IR suppression, and absorbing materials. Thus, the primary tactical implication is that further payload weight will need to be sacrificed to electronic warfare devices carried aboard our platforms and those of the enemy.

References

Commander, Naval Ordnance Systems Command. *Elements of Weapons Systems*. NAVORD OP 3000, vol. 1, 1st Rev. Washington, D.C.: GPO, 1971.

Editor. *High Energy Laser Systems*. Concord, Mass.: General Enterprise, 1978.

Gebbie, H. A., et al. "Atmospheric Transmission in the 1 to 14μ Region," *Proc. Roy. Soc.* A206, 87 (1951).

Hudson, Richard. *Infrared System Engineering*. New York: John Wiley & Sons, 1969.

Kemp, Barron. *Modern Infrared Technology*. Indianapolis, Ind.: Howard W. Sams & Co., 1962.

Meyer-Arenot, Jurgen. *Introduction to Classical and Modern Optics*. Englewood Cliffs, N.J.: Prentice-Hall, Inc., 1972.

Morgan, Joseph. *Introduction to Geometrical and Physical Optics*. New York: McGraw-Hill, 1953.

Naval Operations Department, U.S. Naval War College. *Technological Factors and Constraints in System Performance Study-Electro-Optics*. Vol. I–1, 1975.

RCA Corporation. *RCA Electro-Optics Handbook*. Technical Series EOH-11, 1974.

Wolfe, William L., ed. *Handbook of Military Infrared Technology*. Washington, D.C.: GPO, 1965.

Wolfe, William L., and George T. Ziss, eds. *The Infrared Handbook*. Washington, D.C.: GPO, 1978.

11

Countermeasures

Introduction

Countermeasures are a rapidly growing field, a field that is demonstrating its vital influence on both tactical and strategic decisions. Although countermeasures date back to World War I, the events of recent years (i.e., the Vietnam and Middle East wars) and recent technological advances have rapidly accelerated the development of this facet of modern warfare. Countermeasures include all those means of exploiting an adversary's own activity as a means of determining his intentions or reducing his effectiveness. This involves using energy radiated as a result of an adversary's presence or activity as a means of detection and identification of his weapon systems and platforms. In addition, weaknesses in sensors, fuzes, computer processing, and personnel training are exploited to deceive an adversary as to the actual tactical situation or cause malfunction of his equipment.

Electronic Warfare

An editorial in *Aviation Week & Space Technology* magazine accurately reflects the revolutionary impact of EW.

Electronic warfare has wrought some revolutionary changes in modern military operations. The electronically guided missiles carried by small fast patrol boats, submarines and aircraft have swiftly changed the large aircraft carrier task forces of the surface navy from a powerful offensive asset to a potential defensive liability. The electronic detection, tracking and guidance systems of anti-aircraft missiles have forced attack aircraft into new defenses with electronic countermeasure jamming and deception and "hard kill" missiles that use the electromagnetic radiation of enemy weapons to find and destroy them. The tank, which for so long reigned on the surface battlefield, has become tremendously vulnerable to electronic warfare, both from the ground and from the air.

It is imperative that professional military officers have a basic understanding of electronic warfare. This section is designed to create an awareness and assist the reader in developing an appreciation for some of the capabilities, limitations, and applications of EW. It is included with sensor systems because EW is directly interrelated with sensors and in one sense, are themselves an extremely valuable sensor, frequently providing the commander with the initial enemy detection. The importance of EW in today's highly complex and heavily electronically dependent order of battle cannot be over emphasized.

Basic EW Receivers

The EW receiver is the primary Electronic Support Measures (ESM) equipment and functions as a sensor for, and as a means of identifying, friendly, neutral, and enemy electronic emissions. It provides warning of potential attack, knowledge of enemy capabilities, and an indication of enemy use of active countermeasures to manipulate the electromagnetic spectrum. The design of the electronic warfare receiver provides a special challenge to the engineer, in that no single antenna system or specific receiver circuit can cover the entire range of the electromagnetic spectrum. A set of components can be designed to provide maximum efficiency over a range of up to a few thousand megahertz; however, current requirements demand performance from a few kHz to 50 GHz with a wide range of signal strengths and other parameters such as pulse width, PRF, scan rate, side-band characteristics, and modulation. The solution has been to connect many different frequency-sensitive circuits called tuners and their associated preamplifiers to a common chain of main amplifiers and display or data-storage units. The following are the primary design criteria for EW receivers:

ESM Receiver Design Requirements

The basic problem of EW is obviously to obtain the raw data, which in turn is analyzed to determine the enemy threat. To obtain this data, the collection station will have to have dedicated receiving equipment. The EW receiver differs from an ordinary receiver both in its essential design and in the auxiliary equipment associated with it. The essential requirements are:

Wide spectrum surveillance (wide bandwidth capability). The frequency of the enemy radar is not known beforehand. This means, with present technology, that the frequency spectrum must be searched from 30 kHz to 50 GHz. This range is too large for one receiver to portray, so that either several different ECM receivers with different tuning ranges must be used or one receiver must use different tuning units to cover different parts of the frequency range.

Wide dynamic range. The receiver must be able to receive both very weak and very strong signals without changing its characteristics, for the receiver is not always operating at great distances from a radar, but may in fact be very close. It would be undesirable for the resulting strong signal to disable the analysis capability.

Unwanted signal-rejection (narrow bandpass). Many other signals will exist, with frequencies close to the signal of interest. The receiver should discriminate well between the frequency it is tuned to and signals at other frequencies.

Angle-of-arrival measurement capability. This allows for locating the transmitter by taking bearings at different times (different aircraft/ ship geographical positions). Plotting these different bearings on a chart will locate the transmitter by triangulation. An airborne or ground-based digital computer can also be programmed to perform the same function. In single ship or submarine operations, a location including estimated range can be determined by plotting successive bearing cuts on a DRT or NC2 plotter and employing Target Motion Analysis (TMA) or Eklund ranging methods.

Signal analysis capability. This provides a means of determining the signal modulation, sidebands, pulse width, and PRF. From this information the signal can be identified and associated with a specific threat or platform. This is most effectively performed by a digital computer, but can be done by manual analysis and consulting publications.

Display. The type of display is dictated by the way in which the receiver is used. This varies between the "Fuzzbuster"-type warning light and audio tone device of Vietnam-era fighter aircraft detection systems to very complex signal analysis scopes and computer-controlled alphanumeric displays on CRTs.

Recording system. There is great intelligence value in electronic emissions of all types, including commercial TV, radio, and computer data. For this reason ships, aircraft, submarines, and Marine units are equipped with magnetic tape and other devices to record emissions for further analysis at major intelligence centers.

The basic operational approach is to make a signal collection a three-stage process: *warning*, *sorting*, and *analysis*. *Signal warning*, which alerts the operator to the presence of a signal, may be provided by audio modulation in the operator's earphones, a flashing light, or the presence of a line on a cathode ray tube (CRT). *Signal sorting* often

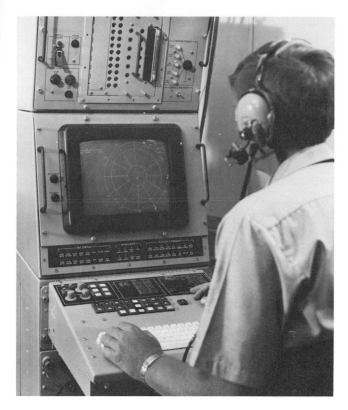

Figure 11–1. AN/SLQ-32 ESM receiver display.

follows immediately after warning and uses the imprecise warning data about the signal frequency and modulation to sort out the signals of immediate interest. (Signal frequency and modulation usually correlate with the degree of threat each signal presents). The amount of data presented to the EW operator depends upon the specific mission requirements, and the amount of equipment that is available. The airborne operator usually has less time and equipment available than a ground-station operator. The airborne operator, however, is more vulnerable to expected threats, so he is provided with more equipment to perform the warning and sorting function. *Signal analysis* includes determining the transmitter's specific capabilities and characteristics for both immediate and future actions. It should not be confused with signal sorting, which usually is to determine only the immediate action required. The current trend appears to be that the airborne data needed for analysis are automatically recorded for later analysis on the ground. Thus, the airborne operator concerns himself primarily with signals that present an immediate threat to the aircraft, unusual signals, and signals of great interest that require immediate

Countermeasures   **329**

analysis. As he is able, the EW operator will analyze signals and record the results as a back-up in case the automatically recorded data are lost. The shipboard operator with additional personnel will be able to analyze the signals almost as they are received.

Electronic Countermeasures

The second major division of Electronic Warfare is ECM, and of the three divisions it is probably the best known. Partly this is because ECM tends to be visualized as "black boxes" that display a visible realization of electronic warfare. Often it appears that if one understands the black boxes, then one has an understanding of ECM, but such an attitude is very narrow because it ignores the total problem of the employment of ECM in warfare. Thus, the approach in this section will be more general; an attempt will be made to lay down the framework within which the black boxes function.

Of the two types of electromagnetic radiating systems against which ECM may be employed—either sensors and/or communications systems—enemy sensors receive by far the greatest attention. The primary reasons for this fact are: (1) the enemy sensor system produces an immediate threat, whereas the communications system does not, and (2) the sensor system is usually specifically directed toward the friendly forces, and communications are not.

The emphasis of ECM employment in this section will be against sensor systems. However, some mention of the theory and practice of employing ECM against communications systems is considered appropriate, particularly in the contemporary Navy, which is so heavily dependent upon communications—including the various computer data links that provide the backbone to the fleet-wide command and control efforts.

From a strategic point of view, using ECM against an enemy communications system is questionable, for by so doing the opportunity to gain valuable information by eavesdropping is lost. Tactically, however, it may be very advantageous to jam the enemy communications system in order to cause a breakdown in his battle plan. This was vividly illustrated during the 1973 Middle East War when the Egyptians successfully jammed the Israeli UHF/VHF radio frequencies, which resulted in a complete disruption of the Israelis' air-to-ground communications and consequently significantly reduced the effectiveness of their close air support.

Typical electronic sensors against which ECM might be used include long-range passive detectors; radar-warning picket ships; airborne radar patrols (AWACS); long-range early-warning radar sets; ground-controlled intercept radar sets; fighter intercept radar; missiles guided by radar or infrared; radio and radar navigation equipment; electronic bombing equipment; electronic identification equipment (IFF); terrain-following radar; antiaircraft artillery (AAA); fire-control radar; and surface-to-air-missile (SAM) control radar, etc. The particular method used will depend upon the tactical situation.

Basic Principles/ECM Effectiveness

The basic purpose of ECM is to interfere with the operation of the sensors of the air/surface defense system, and through them to interfere with the operation of the system itself. Briefly, ECM attempts to make the defense more uncertain as to the threat it faces. The greater the defense uncertainty, the more effective the ECM. To state this principle another way, ECM attempts to reduce the information content of the signals the defense receives with its sensors. The objective of ECM, then, is to force the air/surface defense system to make mistakes or errors.

It is not always possible for the EW operator to determine if the ECM he is using is effective. In some cases it is possible, but not in all cases. To understand this, it is necessary to look at the different radar systems that a defense can use.

The ability of an ECM operator to determine whether his efforts are effective does not depend upon the radar type but upon the system that uses the radar. To describe the system, two different terms will be used: *mono-track* and *track-while-scan* (TWS). The distinction is as follows: A mono-track system follows only one target at a time; the TWS system can follow several. Typically, a mono-track system may use a tracking radar, such as a conical scan or monopulse radar, to align the axis of the antenna mount with the target. The system then measures the azimuth and elevation angles of the mount and combines that information with the radar range to determine target position. By following the change in position over a period of time, the system can measure velocity and acceleration.

The two important features of the mono-track system are that (1) it can only follow one target at a time, and (2) the antenna must be pointed at the target for the system to work. ECM can deny range to the radar, but the antenna can still seek out the direction of the received ECM and thus determine the direction of the target. But deception, specifically certain inverse gain techniques, is capable of causing the antenna not to point at the target. At this point, not only is the defense getting false information, but the target knows it because it can sense that the antenna is pointing somewhere else. Thus, in this instance, the ECM operator has a direct measure of his effectiveness.

Now let us consider the track-while-scan system. Here the system is prepared to track more than one target. It does so by looking at targets in sequence—that is, by covering the total area of interest and noting where it sees targets. For each target detected it remembers the position while it continues its normal scan and compares that with the position it finds on the next scan. After two or three scans, it is not only able to tell the position of each target, but it also generates an accurate track. In this system, some sort of memory—and by implication, a computer—is required.

To the ECM operator the most important problem is that since the TWS system only observes the ECM platform periodically, it gives no indication whether it is tracking him or not. Thus he has absolutely no direct indication as to whether his ECM is effective, even though it may be.

To summarize, only in the case of the mono-track system does the ECM operator have any indication as to whether his efforts are effective. Since mono-track systems usually provide terminal guidance for weapons, such information is more than welcome. But TWS systems provide no such indication, so that the ECM operator is ignorant of the success or failure of the countermeasures employed.

One should always keep in mind that ECM does not have to prevent tracking completely to be effective. In an age where rapid reaction is critical to survival, delaying the establishment of a solid track on a target, causing a moment's confusion, or forcing the decision maker to wait just those few more seconds to be sure of the proper response can enable weapons to penetrate an adversary's defenses.

The Three Classes of ECM

Given that we want to interfere with an enemy air/surface defense radar, how may we go about it? In general there are three fundamental ways, and each designates a class of ECM. (See table 11–1.) We can

1. Radiate active signals to interfere with the radar.
2. Change the electrical properties of the medium between the aircraft/ship and the radar.
3. Change the reflective properties of the aircraft or ship itself.

The first class encompasses most jamming and deception techniques.

Table 11–1.   ECM Techniques by Class and Type

Class	Jamming		Deception
1. Active radiators	Noise radiation	{ Spot { barrage { swept	False target generators Track breakers
2. Medium modifiers	Chaff corridors		Random chaff Chaff bursts
3. Reflectivity modifiers			Vehicle design RAM (Radar Absorbing Materials) Echo enhancers Corner reflectors

The second includes such techniques as chaff dispersion. The third class includes applying radar-absorbing materials to aircraft and both electronic and mechanical echo (BLIP) enhancers for decoys.

Transmitters

The effectiveness of an ECM transmitter (jammer) depends, among other things, upon the power output of the transmitter, losses in the transmission line, antenna gain in the direction of the victim receiver, and transmitter bandwidth. In addition, the amount of the ECM transmitter emission delivered into the victim receiver is a function of the receiver bandwidth, its antenna gain, and the radar cross-sectional area of the target. In order to be effective, the ECM transmitter must be capable of emitting enough power in the bandwidth of the victim receiver to mask (jam) its intended signal or to simulate a deceptive signal realistically.

In order to meet these requirements, most ECM transmitters are designed to be versatile in operation. When the ECM transmitter is used against only one missile, one radar, or one communications device, or against a few such devices grouped closely in frequency, the transmitter can concentrate its available power output into a narrow spectrum. On the other hand, if the ECM transmitter must operate against several devices separated in frequency, it must spread its available power output over a correspondingly increased spectrum. For example, a 1,000-watt transmitter that emits its energy in a 10-MHz spectrum is developing a power density of 100 watts per MHz. If the same transmitter must spread its energy to cover a spread of 100 MHz, its power density is therefore 10 watts per MHz. As indicated previously, the effectiveness of the ECM transmitter depends upon its power density within the bandwidth of the victim receiver, after considering antenna factors and propagation path losses.

Burnthrough

Before addressing the individual ECM techniques, one final principle needs to be discussed—that of radar burnthrough. The principle of burnthrough is usually stated as the range at which the strength of the radar echo becomes equal to or greater than the ECM signal. This phenomenon occurs for all radars at some range; to see why, the inverse square law of electromagnetic wave propagation must be examined.

As you will remember from equation (2–14) of chapter 2, the power density or energy reflected from a target per unit area arriving back at the radar becomes:

$$P_{er} = \frac{P_t \, G\sigma}{(4\pi R^2)^2}$$

Where:

P_{er} = power density of the echo at the radar
P_t = radar transmitted power
σ = radar cross section

A simplified equation for the power density of the jamming signal at the victim radar antenna, disregarding losses, is given by:

$$P_{ECM} = \frac{P_j \, G_j \, B_r}{4\pi \, R^2 \, B_j} \qquad (11\text{--}1)$$

Where:

P_j = jammer transmitted power
G_j = jammer antenna gain
B_j = jammer bandwidth
B_r = victim radar bandwidth

Note that the jamming signal only needs to travel one way to the victim radar, and therefore the inverse square law $1/4\pi R^2$ is only applied once rather than both ways as in equation (2–14) for the victim radar's own signal. This advantage is referred to as "leverage."

In accordance with the definition of burnthrough as stated above, the target will be just barely perceptible through the jamming when $P_{er} = P_{ECM}$. If the self-screening jammer is effective at a specific range, then as the jamming platform closes the victim radar and range decreases, P_{er} will grow more rapidly than P_{ECM}. There will be some separation between the jammer and the radar where $P_{er} = P_{ECM}$, and as the separation continues to decrease, P_{er} eventually becomes greater than P_{ECM}.

If we set $P_{er} = P_{ECM}$ then by setting equation (2–14) equal to equation (11–1) and solving for R we can estimate the burnthrough range R_B.

If

$$\frac{P_t\, G\sigma}{(4\pi R^2)^2} = \frac{P_j\, G_j\, B_r}{4\pi R^2 B_j}$$

then:

$$R_B = \sqrt{\frac{P_t\, G\sigma\, B_j}{P_j\, G_j\, 4\pi B_r}} \qquad (11-2)$$

Note: We have restricted this explanation to the case of a self-screening jammer, though the principles apply to the stand-forward and stand-off jammer as well.

Usually the burnthrough range is calculated for a standard set of conditions and is used to compare the effectiveness of ECM against various radars. But it should be understood that, in practice, the burnthrough range is never a constant. First, the reflective properties of the aircraft or ship can vary over a range of 1,000:1 (radar cross section) depending upon the particular aspect presented to the radar. Second, the ability of the radar to distinguish its echo from the ECM depends upon its design, its condition of maintenance, and on the signal-processing circuits in use at the time. That is, burnthrough to the operator or automatic detection circuit may occur when the echo is either stronger or weaker than the ECM signal, depending upon the radar configuration and condition.

Jamming

Noise jamming. One way of preventing a radar receiver (or any other receiver) from functioning correctly is to saturate it with noise. Noise is a continuous random signal and is dissimilar to the radar signal. The radar signal or echo is a periodic sequence of pulses. Figure 11–2 shows the radar echo first and then the echo with the jamming superimposed. The objective is to conceal the echo. As figure 11–2 illustrates, this means that the average amplitude of the noise must be at least as great as the average amplitude of the radar echo

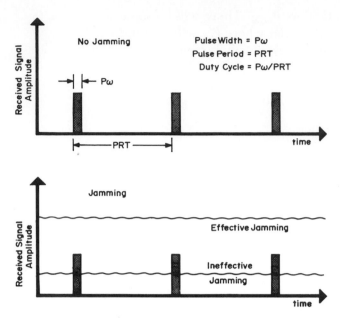

Figure 11–2. Radar signals with and without jamming. (From Aviation Week*)*

to be concealed. This idea can be alternatively expressed by saying that the average power of the jammer must have the same effect as the peak power of the radar echo, or by saying that the noise-to-signal ratio at the input is raised to a level beyond which the receiver can extract intelligence.

Since the jammer must transmit energy continuously while the radar transmits energy in pulses, the jammer requires large average power. This large average power requirement in turn necessitates a transmitter with a correspondingly large size, weight, and power supply, all of which must be carried on the aircraft, ship, or vehicle. Whereas a ship may not be limited by this requirement, an aircraft or small vehicle is limited in the amount of jammer protection it can carry.

Finally, when the radar antenna is pointed toward the jammer, the radar sees signals at all ranges. The effect on a PPI scope is to create a solid line at the azimuth of the jammer. This line, called a strobe, indicates to the operator that a jammer is present and gives its azimuth, but he does not know the range of the jammer if the jamming is effective. Thus, jamming has the bad effect that it can highlight the target's presence and direction and serve to identify it as hostile, but it has the good effect of denying the radar operator the range of the target if sufficient power is used. Figure 11–3 illustrates the idea of a strobe. The left strobe shows the consequence of

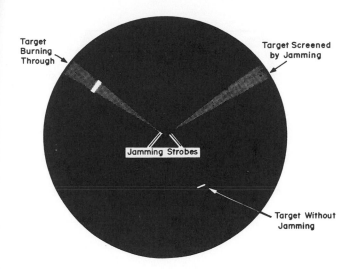

Figure 11–3. Radar PPI scope with jamming.

insufficient jamming power. The target return can be seen "burning through."

Major noise-jamming techniques. Within the general class of jamming, there are three different techniques for generating the noiselike signal to be used. In *spot jamming* all the power output of the jammer is concentrated in a very narrow bandwidth, ideally identical to that of the radar. *Barrage* and *sweep jamming* spread their energy over a bandwidth much wider than that of the radar signal. Thus, spot jamming is usually directed against a specific radar and requires a panoramic receiver to match the jamming signal to the radar signal. The other two techniques, however, can be used against any number of radars and only require a receiver to tell them that there is a radar present.

The difference between barrage and sweep jamming lies in the modulation techniques and size of the frequency band covered. *Barrage jamming* often uses an amplitude-modulated signal covering a 10-percent frequency band (bandwidth equal to 10 percent of the center frequency). *Sweep jamming* often uses a frequency-modulated signal, and the frequency is swept back and forth over a very wide bandwidth. Figure 11–4 illustrates these three types of jamming.

It is nearly impossible to match exactly a jammer frequency to that of a radiating radar; therefore, it is usually necessary to broaden the bandwidth of the noise so that it is greater than the radar bandwidth. A barrage jammer has a very wide bandwidth to cover all radars with frequencies in that band, whereas the spot jammer attempts to match as closely as possible a particular radar frequency.

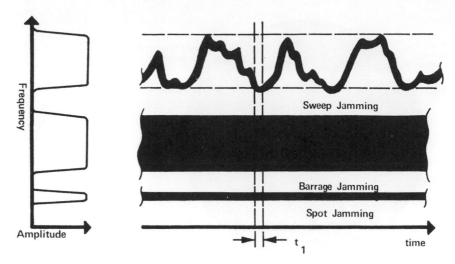

Figure 11–4. Spot, barrage, and sweep jamming.

But this broadening of the jammer bandwidth causes the jammer to require more power than one that is exactly matched, because the power that matters for any radar is the power that is accepted by the receiver. This fact is usually accounted for by specifying the spectral power density that a jammer must have to jam a radar. Power density is the power contained in the jammer output spectrum divided by the bandwidth. Figure 11–5 illustrates this idea by showing that a jammer of a given total power is more effective if its bandwidth is decreased. The usual means of specifying jammer power density is in watts per megahertz (w/MHz).

Since aircraft are limited in the total amount of jammer power they can carry, it is advantageous for the air defense network to use as

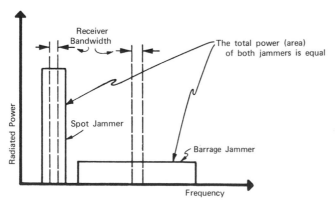

Figure 11–5. The effect of band-width on jammer spectral power density.

many widely different frequencies for its radars as possible. This concept is usually called *frequency diversity*, and it forces the jamming penetrators to either carry a large number of spot jammers or spread their barrage and sweep jammer power in order to cover all the radars. Frequency diversity will also eliminate the mutual interference of integrated forces during large operations. The ability of a single radar to change frequency to counter a spot jammer is called *frequency agility*.

Jamming Tactics

Self-screening jammers (SSJ). In this situation a unit carries jamming equipment for its own protection. This results in a trade-off between weight and space reserved for ECM equipment and that reserved for sensors, weapons, and fuel. The trade-off is most critical in aircraft and least critical in ships. The self-screening method results in maintaining efficient jamming geometry between victim radar target and jammer because the jammer and victim radar are always along the same line.

Stand-off jammers (SOJ). The jamming unit remains just outside the range of enemy weapons, providing screening for attacks units that actually penetrate enemy defenses. Usually the jamming unit will have only that task, although it may be involved in command

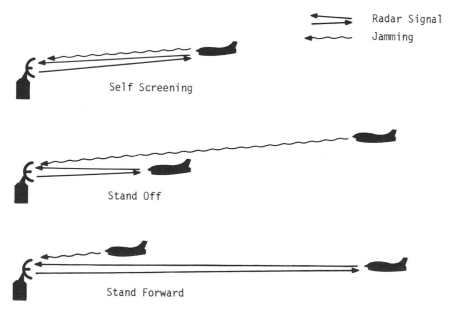

Figure 11–6. Jamming tactics.

and control. The advantage of SOJ is that the jammer is safe from enemy home-on jamming (HOJ) weapons (a submode of nearly all RF homing weapons). The disadvantage of this geometry is that burnthrough occurs earlier on the attack units because the jammer must remain at very long range, while the attack units close the enemy to very short range.

Stand-forward jammers (SFJ). The jamming unit is placed between enemy sensors and the attack units. While maintaining proper geometry between victim sensors, attack units, and the jammer is difficult, this method allows most efficient use of jammer power by reducing spreading and attenuation losses. This situation is most dangerous for the jamming unit because he is a prime target for all weapons systems and well within the capabilities of Home-on-Jam (HOJ) and Anti-Radiation (ARM) weapons.

Deception

The other major type of active ECM is deception. In contrast to noise jamming, deception tries to mimic the radar echo so that the radar will respond as if it is receiving an echo from another aircraft or ship. For a radar to direct a fire control system correctly, it must accurately measure target range, bearing, and elevation. If either range or bearing is misrepresented without the operator's knowledge, the target's location will be incorrectly established. Deception ECM is generally accomplished by repeaters and transponders, and is sometimes also called repeater jamming.

Repeaters. The theory of repeater operation is basically simple. However, actual implementation requires sophisticated circuitry. Basically, the radar signal is received, delayed, amplified, modulated, and retransmitted back to the radar.

Transponders. The transponder differs slightly in that it plays back a stored replica of the radar signal after it is triggered by the radar. The transmitted signal is made to resemble the radar signal as closely as possible. Delay may be employed, but amplification is usually not used. The power requirements for a deception repeater are much lower than for a noise jammer, since the repeater emits its energy in pulses similar to the radar pulses. Its duty cycle is similar to that of the radar.

Range deception. If a repeater were to simply retransmit the received pulse as soon as it was received, it would reinforce the return echo and would help rather than frustrate the radar. But if the received pulse (as opposed to the echo that returns to the radar) could be briefly stored and then transmitted a short time interval later, the radar would first receive the weak natural echo-return followed by an identical but stronger pulse. If a repeater transmitted a series of time-displaced pulses, identical to the radar pulse, it could produce a series of spurious targets, each at different ranges.

In automatic tracking radars, the first step in the process of locking onto a target is for the operator to designate the specific target of interest by positioning the range tracking gate over the target video. Once this is done, the radar's receiver is, in effect, turned off until such time as an echo-return is expected at the approximate range of the designated target, thereby making allowance for the velocity of the target.

This allows the deception repeater to operate in the "range-gate" or track-breaking mode. Initially, the repeater simply repeats back the received radar pulse without any delay, to allow for the radar's automatic gain control to adjust to the stronger signal, which it assumes to be the designated target.

Then the deception repeater begins to introduce increasing amounts of time delay (figure 11–7) before retransmitting back the received radar pulse. Thus, the range-gate circuitry in the radar tracks the stronger pulse and gradually "walks off" from the true target range and makes the target appear to be at a greater range than it really is.

Similarly, the target can be made to appear at a closer range by delaying the received radar pulse long enough such that it can be retransmitted back prior to receiving the next radar pulse. Then the deception pulse will arrive at the radar before the real echo pulse, producing a false target at a closer range.

This false target range information can cause significant aiming and guidance errors for antiaircraft guns and for missiles that require command guidance from ground-based radars.

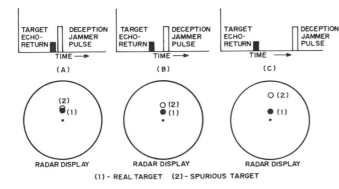

Figure 11–7. Range deception as it would appear on an air-surveillance radar scope. (From Aviation Week & Space Technology)

The simplest remedy that the tracking radar can use is to have its operators switch to a manual mode of operation. This remedy is effective because a man watching a radar scope can see the cover pulse move away from the aircraft return, and he can therefore track the aircraft.

Even though manual tracking will largely counter a repeater, manual tracking is never as smooth as automatic tracking. Thus, the weapon miss distance will increase and increase the probability of aircraft survival against non-nuclear defense weapons.

Angle Deception

Radar and command control systems can be confused by causing the radar to generate incorrect target bearing and elevation information. For this to be successful, the deception device must cause the radar to indicate the presence of a target at some time other than when the radar is at the target's bearing and elevation. There are two primary methods of achieving this effect.

Sidelobe angle deception. First, the sidelobes in the antenna radiation pattern must be evident to the ECM unit. A false target pulse is then transmitted while the ECM unit is at the azimuth of a sidelobe of the victim radar. The radar circuitry is designed to register target angular position in the main lobe only, and therefore displays target video with an angular error equal to the angular displacement between the main lobe and the sidelobe involved. This technique can be applied to any radar with ineffective sidelobe suppression or cancellation. By combining this method with range deception, many false targets at different ranges and bearings can be generated, causing confusion over the entire search volume of the victim radar, with much less required average power than equivalent noise jamming.

Angle tracking circuit deception. Mono-track radars, such as those employing Monopulse, Conical Scan, COSRO, LORO, and Track-While-Scan (TWS) or active tracking radars can be deceived by causing their angle sensitive circuitry to drive in some direction other than that which would correct the existing angular error at any given time. In doing so, the ECM unit will cause errors in solution of the fire control problem and thus induce considerable error and/or delay in weapons employment. Deception of angle-tracking circuits sometimes involves specific equipment tailored to each angle-tracking technique. For instance, the *inverse conical scan (inverse gain)* method mentioned in chapter 5 is only effective against the conical-scan tracker and would not work with the others mentioned above. For all angle-tracking methods, the ECM unit must have knowledge of the scanning and tracking techniques employed by the victim radar. For the conical-scan and lobe-switching radar, this may be obtained by monitoring the radar with an ESM receiver. Monopulse, COSRO, LORO, TWS, and active tracking radars reveal nothing to an ESM operator concerning their tracking methodology. Therefore, good intelligence data is required to build deception devices and properly employ them against these systems. Briefly, two of the techniques that can be employed against all of these systems are:

Blinking. Noise or a sample of the victim radar pulse is amplified and retransmitted from various widely separated points on the ECM unit (or several closely spaced cooperating units) in a random fashion, causing enhancement of the usual movement (wander) of the point on the ECM unit that the radar tracks. For smooth tracking and accurate solution of the fire control problem, the radar should track the centroid of the target. The result of this technique is excessive tracking error.

Crosseye (phase front distortion). Two widely spaced locations on the ECM unit are selected (such as the nose and tail or two wingtips in the case of an aircraft) and interconnected transponders installed. Each of a pair of these locations normal to the direction of the victim radar receives the victim radar pulse and triggers the transponder on the opposite side of the unit, which then transmits a copy of the victim radar pulse with a 180° phase shift. The result is a reversal of the sign of the angular error measured at the victim radar. This causes the radar positioning mechanism to drive in the wrong direction. In the case of a TWS radar or active tracking radar, this technique can result in errors in positioning tracking gates in azimuth and elevation; can prevent the establishment of a smooth track, or can cause problems in acquisition gate, tracking gate, and turn detection gate selection logic.

Continuous Wave Doppler and Pulsed Doppler Deception

CW doppler and pulsed doppler radars were developed to track high-speed, low-flying aircraft in the presence of ground clutter. The echo-return from these radars that enables the target to be tracked is the doppler shift due to the target's velocity.

The deception of the CW doppler requires that the repeater retransmit the received CW signal with a spurious doppler shift, gradually increasing its magnitude to cause velocity track breaking. This will not only cause errors in the fire control solution, but because of the velocity gate walk-off, it can result in loss of target tracking when the repeater is turned off.

Deception of the pulsed doppler radar is much the same. The repeater introduces a similar spurious doppler shift when it retransmits the received pulses.

Echo/Blip Enhancer

Another type of deception repeater is the echo or "blip enhancer." This repeater enlarges the retransmitted pulse in order to make a small radar target, such as a destroyer, appear as a large carrier apparently at formation center. This may also be done mechanically by using properly designed reflectors that will make a small target look like a large one.

Chaff

The primary way to change the properties of the medium between the radar and the target is by the use of chaff. Chaff consists of small metallic (aluminum) dipoles that are designed to resonate at the radar frequency. Half-wave dipoles make very good radar reflectors. Typical dimensions for use against a 10-GHz radar would be 0.6 inch long, 0.01 inch wide, and 0.001 inch thick. Only 0.1 pound is needed to cause an echo equal in size to a large bomber. Thousands of such dipoles are compressed into small packages. When injected into the aircraft slipstream, the chaff packages burst open and the dipoles scatter to form a radar-reflective cloud called a *chaff corridor*.

Each chaff package, dropped independently, can simulate an additional aircraft. A chaff curtain, consisting of thousands of false targets, can be dropped by a small number of aircraft. Such a curtain can so confuse radars that they are unable to locate the real targets within the chaff cloud. Chaff drops so slowly that it normally takes many hours to reach the ground.

When chaff packages are dropped in close sequence, radars viewing the resulting continuous chaff corridor from right angles have difficulty tracking targets within the corridor. If the corridor is viewed nearer to head-on (dispensing aircraft approaching the radar), the radar range gate can be forced to stay on the first return received. Thus, the lead aircraft can be tracked and the chaff echoes gated out. When viewing the corridor tail on, the radar can also track the lead aircraft if the range gate is forced to select the last part of the echo. If the dispensing aircraft uses rockets to fire chaff in front of the aircraft, the problem of maintaining tracking is greatly increased.

Since the chaff particles have considerable aerodynamic drag, their forward velocity quickly drops to near zero. Because of its low velocity, chaff can be regarded as an airborne type of "clutter." Radars such as CW, pulse doppler and MTI (Moving Target Indicator) that can reject clutter are not seriously affected by chaff. Thus, they can continue to track a target within a chaff cloud as long as the target has a radial component of velocity.

The use of chaff by surface units has greatly increased in recent years. Chaff dispensed by a rocket or projectile can be used to decoy or break the track of a missile with active radar guidance.

Chaff is a particularly effective means of defending relatively slow systems such as surface ships. In this situation there is so little difference in velocity between the potential target and the chaff that CW, pulse doppler, and MTI radars have difficulty in separating the target from the chaff clutter. In shipboard defense, chaff rockets can be fired to burst at a specific location, hopefully within the field of view of the weapon RF seeker, creating an alternate target that is more lucrative than the ship itself. The disadvantage of this situation is that it requires an elaborate fire control system and movable launcher to position the chaff burst precisely. The alternative, employing fixed launchers and no fire control system, is to fire several chaff rockets to burst relatively close to the ship. The chaff cloud combines with the ship to form one very large target with a combined centroid somewhere in the chaff cloud. An RF homing weapon that seeks the centroid of its target will thus fly harmlessly past the ship and through the chaff cloud.

Target Masking and Modification (STEALTH)

Techniques for modifying aircraft, ship, and submarine periscope radar cross sections (the variable σ in the radar range equation) have existed since World War II. As previously stated, radar cross section is a function of radar frequency (wavelength), target shape, target aspect, and target composition as well as its physical size. Reduction of radar cross section can be accomplished in three ways:

Alteration of target shape. The configuration of the target must be modified according to the principles of geometrical optics such that the large reflections are diverted to unimportant regions of space (i.e., not back to the radar). The designer should avoid flat, cylindrical, parabolic, or conical surfaces normal to the direction of the radar illumination. These shapes tend to concentrate the energy and provide a large radar return. The target design should include the use of doubly curved surfaces that result in low radar cross section. Unfortunately, in many cases these principles conflict with other important engineering requirements in aircraft and ship design, resulting in increased expense and slow development.

Destructive interference. The object to be protected is coated with material that causes a partial reflection of incident radar energy from the coating surface. If the coating thickness is $\lambda/4$, then the total additional distance traveled between the coating surface and the object's skin surface is $\lambda/2$ or 180°. In this way we achieve destructive interference between the radar energy reflected from the coating surface and that reflected from the skin of the object. Thickness of the coating is not excessive at short wavelengths; however, it is impractical to install coatings thick enough to deal with low-frequency search radars.

Radar absorbent material. In this case the object to be protected is given a coating of successive layers of magnetic composition material such as Ni-Mn-Zn sandwiched with dielectrics that convert 95% of incident RF energy to heat. This material can be made as thin as 1.75 cm, which is practical for aircraft use; however, the weight penalty of 24.9 kg per m^2 is excessive. This would not eliminate their use aboard ship or at ground-based facilities. Another approach, involving continuing research, consists of a phenolic-fiberglass sandwich material. This structure again converts 95% of incident RF energy to heat by using a resistive material consisting of carbon black and silver powder. This material is effective over the range of 2.5 to 13 GHz, which encompasses many fire control and weapon-guidance radars. The disadvantage of this approach is that while it is lightweight and relatively thin, it is not able to handle the high temperature and erosion processes at supersonic speeds. These methods, though promising, still cannot deal with some of the lower radar frequencies.

IR/EO Countermeasures

With the advent of infrared heat-seeking weapons and their increased use, the Department of Defense has been backing an active program for the development of IR Countermeasures Systems. Several countermeasures have been available for years, such as shielding high IR sources from possible detectors, using special nonreflective paints to reduce IR levels radiated, IR decoys, and the tactic of ejecting infrared flares to cause false lock-ons of IR weapons. Recently, however, these techniques have received renewed efforts to improve and refine them. In addition, several new countermeasures systems have been developed, primarily for aircraft.

Electro-optical or laser and TV-guided weapons are also coming into wide use. The uses of lasers for countermeasures vary from range deception to the use of a laser beam to actually blind the operators of visually aimed weapons. Conversely, lasers are being developed to jam enemy range-finding and weapon-guidance lasers. Countermeasures against TV-guided weapons and TV-directed tracking systems are much more difficult to develop, although research is on going in this area.

The requirements for EO countermeasures are dictated by the severity of the EO threat. As the tactical deployment of EO missile seekers, fire control sensors, reconnaissance, surveillance, and other EO systems proliferates, the need for an effective means of countering them will become more urgent. These countermeasures can take the form of active or passive devices, techniques, or procedures. Active devices include such items as flares, modulated radiation, and laser jammers. Passive approaches include such items as camouflage, engine IR suppression, and absorbing materials. Various categories of optical countermeasures are illustrated in figure 11–8. Thus, the primary tactical implication is that further payload weight will need to be sacrificed for electronic warfare devices carried aboard our platforms and those of the enemy.

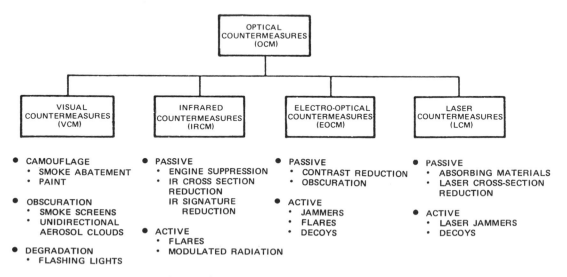

Figure 11–8. Categories of optical countermeasures.

Acoustic Countermeasures

Early sonar operators rapidly discovered that they could passively detect active acoustic devices at ranges greater than the range that the active devices could detect the passive platform. Tacticians reasoned that this counter-detection situation could be exploited much the same as with ESM and radar. The initial underwater threat detection and evaluation capability employed the listening capability of the installed attack sonar set. This was limited to the bandwidth of the sonar receiver until the development of separate interconnected hydrophone arrays for active sonars. By the 1950s, dedicated underwater intercept receivers such as the AN/WLR-2 were developed.

Acoustic countermeasures began with the Pillenwerfer used by German U-boats when the Allied hunter-killer groups began to take their toll in late 1943 and 1944. This device, composed of lithium hydride, acted like a giant Alka-Seltzer tablet, creating thousands of gas bubbles that returned a solid echo similar to a submarine. This was reasonably effective as long as the attacking units didn't see the submarine and the decoy at the same time. The decoy did not cause a doppler shift; therefore, a trained operator could tell the difference.

Dealing with acoustic countermeasures requires the same basic approach as ECCM. Again, the best countermeasure is an experienced and well-trained operator; nevertheless, improvements such as computer signal processing, various filters and delay lines, and automated doppler detection capability are of great help.

Acoustic intercept receivers. Initial attempts at producing underwater intercept receivers were less than satisfactory because the equipments had a high false-alarm rate due to ambient noise. Also, separate receivers were required for initial intercept and for determination of the azimuth of the noise source. Later receivers employed a triangular-shaped array of three hydrophones that determined azimuth by measurement of the time difference between arrival of the signal at each hydrophone. Noise reduction was accomplished by using delay lines and filters that allowed only signals longer than the delay to reach the display. Short noise pulses resulted in no output. A receiver designed in this way could display frequency and azimuth simultaneously after receiving one ping. With the development of active acoustic homing torpedoes, this type of response is required of all acoustic intercept receivers in order to have time to employ torpedo evasion tactics. Modern receivers categorize intercepts and assign priorities according to the potential threat. In this situation torpedoes would have the highest priority, with other intercepts having lesser priority, the least being search sonars in a long-range search mode.

Acoustic countermeasures. The initial approach to acoustic countermeasures had to do with the control of active emissions from sonars and the reduction of self-noise. As with electronic emissions, acoustic emissions should be kept to a minimum and, if possible, only after counter-detection has occurred. However, if analysis of the FOM problem indicates that passive detection of an enemy is not possible, then we are forced to go active. Active operation must take into account the tactical situation. Power levels must be kept down, if possible, to prevent counter-detection. During active sonar attacks, a change to short-range mode will shorten the time between pings and let an adversary know that the ASW unit is in contact. This could result in an unsuccessful attack, with no second opportunity.

Countermeasures for use against underwater acoustic sensors, homing devices, and fuzes developed as these systems evolved. A mine that could be activated by the sounds emanating from a power-driven ship underway was developed by the British in the late stages of World War I, but the first operational use of acoustic mines was by the German Navy against the British in the fall of 1940. There were cases of mines detonating ahead and to the side of ships too far away for the ship's magnetic influence field to have caused the activation. Work started immediately, once these phenomena had been noticed and the mechanism identified, to provide a noisemaker that would project noise far enough ahead of the ship to detonate the mine before the ship was close enough to be damaged by the explosion.

Explosives, compressed air, or electrically operated hammers striking the inside of a watertight case suspended over the side, and parallel pipe devices towed through the water causing the pipes to bang together as the pressure between the pipes was reduced by the faster motion of the water through a constrained space (Bernoulli's Principle) were among the earliest methods developed to counter the acoustic mine. There is a considerable similarity between the early attempts and the present-day U.S. Navy acoustic sweeps. Other early sweep gear consisted of vanes or propellers attached to noisemaking attachments, not too dissimilar from a New Year's Eve whirling ratchet. When towed through the water, the propellers turned and the ratchet device produced noise. Devices similar in principle are still used; for instance, the U.S. Navy's airborne acoustic sweep device depends on a water turbine to produce a turning motion for its noisemaking capability. The early noisemakers were turned on and were kept operating at one intensity while the sweeper was in the field. Subsequently, controllers were added that enabled the intensity of the output to be varied to simulate the approach of a ship target. The same approach can be employed as a means of decoying homing torpedoes. There are noisemakers that can be towed from ships or submarines, providing a lucrative alternate target when the torpedo-target geometry is such that there is wide azimuth separation between the noisemaker and the target. Modern acoustic towed decoys, such as the AN/SLQ-25 NIXIE and the older T-MK6 FANFAIR, employ electronic or electromechanical means to produce the required signals. Submarines employ small torpedo-like mobile decoys that are equipped with transponders capable of returning a realistic signal to active sonars. With noisemaking capability they can simulate submarine passive signatures to some degree. This same technology has been used to provide small expendable training targets (figure 11–9) for ASW forces at much less cost than that for a real submarine providing target services. Though small (about the size of a sonobuoy), the transponders in these targets make them look as large to the detecting sonar as a real submarine.

Acoustic jammers are available that provide random noise or false targets to a hostile active sonar. With the power of today's sonars, a

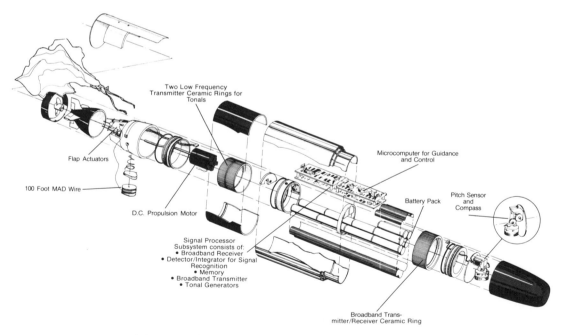

Figure 11–9. Expendable mobile training target. (Courtesy of Sippican Ocean Systems, Inc.)

jammer must have an output SL of at least 200 db (re. 1 µ pa) to be effective when mounted aboard a submarine. The rules governing jammer output, "burnthrough," jammer bandwidth vs. sonar bandwidth, and sonar frequency diversity/agility are similar to those dealing with radar and ECM devices.

Air bubbles can be employed to mask potential targets or to provide alternate targets. The large difference in characteristic impedance (ρc) between the air bubbles and the surrounding water make them very efficient as reflectors of acoustic energy. Very little sound will penetrate a curtain of air bubbles, making them very efficient as masking for noise sources.

Other Countermeasures

Magnetic influence countermeasures. The effect of large ferrous metal bodies such as ship and submarine hulls on the earth's magnetic field has been employed in sensors and fuzes for many years. Countermeasures have for the most part consisted of using electric current to simulate a change in the earth's magnetic field.

Magnetic mines, which were first developed and used in World War I by the British, were used extensively by the Germans in the early days of World War II against the United Kingdom. The Royal Navy created the first magnetic sweeps, both for surface craft and aircraft. The German Navy responded to British magnetic mines with their own sweeps, and whole families of magnetic mine countermeasures were developed. These included the familiar electrode and closed-loop electric current sweeps that we still use today: ships converted to huge magnets to set off mines at some distance from the ship; towed solenoids of several types; and arrays of large magnets towed astern of a sweeper. Although several types of sweeps were built or developed in the United States, main reliance was placed on the straight-tail, open electrode sweep that is common today (figure 11–10). Closed-loop versions of the electrode sweep were also used. The earlier ships relied on large banks of wet-cell batteries for electric power, but the U.S. sweepers are now equipped with powerful generators to provide the electric current.

Influence minesweeping systems operate on the principle of inducing mines to fire in response to influences (simulated signatures of a ship) that are generated in the vicinity of the mine.

All ships act much as magnets with surrounding magnetic lines of

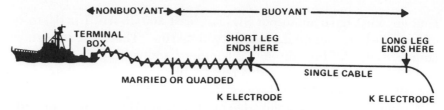

Figure 11–10. Straight-tail magnetic electrode sweep.

force that have both vertical and horizontal components. Magnetic mines can be made to fire on either or both of these components or on the total resultant field. Magnetic minesweeping produces simulations of the ship's magnetic fields.

The same principle can be employed to deceive magnetic anomaly detection equipment. In this case a trailing wire is towed behind a mobile decoy, such as the acoustic decoys described in the last section. Electric current is applied, resulting in an indication on MAD equipment at close range. The general arrangement is similar to that in the mobile training target in figure 11–9.

Pressure influence countermeasures. Ships and submarines cause unique pressure changes in their vicinity while in motion. These pressure changes can be used to trigger mines and cause torpedoes to detonate with a specific geometric relationship to ship and submarine hulls.

Pressure mines were first used operationally in the later stages of World War II by both Axis and Allied forces. The Normandy invasion forces faced the German "oyster" pressure mine in 1944, and the U.S. made liberal use of pressure mines during Operation Starvation against the Japanese homeland in 1945. Despite the many years of scientific effort since their introduction, no operationally acceptable method of sweeping pressure mines is available today. As with any mine, the pressure mine is susceptible to minehunting. Various theories and techniques that provide some limited assistance in countering pressure mines are described in later paragraphs.

As in any influence sweep, the object is to produce a spurious influence in the vicinity of a mine, which will cause the mine mechanism to recognize the spurious influence as a ship and detonate the mine. A ship moving in relatively shallow water creates an area of reduced pressure under the keel, which extends some distance to either side of the ship's track. This phenomenon, an example of Bernoulli's Principle in operation, is illustrated in figure 11–11. A pres-

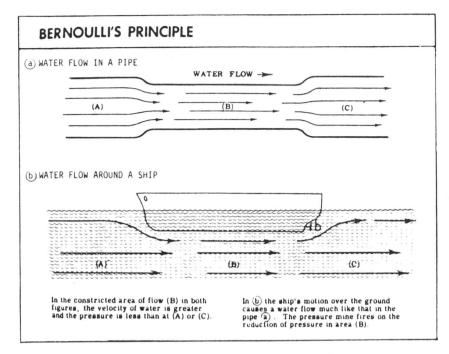

Figure 11–11. Bernoulli principle in pressure mine theory.

sure mine takes advantage of the pressure reduction to actuate a firing mechanism.

Because a pressure mine is susceptible to actuation by the pressure fluctuations from waves and swell, the pressure influence will (in most cases) be combined with either an acoustic or magnetic mechanism to make a combination influence mine. There has been no way found of displacing as large a volume of water as a ship displaces in order to simulate the pressure reduction caused by a ship.

Consequently, much effort has been spent and continues to be spent on the use of ships as pressure sweeps (Guinea Pig Principle) and in attempting to make the ship resistant to the explosion of the mines that it sweeps. Various measures that can be taken to counter the pressure mine partially are discussed in the following paragraphs.

The safe-speed technique is based on the principle that reducing the speed of a ship reduces the amplitude of the pressure field of the ship. This technique is very effective for small ships. For large ships, however, the reduction in speed required may be so great that the ship cannot maintain steerageway. In this case, steerageway may be maintained with the assistance of tugs. The safe speed technique comes under the category of self-protection.

Electronic Counter-Countermeasures (ECCM)

Electronic counter-countermeasures is the art of reducing the effectiveness of an EW threat with the objective of making the cost of effective EW prohibitive for the enemy. As in ECM, ECCM includes both radar design and operator training. The radar ECCM designer must understand the various forms of ECM that his radar is likely to encounter, hence he is very interested in intelligence about the ECM threat. Likewise, the radar operator would like to know what ECM he will be facing. But in both cases detailed intelligence will probably be lacking. Therefore, the designer must provide a variety of options to be used against the expected threats. And the operator must be trained both to recognize the various countermeasures that might be used against him and to select the appropriate combination of options against each of them. The most effective measure to combat ECM is an up-to-date piece of equipment operated by a well-trained operator. Radar design for ECCM can be broken down into three areas: radar parameter management, signal processing techniques, and design philosophy.

Radar Parameter Management

The basic radar parameters are those characteristics that influence the radar's performance. These are: power, frequency, PRF, pulse length, antenna gain, antenna polarization, antenna scan, and antenna sidelobe characteristics. These values, and the means with which they can be manipulated in service, are established in the design phase.

Power. For a ground or surface radar, power is often considered the fundamental ECCM parameter. With this view, ECM becomes a power battle, with the outcome going to the stronger, more powerful opponent. Airborne jamming equipment is limited in size and weight and therefore has a power limitation. Thus, the power advantage lies with the ground or surface radar. In the case of one surface unit versus another, both operate under the same constraint, and the outcome is not obvious.

Frequency. Frequency agility is a significant ECCM design feature. Using components such as frequency synthesizers (something like those employed in radio scanners) instead of conventional crystal-controlled oscillators, some radars are able to change frequency within one pulse repetition time (PRT). This makes deception jamming very difficult. The radar can be designed to change frequency automatically within a certain range, or this can be done manually.

A second way of using frequency as an ECCM technique is the doppler radar, including radars designed for MTI signal processing. The actual ECCM advantage is gained from signal processing in the receiver, but the intention to use the doppler frequency shift must be reflected in the transmitter design. For example, in a pulse-doppler radar the transmitter must often be designed to radiate a very stable frequency. In a pulse compression radar the transmitter must radiate a pulse with an FM slide, sometimes called a chirp pulse due to the change in "tone" as the pulse is transmitted.

Pulse repetition frequency (PRF). In general, high PRF radars are more resistant to ECM because their average power is greater. Changing the PRF in a random fashion is an effective counter to deception because deception ECM depends on predictability of the radar. However, because PRF is related to the basic timing of the radar, this technique results in additional complexity and expense. Random PRF has been employed as a very effective ECCM feature in some radars for many years and has the additional benefit of elimination of MTI radar blind speeds.

Pulse length. An increase in pulse length will increase average power and thus increase detection probability. The trade-off is increased minimum range and degradation of the radar's range resolution capability (the ability to separate targets at the same azimuth and close together in range). This problem can be compensated for by including a pulse compression capability; however, due to receiver blanking during the transmit cycle, the minimum range will stay relatively long. Some modern radars compensate for these difficulties by employing the pulse compression and varying their pulse width depending on mode of operation and expected target range.

Antenna design. Antenna design, as reflected in low sidelobe levels, is an ECCM design technique, because it prevents a jammer or deceiver from affecting the radar at many azimuths. Low sidelobe levels also make the job of antiradiation missiles more difficult, since there is less chance of the missile homing in on the radar unless the radar is pointing at the missile. Sidelobe patterns can be compensated for by employing techniques such as sidelobe cancellation and sidelobe suppression.

Scan pattern. The radar scan pattern can influence ECCM capability because it influences the amount of energy directed toward the radar target. An active tracking phased-array radar is quite ECM resistant because of its ability to rapidly scan its radar beam in a random fashion rather than in the regular circular or sector scan pattern of conventional radars. This irregular beam positioning would give the opposing ECM system little or no warning and make it impossible to predict where and when to transmit false signals. In systems where scanning is performed in the receiver rather than in the transmitted beam, such as those mentioned in the section on angle deception, ECM has no direct access to the radar scan pattern and thus has difficulty using that information to interfere with the radar system operation.

Into this class fall the passive detection and home-on-jam techniques where the "radar" does not transmit, but uses the ECM energy emitted by its victim to determine the victim's location—often by triangulation from two or more separate locations.

Signal-processing techniques

These are usually functions that are incorporated into the radar receiver. Although certain signal-processing techniques may place constraints on the transmitter, many of them have been added to the receiver after the radar has been built. These techniques are called ECCM or *anti-jamming* (AJ) fixes, since they were initially developed as retrofits to improve existing equipment. Radars now tend toward a more sophisticated design concept in which the AJ devices are included in the basic radar system.

Doppler radars, including radars with moving target indicator (MTI) signal processors, although not designed specifically for ECCM purposes, are quite ECM resistant. Since doppler radars (pulse and CW) operate on the frequency shift caused by a moving target, they automatically filter out returns from nonmoving targets and consequently eliminate many unwanted signals, such as those from chaff. They will even discriminate between returns from objects of different velocities such as an aircraft in a chaff cloud. This technique can also make deception more difficult, since the deceiver must imitate the proper frequency shift.

In radar with *automatic threshold detection* (in which the target is said to be present when the receiver output crosses a preset threshold), the presence of a jamming signal can increase the rate of false alarms (false targets) to an intolerable extent. If the radar output data is processed in an automatic device such as a computer, the device might be overloaded by the added false alarms, due to jamming. Thus, it is important that the receiver present a constant false-alarm rate. Receivers designed to accomplish this are called *CFAR* (constant-false-alarm-rate) receivers. Their disadvantage lies in the likelihood that some weak targets will remain below the threshold and be lost.

If an operator were monitoring the radar output, the effect of the additional false alarms could be reduced by having the operator turn down the gain of the receiver during the presence of jamming, or else he might be able to ignore those sectors containing ECM. In an automatic threshold detector, the same effect may be obtained by using the average noise level to provide an automatic gain control, much as an operator would by adjusting a manual gain control. Because the automatic CFAR circuits react faster, they are superior to an operator in keeping the false-alarm rate constant, especially when the radar is subject to noise jamming from only a few azimuth sectors.

A CFAR receiver, no matter whether it is an automatic device or an operator controlling the receiver gain, maintains the false-alarm rate constant by reducing the probability of detection. When the threshold level is raised to maintain a constant false-alarm rate, marginal echo signals that might normally be detected do not cross the higher threshold and are lost. Therefore, CFAR does not give immunity to jamming; it merely makes operation in the presence of jamming more convenient by making the receiver less sensitive. If the jamming were severe enough, the CFAR, for all intents and purposes, could produce the same effect as turning off the receiver.

Other ECCM techniques employ track history to reject false returns such as those discussed in the chapter on track-while-scan radars. The addition of computerized processing of radar video can perform this function as well as correlating echoes returned in several successive radar transmissions as a means to counter the deception jammer.

Radar Design Philosophy

A general rule of thumb for ECCM radar design is to incorporate unpredictable operating parameters. The more orderly a radar is in its operation, the easier it is to predict what the radar is going to do or how it is going to operate; consequently, the job of applying an ECM technique effectively becomes simpler. ECM becomes more difficult, however, if characteristics of the victim radar are constantly changing. The parameter that may most easily be varied to confuse the ECM operator is the frequency. The capability for operator variation of pulse length, PRF, modulation, and antenna characteristics is commonly built into radars to make ECM more difficult.

The most common way to introduce unpredictability into radar design is through frequency diversity. Early radars were all designed to operate in a few specific frequency bands, where narrow-band jamming would render them all ineffective. New radar systems are designed so that each different radar type operates in a different frequency band. The use of a much greater portion of the spectrum, from VHF to SHF (A to J Band), forces ECM operators to cover this total radar spectrum if they are to be effective. This usually results in being able to put less ECM power against a single radar because the airborne platform is limited in its total power capability.

Another aspect of ECCM design philosophy is the relationship between automatic equipment and the human operator. The trained radar operator fulfills a useful and necessary role in a countermeasure environment and cannot be completely replaced by automatic detection and data processors. An automatic processor can be designed to operate only against those interfering or jamming signals known beforehand; that is, any capability against such signals must be programmed into the equipment beforehand. New jamming situations not designed into the data processor might not be readily handled. On the other hand, a human being has the ability to adapt to new and varied situations and is more likely to be able to cope with, and properly interpret, a strange new form of interference than can a machine. *Therefore, a skilled operator is the most important counter-countermeasure for maintaining radar operation in the presence of deliberate and clever countermeasures.*

The Effectiveness of ECM/ECCM

Having understood that electronic warfare is an interaction between friendly and hostile electronic systems, it may be well to ask what is the nature of this interaction? How does electronic warfare interact with electronic systems to reduce their effectiveness or deny their use to the enemy? One traditional way of expressing this is to say that ECM resembles a ladder. That is, an electronic system results in a countering electronic system—ECM; the ECM in turn causes a counter-countermeasure—ECCM—to be implemented; and this process continues endlessly. One can diagram this process as shown in figure 11–12.

This analysis shows that unequivocal superiority can never be achieved through ECM. Unfortunately, this analysis tends to promote a two-valued evaluation of ECM: ECM either works or it doesn't,

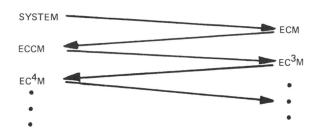

FRIENDLY   ENEMY

SYSTEM

ECM

ECCM

EC^3M

EC^4M

Figure 11–12. The ECM ladder.

depending on what rung of the ladder we are on. However, a more realistic evaluation of this chain yields the following conclusions:

1. The real effectiveness of ECM lies somewhere on a spectrum ranging from completely effective to completely ineffective. The actual evaluation depends both on the position on the ladder and on many other factors, some relating to training and morale and others relating to the uncertainties of combat.

2. ECM techniques normally have only a finite time of superiority. Eventually an adversary will develop a counter technique, and the superiority will pass to him. Thus, one cannot expect a certain ECM technique to give indefinite superiority.

3. As a result of the previous principle, the real advantage of ECM is that it gives relative superiority while an adversary is developing and deploying the countermeasure. Unless an adversary is very perceptive, this relative advantage can be measured by the time delay between the operational employment of two successive steps on the ladder. During this time the succeeding idea is being developed and the necessary equipment built. Therefore, good security is necessary to preserve the relative advantage.

4. One real value of ECM is technological superiority, the ace-in-the-hole idea. However, this concept cannot be extended indefinitely unless a continuing program of development is pursued, because an adversary may anticipate our development and out-distance us if our technology remains static. Furthermore, this concept concentrates on the surprise attendant on the initial use of ECM. Consequently it has much more application to the peacetime development of ECM than to wartime.

5. Finally, a technique should not be discarded because it has a simple counter, for there will be benefits from the inevitable

delay between the time that the enemy is certain that the technique is being used and the time that he can make the counter operational. In that time work can be started on the development of the next step in the ladder to maintain technological superiority.

Although the ECM ladder provides a useful concept of electronic warfare, it does not really help one evaluate the effectiveness of ECM in combat for several reasons. First, as was noted before, it fosters a two-valued measure of effectiveness. Second, it tends to concentrate on the interaction of only two electronic systems rather than consider the complexity of combat where many systems are employed simultaneously. Third, it tends to exclude the human operator, and fourth, it ignores the great difference between peacetime and wartime ECM development.

ECM/ECCM Interaction

Modes of Sensor Operation

In an actual combat engagement an electronic system can have many different modes of operation that will be used depending on the quality of input signal. In an environment devoid of hostile electromagnetic radiation, the system is normally operated in an *automatic mode*. The effectiveness of this mode is often very sensitive to the quality of the input data. If the input data is "clean," i.e., free of enemy ECM, the system has excellent capability; but increasing ECM intensity causes the system to lose effectiveness swiftly (figure 11–13). When the situation becomes impossible, the operator will switch to some *manual mode* of operation, which has less capability in a "clean" environment, but has some capability when the automatic system has failed catastrophically.

The manual mode is also subject to degradation by ECM, although it usually degrades more slowly than automatic operation (figure 11–13). When the input data becomes unusable or unreliable, the system operator will attempt to get data from other electronic sensors or *alternate inputs*. Again, these data sources are subject to degradation although (presumably) less sensitive to degradation than the primary sensor operating in the manual mode. Therefore, it it possible that there would be no reliable electronic data available to the operator, in which case it would be necessary for him to rely on less desirable *backup* systems (optical, sonic, telex, etc.), which are not seriously affected by ECM.

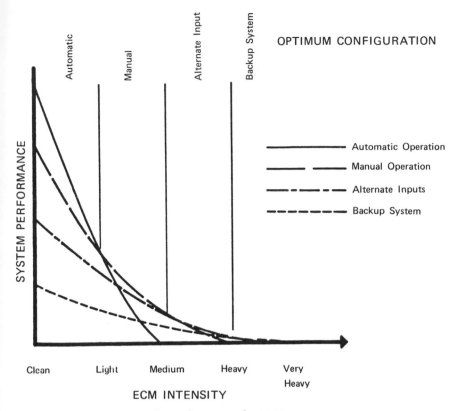

Figure 11–13. System degradation with ECM.

Effect of ECM on Mode of Operation

It is reasonable to expect that the relative performance of the four modes in the face of ECM will be as shown in figure 11–13. In that case the system will obtain the best effectiveness in the face of increasing ECM by switching to successively less capable but more ECM-resistant modes.

Since ECCM is generally the counter to ECM, this sequence of modes of system operation is also an outline of a method of ECCM design to give maximum performance in the face of ECM. Thus, this concept of avoiding a catastrophic failure by "gracefully" falling back to other modes of operation can be called the *ECM/ECCM interaction*.

If all the system modes are not available to the operator, he will not have the maximum possible ECCM capability. For example, if no manual mode were available, the presence of light ECM intensity could lead to complete failure of the automatic mode. Then the op-give him less capability than he would have if he could operate in a manual mode. As a result the use of ECM could lead to a substantial advantage.

This concept can also be applied to the major subsystems of each defense weapon system. With this done, one has the potential for evaluating the performance reduction of any weapon system due to ECM.

If all these options are available, any system has four modes of operation in the face of ECM:

Automatic mode
Manual mode
Alternate input mode
Backup mode

Summary

This chapter has provided the reader with the fundamentals of electronic warfare. In 1969 the JCS issued a policy memorandum setting forth the definition of electronic warfare. Included in this detailed definition were definitions for ESM, ECM, and ECCM. Once it is understood that EW is an interaction between friendly and hostile electronic systems, this interaction and the general theory and effectiveness of ECM and ECCM on sensor operation can be studied.

EW has its own specialized equipment to meet its objectives. In order to gather information, specially designed receivers with such characteristics as wide spectrum surveillance, wide dynamic range,

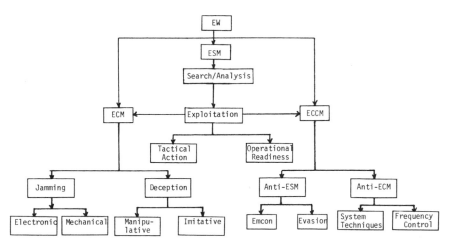

Figure 11–14. Functional relations of EW operations.

good unwanted-signal rejection, and good angle-of-arrival measurement are required. Other equipment includes processors, analyzers, displays, and transmitters and jammers.

The ECM division of EW involves some method or methods of actively preventing or reducing the enemy's use of the electromagnetic spectrum. This may be done by jamming, through deception, or by the use of chaff. All of these methods have varying degrees of success depending on how and when they are used and against which enemy systems they are used. This variance in success is what makes EW a continuous and dynamic interaction.

Finally, ECCM is that division that involves the countering of enemy countermeasures. ECCM is usually accomplished through some type of design feature built into the sensor (e.g., radar). This is done by giving the sensor or radar the capability of altering or changing its basic parameters—such as frequency, power, PRF, etc. Other methods involve special techniques in signal processing and the use of a highly skilled operator.

References

Aviation Week & Space Technology, Vol. 102, No. 4, 27 January 1975.

Bachman, Christian G. *Radar Sensor Engineering*. Lexington, Mass.: D.C. Heath & Co., 1982.

Boyd, J.A., D.B. Harris, D.D. King, and H.W. Welch, Jr. *Electronic Countermeasures*. Los Altos, Cal.: Peninsula Publishing, 1978.

Burns, R.L., Cdr. USN. Unpublished Notes on Mine Warfare, 1983.

Fitts, Richard E. *Fundamentals of Electronic Warfare*. Colorado Springs, Co.: U.S. Air Force Academy, 1972.

Leydorf, G.E., ed. Naval Electronic Systems. Vol 4. Annapolis, Md.: U.S. Naval Academy, 1971.

Nathanson, Fred E. *Radar Design Principles*. New York: McGraw-Hill, 1969.

Sippican Ocean Systems, Inc. *The Expendable Mobile ASW Training Target*. Marion, Mass.: Sippican Ocean Systems, Inc., 1983.

Skolnik, Merrill I. *Introduction to Radar Systems*. New York: McGraw-Hill, 1980.

Van Brant, Leroy B. *Applied ECM*. Vol 1, Dunn Loring, Va.: EW Engineering, Inc., 1978.

12

Military Explosives

Introduction

An explosion is a change in the state of matter that results in a rapid and violent release of energy. From this broad definition, explosions may be divided into three types: mechanical, chemical, and nuclear. Mechanical explosions, such as the disruption of a steam boiler, are of little concern in military applications and are not discussed here. For our purposes, an explosion must be suitable for military use. In this context, chemical and nuclear explosions apply.

An explosive may be defined as a material (chemical or nuclear) that can be initiated and undergo very rapid, self-propagating decomposition, resulting in:

(1) the formation of more stable materials;
(2) the liberation of heat;
(3) the development of a sudden pressure effect through the action of heat on produced or adjacent gases.

One of the basic properties by which a weapon's effectiveness is measured is the quantity of energy, and thus damage potential, it delivers to the target. Modern weapons use both kinetic and potential energy systems to achieve maximum lethality. Kinetic energy systems rely on the conversion of kinetic energy ($\frac{1}{2} MV^2$) into work, while potential energy systems use explosive energy directly in the form of heat and blast or by accelerating the warhead case fragments to increase their kinetic energy and damage volume.

A typical modern projectile might have a mass of 25 kg and contain 20 kg of explosive in a 5 kg case. If the projectile strikes the target going 450 meters per second, the kinetic energy delivered would be $KE = \frac{1}{2} MV^2 = \frac{1}{2} (25)(450)^2 = 2.53 \times 10^6$ joules or about 1.01×10^5 J/kg. If the chemical explosive were detonated on impact, an additional 60×10^6 joules of energy would be released, or 2.5×10^6 J/kg, a factor of 20 increase. For a totally kinetic energy system to impart this energy, it would have to be traveling at approximately 2,245 m/s. These high speeds are difficult to maintain over long ranges, although some armor-piercing shells approach 2,100 m/s; thus, the use of chemical explosives plays a major role in modern warheads.

Chemical Explosive Reaction

A chemical explosive is a compound or mixture which, upon the application of heat or shock, decomposes or rearranges with extreme rapidity, yielding much gas and heat. Many substances not ordinarily classed as explosives may do one, or even two, of these things. For example, a mixture of nitrogen and oxygen can be made to react with great rapidity and yield the gaseous product nitric oxide; yet the mixture is not an explosive since it does not evolve heat, but rather absorbs heat.

$$N_2 + O_2 \rightarrow 2NO \ - \ 43,200 \text{ calories}$$

For a chemical to be an explosive, it must exhibit all of the following:

(1) Formation of gases
(2) Evolution of heat
(3) Rapidity of reaction
(4) Initiation of reaction

Formation of gases. Gases may be evolved from substances in a variety of ways. When wood or coal is burned in the atmosphere, the carbon and hydrogen in the fuel combine with the oxygen in the atmosphere to form carbon dioxide and steam, together with flame and smoke. When the wood or coal is pulverized, so that the total surface in contact with the oxygen is increased, and burned in a furnace or forge where more air can be supplied, the burning can be made more rapid and the combustion more complete. When the wood or coal is immersed in liquid oxygen or suspended in air in the form of dust, the burning takes place with explosive violence. In each case, the same action occurs: a burning combustible forms a gas.

Evolution of heat. The generation of heat in large quantities accompanies every explosive chemical reaction. It is this rapid liberation of heat that causes the gaseous products of reaction to expand and generate high pressures. This rapid generation of high pressures of the released gas constitutes the explosion. It should be noted that the liberation of heat with insufficient rapidity will not cause an explosion. For example, although a pound of coal yields five times as much heat as a pound of nitroglycerin, the coal cannot be used as an explosive because the rate at which it yields this heat is quite slow.

Rapidity of reaction. Rapidity of reaction distinguishes the explosive reaction from an ordinary combustion reaction by the great speed with which it takes place. Unless the reaction occurs rapidly, the thermally expanded gases will be dissipated in the medium, and there will be no explosion. Again, consider a wood or coal fire. As the fire burns, there is the evolution of heat and the formation of gases, but neither is liberated rapidly enough to cause an explosion.

Initiation of reaction. A reaction must be capable of being initiated by the application of shock or heat to a small portion of the mass of the explosive material. A material in which the first three factors exist cannot be accepted as an explosive unless the reaction can be made to occur when desired.

Categories of Chemical Explosions

Explosives are classified as low or high explosives according to their rates of decomposition. Low explosives burn rapidly. High explosives ordinarily detonate. There is no sharp line of demarcation between low and high explosives. The chemical decomposition of an explosive may take years, days, hours, or a fraction of a second. The slower forms of decomposition take place in storage and are of interest only from a stability standpoint. Of more interest are the two rapid forms of decomposition, burning and detonation. The term "detonation" is used to describe an explosive phenomenon of almost instantaneous decomposition. The properties of the explosive indicate the class into which it falls. In some cases explosives may be made to fall into either class by the conditions under which they are initiated. For convenience, low and high explosives may be differentiated in the following manner.

(1) *Low explosives*—These are normally employed as propellants. They undergo autocombustion at rates that vary from a few centimeters per second to approximately 400 meters per second. Included in this group are smokeless powders, which will be discussed in a later chapter, and pyrotechnics such as flares and illumination devices.

(2) *High explosives*—These are normally employed in warheads. They undergo detonation at rates of 1,000 to 8,500 meters per second. High explosives are conventionally subdivided into two classes and differentiated by sensitivity:

   (a) *Primary*—These are extremely sensitive to shock, friction, and heat. They will burn rapidly or detonate if ignited.

   (b) *Secondary*—These are relatively insensitive to shock, friction, and heat. They may burn when ignited in small, unconfined quantities; detonation occurs otherwise.

Characteristics of Military Explosives

To determine the suitability of an explosive substance for *military use*, its physical properties must first be investigated. The usefulness of a military explosive can only be appreciated when these properties and the factors affecting them are fully understood. Many explosives have been studied in past years to determine their suitability for military use and most have been found wanting. Several of those found acceptable have displayed certain characteristics that are considered undesirable and, therefore, limit their usefulness in military applications. The requirements of a military explosive are stringent, and very few explosives display all of the characteristics necessary to make them acceptable for military standardization. Some of the more important characteristics are discussed below:

Availability and cost. In view of the enormous quantity demands of modern warfare, explosives must be produced from cheap raw materials that are nonstrategic and available in great quantity. In addition, manufacturing operations must be reasonably simple, cheap, and safe.

Sensitivity. Regarding an explosive, this refers to the ease with which it can be ignited or detonated—i.e., the amount and intensity of shock, friction, or heat that is required. When the term sensitivity is used, care must be taken to clarify what kind of sensitivity is under discussion. The relative sensitivity of a given explosive to impact may vary greatly from its sensitivity to friction or heat. Some of the test methods used to determine sensitivity are as follows:

(1) Impact—Sensitivity is expressed in terms of the distance through which a standard weight must be dropped to cause the material to explode.
(2) Friction—Sensitivity is expressed in terms of what occurs when a weighted pendulum scrapes across the material (snaps, crackles, ignites, and/or explodes).
(3) Heat—Sensitivity is expressed in terms of the temperature at which flashing or explosion of the material occurs.

Sensitivity is an important consideration in selecting an explosive for a particular purpose. The explosive in an armor-piercing projectile must be relatively insensitive, or the shock of impact would cause it to detonate before it penetrated to the point desired.

Stability. Stability is the ability of an explosive to be stored without deterioration. The following factors affect the stability of an explosive:

(1) Chemical constitution—The very fact that some common chemical compounds can undergo explosion when heated indicates that there is something unstable in their structures. While no precise explanation has been developed for this, it is generally recognized that certain groups, nitro dioxide (NO_2), nitrate (NO_3), and azide (N_3), are intrinsically in a condition of internal strain. Increased strain through heating can cause a sudden disruption of the molecule and consequent explosion. In some cases, this condition of molecular instability is so great that decomposition takes place at ordinary temperatures.

(2) Temperature of storage—The rate of decomposition of explosives increases at higher temperatures. All of the standard military explosives may be considered to be of a high order of stability at temperatures of $-10°$ to $+35°C$, but each has a high temperature at which the rate of decomposition becomes rapidly accelerated and stability is reduced. As a rule of thumb, most explosives become dangerously unstable at temperatures exceeding 70°C.

(3) Exposure to sun—If exposed to the ultraviolet rays of the sun, many explosive compounds that contain nitrogen groups will rapidly decompose, affecting their stability.

Power. The term *power* (or more properly, *performance*) as it is applied to an explosive refers to its ability to do work. In practice it is defined as its ability to accomplish what is intended in the way of energy delivery (i.e., fragments, air blast, high-velocity jets, underwater bubble energy, etc.). Explosive power or performance is evaluated by a tailored series of tests to assess the material for its intended use. Of the tests listed below, cylinder expansion and air-blast tests are common to most testing programs, and the others support specific uses.

Cylinder expansion test—A standard amount of explosive is loaded in a cylinder usually manufactured of copper. Data is collected concerning the rate of radial expansion of the cylinder and maximum cylinder wall velocity. This also establishes the Gurney constant α or $2\sqrt{E}$.

Cylinder fragmentation test—A standard steel cylinder is charged with explosive and fired in a sawdust pit. The fragments are collected and the size distribution analyzed.

Detonation pressure (Chapman-Jouget)—Detonation pressure data are derived from measurements of shock waves transmitted into water by the detonation of cylindrical explosive charges of a standard size.

Determination of critical diameter—This test establishes the minimum physical size a charge of a specific explosive must be to sustain its own detonation wave. The procedure involves the detonation of a series of charges of different diameters until difficulty in detonation wave propagation is observed.

Infinite diameter detonation velocity—Detonation velocity is dependent on landing density (ρ_c), charge diameter, and grain size. The hydrodynamic theory of detonation used in predicting explosive phenomena does not include diameter of the charge, and therefore a detonation velocity, for an imaginary charge of infinite diameter. This procedure requires a series of charges of the same density and physical structure, but different diameters, to be fired and the resulting detonation velocities interpolated to predict the detonation velocity of a charge of infinite diameter.

Pressure versus scaled distance—A charge of specific size is detonated and its pressure effects measured at a standard distance. The values obtained are compared with that for TNT.

Impulse versus scaled distance—A charge of specific size is detonated and its impulse (the area under the pressure-time curve) measured versus distance. The results are tabulated and expressed in TNT equivalent.

Relative bubble energy (RBE)—A 5- to 50-kg charge is detonated in water and piezoelectric gauges are used to measure peak pressure, time constant, impulse, and energy. The RBE may be defined as

$$RBE = \left(\frac{K_x}{K_s}\right)^3$$

where K = bubble expansion period for experimental (x) or standard (s) charge.

Brisance. In addition to strength, explosives display a second characteristic, which is their shattering effect or brisance (from the French meaning "to break"), which is distinguished from their total work capacity. This characteristic is of practical importance in determining the effectiveness of an explosion in fragmenting shells, bomb casings, grenades, and the like. The rapidity with which an explosive reaches its peak pressure is a measure of its brisance. Brisance values are primarily employed in France and the Soviet Union.

Density. Density of loading refers to the unit weight of an explosive per unit volume. Several methods of loading are available, and the one used is determined by the characteristics of the explosive. The methods available include pellet loading, cast loading, or press loading. Dependent upon the method employed, an average density of the loaded charge can be obtained that is within 80–95% of the theoretical maximum density of the explosive. High load density can reduce sensitivity by making the mass more resistant to internal friction. Increased load density also permits the use of more explosive, thereby increasing the strength of the warhead. If density is increased to the extent that individual crystals are crushed, the explosive will become more sensitive.

Volatility. Volatility, or the readiness with which a substance vaporizes, is an undesirable characteristic in military explosives. Explosives must be no more than slightly volatile at the temperature at which they are loaded or at their highest storage temperature. Excessive volatility often results in the development of pressure within rounds of ammunition and separation of mixtures into their constituents. Stability, as mentioned before, is the ability of an explosive to stand up under storage conditions without deteriorating. Volatility affects the chemical composition of the explosive such that a marked reduction in stability may occur, which results in an increase in the danger of handling. Maximum allowable volatility is 2 ml. of gas evolved in 48 hours.

Hygroscopicity. The introduction of moisture into an explosive is highly undesirable since it reduces the sensitivity, strength, and velocity of detonation of the explosive. Hygroscopicity is used as a measure of a material's moisture-absorbing tendencies. Moisture affects explosives adversely by acting as an inert material that absorbs heat when vaporized, and by acting as a solvent medium that can cause undesired chemical reactions. Sensitivity, strength, and velocity of detonation are reduced by inert materials that reduce the continuity of the explosive mass. When the moisture content evaporates during detonation, cooling occurs, which reduces the temperature of reaction. Stability is also affected by the presence of moisture since moisture promotes decomposition of the explosive and, in addition, causes corrosion of the explosive's metal container. For all of these reasons, hygroscopicity must be negligible in military explosives.

Toxicity. Due to their chemical structure, most explosives are toxic to some extent. Since the effect of toxicity may vary from a mild headache to serious damage of internal organs, care must be taken to limit toxicity in military explosives to a minimum. Any explosive of high toxicity is unacceptable for military use.

Mechanism of Chemical Explosive Reaction

The development of new and improved types of ammunition requires a continuous program of research and development. Adoption of an explosive for a particular use is based upon both proving ground and service tests. Before these tests, however, preliminary estimates of the characteristics of the explosive are made. The principles of thermochemistry are applied for this process.

Thermochemistry is concerned with the changes in internal energy, principally as heat, in chemical reactions. An explosion consists of a series of reactions, highly exothermic, involving decomposition of the ingredients and recombination to form the products of explosion. Energy changes in explosive reactions are calculated either from known chemical laws or by analysis of the products.

For most common reactions, tables based on previous investigations permit rapid calculation of energy changes. Products of an explosive remaining in a closed calorimetric bomb (a constant-volume explosion) after cooling the bomb back to room temperature are rarely those present at the instant of maximum temperature and pressure. Since only the final products may be analyzed conveniently, indirect or theoretical methods often used to determine the maximum temperature and pressure values.

Some of the important characteristics of an explosive that can be determined by such theoretical computations and are discussed in this section are:

(1) Oxygen balance
(2) Heat of explosion or reaction
(3) Volume of products of explosion
(4) Potential of the explosive

Oxygen Balance (OB)

Oxygen balance is an expression that is used to indicate the degree to which an explosive can be oxidized. If an explosive molecule contains just enough oxygen to convert all of its carbon to carbon dioxide, all of its hydrogen to water, and all of its metal to metal oxide with no excess, the molecule is said to have a zero oxygen balance. The molecule is said to have a positive oxygen balance if it contains more oxygen than is needed and a negative oxygen balance if it contains less oxygen than is needed. The sensitivity, strength, and brisance of an explosive are all somewhat dependent upon oxygen balance and tend to approach their maximums as oxygen balance approaches zero.

The oxygen balance (OB) is calculated from the empirical formula of a compound in percentage of oxygen required for complete conversion of carbon to carbon dioxide, hydrogen to water, and metal to metal oxide.

The procedure for calculating oxygen balance in terms of 100 grams of the explosive material is to determine the number of gram atoms of oxygen that are excess or deficient for 100 grams of a compound.

$$\text{OB } (\%) = -\frac{1600}{\text{Mol. Wt. of Compound}}\left(2X + \frac{Y}{2} + M - Z\right)$$

where

X = number of atoms of carbon
Y = number of atoms of hydrogen
Z = number of atoms of oxygen
M = number of atoms of metal (metallic oxide produced).

In the case of TNT ($C_6H_2(NO_2)_3CH_3$),

Molecular weight = 227.1
$X = 7$ (number of carbon atoms)
$Y = 5$ (number of hydrogen atoms)
$Z = 6$ (number of oxygen atoms)

Therefore

$$\text{OB } (\%) = -\frac{1600}{227.1}(14 + 2.5 - 6)$$

$$= -74\% \text{ for TNT}$$

Because sensitivity, brisance, and strength are properties resulting from a complex explosive chemical reaction, a simple relationship such as oxygen balance cannot be depended upon to yield universally consistent results. When using oxygen balance to predict properties of one explosive relative to another, it is to be expected that the explosive with an oxygen balance closer to zero will be the more brisant, powerful, and sensitive; however, many exceptions to this rule do exist. More complicated predictive calculations, such as those discussed in the next section, result in more accurate predictions.

One area in which oxygen balance can be applied is in the processing of mixtures of explosives. The family of explosives called amatols are mixtures of ammonium nitrate and TNT. Ammonium nitrate has an oxygen balance of +20% and TNT has an oxygen balance of −74%, so it would appear that the mixture yielding an oxygen balance of zero would also result in the best explosive properties. In actual practice a mixture of 80% ammonium nitrate and 20% TNT by weight yields an oxygen balance of $+1\%$, the best properties of all mixtures, and an increase in strength of 30% over TNT.

Heat of Explosion

When a chemical compound is formed from its constituents, the reaction may either absorb or give off heat. The quantity of heat absorbed or given off during transformation is called the heat of formation. The heats of formations for solids and gases found in explosive reactions have been determined for a temperature of 15°C and atmospheric pressure, and are normally tabulated in units of kilocalories per gram molecule. (See table 12–1). Where a negative value is given, it indicates that heat is absorbed during the formation of the compound from its elements. Such a reaction is called an endothermic reaction. The convention usually employed in simple thermochemical calculations is arbitrarily to take heat contents of all elements as zero in their standard states at all temperatures (standard state being defined as the state at which the elements are found under natural or ambient conditions). Since the heat of formation of a compound is the net difference between the heat content of the compound and that of its elements, and since the latter are taken as zero by convention, it follows that the heat content of a compound is equal to its heat of formation in such nonrigorous calculations. This leads us to the principle of initial and final state, which may be expressed as follows: "The net quantity of heat liberated or absorbed in any chemical modification of a system depends solely upon the initial and final states of the system, provided the transformation takes place at constant volume or at constant pressure. It is completely independent of the intermediate transformations and of the time required for the reactions."

From this it follows that the heat liberated in any transformation accomplished through successive reactions is the algebraic sum of the heats liberated or absorbed in the different reactions. Consider the formation of the original explosive from its elements as an intermediate reaction in the formation of the products of explosion. The net amount of heat liberated during an explosion is the sum of the heats of formation of the products of explosion, minus the heat of formation of the original explosive.

The net heat difference between heats of formations of the reactants and products in a chemical reaction is termed the heat of reaction. For oxidation this heat of reaction may be termed heat of combustion.

Table 12–1.　Heats of Formation from the Elements at 15°C and 760 MM Pressure*

Name	Formula	Molecular Weight	Heats of Formation (Kcal/Mol)		
			Gas	Liquid	Solid
Ammonium perchlorate	NH_4ClO_4	117.5	—	—	78.3
Ammonium picrate	$C_6H_2(NO_2)_3O \cdot NH_4$	246.1	—	—	78.0
Ammonium nitrate	NH_4NO_3	80.0	—		87.8
Carbon dioxide	CO_2	44.0	94.39	—	100.3
Carbon monoxide	CO	28.0	26.43	—	—
Copper picrate	$[C_6H_2(NO_2)_3O]_2Cu$	519.8	—	—	60.4
Cupic oxide	CuO	79.54	—	—	34.89
RDX	$(CH_2)_3N_3(NO_2)_3$	222.13	—	—	24.17
HMX	$C_4H_8N_8O_8$	296	—	—	− 17.9
Hydrochloric acid	HCl	36.46	22.03	—	—
Lead azide	PbN_6	291.3	—	—	− 105.9
Lead oxide	PbO	223.2	—	—	52.47
Lead nitrate	$Pb(NO_3)_2$	331.2	—	—	108.3
Lead picrate	$[C_6H_2(NO_2)_3O]_2Pb$	663.4	—	—	82.2
Lead styphnate	$C_6H(NO_2)_3(O_2Pb)$	450.3	—	—	44.7
Mercuric oxide	HgO	216.6	—	—	21.7
Mercury fulminate	$Hg(CNO)_2$	284.6	—	—	− 64.5
Mercury picrate	$[C_6H_2(NO_2)_3O]_2Hg$	656.3	—	—	42.8
Nitroglycerin	$C_3H_5(NO_3)_3$	227.1	—	85.3	—
Nitromethane	CH_3NO_2	61.0	14.0	27.6	—
PETN	$C(CH_2ONO_2)_4$	316.15	—	—	119.4
Picric acid	$C_6H_2(NO_2)_3OH$	229.1	—	—	56.0
Tetryl	$C_7H_5N(NO_2)_4$	287.1	—	—	− 10.4
Trinitrotoluene (TNT)	$C_6H_2(NO_2)_3CH_3$	227.1	—	—	16.5
Water	H_2O	18.0	57.81	68.38	69.7
Zinc oxide	ZnO	81.4	—	—	84.35
Zinc picrate	$[C_6H_2(NO_2)_3O]_2Zn$	521.6	—	—	102.8

*Data for this tables furnished by Picatinny Arsenal.

Table 12–2.   Order of Priorities

Priority	Composition of Explosive	Products of Decomposition
1	A metal & chlorine	Metallic chloride (solid)
2	Hydrogen & chlorine	HCL (gaseous)
3	A metal & oxygen	Metallic oxide (solid)
4	Carbon & oxygen	CO (gaseous)
5	Hydrogen & oxygen	H_2O (gaseous)
6	CO and oxygen	CO_2 (gaseous)
7	Nitrogen	N_2 (elemental)
8	Excess oxygen	O_2 (elemental)
9	Excess hydrogen	H_2 (elemental)

In explosive technology only materials that are exothermic—that is, have a heat of reaction that causes net liberation of heat—are of interest. Hence, in this text, heats of reaction are virtually all positive. Since reactions may occur either under conditions of constant pressure or constant volume, the heat of reaction can be expressed at constant pressure or at constant volume. It is this heat of reaction that may be properly expressed as "heat of the explosion."

Balancing Chemical Explosion Equations

In order to assist in balancing chemical equations, an order of priorities is presented in table 12–2. Explosives containing C, H, O, and N and/or a metal will form the products of reaction in the priority sequence shown.

Some observations you might want to make as you balance an equation:

(1) The progression is from top to bottom; you may skip steps that are not applicable, but you never back up.
(2) At each separate step there are *never* more than two compositions and two products.
(3) At the conclusion of the balancing, elemental forms, nitrogen, oxygen, and hydrogen, are always found in diatomic form.

Example

TNT: $C_6H_2(NO_2)_3CH_3$; constituents: $7C + 5H + 3N + 6O$

Using the order of priorities in table 12–1, prority 4 gives the first reaction products:

$7C + 6O \rightarrow 6CO$ with one mol of carbon remaining

Next, since all the oxygen has been combined with the carbon to form CO, priority 7 results in:

$$3N \rightarrow 1.5N_2$$

Finally, priority 9 results in: $5H \rightarrow 2.5H_2$.
The balanced equation, showing the products of reaction resulting from the detonation of TNT, is:

$$C_6H_2(NO_2)_3CH_3 \rightarrow 6CO + 2.5H_2 + 1.5N_2 + C$$

Notice that partial mols are permitted in these calculations. The number of mols of gas formed is 10. The product, carbon, is a solid.

Volume of Products of Explosion

The law of Avogadro states that equal volumes of all gases under the same conditions of temperature and pressure contain the same number of molecules. From this law, it follows that the molecular volume of one gas is equal to the molecular volume of any other gas. The molecular volume of any gas at 0°C and under normal atmospheric pressure is very nearly 22.4 liters or 22.4 cubic decimeters. Thus, considering the nitroglycerin reaction.

$$C_3H_5(NO_3)_3 \rightarrow 3CO_2 + 2.5H_2O + 1.5N_2 + .25O_2$$

the explosion of one gram molecule of nitroglycerin produces in the gaseous state: 3 gram molecules of CO_2; 2.5 gram molecules of H_2O; 1.5 gram molecules of N_2; and .25 gram molecule of O_2. Since a molecular volume is the volume of one gram molecule of gas, one gram molecule of nitroglycerin produces $3 + 2.5 + 1.5 + .25 = 7.25$ molecular volumes of gas; and these molecular volumes at 0°C and atmospheric pressure form an actual volume of $7.25 \times 22.4 = 162.4$ liters of gas. (Note that the products H_2O and CO_2 are in their gaseous form.)

Based upon this simple beginning, it can be seen that the volume of the products of explosion can be predicted for any quantity of the explosive. Further, by employing the law of Gay-Lussac for perfect gases, the volume of the products of explosion may also be calculated for any given temperature. This law states that at a constant pressure a perfect gas expands 1/273 of its volume at 0°C, for each degree of rise in temperature.

Therefore, at 15°C the molecular volume of any gas is,

$$V_{15} = 22.4\,(1 + 15/273) = 23.63\,\text{liters per mol}$$

Thus, at 15°C the volume of gas produced by the explosive decomposition of one gram molecule of nitroglycerin becomes

$$V = \left(23.63 \, \frac{\ell}{\text{mol}} \right) (7.25 \, \text{mol}) = 171.3 \, \text{liters}$$

Potential of the Explosive

The potential of an explosive is the total work that can be performed by the gas resulting from its explosion, when expanded adiabatically from its original volume, until its pressure is reduced to atmospheric pressure and its temperature to 15°C. The potential is therefore the total quantity of heat given off at constant volume when expressed in equivalent work units and is a measure of the strength of the explosive.

An explosion may occur under two general conditions: the first, unconfined, as in the open air where the pressure (atmospheric) is constant; the second, confined, as in a closed chamber where the volume is constant. The same amount of heat energy is liberated in each case, but in the unconfined explosion, a certain amount is used as work energy in pushing back the surrounding air, and therefore is lost as heat. In a confined explosion, where the explosive volume is small (such as occurs in the powder chamber of a firearm), practically all the heat of explosion is conserved as useful energy. If the quantity of heat liberated at constant volume under adiabatic conditions is calculated and converted from heat units to equivalent work units, the potential or capacity for work results.

Therefore, if

Q_{mp} represents the total quantity of heat given off by a gram molecule of explosive of 15°C and constant pressure (atmospheric);

Q_{mv} represents the total heat given off by a gram molecule of explosive at 15°C and constant volume; and

W   represents the work energy expended in pushing back the surrounding air in an unconfined explosion and thus is not available as net theoretical heat;

then, because of the conversion of energy to work in the constant pressure case,

$$Q_{mv} = Q_{mp} + W$$

from which the value of Q_{mv} may be determined. Subsequently, the potential of a gram mol of an explosive may be calculated. Using this value, the potential for any other weight of explosive may be determined by simple proportion.

Using the principle of the initial and final state, and heat of formation tables (resulting from experimental data), the heat released at constant pressure may be readily calculated.

$$Q_{mp} = \sum_{1}^{m} v_i Q_{fi} - \sum_{1}^{n} v_k Q_{f_k}$$

where:

Q_{fi} = heat of formation of product i at constant pressure
Q_{f_k} = heat of formation of reactant K at constant pressure
v = number of mols of each product/reactant (m is the number of products and n the number of reactants)

The work energy expended by the gaseous products of detonation is expressed by:

$$W = \int P \, dv$$

With pressure constant and negligible initial volume, this expression reduces to:

$$W = PV_2$$

Since heats of formation are calculated for standard atmospheric pressure ($10.132 \times 10^4 \text{N/m}^2$) and 15°C, V_2 is the volume occupied by the product gases under these conditions. At this point

$$W = \left(10.132 \times 10^4 \frac{\text{Newtons}}{\text{meter}^2} \right) \left(23.63 \frac{\ell}{\text{mol}} \right) (N_{\text{mol}})$$

and by applying the appropriate conversion factors, work is determined in units of kcal/mol.

$$W = \left(10.132 \times 10^4 \frac{N}{m^2} \right) \left(23.63 \frac{\ell}{\text{mol}} \right) (N_{\text{mol}}) \left(\frac{10^{-3} \, m^3}{\ell} \right)$$
$$\left(\frac{\text{Joules}}{\text{Newton-meter}} \right) \left(\frac{1 \, \text{Kcal}}{4185 \, \text{Joules}} \right)$$

Consolidating terms:

$$W = (.572)(N_{\text{mol}}) \frac{\text{kcal}}{\text{mol}}$$

Once the chemical reaction has been balanced, one can calculate the volume of gas produced and the work of expansion. With this completed, the calculations necessary to determine potential may be accomplished. For TNT:

$$C_6H_2(NO_2)_3CH_3 \rightarrow 6CO + 2.5H_2 + 1.5N_2 + C$$

with N_m = 10 mols
Then:

$$Q_{mp} = 6(26.43) - (+16.5) = 142.08 \frac{kcal}{mol}$$

Note: Elements in their natural state (H_2, O_2, N_2, C, etc.) are used as the basis for heat of formation tables and are assigned a value of zero. See table 12–2.

$$Q_{mv} = 142.08 + .572(10) = 147.8 \frac{kcal}{mol}$$

As previously stated, Q_{mv} converted to equivalent work units is the potential of the explosive. (MW = Molecular Weight of Explosive)

$$\text{Potential} = \left(Q_{mv} \frac{kcal}{mol}\right)\left(4185 \frac{Joules}{kcal}\right)\left(\frac{1\ mol}{MW\ gm}\right)\left(\frac{10^3 g}{kg}\right)$$

$$\text{Potential} = \frac{Q_{mv}}{MW}(4.185 \times 10^6)\frac{Joules}{kg}$$

For TNT,

$$\text{Potential} = \frac{147.8}{227.1}(4.185 \times 10^6) = 2.72 \times 10^6 \frac{Joules}{kg}$$

Rather than tabulate such large numbers, in the field of explosives, TNT is taken as the standard explosive, and others are assigned strengths relative to that of TNT. The potential of TNT has been calculated above to be 2.72×10^6 Joules/kg. Relative strength (RS) may be expressed as

$$\text{R.S.} = \text{Potential of Explosive}/2.72 \times 10^6$$

Summary of Thermochemical Calculations

The PETN reaction will be examined as a summary of thermochemical calculations.

$$\text{PETN: C(CH}_2\text{ONO}_2)_4$$

$$MW = 316.15 \qquad \text{Heat of Formation} = 119.4 \frac{Kcal}{mol}$$

(1) Balance the chemical reaction equation. Using table 12–1, priority 4 gives the first reaction products:

$$5C + 12O \rightarrow 5CO + 7O$$

Next, the hydrogen combines with remaining oxygen:

$$8H + 7O \rightarrow 4H_2O + 3O$$

Then the remaining oxygen will combine with the CO to form CO and CO_2.

$$5CO + 3O \rightarrow 2CO + 3CO_2$$

Finally the remaining nitrogen forms in its natural state (N_2).

$$4N \rightarrow 2N_2$$

The balanced reaction equation is:

$$C(CH_2ONO_2)_4 \rightarrow 2CO + 4H_2O + 3CO_2 + 2N_2$$

(2) Determine the number of molecular volumes of gas per gram molecule. Since the molecular volume of one gas is equal to the molecular volume of any other gas, and since all the products of the PETN reaction are gaseous, the resulting number of molecular volumes of gas (N_m) is:

$$N_m = 2 + 4 + 3 + 2 = 11 \; \frac{\text{mol-volume}}{\text{mol}}$$

(3) Determine the potential (capacity for doing work). If the total heat liberated by an explosive under constant volume conditions (Q_m) is converted to the equivalent work units, the result is the potential of that explosive.

The heat liberated at constant volume (Q_{mv}) is equivalent to that liberated at constant pressure (Q_{mp}) plus that heat converted to work in expanding the surrounding medium. Hence, $Q_{mv} = Q_{mp} + \text{Work (converted)}$.

   a. $Q_{mp} = \Sigma Q_{fi}$ (products) $- \Sigma Q_{fk}$ (reactants)

     where: $Q_f = $ Heat of Formation (see table 12–2)

     For the PETN reaction:

$$Q_{mp} = 2(26.43) + 4(57.81) + 3(94.39) - (119.4)$$
$$= 447.87 \; \frac{\text{Kcal}}{\text{mol}}$$

(If the compound produced a metallic oxide, that heat of formation would be included in Q_{mp}.)

b. Work $= .572(N_m) = .572(11) = 6.292 \dfrac{\text{Kcal}}{\text{mol}}$

c. $Q_{mv} = Q_{mp} + \text{Work} = 447.87 + 6.292 = 454.16 \dfrac{\text{Kcal}}{\text{mol}}$

As previously stated, Q_{mv} converted to equivalent work units is taken as the potential of the explosive.

d. Potential $\left(\dfrac{\text{Joules}}{\text{Kg}}\right) = \dfrac{Q_{mv}}{\text{MW}}(4.185 \times 10^6)$

$$= \dfrac{454.16}{316.15}(4.185 \times 10^6)$$

$$= 6.01 \times 10^6 \dfrac{\text{Joules}}{\text{Kg}}$$

This product may then be used to find the relative strength of PETN, which is

e. $\text{RS} = \dfrac{\text{Pot(PETN)}}{\text{Pot(TNT)}} = \dfrac{6.01 \times 10^6}{2.72 \times 10^6} = 2.21$

References

Army Research Office. *Elements of Armament Engineering* (Part One). Washington, D.C.: U.S. Army Material Command, 1964.

Commander, Naval Ordnance Systems Command. *Safety and Performance Tests for Qualification of Explosives*. NAVORD OD 44811. Washington, D.C.: GPO, 1972.

Commander, Naval Ordnance Systems Command. *Weapons Systems Fundamentals*. NAVORD OP 3000, vol. 2, 1st Rev. Washington, D.C.: GPO, 1971.

Departments of the Army and Air Force. *Military Explosives*. Washington, D.C.: 1967.

13

Warheads

Introduction

The basic function of any weapon is to deliver a destructive force on an enemy target. Targets of today include military bases, factories, bridges, ships, tanks, missile launching sites, artillery emplacements, fortifications, and troop concentrations. Since each type of target presents a different physical destruction problem, a variety of general- and special-purpose warheads are required, within the bounds of cost and logistical availability, so that each target may be attacked with maximum effectiveness.

The basic warhead consists of three functional parts:

(1) Fuze (including the safety and arming devices)
(2) Explosive fill
(3) Warhead case

This chapter will address conventional (non-nuclear) warhead characteristics.

The High-Explosive Train

As discussed previously, high explosives comprise one category of chemical explosives. This category is subdivided into primary and secondary explosives. Recall that primary explosives are considerably more sensitive than secondary explosives. The high-explosive train is usually composed of a detonator, booster, and main charge as shown in figure 13–1. The detonator may be initiated electrically or by mechanical shock and may contain an explosive relay, pyrotechnic delay, etc.

Explosive sensitivity decreases from left to right in figure 13–1. The detonator sets up a detonation wave when initiated. The detonation output of the detonator is too low powered and weak to reliably initiate a high-order detonation in the main charge (secondary explosive) unless a booster is placed between the two. Detonation of the booster results in a shock wave of sufficient strength to initiate a high-order detonation of the main explosive charge.

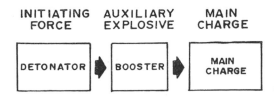

Figure 13–1. High-explosive train.

Explosives are characteristically unstable chemical compounds or mixtures of unstable compounds, and some explosives are formulated with inert binders to achieve variations in the explosive properties. *An explosion of a high-explosive substance is characterized by a chemically reinforced shock wave (detonation wave) travelling at a high velocity.* Figure 13–2 diagrams the principal elements of a detonation reaction. In this figure the detonator has initiated the booster, which has in turn initiated the main charge, with the detonation wave having traveled about two-thirds of the length of the main charge.

If the process were to be stopped momentarily, as diagrammed in figure 13–2, an observer placed inside the unreacted explosive portion would be unaware of what was taking place because he is ahead of the supersonic shock wave. The detonation process, while very rapid, does occur over a finite period of time. The detonation wave is a strong shock wave with pressures as high as 385 kilobars depending on the type of explosive. Levels of shock energy this high are easily capable of breaking the relatively unstable chemical bonds of explosive compounds. Therefore, as the detonation wave passes through the unreacted explosive, atomic bonds within the explosive molecules are

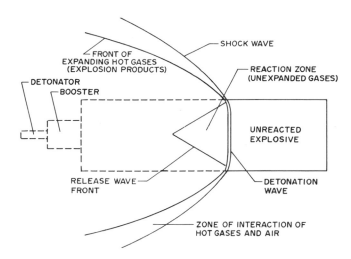

Figure 13–2. Mechanics of detonation.

Warheads   383

broken. There is then a rapid process of chemical recombination into different compounds, principally gases like CO_2, H_2O, N_2, etc., that result in a heat energy release. This release causes rapid expansion of the gases, which reinforces the detonation wave and provides the energy that ultimately produces the destructive effect of a warhead.

The chemical reaction zone, the zone of chemical recombination, is shown in figure 13–2 as a conical zone immediately behind the detonation wave. This high-pressure zone is bounded by a release wave from which expansion of the explosion products occurs. The explosion products expand outwardly in a hot luminous state.

Warhead Characteristics

The warhead is the primary element of the weapon; it accomplishes the desired end result—effective damage to the target. Damage to the target is directly related to the following parameters:

(1) Damage volume—The warhead may be thought of as being enclosed by an envelope that sweeps along the trajectory of the missile. The volume enclosed by this envelope defines the limit of destructive effectiveness of the payload.

(2) Attenuation—As shock and fragments leave the point of origin, a reduction in their destructive potential per unit area takes place. Attenuation can be likened to an expanding sphere, in which the energy available per unit area constantly decreases until it is completely harmless.

(3) Propagation—This is the manner in which energy and material, emitted by the warhead at detonation, travel through the medium in which the blast occurs. When the propagation of a payload is uniform in all directions, it is called isotropic. If not, it is called non-isotropic. See figure 13–3.

Blast Warheads

A blast warhead is one that is designed to achieve target damage primarily from blast effect. When a high explosive detonates, it is converted almost instantly into a gas at very high pressure and temperature. Under the pressure of the gases thus generated, the weapon case expands and breaks into fragments. The air surrounding the casing is compressed and a shock (blast) wave is transmitted into it. Typical initial values for a high-explosive weapon are 200 kilobars of pressure (1 bar = 1 atmosphere) and 5,000 degrees celsius.

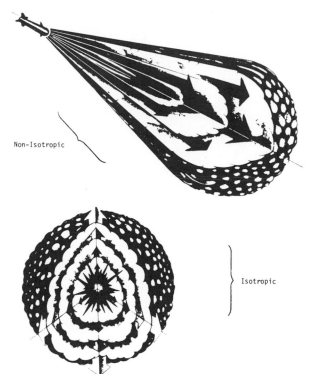

Non-Isotropic

Isotropic

Figure 13–3. Isotropic and non-iso-tropic propagation. (From Weapons Systems Fundamentals)

The detonation characteristics of a few high explosives are presented in table 13–1.

The shock wave generated by the explosion is a compression wave, in which the pressure rises from atmospheric pressure to peak overpressure in a fraction of a microsecond. It is followed by a much slower (hundredths of a second) decline to atmospheric pressure. This portion is known as the positive phase of the shock wave. The pressure continues to decline to subatmospheric pressure and then returns to normal. This portion is called the negative or suction phase. A pressure-time curve is shown in figure 13–4. The durations of these two phases are referred to as the positive and negative durations. The area under the pressure-time curve during the positive phase represents the positive impulse, and that during the negative phase, the negative impulse. The result of this positive/negative pressure variation is a push-pull effect upon the target, which causes targets with large volume to effectively explode from the internal pressure.

For a fixed-weight explosive, the peak pressure and positive impulse decrease with distance from the explosion. This is due to the

Table 13–1. Characteristics of Detonation

Explosive	Loading Density g/cc	Detonation Rate M/S	Heat of Detonation cal/gm	Gurney Constant M/S
Composition B (60% RDX, 40% TNT)	1.68	7840	1240	2402
H-6 (45% RDX, 30% TNT, 20% Al, 5% WAX)	1.71	7191	923	2350
Octol (70% HMX, 30% TNT)	1.80	8377	1074	2560
TNT	1.56	6640	1080	2115
PBX-9404 (93% HMX, 6.5% NITROCELLULOSE, .5% Binder)	1.88	—	—	2637

attentuation of the blast wave. The rate of attenuation is proportional to the rate of expansion of the volume of gases behind the blast wave. In other words the blast pressure is inversely proportional to the cube of the distance from the blast center ($1/R^3$). Blast attenuation is somewhat less than this inside, approximately 16 charge radii from blast center. It should also be noted that there will be fragmentation when the warhead casing ruptures.

Another aspect of overpressure is the phenomenon of Mach reflections, called the "Mach Effect." Figure 13–5 portrays an air burst at some unspecified distance above a reflecting surface, at five successive time intervals after detonation.

When a bomb is detonated at some distance above the ground, the reflected wave catches up to and combines with the original shock wave, called the incident wave, to form a third wave that has a nearly vertical front at ground level. This third wave is called a "Mach Wave"

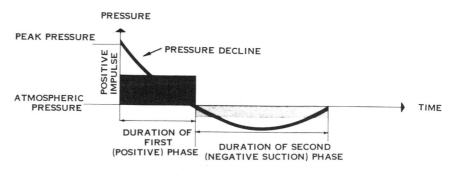

Figure 13–4. Pressure vs time relationship of a blast wave at a given distance from blast center. (From Weapons Systems Fundamentals)

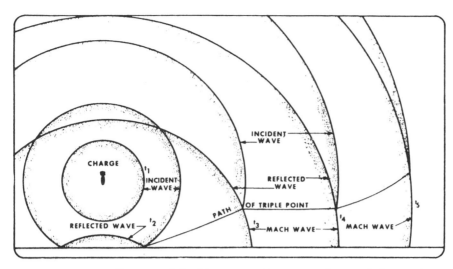

Figure 13–5. Reflection of the blast wave from a surface and the resulting Mach stem. (From Weapons Systems Fundamentals*)*

or "Mach Stem," and the point at which the three waves intersect is called the "Triple Point." The Mach Stem grows in height as it spreads laterally, and as the Mach Stem grows, the triple point rises, describing a curve through the air. In the Mach Stem the incident wave is reinforced by the reflected wave, and both the peak pressure and impulse are at a maximum that is considerably higher than the peak pressure and impulse of the original shock wave at the same distance from the point of explosion.

Using the phenomenon of Mach reflections, it is possible to increase considerably the radius of effectiveness of a bomb. By detonating a warhead at the proper height above the ground, the maximum radius at which a given pressure or impulse is exerted can be increased, in some cases by almost 50%, over that for the same bomb detonated at ground level. The area of effectiveness, or damage volume, may thereby be increased by as much as 100%. Currently only one conventional pure-blast warhead is in use, the Fuel Air Explosive (FAE). Of course, all nuclear warheads are blast warheads, and on most targets they would be detonated at altitude to make use of the Mach Stem effect.

Underwater Blast Warheads

The mechanism of an underwater blast presents some interesting phenomena associated with a more dense medium than air. An underwater explosion creates a cavity filled with high-pressure gas, which pushes the water out radially against the opposing external hydrostatic pressure. At the instant of explosion, a certain amount of gas is instantaneously generated at high pressure and temperature, creating a bubble. In addition, the heat causes a certain amount of water to vaporize, adding to the volume of the bubble. This action immediately begins to force the water in contact with the blast front in an outward direction. The potential energy initially possessed by the gas bubble by virtue of its pressure is thus gradually communicated to the water in the form of kinetic energy. The inertia of the water causes the bubble to overshoot the point at which its internal pressure is equal to the external pressure of the water. The bubble then becomes rarefied, and its radial motion is brought to rest. The external pressure now compresses the rarefied bubble. Again, the equilibrium configuration is overshot, and since by hypothesis there has been no loss of energy, the bubble comes to rest at the same pressure and volume as at the moment of explosion (in practice, of course, energy is lost by acoustical and heat radiation).

The bubble of compressed gas then expands again, and the cycle is repeated. The result is a pulsating bubble of gas slowly rising to the surface, with each expansion of the bubble creating a shock wave. Approximately 90% of the bubble's energy is dissipated after the first expansion and contraction. This phenomenon explains how an underwater explosion appears to be followed by other explosions. The time interval of the energy being returned to the bubble (the period of pulsations) varies with the intensity of the initial explosion.

The rapid expansion of the gas bubble formed by an explosion under water results in a shock wave being sent out through the water in all directions. The shock wave is similar in general form to that in air, although it differs in detail. Just as in air, there is a sharp rise in overpressure at the shock front. However, in water, the peak overpressure does not fall off as rapidly with distance as it does in air. Hence, the peak values in water are much higher than those at the same distance from an equal explosion in air. The velocity of sound in water is nearly one mile per second, almost five times as great as in air. Consequently, the duration of the shock wave developed is shorter than in air.

The close proximity of the upper and lower boundaries between which the shock wave is forced to travel (water surface and ocean floor) causes complex shock-wave patterns to occur as a result of reflection and rarefaction. Also, in addition to the initial shock wave that results from the initial gas bubble expansion, subsequent shock waves are produced by bubble pulsation. The pulsating shock wave is of lower magnitude and of longer duration than the initial shock wave.

Another interesting phenomenon of an underwater blast is surface cutoff. At the surface, the shock wave moving through the water meets a much less dense medium—air. As a result, a reflected wave is sent back into the water, but this is a rarefaction or suction wave. At a point below the surface, the combination of the reflected suction wave with the direct incident wave produces a sharp decrease in the water shock pressure. This is surface cutoff. The variation of the shock overpressure with time after the explosion at a point underwater not too far from the surface is illustrated in figure 13–6.

After the lapse of a short interval, which is the time required for the shock wave to travel from the explosion to the given location, the overpressure rises suddenly due to the arrival of the shock front. Then, for a period of time, the pressure decreases steadily, as in air. Soon thereafter, the arrival of the reflected suction wave from the surface causes the pressure to drop sharply, even below the normal (hydrostatic) pressure of the water. This negative pressure phase is of short duration and can result in a decrease in the extent of damage sustained by the target. The time interval between the arrival of the direct shock wave at a particular location (or target) in the water and that of the cutoff, signaling the arrival of the reflected wave, depends upon the depth of burst, the depth of the target, and the distance from the burst point to the target. It can generally be said that a

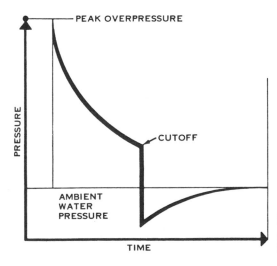

Figure 13–6. Pressure vs time for underwater explosion (near the surface). (From Weapons Systems Fundamentals)

depth bomb should be detonated at or below the target and that a target is less vulnerable near the surface.

Fragmentation Warheads

The study of ballistics, the science of the motion of projectiles, has contributed significantly to the design of fragmentation warheads. Specifically, terminal ballistics studies attempt to determine the laws and conditions governing the velocity and distribution of fragments, the sizes and shapes that result from bursting different types of containers, and the damage aspects of the bursting charge fragmentation.

Approximately 30% of the energy released by the explosive detonation is used to fragment the case and impart kinetic energy to the fragments. The balance of available energy is used to create a shock front and blast effects. The fragments are propelled at high velocity, and after a short distance they overtake and pass through the shock wave. The rate at which the velocity of the shock front accompanying the blast decreases is generally much greater than the decrease in velocity of fragments, which occurs due to air friction. Therefore, the advance of the shock front lags behind that of the fragments. The radius of effective fragment damage, although target dependent, thus exceeds considerably the radius of effective blast damage in an air burst.

Whereas the effects of an idealized blast payload are attenuated by a factor roughly equal to $1/R^3$ (R is measured from the origin), the attenuation of idealized fragmentation effects will vary as $1/R^2$ and $1/R$, depending upon the specific design of the payload. Herein lies the principle advantage of a fragmentation payload: it can afford a greater miss distance and still remain effective because its attenuation is less.

Fragment Velocity

The velocity of the fragments can be looked at in two parts: a) the initial velocity, and b) the velocity attenuation with distance from the origin.

The initial static velocity of the fragments of a cylindrical warhead depends primarily upon two factors:

(1) The charge-to-metal ratio, C/M, where C is the mass of explosive per unit length of projectile and M is the mass of metal per unit length of projectile.

(2) The characteristics of the explosive filler, particularly its brisance and strength. Expressing this quantitatively:

$$V_0 = \sqrt{2E} \sqrt{\frac{C/M}{1 + C/2M}} \qquad (13-1)$$

where the quantity "$\sqrt{2E}$" is known as the Gurney Explosive Energy Constant and is related to the potential energy of the given explosive, as calculated in the military explosives chapter.

Table 13–2 illustrates the relationship between the charge-to-metal ratio and the initial velocities (V_0) of the fragments, and table 13–1 lists typical Gurney Constants.

In this case cylinders of 5.1 cm internal diameter, filled with TNT, were employed. Notice that as the charge-to-metal ratio increases, the fragment velocity also increases.

The fragment velocity as a function of distance(s) is given by the equation:

$$V_s = V_0 e^{-C_D P_a \frac{A}{2m} S} \qquad (13-2)$$

where C_D is the drag coefficient, m is the mass, A is the cross-sectional area of the fragment, and P_a is the density of the atmosphere at the detonation level. Thus, during flight through the air, the velocity of each fragment decays because of air resistance or drag. The fragment velocity decreases more rapidly with distance as the fragment weight decreases. For an assumed initial fragment velocity of 1,825 meters per second, a five-grain (.324 grams) fragment would lose half its initial velocity after traveling 11.25 meters, whereas a 500-grain (32.4 grams) fragment would travel 53.34 meters before losing half its velocity.

Fragment trajectories will follow paths predicted by the principles of external ballistics (chapter 19). For determining the effectiveness

Table 13–2. Fragment Velocity as a Function of Warhead Wall Thickness and C/M Ratio for the Explosive TNT

Wall Thickness (cm)	Charge-to-Metal Ratio (c/m)	Initial Velocity V_0 (M/Sec)
1.27	0.165	875
0.95	0.231	988
0.79	0.286	1158
0.48	0.500	1859

of almost all fragmenting munitions, the subsonic trajectory of the fragments can be ignored. As a result, the density of fragments in a given direction varies inversely as the square of the distance from the weapon. The probability of a hit on some unshielded target is proportional to the exposed projected area and inversely proportional to the square of the distance from the weapon $(1/R^2)$. For an isotropic warhead:

$$P\,(\text{hit}) \propto \text{Frag Density} \times \text{Area Target} \propto \frac{\#\,\text{Fragments}}{4\pi R^2} \times A_T \quad (13\text{--}3)$$

Fragment Flight

The fragments of a warhead travel outward in a nearly perpendicular direction to the surface of its casing (for a cylindrical warhead there is a 7- to 10-degree lead angle). Figure 13–7 portrays a typical fragmentation pattern. The tail and nose spray are frequently referred to separately as the "forty-five degree cone," which is an area of less dense fragmentation. If this payload were to be detonated in flight, the dense side spray would have a slight forward thrust with an increased velocity equal to missile flight velocity.

The angle of the side spray in figure 13–7 would be defined as the beam width of this fragmenting payload. Fragment beam width is defined as the angle covered by a useful density of fragments. Beam width is a function of warhead shape and the placement of the detonator(s) in the explosive charge.

The latest air target warheads are designed to emit a narrow beam of high-velocity fragments. This type of warhead, called an Annular Blast Fragmentation warhead (ABF), has a fragmentation pattern that propagates out in the form of a ring with tremendous destructive

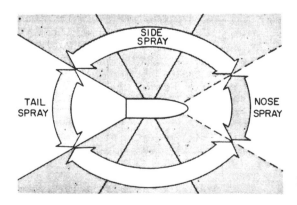

Figure 13–7. Distribution of fragments. (From Weapons Systems Fundamentals)

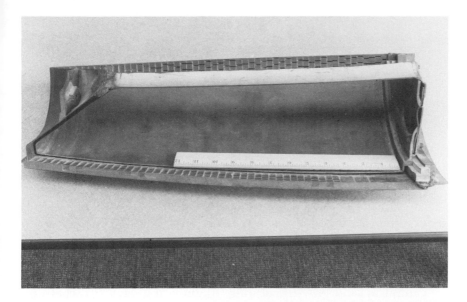

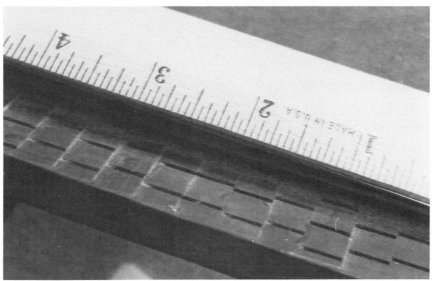

Figure 13–8. An internally scored case for a fragmenting warhead. Note detail in bottom photo.

potential. A newer type of fragmentation warhead is the Selectivity Aimable Warhead (SAW). This "smart" warhead is designed to aim its fragment density at the target. This is accomplished by the fuzing system telling the warhead where the target is located and causing it to detonate so as to maximize the energy density on the target.

Figure 13–9. An externally scored case for a fragmenting warhead.

Fragment Material

The damage produced by a fragment with a certain velocity depends upon the mass of the fragment. It is therefore necessary to know the approximate distribution of mass for the fragments large enough to cause damage. Mass distribution of payload fragments is determined by means of a static detonation in which the fragments are caught in sand pits. In naturally fragmenting payloads where no attempt to control fragment size and number is made, fragmentation may randomly vary from fine, dust-like particles to large pieces. Modern warheads use scored casings and precut fragments to ensure a large damage volume.

Shaped Charge Warheads

The discovery of what is variously referred to as the shaped charge effect, the hollow charge effect, the cavity effect, or the Munroe effect, dates back to the 1880s in this country. Dr. Charles Munroe, while working at the Naval Torpedo Station at Newport, Rhode Island, in the 1880s, discovered that if a block of guncotton with letters countersunk into its surface was detonated with its lettered surface against a steel plate, the letters were indented into the surface of the steel. The essential features of this effect were also observed in about 1880 in both Germany and Norway, although no great use was made of it, and it was temporarily forgotten.

A shaped charge missile consists basically of a hollow liner of metal material, usually copper or aluminum of conical, hemispherical, or other shape, backed on the convex side by explosive. A container, fuze, and detonating device are included.

When this missile strikes a target, the fuze detonates the charge from the rear. A detonation wave sweeps forward and begins to collapse the metal cone liner at its apex. The collapse of the cone results in the formation and ejection of a continuous high-velocity solid jet of linear material. Velocity of the tip of the jet is on the order of 8,500

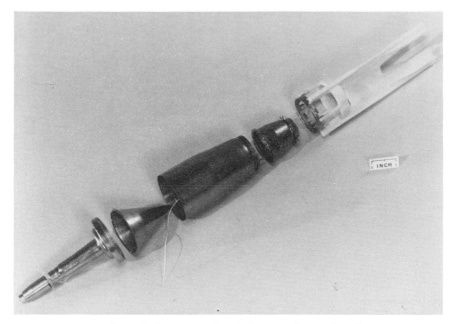

Figure 13–10. Shaped charge warhead from a cluster bomb.

meters per sec, while the trailing end of the jet has a velocity on the order of 1,500 meters per sec. This produces a velocity gradient that tends to stretch out or lengthen the jet. The jet is then followed by a slug that consists of about 80% of the liner mass. The slug has a velocity on the order of 600 meters per sec. This process is illustrated in figure 13–11.

When the jet strikes a target of armor plate or mild steel, pressures in the range of hundreds of kilobars are produced at the point of contact. This pressure produces stresses far above the yield strength of steel, and the target material flows like a fluid out of the path of the jet. This phenomenon is called hydrodynamic penetration. There is so much radial momentum associated with the flow that the difference in diameter between the jet and the hole it produces depends on the characteristics of the target material. A larger diameter hole will be made in mild steel than in armor plate because the density and hardness of armor plate is greater. The depth of penetration into a very thick slab of mild steel will also be greater than that into homogeneous armor.

In general, the depth of penetration depends upon five factors:

(1) Length of jet
(2) Density of the target material

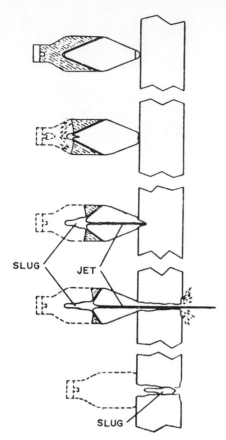

SLUG

JET

SLUG

Figure 13–11. Shaped charge sequence.

(3) Hardness of target material
(4) Density of the jet
(5) Jet precision (straight vs. divergent)

The longer the jet, the greater the depth of penetration. Therefore, the greater the standoff distance (distance from target to base of cone) the better. This is true up to the point at which the jet particulates or breaks up (at 6 to 8 cone diameters from the cone base). Particulation is a result of the velocity gradient in the jet, which stretches it out until it breaks up.

Jet precision refers to the straightness of the jet. If the jet is formed with some oscillation or wavy motion, then depth of penetration will be reduced. This is a function of the quality of the liner and the initial detonation location accuracy.

The effectiveness of shaped charge warheads is reduced when they are caused to rotate. (Degradation begins at 10 RPS). Thus, spin-stabilized projectiles generally cannot use shaped-charge warheads.

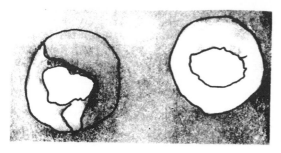

Figure 13–12. Spalling of armor plate (rear face).

The effectiveness of a shaped charge payload is independent of the striking velocity of the warhead. In fact, velocity of the warhead must be taken into consideration to ensure that detonation of the payload occurs at the instant of optimum stand-off distance. The jet can then effectively penetrate the target. Damage incurred is mostly a function of the jet and material from the target armor spalled off the rear face. This action of target material joining with the shaped charge jet is known as spalling. The extent of spalling is a function of the amount of explosive in the payload and the quality of the target armor. Figure 13–12 illustrates the results of armor plate spalling.

Continuous-Rod Warheads

Early warhead experiments with short, straight, unconnected rods had shown that such rods could chop off propeller blades, engine cylinders, and wings, and in general, inflict severe damage to a fighter aircraft. However, rod warheads were ineffective against larger planes because the nature of most bomber aircraft structures permits a number of short cuts in their skin without lethal damage occurring. It was found, however, that long, continuous cuts would do considerable damage to a bomber; therefore, the continuous-rod warhead was developed.

Upon detonation, the continuous-rod payload expands radially into a ring pattern. The intent is to cause the connected rods, during their expansion, to strike the target and produce damage by a cutting action (see figure 13–13).

Each rod is connected end-to-end alternately and arranged in a bundle radially around the main charge. The burster is designed such that upon detonation the explosive force will be distributed evenly along the length of the continuous-rod bundle. This is important in order to ensure that each rod will maintain its configuration and consequently result in uniform integrity of the expanding circle. Fig-

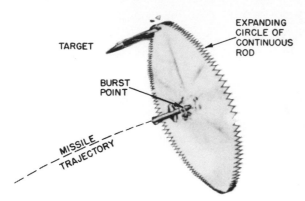

TARGET

EXPANDING
CIRCLE OF
CONTINUOUS
ROD

BURST
POINT

MISSILE
TRAJECTORY

*Figure 13–13. Expansion of continuous-
rod warhead.*

ure 13–14 serves to illustrate the arrangement of the bundle on a
section of the main charge, and its accordion-like appearance as the
section begins expansion.

The metal density of a normal fragmentation warhead attenuates
inversely with the square of the distance ($1/R^2$). However, because
it is non-isotropic, the metal density of a continuous-rod payload
attenuates inversely as the distance from the point of detonation
($1/R$).

To ensure that the rods stay connected at detonation, the maximum
initial rod velocity is limited to the range of 1,050 to 1,150 meters
per second. The initial fragment velocities of fragmentation warheads
are in the range of 1,800 to 2,100 meters per second. Thus, in comparison, continuous-rod warheads cannot produce as much destructive energy potential as fragmentation warheads.

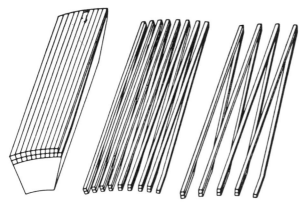

*Figure 13–14. Section of continuous-rod
bundle.*

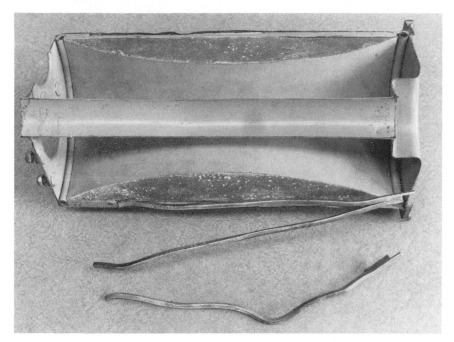

Figure 13–15. Continuous-rod warhead (cutaway).

Special-Purpose Warheads

There are other means of attacking targets than with blast, fragmentation, shaped charge, or continuous rod payloads. Several types of payloads are more specialized in nature, designed to perform a specific function. A few of these will be described.

(1) *Thermal warheads*—The purpose of thermal warheads is to start fires. Thermal payloads may employ chemical energy to kindle fires with subsequent uncontrollable conflagrations, or nuclear energy to produce direct thermal destruction as well as subsequent fires. Thermal payloads of the chemical type may be referred to as incendiary or fire payloads. Many area targets are more effectively attacked by fire than by blast or fragmentation. Thermal warheads, principally in the form of aircraft bombs (Napalm), have been developed for use against combustible land targets where large and numerous fires will cause serious damage.

(2) *Biological and chemical warheads*—A biological warhead uses bacteria or other biological agents for accomplishing its pur-

Figure 13–16. Detonation of a continuous-rod warhead.

poses of causing sickness or death, and is of extreme strategic importance since it is capable of destroying life without damaging buildings or materials. The poisoning of water supplies is probably the single most efficient way of destroying enemy personnel. The war potential of the enemy, such as guns, missile launching sites, etc., are thus left intact and at the disposal of the attacker. The biological agent may be chosen so that it causes only temporary disability rather than death to enemy personnel, thereby making it relatively simple to capture an enemy installation. A small explosive charge placed in a biological payload is useful in effecting the initial dispersion of biological agents. A chemical warhead payload is designed to expel poisonous substances and thus produce personnel casualties.

(3) *Radiation warheads*—Radiological material may be employed as the payload in warheads in the same manner as chemical and biological agents. The payload may consist of matter prepared especially for the purpose, radioactive by-products of another process, or an atomic warhead designed to produce an abnormally large amount of radioactive material. The neu-

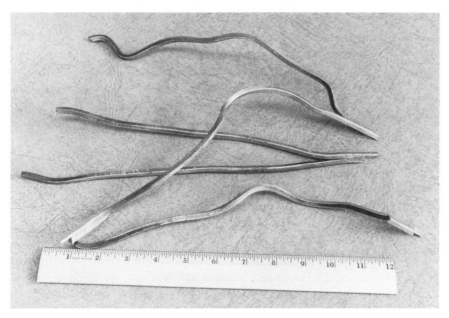

Figure 13–17. Continuous-rod warhead fragments.

tron bomb produces more damaging neutron radiation than a normal blast atomic bomb and thereby achieves the same destructive area with a smaller blast yield and thus actually decreases physical damage.

(4) *Pyrotechnic warheads*—Pyrotechnics are typically employed for signaling, illuminating, or marking targets. In the simplest form they are hand-held devices. Some examples of more elaborate warhead payloads are as follows:

(a) Illumination—These warheads usually contain a flare or magnesium flare candle as the payload, which is expelled by a small charge and is parachuted to the ground. During its descent the flare is kindled. The illuminating warhead is thus of great usefulness during night attacks in pointing out enemy fortifications. Illumination projectiles are used with great effectiveness in shore bombardment. Illuminating warheads are also used as aircraft flares and flare rockets to assist in the attack of the ground targets and submarines. Because these flares are difficult to extinguish if accidentally ignited, extreme caution in their handling is required.

(b) Smoke—These warheads are used primarily to screen troop movements and play a vital role in battlefield tactics. A black powder charge ignites and expels canisters that may be designed to emit white, yellow, red, green, or violet smoke.

(c) Markers—White phosphorus is commonly employed as a payload to mark the position of the enemy. It can be very dangerous, especially in heavy concentrations. The material can self-ignite in air, and though it can be extinguished by water, it will rekindle upon subsequent exposure to air. Body contact can produce serious burns. Copper sulphate prevents its re-ignition.

(5) *Anti-personnel warheads*—Such warheads are designed to destroy or maim personnel or to damage material enough to render it inoperable. In the area of field artillery, the flechette or beehive round is an example of an anti-personnel warhead. The payload in this projectile consists of 8,000 steel-wire, fin-stabilized darts. Upon detonation the darts, or flechettes, are sprayed radially from the point of detonation, normally within sixty feet of the ground. It is effective against personnel in the open or in dense foliage.

(6) *Chaff warheads*—Chaff may be employed to decoy enemy weapons or blind enemy radar. The payload typically consists of metal-coated fiberglass strands cut in lengths determined by wavelength of the RF energy to be countered. Chaff may be dispensed in a variety of warheads, including projectiles and rockets.

(7) *Cluster bomb units (CBU)*—CBUs are air-delivered weapons that are canisters containing hundreds of small bomblets for use against a variety of targets, such as anti-personnel, armored vehicles, or ships. Once in the air the canisters open, spreading the bomblets out in a wide pattern. The advantage of this type of warhead is that it gives a wide area of coverage, which allows for a greater margin of error in delivery. Rockeye is a CBU that contains over 225 bomblets. APAM is an improved Rockeye type CBU that contains over 500 bomblets. Like Rockeye, each bomblet contains a shaped charge warhead. The APAM bomblet also has an anti-personnel/soft target detonation mode.

(8) *Mines*—Mine warheads use the underwater blast principles described earlier to inflict damage on the target ship or submarine. The damage energy transmitted is approximately equally divided between the initial shock wave and the expanding gas

bubble. If the target is straddling the gas bubble, then it will have unequal support and may be broken in two. As the detonation depth increases, particularly in excess of 180 feet, the effect of the gas bubble causing damage is greatly diminished; therefore, bottom mines are rarely used in waters exceeding 180–200 feet. Mines typically use the highest potential explosives, generally 1.3 to 1.75 relative strength. Mines have also been developed that actually launch a smart torpedo that then passively and actively homes in on the target before detonation.

(9) *Torpedoes*—Torpedo warheads must be capable of damaging both ships and submarines. Homing in on the screws can achieve a mobility kill. Detonation under the keel at midships can cause the severe gas-bubble damage mentioned with mines, and if the depth is less than 300 feet, the reflected shock wave can substantially increase the damage effects. Torpedoes that actually impact the hull of a ship or submarine have to overcome the double hull/void structure. Deep-diving submarines with especially thick hulls require highly specialized warheads.

(10) *Anti-tank warheads*—Because of extensive innovative advances in tank armor, shaped charge warheads have grown in diameter and other types of warheads developed.

(a) The kinetic energy defeat mechanism employs a very heavy, hard, metal-core penetrator traveling at extremely high velocity. The penetrator is fin stabilized and uses a discarding sabot to increase its size to fit the gun barrel diameter when fired. The armor plate is thus defeated by either: (1) ductile or plastic flow failure, or (2) by shearing or plugging such as a "cookie cutter" would do. The shape of the penetrator tip on this weapon (or any other weapon) is the determining factor.

(b) The high-explosive, plastic defeat mechanism uses a high-explosive plastic filler in a shell that deforms on impact to effectively put a large glob or cone of plastic explosive against the side of the armor. The timing of the base detonator is critical for maximum effect. The armor is not actually penetrated, but extensive spalling is caused on the opposite side of the armor. This warhead is limited to lighter armor than the shaped-charge or armor-piercing kinetic energy warheads.

Summary

High explosives are basically employed in warheads to produce damage. Initiation of the reaction is achieved through the high-explosive train. Rapidity of the reaction is enhanced by the phenomenon of detonation. The generation of heat and the evolution of gases produce pressure effects and radiation, which constitute the damage potential of the warhead.

This chapter has presented a number of ways in which these principles may be applied to produce an explosive force. Through a basic description of warheads, it may be seen how a specific target may determine the warhead characteristic to be employed in order to counter that target. Variation upon the four basic types of warheads results in more specialized designs developed to provide the military arsenal with greater flexibility.

References

Commander, Naval Air Systems Command, *Joint Munitions Effectiveness Manual, Basic JMEM A/S*. NAVAIR 00-130-AS-1. Washington, D.C.: GPO, 1974.

Commander, Naval Ordnance Systems Command. *Weapons Systems Fundamentals*. NAVORD OP 3000, vol. 2, 1st Rev. Washington, D.C.: GPO, 1971.

Departments of the Army and Air Force. *Military Explosives*. Washington, D.C., 1967.

14

Fuzing

Introduction

A fuze is a weapon subsystem that activates the warhead mechanism in the vicinity of the target and also maintains the warhead in a safe condition during all prior phases of the logistic and operational chain.

The fuze is essentially a binary state mechanism. In the context of weapon system hardware, a fuze and warhead are unique in that they are expected to remain functionally quiescent until a bona fide target is encountered, and then to function as intended in a fraction of a millisecond. Guidance systems may recover from transient malfunctions; target-tracking radars may experience numerous false alarms without significantly compromising their utility; and missile airframes may flex and recover, but the fuze-warhead process is singular and irreversible. The quality required of fuze designs is usually specified by two values: functional reliability, which ranges typically from 0.95 to 0.99 for complex missile fuzes, and to 0.999 for projectile and bomb contact fuzes; and safety reliability, for which a failure rate not greater than 1 in 10^6 must be proved prior to release of items for service usage.

Function of the Fuze System

The weapon fuze system has five basic functions that it can perform:

(1) Keep the weapon safe
(2) Arm the weapon
(3) Recognize or detect the target
(4) Initiate the detonation of the warhead
(5) Determine the direction of detonation (special fuzes only)

A typical fuze system that incorporates these five basic functions is depicted in figure 14–1. These functions will be described in greater detail in the following sections.

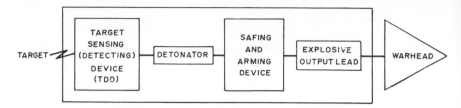

Figure 14–1. Basic fuze system.

Target Detection and Recognition

Target detection and recognition must occur either when the target is close enough to be contained within the lethal envelope of the warhead, or such that the proximity fuze can predict when this condition will occur. This function can be accomplished by several types of mechanical or electrical sensor devices. The specific device used classifies the type of fuzing system. Once the target has been detected or "sensed," the detection or recognition device either sends, or predicts when to send, a fire signal to the detonator. There are four basic categories of these devices:

(1) *Impact or contact*—This sensing device detects the first impact of the weapon with an object. Its output initiates the detonator. Typical sensor mechanisms include displacement of an inertial mass, stressing of a piezoelectric crystal, short-circuiting of a coaxial transmission line, and interruption of an electrical circuit. Point detonating fuzes are of this type. A delay mechanism can also be incorporated that provides a short detonation delay (in microseconds) after weapon contact and allows for weapon penetration of the target to maximize damage effect.

(2) *Ambient*—Although not able to detect the physical presence of the target, it can sense the unique environment in which the target can be found, such as water depth. This type of sensing devices would normally be found on depth-bomb and depth-charge weapons.

(3) *Timer*—After a predetermined elapsed time, a timing device will send a fire signal to the detonator. The "sensing" or "detecting" of the target is predetermined by the user in that a preset elapsed time is based on calculations of when the target is expected to be within the damage volume. Gun projectiles use this type of fuzing. Bombs can have variable time fuzes that can be set to go off from minutes to hours after striking the ground.

(4) *Proximity*—This device does not require target contact, but

will sense the physical presence of the target at some distance. It sends a fire signal to the detonator when the target is predicted to be within the damage volume of the warhead. Proximity fuzes are called target-detecting devices or TDDs.

Warhead Initiation

A warhead usually contains a powerful but relatively insensitive high explosive that can only be initiated by the heat and energy from a primary explosive. This primary explosive is a component of the fuze subsystem and is normally loaded in the detonator. If the detonator is designed properly, it can only be activated by a unique fire signal received from the target-sensing device. A detonator can be designed to activate when it receives either electrical energy (high voltage) or mechanical energy (shock or stab) from the target sensor.

Fuze System Classification

Several fuze system classification conventions are employed in present Navy practice. Since fuze designs vary widely according to weapon characteristics and mission, one classification convention groups them by weapon application:

(1) Gun projectile fuzes
    (a) For rotating ammunition
    (b) For nonrotating ammunition
(2) Rocket fuzes
(3) Bomb fuzes
(4) Mine fuzes (called "exploders")
(5) Missile fuzes
    (a) Air-to-air
    (b) Air-to-surface
    (c) Surface-to-air
    (d) Surface-to-surface (subsurface to surface)
(6) Torpedo fuzes (called "exploders")

A second classification system is used that reflects the manner of fuze operation:

(1) Proximity fuzes (VT fuzes)
    (a) Active
    (b) Semi-active
    (c) Passive

(2) Time fuzes
(3) Point detonating fuzes (impact)
(4) Delay fuzes
(5) Command detonate fuzes

Proximity Fuzes

Proximity fuzing had its origins in England early in WWII. Operations research analysts, pondering how to increase the effectiveness of their antiaircraft artillery, calculated that a proximity-sensing fuze carried on the projectile could make the German bomber effectively 10 times as large as its physical size by detonating the projectile in the vicinity of the target rather than at a fixed flight time of the projectile. Thus, of those projectiles that would intercept the target at a range where damage could be inflicted, ten times as many would be effective in damaging or destroying the target in comparison to time-fuzed projectiles. The enemy nomenclature ascribed to these fuzes was variable-time, or VT, fuzes, although they actually did not work on a timing principle. Today, the incidence of direct hits by guided missiles is higher than for unguided projectiles, but the original principles still hold true.

Proximity fuzes accomplish their purpose through "influence sensing," with no contact between the warhead and target. These fuzes are actuated by some characteristic feature of the target rather than physical contact with it. Initiation can be caused by a reflected radio

Figure 14–2. An aircraft bomb time fuze.

Figure 14–3. An RF proximity fuze for a gun projectile.

signal, an induced magnetic field, a pressure measurement, an acoustical impulse, or an infrared signal.

A proximity fuze is classified by its mode of operation, of which there are three: active, semi-active, and passive. These three modes are illustrated in figure 14–4.

Electromagnetic proximity fuzing. Conceivably, all portions of the electromagnetic spectrum could be used for target detection. Practically, however, considerations of propagation, attenuation, and other parameters affected by the radiation determine the applicability. The portions of the spectrum having the greatest utility are radio, radar (microwaves), and infrared. An electromagnetic fuze, operating par-

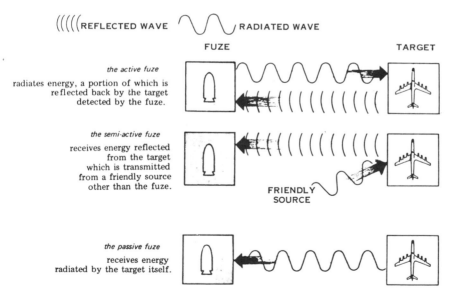

Figure 14–4. Fuze classification by mode of operation.

ticularly in the radio and radar region, may be constructed to operate much like a miniature radar set. It must transmit, receive, and identify electromagnetic pulses. The proper received signal initiates the detonator. The basic active electromagnetic proximity TDD has the following components:

(1) A transceiver composed of solid-state electronics assemblies, which is capable of delivering the required power for transmission and sensitive enough to sense the weak signal return.
(2) Amplifying circuitry to magnify the return signal, so that it will activate the firing circuit and initiate the detonator. The receiver and amplifier circuits are designed to select the correct signal.
(3) A power supply to generate and provide electrical power for the fuze.

Surface weapon applications. Some weapons used against surface targets, such as bomblets delivered to the target area in canisters called cluster bomb units (CBU) and fuel-air-explosive (FAE) weapons, employ proximity fuzes to deploy and disperse the payload at a predetermined height. Anti-personnel weapons having unitary warheads are more effective when detonated above the target area than on contact. Proximity fuzes for these applications may function as radio or electro-optical altimeters or as slant-range-sensing devices that measure range to the surface at the projected point of weapon impact.

One means of signal selection makes use of the radar principle, in which the elapsed time between a transmitted and received pulse is a function of range between target and weapon. A range-gate circuit set for a given distance will pass the signal to initiate the warhead when the elapsed time reduces to a predetermined value. The maximum range gate, which renders the fuze insensitive to effects that are farther away in range, is called the range cut off (RCO) of the TDD sensor. For example, with respect to backscatter from precipitation, the magnitude of fuze response is proportional to the volume of rainfall interrogated within an "in integration period." When this volume is restricted by the range cutoff, fuze response to rain return is reduced by an amount proportional to the reduction in volume of rain interrogated. This mechanism is especially important in the engagement of a low-altitude target, where the sea surface is a highly efficient reflector of radar waves.

Another means makes use of the doppler principle, in which the frequency of the received signal varies as a function of the relative velocity between the weapon and target. This permits the classification of targets according to their radial velocities, which is useful in the selection of a primary target within a group of signals from a variety of sources. The doppler frequency an also be used to determine when to detonate the warhead. If the encounter is head-on, the doppler would be a relatively high up-shift, in comparison to predetermined levels set within the fuze circuitry, and detonation of the warhead would need to be immediate to ensure hitting the target and not going behind it. If the encounter is from the rear, as in a chasing situation, the doppler shift would be relatively low, and therefore a delay in detonation might be desired to ensure a hit. The point of detonation could occur when the doppler shifts from an up to a down doppler or at the point of closest approach.

Missile fuze applications. In air-target weapon applications, the main function of the proximity fuze is to compensate for terminal errors in weapon trajectory by detonating the warhead at a point calculated to inflict a maximum level of damage on the target. Because of the kinematic relationships of the weapon, the target, and the warhead kill mechanism following detonation, the preferred point of detonation is not, in general, the point of closest approach of the weapon to the target. Instead, the system engineer strives for a fuze design that will adaptively initiate the warhead within the so-called "lethal burst interval" for each trajectory that his weapon is likely to experience in future operational usage. The lethal burst interval is defined as that interval along the trajectory in which the warhead can be detonated so as to hit the target in the vulnerable area. That ideal state is of course never realized in practice, where idealism must be tempered by practicality. As a compromise, the engineer derives a design that is practical, affordable, and that will maximize the number of lethal detonations in a representative sample of all postulated encounters. The actual point of detonation realized in a given encounter is the result of fuze design parameters, weapon vector velocity and angle of attack at encounter, target geometry and vector velocity, location of the encounter in the weapon performance envelope, burst control logic, and a wide variety of other contributing factors such as active or passive countermeasures and environmental effects.

As an example of this, realize that tactical missile warheads are not so powerful that they will devastate the target if detonated anywhere in its vicinity. Also, warheads cannot be made larger and heavier without seriously compromising missile speed, altitude, range, and maneuverability. Therefore, the fragments ejected by the warhead must be delivered onto those areas of the target that are most vulnerable to damage: the cockpit, the engine compressor stages, and the flight control system. This requires sophisticated fuzing, with precise burst control.

Furthermore, to maximize its lethal range, the warhead is designed such that ejecta are confined to a narrow zone in the missile pitch plane. Thus, a lethal density of fragments is maintained to ranges much greater than if the fragments were dispersed isotropically. The proximity fuze is called upon to solve this convergence problem—i.e., converging the narrow fragment pattern and the limited vulnerable regions of the target. Figure 14–5 illustrates how this is accomplished. The figure represents a missile approaching the target from the rear and passing either above or below the target (i.e., not a direct hit). Target vulnerable areas or regions that must be hit to ensure a kill are also depicted.

At Point A the proximity fuze detects the first extremity of the target that penetrates its sensory pattern. This initiates a series of events that will result in warhead detonation at Point B. The time delay that permits the missile to traverse from Point A to Point B is varied as a function of closing velocity in accordance with the equation

$$T = \frac{M}{V_c} - N$$

where V_c is the closing velocity in meters per second, T is in milliseconds, and M and N are either constants or variables, depending on the complexity of the fuze, with their units chosen accordingly. When the warhead is detonated at Point B, the vector sum of missile velocity, warhead expansion velocity, and target velocity will cause

 - region of target receiving fragment impacts

■ - sample vulnerable regions in the target

✳ - location of target penetration into sensory pattern

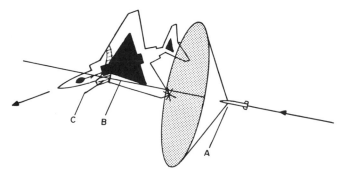

Figure 14–5. Representative terminal engagement situation.

the warhead ejecta to impact the target in Region C. This illustrates a successful warhead detonation, as the fragments impact some of the vulnerable regions of the target.

It should be evident immediately that the terminal encounter situation involves the interplay of many parameters that are dependent upon target characteristics, missile characteristics, and positional relationships at the time of missile launch. The degree of variability and uncertainty in these parameters is increased by the maneuverability and countermeasures capability of the target. Since most missiles are capable of all-aspect attack, and the target's velocity can vary over a wide range of values, the closing velocity used in the time delay equation may range from 180 to 1,800 meters per second, or more. The spectrum of targets intended for the missile will encompass targets that may be small, medium, or large in physical size, but their velocity capabilities overlap to such an extent that a time delay selected for a given V_c might be successful for one target and a failure for another. Furthermore, it is possible for very long targets in high-crossing-angle encounters to present only a square meter or less of vulnerable area to the warhead. Thus, gross target dimensions are not very useful as measures of where the warhead should best be detonated.

Being sensor devices by nature, fuzes are subject to a wide spectrum of disturbing influences in the real-world tactical environment. One of the foremost prerequisites of good fuze design, therefore, is to devise a sensor system that discriminates bona fide target return from all distracting influences, whether they take the form of electronic or optical countermeasures, intense electromagnetic radiation levels characteristic of fleet environments, chaff, precipitation, out-of-range targets, or radar clutter such as occurs in missile flight at low altitude.

Reasonably effective and affordable solutions to all of these problems have been developed. Today every air-target guided missile in the Navy carries a proximity fuze.

Magnetostatic fuze applications. Magnetic sensors, such as magnetic anomaly detection (MAD), measure changes in the earth's magnetic field or the presence of a source of magnetic flux. In the case of fuze systems, a magnetic sensor is designed to recognize an anomaly and ultimately cause the fuze and safety and arming (S&A) device to function. Such a target detection device may be designed that will close a firing circuit upon a disturbance of the earth's magnetic field by one of the magnetic components of a ship, as described in chapter 9. The target does not necessarily have to be moving, although an

S&A device may be employed that requires a certain rate of target movement. Mines that employ this principle of fuzing are commonly used. They are known as dip-needle, influence mines.

Another type of TDD employed with mines is an inductor mechanism, frequently called a search cell. This device employs the principle that a magnetic field induces current flow in a conductor as the field changes relative to the conductor. The small voltage induced in the search cell is amplified and then caused to energize the firing circuit, which in turn initiates the detonator. The extreme simplicity of this device makes it highly reliable and difficult to counter.

Magnetostatic fuzing is also used for subsurface targets. The magnetic field disturbance fuze for subsurface targets is also actuated by a change in the surrounding magnetic field. Any change in the magnitude of the magnetic field activates the fuze. A magnetic-type fuze provides the possibility of damaging a target without a direct hit. This is important, as the damage potential is greater when the explosion of the warhead takes place several feet below the hull, rather than at the side near the surface of the water. The most advanced methods of fuze initiation operated by a ship's magnetic field employ an electromagnetic detecting system. Such a system operates on what can be called the "generator principle." Essentially an electric generator consists of a coil of wire rotated in a magnetic field to produce a voltage. Similarly a small voltage is developed across a coil of wire (the search coil) when it comes in contact with a moving or changing magnetic field. However, a complex problem can occur, due to the fact that the movement of the interceptor itself (torpedo) through the water creates its own change in the field gradient and initiates the fuze at an earlier time than intended. This has led to the development of the gradiometer, a device attached to the torpedo, which has two search coils approximately one foot apart and connected in opposing series. As the now magnetically balanced torpedo moves in earth's magnetic field, equal and opposite voltages are induced in the coils, and no net voltage results. In the vicinity of a steel vessel, the situation is different. One of the two coils is slightly closer to the vessel than the other, and a slightly different voltage will therefore be induced in it. This difference is small, but when properly amplified, it causes the detonator to explode the warhead.

Acoustic fuze applications. Acoustic disturbances, such as propeller and machinery noises or hull vibrations, invariably accompany the passage of a ship through the water. The intensity or strength of the sound wave generated depends upon several factors, such as ship size, shape, and type; number of propellers; type of machinery, etc.

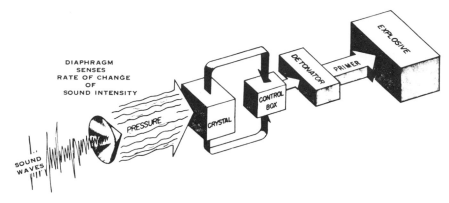

Figure 14–6. Acoustic mine mechanism.

Therefore, a ship's acoustic signal is variable, and acoustic fuzes must be designed to prevent an intense signal from actuating the fuze at distances well beyond the effective explosive radius of the payload. Figure 14–6 illustrates a basic acoustic mine mechanism.

This system employs a hydrophone as a detector to sense the presence of a target. A typical hydrophone functions much the same as the human ear. A diaphragm (corresponding to an eardrum) vibrates from the impact of underwater sound waves. These vibrations are transmitted through an oil medium to a crystal, which converts the mechanical energy to the electrical energy required to initiate the firing mechanism. The selectivity of the firing mechanism is so critical that only the pulses of the required characteristics are sent to the detonator. Selectivity is necessary because of the varied sounds that are received by the mine. To distinguish among these many sounds, acoustic firing mechanisms must possess a very selective type of hearing. For example, a 2,000-ton tramp steamer may have one large propeller turning over rather slowly, and a 2,000-ton destroyer may have two propellers turning over much faster. An acoustic firing mechanism can distinguish between the steamer and the destroyer, and fire on the selected target. When the firing mechanism detects a sound that has the required characteristics (including intensity and rate of change of intensity), the mechanism initiates the firing circuitry and fires the detonator.

Acoustic fuze mechanisms are used in torpedoes as well as mines. There are two operating modes of acoustic torpedoes, the active and passive types. The passive type has a homing device that guides the torpedo in the direction of the strongest target noise. The active type employs a sonar set that emits a series of sonic pings that are reflected back to a receiver in the torpedo. The principle is similar to that of a radar set. As the torpedo approaches the target, less time is required for a signal to travel to the target and return. At a predetermined critical distance, initiation of the firing circuit begins.

Seismic Fuzing

A similar type of acoustic influence sensor used in some types of mines is the "seismic" firing mechanism. This sensor is essentially an acoustic fuze, but receives its threshold signal in a lower bandwidth through weapon-case vibration. These sensors can be made extremely sensitive and may provide for both land-based or in-water application. They offer advantages over the pure acoustic mine fuze in that they may be set over a wider range of selectivity and may incorporate some countermeasure features. Most new mines will use a seismic fuze with other influence fuzes as a means of ensuring weapon activation on a valid target and to reduce the effectiveness of mine sweeping efforts.

Hydrostatic (pressure) fuzing. Oceans swells and surface waves produce pressure variations of considerable magnitude. Moving ships displace water at a finite rate. This continuous water flow is measurable at considerable distances from the ship as pressure variations that normally exist in the water. Various pressure-measuring mechanisms can be used in fuzes to detect such variations. The pressure differential becomes more pronounced when the ship is moving through confined waters, but is still appreciable in the open sea, even at a considerable depth. This pressure variation, called the "pressure signature" of a ship, is a function of ship speed and displacement and the water depth. Therefore, to avoid premature firing because of wave action, pressure-firing mechanisms are designed so as to be unaffected by rapid pressure fluctuations. Pressure sensors are commonly associated with bottom mines and are extremely difficult to counter through normal influence-mine countermeasure techniques. Pressure-firing mechanisms are seldom used alone, but are generally combined with other influence firing devices.

Combination fuzing. Systems involving a combination of influences are available in most mine firing devices. The combinations of magnetic, pressure, and acoustic/seismic systems are used to compensate for the disadvantages of one system with the advantages of another. Mine countermeasure effectiveness can be greatly reduced through use of combination fuzing.

Mine performance data. Minefield theory involves detailed and complex analysis, which is beyond the scope of this text. The entire minefield must be considered as a weapon in a mining scenario, and multiple transistors are programmed against it to determine the overall effectiveness. For the sake of simplicity, our discussion will be restricted to a single mine against a single target. The influence sensors described earlier may be considered individually or as a combination. Regardless of the particular influence, there is a threshold level that will activate the mine based on the sensitivity setting for the weapon. This will obviously occur at some distance from the target—the distance being greater the more sensitive the mine setting. This distance is referred to as actuation distance and is depicted in figure 14–7.

It should be obvious that a mine could be so sensitively set that it could be made to detonate on a target influence such that the explosion would be outside of the range at which the mine could do damage to the target. The range at which a mine will damage a target is referred to as the "damage distance." This would also be described as similar to the circular pattern of figure 14–7. From a minefield planning standpoint, it is most important to optimize the mine setting such that the weapon does not actuate until the target is within damage range. Obviously, the actuation distance should be less than or equal to the mine damage distance. The problem becomes much more complex in actual planning. Each target class has its own associated signature as well as relative toughness against damage, and the ship-mine encounter is greatly influenced by such factors as ship heading and speed, environmental state, and orientation of mine and ship. It

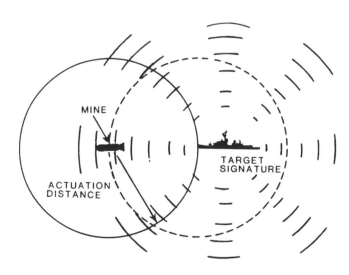

Figure 14–7. Mine actuation distance.

is impossible to determine all of these factors precisely; therefore, approximations are made at varying levels of accuracy. Mine actuation probabilities and damage probabilities have been computed based on various target and mine types, water depths, ship speeds, mine sensitivities, etc., and are published as classified information for use in minefield planning methodology.

Safing and Arming

When prehistoric man first dropped his club on his toe, he realized that his own weapon could be dangerous to himself as well as to his enemies. With today's highly destructive weapons, there must be a high degree of assurance that the weapon will not detonate until it has reached the target that it is intended to destroy. This assurance is provided by the safing and arming device (S&A).

The S&A device is a fuze component that isolates the detonator from the warhead booster charge during all phases of the weapon logistic and operational chain until the weapon has been launched in the intended mode and has achieved a safe displacement from the launch vehicle. Then, at that point in the trajectory, the S&A device removes a barrier from the explosive train, allowing the detonator thereafter to initiate the warhead.

Some S&A devices function by measuring elapsed time from launch, others ascertain distance traveled from the launch point by sensing and doubly integrating the acceleration experienced by the weapon. Some devices sense and integrate air speed or projectile rotation (centrifugal force), while still others may sense several stimuli characteristic of the weapon trajectory, such as rocket motor gas pressure and acceleration.

The safety and arming device. To maximize the safety reliability of a fuze, the S&A device must ensure that the forces it senses will be unique to the weapon when deployed, and cannot be intentionally or accidentally duplicated during ground handling or prelaunch operations.

As an example, most missiles incorporate an S&A device that utilizes acceleration-sensing. This device senses the acceleration from the rocket motor. The rocket motor boost may only induce a 10-g force, while the weapon dropped from a sling may easily experience 500-g shock forces. Therefore, another feature must be used to prevent arming should the weapon be dropped. This salient feature is that acceleration-sensing systems must experience acceleration for a protracted period of time, such as for at least one second or at least 10 seconds. Such a system is illustrated in figure 14–8.

In this device, a g-weight within the S&A drives the "out-of-line" explosive lead into alignment at a rate controlled (typically) by a Geneva escapement, the rate of which is not very sensitive to the acceleration magnitude. The "intent to launch" signal, by operating on the armature of a solenoid, retracts the launch latch as the weapon experiences forward acceleration. The g-weight tends to move aft against the spring, but its rate of movement is retarded by the Geneva escapement, which functions like the escapement of an alarm clock. After a period of time the detonator, the "out-of-line" explosive lead, and the output explosive lead align and form a continuous explosive chain from the detonator to the warhead booster charge. When the g-weight reaches that position, a second pin is pushed by a spring into a detent in the g-weight and locks it in the armed position.

If the rocket motor is faulty or such that sufficient acceleration is not sustained for the expected time, then the aft spring will return the g-weight rapidly to its original position (the Geneva escapement has, in effect, a ratchet that permits rapid reverse movement), and the launch latch will be inserted into the g-weight again, locking it into the safe position. This ensures that the warhead will not detonate should it unexpectedly fall short, due to motor failure.

The linear-motion g-weight acceleration integrator, while very rugged, has the functional disadvantage that during lateral acceleration of the missile, which may exceed 30-g in magnitude, the frictional force between the g-weight and the tube is high. This retards the

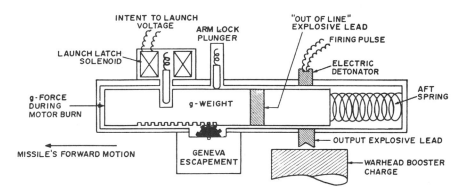

Figure 14–8. Example demonstrating the principle of an acceleration-integration S&A device.

axial motion of the g-weight and extends the arming distance. In a more efficient design, linear motion is converted into rotary motion of the g-weight. A metal disk mounted eccentrically on a transverse shaft rotates as the missile accelerates, aligning the explosive train.

To obtain the desired safety reliability in this example, there are several redundant components: the launch latch, the Geneva escapement, and the g-weight with its spring. If any one should fail (e.g., should the launch latch shear if the weapon were dropped), another would still prevent inadvertent arming (the Geneva escapement would prevent the g-weight from moving aft). This is the type of redundancy that is found in all S&A devices.

Thus, a fundamental principle in fuze design can be stated as:

A redundant increase in the number and types of devices placed in series in the firing path increases the safety reliability of a fuze.

S&A devices are made of extremely high quality and are designed to have a probability of safety failure of not greater than 1 in 10^6. That is the usual safety level required of Navy missile S&As. Approximately 350,000 have been fielded for fleet use without a single safety failure.

The discussion so far has emphasized keeping the weapon safe before it reaches the target. It may be necessary to include an additional S&A device in the firing path to safe the weapon if the intended target is missed. An example would be an antiaircraft projectile or SAM that could fall on friendly territory if an airborne target were missed. To preclude this possibility, a surface-to-air missile could have an additional timer S&A device that would normally arm. This would allow firing path continuity until the expected elapsed time from launch to target intercept is exceeded, at which time the device will safe the missile.

An alternative to using a timer S&A device would be to place an additional timer firing device in the fuze system in addition to the normal target-sensing device. If the target is missed, then the alternate timer device would send the fire signal for detonation. The timer setting would be based on a time greater than normal intercept, but would detonate while the weapon was still safely airborne. This alternative design method of increasing the safety reliability is found in most antiaircraft projectiles.

Although the fuze with its S&A device is the primary safety component of the weapon, it must be realized that the warhead is not insensitive to influences other than fuze initiation. The chemical high explosives used in both conventional and nuclear warheads can be detonated if subjected to enough heat and energy from external sources.

Combat or accidental detonations or fire can provide this required energy.

Reliability

The reliability of the basic fuze functions of target sensing, arming, and payload initiation is obviously contrary to the weapon safety function of a fuze. A fuze detonator that will reliably detonate the payload at target impact presents a safety reliability problem if it also detonates when dropped during handling.

To design a fuze to be reliably safe, a designer may compromise arming and firing reliability. A fuze detonator designed not to detonate from rough handling may also be so insensitive that the contact fuze would dud at target impact. An S&A pressure device that is designed to sense too high an airspeed may not arm in time when deployed against short-range targets. There are several methods available to the designer to increase arming and initiation reliability and also increase safety reliability without compromising the reliability of each of these paradoxical functions.

Functional Reliability. Although fuze design must emphasize safety,

Figure 14–9. Safety and arming device.

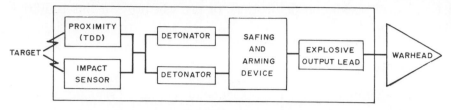

Figure 14–10. Fuze system redundancy.

the primary objective of the warhead is to detonate at the proper time. Therefore, the sequence of S&A and target-sensing devices must have a high probability of functioning correctly when they receive their unique arming signal. Functional failure of any one of the devices in figure 14–1 would result in a dud warhead. As with any man-made device, the fuze components must be based on a sound design, avoiding an overly complex function requirement. Before the reliability criteria can be assured, every new S&A device must be extensively tested. Sophisticated weapons will have S&A devices that sense and arm with such a high reliability that less than one in a thousand is expected to fail functionally. Note that a functional failure is *not* the same as a safety failure, but occurs when the component fails to operate as designed when proper environmental conditions exist.

Reliability of the entire fuze system can be increased by having more than one type of target sensor placed in parallel and more than one detonator in the S&A device, as shown in figure 14–10. Most missile fuze systems have one or more backup contact sensors in addition to their proximity sensor. Thus, the probability of warhead functioning is increased. This leads to another basic principle in fuze design, which can be stated as:

> *A redundant increase of the number of similar components placed in parallel in the firing path will increase the arming and firing reliability.*

The performance of complex systems such as weapon fuzes can be determined through application of probability theory. The principles of parallel operation as stated above, as well as those of series systems, lead to a method of determination of total system reliability regardless of the number or arrangement of components.

Two fundamental principles of probability theory are used in determining fuze reliability:

(1) The probability of several statistically independent events oc-

curring simultaneously is the product of the probabilities that the individual events occur. Two events, A and B, are independent if the probability that A occurs is unaffected by the occurrence or nonoccurrence of B, and vice versa. Thus, the probability that events A and B both occur, given that their probabilities of occurrence are $p(A)$ and $p(B)$ is

$$p(A \text{ and } B) = P(A) \times p(B)$$

(2) The probability of several mutually exclusive events occurring is the sum of the probabilities of each event. Two events are said to be mutually exclusive if the occurrence of one event prevents the occurrence of the other. If events A and B are mutually exclusive and if their probabilities of occurrence are $p(A)$ and $p(B)$, then the probability that either A or B will occur is

$$p(A \text{ or } B) = p(A) + p(B)$$

Mutually exclusive events are not independent since, by definition, if one occurs, the other cannot, or $p(A \text{ and } B) = 0$.

Series Systems. Suppose that a system consists of two independent components arranged in series. That is, for the system to operate properly or be successful, each of these independent components must operate properly and in sequence. Schematically this system can be depicted as follows:

The effect of each component's success or failure on total system performance can be tabulated as follows:

Component 1	S	S	F	F
Component 2	S	F	S	F
System	S	F	F	F

Notice that the system is successful only if both of the components are successful. All other possible situations lead to system failure. In order to calculate the probability of this system's success, it is only necessary to calculate the probability that both components are successful. Letting S_1 and S_2 stand for the probability that component 1 and component 2 are successful respectively and noting that these components are independent, a simple expression for the probability of system success results:

$$p(S) = S_1 \times S_2$$

Also, since the qualities of success and failure are mutually exclusive and cover *all* possible system outcomes.

$$p(S) + p(F) = 1$$

or

$$p(F) = 1 - p(S) = 1 - (S_1 \times S_2)$$

If a system has more than two components in series, its probability of success is again simply the product of the individual component success probabilities:

$$p(S) = S_1 \times S_2 \times S_3 \times \ldots$$

and

$$p(F) = 1 - p(S) = 1 - (S_1 \times S_2 \times S_3 \times \ldots).$$

As an example, the S&A device of figure 14–2 has three independent components that must operate in series for arming to occur. The system can be modeled as follows:

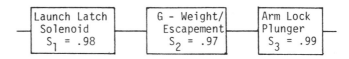

The probability of successful arming for this device can be calculated as

$$p(S) = S_1 \times S_2 \times S_3 = .98 \times .97 \times .99 = .9411$$

Also, the probability of failure is

$$p(F) = 1 - p(S) = 1 - .9411 = .0589.$$

Parallel Systems. Suppose that a system consists of two independent components arranged in parallel. This means that for the system to be successful, only one of the components must be successful. Schematically, this system can be depicted as follows:

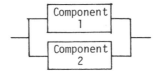

The effect of each component's success or failure is illustrated in the following table:

Component 1	S	S	F	F
Component 2	S	F	S	F
System	S	S	S	F

Notice that for a parallel system, the only way that the system can fail is if all the individual components fail simultaneously. Calculating the probability of system success is rather complicated since it is the probability that component 1 and component 2 are successful *or* component 1 is successful and component 2 fails *or* component 1 fails and component 2 succeeds. It is much easier to calculate the probability that the system fails, which is:

$$p(F) = F_1 \times F_2$$

Then, since system success and failure are mutually exclusive,

$$p(S) = 1 - p(F) = 1 - (F_1 \times F_2)$$

For example, consider a system consisting of two detonators placed in parallel, each with a success probability of .95.

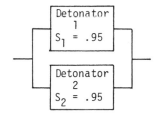

The probability of success for this system is given by

$$p(S) = 1 - (F_1 \times F_2)$$

Now, since the qualities of success or failure for each individual component are mutually exclusive

$$S + F = 1$$

or

$$F = 1 - S$$

thus,

$$p(S) = 1 - (F_1 \times F_2) = 1 - [(1 - S_1) \times (1 - S_2)]$$
$$= 1 - [(1 - .95) \times (1 - .95)]$$
$$= 1 - (.05 \times .05)$$
$$= 1 - .0025$$
$$= .9975.$$

Fuze system reliability: an example. A particular type of ammunition used for shore bombardment against troops in the open is designated as VT-NSD (variable time–non-self-destruct). The fuze system for this type of projectile has a proximity sensor designed to detonate 100 feet from the ground and an impact sensor as a backup, should the proximity sensor fail. The following diagram is a schematic representation of the entire fuze system, and each component's probability of operating successfully is given.

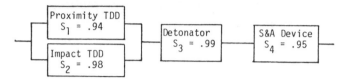

To calculate the fuze system reliability (probability of success), it should first be noted that this is a combination of parallel and series elements. If the probability of the TDD function success is first calculated, then this system is reduced to three functional elements in series. Calculating the probability of the TDD function success,

$$p_{\text{TDD}}(S) = 1 - p_{\text{TDD}}(F) = 1 - (F_1 \times F_2) = 1 - [(1 - S_1) \times (1 - S_2)]$$
$$= 1 - [(1 - .94) \times (1 - .98)] = .9988$$

Now, calculating the overall success probability of three functional elements in series,

$$p(S) = p_{\text{TDD}}(S) \times S_3 \times S_4 = (.9988)(.99)(.95)$$
$$= .9394$$

Thus, this fuze system will successfully detonate the warhead 94% of the time.

Safety reliability. As previously discussed, a safety failure is different from a functional failure. A safety failure occurs when the components, for some reason, fail to keep the fuze in a safe condition when so desired, and premature arming occurs. Thus, a safety failure is said to have occurred if the weapon becomes armed other than through its normal firing sequence. From this definition, it can be seen that a safety failure is solely a function of the safety and arming device. For a safety failure to occur, the series components of a safety and arming device must simultaneously malfunction in such a manner that the weapon is armed. Since the probability of a component of an S&A device having a safety failure is normally very small, the probability of three or four components having a safety failure simultaneously is minute. Thus, again, *series redundancy leads to safety reliability*.

Summary

The fuze is that functional subsystem of the ordnance system that actuates the warhead in the vicinity of the target and maintains the weapon in a safe condition during all prior phases of handling and launching. All fuzing systems perform four basic functions: safing, arming, recognition or sensing of the target, and initiation of the warhead. All fuzes contain some type of target-sensing device, with all missiles having an electromagnetic proximity sensing device called a TDD. TDDs are classified according to their mode of operation: active, semi-active, or passive. All fuzes contain S&A devices that keep the weapon safe through a series of redundant components until the weapon has sufficient separation from the launch point. At that point the S&A device removes a barrier from the explosive train, arming the weapon. The redundant components provide a measure of safety reliability for the weapon.

References

Bulgerin, H. A. "Comments of Fuze Technology." Unpublished notes.

Burns, R. L., Cdr., USN. "Notes on Mine Warfare." COMMINWARCOM, Charleston, S.C., 1983.

Commander, Naval Ordnance Systems Command. *Weapons Systems Fundamentals*. NAVORD OP 3000, vol. 2, 1st Rev. Washington, D.C.: GPO, 1971.

Weapons and Systems Engineering Department. *Weapons System Engineering*. 6th ed. Annapolis, Md.: U. S. Naval Academy, 1984.

15

Guidance and Control

Introduction

The term *missile* in the post–World War II era has generally been used synonymously with "guided missile," due to the wide impact of guided missile technology upon the weapons field. In the unguided case, initial conditions (such as train, elevation, powder charge in naval guns) and exterior ballistic effects are parameters that, along with normal distribution, affect the "fall of shot." As advances in technology permitted (paralleled by increasing threat complexity), the development of guided missiles made possible a significant increase in terminal accuracy of military weaponry. The application of automatic control is prevalent in broad regions of missile technology including:

Underwater Homing Torpedoes
Surface-to-Surface Aerodynamic Guided Missiles
Inter-Continental Ballistic Missiles
Air-to-Air Guided Missiles
Surface-to-Air Guided Missiles
Guided Projectiles

This chapter will deal primarily with the aerodynamic guided missile. Various aerodynamic missile flight paths will be introduced and a simplified analysis included to demonstrate the relative advantages/disadvantages of each.

Purpose and Function

Every missile guidance system consists of an attitude control system and a flight path control system. The attitude control system functions to maintain the missile in the desired attitude on the ordered flight path by controlling the missile in pitch, roll, and yaw. The attitude control system operates as an autopilot, damping out fluctuations that tend to deflect the missile from its ordered flight path. The function of the flight path control system is to determine the flight path necessary for target interception and to generate the orders to the attitude control system to maintain that path.

It should be clear at this point that the concept of "Guidance and Control" involves not only the maintenance of a particular vehicle's path from point A to B in space, but also the proper behavior of the vehicle while following the path. A missile that follows a prescribed path half the way to a target and then becomes dynamically unstable is then incapable of remaining upon the path (or else fails structurally due to aerodynamic loading). Such a vehicle, in order to perform properly, must be "piloted" and capable of responding to control signals.

The operation of a guidance and control system is based on the principle of feedback. The control units make corrective adjustments of the missile control surfaces when a guidance error is present. The control units will also adjust the control surfaces to stabilize the missile in roll, pitch, and yaw. Guidance and stabilization corrections are combined, and the result is applied as an error signal to the control system.

Accelerometers

The heart of the inertial navigation system for ships and missiles is an arrangement of accelerometers that will detect any change in vehicular motion. To understand the use of accelerometers in inertial guidance, it is helpful to examine the general principles involved.

An accelerometer, as its name implies, is a device for measuring acceleration. In their basic form such devices are simple. For example, a pendulum, free to swing on a transverse axis, could be used to measure acceleration along the fore-and-aft axis of the missile. When the missile is given a forward acceleration, the pendulum will tend to lag aft; the actual displacement of the pendulum from its original position will be a function of the magnitude of the accelerating force. Another simple device might consist of a weight supported between two springs. When an accelerating force is applied, the weight will move from its original position in a direction opposite to that of the applied force. The movement of the mass (weight) is in accordance with Newton's second law of motion, which states that the acceleration of a body is directly proportional to the force applied and inversely proportional to the mass of the body.

If the acceleration along the fore-and-aft axis were constant, the speed of the missile at any instant could be determined simply by multiplying the acceleration by the elapsed time. However, the acceleration may change considerably over a period of time. Under these conditions, integration is necessary to determine the speed.

If the missile speed were constant, the distance covered could be calculated simply by multiplying the speed by time of flight. But because the acceleration varies, the speed also varies. For that reason, a second integration is necessary.

The moving element of the accelerometer can be connected to a potentiometer, or to a variable inductor core, or to some other device capable of producing a voltage proportional to the displacement of the element.

Usually there are three double-integrating accelerometers continuously measuring the distance traveled by the missile in three directions—range, altitude, and azimuth (figure 15–1). Double-integrating accelerometers are devices that are sensitive to acceleration, and by a double-step process measure distance. These measured distances are then compared with the desired distances, which are preset into the missile; if the missile is off course, correction signals are sent to the control system.

Accelerometers are sensitive to the acceleration of gravity as well as missile accelerations. For this reason, the accelerometers that measure range and azimuth distances must be mounted in a fixed position with respect to the pull of gravity. This can be done in a moving missile by mounting them on a platform that is stabilized by gyroscopes or by star-tracking telescopes. This platform, however, must be moved as the missile passes over the earth to keep the sensitive axis of each accelerometer in a fixed position with respect to the pull of gravity. These factors cause the accuracy of the inertial system to decrease as the time of flight of the missile increases.

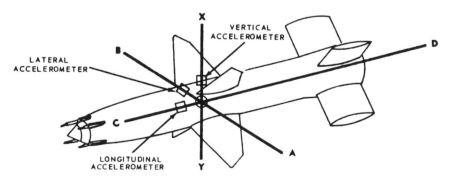

Figure 15–1. Accelerometers in guided missiles.

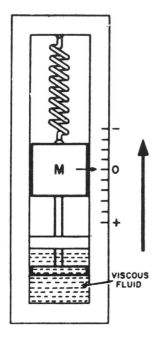

Figure 15–2. Liquid-damped system.

To eliminate unwanted oscillations, a *damper* is included in the accelerometer unit. The damping effort should be just great enough to prevent any oscillations from occurring, but still permit a significant displacement of the mass. When this condition exists, the movement of the mass will be exactly proportional to the acceleration of the vehicle.

Figure 15–2 shows a mass suspended by a spring in a liquid-damped system. If the case experiences an acceleration in the direction indicated by the arrow, the spring will offer a restraining force proportional to the downward displacement of the mass, while the viscous fluid will serve to dampen any undesirable oscillations.

Figure 15–3 shows a system that is electrically damped. The mass (M) is free to slide back and forth in relation to the iron core (C). When the vehicle experiences an acceleration, the voltage (E), which is proportional to the displacement of the mass, is picked off and amplified. The current (I) (still proportional to the displacement) is sent back to the coil around the core. The resulting magnetic field around the coil creates a force on the mass, which damps the oscillations. In this system the acceleration could be measured by the displacement of the mass (X), by the voltage (E), or by the current (I).

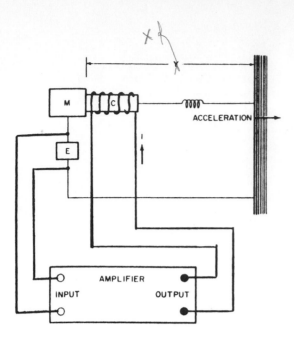

Figure 15–3. Electrically damped acceler-ometer.

Sensors

The guidance system in a missile can be compared to the human pilot of an airplane. As a pilot guides his plane to the landing field, the guidance system "sees" its target. If the target is far away or otherwise obscured, radio or radar beams can be used to locate it and direct the missile to it. Heat, light, television, the earth's magnetic field, and Loran have all been found suitable for specific guidance purposes. When an electromagnetic source is used to guide the missile, an antenna and a receiver are installed in the missile to form what is known as a sensor. The sensor section picks up, or senses, the guidance information. Missiles that are guided by other than electromagnetic means use other types of sensors, but each must have some means of receiving "position reports."

The kind of sensor that is used will be determined by such factors as maximum operating range, operating conditions, the kind of information needed, the accuracy required, viewing angle, and weight and size of the sensor, and the type of target and its speed.

Phases of Guidance

Missile guidance is generally divided into three phases — boost, midcourse, and terminal. These names refer to different parts of the flight path. The boost phase may also be called the launching or initial phase.

Boost phase. Navy surface-to-air missiles accelerate to flight speed by means of the booster component. This booster period lasts from the time the missile leaves the launcher until the booster burns its fuel. In missiles with separate boosters, the booster drops away from the missile at burnout. The objective of this phase is to place the missile at a position in space from where it can either "see" the target or where it can receive external guidance signals. During the boost phase of some missiles, the guidance system and the aerodynamic surfaces are locked in position. Other missiles are guided during the boost phase.

Midcourse phase. The second, or midcourse, phase of guidance is often the longest in both distance and time. During this part of the flight, changes may be required to bring the missile onto the desired course and to make certain that it stays on that course. During this guidance phase, information can be supplied to the missile by any of several means. In most cases, the midcourse guidance system is used to place the missile near the target, where the system to be used in

Figure 15–4. Launch and boost phase of Tomahawk missile. Note that control surfaces have not yet deployed.

Guidance and Control   **433**

the final phase of guidance can take over. In other cases, the mid-course guidance system is used for both the second and third guidance phases.

Terminal phase. The last phase of missile guidance must have high accuracy as well as fast response to guidance signals. *Missile performance becomes a critical factor during this phase.* The missile must be capable of executing the final maneuvers required for intercept within the constantly decreasing available flight time. The maneuverability of the missile will be a function of velocity as well as airframe design. Therefore, a terminal guidance system must be compatible with missile performance capabilities. The greater the target acceleration, the more critical the method of terminal guidance becomes. Suitable methods of guidance will be discussed in later sections of this chapter. In some missiles, especially short-range missiles, a single guidance system may be used for all three phases of guidance, whereas other missiles may have a different guidance system for each phase.

Types of Guidance Systems

Missile guidance systems may be classified into two broad categories: missiles guided by man-made electromagnetic devices, and those guided by other means. In the first category are those missiles controlled by radar, radio devices, and those missiles that use the target as a source of electromagnetic radiation. In the latter category are missiles that rely on electromechanical devices or electromagnetic contact with natural sources, such as the stars (self-contained guidance systems).

All of the missiles that maintain electromagnetic radiation contact with man-made sources may be further subdivided into two subcategories.

(1) Control guidance missiles
(2) Homing guidance missiles

Control Guidance

Control guidance missiles are those that are guided on the basis of direct electromagnetic radiation contact with friendly control points. Homing guidance missiles are those that are guided on the basis of direct electromagnetic radiation contact with the target. Control guidance generally depends on the use of radar (radar control) or radio (radio control) links between a control point and the missile. By use

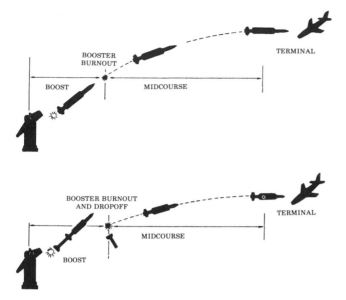

Figure 15–5. Guidance phases of missile flight.

of guidance information transmitted from the control point via a radio or radar link, the missile's flight path can be guided. This chapter will use radar control guidance as a model for discussion because it is by far the most common application of control guidance methods. The principles discussed may be readily applied to radio (including television) control guidance.

Radar control guidance. Radar control guidance may be subdivided into two separate categories. The first category is simply referred to as the command guidance method. The second is the beam-rider method, which is actually a modification of the first, but with the radar being used in a different manner.

(1) *Command guidance*—The term *command* is used to describe a guidance method in which all guidance instructions, or commands, come from sources outside the missile. The guidance system of the missile contains a receiver that is capable of receiving instructions from ship or ground stations or from aircraft. The missile flight-path control system then converts these commands to guidance information, which is fed to the attitude control system.

In the command guidance method, one or two radars are used to track the missile and target. Figure 15–6 is a block diagram of how this method works in actual practice. As soon as the radar is locked on the target, tracking information is fed into the computer. The missile is then launched and is tracked by the radar. Target and missile ranges, elevations, and bearings are continuously fed to the computer.

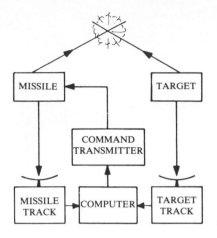

Figure 15–6. Command guidance system.

This information is analyzed and a missile intercept flight path is computed. The appropriate guidance signals are then transmitted to the missile receiver. These signals may be sent by varying the characteristics of the missile-tracking radar beam, or by way of a separate radio transmitter. The radar command guidance method can be used in ship, air, or ground missile delivery systems.

A relatively new type of command guidance by wire is now operational in some short-range antitank-type weapons. These systems use an optical sight for tracking the target while the weapon emits a characteristic infra-red signature, which is used for tracking the weapon with an IR sensor. Deviation of the weapon from the line of sight (LOS) to the target is sensed, and guidance commands are generated that are fed to the weapon control system in flight via a direct wire link. Each weapon contains wire spools that pay out as the warhead flies out the line of sight to the target. Current usage of these systems is in relatively lightweight, portable, short-range battlefield environments against armored targets where their high accuracy and substantial warheads are most efficiently employed.

(2) *Beam-rider method*—The main difference between the beam-rider method and the radar command guidance method is that the characteristics of the missile-tracking radar beam are not varied in the beam-rider system. The missile has been designed so that it is able to formulate its own correction signals on the basis of its position with respect to the radar scan axis. The technique is best understood after reviewing the principles of conical-scan tracking in chapter 5. The missile's flight path control unit is sensitive to any deviation from the scan axis of the guidance radar and is capable of computing the proper flight path correction. An advantage of this type of system is

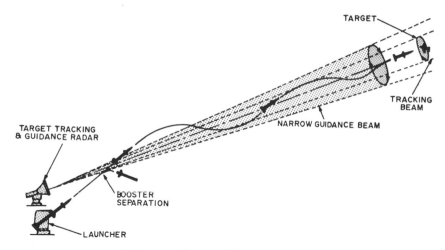

Figure 15–7. Simple beam-rider guidance system.

that it requires only one radar. This radar must, of course, have a conical-scan feature in order to provide both target-tracking capability and a missile flight-path correction reference axis. A second advantage is that since the missile formulates its own directional commands, several missiles may be launched to "ride" the beam simultaneously, without the need for a cumbersome and complicated multiple-missile command system.

Figure 15–7 illustrates a simple beam-rider guidance system on a typical LOS course. The accuracy of this system decreases with range because the radar beam spreads out, and it is more difficult for the missile to remain in its center. If the target is moving, the missile must follow a continuously changing path, which may cause it to undergo excessive transverse accelerations.

Homing Guidance

Homing guidance systems control the flight path by employing a device in the weapon that reacts to some distinguishing feature of the target. Homing devices can be made sensitive to a variety of energy forms, including RF, infrared, reflected laser, sound, and visible light. In order to home on the target, the missile or torpedo must determine at least the azimuth and elevation of the target by one of the means of angle tracking mentioned previously. Active homing missiles will also have the means of determining range of the target if necessary. Tracking is performed by a movable seeker antenna or an array with stationary electronically scanned arrays in development for missiles and operational in some torpedoes. Determination of angular error by amplitude comparison monopulse methods is preferred over the older COSRO systems because of the higher data rate and faster response time; however, phase comparison monopulse or interferometer methods have advantages in some applications. Homing guidance methods may be divided into three types: *active*, *semiactive*, and *passive* homing (figure 15–8). These methods may be employed in seekers using any of the energy forms mentioned above, although some methods may be excluded by the nature of the energy form; for example, one would not build a passive *laser* seeker or an active or semi-active infrared seeker.

Active homing. In active homing, the weapon contains both the transmitter and receiver. Search and acquisition are conducted as with any tracking sensor. The target is tracked employing *monostatic* geometry in which the returning echo from the target travels the same path as the transmitted energy (figure 15–8). An onboard computer calculates a course to intercept the target and sends steering commands to the weapon's autopilot. The monostatic geometry allows the most efficient reflection of energy from the target, but the small

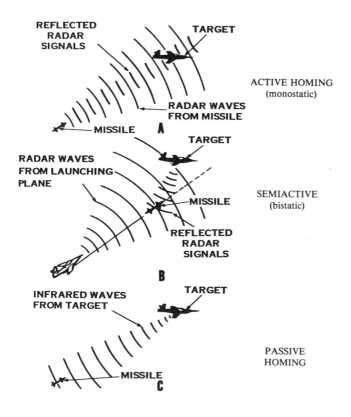

Figure 15–8. Homing guidance.

size of the missile restricts the designer to high frequencies and low power output from the transmitter, resulting in short seeker acquisition range.

Semiactive homing. In semiactive homing, the target is illuminated by a tracking radar at the launching site or other control point. The missile is equipped with a radar receiver (no transmitter) and by means of the reflected radar energy from the target, formulates its own correction signals as in the active method. However, semiactive homing uses *bistatic* reflection from the target, meaning that because the illuminator platform and weapon receiver are not co-located, the returning echo follows a different path than the energy incident to the target. Due to its shape and composition, the target may not reflect energy efficiently in the direction of the weapon. In extreme cases the weapon may lose the target entirely, resulting in a missed intercept. This disadvantage is compensated for by the ability to use greater power and more diverse frequency ranges in an illumination device in a ship, aircraft, or ground station.

Passive homing. Passive homing depends only on the target as a source of tracking energy. This energy can be the noise radiated by a ship or submarine in the case of a passive homing torpedo, RF radiation from the target's own sensors in the case of an anti-radiation (ARM) weapon, heat sources such as ship, aircraft, or vehicle exhausts, contrast with the temperature or visible light environment, or even the radiation all objects emit in the microwave region. As in the other homing methods, the missile generates its own correction signals on the basis of energy received from the target rather than from a control point. The advantage of passive homing is that the counter detection problem is reduced, and a wide range of energy forms and frequencies are available. Its disadvantages are its susceptibility to decoy or deception and its dependence on a certain amount of cooperation from the enemy.

Accuracy. Homing is the most accurate of all guidance systems because it uses the target as its source for guidance error signals. Its superior accuracy is shown when used against moving targets. There are several ways in which the homing device may control the path of a missile against a moving target. Of these, the more generally used are *pursuit* flight paths and *lead* flight paths, which are discussed in Part II of this chapter. Because monopulse methods in weapons seekers are advantageous and are becoming the method of choice in current weapons, it is necessary to address the two basic types:

Amplitude comparison monopulse. This method, described in chapter 5, requires a gimballed seeker antenna covered by a radome at the nose of the weapon. Because of aerodynamic requirements, the radome shape is normally not optimal for radar performance. Very precise orders to the antenna are required to achieve target acquisition due to the single antenna's limited field of view. In these systems the size of the antenna directly determines the limits of the frequency range of the seeker. Its primary advantage is its consistent performance throughout the potential speed and maneuverability range of potential targets.

Interferometer (phase comparison monopulse). The interferometer eliminates the requirement for a movable antenna, having instead fixed antennas mounted at the edge of the airframe or on the wing tips, the result being reduced complexity and a wider field of view. As depicted in figure 15–9, two antennas separated by a known distance are installed for each mobility axis of the weapon. In the diagram the antennas A and B, separated by the distance d, receive energy emitted (passive homing) or reflected (semiactive homing) from the target.

Because the distance to the target is relatively large, it is assumed that the RF energy arrives as a series of planar waves with wavelength λ. In accordance with the discussion of electronic scanning in chapter 7 and towed acoustic arrays in chapter 9 it is evident that for the geometry pictured, the phase sensed by antenna B will lag that sensed

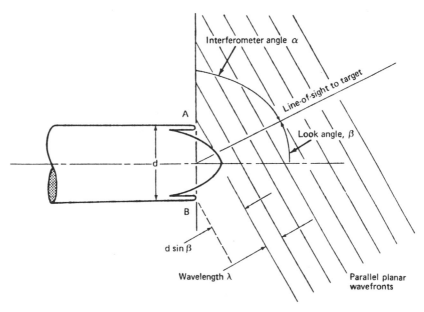

Figure 15–9. Body-fixed RF interferometer. (From Gulick and Miller)

by antenna A by some phase angle θ which is proportional to $d \sin \beta$; therefore:

$$\theta = \frac{2\pi d}{\lambda} \sin \beta \qquad (15-1)$$

If λ is known and the phase angle θ can be determined, then the look angle, β, can be calculated.

The interferometer provides the advantage of wide field of view, flexibility in airframe design, unobstructed use of weapon interior space, and the ability to cover broad frequency bands without constraints imposed by limited antenna size. The separation between the antennas governs the performance of the system, with missile body diameter or fin spread separation as the usual arrangement. The disadvantage of the interferometer is the angular ambiguity that may exist for wavelengths less than the separation between the antennas at a specific angle of incidence. If the distance between the antennas at an angle of incidence β is $d \sin \beta$, and λ is less than $d \sin \beta$, then it is not possible to determine if the phase angle θ measured is just that or $\theta + n2\pi$ radians, where n is any integer. However, this is a minor problem in most homing systems because the absolute look angle β is not as important as the rate of change of that angle.

The interferometer has an advantage in resolving multiple targets at twice the range of a typical amplitude comparison monopulse seeker in the same size weapon. This gives the missile twice the time to respond to the changeover from tracking the centroid of the group to tracking one specific target, thus increasing the hit probability.

Composite systems. No one system is best suited for all phases of guidance. It is logical then to combine a system that has good midcourse guidance characteristics with a system that has excellent terminal guidance characteristics, in order to increase the number of hits. Combined systems are known as composite guidance systems or combination systems.

Many missiles rely on combinations of various types of guidance. For example, one type of missile may use command guidance until it is within a certain range of a target. At this time the command guidance may become a back-up mode and a type of homing guidance commenced. The homing guidance would then be used until impact with the target or detonation of a proximity-fuzed warhead.

The device that switches guidance systems is called a control matrix. It automatically transfers the correct signals to the control system regardless of conditions. If the midcourse guidance system should fail, the matrix switches to an auxiliary guidance system to hold the missile on course. Should the original midcourse guidance system become active again, the matrix will switch control from the auxiliary back to the primary system.

If a target uses jamming (deceptive interference) devices, the matrix can switch to another guidance method, even in the terminal phase of flight. Many operational missiles have such sophisticated guidance systems.

Hybrid guidance. A combination of command guidance and semi-active homing guidance is a type of hybrid guidance. It achieves many advantages of both systems. It attains long-range capabilities by maintaining the tracking sensors on the delivery vehicle (ship, aircraft, or land base) and transmitting the data to the missile. By having the missile compute its own weapon line drive orders, the entire mechanization of the fire control problem can be simplified.

Self-Contained Guidance Systems

The self-contained group falls in the second category of guidance system types. All the guidance and control equipment is entirely within the missile. Some of the systems of this type are: *preset, terrestrial, inertial,* and *celestial navigation.* These systems are most commonly applicable to surface-to-surface missiles, and electronic countermeasures are relatively ineffective against them since they neither transmit nor receive signals that can be jammed.

Preset guidance. The term *preset* completely describes one guidance method. When preset guidance is used, all of the control equipment is inside the missile. This means that before the missile is launched, all information relative to target location as well as the trajectory the missile must follow must be calculated. After this is done, the missile guidance system must be set to follow the course to the target, to hold the missile at the desired altitude, to measure its air speed and, at the correct time, cause the missile to start the terminal phase of its flight and dive on the target.

A major advantage of preset guidance is that it is relatively simple compared to other types of guidance; it does not require tracking or visibility.

An early example of a preset guidance system was the German V-2, where range and bearing of the target were predetermined and set into the control mechanism. The earliest Polaris missile was also designed to use preset guidance during the first part of its flight, but this was soon modified to permit greater launch flexibility.

The preset method of guidance is useful only against stationary targets of large size, such as land masses or cities. Since the guidance information is completely determined prior to launch, this method would, of course, not be suitable for use against ships, aircraft, enemy missiles, or moving land targets.

Navigational guidance systems. When targets are located at great distances from the launching site, some form of navigational guidance must be used. Accuracy at long distances is achieved only after exacting and comprehensive calculations of the flight path have been made. The mathematical equation for a navigation problem of this type may contain factors designed to control the movement of the missile about the three axes—pitch, roll, and yaw. In addition, the equation may contain factors that take into account acceleration due to outside forces (tail winds, for example) and the inertia of the missile itself. Three navigational systems that may be used for long-range missile guidance are inertial, celestial, and terrestrial.

Inertial guidance. The simplest principle for guidance is the law of inertia. In aiming a basketball at a basket, an attempt is made to give the ball a trajectory that will terminate in the basket. However, once the ball is released, the shooter has no further control over it. If he has aimed incorrectly, or if the ball is touched by another person, it will miss the basket. However, it is possible for the ball to be incorrectly aimed and then have another person touch it to change its course so it will hit the basket. In this case, the second player has provided a form of guidance. The inertial guidance system supplies the intermediate push to get the missile back on the proper trajectory.

The inertial guidance method is used for the same purpose as the preset method and is actually a refinement of that method. The inertially guided missile also receives programmed information prior to launch. Although there is no electromagnetic contact between the launching site and the missile after launch, the missile is able to make corrections to its flight path with amazing precision, controlling the flight path with *accelerometers* that are mounted on a gyro-stabilized platform. All in-flight accelerations are continuously measured by this arrangement, and the missile attitude control generates corresponding correction signals to maintain the proper trajectory. The use of inertial guidance takes much of the guesswork out of long-range missile delivery. The unpredictable outside forces working on the missile are continuously sensed by the accelerometers. The generated solution enables the missile to continuously correct its flight path. The inertial method has proved far more reliable than any other long-range guidance method developed to date.

Celestial reference. A celestial navigation guidance system is a

Figure 15–10. The Tomahawk missile employs inertial guidance with updates from a radar altimeter. The altimeter matches measured terrain height with stored values in a computer.

system designed for a predetermined path in which the missile course is adjusted continuously by reference to fixed stars. The system is based on the known apparent positions of stars or other celestial bodies with respect to a point on the surface of the earth at a given time. Navigation by fixed stars and the sun is highly desirable for long-range missiles since its accuracy is not dependent on range. Figure 15–11 sketches the application of the system as it might be used for a guided missile.

The missile must be provided with a horizontal or a vertical reference to the earth, automatic star-tracking telescopes to determine star elevation angles with respect to the reference, a time base, and navigational star tables mechanically or electrically recorded. A computer in the missile continuously compares star observations with the

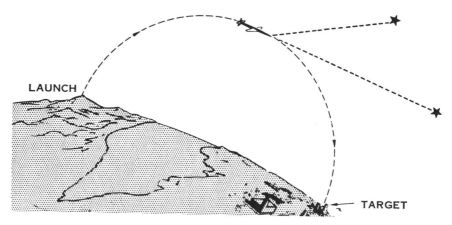

Figure 15–11. Celestial guidance.

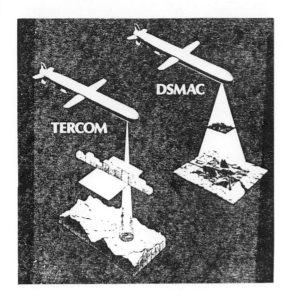

Figure 15–12. Terrestrial guidance.

time base and the navigational tables to determine the missile's present position. From this, the proper signals are computed to steer the missile correctly toward the target. The missile must carry all this complicated equipment and must fly above the clouds to assure star visibility.

Celestial guidance (also called stellar guidance) was used for the Mariner (unmanned spacecraft) interplanetary mission to the vicinity of Mars and Venus. No guided missile system at present uses celestial guidance.

Terrestrial guidance method. Various picture and mapmatching guidance methods have been suggested and devised. The principle is basically the same for all. It involves the comparison of a photo or map of the terrain over which the missile is flying with observations of the terrain by optical or radar equipment in the missile. On the basis of the comparison (figure 15–12), the missile is able to cause the actual track to coincide with the desired track. The system is, of course, quite complicated and is usable only against stationary targets such as large land masses and industrial areas.

Guided Flight Paths

A guided missile is usually under the combined influence of natural and man-made forces during its entire flight. Its path may assume almost any form.

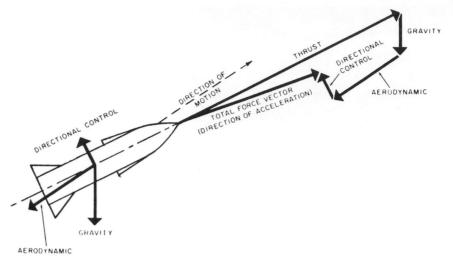

Figure 15–13. Vector sum diagram.

Man-made forces include thrust and directional control as shown in figure 15–13. The vector sum of all the forces, natural and man-made, acting on a missile at any instant, may be called the total force vector. It is this vector, considered as a function of time in magnitude and direction, that provides velocity vector control. Paths along which a guided missile may travel may be broadly classified as either preset or variable. The plan of a preset path cannot be changed in mid-flight; the plan of a variable path is altered according to conditions occurring during flight.

Preset Guided Paths

Constant. A preset guided missile path has a plan that has been fixed beforehand. This plan may include several different phases, but once the missile is launched, the plan cannot be changed. The phases must follow one another as originally planned. The simplest type of preset guided missile path is the *constant* preset. Here, the missile flight has only one phase.

The term *constant preset* may be broadened to include flights that are constant after a brief launching phase that is different in character from the rest of the flight. During the main phase of a constant preset guided-missile flight, the missile receives no control except that which has already been built into it. However, it receives this control throughout the guided phase of flight. Often it is powered all the

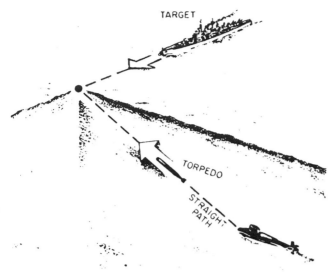

Figure 15–14. Constant preset guided path.

way. The nature of a constant preset guided-missile flight path depends on how it is powered, and the medium through which it travels.

A torpedo fired from a submarine to intercept a surface target, figure 15–14, may describe a straight line — a constant preset guided path.

Programmed. A missile could be guided in a preset path against a fixed target; the joint effect of missile power and gravity would then cause the path to become a curve. A missile following a preset path may be guided in various ways—for instance, by an autopilot or by inertial navigation. The means of propulsion may be motor, jet, or rocket. A more complex type of preset guided-missile path is the *programmed* preset. Here, the missile flight has several phases: for example: a torpedo, as illustrated in figure 15–15, executing a search pattern. During the first phase, the torpedo, having been launched in some initial direction other than the desired ultimate direction, gradually finds the desired direction by control mechanisms such as gyros and depth settings. The torpedo then maintains this direction for the remainder of this first phase, at the end of which it is presumed to be in the neighborhood of a target. During the second phase, the torpedo executes a search pattern, possibly a circular or helical path.

Variable Flight Paths

The guided flight paths of greatest interest are those that can vary during flight. In general, the heading of the weapon is a function of target position and velocity. These parameters are measured by con-

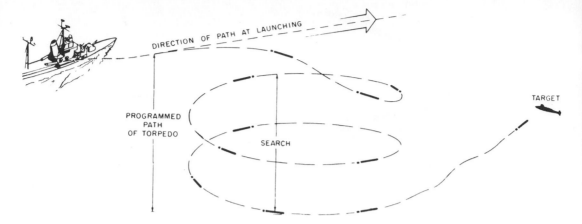

Figure 15–15. Torpedo programmed path.

tinuous tracking, and the resultant missile flight path is determined, assuming that the target motion will remain unchanged until new data is received. There are four basic types of variable flight paths in common use: pursuit, constant-bearing, proportional navigation, and line of sight.

Pursuit. The simplest procedure for a guided missile to follow is to remain pointed at the target at all times. The missile is constantly heading along the line of sight from the missile to the target, and its track describes a pursuit path with *the rate of turn of the missile always equal to the rate of turn of the line of sight.* Pure pursuit paths are highly curved near the end of flight, and often the missile may lack sufficient maneuverability to maintain a pure pursuit path in the terminal phase of guidance. When this is the case, the missile can be designed to continue turning at its maximum rate until a point is reached where a pursuit course can be resumed. The most common application of the pursuit course is against slow-moving targets, or for missiles launched from a point to the rear of the target.

> *Pursuit:* Lead or deviated pursuit course is defined as a course in which the angle between the velocity vector and line of sight from the missile to the target is fixed. For purposes of illustration, lead angle is assumed to be zero, and only pure pursuit is described. ($\theta_M = \beta$). (See figure 15–16.)

Constant bearing. At the opposite extreme to a pursuit path is a constant-bearing or collision path. The missile is aimed at a point ahead of the target, where both the missile and target will arrive at the same instant. The line of sight to this point does not rotate relative

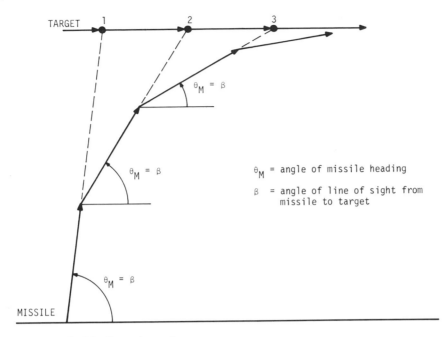

Figure 15–16. Pursuit path.

θ_M = angle of missile heading

β = angle of line of sight from missile to target

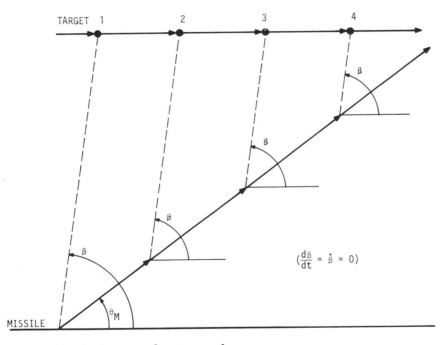

$$\left(\frac{d\beta}{dt} = \dot{\beta} = 0\right)$$

Figure 15–17. Constant bearing path.

to the missile. The missile path is as linear as the effect of gravity and aerodynamic forces allow. If the target makes an evasive turn or if the target's velocity changes, a new collision course must be computed and the missile flight path altered accordingly. The outstanding feature of this course is that for a maneuvering constant-speed target, the missile lateral acceleration never exceeds the target's lateral acceleration. The major drawback lies in the fact that the *control system requires sufficient data-gathering and processing equipment to predict future target position.*

Constant Bearing: A course in which the line of sight from the missile to the target maintains a constant direction in space. If both missile and target speeds are constant, a collision course results. (See figure 15–17.)

$$\left(\frac{d\beta}{dt} = \dot{\beta} = 0\right)$$

Proportional navigation. The more advanced homing missiles will employ some form of proportional navigation. The missile guidance

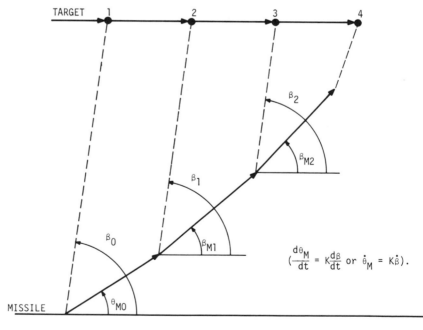

Figure 15–18. *Proportional navigation flight path.*

receiver measures the rate of change of the line of sight (LOS) (bearing drift, if you will) and passes that information to the guidance computer, which in turn generates steering commands for the autopilot. The missile rate of turn is some fixed or variable multiple of the rate of change of the LOS. This multiple, called the *navigation ratio*, can be varied during missile flight to optimize performance. A missile employing this method is said to use proportional navigation with a variable navigation ratio (VNR). The navigation ratio may be less than 1:1 early in the flight to conserve velocity and increase range. As the flight proceeds, the navigation ratio will increase to 2:1, 4:1, or even more to ensure that the missile will be agile enough to counter target maneuvers in the terminal phase of flight.

Proportional: A course in which the rate of change of the missile heading is directly proportional to the rate of rotation of the line of sight from missile to target. (See figure 15–18.)

$$\left(\frac{d\theta_M}{dt} = K\frac{d\beta}{dt} \text{ or } \dot{\theta}_M = K\beta \right)$$

Line of Sight. Here, the missile is guided so that it travels along the line of sight from the *launching station* to the target. This is, of

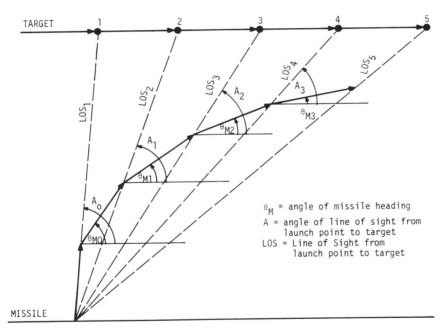

Figure 15–19. *Line of sight path.*

course, the flight path flown by a beam-riding missile. An alternative form of a beam-riding path is the *constant lead angle path*. Here the beam that the missile follows is kept ahead of the line of sight by a constant offset. The major advantages of the line of sight path are its flexibility and the minimal complexity of the equipment that must be carried in the missile, since the major burden of guidance is assumed at the launching station.

> *Line of Sight:* Defined as a course in which the missile is guided so as to remain on the line joining the target and point of control. This method is usually called "beam riding." (See figure 15–19.)

Table 15–1.   Guidance Law Comparison

Law	Advantage	Disadvantage
Pursuit	Simple Mechanization	Poor Against Maneuvering Targets
		Launch Geometry Restrictions
Fixed Lead Angle Line-Of-Sight	Simple Mechanization	Poor Against Maneuvering Targets
	Less Geometry Restricted Than Pursuit	Lead Angle Correct for Fixed Geometry Only
Constant Bearing Collision	Requires Minimum Maneuver Capability	Requires Infinite Gain and No Time Lags—Most Complex in Data Gathering and Processing
Proportional Navigation	Good Against Maneuvering Targets	More Complex Mechanization
	All-Aspect Capability	
Optimal Homing	Solves Specific Problems Such As Long Range	More Complex Mechanization
	May Improve Proportional Navigation Shortcomings	

Table 15–2. Current Guidance System Examples

Weapon	Guidance
Air-to-Air	
Phoenix	Semiactive/Active/Command
Sparrow	Semiactive
Sidewinder	Passive (IR)
Air-To-Surface	
Harpoon	Active Radar
Maverick	T.V. (passive)
Walleye	T.V. (passive)
Shrike	Passive (RF)
Sram	Inertial
Standard Arm	Passive (RF)
Antisubmarine	
Subroc	Inertial
Asroc	Ballistic
Surface-to-Air	
Sea Sparrow	Semiactive
Hawk	Semiactive
RAM	Passive IR/RF (Interferometer)
Patriot	Command; Semiactive (retransmission)
Standard MR (SM-1)	Semiactive
Standard ER (SM-1)	Semiactive
Standard SM-2 MR (Aegis)	Command; Semiactive
Standard SM-2 ER	Command; Semiactive
Surface-to-Surface	
Poseidon	Inertial
Tomahawk (Land Attack)	Terrestrial (terrain following)
Trident	Inertial
Standard	Semiactive
Harpoon	Active-Radar
Tomahawk (Antiship)	Inertial/Active Radar
Battlefield Support	
Lance	Inertial
Tow	Wire-Guided (command), Optically Tracked
Dragon	Wire-Guided
Stinger	Passive (IR); Proportional Navigation

Table 15–3. Guidance System Categories

| Guidance Systems that Use Man-Made Electromagnetic Devices | | Self-Contained Guidance Systems | |
Radar Control	Homing	Preset	Navigational
a. Command	a. Active		a. Inertial
b. Beam-Rider	b. Semiactive		b. Celestial
c. Modified Beam-Rider	c. Passive		c. Terrestrial
Composite Systems Hybrid (Command/Semiactive)			

Summary

The three phases of guidance are boost, midcourse, and terminal. The distinction between phases is primarily based upon a breakdown of the flight path rather than in any change-over points in guidance methods. The terminal phase is, however, the most critical and demands peak performance from the guidance system.

Guidance systems are divided into two broad categories; those that use man-made electromagnetic devices and those that use some other means. The various subcategories of guidance systems are shown below in table 15–3.

Guided missile paths may be classified as either preset or variable. Preset guided paths have planned flight routines that cannot be changed in mid flight on the basis of updated data. A preset plan may be for a one-phase flight (constant preset) or a flight of several phases (programmed preset). Variable guided flight paths have plans that can be changed in mid flight; thus they make possible the successful pursuit of a target that makes evasive maneuvers. Prediction of target position is continuously reappraised and the missile course is recomputed in the light of new target data. Variable guided flight paths include pursuit, constant bearing, proportional navigation, and line of sight.

The interception by a missile of a moving target depends on the prediction of future target position, and requires certain assumptions. When using bullets, ballistic missiles, or preset guided missiles, it is assumed that the target motion measured while tracking will remain unchanged during missile flight. When using variable guided missiles, it is assumed that the target motion, measured at any instant by almost continuous tracking, will remain unchanged over a short time interval.

References

Bureau of Naval Personnel. *Principles of Guided Missiles and Nuclear Weapons*. NAVPERS 10784-B, 1st Rev. Washington, D.C.: GPO, 1972.

Commander, Naval Ordnance Systems Command. *Weapons Systems Fundamentals*. NAVORD OP 3000, vols. 2 & 3, 1st Rev. Washington, D.C.: GPO, 1971.

Gulick, J. F., and J. S. Miller, *Missile Guidance: Interferometer Homing Using Body Fixed Antennas*. Technical Memorandum TG1331 (TSC-W36-37), Laurel, Md.: Johns Hopkins University Applied Physics Laboratory, 1982.

16

Weapon Propulsion and Architecture

Propulsion

Every weapon requires some type of propulsion to deliver its warhead to the intended target. This chapter will be a study of the propulsion systems used to propel weapons to their targets. The underlying principle of propulsive movement has been stated by Newton in his Third Law of Motion: *To every action there is an equal and opposite reaction.* Every forward acceleration or change in motion is a result of a reactive force acting in the opposing direction. A person walks forward by pushing backwards against the ground. In a propeller-type airplane, the air through which it is moving is driven backward to move the airplane forward. In a jet-propelled plane or a rocket, a mass of gas is emitted rearward at high speed, and the forward motion of the plane is a reaction to the motion of the gas. Matter in the form of a liquid, a gas, or a solid may be discharged as a propellant force, expending its energy in a direction opposite to the desired path of motion, resulting in a predetermined acceleration of the propelled body along a desired trajectory.

Types of Propulsion

The power required to propel a warhead to its target is obtained through the controlled release of stored energy. Usually types of propulsion are considered from two viewpoints. The *energy source* may be the end product of:

(1) a chemical reaction
(2) a compression of gases or liquids
(3) the effect of gravity

By *method of launch*, weapon propulsion systems are normally classified as:

(1) impulse-propulsion or gun-type—a projectile
(2) reaction—a missile or torpedo
(3) gravity—a bomb

Impulse Propulsion

Impulse propulsion systems include all weapons systems in which a projectile is ejected from a container (usually a long tube) by means of an initial impulse. Also included in this classification are systems that employ compressed gases (torpedo and Polaris/Poseidon launching systems) to provide the initial impulse propulsion until they have cleared the launching vehicle.

The expulsion of a projectile at the high velocities demanded by modern warfare requires tremendous forces. The study of these forces and of the action within a gun at the time of fire is referred to as *interior ballistics*. It comprises a study of a chemical energy source, a working substance (high-pressure gas), and the equipment to release and direct the working substance. To provide the high speed of response needed in a gun, the propellant must transfer its energy of reaction to the projectile by means of the expanding gaseous products of combustion, which are considered the working substances.

Explosive propellant train. The gas that causes the pressure that propels the projectile is generated by the ignition of an explosive train. This explosive train is termed a propellant train and is similar to the high-explosive train discussed previously. The difference is that the propellant train consists primarily of low explosives instead of high explosives and has a primer, an igniter or igniting charge, and a propelling charge. Ignition of a small quantity of sensitive explosive, the primer (lead azide), is initiated by a blow from the firing pin and is transmitted and intensified by the igniter so that the large, relatively insensitive propelling charge burns in the proper manner and launches the projectile. Figure 16–1 shows the elements just mentioned.

Propellants. All guns and most rocket-powered weapons use solid propellants to provide their propulsion. The first solid propellant used

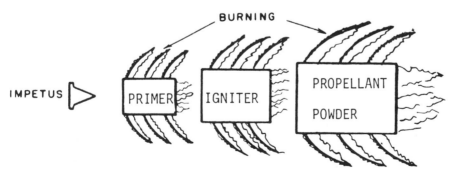

Figure 16–1. Explosive propellant train.

by man was black powder in the thirteenth century. Black powder is no longer considered suitable for use as a propellant for several reasons: it burns incompletely, leaving large amounts of residue; it creates high temperatures resulting in rapid bore erosion; it creates great billows of black smoke; and it detonates rather than burns.

Gunpowders or smokeless powders are the propellants in use today. This substance is produced by combining nitrocellulose (nitric acid and cotton) with ether and alcohol to produce a low explosive. Although called smokeless powders, they are neither smokeless nor in powder form, but in granule form. Smokeless powders may be considered to be classed as either single or multibase powders.

In single-base powders, nitrocellulose is the only explosive present. Other ingredients and additives are added to obtain suitable form, desired burning characteristics, and stability. The standard single-base smokeless powder used by the Navy is a uniform colloid of ether-alcohol and purified nitrocellulose to which, for purposes of chemical stability, is added a small quantity of diphenylamine.

The multibase powders may be divided into double-base and triple-base powders, both of which contain nitroglycerin to facilitate the dissolving of the nitrocellulose and enhance its explosive qualities. The nitroglycerin also increases the sensitivity, the flame temperature, burning rate, and tendency to detonate. The higher flame temperature serves to decrease the smoke and residue, but increases flash and gun-tube erosion. Double-base propellants have limited use in artillery weapons in the United States due to excessive gun-tube erosion, but are the standard propellants in most other countries. Double-base propellants are used in the United States for mortar propellants, small rocket engines, shotgun shells, the 7.62-mm NATO rifle cartridge, recoilless rifles, and the Navy's 5"/54-caliber gun.

Triple-base propellants are double-base propellants with the addition of nitroguandine to lower the flame temperature, which produces less tube erosion and flash. The major drawback is the limited supply of the raw material nitroguandine. At present, triple-base propellants are used in tank rounds and are being tested for new long-range artillery rounds.

Solid propellants are designed to produce a large volume of gases at a controlled rate. Gun barrels and some rocket casings are designed to withstand a fixed maximum gas pressure. The pressure generated can be limited to this maximum value by controlling the rate of burning of the propellant. The burning rate is controlled by varying the following factors:

(1) The size and shape of the grain, including perforations.

(2) The web thickness or amount of solid propellant between burning surfaces; the thicker the web, the longer the burning time.
(3) The burning-rate constant, which depends on the chemical composition of the propellant.
(4) The percentages of volatile materials, inert matter, and moisture present. A 1% change in volatiles in a low-volatile-content propellant may cause as much as a 10% change in the rate of burning.

When a propellant burns in a confined space, the rate of burning increases as both temperature and pressure rise. Since propellants burn only on exposed surfaces, the rate of gas evolution or changes in pressure will also depend upon the area of propellant surface ignited. Propellants are classified according to variations in the rate of burning due to changes in the quantity of ignited surface; for example, grains are:

(1) Degressive or regressive burning—as burning proceeds, the total burning surface decreases. Propellants formed in pellets, balls, sheets, strips, or cord burn degressively. (See figure 16–2.) Degressive grains are used in weapons with short tubes.
(2) Neutral burning—as burning proceeds the total burning surface remains approximately constant. Single perforated grains and star perforations result in neutral burning. (See figure 16–3.)
(3) Progressive burning—as burning proceeds, the total burning surface increases. Multi-perforated and rosette grains burn progressively.

Compressed air/gas. One final propellant that needs mentioning is compressed air or gas. Compressed air or a compressed gas is used for the ejection of torpedoes and missiles. Particularly useful in submarines, compressed air has the advantage of being available and

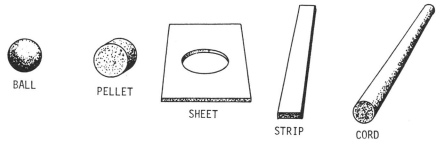

BALL   PELLET   SHEET   STRIP   CORD

Figure 16–2. Degressive burning grains.

Weapon Propulsion and Architecture   **459**

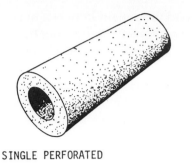

SINGLE PERFORATED

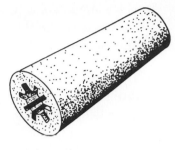

STAR PERFORATED

Figure 16–3. *Neutral burning grains.*

MULTI-PERFORATED

ROSETTE

Figure 16–4. *Progressive burning grains.*

easily controllable without the obvious disadvantages of explosives. In addition, the high pressures obtainable from gunpowder are not needed in these applications, since the expanding gas serves primarily as a booster, with a sustaining propulsion system taking over once the missile is clear of the submarine or torpedo launcher. Its disadvantage is the requirement to maintain a high-pressure air compressor with its associated high noise level.

Interior Ballistics

Action inside the gun. When the charge is ignited, gases are evolved from the surface of each grain of propellant, and the pressure in the chamber rises rapidly. Due to friction and resistance of the rotating band, the projectile does not move until the pressure behind it reaches several hundred pounds per square inch. For a time after the projectile starts to move, gases are generated more rapidly than the rate at which the volume behind the projectile is increased, and the pres-

Figure 16–5. Note the powder grains (simulated) in this cutaway of 76-mm semi-fixed ammunition for the Mk. 75 gun.

sure continues to rise. As the propellant burning area decreases, the pressure falls; however, the projectile continues to accelerate as long as there is a net force acting on it. When the projectile reaches the muzzle, the pressure inside the tube has fallen to about a tenth to a third of the maximum pressure. Gas pressure continues to act on the projectile for a short distance beyond the muzzle, and the projectile continues to accelerate for a short time. Figure 16–6 shows the relationship of pressure and velocity versus distance of projectile travel.

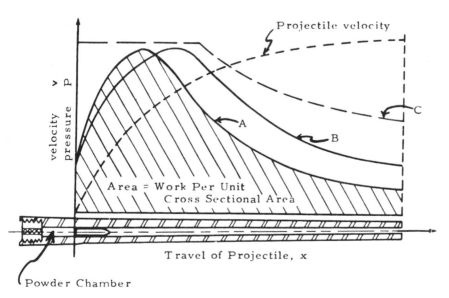

Figure 16–6. Interior ballistics. Pressure-travel (solid lines) and velocity-travel (dotted lines) curves.

Since the work performed on the projectile is a function of the area under the pressure-travel curve, the muzzle velocity produced by the propellant can be determined.

$$\text{Work} = \triangle KE = \frac{1}{2}mv^2, \text{ if the Initial Velocity is zero.}$$

Should it be desired to increase the muzzle velocity of a projectile, the work performed or the area under some new curve must be greater than the area under a curve giving a lower muzzle velocity. Such an increase in velocity is indicated by curve B, whose maximum pressure is equal to that of curve A, but whose area is greater than that under A. It appears that the ideal pressure-travel curve would be one that coincided with the curve of permissible pressure. If it were possible to design such a propellant, it would have undesirable characteristics. In addition to producing excessive erosion (which would materially decrease the accurate life of the gun), brilliant flashes and non-uniform velocities due to high muzzle pressure would result. The powder chamber would also have to be enlarged, thus increasing the weight and decreasing the mobility of the gun. Curve C is the gun strength curve, which indicates maximum permissible pressure and is a function of gun tube thickness. (See chapter 19).

Note: Often the pressure-travel curve is the *given* variable, and the gun tube thickness is then dictated by the pressure-travel curve.)

There are several methods available for changing the pressure-travel curves for a given gun. The easiest method is to change the type of propellant grain. Figure 16–7 illustrates the effect that the three types of powder grains have on the pressure-travel curve. As can be seen, a progressive powder reaches maximum pressure much later than a degressive powder and loses pressure much more gradually. The degressive powder reaches a much larger maximum pressure as shown below. Thus, it stands to reason that degressive powders

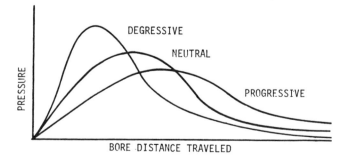

Figure 16–7. Pressure-travel curve.

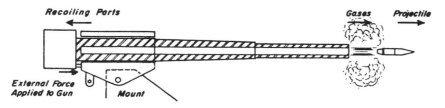

Figure 16–8. A conventional gun system.

are used in weapons with short tubes, and increasingly progressive powders are used in weapons with longer tubes.

Other methods of changing the pressure-travel curve are by altering the burning rate of the powder, changing the loading density of the propellant, or by changing the grain size.

The energy developed by the burning of the propellant in a typical medium-caliber gun, assuming complete combustion, is distributed as follows:

Energy Absorbed	% of Total
Translation of projectile	32.00
Rotation of projectile	00.14
Frictional work on projectile	2.17
(Due to engraving of rotating bands, wall friction, and effects of increasing twist)	34.31
Translation of recoiling parts	00.12
Translation of propellant gases	3.14
Heat loss to gun and projectile	20.17
Sensible and latent heat losses in propellant gases	42.26
	65.69
Propellant potential	100.00%

(Reflected in the area generated under a pressure-travel curve for the cannon, figure 16–6.)

Reaction Propulsion

Introduction. Contrary to popular belief, reaction motors do not obtain thrust by "pushing" against the medium in which they are operating. Thrust is developed by increasing the momentum of the working fluid and creating a pressure differential therein. Newton's

Third Law of Motion states that for every action, there is an equal and opposite reaction. This principle forms the basis for the motion of all self-propelled objects. Pressure differentials are employed to move propeller-driven aircraft as well as rockets and jet-propelled missiles. By definition, a reaction-propelled vehicle is one containing within its structure its own source of propulsion, i.e., a reaction-type motor. The mediums in which reaction motors operate and the types that have been used in weapon systems are:

air: propeller engines, turbojets, ramjets, rockets
vacuum: rockets
water: screws, hydrojets, rockets

The performance required of modern propulsion systems, insofar as range, velocity, and control are concerned, is considerably in excess of that which can be accomplished by heretofore conventional methods. Until the advent of guided missiles that travel at supersonic speeds to lessen the probability of interception, the reciprocating engine–propeller combination was considered satisfactory for the propulsion of aircraft. The generation of shock waves as the speed of sound is approached limits the development of thrust and thus the speed of propeller-driven craft. Although future developments may overcome the limitations of propeller-driven vehicles, it is necessary at the present time to use jet propulsion for missiles traveling at high subsonic and supersonic speeds. A minor disadvantage of jet propulsion is that tremendous quantities of fuel are consumed per second of flight time. The efficiency ratings of jet engine types, however, are so superior to those of propeller-driven types that the disadvantage as a measure of degree is minimal. Also, the only means of self-propulsion that will operate in a vacuum is jet propulsion with rockets.

Classification of jet propulsion engines. Jet propulsion is a means of locomotion obtained from the momentum of matter ejected from within the propelled body in the form of a fluid jet. The fluids used for producing the jet include water, steam, heated air, and gases produced by chemical reaction. The fluid may be drawn into the body from the very medium in which the body is moving, such as air in a jet engine or water in a hydrojet engine, or it may be self-contained, as in the case of rocket engines, where the working fluid is composed of the gaseous products of rocket fuel combustion. A jet-propulsion engine consists essentially of an air inlet section (diffuser) for air-breathing jets, a propellant supply system, a combustion chamber, and an exhaust nozzle. The purpose of the propellant system and the combustion chamber is to produce large volumes of high-temperature, high-pressure gases. The exhaust nozzle then converts the heat energy into kinetic energy as efficiently as possible. In jet engines and in liquid-fuel rockets, the fuel is pumped into the combustion chamber to be burned. In a solid-propellant rocket, the combustion chamber already contains the fuel to be burned.

Popular terminology makes a distinction between jets and rockets: a jet takes in air from the atmosphere; a rocket needs no air supply, as it carries its own supply of oxygen. Both types of engines operate by expelling a stream of gas at high speed from a nozzle at the after end of the vehicle. For purposes here, a rocket can be considered a type of jet engine. Jet-propulsion systems used in missiles may be divided into two classes: thermal jet engines and rockets.

In a thermal jet engine (air breathing), the missile breathes in a quantity of air at its input end and compresses it. Liquid fuel is then injected into the compressed air and the mixture is ignited in a combustion chamber. As the resulting hot gases are expelled through a nozzle at the rear of the vehicle, heat energy is transformed into kinetic energy, and thrust is created. Missiles using air-breathing propulsion systems are incapable of operating in a vacuum.

As previously mentioned, the basic difference between a rocket and a thermal jet engine is that the rocket carries its own oxidizer and needs no outside air for the combustion process. In addition, the thrust developed by an air-breathing engine is dependent on the momentum change between the fluid (air) entering the engine and the fluid (hot gases) exiting the engine, whereas in a rocket the thrust depends only on the momentum or velocity of the jet of exhaust gases. Furthermore, the thrust developed by a rocket per unit-of-engine frontal area and per unit-of-engine weight is the greatest of any known type of engine. Rockets are distinguished by the means used to produce exhaust material. The most common type of rocket engine obtains its high-pressure gases by burning a propellant. This propellant consists of both fuel and oxidizer and may be solid or liquid.

Propellants. The fuels and oxidizers used to power a jet/rocket engine are called propellants. The chemical reaction between fuel and oxidizer in the combustion chamber of the jet engine produces high-pressure, high-temperature gases. These gases, when channeled through an exhaust nozzle, are converted into kinetic energy creating a force acting in a direction opposite to the flow of the exhaust gases from the nozzle. This propulsive force, termed thrust, is a function primarily of the velocity at which the gases leave the exhaust nozzle and the mass flow rate of the gases.

In order to develop a high thrust with a solid propellant, grains or

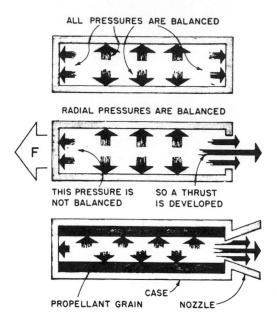

ALL PRESSURES ARE BALANCED

RADIAL PRESSURES ARE BALANCED

F

THIS PRESSURE IS NOT BALANCED

SO A THRUST IS DEVELOPED

PROPELLANT GRAIN   CASE   NOZZLE

Figure 16–9. Development of thrust in rocket motor.

charges of propellant are employed with large burning surfaces so that a high rate of mass flow is developed. The duration of burning of a propellant charge is determined by the web of the grain and the burning rate. Since the combustion chamber has fixed dimensions and capacity for propellant, the thrust may be either great, but of short duration, or low, but of long duration. The thrust developed by a reaction motor is the resultant of static pressure forces acting on the interior and exterior surfaces of the combustion chamber. This force imbalance is shown graphically in the following illustrations.

The static pressures acting upon the interior surfaces depend upon the rate at which propellants are burned, the thermochemical characteristics of the gases produced by their combustion, and the area of the throat of the dispersing nozzle. As the internal forces are several times greater than the external forces, and as the forces acting normal to the longitudinal axis of the combustion chamber do not contribute to the thrust, the thrust developed is primarily the resultant axial component of the pressure forces.

If the thrust-time curve (figure 16–10) obtained from firing a rocket is integrated over the burning duration, the result is called total impulse and is measured in Newton-seconds. Then

$$I_t = \int_o^{t_b} T dt = T_{av} t_b$$

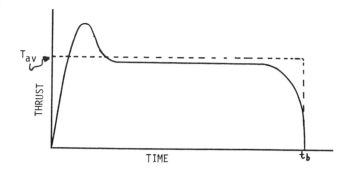

Figure 16–10. Thrust-time curve.

where

    I_t is total impulse Newton-sec (N-sec)
    t_b is burn time (sec)
    T_{av} is average thrust in Newtons (N)

The performance characteristics of a specific propellant is called the specific impulse of the propellant (solid-fuel) or specific thrust of the propellant (liquid-fuel). The specific impulse is a measure of the "quality" or "merit" of the fuel and is defined as:

$$I_{sp} = \frac{T_{av}\, t_b}{m_p g} = \frac{I_t}{m_p g}$$

where

    I_{sp} is specific impulse (sec)
    m_p is mass of solid propellant (kg)
    g is the force of gravity (9.8 M/sec^2)

Although the units of specific impulse are seconds, the I_{sp} of a fuel is actually the amount of impulse per kg of fuel. In other words it reflects the specific energy of the fuel. Thus, the fuel with the highest I_{sp} will produce the greatest performance.

Propellants are classified as either solid propellants or liquid propellants. Nearly all of the rocket-powered weapons in use by the United States use solid propellants. Liquid propellants are still used in some of the older ICBMS and will be used in future cruise missiles. Of course, all thermal jet engines burn a liquid fuel.

Solid propellants consist of a fuel (usually a hydrocarbon) and an oxidizer, so combined as to produce a solid of desired chemical potential. The burning rate, which directly affects the amount of thrust produced, is the velocity in meters per second at which the grain is consumed. Burning rates of propellants depend upon the chemical composition of the propellant, the combustion chamber temperature and pressure gradient, gas velocity adjacent to the burning surface, and the size and shape of the grain or the geometry of the charge. The propellant charges are cast to obtain the types of burning previously discussed: neutral, progressive, or degressive burning. Propulsive specifications will determine which type is to be used. Normally a uniform burning rate is desired so that a constant thrust is produced. Most Navy propellants use either a cruciform grain or a cylindrical grain with an axial hole and radial perforations. (Figure 16–11.) The cruciform grain in cross section is a symmetrical cross. If all of the exterior surface of this grain were permitted to burn,

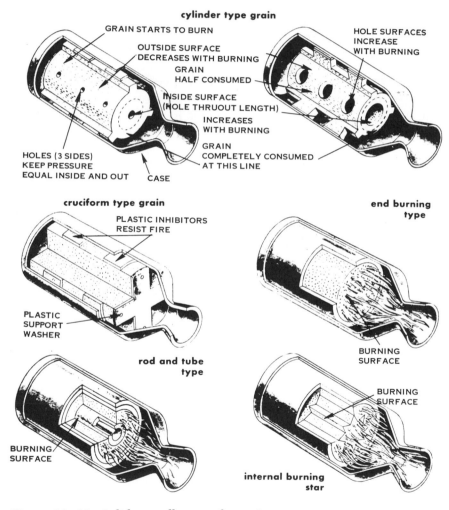

Figure 16–11. Solid propellant configurations.

there would be a gradual decrease of area, and the burning rate would be regressive. Since a uniform burning rate is desired, a number of slower-burning plastic strips or inhibitors are bonded to certain parts of the area exposed on the outer curved ends of the arms. These control or slow the initial burning rate, and gas-production rate is approximately uniform over burning time. Other cylinder grain types are shown in figure 16–11.

Liquid propellants are normally stored in tanks outside the combustion chamber and are injected into the combustion chamber. The injector vaporizes and mixes the fuel and oxidizers in the proper proportions for efficient burning. Liquid propellants are classified as either monopropellant or bipropellant. The monopropellant has the fuel and oxidizer mixed, and the bipropellant has the fuel and oxidizer separated until firing.

Liquid fuels are more powerful than solid fuels; but other than this advantage, a liquid-fuel rocket is not ideally suited as a weapon-propulsion system. Because of their high volatility and corrosive nature, liquid fuels cannot be stored for long periods of time, which usually means the system must be fueled just prior to launch. This negates its ability to be a quick-reaction weapon, which is usually required in combat situations.

Solid-fuel rocket engines do not require complex plumbing systems and are fairly simple systems as illustrated in figure 16–12. Storage problems are minimized, and the propellant is usually very stable. For these reasons, solid-fuel rockets are almost in exclusive use.

Elements of propulsion subsystems. A jet-/rocket-propelled engine is basically a device for converting a portion of the thermochemical energy developed in its combustion chamber into kinetic energy associated with a high-speed gaseous exhaust jet. The basic elements

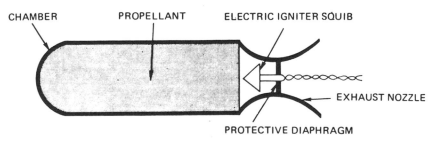

Figure 16–12. Elements of solid rocket motor.

of the engine are: 1) the combustion chamber, wherein the transformation of energy from potential to heat occurs; 2) the exhaust nozzle, wherein thermochemical energy is converted into the kinetic energy necessary to produce an exhaust jet of propulsive potential; and 3) the diffuser (for air-breathing jets only) or intake duct, wherein the high-speed air intake is converted into low-speed, high-pressure air for entry into the combustion chamber as an oxidizing agent.

The combustion chamber is the enclosure within which high-temperature, high-pressure gases are produced and potential energy is converted to kinetic energy. For liquid-fuel engines, injectors bring the fuel and oxidizers together in the chamber, and for solid-fuel engines the propellant is already contained in the chamber. Also contained in the combustion chamber is some type of ignition device to initiate the burning of the propellant.

An exhaust nozzle is a mechanically designed orifice through which the gases generated in the combustion chamber flow to the outside. The function of the nozzle is to increase the exit velocity of the hot gases flowing out of the engine so that maximum thrust is extracted from the fuel. A nozzle consists of a mouth, throat, and exit as illustrated below.

Under conditions of steady flow, the mass flow rate, by Bernoulli's Theorem, remains constant. Thus, in subsonic flow, where the density of the gas/fluid is considered to remain constant, the velocity must increase at any point where the cross-sectional area decreases in order to accommodate a constant mass flow rate. If flow remains subsonic, then as the cross-sectional area increases, the velocity will decrease.

It is possible to reduce the cross-sectional area of the nozzle throat to the point that the velocity will reach a maximum and become sonic. Then, with proper design of the divergent section of the nozzle, the flow velocity can be expanded supersonically as the cross-sectional area increases.

Since thrust from a rocket motor is proportional to the momentum of the exhaust gases ejected per second and momentum is equal to mass times velocity, the thrust efficiency can be increased at no extra

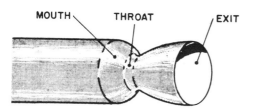

MOUTH   THROAT   EXIT

Figure 16–13. Nozzle components.

cost in fuel consumption if the exhaust velocity is maximized by proper nozzle design.

One of the more efficient designs in common use is the De Laval nozzle. The De Laval nozzle converges to a throat at which the velocity becomes sonic, and then the nozzle diverges such that the flow is expanded supersonically.

Turbojet engines. A turbojet engine derives its name from the fact that a portion of its exhaust output is diverted to operate a turbine, which in turn drives the air compressor used to compress the input air flow. Modern turbojets are of the axial-flow design as depicted in figure 16–14. An axial flow compressor is similar in operation to a propeller. As the rotor of the axial compressor turns, the blades impart energy of motion in both a tangential and axial direction to the air entering the front of the engine from the diffuser. The function of the diffuser or intake duct is to decelerate the velocity of the air from its free stream velocity to a desired velocity at the entrance of the compressor section or combustion chamber, with a minimum of pressure loss. For both subsonic and supersonic diffusers, the flow is decelerated from inlet to the engine compressor section. It is important to note that the air flow must be subsonic before it enters the engine. The stator is set in a fixed position with its blades preset at an angle such that the air thrown off the first-stage rotor blades is redirected into the path of the second-stage rotor blades. The added velocity compresses the air, increasing its density and, as a result, its pressure. This cycle of events is repeated in each stage of the compressor. Therefore, by increasing the number of stages, the final pressure can be increased to almost any desired value.

The combination of the air-intake system, air compressor, combustion system, and turbine is essentially an open-cycle gas turbine combined with a jet stream. In operation, the compressor, driven by

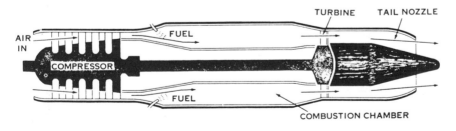

Figure 16–14. Axial-flow turbojet.

the gas turbine, supplies air under high pressure to the combustion chamber, where the fuel and air are mixed and burned. The turbine absorbs only part of the energy, while the remainder is employed for the production of thrust. Once started, combustion is continuous.

Without proper intake or diffuser design, the turbojet is limited to less than the speed of sound. As velocity approaches Mach 1, shock waves develop on the compressor blades and severely interfere with its operation. However, with *variable-geometry inlets* (the shape of inlet can be changed with changes in velocity) and improved diffuser designs, the turbojet engine's capabilities can be extended into the supersonic region. A turbojet can develop large static thrust, carry its own fuel, and its thrust is practically independent of speed.

The turbojet engine can be modified into three other major engine types: turboprop, turboshaft, and turbofan. These engines extract additional energy from the exhaust gases aft of the gas compressor turbine by adding a second stage of turbine blades. This second stage, the power turbine, propels a shaft attached to a propeller (turboprop), helicopter rotors (turboshaft), or fan blades (turbofan). The direct thrust produced by the flow of exhaust gases rearward is converted to a torque that drives the propeller, rotors, or fan. These types of engines are more efficient than the turbojet engine.

Currently several missiles use turbojets and turbofans for main propulsion plants. These are generally longer-range missiles and include the Harpoon, Tomahawk, and the Air-Launched Cruise Missile (ALCM).

Ramjet engines. The most promising jet engine, from the standpoint of simplicity and efficiency at supersonic speed, is the ramjet—so called because of the ram action that makes possible its operation.

The ramjet, as illustrated in figures 16–15, 16–16, and 16–17, has no moving parts. It consists of a cylindrical tube open at both ends, with an interior fuel-injection system. As the ramjet moves through the atmosphere, air is taken in through the front of the diffuser section, which is designed to convert high-speed, low-pressure air flow into low-speed, high-pressure air flow. Thus, a pressure barrier is formed and the escape of combustion gases out of the front of the engine is prevented.

The high-pressure air then mixes with the fuel, which is being sprayed continuously into the engine by the fuel injectors. Burning is initiated by spark plug action, after which it is uninterrupted and self-supporting—i.e., no further spark plug assistance is required. The flame front is kept from extending too far toward the rear of the

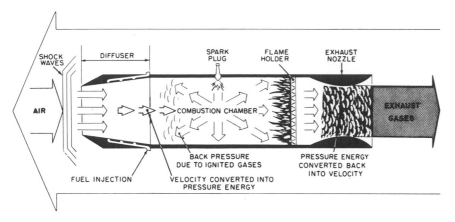

Figure 16–15. Low-supersonic ramjet.

engine by a device called the flameholder. By restricting burning to the combustion chamber, the flameholder maintains the combustion chamber temperature at a point high enough to support combustion. The combustion gases bombard the sides of the diffuser and the ram air barrier, exerting a force in the forward direction. Since the gases are allowed to escape out of the rear through the exhaust nozzle, the force in the forward direction is unbalanced. The degree to which this force is unbalanced depends on the efficiency with which the exhaust nozzle can dispose of the rearward-moving combustion gases by converting their high-pressure energy into velocity energy.

Ramjets operate in the subsonic, supersonic, and hypersonic ranges. Theoretically, there is no limit to the speed they can attain. However, because of the intense heat generated by air friction, present-day

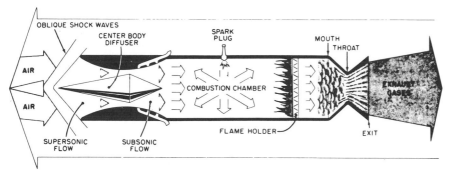

Figure 16–16. Hypersonic ramjet.

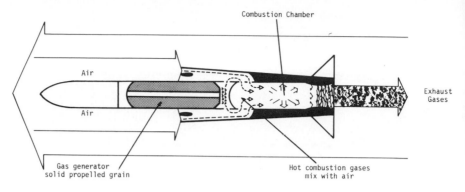

Figure 16–17. Solid-fuel ramjet.

materials are unable to withstand speeds in excess of Mach 5.0 in the atmosphere.

The main disadvantage of ramjet engines lies in the fact that they are, by the nature of their operation, unable to develop thrust at rest (static thrust). If fired at rest, high-pressure combustion gases would escape from the front as well as the rear. Consequently, before a missile with a ramjet engine can function properly, it must first be boosted by some other propulsion system to a speed approximately equal to that at which it was designed to operate. Ramjet engines are also restricted to use in altitudes below approximately 90,000 feet, since they must have air to operate.

A new variant of the ramjet, an integral rocket/ramjet, is under development for advanced cruise missiles. The rocket propellant is carried in the combustion chamber of the ramjet and provides the boost to get the ramjet up to high speed. When the propellant has burned leaving the chamber empty, the ramjet begins operation.

By burning a solid fuel containing insufficient oxidizer and combining the oxygen-deficient combustion products with air from outside the missile, engineers have been able to build a solid-fuel ramjet. This is especially promising when the advantages of solid fuel are combined with the increased range potential realized when using ambient air rather than an onboard oxidizer. The solid-fuel ramjet (figure 16–17) shows great potential to increase both the speed and the range of surface-to-air and cruise missiles.

Gravity-Type Propulsion

Gravity-type propulsion is the propulsion system used for free fall and glide bombs, and for missiles once their reaction propulsion system has ceased functioning. In either case, the missile or bomb has

Table 16-1.   Reaction Motor Advantages

Solid-fuel Rocket	*Liquid-fuel Rocket*	*Ramjet*	*Turbojet*
Very simple	Relatively simple	Very simple	Develops large static thrust
Unlimited speed	Practically unlimited speed	No wearing parts. Gets oxygen from air	Consumes fuel only; gets oxygen from air
Operates in any medium or in a vacuum	Operates in any medium or in a vacuum	Lightweight	Thrust practically independent of speed
No moving parts	Relatively few moving parts	Relatively inexpensive to construct and operate	Uses common fuels (liquid)
Full thrust on take off	Develops full thrust on take off	Easy to build	
Requires no booster	Has less need for a booster than air-breathing engine	Uses common fuels. Can be solid-fueled	
Can be used in stages or clusters	Can be staged in combination with liquid or solid rockets	Efficient at high speeds and altitudes	
Can be stored fully fueled		Supersonic	
Ready to fire anytime			

Source: NAVORD OP 3000

some initial velocity given to it from its launching platform (e.g., for a bomb it would be the aircraft velocity). Once it has been released, the only forces acting on it are gravity, drag, and lift in the case of a glide bomb. The potential energy of the weapon (its altitude) is converted to kinetic energy (velocity) as it falls due to the force of gravity.

Weapon Architecture

The structure of a missile or torpedo is designed to support and protect the warhead, guidance, and propulsion subsystems. It must

Table 16–2.   Reaction Motor Disadvantages

Solid-fuel Rocket	Liquid-fuel Rocket	Ramjet	Turbojet
High rate of fuel consumption	High rate of fuel consumption	Must be boosted to high speed before it can operate	Limited to low supersonic speeds usually less than Mach 3
Short burning time	Short burning time	Limited to operation in atmosphere	Complicated engine with many moving parts
Comparatively short range unless staged	Comparatively short range unless staged	Speed presently limited to about 3,600 mph	Power limited by stresses on turbine blades
Fragile and sensitive to environmental conditions	Cannot be stored fully fueled for long periods of time		Limited to operation in earth's atmosphere
	Long checkout procedure at launching		

Source: NAVORD OP 3000

withstand environmental forces as well as accelerations imposed by motion of the weapon. It must be lightweight in order to attain useful velocity easily and have adequate range, while having sufficient strength to resist bending or outright structural failure during high-speed turns. Additionally, its physical shape must be aerodynamically or hydrodynamically sound to ensure efficiency, while being compatible with storage facilities, launch mechanisms, and platforms. The architecture of the weapon can, to a large measure, determine its success or failure.

Missiles

The size and type of a missile selected for a particular function are based on the target, the launch vehicle or platform, range and maneuverability requirements, altitude envelope, and storage requirements. Minimum size and weight may not be the most efficient architecture, and it is often best to employ various types of structures for different sections of the missile to obtain certain design or maintenance advantages. Before addressing missile architecture, consid-

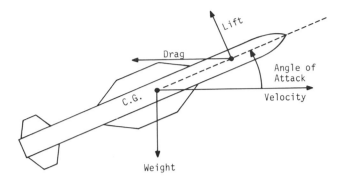

Figure 16–18. Missile force diagram.

eration must be given to forces experienced by a missile in flight (figure 16–18).

Drag and Lift

These aerodynamic forces are handled analytically by resolving them into two planar components—parallel to, and at right angles to, the direction of flow of the medium being traversed. The lift and drag forces are considered to act at a point called the Center of Pressure, C.P. (figure 16–18).

Lift is supplied by airfoils due to pressure distributions caused by their shape and inclination to the passing medium (angle of attack). The entire body of the missile supplies lift when inclined to the airstream and sometimes provides a major contribution to this force at high velocities. The amount of lift provided is directly related to the density of the medium in addition to the missile's velocity. Thus, because the size of missile airfoils cannot be increased at high altitudes, loss of lift due to lower air density must be compensated for by an increased angle of attack.

Parasitic drag is a force that opposes motion of the missile, due to displacement of the air in front of it, and to friction from the flow of air over its surface. All exposed missile surfaces resist this flow and contribute to drag. Drag is directly proportional to the velocity squared, thus streamlining of the missile becomes paramount as velocity increases. If the surface is rough or irregular, turbulence in the flow will increase and counteract the effect of streamlining. By minimizing these irregularities, the layers of air close to the surface of the missile flow smoothly (laminar flow), and drag is minimized for that particular configuration. Induced drag is caused by inclination of the wings or control surfaces to the airstream thus increasing the amount of air displaced in front of the missile.

Stability

While the weight of the missile is considered to act at the center of gravity (C.G. in figure 16–18), the lift and drag forces are considered to act at a point called the center of pressure (C.P. above). Lift and drag-force vectors intersect at this point, and if the center of gravity and the center of pressure are not located at the same point, as is often the case, the resulting moment of the forces acting at these points may cause unstable flight conditions. Therefore, the location of the center of pressure, determined by the configuration of the missile's structure, is an important factor in missile stability. In addition to the moments tending to produce rotation about the center of gravity (roll, pitch, and yaw), there are moments applied about the hinges or axes of the missile control surfaces. When force vectors representing these pressures have their origin at the center of gravity, it is then possible to describe the rotation of the missile in terms of angular displacements about these axes. When all forces acting on the missile are resolved into component forces along the three axes, we can completely specify the resultant motion of the missile with respect to its center of gravity. The angle of attack of the missile is identified as the angle between the longitudinal axis and the direction of flow of the undisturbed medium; it is generally taken to be positive when the direction of rotation is as shown in the illustration of forces acting on a missile in motion. A missile in flight encounters various forces that may be characterized as disturbing forces or moments, inasmuch as they tend to cause undesired deviations from the operational flight path. They may be random (wind, gusts, etc.) or systematic (misalignment of thrust components). When a missile is design-stable, it will return to its former position after being disturbed by an outside force. Guided missiles have the great advantage over unguided missiles in being able to correct, to some degree, both random and systematic disturbances that may occur during flight.

Control Surface Configuration

In guided missiles it is desirable to have a method of altering the direction of motion. By including airfoils with variable angle of attack, forces can be applied to alter the orientation of the missile in a plane at right angles to the plane of the airfoil, just as the rudder of a ship alters its angle to the flow of water. In both cases, it is this change in angle of attack of the body (hull) of the vehicle that results in the turn. Variation of the location of the control surfaces and other airfoils can significantly change the performance characteristics of the missile.

Canard control. The canard type is characterized by small control surfaces well forward on the body, while the main lifting surface is well aft (figure 16–19). These control surfaces are deflected in a positive manner; that is, the leading edge is raised to provide for a positive attack angle. To apply sufficient force, the canards must be positioned at a large angle of attack, causing large loads on hinges and missile structure. Therefore, large amounts of power are required to position these surfaces rapidly in order to reduce the total time that the force and additional drag are experienced. Canards require relatively large fixed surfaces aft on the missile airframe to improve stability.

Wing control. The wing-control type has control surfaces near the center of the airframe, which are also the main lifting surfaces. The entire lift surface is controllable, increasing or decreasing lift in response to control signals. This produces rapid missile maneuvers without requiring large inclinations to the airstream, resulting in minimum drag and minimum change in missile attitude or orientation in space. Maneuvers are initiated at the instant the wings are deflected and are not dependent upon an increase in body angle. Delay in change of missile orientation may be detrimental to some guidance means because the missile seeker may not be able to maintain contact with the target during maneuvers.

Tail control. The control surfaces in this case are at the rear of the body. Lift, supplied by fixed airfoils at the midsection, and deflection of the tail control surfaces are used to alter the missile angle of attack. With this configuration, control surface deflections are in a direction

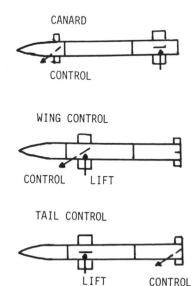

Figure 16–19. Control surface placement.

opposite to that of the angle of attack. Deflections are minimized, resulting in low control surface and body-bending loads as well as in little force on control surface pivots or hinges. Since the main lifting airfoils are not deflected, wing-tail interference effects are minimized. Because of the distance from the center of gravity (long lever arm), control surface size can be reduced, resulting in minimum drag. High power is required for the same reason as in canard control. Control-mechanism design problems are compounded by the small volume available and the severe heat conditions that may be encountered when the control surfaces are located aft in the vicinity of the propulsion-system exhaust nozzle.

Missile Architecture

The components of a missile are located in four major sections: the guidance section, warhead section, autopilot section, and control and propulsion sections. The functional systems of the missile are:

1. The guidance system
2. The warhead section
3. The autopilot
4. The propulsion system
5. The control system

The guidance system. The guidance system for a homing missile consists of an antenna assembly or electro-optical device protected by an optically transparent cover or a radome in the case of the radio frequency system, and electronic components that analyze signals from the target and compute orders for use by the autopilot. The sensor employed is usually a gimbal-mounted automatic tracking sensor (except the interferometer method) that tracks the target line-of-sight (LOS) and sends signals about the target's movement to the guidance electronics.

The warhead. The warhead consists of the fuze assembly, warhead, safety and arming device, and fuze booster. The fuze assembly usually contains a contact and proximity fuze. The contact fuze is enabled at all times, and the proximity fuze is actuated electronically. Its circuitry works in conjunction with the guidance section to ensure that the target detection device (TDD) remains unarmed until just prior to intercept, minimizing vulnerability to jamming. The safety and arming device prevents arming of the warhead until the missile is a safe distance from the firing platform.

The autopilot. The autopilot is a set of electronic instruments and electrical devices that control the electric actuators (motors) of aero-

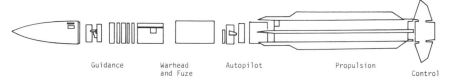

Guidance   Warhead   Autopilot   Propulsion
              and Fuze   Control

Figure 16–20. Functional systems of a guided missile.

dynamic control surfaces (tails). In the absence of signals from the guidance computer, the autopilot maintains the correct missile attitude and maintains the missile flight in a straight line. Called-for-acceleration signals from the guidance computer will cause the autopilot to command corresponding changes in flight path, while continuing to stabilize the missile.

The propulsion system. Any of the methods of propulsion previously described may be used as long as the missile has sufficient speed advantage over the target to intercept it. The propulsion system must accelerate the missile to flying speed rapidly to allow a short minimum range and achieve sufficient velocity to counter target maneuvers. Powered flight may occur for most of the operational range of the weapon or only at the beginning (boost-glide). Boost-glide weapons are limited in their ability to engage at long range targets that have significant altitude difference or perform rapid maneuvers.

The control system. The steering or control unit may be located forward, in the midsection, or aft on the missile, depending on where the control surfaces are located. Movement of control surfaces may be electrical or hydraulic, with electrical actuation becoming the dominant method. Some weapons are limited in allowable locations for the control actuators because of size limitations or difficulty in passing signals from the autopilot to remote points on the airframe.

Architecture of Gun Ammunition

Gun projectiles are similar in function to missiles, but differ in the means of propulsion and stabilization. Their external shape is designed to obtain maximum stability while experiencing minimum drag. The internal structure of the projectile is dictated by the type and strength of the target, gun pressure characteristics, and the type of trajectory desired. The distribution of weight is a matter of considerable importance in that the center of gravity should be on the longitudinal axis and forward of the center of pressure to ensure maximum stability. High standards of accuracy are required in gun manufacture to ensure

Figure 16–21. Air-to-air infrared homing missile components. Note that this Sidewinder employs canard control.

uniform flight characteristics and therefore predictable hit patterns. A detailed discussion of the forces affecting projectiles and missiles in general is contained in chapter 19.

Projectiles. Small arms and machine-gun projectiles are made of solid metal; however, projectiles of 20-mm guns and larger have many components. The external features of projectiles are depicted in figure 16–23. The form of the forward end of the projectile is an ogival curve (generated by revolving an arc of a circle about a chord) that is aerodynamically efficient. Behind the ogive, the projectile is cylindrical with the exception of the bourrelet, which is slightly larger than the diameter of the body to reduce the surface area (and thus the friction) of the projectile contacting the gun bore. Near the after end of the projectile is the rotating band, which is actually larger than gun bore diameter to engage the rifling grooves and seal the bore while supporting the aft end of the projectile. The rifling actually engraves the rotating band to ensure a gas-tight seal. Aft of the rotating band the cylindrical shape may continue to the base of the projectile or it may be tapered to a "boat tail." A square aft section is more efficient in sealing propellant gases and converting pressure to kinetic energy; however, the boat tail provides better aerodynamic characteristics. Newer projectiles such as that in figure 16–25 incorporate

Figure 16–22. Air-to-air radar homing missile components.

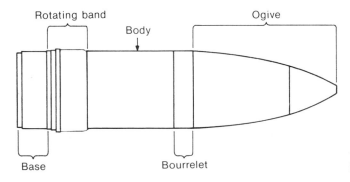

Figure 16–23. Details of the gun projectile.

Figure 16–24. Lands and grooves of rifling in a gun barrel.

a plastic rotating band and rear section that discards in flight, leaving a boat tail rear section and reducing air friction due to the rough surface of the rotating band. This projectile has less drag and therefore more range than similar projectiles without this capability. There are three general classes of projectiles:

1. Penetrating
2. Fragmenting
3. Special-purpose

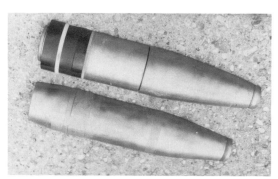

Figure 16–25. A 5"/54-cal. projectile incorporating the discarding aft section (above) and a conventional 5"/54-cal. projectile (below). Note the more pronounced taper of the rear section of the new projectile once the rotating band is discarded.

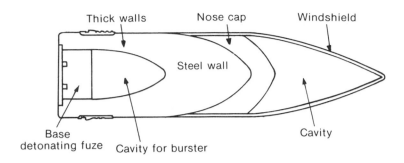

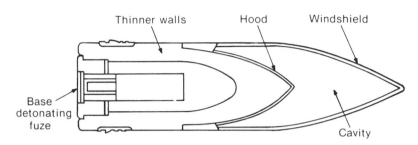

Figure 16–26. Penetrating projectiles.

Penetrating projectiles. These include armor-piercing (AP) and common (COM). They employ kinetic energy to penetrate, respectively, heavy and light armor. The bursting charge employed must be insensitive enough to permit penetration without premature detonation. Figure 16–23 shows the architecture of AP and COM projectiles. Both have thick steel walls and the AP projectile includes a hardened nose cap to penetrate armor or concrete, thus reducing the amount of space for explosives. Because efficient penetrating shapes are not good aerodynamically, an ogival-shaped thin steel windshield is included to reduce drag. These are the heaviest projectiles and therefore have the lowest initial velocity, but their velocity does not decay as rapidly as other projectiles due to the additional mass (see equation 13–3).

Fragmenting projectiles. As presented in chapter 13 these projectiles inflict damage by high-velocity fragments. They have relatively thin walls that may be scored and have a large cavity for the bursting charge. In use today, fragmenting projectiles are classified as high-capacity (HC) or antiaircraft common (AAC), which differ primarily in the type of fuze employed. As newer types of multi-purpose fuzes are employed, one projectile can serve both of these purposes.

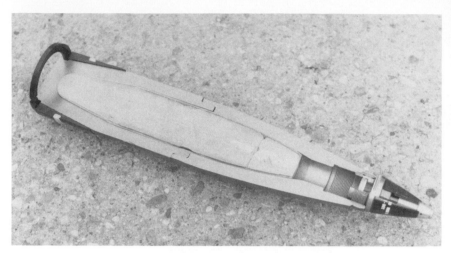

Figure 16–27. A 5″/54-cal. high-capacity projectile with contact fuze. Note the wall thickness versus the size of the explosive charge.

Special-purpose projectiles. These are designed to support the destruction of targets, such as providing illumination or screening smoke. If the payload includes any explosive, it is a small charge designed to expel the contents of the projectile (figure 16–29).

Guided projectiles. The idea of guided projectiles came from the

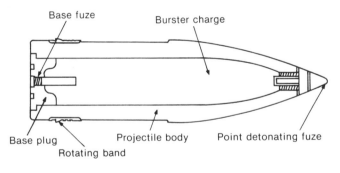

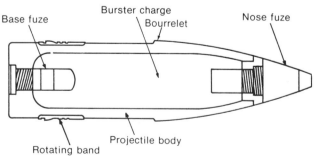

Figure 16–28. Fragmenting projectiles.

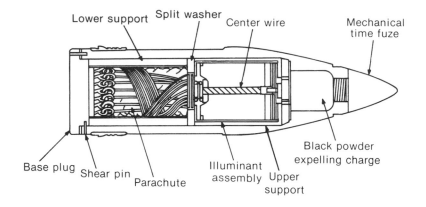

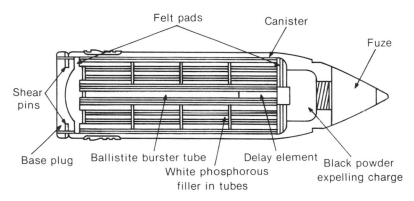

Figure 16–29. Special-purpose projectiles: illumination above, white phosphorous below.

outstanding performance of the laser-guided bombs used in Vietnam. They employ a miniature shock resistant semiactive laser seeker in the projectile for terminal guidance and may or may not include a rocket assist (RAP) motor. The Navy, in conjunction with the Army and Marine Corps, developed a family of 5-inch, 155-mm, and 8-inch projectiles that provide greatly increased hit probability at much less cost than a guided missile in some applications.

Gun propellant configuration. Case guns are those that employ propellant encased in a metal shell, while bag guns are those that employ propellant charges packed in silk bags. The use of bags is confined to large guns where the total propellant powder required to attain the required initial projectile velocity is too great in weight and volume to be placed in a single rigid container. By packing the powder grains in bags, it is possible to divide the total charge into units that can be handled expeditiously by one man.

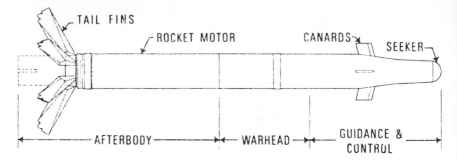

Figure 16–30. Guided projectile.

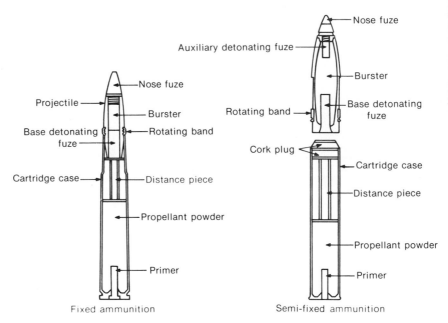

Figure 16–31. Cross sections of case ammunition.

Torpedo Architecture

The technology acquired in the development of advanced guided missiles is generally applicable to the torpedo. There is, in fact, a direct analogy between the homing missile and the homing torpedo, which allows a similar approach in their discussion by substituting the theories of hydrodynamics for those of aerodynamics. Air and water are fluids that display some of the same properties when allowances are made for differences in density, mass, and the general lack of compressibility of water. The force diagram for the torpedo as depicted in figure 16-33 is similar to that for the missile, except buoyancy is included.

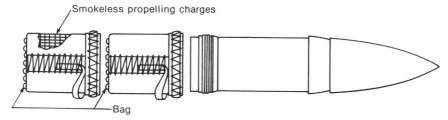

Smokeless propelling charges

Bag

Figure 16–32. Bag ammunition.

Torpedoes consist of a large number of components located in four structural sections, the nose section, warhead (or exercise head), center section, and afterbody and propellers (or hydrojet). To understand how the torpedo operates, a study of the functional systems is required; these are:

(1) the propulsion system
(2) the control and guidance system
(3) the warhead and fuze

Some of the major components of liquid fuel and electric torpedoes are shown in figure 16-34.

The propulsion system. The components of the propulsion system are physically located in the torpedo center and afterbody sections. Upon water entry the torpedo propulsion system is activated, allowing liquid fuel to flow to the combustion chamber. The hot gases produced from the burning fuel drive the engine, which turns an alternator to provide electrical power and also propels the torpedo via two counter-rotating propellers. The engine is usually an external combustion (i.e.,

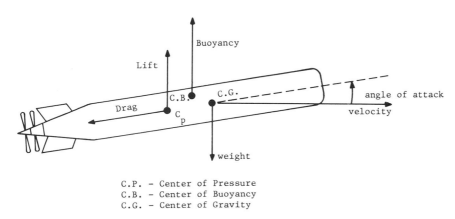

Buoyancy

Lift

C.B.

C.G.

Drag

C_p

angle of attack

velocity

weight

C.P. – Center of Pressure
C.B. – Center of Buoyancy
C.G. – Center of Gravity

Figure 16–33. Torpedo force diagram.

Weapon Propulsion and Architecture   **489**

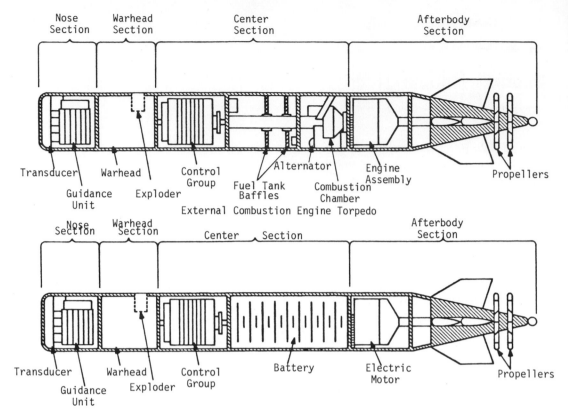

Figure 16–34. Electric torpedo.

the fuel is burned outside the cylinders), axial piston reciprocating type that burns liquid fuel. This fuel is a monopropellant; i.e., it contains the oxygen necessary for its combustion. In some torpedoes a solid fuel similar to that described for rockets is used to supply hot gas to the engine. This fuel, as with most liquid propellants, is very toxic, combustible, and corrosive.

Torpedoes that employ electric motors for propulsion merely substitute a battery and motor for the engine and fuel tank described above. They are characterized by shorter range and lower speed than torpedoes propelled by heat engines. Because propulsion power requirements increase as a function of depth, it is necessary to increase engine output as depth increases to maintain exhaust flow due to higher ambient pressure. To accomplish this, a hydrostatic device on the fuel pump increases the quantity of fuel supplied to the combustion chamber, which increases hot gas production and engine output. This increased fuel consumption causes a loss of torpedo running time and range at greater depths.

Control and Guidance System

The torpedo can employ either active and/or passive homing and in some cases can receive command guidance via a trailing wire. In active homing the torpedo transmits sound and listens for a returning echo. In passive homing the torpedo detects target radiated noise. If no signal is received, the torpedo can shift automatically to active search. After reaching its operational depth, the torpedo can search in a circular pattern or other pre-programmed path. The type of search conducted depends on the launch platform, torpedo type, and target category.

Tranducers. The torpedo detects targets by receiving acoustic signals that can be evaluated to determine the validity of the contact and target bearing and range. The transducer array consists of many elements that operate by employing the electronic scanning principles in chapter 7 to create a directional beam and change its direction. A narrow vertical beam is used in shallow water and during the attack phase to minimize surface and bottom reverberation, while a broad vertical beam is used in deep water for better target acquisition. The computer (or automatic pilot) decides which beam width is appropriate.

Transmitter. Whenever the torpedo is searching in the active mode, the transmitter is controlled by the computer and, when directed, generates a pulse of energy that is sent to the transducer through a series of amplifiers. Computer inputs control the characteristics of the pulse, such as its power, duration, and interval.

Receiver. The basic functions of the receiver are to receive target information from the transducer, determine if the contact is a valid target, and supply valid target signals to the computer. Self-noise and reverberation are detrimental to target detection, but can be suppressed by special circuits that distinguish targets from the background.

Computer. The computer provides control signals and a time base for the transmitter, receiver, and automatic pilot. When the torpedo reaches its search depth, the automatic pilot sends a signal, enabling the computer to function. At the same time it informs the computer whether homing is to be active or passive, and the type of search pattern. Upon receipt of a valid signal, it determines range by calculating the time interval between transmission and reception. Next, it sends a range gate back to the receiver that inhibits reception of any echo not at approximately the same range as the previous valid one. After transmission of the range gate, the yaw angle signal from the receiver is converted to right or left commands to the autopilot.

This command starts the torpedo steering towards the target bearing. The computer updates its command signals after every echo in order to guide the torpedo to the target. At appropriate times during this attack phase, information is sent to the transmitter to change its power, vertical beam width, and beam axis.

Autopilot. The automatic pilot receives torpedo programming information before launch, transmits part of this information to other components in the control and guidance system, controls certain depth functions, and combines command signals with existing conditions to control a steering actuator. A course gyro is contained in the autopilot, which senses the torpedo heading in relation to a programmed heading set in at launch.

The autopilot also contains the yaw, pitch, and roll integrating gyros. Steering commands for pitch and yaw, whether generated by the computer or autopilot itself, are combined with the rate gyro's outputs so that correct command signals are sent to the actuator controller. That is, the autopilot combines desired results with existing conditions of motion and orders the fin controllers to reposition the fins.

Steering unit. The steering control actuator contains three motors controlled by signals from the power unit. The outputs of the motors move four fins that control the movement of the torpedo; the upper and lower rudder fins are operated individually by separate actuators to control yaw and roll; the port and starboard elevator fins are operated simultaneously by a common actuator to control pitch.

Warhead Section

Torpedo warheads are either pure blast devices or special warheads designed to penetrate well-protected targets. Warheads and fuzes are covered in chapter 13 and will not be further addressed here.

Summary

The first part of this chapter has presented a study of the propulsion systems used to propel weapons to their targets. The three main types of propulsion systems are: impulse or gun-type, reaction, and gravity. Impulse propulsion includes the study of interior ballistics and the propellants used in today's guns and impulse-propelled weapons. Reaction propulsion deals with systems that internally carry their own propulsion. Rocket engines and thermal jet (air-breathing) engines are two types of reaction propulsion systems. Within the rocket engine category are both liquid and solid-fueled engines, and within the thermal jet engine category fall the turbojet and ramjet engines. Finally, gravity propulsion is the type of propulsion system used for the dropping of bombs and relies on the principle of converting potential energy to kinetic energy.

References

Commander, Naval Ordnance Systems Command. *Weapons Systems Fundamentals*. NAVORD OP 3000, vol. 2, 1st Rev. Washington, D.C.: GPO, 1971.

Department of Engineering, U.S. Military Academy. *Weapons Systems Engineering*. Vol. 1, West Point, N.Y.: U. S. Military Academy, 1975.

Fox, J. Richard, ed. *Shipboard Weapon Systems*. Annapolis, Md.: U.S. Naval Academy, 1975.

Mason, L., L. Devan, F. G. Moore, and D. McMillan. *Aerodynamic Design Manual for Tactical Weapons*. Dahlgren, Va.: Naval Surface Weapons Center, 1981.

17

Launching Systems

Introduction

The purpose of a launching system is to place a weapon into a flight path as rapidly as the situation demands. Launching must occur at the optimum moment so that the weapon system may function effectively. The launching system must safely withstand the propulsive forces of the weapon, and it must be highly reliable in order for the weapon to achieve the kill probability for which it is designed. The most significant general requirements of launching systems are as follows:

1) *Speed*—The launcher must be capable of rapid initial employment and a subsequent high rate of fire.
2) *Reliability*—No matter what the degree of sophistication adopted in the design of a launcher, it must be capable of a certain level of repeated use without failure. It must also be repairable.
3) *Safety*—The vehicle upon which the launcher is mounted and the personnel who operate and control the launcher must be able to function without damage or injury.
4) *Compatibility*—The launching system must complement the mission of the delivery vehicle and consequently other weapon systems installed. It must be designed to withstand the particular rigors of deployment associated with the mission of the delivery vehicle as well (corrosive environment, strong dynamic forces, vibration).

Any launching system must perform certain distinct functions in order to successfully launch the weapon associated with it. In the operational configuration, these functions do not necessarily occur in isolation, but frequently integrate as processes in achieving the designed goal of the system. These basic functions are as follows:

1) *Storage*—A safe and readily accessible area must be provided for the storage of weapons until they are needed.
2) *Transfer*—The weapons must be moved from the storage position to the loading position and vice versa.

3) *Loading*—Before the weapon may be put into flight, it must be placed on the launching device in a ready-to-fire position.

4) *Control*—Once the weapon has been loaded, it must be oriented in space. Typically a launching system functions in response to the solution of the fire control problem. Specifically, the launcher receives the position error signal from the computational systems, in the form of a DC voltage. Most launching systems are configured with angle-tracking servo systems for train and elevation. The angle-tracking servo system responds to the analog (DC voltage) input in a manner identical to the angle-tracking system described in chapter 5.

5) *Launching*—Flight initiation occurs during the process of launching as a result of a propelling force provided to the weapon by gravity, an impulse, or a reaction. A launching system is classified by the propelling force employed.

Gravity Launching Systems

Gravity launchers are characteristically simple in design because they rely upon gravity to cause separation of the weapon from the launcher. Since the initial velocity and orientation of the weapon is supplied by the delivery vehicle, no additional forces are applied to

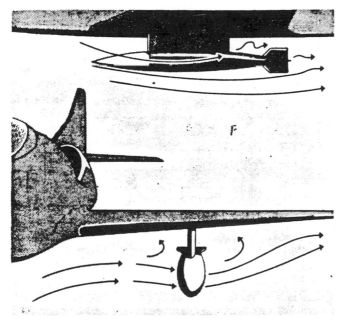

Figure 17–1. Air flow about a high-speed gravity launcher.

the weapon at release, and the launcher incurs no sudden shock. Airborne platforms used this type of system in the past. However, with the high speeds of high-performance aircraft, gravity launching of all but small practice weapons has become unfeasible. Because of the air-flow patterns about the weapon and launch platform, aerodynamic forces are created that can result in the weapon not separating from the aircraft or separating and then striking the aircraft. Therefore, pure gravity-launching systems are seldom used.

Impulse Launchers

In this case a force is applied to the weapon either to project it along the entire path of its trajectory or, to a lesser degree, to clear the weapon from the delivery vehicle. Two basic launcher types employ this method: cannon launchers and ejector launchers. Cannon launchers may be further subdivided into guns, howitzers, and mortars. The basic differences among these subdivisions are trajectory, initial velocity, and size of the launcher, with guns having the highest muzzle velocities and flattest trajectories. Since the functional operations of the three cannon-launcher types are similar, gun launchers will be examined.

Gun-type launchers. A gun launcher not only imparts *Initial Velocity* or *IV* to the weapon (more commonly referred to as a projectile), but it also provides projectile flight guidance in the most simple application. Specially designed projectiles may be fitted with a rocket motor (rocket assisted projectile—RAP) or with a guidance package (Laser, IR). A major consideration in gun launcher design is energy dissipation of the reaction force (recoil) created by the impulse employed to propel the projectile.

In chapter 16, various propulsion principles were discussed, all of which led to the generation of heat and gas in a confined space. Gun barrels must be constructed with enough inherent strength to withstand the pressures developed by propellant heat and gas. Additionally, most gun launchers are characteristically large and heavy since the reactive force of the initial impulse is largely absorbed by the launcher in conjunction with its recoil/counter-recoil system.

A gun barrel is normally thickest at the powder chamber where the greatest pressure effects occur. The gun barrel then tapers in thickness proportional to the pressures exerted by the propellant. To gain an appreciation of the basic principles involved in gun design, see figure 17–2.

Gun strength must exceed the powder pressure at every point by

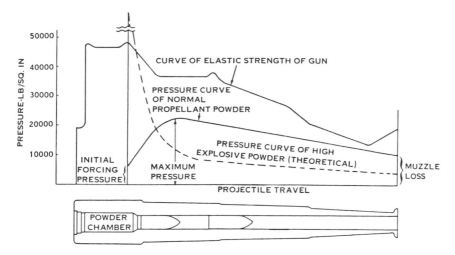

Figure 17–2. Relation between gun barrel cross section and strength/pressure curves.

an amount that will provide a sufficient margin of safety. The pressure curves in figure 17–2 show pressure beginning at a value well above zero. This indicates the pressure build-up that occurs after the propelling charge begins to burn but before the projectile begins to move. (The x-axis in the figure represents projectile movement in the bore, not time or bore length.)

Note that the gun strength curve does not vary in parallel with the powder pressure curve. The reason is that the same pressure that the expanding gases exert against the base of the projectile is exerted equally against all interior surfaces of the gun behind the projectile. Hence, the breech part of the barrel must be designed for the maximum stress. After the projectile passes the point of maximum pressure, it continues to be accelerated by gas pressure until it leaves the muzzle. The total area under the curve, up to the point where the projectile leaves the gun, is a rough measure of initial velocity, and the pressure remaining at the muzzle is an indication of the muzzle loss. A high muzzle pressure increases muzzle flash. As can be seen in the figure, employment of a high explosive would exceed the strength of the gun almost instantaneously upon detonation. In fact, the release of energy would be so rapid that the greater portion would be expended in rupturing the gun rather than in translating the projectile through the barrel.

The gun barrel is subject to two principle stresses:

1. A tangential stress or tension, coupled with a radial stress, tending to split the gun open longitudinally.

2. A longitudinal stress tending to pull the gun apart in the direction of its axis.

The greatest stress is in a direction tangent to a radius of the barrel due to gas pressure, and thus the longitudinal stress can be neglected without significant error. Lames' Law states: "At any point in a cylinder under fluid pressure, the sum of the tangential tension and the radial pressure varies inversely as the square of the radius." This means that in a cylinder under internal pressure, points in the metal close to the bore experience a large proportion of the stress, while those at a greater radius experience progressively less stress. The result is that there is a limit beyond which any additional wall thickness will not add much in strength. Therefore, construction methods must be employed that will cause the outer layers of metal to absorb more stress.

All modern gun barrels are made of steel, and they are generally prestressed to make them more resistant to internal (bursting) pressures. The object of prestressing is to make the outer layers of metal in the barrel bear a greater proportion of the bursting load. The built-up method of prestressing is to heat steel ring-shaped jackets, or hoops, to high temperatures, then slip them over the gun tube and allow them to cool. As the hoops cool, they contract, until at the end of the process they squeeze the tube with a pressure of thousands of pounds per square inch.

Most modern gun barrels are of one-piece or monobloc construction. They are prestressed by a process of radial expansion. In this process, a gun tube with bore slightly smaller than the caliber desired is expanded by hydraulic pressure. When the pressure is released, the outer layers of the tube tend to return to their original dimensions, while the enlarged inner layers tend to maintain their enlargement. Thus, the inner layers of metal are severely compressed by the contraction of the outer layers, as if a hoop had been shrunk on them. The built-up and radially expanded methods may be incorporated in a single gun. The 8″/55-caliber gun, for example, has a jacket shrunk on a radially expanded tube. Smaller guns are made from a single steel forging with neither radial expansion nor hoops. The pressure per unit area may be higher in small guns than in large guns; however, the tube walls may be made thicker and more massive in small guns without resulting in an excessively large forging. This type of construction is limited to guns of 3-inch caliber and smaller.

Recoil/Counter-recoil systems. Recoil is the rearward movement of the gun and connected parts during and after firing. It is caused by reaction to the forward motion of the projectile and propellant gases.

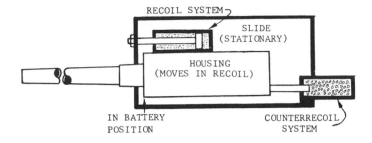

*GUN FIRES-THRUST OF RECOIL MOVES HOUSING REARWARD.

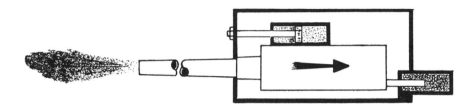

*COUNTERRECOIL PRESSURE CAUSES HOUSING TO MOVE FORWARD.

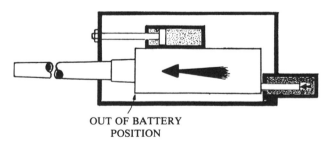

Figure 17–3. Recoil/counterrecoil of a medium-caliber gun.

After recoil, the gun and connected parts return to the in-battery, or firing position. This forward movement is called "counter recoil."

If the gun were mounted rigidly, without any recoil system, it would be practically impossible to build a carriage to withstand the loads imposed upon it, without rupturing, overturning, or displacing it. To bring the carriage stresses down to a reasonable value and to ensure stability, a recoil system is interposed between the gun and

Launching Systems   **499**

the carriage. The recoil mechanism absorbs the energy of the recoiling parts over a certain convenient length and returns the gun to battery for further firing. The recoiling parts are the gun and those parts of the recoil mechanism and carriage that move with the gun in recoil and counter recoil. A recoil mechanism usually consists of three components—a *recoil brake,* which controls the recoil and limits its length; a *counter-recoil mechanism,* which returns the recoiling parts to in-battery position; and a *counter-recoil buffer,* which slows the end of counter-recoil motion and thereby prevents shock of the recoiling parts (figure 17–3).

In most naval guns the recoil brake is hydraulic and consists of four elements: a cylinder; a piston; a liquid, such as glycerin and water; and some form of orifice in the piston that allows the liquid to flow from one side of the piston to the other. The motion of the piston within the cylinder forces the liquid through the orifices, absorbing the energy of recoil and controlling the return of the gun to battery during counter recoil. The work required to force a liquid through a given orifice can be definitely determined from the laws of hydraulics and depends on the area of the orifice, the area of the piston, the velocity of the piston, and the weight of the liquid. The work done on the piston is used to overcome the movement of the gun during recoil, whereas the work done on the liquid during the same time is indicated by a rise of temperature of the liquid. It can be shown that the work absorbed by the hydraulic brake can be fully accounted for in the rise of temperature of the liquid. Under rapid-fire conditions, the temperature rise is accumulative from shot to shot and results in a considerable rise in temperature, which must be taken into account in designing a recoil system.

Another method of reducing the forces of recoil is the muzzle brake. A muzzle brake is a device consisting of one or more sets of baffles attached to the muzzle end of the gun barrel (figure 17–4). As the projectile leaves the muzzle, the high-velocity gases following the projectile through the tube strike the baffles of the brake and are deflected rearward and sideways into the atmosphere (figure 17–5). In striking the baffles, the gases exert a forward force that partially counteracts the force of recoil. The muzzle brake also acts as a blast deflector and reduces obscuration of the target, an important function in direct-fire weapons (tanks).

Soft recoil systems. In the development of gun launchers for aircraft, it was found that the high-velocity projectiles used caused excessive reaction forces at the gun trunnions. Consequently, additional structural strength had to be built into the airframe to absorb the

Figure 17–4. Medium-caliber howitzer muzzle brake.

stresses transmitted to the aircraft structure. To reduce these reactive forces, the principle of soft recoil was applied to these weapons. Another term for this principle is out-of-battery firing.

The soft recoil system differs from the conventional recoil system in that the recoiling parts are mechanically held against a gas spring force acting in the direction of firing. Upon release, the expanding gas accelerates the housing forward in the direction of fire; propellant ignition occurs automatically when proper velocity is attained. The

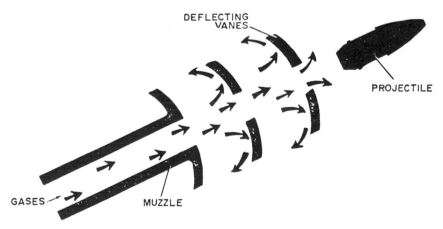

Figure 17–5. Functioning of a muzzle brake.

firing impulse overcomes the forward momentum of the recoiling parts, reverses their direction, and forces them back against the gas spring until they are latched into the battery position. Figure 17–6 illustrates the difference between the conventional and soft recoil systems.

The advantages of the soft recoil system are that it greatly reduces the horizontal forces on the gun platform or trunnions and the total recoil cycle time is reduced, allowing for higher rates of fire. In addition to aircraft guns, this system is currently employed on the 105-mm light towed howitzer.

Recoilless systems. Another solution to the recoil problem is the recoilless principle. The recoilless rifle operates on the basis that if the momentum of the propellant gases discharged to the rear is equal to the gases expelled forward, then the launcher will have no momentum imparted to it. Considering the four movable parts of the system to be the projectile, the gases forward, the gases rearward, and the gun itself, and representing the mass of each as m_1, m_2, m_3, and m_4, respectively, and the velocities of each as v_1, v_2, v_3, and v_4, then:

$$m_1v_1 + m_2v_2 + m_3v_3 + m_4v_4 = 0.$$

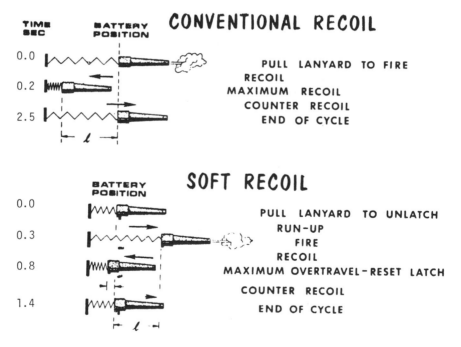

Figure 17–6. Comparison of cycles.

If the gun is recoilless, then $v_4 = 0$, and the equation reduces to:

$$m_1v_1 + m_2v_2 + m_3v_3 = 0$$

or

$$m_3v_3 = -m_1v_1 - m_2v_2.$$

That is, the combined momentum of the projectile and the forward-moving gases is equal, but opposite in direction, to the momentum of the gases discharged through the breech. If this is true for all instants during the weapon's firing period, which is about a hundredth of a second, then the momentum of the weapon must equal zero at all times during firing, and the weapon can be considered perfectly recoilless. In practice, however, this is generally not the case. A recoilless weapon is usually recoilless in the mean; i.e., although the total momentum applied to it over the firing period is zero, the sum of the momentums at any instant is not necessarily zero. The weapon undergoes large unbalanced forces during some parts of the pressure interval, and oppositely directed forces during other parts of the pressure interval. Thus, its recoillessness is an average rather than an absolute value. Figure 17–7 illustrates the basic considerations associated with a recoilless rifle.

The main advantage of recoilless rifles over conventional guns of comparable caliber is their much lighter weight, which gives them greater mobility. The price paid for this advantage is a slight reduction in velocity and range, and a large (2.5 to 3 times as much) increase in the quantity of propellant required. The main drawback of recoilless launchers is the tremendous blast to the rear of the gun (back blast) caused by the escaping gas. The danger zone for a comparatively low caliber (57-mm) rifle is a conical section 17 meters long and 14 meters wide diverging rearward from the breech. Because of these disadvantages and the fact that techniques for achieving greater mobility of conventional guns have been developed, recoilless rifles are not as prevalent in the ground arsenal as in the past.

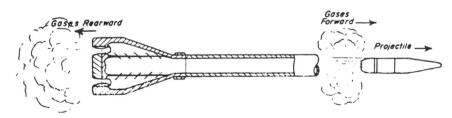

Figure 17–7. Recoilless rifle.

Ejector-type launchers. Impulse launchers for weapon ejection are employed for both free-fall and self-propelled weapons. Their main purpose is to ensure that the weapon safely clears the delivery vehicle. Ejection is usually accomplished by the expansion of high-pressure gases from a compressed air supply or from ignition of a propellant charge. Because it is used for ejection purposes only, the impulse is small, and the launcher can be built to withstand the shock of launching without the need for excessive structural strength or special devices. Thus, launchers of this type are fairly light and simple in design.

Self-propelled weapons, which are impulse launched, frequently are large and heavy, making transfer and loading a slow, laborious process. A launcher of this type usually has several launching tubes, and the weapons are stored within the tubes until needed. The most common launcher of this type is the torpedo tube. Torpedo tubes are installed in ships and submarines and may be of fixed or trainable design. Torpedo ejection is caused by expanding gas from a gas-generating chemical or from a compressed air supply. In earlier submarines, fixed torpedo tubes were installed in the bow and stern; in most U.S. Navy submarines, however, they are located only in the forward section. Fixed tubes are also found in certain surface combatants. These nontrainable tubes are mounted within enclosed spaces singly or in groups of two or more on each side of the ship. To preclude the launch vehicle having to maneuver radically to provide ideal orientation for the torpedo relative to the target at launch, torpedoes deployed from fixed tubes are equipped with guidance features to compensate for this restriction. The interior location permits all tubes to be located in a torpedo compartment where they may be readily maintained, regardless of weather or topside activities.

Trainable tubes are installed aboard surface ships in a clear deck area so that they may be oriented as required. The triple-tube launcher, illustrated in figure 17–8, is most commonly found on destroyer-type combatants.

To reduce space, the tubes are stacked one above the other. By fabricating the tubes of reinforced fiberglass, weight is reduced to a minimum, and maintenance due to topside exposure is less. In this figure, note the air flasks at the breech. Removable covers are provided at the muzzle when the launcher is in a stowed configuration.

One method in which missile-equipped submarines launch their missiles is by compressed-air ejection. Compressed air is stored in a launch and flask until missile launch. At this time the compressed air is released into an eject pressure chamber beneath the missile where

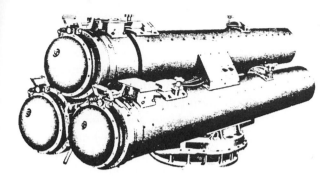

Figure 17–8. Mk 32 torpedo tubes employed aboard most surface combatants as a launcher for the Mk 46 ASW torpedo.

the pressure is built up at a programmed rate. This results in a smooth, rapid acceleration of the missile to the required ejection velocity.

Employing principles similar to that described above, ejection may be accomplished by burning a propellant grain. In this case, the hot gases generated by the propellant grain may be used to flash water to steam. The steam-gas mixture can then be introduced to the eject pressure chamber to accomplish missile ejection. This steam eject system is found aboard newer submarine classes. In either case, the result is a flameless launch, with rocket motor ignition of the missile occurring at a safe distance from the submarine.

In addition to ejecting large ballistic missiles from missile tubes, submarines can also ejection-launch smaller missiles from their torpedo tubes. Harpoon and Tomahawk can be launched in this manner.

Ejection launchers are also employed aboard aircraft. Nearly all free-fall and glide weapons carried by naval aircraft are ejection-launched. At the time of launch, an explosive cartridge(s) is detonated. This produces a high-pressure gas that acts on a piston, thus forcing the hooks holding the weapon to open, and simultaneously forcing a metal rod or ejection foot against the weapon. This action physically ejects the weapon away from the aircraft, ensuring that it is clear of the aerodynamic flow around the aircraft.

In addition to free-fall weapons, missiles are also ejection-launched to clear them from the aircraft prior to motor ignition. Phoenix and Sparrow are examples of this.

Reaction Launchers

This third general type of launcher is one in which the force separating the weapon from the launcher is contained within the weapon. These weapons are normally rockets or missiles. The propulsion system of the missile itself may be used to provide the necessary force. Thus, most self-propelled weapons, if not launched by ejection, are put into flight by reaction launchers.

Reaction launchers provide static support for the weapon and initial flight orientation. They are characteristically small and light since they are not required to sustain large moments of force upon weapon launch. Reaction-propelled weapons often depend upon wings or fins to provide lift, and must use rocket thrust to overcome gravity temporarily and to propel the weapon to desired flight speed. If, during the development of thrust, a weapon is free to move along the launcher, it might not have sufficient thrust or lift to overcome gravity at the time it leaves the launcher. Thus, the missile could fall to the deck of a launching ship or become completely disoriented before sufficient thrust or lift had been developed to sustain its flight. To prevent this from happening, the weapon is restrained on the launcher until sufficient thrust is generated. The restraining device may be simply a pin that is sheared when the weapon develops the required thrust, or it may be a more complicated, reusable device that releases the weapon when the required thrust is exerted.

The launcher must be protected from the blast and subsequent corrosive effects of the propellant exhaust stream. This is usually achieved by a protective covering of the launcher and by blast deflection plates or shields. The launcher structure must be able to resist the deteriorating effects of the propellant gases, and the structural design of the launcher should be such as to minimize loading or stresses due to propellant blast or recoil momentum. As with any launcher, the reaction launcher must be compatible not only with the space and weight limitations imposed by the delivery vehicle, but with the environment in which the vehicle operates as well. Launcher design is influenced by the degree of control and guidance required of the weapon system. An uncontrolled rocket may require a considerable amount of flight control by the launcher before it is released into free flight, while a guided missile does not require this initial control to the same degree. Consequently, reaction launchers are divided into three classes as illustrated in figure 17–9.

Launcher Cutouts. Due to obstructions, guns and missile launchers aboard ship and ashore are subject to constraints in their coverage. Shore-based systems must deal with terrain features and man-made structures when a clear, flat emplacement area cannot be found. Shipboard weapons systems are subject to deckhouses, antennas, lifelines, boats, and other weapons in their firing arcs. All systems employ some type of mechanical linkage that inhibits the firing circuit at

Figure 17–9. Nike missiles on rail launcher.

values of azimuth and elevation that would cause the weapon to damage structures or be damaged or deflected during launch. These firing cutout mechanisms can also be constructed so that the launcher or gun will automatically elevate to a safe firing elevation at azimuths where obstructions are located, while notifying the controlling weapon system of the circumstances.

Rail launchers. The term *rail launcher* may be applied to launchers making use of rails, tubes, long ramps, and even tall vertical towers. All provide, to a varying degree, constraint to the weapon while it is moving on the launcher, and they thus provide a considerable amount of flight control. For uncontrolled weapons, such as rockets, the rails must be fairly long so that the rocket is constrained for a longer portion of the rocket motor burning time to provide the necessary initial velocity vector control. If the missile is equipped with a guidance system, the rail length can usually be reduced. Long-range weapons, guided or unguided, normally require a longer rail since their initial acceleration is comparatively low relative to short-range weapons. A rocket booster may be employed, however, to provide sufficient acceleration to permit reduction of rail length. This is the case with the surface-launched Harpoon.

Thrust developed parallel to the axis of the rail or tube will propel the weapon along the rail and into a proper trajectory. Vertical components of the thrust will force the weapon against the rails or tube and thus against the launcher. The launcher must, therefore, be capable of withstanding a portion of the weapon thrust as well as of supporting the weapon. Lateral constraint of the weapon is necessary in order to prevent the weapon from lifting from the rails or wandering during its motion along the launcher rail. This is usually achieved by lugs on the weapon, which ride in slots on the launcher rail. In general, the longer the launcher rails, the better the initial flight control and the less the launching dispersion.

However, long rails, like long beams, can sag and bend. The longer the beam, the greater the possible deflection, unless the rail is well supported along its entire length. This kind of support is not practical in tactical launchers, so a certain amount of beam deflection or droop will occur at the end of long rail launchers. This droop and the effects of vibrations set up as the missile moves along the rail cause the rail to whip and produce unwanted deviations in the missile orientation. These effects can be minimized by reducing the length of the launcher rails. Thus, material and structural characteristics will limit the length of a rail launcher for tactical usage. This necessary restriction in rail length is not as serious as it might seem because the effectiveness of a rail launcher in constraining weapon travel to the direction of the rails varies as the ratio of time of rail travel to the total time of boosted uncontrolled flight. Since a weapon starts from rest on the launcher, the time of rail travel will vary as the square root of its length.

Since

$$S = \frac{1}{2}at^2 \qquad (17\text{--}1)$$

Then

$$t = \frac{\sqrt{2S}}{a} \qquad (17\text{--}2)$$

Where

S = rail length
a = missile acceleration
t = elapsed time of travel

Therefore, a relatively short rail will still provide considerable initial flight control to a weapon.

Rail launchers may be fixed or movable. They may serve as ready service storage for missiles and provide facilities for fueling and servicing. The simplicity of design of rail launchers also promotes reliability and ease of maintenance and repair. Airborne launcher rails, because of space and air flow-field problems, are usually very short. As a rule, the greater the speed the missile had achieved at separation from the launcher, the less the air-flow field effects will influence missile flight. Rail launchers are deployed aboard ships, submarines, aircraft, and in the field.

Zero-length launcher. Through common usage, the classification "zero-length launcher" has come to mean any rail launcher where

Figure 17–10. Shrike missile on aircraft zero-length launcher.

the weapon travels less than eight centimeters before it is released from the rail. Since the weapon separates from the launcher shortly, or even immediately, after it begins to move, little or no effective flight control is provided by the launcher. Therefore, the launchers are used with weapons that can immediately assume stable flight. The chief advantages of zero-length launchers are their small size, light weight, comparative simplicity, and ease of maintenance and repair. Because of their small size and weight, the zero-length launchers require a minimum of deck space and are easily moved in train and elevation. Therefore, they are used extensively in shipboard, ground, and airborne installations for the launching of guided missiles. Figure 17–10 shows an aircraft version.

Platform launcher. A platform launcher is relatively simple in construction and is employed where the rocket or missile must achieve high altitude as soon as possible for most efficient operation. In the rarefied air of the upper atmosphere, velocity loss due to aerodynamic drag is minimized, resulting in greater final velocity and longer range. Long-range ballistic missiles are built as light as possible and are

Figure 17–11. Trailer-mounted zero-length rail launcher for Improved Hawk missile.

Figure 17–12. Shipboard zero-length rail launcher with Standard missile.

stressed primarily for longitudinal loads. ICBMs and similar missiles are normally launched vertically from a platform. At present, there are no platform launchers employed in Naval and Marine Corps weapon systems.

Canister launchers. With the advent of solid-state guidance, all-electric controls, and solid-fuel rocket motors with a long service life, guided missile storage requirements have been greatly simplified. These advances, combined with missile flight characteristics that allow the use of zero-length launchers, make it possible to include the shipping container of the weapon as an integral part of the launcher. The resulting canister launcher contains the missile, which is supported by zero-length rail segments or by the surface of the container for lightweight weapons. The canister may be hand-held, as in the Stinger and Dragon employed by the Marines. For larger missiles such as Harpoon, the canister containing the weapon is installed on or within a support structure or launch tube that may be fixed or mobile. In either case the weapon remains within a sealed container until launch. This minimizes direct handling of the weapon and limits its exposure to adverse environments.

Figure 17–13. Harpoon missile emerging from a canister launcher.

The Vertical Launch System (figure 17–14) employs a standard canister that may contain a variety of missile types, deployed in eight-cell modules aboard ship. The result is a net increase in weapon stowage as well as rate of fire. Each cell and canister acts as a separate launcher independent of the others, except for the exhaust-gas management system that is common to each eight-cell module. There is no launcher reload time, and thus a much higher rate of fire can be maintained.

The canister launcher, though advantageous in many ways, places additional stress on the weapon because of the interior ballistics of the system. The canister confines the weapon for a short period of time after rocket motor light off, subjecting it to shock waves due to the flow of high-velocity combustion products prior to the rupture of the canister end closures and the weapon's emergence. Ignition of the rocket motor causes a shock wave to develop between the weapon and the inner wall of the canister. This shock wave is re-transmitted from the forward closure back to the missile radome. The net result is a pulsating axial load on the weapon due to dynamic gas phenomena in the canister during launch. The effects of these forces vary with the specific system, but have been known to reach 1,000 kg in the VLS employing the Standard missile.

In the special case where the canister is stored and fired from

Figure 17–14a. Launch of a Standard missile from a Vertical Launch System (VLS) canister.

within a ship hull, such as in VLS, exhaust-gas management is a significant problem. The exhaust stream typically has a temperature of 2,400° Kelvin and a velocity of over 2,500 meters per second. Additionally, it includes highly abrasive particles and active chemical agents. Whatever system is used to dissipate the missile exhaust, it must be able to withstand strong pressure waves, not only for the brief time between motor ignition and weapon departure, but it must

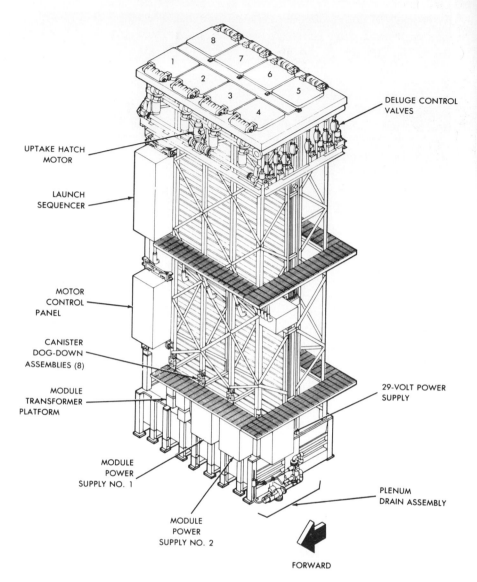

Figure 17–14b. Vertical Launch System (canister launcher).

also be able to handle the complete burn of the rocket motor with
the weapon restrained in the canister in the event of accident. The
ability to handle restrained rocket motor burn has been a missile-
magazine design constraint since missiles were first placed aboard
ship; the intent in VLS, however, was to make sure that not only
would the ship survive, but that the remaining missiles were still
operable as well. Steel surfaces are protected from melting or being

weakened by a replaceable ablative coating that dissipates heat by vaporization during exposure to rocket-motor exhaust. The exhaust stream is routed to the atmosphere by a duct system that avoids impingement on unprotected surfaces.

Storage

To achieve and sustain optimum firing, the launching system selected for a given weapon system must include a storage subsystem capable of performing its allotted functions in a minimal period of time. The capacity of the subsystem must be adequate to sustain the desired firing operation and the facilities must be readily accessible. A magazine is a term used to denote a storage area needed to provide the space and the safety facilities for storage of large quantities of gravity, gun, or reaction-type weapons. Magazines are classified in three categories:

Primary magazines. This category is designed to stow the delivery vehicle's complete peacetime allowance of ammunition. Primary magazines are typically well-protected and equipped with thermal insulation, ventilation, and sprinkling systems designed to cool the weapons below a programmed upper temperature limit. A method of ensuring

Figure 17–15. Ground-launched cruise missile fired from a mobile canister launcher.

Figure 17–16. Stinger missile launched from canister launcher.

security, both physical and environmental, is associated with the primary magazine, such as locking devices and alarm systems, local and remote. In the case of reaction-type weapons, restraining equipment for the weapon is incorporated to prevent an ignited propulsion motor from moving the weapon. Vents are also provided to prevent disruptive pressures from developing within the magazine in the event of inadvertent propulsion motor ignition.

Ready-service magazines. This type of storage designates the ammunition storage facilities in the immediate vicinity of the launcher. This storage is used only when ammunition is required to immediately service the launcher. Under this classification scheme, certain gravity and reaction-type launching systems do not have primary magazines as such, and may be said to have only ready service magazines. However, the characteristics of primary magazines are normally incorporated in the design of these storage facilities.

Lockers. These are compartments designed for storing sensitive or

Figure 17–17. Pershing II missile on platform launcher.

special types of ammunition such as fuzes, pyrotechnics, blasting caps, hand grenades, and explosive chemicals. Lockers are normally located above the damage control deck and on a weather deck if possible to localize and minimize the effects of fire or other adverse environment.

Most magazines are single-purpose. That is, they are designed for a homogeneous quantity of ammunition. Multipurpose magazines may be required because of space limitations in the delivery vehicle. In this case different types of ammunition will be stored. Such mixed storage will not include special types of ammunition designated for locker storage. Where mixed storage is employed in the multipurpose magazine, the various types of ammunition will be segregated for ease of identification and accessibility. Very specific requirements exist specifying ammunition types that may be stored in the same magazine or locker and those which are incompatible. These regulations are listed in OP5 for shore stations and in OP4 or OP3347 for ships.

Figure 17–18. Transfer system for reaction launcher.

Transfer Equipment

Weapon transfer equipment is designed to move weapons and associated components (fuzes, special payloads) from the primary magazine to ready-service lockers and then to the launcher. In addition, the transfer system is normally capable of returning the weapon to the magazine. To achieve rapid initial employment, the transfer system must be capable of moving the weapons at a rate commensurate with the launcher rate of fire. If a transfer line or channel has a transfer rate less than the required rate of fire, then two, or even three transfer lines may be necessary to feed the launcher. When transferring weapons to rotating launchers, it is necessary at some point along the line to shift from nonrotating transfer equipment to equipment rotating with the launcher. This becomes a problem of considerable magnitude for a high-rate-of-fire system where the weapon must be transferred while the launcher is rotating. This can be accomplished by a manual transfer, or by complex automatic equipment, as in high-rate-of-fire naval guns. When the weapons to be transferred are large, it is often necessary to have the rotating launcher return to a specified position before a weapon is transferred to it. Weapon flight preparation facilities are often found in the transfer system. En route to the launcher, operations such as weapon assembly, checkout, servicing, and even programming of the weapon may be performed. To prevent damage to operating personnel and to the delivery vehicle in the event of weapon explosion or ignition, the transfer system must be designed to localize and contain detonations, fires, propulsion-motor blast, etc. In addition to the lethal effects of the weapon itself, personnel can be injured by the moving and rotating machinery of the launching system. Thus, in the transfer system, as well as in every component of a launching system, careful attention must be given in the design of equipment to minimize the danger of accidents.

The transfer of gun ammunition and reaction ammunition can be as simple as moving an airborne missile on a dolly from the primary magazine, via elevators, to the launcher mounted on an aircraft, or it can be as complex as a system that provides for the automatic transfer to a dual-rail launcher of large guided missiles weighing in excess of one ton. In the more complex transfer systems, hydraulic, pneumatic, and electrical servo systems are employed to accomplish the task in such a manner that operating personnel must only monitor system functions from a local or remote-control panel.

Loading Equipment

Weapon loading equipment is needed to place the weapon in firing position on the launcher in a rapid, reliable, and safe manner. The loading operation consists of moving the weapon from the transfer equipment to the launcher and positioning it on the launcher. This operation involves a transfer to the launcher and the moving or ramming of a weapon along rails or trays into firing position on the launcher. The transfer and ramming functions can be performed manually, mechanically with human operator control, or automatically with human monitoring. In some types of fixed launchers with low rates of fire, the ramming operation is not necessary. The weapon is simply hoisted or lowered into position on the launcher. However, loading high-rate-of-fire launchers requires a fast, precise ramming cycle. Some means must be provided for the unloading of unfired but usable weapons and for the jettisoning of unsafe and dud weapons. In most cases, the loading equipment is designed to accomplish these functions when it is not desirable that they be accomplished by hand. In some cases, special equipment must be provided to perform the jettisoning function. To achieve rapid weapon employment and to maintain a high rate of fire, the loading rate must be commensurate with the required launcher rate of fire. As with transfer equipment, this often requires the use of more than one loading unit per launching tube or rail, or more than one line or channel feeding weapons to the ramming equipment.

The majority of automatic loading systems employ a catapulting device, a rail spade, or chain device.

(1) *Catapult ramming*—This method is found in gun launchers employing fixed ammunition. A round is received from the transfer system and aligned with the gun bore. The tray in which the round is resting is then moved toward the breech rapidly, and abruptly stopped. At the end of the tray travel, the round is released and catapulted into the chamber, whereupon the breechblock seals the breech. Figure 17–19 portrays this loading method.

(2) *Rail-spade ramming*—This method is frequently employed in the ramming of semi-fixed and separate loading ammunition, and in the loading of torpedoes and reaction weapons where the weapon is housed in a ready-service magazine (the launcher itself). Figure 17–20 depicts rail-spade loading of a torpedo/booster configuration.

The size of many reaction weapons require the use of manually controlled loading equipment. The weapon is supported by the loader, which may be fixed or portable, in the vicinity of the launcher and slowly rammed into position. This is a

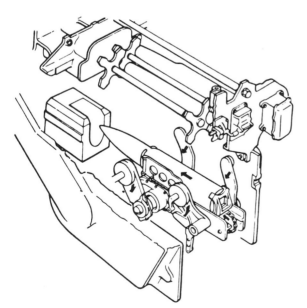

Figure 17–19. Catapult ramming of field ammunition in a gun launcher.

Figure 17–20. Rail-spade ramming ASROC.

comparatively slow process and is suitable only for launchers that are not expected to engage a large number of targets between reloading.

(3) *Chain ramming*—A flexible-link chain is frequently employed in the previous two categories of ramming, but in this category, the end of the chain is provided with a buffer pad that engages the base of the weapon. The chain is driven by a sprocket along a track, where it is free to move forward or retract, as required. In figure 17–21 notice that the chain can flex in only one direction. The buffer serves to protect the weapon from damage since velocities of more than three meters per second may be achieved by this ramming method in some designs.

Control

Once the weapon has been loaded in the launcher, the final step of engaging a target may take place—the delivery of the weapon. For this to occur, the launcher must be positioned along a line that will ultimately result in the weapon intercepting the target. This line is, appropriately, the line-of-fire (LOF). In general, the launching

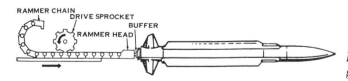

Figure 17–21. Chain ramming of a guided missile in a reaction launcher.

Launching Systems **521**

system is subordinate in weapon-system dynamics in that it must respond to certain types of orders. Depending upon the weapon system employed, these orders are known as gun orders, launcher orders, torpedo orders, missile orders, etc. The specific nature of these orders will vary from system to system. For instance, a typical set of gun orders may be: gun train (Bdg'), elevation (Edg'), sight angle (Vs), sight deflection (Ls), parallax (pl), and fuze time (T5). The alphanumeric figures associated with each of the orders are known as fire control symbols. They are often employed as a shorthand device for describing information/data flow in weapon systems. Following is an example of a set of missile orders: seeker head orders, doppler predict, ship roll correction, channel select, gravity bias, and target select. Each of these orders will be transmitted from the computational system to the launching system and/or to the weapon itself continuously during the interval between launcher assignment and weapon launch or until the launcher has been taken out of the system electronically.

A launching system will often have several types of weapons stored within its confines, so it must receive orders regarding the type or types of weapons to be launched. For example, in a shipboard gun-launching system, several types of projectiles are in the magazines. Control station personnel must select the type of projectile to be fired and notify the launching system of its choice. In a shipboard guided-missile launching system, both homing and beam-riding missiles may be available. The launching system must receive orders regarding which type of missile to launch. In addition to the type of missile, the launching system must know how many missiles to launch. For example, a submarine launching system may fire one, two, or a whole spread of torpedoes. A guided-missile launching system may fire a one- to two-round salvo, and a gun-launching system may fire continuously until a target is destroyed or out of range.

Basically, however, the most important function of the launcher is to provide initial flight orientation to the weapon. In cases where the launcher is fixed rigidly to the delivery vehicle, the whole vehicle must be maneuvered to provide this orientation. When a launching system is mounted in a vehicle that is not suitably maneuverable, a launcher that may be rotated about one or more axes is normally employed. As discussed in previous chapters, a sensor system will detect, classify, and locate a target such that present target position is continuously entered into the computational system. It is the output of the computational system that provides the orders that cause movement of the launcher to the LOF. As discussed in chapter 5, once the line-of-sight (LOS) is defined by the tracking system, the weapon launch lead angle may be computed. The gross measure of this angle is between the LOS and the LOF. Movement of the launcher is azimuth (train), and elevation to the LOF is accomplished by respective analog signals in the form of DC error voltages representing magnitude and direction. The launcher is normally referenced to the delivery vehicle (reference frames will be discussed further in chapter 18). The error signals are entered into the train and elevation servo systems of the launcher. The resulting drive signals cause the launcher to respond in train and elevation, while employing position and velocity feedback in a manner identical to that described in chapter 3.

In order to carry out control of a launching system effectively, a scheme of communications must be incorporated. Physical movement of the launcher and transfer/loading functions may be directed by simple voice commands, followed by an appropriate action response. In more complex systems where multiple weapons are employed against various, simultaneous targets, communications are accomplished by information systems using electronic data-processing components. In the more extreme order of complexity, communication and control may be initiated by the operator, whereafter the complete cycle of transfer, loading, positioning, and launching will occur without further human operator input.

Launching Systems

In the case of impulse and reaction systems, launching of the weapon is brought about by the activation of the propelling charge in such a manner that expanding gases result in the explosion of the weapon. Launching for gravity systems is brought about by the simple release of the weapon. Launching systems must provide for the safety of operating personnel and the vehicle in which the systems are installed. A great number of safety features are included in the various components that make up the entire system. Most launchers are equipped with mechanisms that prevent the launcher from pointing or firing at the delivery vehicle. Mechanical devices, such as firing cut-out cams and electrical circuitry programmed to cause arbitrary launcher movement upon approaching blind or non-firing zones, are employed to ensure that the line-of-fire never occurs within a danger zone without warning to operating personnel.

Methods to evacuate or re-direct propellant gases are a design feature of launchers to prevent physical harm to personnel and damage to components (gas ejectors in guns, blast deflectors and diffusers

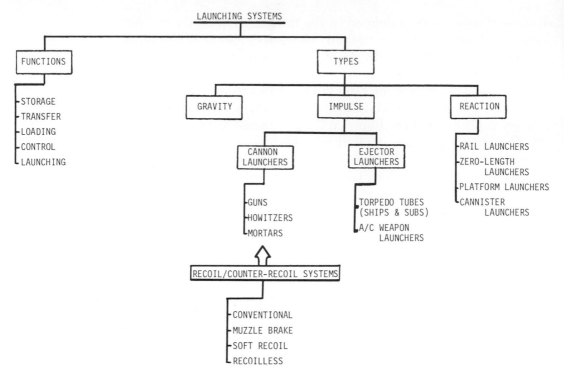

Figure 17–22. Launching system functional relationships.

in reaction launchers). Generally, however, the delivery vehicle is protected from exhaust damage by the design and location of the launcher on the vehicle as well as by the maintenance of an unobstructed area around the launcher and the use of protective materials.

Summary

The purpose of a launching system is to place a weapon into a flight path, the LOF, as rapidly as required. Launching systems must perform with speed and reliability, while displaying weapon system compatibility and safety. The basic functions of the launching system are weapon storage, transfer, loading, control, and launching. The three basic types of launchers are gravity, impulse, and reaction. The lightest and least complex type is the gravity launcher, while the impulse launcher is characteristically heavy and bulky. The requirement to contain the reactive propellant gases and to dissipate the reactive energy of the propellant through a recoil system contributes to the size requirement of impulse launchers. Reaction launchers have significantly minimized these disadvantages. Weapons employed with reaction launchers are characteristically more complex than weapons associated with gravity and impulse launchers. Launchers, once assigned to the weapon system, respond to error signals, called orders, from the computational system; these orders are derived from present target position as established by the sensor system.

References

Bureau of Naval Personnel. *Navy Missile Systems*. Washington, D.C.: GPO, 1971.

Commander, Naval Ordnance Systems Command. *Weapons Systems Fundamentals*. NAVORD OP 3000, vol. 2, 1st Rev. Washington, D.C.: GPO, 1971.

Naval Education and Training Command. *Gunner's Mate G 3 & 2*. Washington, D.C.: GPO, 1974.

Naval Education and Training Support Command. *Principles of Naval Ordnance and Gunnery*. Washington, D.C.: GPO, 1974.

Yagi, Jon J. "Internal Ballistics of Weapon Launching Systems." *Naval Engineers Journal*, Vol. 95, No. 3, May 1983, pp. 178–91.

18

Reference Frames and Coordinate Systems

Introduction

The solution to the weapon control problem involves the gathering and processing of information relating to the position and motion of a target. In order to be useful, position and motion data must be related to a known reference. For example, an aircraft's velocity does not provide any meaningful information unless it is known whether the velocity is relative to the air in which it is flying, the ground over which it travels, or perhaps even to the distant fixed stars.

Frames of reference are characterized by several major properties: an origin, reference lines, reference planes, and stability.

Origin. To be useful for measuring linear distances, a reference frame must have a reference point of origin that establishes the zero point for the frame. A distance of 100 yards has meaning within the frame since it is understood that the measured distance is relative to the frame's origin.

Reference lines. Simply measuring distance is not sufficient to establish position within a particular reference frame. In weapon systems, target *direction* from the origin is measured in angular quantities. To give meaning and a zero reference to angular quantities, reference lines are established. Reference lines pass through the origin and establish the axes of the reference frame.

Reference planes. In addition to reference lines, angular measurements require the definition of planes in which angles are to be measured. For example, an object located a distance of 100 yards from the origin and 45° from a reference line has virtually an infinite possibility of actual locations unless the plane in which the angle is measured is defined. Figure 18–1 illustrates two possible locations based upon a distance and an angle measured in two different planes.

A general reference frame can now be constructed based upon the three properties described above. Since it is desired to express position both with linear and angular quantities, the general reference frame is comprised of three reference axes (X, Y, Z), with the azimuth reference line arbitrarily chosen as the X axis. A horizontal reference plane is established and is that plane that contains the X and Y axes.

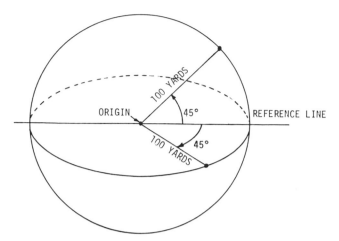

Figure 18–1. Position of an object in two different planes.

A vertical reference plane is also employed and is defined as that plane that contains the target and the Z axis. Figure 18–2 illustrates this general reference frame.

Stability. The property of reference frame stability directly affects the description of target motion within the reference frame. A truly stable or inertial reference frame is one that is held fixed or nonrotating with respect to the distant stars. In this type of reference frame, target motion is very easily described since all changes in target position within the frame are due only to the motion of the target itself. An unstable or non-inertial reference frame is one that is constantly rotating in a random manner, and therefore changes in target position within such a reference frame are the result of *both* target motion *and* reference frame rotation.

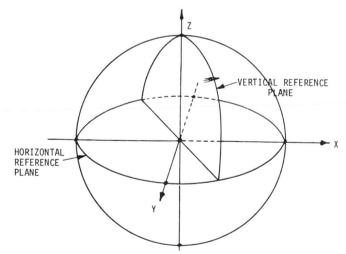

Figure 18–2. General three-dimensional reference frame.

A reference frame may have virtually any point in the universe as its origin. Reference frames useful in weapons control originate either at the center of the earth or at the weapon station itself. In this text, attention will be concentrated on reference frames that originate at the weapon station.

Weapon Station Reference Frames

Weapon station reference frames are fixed to, and move with, weapon platforms, such as ships, aircraft, submarines, and controlled missiles. The frames of reference used in weapon control are of two general types: those that are unstable and thus non-inertial; and those that are stabilized and considered inertial for the computation of target motion.

The *unstabilized weapon station frame* has as its origin one of the sensors of the fire control system. The reference axes are defined by the architecture of the weapon platform. One axis is oriented fore and aft, another horizontally and perpendicular to the fore-and-aft axis, and a third is oriented vertically, perpendicular to the other two. The major characteristic of the unstabilized reference frame is that it rotates about all three of its axes as the weapon station rotates in pitch, roll, and yaw. For this reason, it is considered non-inertial and thus not suitable for the description of target motion.

The origin of the *stabilized weapon station frame* is again at the weapon station. However, the reference axes are no longer coincident with the structure of the vehicle. This is due to the incorporation of inertial elements (gyroscopes) within the weapon station, which establish the axes for this frame of reference. One such element is made to track the axis of rotation of the earth, thus establishing a permanent north-south horizontal reference line. A second horizontal reference line is established by the perpendicular east-west line derived from the same inertial element as the N-S line. Another inertial element is made to track the center of the earth and thus establish a fixed vertical axis. Because the axes of this reference frame are fixed to true north and the center of the earth, the stabilized weapon station frame is considered inertial during the flight times of most weapons. For this reason, the stabilized reference frame is employed for the description of target motion and the computation of lead angles.

Figure 18–3 illustrates that in any given weapon system there may be several functional reference frames. A surface combatant is used here as an example because it is on this type of weapon station that this concept of multiple reference frames is most pronounced. The

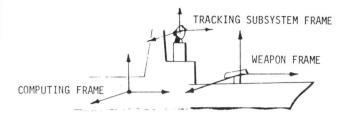

TRACKING SUBSYSTEM FRAME

WEAPON FRAME

COMPUTING FRAME

Figure 18–3. Several weapon-station frames in a single-weapon control system.

sensor and tracking systems may gather target information in one weapon station frame (unstable) while the computational system computes lead angles in another (stable), and the launching system is positioned in still a third (unstable). Note that these related frames of reference are displaced from one another and will rotate with respect to one another.

Coordinate Systems

A system of coordinates must be established to uniquely describe a position in space or to describe the magnitude and direction of target velocity with respect to a specified reference frame. For the location to have meaning we must designate a starting point or a reference point and a system of measure, such as length, time, weight, etc. In order to give the measuring system a zero point and to describe more easily the coordinate system, a reference frame will be established, as previously mentioned, consisting of three mutually perpendicular lines. The point from which these lines originate is the starting point, a zero position. In actual weapon systems, this zero position is generally the pivotal axes of the sensor and tracking subsystem since all initial target data is generated there. A coordinate, then, is one of a set of values used to locate a point relative to a reference system of lines or surfaces. (See figure 18–4.)

Any weapon system can be subdivided by function into three general categories: *data measurement*, *computation*, and *data utilization*. By the nature of the hardware design constraints, each functional category employs a coordinate system that allows the simplest expression of the problem and the easiest method of actual implementation.

Spherical Coordinate System

A *spherical* coordinate system is ideal for use in the process of actually measuring target parameters. This is due to the fact that sensor and tracking systems rotate about their coordinate axes and measure distance along a straight line to the target. A generalized

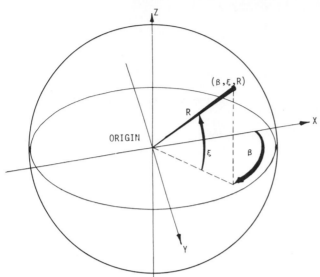

Figure 18–4. Generalized spherical coordinate system.

spherical coordinate system consists of two angles and a linear distance. This system can therefore be represented by an ordered triple of characters (β, ε, R), which describe any point in the reference frame (figure 18–4). Specific examples of the use of the spherical coordinate system on two diverse real-world weapons platforms is illustrated in figure 18–5.

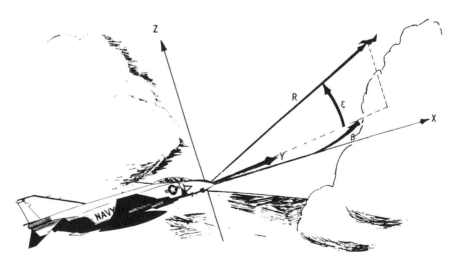

Figure 18–5a. Fighter aircraft employment of a spherical coordinate system.

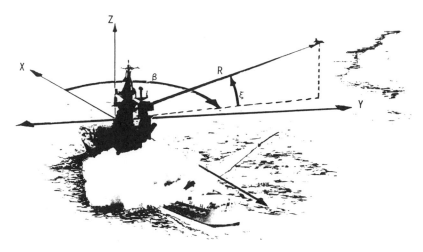

Figure 18–5b. Surface combatant employment of a spherical coordinate system.

Cylindrical Coordinate System

Most weapon control computation is accomplished using a rectangular coordinate system, although some older gun fire control systems remain that use a cylindrical coordinate system. A cylindrical coordinate system employs an angle of azimuth, a vertical linear distance, and a horizontal linear distance (figure18–6).

Rectangular Coordinate System

The *Rectangular* or *Cartesian* coordinate system employs the target's range in the true north/south direction as the Y-axis distance,

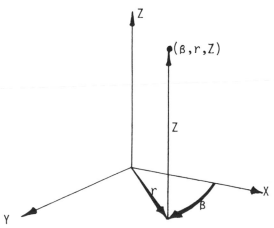

Figure 18–6. A cylindrical coordinate system.

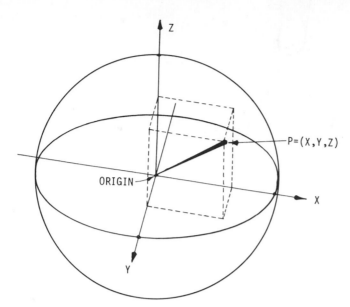

Figure 18–7. Generalized rectangular coordinate system.

the target's range in the east/west direction as the X-axis distance, and the vertical height as the Z-axis distance. The rectangular coordinate system is illustrated in figure 18–7. Calculation of target velocity and prediction of future target position is made easier in cartesian coordinates, thus reducing the time required for computer solution of the fire control problem. For this reason, and the ease with which data can be shared by widely separated forces, the cartesian coordinate system is used by most modern fire control systems and command and control facilities.

Coordinate Conversion

Coordinate conversion is the process of changing from one system of characters that describe a point within a reference frame to another system of characters describing the same point in the same reference frame. Figure 18–8 illustrates the relationship between the spherical coordinate system and the rectangular coordinate system. The equations that govern the conversion are as follows:

$$X = R \cos Z \cos \beta \qquad (18\text{–}1)$$
$$Y = R \cos Z \sin \beta \qquad (18\text{–}2)$$
$$Z = R \sin Z \qquad (18\text{–}3)$$

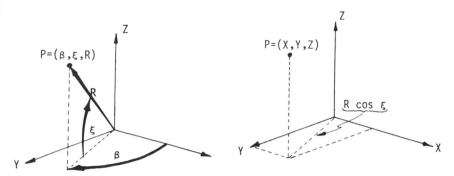

Figure 18–8. Relationship between spherical and rectangular coordinates within the same reference frame.

Coordinate Transformation (Reference Frame Rotation)

The process of stabilization of the target coordinates is one of transforming the target coordinates from one *reference frame* to another using the *same coordinate system*. The reference frame rotation results from the roll and pitch of the weapon station. The process of transformation then involves the rotation of the coordinates in the unstabilized frame through the angles of pitch and roll to obtain the coordinates in a stabilized frame. Figure 18–9 provides a synopsis of coordinate conversion and transformation.

Consider first a simplified two-dimensional case where the unstabilized coordinates (R, E) and the angle of pitch, ϕ, have been measured. The task is to first convert the measured coordinates into

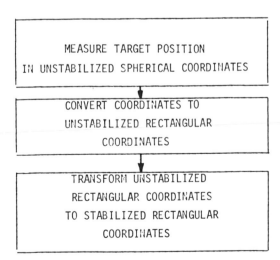

Figure 18–9. Coordinate conversion and transformation.

unstabilized rectangular coordinates and then rotate the unstabilized reference frame through the angle of pitch to obtain rectangular coordinates in a stabilized reference frame.

The basic relationships governing this transformation are:

$$X' = R \cos Z \tag{18-4}$$
$$Z' = R \sin Z \tag{18-5}$$
$$X = R \cos (Z + \phi) \tag{18-6}$$
$$Z = R \sin (Z + \phi) \tag{18-7}$$

Using the formulas for the cosine and sine of the sum of two angles we have:

$$
\begin{aligned}
X = R \cos (\xi' + \phi) &= R (\cos Z' \cos \phi - \sin Z' \sin \phi) \\
&= (R \cos Z') \cos \phi - (R \sin Z') \sin \phi \\
&= X' \cos \phi - Z' \sin \phi \tag{18-8}
\end{aligned}
$$

$$
\begin{aligned}
Z = R \sin (Z' + \phi) &= R (\sin \phi \cos Z' + \cos \phi \sin Z') \\
&= (R \cos Z') \sin \phi + (R \sin Z') \cos \phi \\
&= X' \sin \phi + Z' \cos \phi \tag{18-9}
\end{aligned}
$$

Example: (TWO-DIMENSIONAL CASE)
Target Parameters

$$R = 20,000 \text{ meters}$$
$$\xi' = 35° (.6108 \text{ radians})$$

Angle of Pitch
$$\phi = +8° (.1396 \text{ radians})$$

(1) Convert unstable spherical coordinates to unstable rectangular coordinates:

$$
\begin{aligned}
X' &= R \cos \xi' \\
&= 20,000 \cos (35°) \\
&= 20,000 (.819) \\
&= 16,383.04 \text{ meters} \\
Z' &= R \sin \xi' \\
&= 20,000 \sin (35°) \\
&= 20,000 (.573) \\
&= 11,471.53 \text{ meters}
\end{aligned}
$$

Note: A starboard roll and down-pitch angle will both be considered as negative angles.

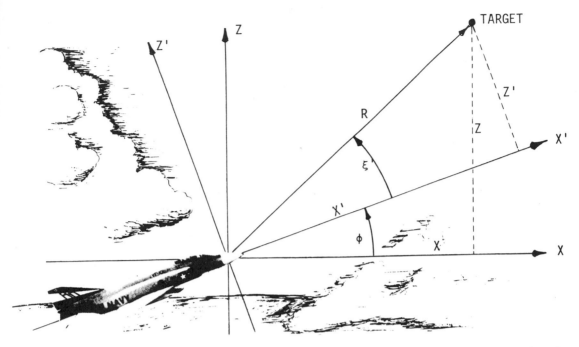

Figure 18–10. Two-dimensional relationship between unstabilized reference frame (X',Z') and the stabilized reference frame (X,Z), considering only the angle of pitch (ϕ).

(2) Rotate the unstable coordinates through the angle of pitch using equations (18–8) and (18–9):

$$X = X' \cos \phi - Z' \sin \phi$$
$$= 16{,}383.04 \cos (8°) - 11{,}471.53 \sin (8°)$$
$$= 16{,}383.04\,(.99) - 11{,}471.53\,(.139)$$
$$= 14{,}627.07 \text{ meters}$$
$$Z = X' \sin \phi + Z' \cos \phi$$
$$= 16{,}383.04 \sin (8°) + 11{,}471.53 \cos (8°)$$
$$= 16{,}383.04\,(.139) + 11{,}471.53\,(.99)$$
$$= 13{,}639.96 \text{ meters}$$

Equations (18–8) and (18–9) represent the rectangular coordinates in the stabilized reference frame in terms of the coordinates in the unstabilized reference frame. These equations are general in nature and serve to illustrate a fundamental concept in analytic geometry, which can be stated as follows:

Rectangular coordinates in a reference frame that is rotated with respect to a second reference frame, can be expressed in terms of

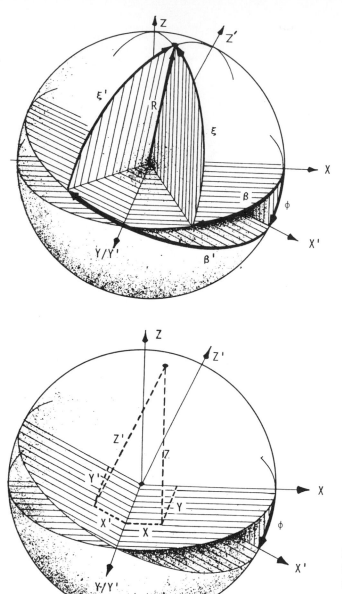

Figure 18–11. Relationships between reference frames and coordinate systems when azimuth is not zero and rotation is through the angle of pitch (ϕ).

the rectangular coordinates of the second reference frame and *sine* and *cosine* functions of the angle of rotation.

For our purposes the *angles of rotation* are the angles of pitch and roll of the weapon station. Once rectangular coordinates are generated for the unstable system, direct applications of the above principle and the general forms of equations (18–8) and (18–9) for the angles of pitch and roll will yield rectangular coordinates in the stable system. Figure 18–11 illustrates the relationship between the stable and unstable coordinates when only the angle of pitch is considered.

In the general case where roll is non-zero, the coordinates (X, Y, Z) derived above would be an intermediate set of coordinates and would be used to rotate about the X axis or the roll axis as follows:

θ = Roll angle

X stable = X (rotation is about axis of roll)   (18–10)

Y stable = $Y \cos (\theta) - Z \sin (\theta)$ (18–11)

Z stable = $Y \sin (\theta) + Z \cos (\theta)$ (18–12)

The general scheme for reference frame rotation is as follows:

Convert unstable spherical coordinates
to unstable rectangular coordinates

$$X' = R \cos \xi' \cos \beta'$$
$$Y' = R \cos \xi' \sin \beta'$$
$$Z' = R \sin \xi'$$

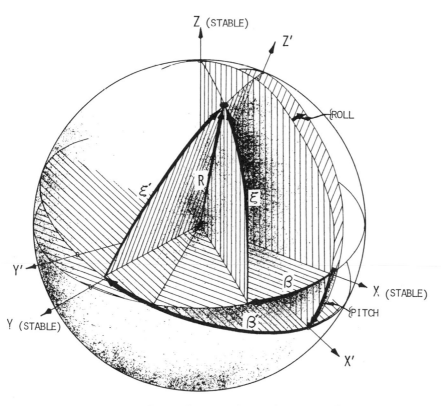

Figure 18–12. Spherical coordinate relationships considering both pitch and roll.

Rotate through the angle of pitch

$X = X' \cos \phi - Z' \sin \phi$
$ = (R \cos \xi' \cos \beta') \cos \phi - (R \sin \xi') \sin \phi$
$Y = Y'$ (rotation is about the Y' axis)
$Z = X' \sin \phi + Z' \cos \phi$
$ = (R \cos \xi' \cos \beta') \sin \phi + (R \sin \xi') \cos \phi$

Rotate through the angle of roll

X stable $= X$ (Rotation is about axis of roll)
Y stable $= Y \cos \theta - Z \sin \theta$
Z stable $= Y \sin \theta + Z \cos \theta$

Reference Frame Translation

Reference frame translation can be defined as the location of a point (target) with respect to two different reference frames whose origins are physically displaced from one another. Figure 18–13 illustrates this relationship for two coplanar reference frames, A and B, which are displaced linearly by distance h. The point T (target) may be located in direction and distance from reference frame A by the angle ϕ_1 and the range R_1. In order to transform target coordinates from reference frame A to reference frame B, the angle P_h must be taken into consideration to provide the coordinates ϕ_2 and R_2.

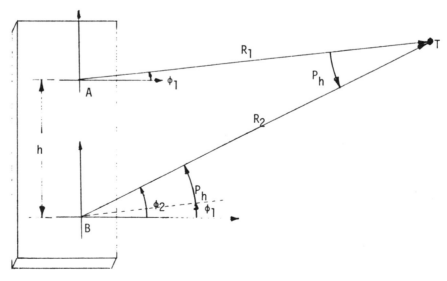

Figure 18–13. The effect of translation on target location.

This displacement of reference frames is common aboard ships. It is necessary, for example, to describe a target's location accurately in both the reference frame of a missile director and in the frame of its associated missile launcher. The term *parallax correction* is used to describe the data conversion needed to compensate for this translation of reference frames. In addition to the horizontal displacement, illustrated in figure 18–13, a vertical displacement also exists due to the general configuration of directors and launchers (or guns) being mounted on different deck levels.

Weapons System Alignment

Modern weapons systems ashore and afloat include many elements that are physically displaced from one another. To function as an effective system, these elements must be aligned to one another in azimuth and elevation and must rotate in parallel planes. When this is accomplished, the following requirements will be met:

(1) All weapon bores, launcher rails, sight telescopes, and radar beams are parallel and remain parallel throughout any operating motion (when no parallax or ballistic corrections are made).
(2) All related readouts of movement are correct with respect to the established reference.
(3) All intra-element angle transmissions are correct.

These requirements are met when the following are accomplished:

(1) All readouts and transmission systems are aligned so that the zero-degrees train reference lines of the elements are parallel.
(2) The planes of rotation (roller-path planes) of the elements are parallel or effectively parallel.
(3) All readouts and transmission systems are aligned so that when the pointing lines are parallel in train, the zero elevation references are parallel.

Alignment. Alignment of weapons system elements begins with establishment of parallel planes of rotation of the system elements. Ashore, in Marine systems, surveyors and combat engineers will determine the suitability of the chosen site with reference to slope of the ground, physical space available, and the presence of obstructions. Truck or trailer mounted elements must be firmly emplaced and then leveled using adjustable braces provided for that purpose. Once this has been done, the only error would result from defects in the machined surface of the truck or trailer frame upon which the element rotates.

Because a ship changes shape when afloat, due to loading, and is in constant motion, due to wind and wave action, the initial phase of alignment of launchers, sensors, and navigational references is performed in dry dock. Once parallel roller-path planes are established with the ship constrained by keel blocks, the ship is floated, loaded to specified displacement, and the data re-checked. Sometimes machining of the roller path is required afloat due to the ship's bending or sagging when waterborne.

Whether aboard ship or ashore, one element is selected as a reference, and all others are aligned to it. Aboard ship, a forward gun director or, in the absence of a gun director, the lowest forward missile director is selected. Ashore, the element with greatest precision (such as the CW acquisition radar in a Hawk missile battery) is made the reference. In any case, it is helpful if the reference element is in visual sight of the other elements for train and elevation alignment.

Once parallel planes of rotation have been established, the zero degrees train and elevation reference must be established for each element, and display of angular measurements must be calibrated. Transmission of this data between elements must be verified for accuracy, and a correction applied if necessary. Ships or shore-based elements will employ calibrated metal bars or yokes called tram bars

Figure 18–14. Horizontal and vertical parallax considerations. Fire control system to weapon (h_1V_1) search radar to fire control system (h_2V_2).

as gauges to verify the accuracy of angular measurement in periodic re-checks after alignment has been performed. The tram bar is placed between metal pads, one of which is located on the stationary base and the other on the rotating part of the element. This establishes a calibrated angle of rotation that is compared with readouts of the angle and transmitted data. If there is an error, the readouts and transmission systems are adjusted to read the calibrated angle that should correct the error throughout the range of motion of the element.

One of the best ways to verify alignment between elements is by performing the star check. In this case a star is selected of proper elevation at a convenient bearing, and all system elements are trained and elevated to it. Launchers and guns will have temporary boresights installed so that they can be checked also. Stars are such a great distance away that the parallax between elements is essentially zero; therefore, all elements should have the same measurement of train and elevation when sighted on the same star (figure 18–15).

Collimation. Many system elements such as missile fire control radars may employ several different radar beams plus an optical line-of-sight (LOS) reference. The parallelism between beams radiated by a single element is achieved by the process of collimation. At a specified distance, the element is sighted in on an optical target that has radar-receiving antennas displaced from it such that each will be located exactly in the center of the beam that antenna was designed to receive if that beam is properly aligned (figure 18–16). The element is trained and elevated back and forth across the target while power measurements are taken. If maximum signal strength is measured at some time other than when the optical target is in the center of the boresight telescope, a mechanical or electrical adjustment is made to the antenna to correct it.

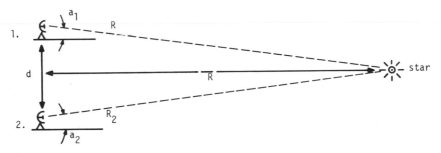

Figure 18–15. As R goes to infinity, d becomes much less significant; therefore, the angles measured by 1 and 2 will approach equality.

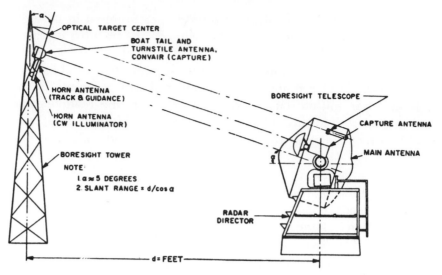

Figure 18–16. Collimation of a multiple-beam fire control radar.

Aircraft system boresighting. The boresighting process performs the same function for aircraft as battery alignment and collimation do for ship and land-based systems. Its purpose is to establish a relationship between the flight attitude of the aircraft, the bore axes of guns and weapon-releasing equipment, radar beam axes, and those of optical sights and Head-Up Displays (HUD). The process is designed to employ pertinent ballistics and mechanical data in establishing the relationship between the sight line of the optical or radio frequency aiming device and the trajectory of the weapon being fired or ejected, in order to predict its mean point of impact at predetermined ranges. The boresighting procedure is carried out in two phases: electrical boresighting and harmonization. Electrical boresighting will require that RF energy be radiated, but harmonization can be accomplished without radiation if the antenna's optical axis is in proper agreement with its RF axis (collimated).

Electrical boresighting. This procedure is the equivalent of collimation as presented previously. The aircraft's installed radar or radars are made parallel to the optical axis of the antenna. A portable frame is attached to the aircraft (figure 18–17), which incorporates radar and optical targets for various armament and sensors. This frame is employed much like the collimation tower in figure 18–16.

Harmonization. This procedure brings the radar optical axis into a parallel relationship with a baseline in the aircraft structure called the *armament datum line.* This is the equivalent of the process of

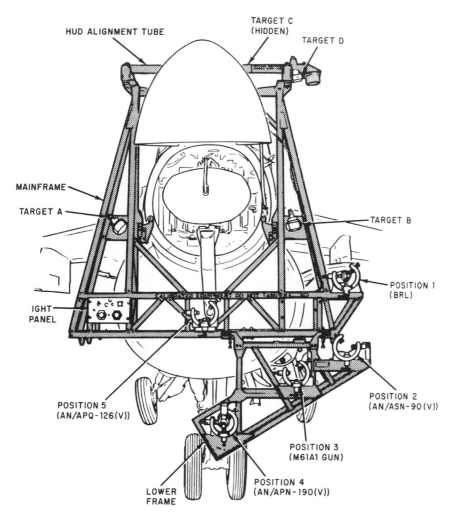

Figure 18–17. Short-range boresighting equipment.

roller-path plane-of-rotation adjustment for ships in addition to the establishment of zero train and elevation. Harmonization also includes alignment of the weapon-releasing equipment and optical sights or head-up displays (HUD).

Summary

In this chapter we have presented the concepts of reference frames and coordinate systems as applied to the field of weapon control. Various types of reference frames were investigated with emphasis upon the weapon station reference frames. Non-inertial reference frames, those that partake in the rotational motions of the weapon station, are suitable for target data measurement and utilization but extremely cumbersome for computation. Target motion is most easily described and computations are facilitated by the employment of an inertial (stable) reference frame.

The transition from the non-inertial to the inertial frame necessitated the use of several different coordinate systems. These coordinate systems, *Spherical, Cylindrical,* and *Rectangular* facilitate the description of target position and velocity. Finally the problems of reference frame rotation and translation were investigated and examples given.

References

Commander, Naval Ordnance Systems Command. *Weapons Systems Fundamentals*. NAVORD OP 3000, vol. 2, 1st Rev. Washington, D.C.: GPO, 1971.

Naval Education and Training Command. *Aviation Firecontrolman* 1 & C. Washington, D.C.: GPO, 1977.

19

Ballistics and the Fire Control Problem

Introduction

In the previous chapter it was shown that a weapon system measured target coordinates and stabilized that measured data to an inertial reference frame suitable for computation. Target information, however, comprises only part of the input data necessary for calculation. An accurate description of the flight path of the weapon is also necessary if the weapon is to be delivered accurately to the target. Weapons, in general, do not follow straight paths to the point of target intercept. Physical phenomena acting on the weapon during its time of flight cause it to miss its target if the weapon were aimed directly at the target. The fire control problem can then be divided into two major categories:

(1) The effect of relative target motion during the time of weapon flight.
(2) The physical phenomena collectively called ballistics, which produce a curved weapon trajectory.

These are illustrated in figure 19–1.

Relative Motion

The effect of relative motion results in the requirement to aim a weapon at some point in space that is displaced from the present target position. The amount of displacement or lead depends on the relative velocity and on the time of flight (TOF) of the weapon from the launch point to the target. The point of collision between the weapon and the target is the future target position. A basic assumption that is made when computing the effect of relative motion is that the target will not accelerate during the time of flight of the weapon. Thus, by following a straight-line path, the target simplifies our problem of prediction and thus lowers the target's chances of survival. It might be presumed that a target would avoid this path and use diversionary tactics such as zig-zags, curved paths, etc. Certain factors oppose these choices of target paths. The first is that the shortest

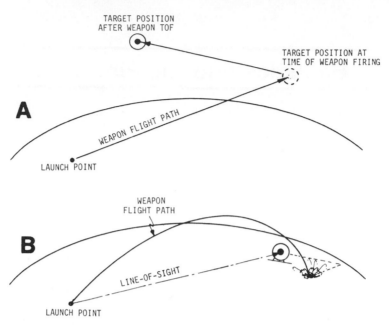

Figure 19–1. A. Miss-producing effect of target relative motion with straight weapon flight path.
B. Miss-producing effect of a curved flight path considering a stationary target.

distance between two points is a straight line; therefore, a target following a straight-line course will be exposed to danger for a shorter period of time. The target being in danger for a shorter period of time may be more important than the increased danger for that time. Also, most targets tend to follow a straight-line path. It must be noted that an attacking vehicle must press home its attack. If our presence and the fact that we are prepared to launch a counter weapon causes an attacker to make such radical maneuvers that would cause our weapon to miss, then there is a high probability that his weapon will miss also. Therefore, even if evasive maneuvers are taken by a target, these maneuvers will average over time to a straight-line course or one with a slight curve. Secondly, it should be realized that even if the target accelerates and/or turns, the shorter the TOF, the less the error. With the above assumptions in mind, the relative-motion calculation is reduced to a simple linear function of time:

$$P_2 = P_1 + VT \qquad (19–1)$$

where:

P_2 is the future position of the target

P_1 is the present position of the target as measured by the sensor subsystem

V is the total relative target velocity

T is the time of flight of the weapon.

As figure 19–2 illustrates, this relationship in a stabilized reference frame actually must be expressed in each dimension:

$$X_2 = X_1 + \frac{\Delta x}{\Delta t} T \tag{19-2}$$

$$Y_2 = Y_1 + \frac{\Delta y}{\Delta t} T \tag{19-3}$$

$$Z_2 = Z_1 + \frac{\Delta z}{\Delta t} T \tag{19-4}$$

The future target position derived from the above calculations generally comprises the most significant component of the lead angle. The final aiming angles for the weapon are the angles of azimuth and elevation, which include the target motion effect and the corrections as a result of trajectory curvature. The calculation of the relative-motion effect therefore solves only part of the weapon control problem, which answers the following question:

For a *known* weapon time of flight, what is the position of the target at the end of the time of flight?

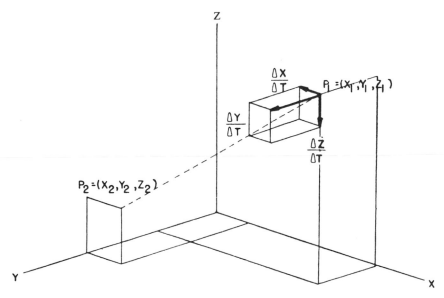

Figure 19–2. Relative motion in Cartesian coordinates.

Only when a knowledge of target position is gained can the effects of weapon-path curvature be computed.

Exterior Ballistics

Exterior ballistics is a generic term used to describe a number of natural phenomena that tend to cause a weapon in flight to change direction or velocity or both. These phenomena are:

Gravity
Drag
Wind
Drift (when considering spin-stabilized weapons)
Coriolis effect

The computation of relative-motion effects produces the actual point of collision between the weapon and the target. The computation of the effects of ballistics produces aiming corrections as a result of the curvature of the weapon's flight path. These corrections don't change the final collision point, but cause the trajectory of the weapon to intersect the flight path of the target. The ultimate aim of ballistic computation, then, is to produce angular corrections to the azimuth and elevation values derived from the relative-motion results. Inherent in these calculations is the computation of time-of-flight of the weapon, which in turn is used to facilitate the relative-motion computation.

Ideally, it is desired to produce a procedure that totally describes the complex trajectory of a weapon. When provided the coordinates of the future target position as input data, this procedure would produce angles of launch and weapon time-of-flight as output. Figure 19–3 illustrates the conceptual goal of a ballistic solution. It must be emphasized here that the central problem of weapon delivery is the solution of the intersection of two curves, one described by the motion of the target and the other described by the motion of the weapon.

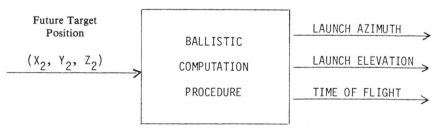

Figure 19–3. Input/output relationships of a ballistic procedure.

Gravity. The force of gravity always tends to accelerate an object downward toward the center of the earth. The effects of this force on the trajectory of a weapon are well known and if considered alone result in a very simple solution to the trajectory problem. Figure 19–4 is an illustration of the trajectory of a weapon in a vacuum and the effect of gravity upon the weapon. In a vacuum on a "flat" nonrotating earth, the horizontal component of the initial velocity of the weapon ($V_0 \cos \theta$) remain unchanged. However, the vertical component ($V_0 \sin \theta$) is continuously changed as a result of the acceleration due to gravity. This changing vertical velocity results in a parabolic trajectory. A ballistic procedure that will provide an approximation to the desired output can be developed from the equations that describe this trajectory. A two-dimensional example will serve to illustrate this procedure.

The differential equations of motion are:

$$\frac{d^2x}{dt^2} = 0 \qquad\qquad (19\text{–}5)$$

$$\frac{d^2z}{dt^2} = \frac{d\dot{z}}{dt} = \ddot{z} = -g \qquad\qquad (19\text{–}6)$$

subject to the initial conditions,

$$x(t = 0) = 0$$
$$\dot{x}(t = 0) = v_0 \cos \theta$$
$$\dot{z}(t = 0) = v_0 \sin \theta$$
$$z(t = 0) = 0$$

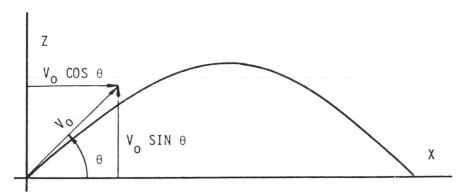

Figure 19–4. Weapon trajectory considering gravity alone acting on the weapon.

These are solved by separating variables, and integrating and evaluating constants of integration (through use of initial conditions). Thus, from equation (19–5):

$$\frac{dx}{dt} = \dot{x} = \text{Constant} = v_0 \cos \theta$$

$$\int dx = v_0 \cos \theta \int dt = x = (v_0 \cos \theta)\, t + C_1$$

Evaluate constant of integration, C_1:

$$x(0) = 0 + C_1 \text{ hence, } C_1 = 0 \text{ and } x = tv_0 \cos \theta \text{ or}$$

$$t = \frac{x}{v_0 \cos \theta} \tag{19–7}$$

Solve equation (19–6) for z:

$$d\dot{z} = -g\,dt \text{ hence, } \dot{z} = -gt + C_2$$

Evaluate constant of integration, C_2:

$$\dot{z}(0) = 0 + C_2 = v_0 \sin \theta \therefore C_2 = v_0 \sin \theta$$

$$\dot{z} = \frac{dz}{dt} = -gt + v_0 \sin \theta$$

Solve for z:

$$\int dz = \int (-gt + v_0 \sin \theta)dt$$

$$z = gt^2/2 + t(v_0 \sin \theta) + C_3$$

Evaluate constant of integration, C_3:

$$z(0) = 0 + 0 + C_3 = 0 \text{ hence, } C_3 = 0$$

$$z = -\frac{g}{2} t^2 + (v_0 \sin \theta)t$$

or

$$\theta = \arcsin \left(\frac{z + .5g\, T^2}{v_0 T} \right) \tag{19–8}$$

The procedure for the solution of equations (19–7) and (19–8) is one of successive approximations. The concept is to compute a first approximation to T by using equation (19–7) and $\theta = \text{ARCTAN } (z/X)$. Next compute the effect of gravity on θ using equation (19–8). Use the results of equation (19–8) to compute a new value for T. Continue this alternate substitution of variables until the values of T

and θ converge to a final value accurate enough for use. This procedure is common to all fire control systems and must be well understood. Sufficient accuracy can be determined by testing the absolute difference between T_n and T_{n-1} as it approaches zero, where n is the number of iterations. Figure 19–5 is an annotated flow diagram of this procedure. The above ballistic procedure is valid regardless of the elevation of the target's future position, since equations (19–7) and (19–8) describe the trajectory that passes through the point (X, Z), which defines this position. This validity (in a vacuum) can be shown

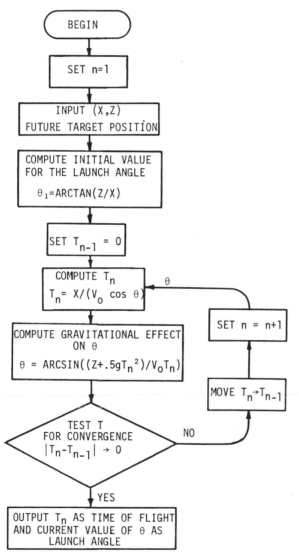

Figure 19–5. Flow diagram for ballistic procedure considering only gravity.

by comparing the trajectories of a surface target ($Z = 0$) and one for an air target ($Z > 0$). (Refer to figure 19–6.)

Drag. In the vacuum trajectory situation, the solution was easily obtained because of the simplifications and assumptions made in formulating the problem. When the effects of the atmosphere are considered, forces other than gravity act on the weapon, which cause it to deviate from a pure parabolic path. This deviation results specifically from the dissipation of energy as the weapon makes contact with the atmosphere. It has been found that the loss of energy of a projectile in flight is due to:

(1) *Creation of air waves*—The magnitude of this effect is influenced by the form (shape) of the weapon as well as by the cross-sectional area.

(2) *Creation of suction and eddy currents*—This phenomenon is chiefly the result of the form of the weapon and in gun projectiles specifically, the form of the after body.

(3) *Formation of heat*—Energy is dissipated as a result of friction between the weapon and the air mass.

The combined effect of energy loss is a deceleration of the projectile during its time-of-flight. This deceleration acts to decrease the velocity of the weapon as it travels through the atmosphere. For a given projectile form, the retardation in velocity is directly proportional to the atmospheric density and to the velocity itself. This deceleration called *parasitic drag* is given by the following relationship:

$$D = C\rho AV^2/2 \qquad\qquad (19\text{–}9)$$

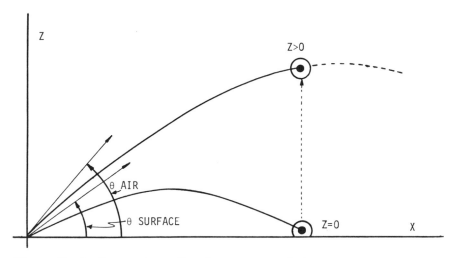

Figure 19–6. *Comparison of surface-target and air-target trajectories.*

where:

C is the drag coefficient derived from empirical data.

ρ is the atmospheric density that is a function of the altitude and the temperature of the atmosphere at any given height.

A is the cross-sectional area of the projectile.

V is the velocity of the projectile at any instant of time during the flight.

Parasitic drag always acts in a direction opposite to that of the motion of the weapon, as shown in figure 19–7. As a result, two fundamental interdependent actions take place while a weapon is in flight. First, as illustrated in equation (19–9), the force of drag at any point in the weapon's trajectory is a direct function of the velocity at that point. Because the drag force is continuously retarding the velocity of the weapon, the *force of drag itself* is continuously changing over the entire time-of-flight of the weapon, with drag dependent upon velocity and in turn velocity dependent upon drag. *Thus, the magnitude of both the velocity and the drag are changing with each dependent upon the other.* Second, as the weapon travels the curved path of the trajectory, the angle δ (figure 19–7) is never constant, which results in the force of drag continuously changing direction throughout the entire flight of the weapon.

The force of drag constantly changes in magnitude as a function of velocity and in direction as a function of the direction of motion of the weapon.

The end result of drag is to slow the projectile over its entire trajec-

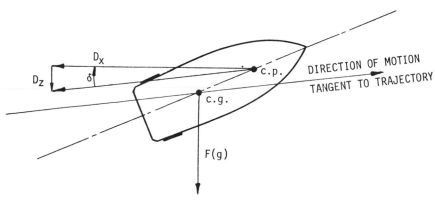

Figure 19–7. Parasitic drag and gravity acting on a projectile in flight. The relative position of the center of gravity (C.G.) and the center of pressure (C.P.) is dependent on the projectile configuration.

Ballistics and the Fire Control Problem   **553**

tory, producing a range that is significantly shorter than that which is achievable in a vacuum.

A discussion of the vacuum and atmospheric trajectories is warranted. While the vacuum trajectory is symmetric about the mid-range value, with the angle of fall equaling the angle of departure, the atmospheric trajectory is asymmetric. The summit of the trajectory is farther than mid-range, and the angle of fall is greater than the angle of departure. Additionally, the atmospheric trajectory is dependent on projectile mass due to external forces—which also, unlike the vacuum case, causes the atmospheric trajectory's horizontal component of velocity to decrease along the flight path. This results in a computation of the necessary departure angle to effect maximum range, whereas in a vacuum the maximum range's departure angle is 45°.

In consideration of the elevation at which maximum range is achieved, there are two offsetting effects: the change in drag with projectile velocity and the atmospheric density. A projectile's velocity is greatest immediately upon leaving the gun, thus drag is greatest at this time also. For small, lightweight projectiles, deceleration is greatest at the beginning of flight; therefore, to take advantage of improvement in horizontal range while the velocity is greatest, it is necessary to shoot at elevations less than 45°. In large projectiles such as those employed on battleships it is best to employ elevations above 45° to enable the projectiles to quickly reach high altitudes where air density and thus drag are decreased. Range increases result from the approximation of vacuum trajectory conditions in the high-altitude phase of projectile flight.

Wind. The effects of wind can be divided into two components: *range wind* and *cross wind*. *Range wind* is that component of wind that acts in the plane of the line of fire. It serves to either retard or aid the projectile velocity, thus either increasing or decreasing range.

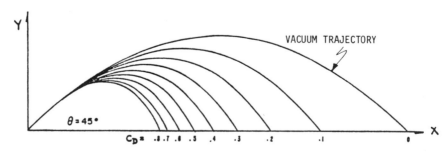

Figure 19–8. Comparison of vacuum and atmospheric trajectories. (Courtesy of Schmidt)

Cross wind acts in a plane perpendicular to the line of fire and serves to deflect the projectile either to the right or left of the line of fire.

Wind acts on the projectile throughout the time of flight; therefore, the total deviation in range and azimuth is a function of the time-of-flight.

Drift. Drift of a gun projectile is defined as the lateral displacement of the projectile from the original plane of fire due *only* to the effect of the rotation of the projectile. The principal cause of the drift lies in the gyroscopic properties of the spinning projectile. According to the laws of the gyroscope, the projectile seeks, first of all, to maintain its axis in the direction of its line of departure from the gun. The center of gravity of the projectile, however, follows the curved path of the trajectory, and the instantaneous direction of its motion, at any point, is that of the tangent to the trajectory at that point. Therefore, the projectile's tendency to maintain the original direction of its axis soon results in leaving this axis pointed slightly above the tangent to the trajectory. The force of the air resistance opposed to the flight of the projectile is then applied against its underside (figure 19–7). This force tends to push the nose of the projectile up, upending it. However, because of the gyroscopic stabilization, this force results in the nose of the projectile going to the right when viewed from above. The movement of the nose of the projectile to the right then produces air resistance forces tending to rotate the projectile clockwise when viewed from above. However, again because of the gyroscopic stabilization, this force results in the nose of the projectile rotating down, which then tends to decrease the first upending force. Thus, the projectile curves or drifts to the right as it goes toward the target. This effect can easily be shown with a gyroscope.

A more detailed analysis of gyroscopic stability would show that a projectile is statically unstable, but because of the gyroscopic effects, becomes dynamically stable. These effects actually cause the axis of the projectile to make oscillatory nutations about its flight path. Also the Magnus Effect, where a rotating body creates lift (figure 19–9) must be considered. The Magnus Effect is what causes a pitched baseball to curve.

Coriolis effect. The preceding effects have all considered the earth to be flat and non-rotating. Actually this is not the case, and centripetal acceleration and coriolis acceleration caused by the rotating earth must be considered. The centripetal acceleration of a point on the earth's surface will vary with its distance from the rotation axis. Thus, the difference in the velocities of the launcher and the target because of their different locations on the earth's surface must be considered.

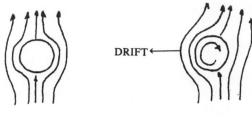

streamlines w.o.
spin

streamlines with
spin

*Figure 19–9. The Magnus Effect
(Courtesy of Schmidt).*

The coriolis acceleration force is created when a body or projectile moves along a radius from the axis of rotation of the earth (or a component of it). This force tends to curve an object to the right in the Northern Hemisphere and to the left in the Southern Hemisphere. An observable example would be that the air moving outward from a high becomes clockwise wind and air moving into a low becomes counterclockwise wind.

Ballistics Procedure

The ballistics procedure described earlier is a highly simplified illustration of a concept of trajectory calculations. The calculations involved in a practical trajectory procedure are extremely complex and must take into account factors such as drag, lift, drift, and wind as well as the force of gravity. The two basic equations, (19–7) and (19–8), must be expanded to include all of the forces acting on the weapon over the time-of-flight. Although a practical ballistic procedure is very complex in detail, the logic flow is identical to that described in figure 19–5. The output answers the second major question in the solution of the fire control problem:

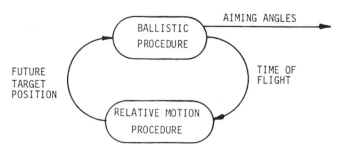

Figure 19–10. Prediction procedure closed-loop flow diagram.

For a known point in space, what will be the launch angle and time-of-flight of a weapon to that point?

Prediction Calculation of Future Target Position

Now that relative motion and ballistic procedures have been investigated separately, it must be pointed out that in reality each is dependent upon the other. In the statements of the relative-motion and ballistics problems given above, it will be noted that the solution for future target position depends on time-of-flight, and in turn, the solution for the ballistic trajectory and time-of-flight depends upon the future target position. To illustrate the problem a bit further: for any given point in space a trajectory and time-of-flight can be computed, but the correct point in space for intercept cannot be given directly since that point depends upon time-of-flight for its calculation. In this context, time-of-flight is a generic term for the time of travel of the weapon. The prediction algorithm described below is general in nature and is directly applicable to *all* weapons systems. The prediction procedure incorporates both the relative-motion procedure and a ballistic procedure in a closed loop manner. Since at the outset neither the future target position nor consequently the final time-of-flight are known, the solution is an application of the principle of successive approximations. Since the measured present target position is the first-known point in space, this position can be employed to produce a first approximation to the launch angle and time-of-flight. (Trajectory #1 in figure 19–11).

If the weapon were fired based upon this first approximation, it would obviously pass well behind a moving target. Now compute just how far behind the target the projectile would pass. In other words, where is the target at the end of the time-of-flight computed to the present position? Compute the new position and a new point. If the weapon were fired at this new point, it would pass well ahead of the target. Using the time of trajectory #2, compute a new target position, a third trajectory and time (trajectory #3). Continue computing alternate target positions and times until the difference between the two most recently computed times is very small, say 10^{-5} sec. When this occurs, the point in space used to compute the time-of-flight will be the same point that results when time-of-flight is applied to the relative motion solution and the fire control problem is solved. The above scheme as outlined can be applied to either an analog computer with electro-mechanical feedback loops or to a digital computer that

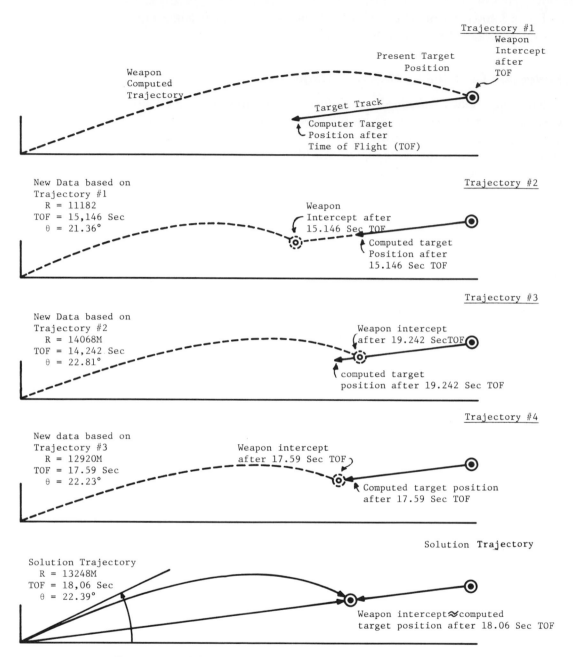

Figure 19–11. Illustration of the iterative procedure employed in a fire control solution. Only four of ten iterations are shown, along with the solution trajectory that passes through the future target position.

employs numerical techniques and software. Both implementations exist in the Navy today.

Summary

This chapter has described general procedures for the solution of a weapon control problem. The overall prediction procedure was divided into sub-procedures of relative motion and weapon ballistics. As input, the relative-motion procedure receives present target position, relative target velocity, and weapon time-of-flight and yields

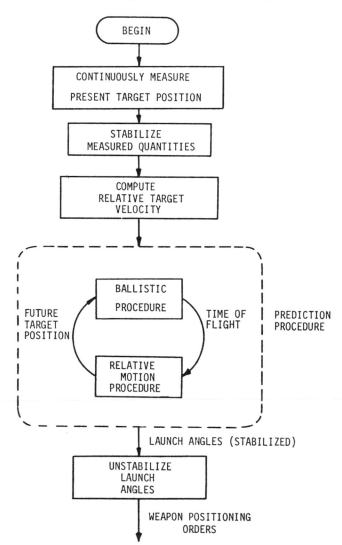

Figure 19–12. Summary of the solution to the fire control problem.

as an output successive approximations to future target position. A ballistics procedure receives as input the approximations to future target position, and its output is successive approximations to the launch angle and time-of-flight. The overall iterative process is terminated when $T_n - T_{n-1} \to 0$ (figure 19–5) which indicates that the refinement of future target position is becoming precise. Figure 19–12 provides the summary of the weapon control problem in flow chart form.

References

Bliss, Gilbert Ames. *Mathematics for Exterior Ballistics*. New York: John Wiley and Sons, 1944.

Herrmann, Ernest E. *Exterior Ballistics 1935*. Annapolis, Md.: U.S. Naval Institute, 1935.

Schmidt, Edward M. *Notes on Exterior Ballistics*. Ballistic Research Laboratories, 1982.

Wrigley, Walter, and John Hovarka. *Fire Control Principles*. New York: McGraw-Hill, 1959.

20

Command, Control, and Communication

Introduction

Throughout this text, attention has been directed toward principles and technologies associated with the hardware of weapons systems. Underlying these weapons systems and the methods by which they are caused to function, is the fundamental concept that they are simply devices or processes that serve as tools to augment the capabilities of a human being. For example, an electromagnetic sensor may augment the visual and audio sensor of an individual; a weapon enhances the individual's ability to inflict damage; a combat direction system expands the decision making capacity of a person; and so forth. At the functional center, no matter how remote, of every weapon system, combat system, or combat direction system is a human being who is engaged in the employment of that system or grouping of systems.

Definitions

Data is the raw material from which information is made. In isolation, data is meaningless. Information is an ordered or sorted grouping of data that conveys rationality. The purpose of any information system is to process data in aggregation to provide knowledge or intelligence. This information may very well be data for some user on a higher level who may, in turn, process it to produce more comprehensive information and so on, until the final user is served. A command, control, and communication (C^3) system is an information system employed within a military organization. It is a general phrase that incorporates strategic and tactical systems. Consequently, a combat direction system, tactical data system, or warning and control system may each be considered C^3 systems. The following definitions of terms are commonly accepted in the military context.

(1) *Command*—The functional exercise of authority, based upon knowledge, to attain an objective or goal.
(2) *Control*—The process of verifying and correcting activity such that the objective or goal of command is accomplished.
(3) *Communications*—The ability and function of providing the

necessary liasion to exercise effective command between tactical or strategic units of command.

(4) *Strategic*—Broadly defined methods of accomplishing a goal.

(5) *Tactical*—Narrowly defined methods of accomplishing objectives en route to a strategic goal. There are normally a number of tactics that make up a single strategy.

Therefore, command, control, and communications may be succinctly defined as:

The knowledgeable exercise of authority in accomplishing military objectives and goals.

An important point to realize is that C^3 is a human function. The method by which command and control is carried out is the C^3 *system*, which serves to augment the cognitive functions of the individual engaged in command and control. A complex C^3 system is an integrated combination of people, procedures, and hardware used to enhance the ability of the individual performing command and control.

The commander may be the President of the United States or he may be the mount captain of a naval gun. The nature of his mission may be strategic or tactical. Consequently, the C^3 system employed must necessarily complement the needs of the commander. Just as one person's information may be another's data, the tactical considerations of one person may be the strategy of another. C^3 systems will normally reflect the complexity or simplicity required by the circumstances.

Communications

Command and control cannot be accomplished without the existence of two-way communications. Commands could not be passed from the commander to subordinates. Control would be impossible unless feedback in some form could take place. Basic to any control system is the incorporation of a reliable communications network. In reality, the more remote the commander is from the scene of action the more dependent he becomes upon rapid, reliable communications.

The majority of long-range communications today are being transmitted electronically via satellite with high-frequency sky-wave propagation as a backup. Automation is achieved at communications centers and substations located throughout the world using machine and computer-controlled processing and re-transmission systems. These stations, ashore and afloat, provide relatively efficient global coverage for strategic and tactical systems. Electronic reproduction, distribution, and display devices are available on ships that have greatly reduced manual message processing. These equipments, such as NAVMACCS, automatically monitor the fleet broadcast and record messages addressed to the ship or embarked unit commander in digital format for retrieval on a CRT display or printout on a high-speed printer. Just as combat direction systems display real-time tactical information, management-oriented information is accessible on a near real-time basis as well. In some cases the communications center can route messages directly to small CRT displays variously located about the unit. Manual processing has been reduced to a minimum, freeing human resources to perform more important functions.

With Fleet Satellite Communications (FLTSATCOM), the UHF spectrum has become the primary carrier of global military communications. The existing HF network has assumed a secondary, but important, backup rule.

Environment

The increasing need for responsive C³ systems is being driven by the rapidity with which weapons can be deployed. Figure 20–1 reveals that this rate has become exponential since the turn of the century. Figure 20–2 displays the compression of reaction time to counter incoming weapons from the instant of initial detection. Figure

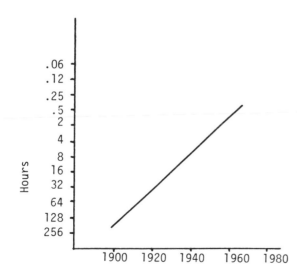

Figure 20–1. Weapon deployment at a nominal range of 2,000 nm.

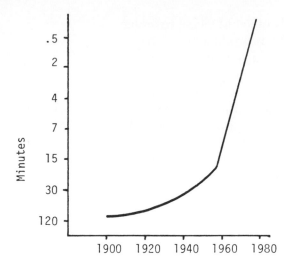

Figure 20–2. Nominal defensive reaction time.

20–2 becomes meaningless, of course, when the detection system fails to detect the inbound weapon. At the unit combat system level, the C^3 system has become relatively efficient in dealing with short reaction times. NTDS and other comparable tactical C^3 systems have begun to satisfy the requirements of on-scene commanders. As these systems expand in capability, remote commanders will become increasingly involved at the tactical level, especially where the engagement has strategic significance. Current technology has already placed heads of government in direct communication with one another. Proliferation of information systems at this level is resulting in political considerations having immediate impact upon military deployment of forces. In this environment it is conceivable that a fighter pilot en route to a tactical objective may be diverted from his target by a direct order from the commander-in-chief. Melodramatic as this may seem, C^3 systems have achieved that degree of efficiency.

In today's environment and with all other considerations assumed equal, the commander who has the "best" information (timely and accurate) will prevail in a conflict of military forces. The key phrase in the definition of command and control is "knowledgeable exercise of authority." The commander who commands without the benefit of information pertinent to the goal or objective, increases the probability of failing to control his resources optimally. Where that goal is both tactical and strategic in nature involving both military and political considerations, the on-scene commander may not have the information pertinent to that goal.

A constantly changing environment is shaping the structure of C^3 systems. That structure is incorporating all branches of the armed services and is gradually centralizing command and control at the seat of government.

In effect, technological developments in weaponry have reduced the time within which to receive and analyze information. In a broader spectrum, increasing events (political and military) per unit time have further complicated the decision process. An isolated conflict can rapidly become international in scope.

Structure

In this chapter a variety of C^3 systems, mostly tactical in function, are discussed. This suggests the fact that C^3 systems in today's military were not systematically designed. In many cases, isolated systems were introduced in response to perceived needs or to take advantage of existing technology. The Vietnam War played a significant role in highlighting the need for a more broadly structured, integrated C^3 system. Today, C^3 systems are being developed to incorporate the following areas in support of commanders engaged in command and control:

(1) Reconnaissance and surveillance
(2) Environmental observation and forecasting
(3) Intelligence analysis
(4) Electronic warfare
(5) Navigation
(6) Management
(7) Strategic and tactical weapons deployment
(8) Logistics and supply

In describing C^3 system structure, the practice in the past has been to present a hierarchical chain of command where information is depicted flowing up and down. Owing to the environment within which the C^3 system must perform in this era, the traditional hierarchy is diminishing in actual practice. In its place a *network* of command and control is evolving. Figure 20–3 illustrates the basic form of this network on a broad scale.

In this case, the National Command Authority (NCA) interacts with two shore-based Fleet Command Centers (FCC) and one Afloat Tactical Flag Command Center (TFCC).

(1) NCA—The President and Secretary of Defense
(2) FCC—CINCLANTFLT, CINCPACFLT, CINCUSNAVEUR
(3) TFCC—Numbered fleet commanders or task force commanders, normally on-scene.

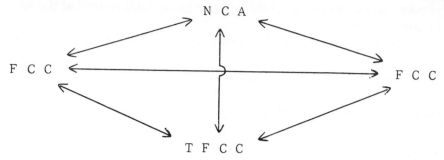

Figure 20–3. C³ network on a macro-scale.

A considerable number of intermediate commanders have not been included. In fact the trend in C³ systems is toward a reduction in the number of subordinate commanders in order to increase the efficiency of the system. Extrapolating the C³ system network further, it is apparent that weapon platform commanders will play a significant role in strategic matters as well as tactical. With command and control considerations ranging from the political realm to specific military employment of force, it is unlikely that a commander will possess all of the skills and information required to singularly engage in C³. The network system in figure 20–3 suggests that an interdisciplinary team concept may be required.

Automated Combat Direction Systems

In a complex multi-threat combat environment, automated combat direction systems such as NTDS make it possible for men to deal with the massive number of targets and compressed reaction times of modern warfare. The complex C³ functions required to keep track of hundreds of friendly, neutral, and enemy ships, aircraft, and weapons, while engaging only those permitted by the current rules of engagement, would be impossible by manual methods.

Joint operations between the Navy, Marine Corps, and U. S. Air Force in the Gulf of Tonkin in the late sixties and early seventies underscored the potential for increased effectiveness that existed when automated C³ systems were available to all participants in an objective area employing a means of rapid data exchange.

The Tonkin operation was the first serious attempt at inter-operability that met with some success. However, data exchange had to be accomplished via the Marine Corps Tactical Data System ashore at Da Nang.

In order to overcome and correct the compatibility problems discovered through this early attempt at joint CDS operations, the Tactical Air Control System/Tactical Air Defense System (TACS/TADS) was evaluated in 1977 to test the digital exchange of information between the semiautomated tactical data systems. The TACS/TADS interface provided U.S. joint and unified commanders with longer range radar detection, continuous tracking, identification, and surveillance of aircraft and ships, more time for threat evaluation and weapon assignment, quicker responses to tactical situations, and a capability to avoid mutual interference through real-time exchange of information regarding own-force activities. These and many other advantages accrue when automated tactical systems are integrated through digital links. The systems currently able to transfer information in joint operations are:

(1) The U.S. Army Air Defense Command and Control Systems, designated the AN/TSQ-73;
(2) The U.S. Navy Tactical Data System, or NTDS, which is the central command and control system on U.S. Navy combatants;
(3) The U.S. Navy airborne tactical data systems available in the E-2, P-3, and S-3 aircraft;
(4) The U.S. Air Force Tactical Air Control System Control and Reporting Center (CRC), designated the AN/TSQ-91;
(5) The U.S. Air Force Airborne Warning and Control System (AWACS) Aircraft (E-3);
(6) The U.S. Marine Corps Air Command and Control System, designated the MACCS;
(7) Various allied ships and aircraft able to operate with U.S./NATO Link standards;
(8) The NATO Air Command and Control System (ACCS) which, when complete, will include the older NADGE (NATO Air Defense Ground Environment), The French STRIDA (Systéme de Traitement et de Represèntation des Informations de Défense Aerienne), The British UKAGE, the German GEADGE, the Spanish *Combat Grande*, and the NAEWS (NATO Early Warning System) which includes AWACS and *Nimrod* airborne early warning aircraft.

When the systems are deployed together, their combined radar coverage can exceed an area of over a million square miles. By exchanging data on radar-held targets, each system can have the benefit of radar coverage of the other systems, and the joint tactical commander can more effectively control the overall efforts of the forces available. Thus, when interfaced, the overall surveillance capability of the total complex of systems should exceed the sum total of the individual system capabilities. In addition, joint operations are less sensitive to outages and countermeasures when the systems operate as a team, because alternate means will be available to achieve tactical objectives.

To achieve these objectives an automated combat direction system must perform the following functions:

(1) Data collection and storage
(2) Target tracking and prediction
(3) Command and control
(4) Communications
(5) Display

Data Collection and Storage

From the point of view of the command and control system, there are really only two categories of information: that obtained from sensors co-located with the system or local tracks; and that obtained from sensors not co-located with the system or remote tracks. The sensors and sources include radar, ESM, IFF, sonar, visual observations, and intelligence data. Both the local and the remote information are stored in a track file similar to that described for TWS systems in chapter 6 and are listed in table 20-1.

These data may be stored by any of the means described in chapter 4, e.g., magnetic tape, disk, drum, core, or semiconductor memory.

Reference frames. Obviously there must be a single reference frame if several combat direction systems are operating together. These systems will operate in a stabilized cartesian coordinate system with an easily identifiable origin, such as a geographic feature or the intersection of whole-number latitude and longitude lines (i.e., 42°N/75°W), which is referred to as the Data Link Reference Point or DLRP. In the event that any unit does not accurately measure its

Table 20-1. Simplified Combat Direction System Track File

Track Number	Weapon Order
Position History (X,Y,Z)	Course and Speed
Identity	Data Source
IFF Response	Side Number
Track Category (Surface, Air, Sub)	Engagement Priority
Current Mission	Controlling Unit (i.e., for CAP)
Weapon Load	

position relative to DLRP, its track position reports for targets held mutually with other units will not correlate. The result will be two track files and separate track numbers for the same target, resulting in ambiguity and confusion. This type of track ambiguity is called dual designation and is in some ways similar to that described for TWS systems in chapter 6. Dual designation is detrimental in that it affects the operation of all command and control systems involved in the data exchange. Other causes of dual designation include problems with relative sensor alignment (chapter 18), platform relative movement, and navigation error.

Gridlock. While it is desirable to eliminate these sources of reference frame error, error must eventually appear over time and will grow unless compensation is introduced in a procedure called gridlock. First, a determination is made that gridlock error and dual designations exist, then a target is selected that is held on radar by all participants. A comparison is made manually or as a computer subroutine to determine that the tracks are in fact the same (correlation). One system is selected as a reference, usually the one considered to have the best navigation data. Finally, all other systems cause a bias to be included in their computer's position reports such that their display of the target is superimposed over that of the ref-

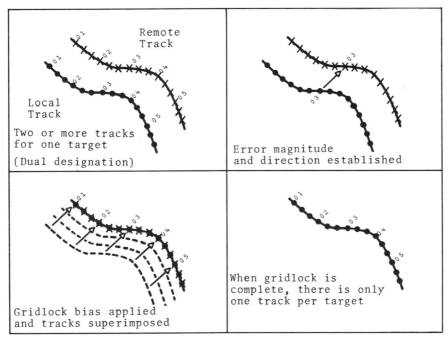

Figure 20–4. Dual designation and gridlock.

erence system. This bias is the same for all tracks reported for one specific system, but obviously is different between systems and is zero for the reference because its reports are assumed to have no error. Gridlock is depicted in figure 20–4.

Target Tracking and Prediction

Information from local data sources can be entered manually or it can come in the form of digital position reports from a TWS or active tracking radar. Fire control system data (called repeatback data) is usually an automatic digital or analog input that must be converted to digital data compatible with the Combat Direction System com-

Figure 20–5. Operator of a non-acoustic sensor operator in a P-3C aircraft. Note radar video superimposed over symbology.

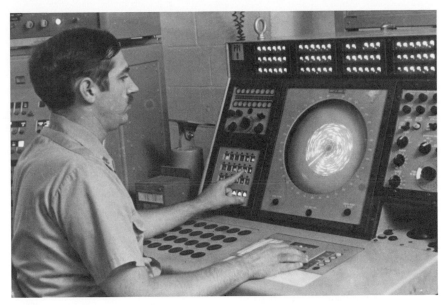

Figure 20–6. Sonar PPI presentation on an NTDS operator display console.

puter. Fire control system data includes that from sonar and from gun-system optics. In the case of ground-based systems, fire control data may be classified as remote data such as that obtained from radars associated with a Hawk or Patriot missile fire unit not co-located with the CDS.

The CDS will normally include equipment to convert data to a format usable by its digital computer including Analog to Digital converters, digital formating equipment, and external buffers if necessary. The purpose of the buffer is to store data from several low data rate sources such as sonar or gyro references until the computer needs it. Without the buffer these low-rate sources would slow down the computer and make it inefficient. With the buffer the computer can cycle through several input/output channels in order as required without having to wait for data.

The CDS will perform tracking and prediction functions similar to those of a TWS radar but using many other data sources. The purpose of the CDS is to provide data and assist in its evaluation rather than to solve the fire control problem. Therefore, the functions it performs will be optimized for communication with operators. The system will include some type of tracking algorithm, similar to that in chapter 6, which may or may not include hostile target parameters and rules of engagement criteria for target evaluation. Outputs for display to humans would include course, speed, CPA, intercept geometry, and evaluated data such as target probability areas or weapon danger areas.

Command and Control

The most important function of the automated combat direction system is in augmenting and assisting the commander in the decision-making process during combat. In performing this function, the system will make various calculations in order to provide graphic and alphanumeric displays that may be clearly interpreted and evaluated by decision makers. In addition, the system may make preprogrammed evaluations and actually automatically assign sensors or weapons as permitted by the rules of engagement.

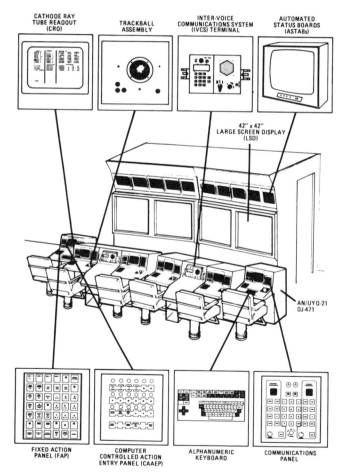

Figure 20–7. Operator-CDS computer communications devices.

Figure 20–8. NTDS operator display with CRT readout.

Force orders. In addition to providing the means with which an individual unit commander can employ the weaponry and sensors assigned him, the force commander can direct conditions of readiness and weapon pairing by secure (i.e., encrypted) intracomputer communications. Commanders at each level are provided confirmation of action taken through graphics and alphanumeric data.

Rules of engagement. Most automated combat direction systems provide some means of automatic threat reaction. The degree to which this response can be tailored to the specific tactical situation varies considerably from system to system. Though the degree of sophistication of response logic varies, the actual modes of response can in general be summarized as follows:

(1) *Automatic*—The combat direction system makes decisions as programmed, up to and including weapons firing.
(2) *Semiautomatic*—The combat direction system performs all functions up to weapon firing; however, an operator must close a firing key. Countermeasures such as ECM and chaff may still be automatic.
(3) *Manual*—Each step is performed by an operator in classical sequence; however, track data may still be provided by an automatic tracking system such as a TWS radar.

Command, Control, and Communication   **573**

The more sophisticated systems allow programming of specific weapons and sensor response, using the location of the system or some other designated position as the defended zone. In addition, zones can be established in bearing and range within which specific types of response can be prearranged.

Communication Links

Digital communications between computers allows much more rapid exchange of data than would be possible using human language. Indeed, it is the only way that complete information can be made available to all involved in the decision-making process. In order for all services and agencies, including those from allied countries, to mutually support one another, a series of data-link standards have been agreed upon that apply to all systems and are implemented regardless of the communications method employed.

A series of standard formatted messages are used to exchange digital data between the computers associated with the systems. These messages contain the various elements of information required for digital exchanges. The messages are interpreted by the computers and converted into display information for use by systems operators.

(1) Tactical Data System Base Information is exchanged to identify the units in the interface.

(2) Track Information is exchanged so that information on all aircraft, surface ships, and subsurface tracks that are within detection range of the systems are available to all participants, though this data may not be displayed if not applicable (i.e. the AN/TSQ-73 would not display subsurface tracks).

(3) Electronic Warfare Information is exchanged so that jamming sources can be located and identified and other electronic warfare data can be shared.

(4) Command Information is exchanged so that the systems can coordinate their efforts in combat operations and tactical commanders can have detailed information on the forces at their disposal.

(5) Specific Control Information is exchanged on friendly aircraft under the direction of the air-control systems. This information keeps all systems informed on the details of combat missions being flown.

(6) Data Management Information is exchanged to control the large volume of information involved, and to minimize mutual interference. For example, aircraft and surface tracks no longer

Figure 20–9. Operator display from an E-3 Airborne Warning and Control (AWAC) aircraft. (Courtesy Boeing Aerospace)

active in the systems complex are deleted, and all systems are notified. Or if conflicts in data occur, information is exchanged between systems so that operators can resolve the conflict situation. The exchange of this information permits continuous coordination and harmonization between the tactical air control and tactical air defense systems involved. It minimizes mutual interference and significantly increases the effectiveness of the systems in a joint operations area.

These link messages are employed in the various Tactical Digital Links (TADLs) that incorporate and include the various numbered links used by the Navy.

(1) *TADL "A" (Link 11)*—Link 11 is a two-way, real-time encrypted data transmission over either UHF or HF radio frequencies. Essential in its importance is the two-way data exchange. Link 11-equipped aircraft or ships, or ships and aircraft, can relay secure tactical sensor information in addition to weapon deployment and engagement status. Coupled with a central memory and processing unit, multiple stations can either receive information or actively enter the net and send and receive data. One station will be designated as NCS (Net Control Sta-

Figure 20–10. Large-screen displays.

tion) to provide a synchronizing sampling of each transmitting unit's data. Transmissions can be in the UHF range to limit detection to line-of-sight ranges or HF when over-the-horizon ranges are desired.

(2) *TADL "B"*—This is a highly directional two-way line-of-sight microwave transmission similar to microwave telephone communications. The units involved must have antennas pointed directly at each other, as the transmission employs a very narrow directional beam. Due to antenna aiming requirements, this method is employed by ground-based systems only.

(3) *TADL "C" (Link 4)*—This is a one- or two-way link used to exchange information with and control specially configured fighter aircraft. This enables the console operator at a surface or airborne CDS to direct the aircraft remotely. In addition, data on target location and identity can be transferred from the fighter to the controlling unit who in turn can distribute that information on the other links.

(4) *Link 14*—Link 14 is a one-way data transmission system pro-

viding non-NTDS-equipped surface platforms with data made available from NTDS platforms. NTDS Link 11-equipped platforms can transmit encrypted data to platforms lacking this capability. This raw data is then transcribed manually and presented to local commanders for possible action. Tactical and strategic conditions presented to non-NTDS platforms, even though done manually, can provide the C^3 necessary in a contemporary battle. Information can be received by a standard radio receiver and teletype.

Display

Automated Combat Direction Systems (CDS) have replaced the relatively slow manual target plotting and data processing of World War II and the 1950s with the nearly instantaneous recognition, reaction, and distribution capability of the high-speed digital computer. The CDS operator has symbology available to him in real-time that represents the entire tactical situation, including all surface, subsurface, air, and land assets supporting him, plus the platforms, facilities, and weapons of his adversary.

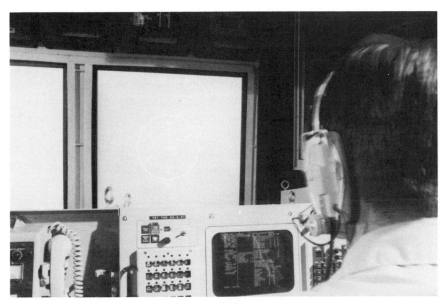

Figure 20–11. Cathode ray tube (CRT) readout of computer alphanumeric data.

For purposes of this discussion we will divide CDS displays into three functional areas:

(1) *Operator displays*—Those displays provide sensor data (including sonar if applicable) and enable the individual to enter, readout, and make use of computer data via graphics and alphanumeric displays.

(2) *Command/evaluation displays*—These are for the use of the force commander or unit commander and his staff. The displays are larger (called Large Screen Displays) and usually allow only limited raw data input. Their primary purpose is evaluation of data and employment of weapons.

(3) *Automated status displays*—These provide information of a general nature for large numbers of tracks of the same general category, such as that provided by manual status boards found in conventional CICs.

Operator displays. This type of display is usually standardized for economy and to make training, repair, and supply easier. It is adapted to specific jobs by the CDS computer program. Usually it contains a 30- to 37-cm CRT employing two separate guns and allows the display of raw sensor video as well as symbology, graphics, and alphanumerics. Communications with the computer are accomplished via fixed action buttons, computer-controlled action buttons, an alphanumeric keyboard (like a personal computer), and a communications panel. Positions on the main CRT are indicated by moving a marker on the scopeface with a ball-shaped roller, a joystick, or by touching the face of the CRT. Computer-supplied lists of alphanumeric data are provided by a smaller auxiliary CRT placed above or beside the main CRT. Generation of symbology may be done at each display or by a centralized symbol generator.

Command/evaluation displays. In the evolution from the large-area status boards and vertical polar coordinate plots to the automated display provided by CDS, a 20-fold increase in target-handling capability was realized, but the greatest advantage of the manual displays—that of general availability to decision making made possible by the size of the manual plot was lost. Where the vertical plot provided a large display for use by several persons simultaneously, the 37-cm plan position indicator (PPI) of the operator display was inaccessible to more than one or two persons and did not provide sufficient detail over a large enough display area for the commander and his staff. Early large screen displays could not provide real-time update of data and therefore were little better than manual methods.

Figure 20–12. Operations Summary Console (NTDS).

Later displays were built employing large (53-cm diameter) CRTs that were essentially enlarged Operator Displays such as the navy's Operations Summary Console (OSC) (figure 20–12).

Shore-based systems such as the Marine Air Command and Control System (MACCS) employed large projection type displays that operated from CDS computer data in real time quite like large-screen commercial television. These displays were used primarily for high-level command and control employing symbology graphics and alphanumerics with no access to raw sensor data.

With the advent of liquid-crystal light valve technology in the early 1980s, displays over one square meter in area became available that had the advantage of acceptability for viewing under ambient light, unlike the CRTs that require a darkened room. These displays provide multi-color computer-controlled displays on a full-color map or chart background.

Automated status displays. One of the last manual functions in automated CDS is that of tabular data. With modern track loading it is unlikely that men can keep up with available data; therefore, modern CDSs provide for a TV monitor display of status board data much like flight schedule displays in modern commercial airports.

Display Reference

The Operator Display retained some of the same limitations of noncomputerized radar repeaters in that the display provided was not corrected for the course and speed of the platform within which it was installed. This characteristic is not a problem in most situations and is even desirable in some circumstances; however, it has been a significant drawback to the automation of antisubmarine warfare, ASCM targeting, navigation, and other activities requiring true-motion displays or geographically fixed plot.

Command/Evaluation displays beginning with the Operations Summary Console (OSC) have been designed with the capability of providing a geographically fixed true-motion display in addition to the conventional relative-motion display provided by radarscopes. While prosecuting sonar contacts, it is imperative that a plot of the geographic position of the attacking ship, assist units, and submarine be maintained in order to evaluate the target submarine's maneuvers and aspect. Without a geographically fixed plot it can be extremely difficult to separate the submarine from underwater geographic features, decoys, and even the wake turbulence of the prosecuting ships. This need has been filled by the dead-reckoning tracer (DRT), and more recently by varieties of the NC-2 plotter, each requiring several men to operate. The DRT and the more advanced NC-2 are limited by the requirement to plot manually all contacts with pencil on paper. This eventually results in a complex mass of lines and requires that target processing and evaluation stop while the paper is changed and the plotting "bug" or "bugs" reset. Under those conditions, 80 percent of the effort was devoted to manual processing and only 20 percent to the actual consideration of tactics.

Using the OSC or some of the other evaluation displays, the operator may select the frame of reference within which information is to be displayed. In a sector-screening situation with the guide as a reference and track history enabled on own ship, the operator may observe his ship's position within its assigned sector for the previous 30 minutes to verify complete coverage. Once sonar contact is gained, he chooses a position near but not directly over the submarine and enters a symbol for a geographically fixed point, which is then used as a reference to orient the OSC geographic display. Once this is accomplished, the scope presentation shifts to center on the geographic point. The own-ship symbol can be observed to move across the scope face in the manner of a DRT bug. OSC track history is then enabled for the submarine, and all surface and air assist units. The geographic plot that results is maintained automatically as long as the operator desires without the delays and inconvenience inherent in manual plotting.

Inherent Problems

Command, control, and communications systems span a continuum from the issuing of simple verbal orders and the direct observation of activity, to remote directives and synthetic representation of resulting activity. Command and control systems are approaching the point where the more complex case may occur within the same span of time as the simplest one. In the following paragraphs some of the more controversial problems are addressed.

(1) *Evaluation*—The digital computer is supremely capable of processing large volumes of data and performing a remarkable degree of evaluation, given a suitable program set. There may be, however, a tendency for users to place inordinate significance upon the results. C^3 is characteristically uncertain and unpredictable, involving considerable subjective evaluation.

(2) *Orientation*—There has been a tendency to employ technology merely because it was available, not because it was needed. Commanders are often faced with a C^3 system unsuited to his or her needs. In most cases the tendency is to adjust to the system even though it may waste resources and restrict effectiveness. C^3 systems should be designed with sufficient flexibility to accommodate the needs of different human beings. Emphasis in system design should favor the commander rather than the technology employed.

(3) *Cost*—Hardware and supporting equipment and processes are expensive. The economics of the military environment will always be a strong factor in deciding which C^3 system will be employed.

(4) *Decision making*—In the attempt to expand the capabilities of general-purpose computers and make them as flexible in use as possible, unnecessarily detailed information is frequently provided. *Too much information can create indecision, just as can too little information.* The C^3 system must be structured and operated to reduce variables and define alternatives for commanders, while concurrently avoiding an information glut at the decision-making level.

(5) *Discipline*—Where high-level commanders possess the capability to engage in evaluation at the on-scene commander level, erosion of authority of the on-scene commander will take place.

If a number of commanders in the C³ system are capable of interacting, confusion may occur. The senior commander with the most pertinent information should take precedence. Multiplicity of evaluation can provide consistently better results than the evaluation of a single commander. Those in command at all echelons must know what their seniors are thinking, when to act, when to question, and when to give orders. Command and control of the near future will require a rational discipline on the part of informed commanders who work together as a team to accomplish objectives and goals. On-scene commanders must be constantly sensitive to orders from higher authority while maintaining the mental freedom of action necessary when it is required that they act, but being careful not to include action contrary to the national interest. This concept of mental discipline is perhaps the most critical—and controversial—area in this new age of command and control.

(6) *Survivability*—Beyond the level of direct command and control, communications plays the key role in maintaining the integrity of the C³ system. Reliability through system design (redundancy, ruggedization, miniaturization, etc.) is essential to ensuring survivability, particularly in a time of escalating conflict. An ironic aspect of communications survivability at the highest C³ levels also exists. An opposing government's control over its own military forces is also normally dictated by its having intact communications. Destruction of its communications system would preclude stopping a conflict once its forces were committed. This consideration can impact significantly upon the tactical employment of own forces.

References

Frieden, Lieutenant D. R. "The Operations Summary Console." *Surface Warfare* (July 1978): 20–22.

Grant, Lieutenant Peter M. "Getting the Big Picture into Our CICs." U.S. Naval Institute *Proceedings* (January 1984): 109–11.

Moran, M.J. "Winning in the Computer Age." *Surface Warfare* (March/April 1976): 24–28.

Naval Operations Department, U.S. Naval War College. *Technological Factors and Constraints in System Performance Study—Command and Control.* Vol. 1–2, 1975.

Peet, Vice Admiral Ray, USN, and Michael F. Melich. "Fleet Commanders: Ashore or Afloat?" U.S. Naval Institute *Proceedings* (June 1976): 25–33.

Staff. "Task Force Survival Relies on Early Detection." *Military Electronics/Countermeasures* (March 1983): 24–36.

Tennent, Lieutenant J.H. "Aegis Display System: The Commander's Battle Picture." *Surface Warfare* (March 1982): 2–6.

Ward, J.W.D., and G.N. Turner. *Military Data Processing and Microcomputers.* Oxford, U.K.: Brassey's Publishers Limited, 1982.

A

Table of the Joint Electronics Type Designation System

Electronic equipment is designated with the prefix A/N followed by three letters from the columns below (e.g., A/N-SPS-10)

First Letter (Designed Installation Classes)	Second Letter (Type of Equipment)	Third Letter (Purpose)
A—Piloted aircraft	A—Invisible light, heat radiation	A—Auxiliary assemblies (not complete operating sets used with or part of two or more sets or sets series)
B—Underwater mobile, submarine	B—Pigeon (do not use)	
C—Air transportable (inactivated, do not use)	C—Carrier	B—Bombing
	D—Radiac	C—Communications (receiving and transmitting)
D—Pilotless carrier	E—Nupac	
F—Fixed ground	F—Photographic	D—Direction finder, reconnaissance, and/or surveillance
G—General ground use	G—Telegraph or teletype	
K—Amphibious	I—Electromechanical or inertial wire-covered	E—Ejection and/or release
M—Ground, mobile		G—Fire-control, or searchlight directing
P—Portable	K—Telemetering	
S—Water surface	L—Countermeasures	H—Recording and/or reproducing (graphic, meteorological, and sound)
T—Ground, transportable	M—Meteorological	
U—Ground, vehicular	N—Sound in air	
W—Water surface and underwater combination	P—Radar	K—Computing
	Q—Sonar and underwater sound	L—Searchlight control (inactivated, use G)
	R—Radio	M—Maintenance and/or test assemblies (including tools)
	S—Special types, magnetic, etc., or combinations of types	N—Navigational aids (including altimeters, beacons, compasses, racons, depth, sounding, approach, and landing)
	T—Telephone (wire)	
	V—Visual and visible light	
	W—Armament (peculiar to armament, not otherwise covered)	P—Reproducing (inactivated, use H)
		Q—Special, or combination of purposes
	X—Facsimile or television	R—Receiving, passive detecting
	Y—Data processing	S—Detecting and/or range and bearing, search
		T—Transmitting
		W—Automatic flight or remote control
		X—Identification and recognition

Example: AN/SPS-10   Y — Surveillance & control
  S-Surface; P-Radar; S-Detecting and range and bearing search

Weapon Designation Symbols

Missiles are designated with three symbols from the columns below plus a number (e.g., RIM-2F)

Launch Environment Symbols	Mission Symbols	Vehicle Type Symbols	
A Air	D Decoy	M Guided missile	Unmanned, self-propelled vehicles
B Multiple	E Special electronic		
C Coffin			
H Silo stored	G Surface attack	N Probe	Non-orbital instrumented vehicles
L Silo launched	I Intercept-aerial		
M Mobile			
P Soft pad	Q Drone	R Rocket	Self-propelled vehicles without installed or remote-control guidance mechanisms
R Ship	T Training		
U Underwater	U Underwater attack		
	W Weather		

Example: The Phoenix missile is the AIM-54

A—Air launched; I—Intercept-aerial; M—Guided missile

Example: The ASROC missile is the RUR-5

R—Ship-launched; U—Underwater attack; R—Rocket unguided

C

Glossary of Weapons Systems Terms

Acquisition Gate—A small volume of space centered on the first instantaneous target position, which will be monitored on each scan for the presence of target information.

Aerodynamics—That field of dynamics that treats of the motion of air and other gaseous fluids and of the forces acting on solids in motion relative to such fluids.

Afterburning—(1) The characteristic of certain rocket motors to burn irregularly for some time after the main burning and thrust have ceased. (2) The process of fuel injection and combustion in the exhaust jet of a turbojet engine (after the turbine).

Aileron—A hinged or movable surface on an airframe, the primary function of which is to induce a rolling moment on the airframe. It usually is part of the trailing edge of a wing.

Airfoil—A thin body, such as a wing, aileron, or rubber, designed to obtain reaction from the air through which it moves.

Airframe—Concerning guided missiles, the assembled principal structural components, less the propulsion system, control and electronic equipments, and payload.

Air Speed, True—Calibrated air speed corrected for altitude effects, i.e., pressure and temperature, and for compressibility effects where high speeds are concerned. Not to be confused with ground speed.

Ambient Noise—Noise present as background noise in the ocean such as seismic, biological, ocean traffic, tide, wind, and storm noise.

Analog Computer—A computer that uses electrical or mechanical devices to develop an analogy to a real problem to simulate the problem in order to obtain a solution to the problem.

Arming—As applied to fuzes, the changing from a safe condition to a state of readiness for initiation. Generally a fuze is caused to arm by acceleration, rotation, clock mechanism, air speed, or by combinations of these.

Artificial Horizon—(1) A device that indicates the attitude of an aircraft with respect to the true horizon. (2) A substitute for a natural horizon, such as a liquid level, pendulum, or gyroscope incorporated in a navigating instrument.

Attenuation Loss—The reduction of the intensity of a sound pulse due to absorption and scattering properties of seawater.

Attitude—The position of an aircraft as determined by the inclination of its axes to some frame of reference. If not otherwise specified, this frame of reference is fixed to the earth.

Ballistics, Exterior—The study of the forces that cause a projectile in flight to change direction and velocity.

Ballistics, Interior—The study of the forces and action within a gun that is firing.

Beacon, Radar—Generally, a nondirectional radiating device, containing an automatic radar receiver and transmitter, that receives pulses (interrogation) from a radar, and returns a similar pulse or set of pulses (response). The beacon response may be on the same frequency as the radar, or may be on a different frequency.

Blast Warhead—A warhead that is designed primarily to cause blast damage.

Booster—(1) A high-explosive element sufficiently sensitive to be actuated by small explosive elements in a fuze and powerful enough to cause detonation of the main explosive filling. (2) An auxiliary propulsion system that travels with the missile and may or may not separate from the missile when its impulse has been delivered.

Bottom Bounce—A phenomenon in which the bottom of the ocean is smooth enough to reflect a sound beam at an angle back to the surface of the ocean.

Bottom Loss—The reduction of the intensity of a sound pulse due to the roughness of the ocean bottom and the formation of a bottom wave that travels in the ocean floor.

Brisance—The rapidity with which an explosive reaches its peak pressure.

Burning, Degressive (or Regressive)—As the burning proceeds, the total burning surface decreases. Shapes of such propellants are pellets, balls, sheets, strips, or cord.

Burning, Neutral—As burning proceeds, the total burning surface remains approximately the same. Shapes of such propellants are single and star perforations.

Burning, Progressive—As burning proceeds, the total burning area increases. Shapes of such propellants are multi-perforated and rosette grains.

Burnthrough—The range at which the radar echo can just barely be discerned through the jamming.

Burster—The last charge in a high-explosive train that contains secondary high explosive and is set off by the booster.

Catapult—A fixed structure that provides an auxiliary source of thrust to a missile or aircraft; must combine the function of directing and accelerating the missile during its travel on the catapult; serves the same function for a missile as does a gun tube for a shell. (See launcher.)

Cavitation—The formation and collapse of vapor pressure bubbles owing to the movement of a body through water, or the effects of this action.

Closed Loop—A type of control system in which feedback from the output is used as part of the input. The output is compared with the input.

Conical Scanning—A radar scanning system wherein the radar beam is caused to rotate so that the beam axis forms a circle about a point in space (target). May be performed passively with a receiver nutating its antenna.

Continuous Rod Warhead—A warhead that is designed to eject an expanding ring of connected rods that can cut through aircraft or structures.

Control—(1) Concerning missiles in general, the entire processes of intelligence and maneuver intended for reaching a specified destination, and special connotation on changes in course owing to data that may be observed and computed either in the missile or externally. (2) Concerning an airframe, a device for effecting a change in motion.

Convergence Zone—An area formed in the water due to temperature and pressure changes that causes an initially downward refracted sound beam to be refracted upward to the surface.

Correction, Curvature—Correction of the prediction angle for the ballistic deviations due to gravity and wind.

Correction, Jump—Correction of the prediction angle for movements of the weapon station and launcher.

Correction, Lead—Correction of the prediction angle for leading the target to ensure interception at a future time.

Countermeasures—All those means of exploiting an adversary's own activity as a means of determining his intensions or reducing his effectiveness. This involves using energy radiated as a result of an adversary's presence or activity as a means of detection and identification of weapon systems and platforms. In addition, weaknesses in sensors, fuzes, computer processing, and personnel training are exploited to deceive an adversary as to the actual tactical situation or cause malfunction of his equipment.

Critically Damped—The amount of restraint in a system that allows the oscillation to die down to the desired level as rapidly as possible without overshooting the desired level.

Damping—The restraint introduced into a control system to cause oscillations in the system to die down to a desired level.

Deception—The deliberate radiation, reradiation, alteration, absorption, or reflection of electromagnetic energy in a manner intended to mislead the enemy in the interpretation or use of information received by his electronic systems.

Definition—Refers to the fidelity with which a visual recording device forms an image. Definition is good when the image is sharp and clear.

Density—Density of loading is the unit weight of an explosive per unit volume and depends on how the explosive is packed.

Detector, Infrared—Two classes of IR detectors: (1) Thermal detectors, which depend on the heating effect of IR radiation to sense or measure the IR radiation. Types include radiometers, thermocouples and thermopiles, thermometers, bolometers, and heat cells. (2) A second type that depends on the quantum nature of photons to measure infrared radiation. These are made of semiconductors.

Detonator—The initial and most sensitive charge in the high-explosive train, which when detonated causes detonation of the booster charge.

Digital Computers—A computer that employs arithmetic and logical functions on numbers in order to solve complex equations rapidly and store the numbers in a memory for retrieval at any time.

Dive—(1) A steep descent, with or without power, in which the air speed is greater than the maximum speed in horizontal flight. (2) In stress analysis, a design condition for the wings, representing a steady state of flight characterized by high speed and an angle of attack approximately that of zero lift.

Doppler Effect—An apparent change in the frequency of sound or radio waves, occurring when the source and observer/target are in motion relative to one another; frequency increases when source and observer approach one another and decreases when they move apart.

Drag—That component of the total forces on a body, in excess of the forces owing to ambient atmosphere, and parallel to the free-stream velocity but opposing the direction of motion. It is composed of skin-friction-, profile-, induced-, interference-, parasite-, and base-drag components.

Drag-Weight Ratio—The ratio of the drag of a missile to its total weight.

Drone—A remote-controlled aircraft.

Ducting—The extension of the range that an electromagnetic wave will travel due to a temperature inversion in the atmosphere that forms a channel or duct for the wave to travel in.

Electromagnetic—Pertaining to the combined electric and magnetic fields associated with radiation or with movements of charged particles.

Electronic Countermeasures (ECM)—Division of electronic warfare involving actions taken to prevent or reduce an enemy's effective use of the electromagnetic spectrum.

Electronic Counter Countermeasures (ECCM)—Division of electronic warfare involving actions taken to ensure friendly effective use of the electromagnetic spectrum despite the enemy's use of EW.

Electronic Warfare (EW)—Military action involving the use of electromagnetic energy to determine, exploit, reduce, or prevent hostile use of the electromagnetic spectrum and action that retains friendly use of the electromagnetic spectrum.

Electronic Warfare Support Measures (ESM)—Division of electronic warfare involving actions taken to search for, intercept, locate, record, and analyze radiated electromagnetic energy, for the purpose of exploiting such radiations in support of military operations.

Error Signal—(1) In servomechanisms, the signal, frequently a voltage, applied to the control circuit that indicates the misalignment between the controlling and the controlled members. (2) In tracking systems, a voltage, depending upon the signal received from the target, whose sign and magnitude depend on the angle between the target and the boresight axis of the system.

Explosive, High—A detonating explosive used normally in warheads. Two types of high explosive are primary and secondary. A primary high explosive will detonate when ignited, while a secondary type, which is relatively insensitive, may burn if ignited in small quantity.

Explosive, Low—A slow-burning explosive used normally as a propellant.

Feedback—That portion of the output of a system that is returned to modify the input to the system.

Flux Lines—Lines about which the electric and magnetic fields flow.

Fragment Warhead—A warhead designed to do most damage from fragments ejected from the warhead at detonation.

Frequency, Electronic—The number of recurrences of a periodic phenomenon in a unit of time. In specifying electrical frequency, the customary unit of time is the second. For example, 15 Hz is understood to mean 15 cycles per second.

Frequency, Infrared—The range of visible radiation frequencies that adjoins the visible-red spectrum and extends to microwave radio frequencies. The IR spectrum is from .76μ to 1,000μ.

Fuselage—The body of approximately streamline form, to which the wings and tail unit of an aircraft are attached.

Future Line-of-Sight—An imaginary line between the weapon station and the position of the target at the instant of interception.

Fuze—A device designed to initiate a detonation under the conditions desired, such as by impact, elapsed time, proximity, or command. A fuze must also keep the weapon safe until clear of the launching platform through the use of its safing and arming device.

Gimbal—A mechanical frame containing two mutually perpendicular intersecting axes of rotation (bearings, shafts, or both).

Ground Speed—The horizontal component of the velocity of an aircraft relative to the ground.

Ground Wave—That portion of a transmitted electromagnetic wave that travels in the atmosphere immediately above the surface of the earth.

Guidance—Concerning missiles, the entire processes of intelligence and maneuver intended for reaching a specified destination, with special connotation on the flight path and on the information for determining the proper course.

Guidance, Beam Rider—A system for guiding missiles that uses a beam directed into space, such that the center of the beam axis forms a line along which it is desired to direct a missile. The beam, which may be either fixed in elevation and azimuth or moving, may be a radar beam, a light beam, or a beam of some other type. Equipment is built into the missile, such that the missile can determine when it is in the center of the beam or can determine the direction and magnitude of the error when it has deviated from the center of the beam. Also built into the missile are suitable electronic circuits, servomotors, aerodynamic surfaces, and/or other equipment, such that the missile, by its own initiative, will return toward the center of the beam when it has deviated therefrom for any reason.

Guidance, Command—A guidance system wherein intelligence transmitted to the missile from an outside source causes the missile to traverse a directed path in space.

Guidance, Homing—A system by which a missile steers itself toward a target by means of a self-contained mechanism that is activated by some distinguishing characteristic of the target. Depends upon the maintenance of electromagnetic radiation contact between the missile and target.

Guidance, Active Homing—A system of homing guidance wherein both the source for illuminating the target and the receiver are carried within the missile.

Guidance, Passive Homing—A system of homing guidance wherein the receiver in the missile uses electromagnetic radiations from the target.

Guidance, Semiactive Homing—A system of homing guidance wherein the receiver in the missile uses electromagnetic radiations from the target, which has been illuminated from a source other than in the missile.

Guidance, Inertial—A system independent of information obtained from outside the missile, the sensitive elements of which system make use of the principle of Newton's second law of motion.

Guidance, Midcourse—The guidance applied to a missile between the termination of the launching phase and the start of the terminal phase of guidance.

Guidance, Preset—A technique of missile control wherein a predetermined path is set into the control mechanism of the vehicle and cannot be adjusted after launching.

Guidance, Terminal—The guidance applied to a missile between the termination of the midcourse guidance and impact with, or detonation in close proximity of, the target.

Guidance, Terrestrial Reference—A technique of missile control wherein the predetermined path set into the control system of a missile can be followed by an optical or radar device that compares observed terrain features with a preset terrain map.

Guided Missile—An unmanned vehicle moving above the earth's surface, whose trajectory or flight path is capable of being altered by a mechanism within the vehicle.

Gyroscope—A wheel or disk, mounted to spin rapidly about an axis and also free to rotate about one or both of two axes perpendicular to each other and to the axis of spin. The spinning gyroscope either offers considerable resistance, depending upon its angular momentum, to any torque, which would tend to change the direction of the spin axis, or if free, changes its spin axis in a direction perpendicular both to the torque and to the original spin axis.

Hangfire—The delayed ignition of the propellant or the igniter.

High-Resolution Sonar—A sonar that uses high frequencies to get short-range, high-resolution capabilities. Useful for searching for small underwater objects and bottom mapping.

Hybrid Computers—Computers that have both analog and digital components connected by analog/digital and digital/analog interfacing devices.

Hygroscopicity—The moisture-absorbing tendency of an explosive.

Input—Stimulus or excitation applied to a control system from an external source, usually in order to produce a specified response from the system.

Interference—(1) The aerodynamic influence of two or more bodies on one another. (2) In physics, the effect of superimposing two or more trains of waves. The resulting amplitude is the algebraic sum of the amplitudes of the interfering trains. When two sets of spherical waves interfere, a system of stationary nodes and anti-nodes is formed, which in optics is known as *interference fringes*. (See Interferometer.) (3) In radio communication, the disturbance of reception owing to strays or undesired signals. (4) In radar, confusing signals accidentally produced on the indicator by the effects of either friendly or enemy electrical apparatus or machinery or by atmospheric phenomena.

Interferometer—An apparatus used to produce and show interference between two or more wave trains coming from the same luminous area, and also to compare wavelengths with observable displacements of reflectors, or other parts, by means of interference fringes. An interferometer is frequently used to obtain quantitative information on flow around bodies in wind tunnels. (See Interference.)

Ionosphere—That portion of the earth's atmosphere, beginning about 30 miles above the earth's surface, which consists of layers of highly ionized air capable of bending or reflecting certain radio waves back to the earth.

Isothermal Layer—A layer in which the temperature of the seawater is constant with depth.

Jamming—The deliberate radiation, reradiation, or reflection of electromagnetic energy, with the object of impairing the use of electronic devices, equipment, or systems by an enemy. An ECM measure.

Jet—The exhaust stream or rapid flow of fluid from a small opening or nozzle.

Jet Vane—A vane made of some highly heat-resisting material placed in the jet stream for use in guidance of a missile.

Launcher—A mechanical structure that forces a missile or projectile to move in the desired direction of flight during initial motion, but does not itself propel the missile. (See Catapult.)

Launcher, Zero Length—A launcher that supports the missile in the desired attitude prior to ignition, but which exercises negligible control on the direction of the missile's travel after ignition.

Line-of-Sight—An imaginary line between the weapon station and the instantaneous target position.

Mach Number—The ratio of the velocity of a body to that of sound in the medium being considered. Thus, at sea level, in air at the Standard U.S. Atmosphere, a body moving at a Mach number of one (M = 1) would have a velocity of approximately 340.2m/sec (the speed of sound in air under those conditions).

Magnetic Anomaly Detector (MAD)—A means of detecting changes in the earth's magnetic field caused by the presence of ships and submarines.

MIL—(1) A unit of angular measurement. In artillery and guided missile usage, a mil is equal to 1/6400 of a circle. In infantry usage, a mil is the angle subtended by 1 meter at 1,000 meters distance. (100 artillery mils equals 98.2 infantry mils.)

Navy Tactical Data System—A hybrid computing system that connects ships, submarines, and aircraft into one sensor and weapons system by using a digital computer to maintain track of all targets and weapons assignments.

Navigation, Celestial—Navigation by means of observations of celestial bodies. A system wherein a missile, suitably instrumented and containing all necessary guidance equipment, may follow a predetermined course in space with reference primarily to the relative positions of the missile and certain preselected celestial bodies. Determination of the vertical to the earth's surface may be necessary in addition.

Open Loop—A type of control system in which no feedback is used.

Output—The actual response obtained from the system.

Overdamped—The amount of restraint in a system that allows the oscillations to take an excessive amount of time to reach, but not overshoot, the desired level.

Payload—Warhead, fuze, and container. In the case of research and test vehicles, this includes equipment for taking data and transmitting or recovering it.

Phase Angle—The number of radians through which a point on an oscillating wave has passed after some given time.

Phased Array Radar—A radar system in which the antenna does not move, but instead electronic steering of the radar beam is used by closely spaced radiating elements that form wave fronts of maximum energy as a function of the phase relationship between the radiating elements.

Phase Difference—The number of radians through which a point on an oscillating wave must pass to have the same relative amplitude as some reference point on a reference wave.

Pitch—An angular displacement about an axis parallel to the lateral axis of an airframe.

Plane Wave—Type of wave in which the wave fronts form planes perpendicular to the direction of propagation.

Precession—A change in the orientation of the axis of a rotating body, such as a spinning projectile or gyroscope, the effect of which is to rotate this axis (axis of spin) about a line (axis of precession) perpendicular to its original direction and to the axis (axis of torque) of the moment producing that change.

Prediction Angle—The angle between the line-of-sight and the weapon line. The prediction angle takes into consideration the relative motion of target and weapon station, environmental forces, and launcher movements.

Preset Guided Paths—The path that has been fixed before the missile is launched. The preset path may be constant or preprogrammed.

Propellant—Material, consisting of fuel and oxidizer, either separate or together in a mixture or compound, which, if suitably ignited, changes into a large volume of hot gases, capable of propelling a rocket or other projectile.

Propulsion, Impulse—Propulsion is provided by a single, initial impulse or explosion.

Propulsion, Reaction—Propulsion is provided by increasing the momentum of the working fluid and creating a pressure differential in the fluid.

Pulse Jet—A compressorless jet-propulsion device that produces thrust intermittently, with an operating frequency determined by the acoustic resonance of the engine. Consists of a pulsating or intermittent inlet-valve system, a combustion chamber, and a discharge nozzle. Owing to the partial vacuum created for a short time in each cycle by the pulsating nature of the combustion and exhaust, this device can take in air and produce thrust even under static conditions.

Pulse Length—The time duration of the transmission of a pulse of energy, usually measured in microseconds or in the equivalent distance in meters, miles, etc., represented by the pulse signal on a radarscope.

Pulse Repetition Frequency (PRF)—Frequency with which the pulses are repeated. PRF is related to the pulse repetition time.

Pulse Repetition Time (PRT)—Time between the beginning of one pulse and the beginning of the next.

Radar, Continuous-Wave—A system in which a transmitter sends out a continuous flow of radio energy to the target, which reradiates (scatters) the energy intercepted and returns a small fraction to a receiving antenna. Because both the transmitter and receiver are operating simultaneously and continuously, it is impractical to employ a common antenna, and usually two similar structures are employed side by side and so oriented that only a small fraction of the transmitted power leaks directly into the receiver. The reflected wave is distinguished from the transmitted signal by a slight change in radio frequency. The CW method has interesting properties—(1) its ability to distinguish moving targets against a stationary reflecting background; (2) it is more conservative of bandwidth than pulse radar.

Radar, Pulse—Radar in which sharp pulses of radio energy are sent out from the transmitter. When these "pulses" encounter a reflecting object, they are reflected as discrete echoes that are detected by the radar receiver during the interval between the transmitted pulses. The pulse method has the ability to measure distances and engage several targets simultaneously.

Radome—A contraction of the words radar dome. The housing for a radar antenna, transparent to radio frequency radiation. It may include some nontransparent areas, however.

Ramjet—A compressorless jet-propulsion device that depends for its operation on the air compression accomplished by the forward motion of the unit. Must have some initial velocity before it can be started. Cannot produce thrust while at rest.

Range, Slant—The distance, in a straight line, from a gun, a point of observation, or a radar set to a target.

Reference Frame—A system characterized by the major properties of an origin, reference lines, reference planes, and stability. Used to measure the distance and angular position of an object relative to some point in space.

Reflection—When an electromagnetic wave encounters a conductor, it is reflected such that the angle of incidence of the wave with the conductor equals the angle of reflection.

Refraction—The bending of an electromagnetic wave when it encounters a boundary where the velocity of light differs. Such a boundary may be caused by variations in air density.

Resolution—In radar, the minimum separation in angle or in range between two targets that the equipment is capable of distinguishing.

Rocket—A thrust-producing system or a complete missile, which derives its thrust from ejection of hot gases generated from material carried in the system, not requiring intake of air or water.

Roll—An angular displacement about an axis parallel to the longitudinal axis of an airframe.

Rudder—A hinged or movable auxiliary airfoil on an aircraft, the function of which is to impress a yawing moment on the aircraft.

Safety & Arming Device—A device in the fuze of a warhead to keep the warhead safe until it is a safe distance from the launcher or until it is desired that the warhead be armed. At that time the S&A device arms the warhead.

Scan, Radar—Denotes the motion of a radio-frequency beam through space in searching for a target. There are many types of scanning used that are denoted by the path described in space by a point on the radar beam, such as circular, conical, spiral, and helical.

Self-Destruction Equipment—Primacord, or some other type of explosive, in a circuit such that it may be exploded by (a) a time-delay mechanism, (b) a radio-command link, (c) an automatic trip mechanism on the roll-stabilization gyro, or other signal.

Self-Noise—Noise produced by the ship itself such as machinery, flow, and electrical component noise.

Sensitivity—The ease with which an explosive can be ignited or detonated.

Shadow Zone—A zone in which the sound intensity is theoretically negligible due to the refraction or bending of sonar pulses in water, leaving the area unsonified.

Shaped-Charge Warhead—A warhead used against hardened and armored targets. As the warhead strikes the target, a detonation wave sweeps forward from the rear and collapses a metal cone liner, causing the formation and ejection of a continuous high-velocity solid jet of liner material. This jet has the capability of penetrating almost any material.

Simulator—Concerning missiles, a device that solves a problem by use of components that obey the same equations as the system being studied. Frequently, an electrical analog or rotation instead of translation is used for mechanical problems. In general, a simulator is an alternative means of determining the effects of changing each of several design parameters at much less expense than building and testing complete missiles or systems.

Simulator, Yaw (Pitch)—A test instrument used to derive and thereby permit study of probable aerodynamic behavior in controlled flight under specific initial conditions. Certain components of the missile guidance system, such as the receiver and the servo loop are connected into the simulator circuitry. Also, certain aerodynamic parameters of the specific missile must be known and set into the simulator. Most simulators are applicable to a single plane. In the case of the yaw simulator, this plane is the yaw plane. The missile is assumed to be completely roll stabilized.

Simultaneous Scanning—The radar scanning system that is capable of obtaining the range, bearing, and elevation of a target from a single pulse.

Skywave—That portion of a transmitted electromagnetic wave that travels upward and outward and is not in contact with the ground. Part of the sky wave is refracted by the ionosphere and returns to earth.

Sonar—Sound Navigation Ranging, the use of acoustic pulses to determine the range and direction of a target in the water.

Sonic, Hyper-(Hypersonic)—(1) High supersonic velocities, of the order of Mach 5, or greater. (2) Velocities at which time of missile passage is of the order of the relaxation time—that is, the time for gas molecules to reach equilibrium after a sudden change in conditions. In such a domain, gases must be treated as discrete particles rather than continuum. Measurements of relaxation times of gases are incomplete, but there are indications that Mach numbers of the order of ten must be regarded as hypersonic. Velocities that are not hypersonic at sea level may become so at high altitude, as relaxation times will be longest where densities are relatively low.

Sonic Speed—The speed of sound locally. A value that is variable depending on the pressure and temperature of the air or water.

Sonic, Sub-(Subsonic)—Less than the speed of sound or less than Mach number one.

Sonic, Super-(Supersonic)—Faster than the speed of sound. When supersonic speed is attained by a moving object, no advance information in the form of advance pressure waves can be given to the advancing air, as the body is moving faster than the pressure waves emanating from the body can propagate themselves forward. As a result, shock waves are formed that move with the body, attached or unattached depending on the condition.

Sonic, Tran-(Transonic)—The intermediate speed in which the flow patterns change from subsonic flow to supersonic—i.e., from Mach numbers of about 0.8 to 1.2, or vice versa.

Sonobuoy—An expendable device designed to be dropped from aircraft and ships and used to detect underwater sounds and to transmit these sounds to nearby aircraft.

Sound Channel—An area formed in the water due to temperature and pressure changes, which causes any sound signal traveling in the area to be refracted back and forth so that it becomes horizontally channeled.

Space Wave—At frequencies of greater than 30 MHz, the ionosphere has no effect on electromagnetic waves, thus allowing the waves to travel in straight lines eventually reaching space. The space wave is limited to line-of-sight transmission.

Special-Purpose Warhead—Warheads designed to use special effects such as heat, light, biological, chemical, smoke, chaff, and radiation to mark or destroy a target.

Spreading Loss—The reduction of the intensity of an acoustic or RF pulse as it spreads out and expands away from the source.

Stability—That property of a system that causes it, when its equilibrium is disturbed, to develop forces of moments tending to restore the original condition. Also the ability of an explosive to be stored without deterioration.

Strength—The quantity of energy released when the explosive is detonated.

Surface Layer—A layer that is affected by daily and local changes of heating and cooling and wind action.

Target Detection Device (TDD)—Device in the fuze of a warhead that detects the presence of the target or specific environmental factors where the target is expected.

Telemetering System—The complete measuring, transmitting, and receiving apparatus for remotely indicating, recording, and/or integrating information.

Temperature, Absolute—Scales based upon zero degrees as the lowest temperature attainable even theoretically. Absolute zero is approximately $-273.18°C$. The absolute temperature scale is in degrees Kelvin (°K).

Test, Engineering—Tests conducted by a developing agency comprising examinations, investigations, or other observations necessary to determine the technical adequacy of the material undergoing test. Pilot or experimental models are subjected to those tests at the various laboratories and proving grounds prior to initiation of procurement of a production model.

Thermocline—A layer in the ocean in which the termperature changes rapidly with depth. There are both seasonal and permanent thermoclines.

Towed Array Sonar System (TASS)—A passive sonar system in which the energy-sensing element is a line of hydrophones towed astern of the vessel. Allows sensing elements to be farther from machine noise.

Tracking, Automatic—The process of using range data and/or angular data in such a manner as to obtain error signals, which are then used to drive devices that keep the tracking system locked on a target.

Track File—A file stored in the computer memory of a track-while-scan system that contains window, position, velocity, and acceleration data.

Tracking Line—The line that forms the axis of symmetry of the radiated energy commonly called the antenna boresight axis.

Track-While-Scan—A radar system that has the capability of simultaneously searching and tracking multiple targets through the use of a digital computer, which continuously updates each target position with each scan in a target-track file.

Tracking Gate—A small volume of space whose size and position are determined by the acquisition window and subsequent scans during which target information is monitored. Size of tracking window describes tracking accuracy of the system.

Transducer—A device that converts the energy of one transmission system into the energy of another transmission system. A loudspeaker and a phonograph pickup are two examples of transducers; the former changes electrical energy into acoustical energy, and the latter changes mechanical energy into electrical energy.

Transmission Line—A system of material boundaries forming a continuous path from one place to another and capable of directing the transmission of electromagnetic energy along this path.

Trim—(1) In electronics, denotes a small change or necessary adjustment of the tuning capacity. (2) Concerning aircraft, the attitude with respect to wind axes at which balance occurs in rectilinear flight with free controls.

Tumbling—(1) The act performed by a two-frame free gyroscope when both frames become coplanar. Under these circumstances, the gyro wheel rotates about a diameter as well as about its polar axis, resulting in loss of control. (2) Concerning missiles and projectiles in flight, turning end-over-end about the transverse missile axis.

Turbojet—A jet motor whose air is supplied by a turbine-driven compressor, the turbine being activated by exhaust gases from the motor.

Umbilical Cord—A cable fitted with a quick disconnect plug at the missile end, through which missile equipment is controlled and tested while the missile is still attached to launching equipment or parent plane.

Underdamped—The amount of restraint in a system that allows the oscillations to overshoot the desired level and continue for a relatively long period of time.

Variable Depth Sonar (VDS)—Sonar that can be lowered to different depths to eliminate the effects of shadow zones.

Variable Flight Path—The path can vary during flight with changes in target position and motion. Variable paths include pursuit, collision, proportional navigation, and beam-riding paths.

Vector Quantity—A quantity that requires for description both magnitude and direction, such as displacement or velocity of a particle.

Video—The term *video* is applied to the frequency band of circuits by which visual signals are transmitted.

Volatility—The readiness with which a substance vaporizes.

Warhead—The portion of a weapon intended to be lethal or incapacitating (the payload); normally the warhead casing, explosive, and/or chemical or incendiary agents, etc.

Wave Guide—A guide, consisting either of a metal tube or dielectric cylinder, capable of propagating electromagnetic waves through its interiors. The widths or diameters of such guides are determined by the frequency to be propagated. The metal guides may be evacuated, air-filled, or gas-filled, and are generally rectangular, oval, or circular in cross section. The dielectric guides consist of solid dielectric cylinders surrounded by air.

Weapon Line—A line along which a weapon should be launched to ensure target interception after a predetermined time of flight.

Weapon Station—Platform from which a weapon is launched, such as a ship, shore station, or aircraft.

Weapon Velocity Vector—The speed and direction vector for a weapon in flight.

Yaw—An angular displacement about an axis parallel to the normal axis of an aircraft.

Index